CONSTITUTIONAL DOCUMENTS

OF THE

PURITAN REVOLUTION

1625—1660

SELECTED AND EDITED

BY

SAMUEL RAWSON GARDINER, M.A., D.C.L.

THIRD EDITION. REVISED

OXFORD

AT THE CLARENDON PRESS

Oxford University Press, Walton Street, Oxford OX2 6DP

OXFORD LONDON GLASGOW
NEW YORK TORONTO MELBOURNE WELLINGTON
KUALA LUMPUR SINGAPORE HONG KONG TOKYO
DELHI BOMBAY CALCUTTA MADRAS KARACHI
NAIROBI DAR ES SALAAM CAPE TOWN

ISBN 0 19 822629 2

First published 1889
Second edition 1899
Third edition 1906
Reprinted 1912, 1920, 1927
1936, 1947, 1949, 1958, 1962, 1968
Reprinted in paperback 1979

British Library Cataloguing in Publication Data

The constitutional documents of the Puritan Revolution,
   1625–1660. – 3rd ed., revised
   1. Great Britain – Constitutional history – Sources
   2. Great Britain – Politics and government –
   1625–1649 – Sources
   3. Great Britain – Politics and government –
   1649–1660 – Sources
   I. Gardiner, Samuel Rawson
   342′.41′029   JN193   79–40848
   ISBN 0-19-822629-2

*Printed in Great Britain
at the University Press, Oxford
by Eric Buckley
Printer to the University*

PREFACE TO THE SECOND EDITION

THE documents in this volume are intended to serve either as a basis for the study of the Constitutional History of an important period, or as a companion to the Political History of the time. By far the greater number of them are printed in books which, though commonly to be found in large libraries, are, on account of their size and expense, not readily accessible to students in general. The MS. of the Constitutional Bill of the first Protectorate Parliament, in the handwriting of John Browne, Clerk of the Parliaments, is preserved at Stanford Hall in the possession of Lord Braye, with whose kind permission the copy used in this volume has been taken. It is possible that a great part of the document might have been recovered from the entries of clauses and amendments in the Journals of the House of Commons, but, as far as I know, this is the only complete copy in existence.

The documents in Part I of the present edition have been added at the suggestion of Professor Prothero, who very generously placed at my disposal the copies he had made with the intention of adding them to his own *Statutes and other Constitutional Documents illustrative of the reigns of Elizabeth and James I* (Clarendon Press, 1894). Though the Navigation Act of the Commonwealth has no claim to a place amongst Constitutional Documents, it is of sufficient importance to be printed in the Appendix.

S. R. G.

CONTENTS

PART I.

From the Accession of Charles I to the Meeting of the Third Parliament of his Reign.

PAGE

1. Speech of Sir Nathaniel Rich, proposing terms on which the House of Commons may be prepared to grant Supply .   1

2. Protestation of the Commons   2

3. Documents relating to the Impeachment of the Duke of Buckingham   3

4. The Restraint of the Earls of Arundel and Bristol . .   44

5. The King's Letter and Instructions for the collection of a Free Gift   46

6. Commission for raising Tonnage and Poundage with Impositions   49

7. The Commission and Instructions for raising the Forced Loan in Middlesex   51

8. The case of the Five Knights, before the Court of King's Bench   57

PART II.

From the Meeting of the Third Parliament of Charles I to the Meeting of the Long Parliament.

9. Notes of a Bill brought in by Sir Edward Coke to secure the liberties of the subject   65

10. The Petition of Right   66

11. The Remonstrance against Tonnage and Poundage . .   70

12. The King's Speech at the Prorogation of Parliament at the end of the Session of 1628   73

13. The King's Declaration prefixed to the Articles of Religion .   75

14. Resolutions on Religion drawn by a Sub-Committee of the House of Commons   77

15. Protestation of the House of Commons   82

16. The King's Declaration showing the causes of the late Dissolution   83

17. The Declaration of Sports   99

18. Act of the Privy Council on the position of the Communion Table at St. Gregory's   103

19. Specimen of the first Writ of Ship-money . . .   105

20. The King's Case laid before the Judges, with their Answer .   108

21. Extracts from the Speech of Oliver St. John in the Ship-money Case   109

PAGE

22. Extracts from the Argument of Sir Robert Berkeley, Justice
    of the King's Bench 115
23. The Scottish National Covenant 124
24. Petition of Twelve Peers for the summoning of a new Parliament 134
25. The King's Writ summoning the Great Council . . . 136

PART III.

FROM THE MEETING OF THE LONG PARLIAMENT TO THE OUTBREAK OF THE CIVIL WAR.

26. The Root and Branch Petition 137
27. The Triennial Act 144
28. The Protestation 155
29. Act for the Attainder of the Earl of Strafford . . . 156
30. Act against Dissolving the Long Parliament without its own
    consent 158
31. The Tonnage and Poundage Act 159
32. The Ten Propositions 163
33. Bill on Church Reform read twice in the House of Lords . 167
34. Act for the Abolition of the Court of Star Chamber . . 179
35. Act for the Abolition of the Court of High Commission . 186
36. Act declaring the illegality of Ship-money 189
37. Act for the limitation of Forests 192
38. Act prohibiting the exaction of Knighthood Fines . . 196
39. Resolutions of the House of Commons on Ecclesiastical Innovations 197
40. Order of the House of Lords on the Services of the Church . 199
41. Extract from the Instructions to the Committee in Scotland,
    proposed by the House of Commons 199
42. The King's Speech to the Recorder of the City of London . 201
43. The Grand Remonstrance, with the Petition accompanying it 202
44. The King's Proclamation on Religion 232
45. The King's Answer to the Petition accompanying the Grand
    Remonstrance 233
46. The Impeachment of one member of the House of Lords, and
    of five members of the House of Commons 236
47. A Declaration of the House of Commons touching a late
    breach of their Privileges 237
48. The Clerical Disabilities Act 241
49. The Impressment Act 242
50. The Militia Ordinance 245
51. The Declaration of the Houses on Church Reform . . . 247
52. The King's Proclamation condemning the Militia Ordinance 248

PAGE

53. The Nineteen Propositions sent by the two Houses of Parliament to the King at York **249**

54. Declaration of the Houses in Defence of the Militia Ordinance   254

55. The King's Letter sent with the Commissions of Array to Leicestershire 258

56. The Votes of the Houses for raising an Army . . . 261

PART IV.

From the Outbreak of the Civil War to the Execution of the King.

57. The Propositions presented to the King at the Treaty of Oxford 262

58. The Solemn League and Covenant 267

59. The Ordinance appointing the First Committee of both Kingdoms 271

60. The Ordinance appointing the Second Committee of both Kingdoms 273

61. The Propositions of the Houses presented to the King at Oxford, and subsequently discussed at the Treaty of Uxbridge 275

62. The King's Propositions to be discussed at Uxbridge . . 286

63. The Self-denying Ordinance 287

64. The Negative Oath 289

65. Order of the two Houses for taking away the Court of Wards   290

66. The Propositions of the Houses sent to the King at Newcastle   290

67. The King's first answer to the Propositions presented at Newcastle 306

68. The King's second answer to the Propositions presented at Newcastle 308

69. Suggested answer to the Propositions drawn up for the King by the leading Presbyterians and a small number of the Independents, and forwarded by the French Ambassador to Cardinal Mazarin to be laid before Queen Henrietta Maria   309

70. The King's third answer to the Propositions presented at Newcastle 311

71. The Heads of the Proposals offered by the Army . . . 316

72. The King's answer to the Propositions of Parliament . . 326

73. Letter of Charles I to the Speaker of the House of Lords . 328

74. The Agreement of the People, as presented to the Council of the Army 333

75. The Four Bills, with the Propositions accompanying them . 335

76. The Engagement between the King and the Scots . . . 347

77. Additional Articles of the Engagement 353

78. The King's reply to the Four Bills and the accompanying Propositions 353

PAGE

79. The Vote of No Addresses 356
80. The Act erecting a High Court of Justice for the King's Trial 357
81. The Agreement of the People 359
82. The Charge against the King 371
83. The King's reasons for declining the jurisdiction of the High
    Court of Justice 374
84. The Sentence of the High Court of Justice upon the King . 377
85. The Death Warrant of Charles I 380

PART V.

The Commonwealth and Protectorate.

86. Act appointing a Council of State 381
87. Engagement taken by the members of the Council of State . 384
88. Act abolishing the office of King 384
89. Act abolishing the House of Lords 387
90. Act declaring England to be a Commonwealth . . 388
91. Act declaring what offences shall be adjudged Treason . 388
92. Engagement to be taken by all men of the age of eighteen . 391
93. Act repealing several clauses in Statutes imposing penalties
    for not coming to church 391
94. Act for the Settlement of Ireland 394
95. Declaration by the Lord General and the Council on the dis-
    solution of the Long Parliament 400
96. Summons to a Member of the so-called Barebones Parliament 405
97. The Instrument of Government 405
98. An Ordinance by the Protector for the Union of England
    and Scotland 418
99. An Ordinance by the Protector for Elections in Scotland . 422
100. An Ordinance by the Protector for Elections in Ireland . 425
101. The Constitutional Bill of the First Parliament of the
    Protectorate 427
102. The Humble Petition and Advice 447
103. The Additional Petition and Advice 459
104. Writ summoning Richard Cromwell to the House of Lords
    of the Protectorate 464
105. The Declaration of Breda 465

APPENDIX.

The Navigation Act 468

INDEX 472

INTRODUCTION

I. To the meeting of the Third Parliament of Charles I.

[—— 1628.]

REVOLUTIONS, no less than smaller political changes, are to be accounted for as steps in the historical development of nations. They are more violent, and of longer duration, in proportion to the stubborn resistance opposed to them by the institutions which stand in their way ; and the stubbornness of that resistance is derived from the services which the assailed institutions have rendered in the past, and which are remembered in their favour after they have ceased to be applicable to the real work of the day, or at least have become inapplicable without serious modification.

On the other hand, many who, throwing off the conservatism of habit, have bent themselves to sweep away the hindrances which bar the path of political progress, show an eagerness to put all established authority to the test, and to replace all existing institutions by new ones more in accordance with their ideal of a perfect State—an ideal which, under all circumstances, is necessarily imperfect. Revolutions, therefore, unavoidably teem with disappointment to their promoters. Schemes are carried out, either blundering in themselves or too little in accordance with the general opinion of the time to root themselves in the conscience of the nation ; and, before many years have passed away, those who were the most ardent revolutionists, looking back upon their baffled hopes, declare that nothing worthy of the occasion has been accomplished.

The historian writing in a later generation is distracted neither by these buoyant hopes, nor by this melancholy despair. He knows, on the one hand, that, in great measure, the dreams of the idealists were but anticipations of future progress ; and on the other hand, that the conservative misgivings of those who turned back were but the instrument through which the steadiness of progress indispensable to all healthy growth was maintained. A Revolution, in short, as an object of study, has an unrivalled attraction for him, not because it is exciting, but because it reveals more clearly than smaller changes the law of human progress.

One feature, therefore, is common to all Revolutions, that the nation in which they appear is content, perhaps after years of agitation, with just so much change as is sufficient to modify or abolish the institution which, so to speak, rankles in the flesh of the body politic. In the French Revolution, for instance, the existence of privileged classes was the evil which the vast majority of the nation was resolved to eradicate ; and after blood had been shed in torrents, the achievement of equality under a despot satisfied, for a time at least, this united demand of the nation. Not the taking of the Bastille nor the execution of Louis XVI, but the night of August 4, when feudal privileges were thrown to the winds, was the central fact of the French Revolution. It was of the essence of the movement that there should cease to be privileged orders. It was a secondary consequence that the King's authority was restricted or his person misused.

In the English Revolution, on the other hand, it was of the essence of the movement that the authority of the King should be restricted. The Kingship had done too much service in the recent past, and might do too much service again, to be absolutely abolished, and there was no widespread desire for any social improvements. The abolition of the House of Lords and the sweeping away of Episcopacy were secondary consequences of the movement. Its central facts are to be traced in the legislation of the first months of the Long Parliament, especially in the Triennial Act, the Tonnage and Poundage Act, and the Acts for the abolition of the Star Chamber and the High Commission. Then, just as in the French Revolution the Reign of Terror followed upon the abolition of privileges on account of the suspicion that those who had lost by the change were conspiring with foreign armies to get them back; so in the English Revolution there followed, first the Civil War and then the trial and execution of the King, on account of the suspicion that Charles was personally unwilling to consent to the loss of power and was conspiring with foreign armies to recover it.

The authority inherited by Charles at his accession was derived from the Tudor monarchy, which had come into power in defence of the middle classes against the great landowners, and had maintained itself in power as the champion of a National Church against a foreign ecclesiastical organisation backed by foreign governments. No such conflict could be successfully waged without reliance on spiritual forces, as well as on the craving for the material advantages to be obtained by casting off the oppressions of the nobility at home or by repelling invaders from abroad. To some extent the spiritual force grew out of the struggle itself, and the exaggerated expressions of loyalty to the wearer of the crown, which fall so strangely on modern ears, were but the tokens of a patriotic tide of feeling which was indeed very far from clearing away evil passions, but which at all events did something to elevate the men who were subject to them. In the main, however, the spiritual force which bore Elizabeth to triumph was religious zeal, or at least zeal which was permeated by the influence of religion.

Of this combined effort of patriotism and religion the Tudor institutions bore the impress. Not only were the judges removable by the Crown, but the Court of Star Chamber, which could fine, imprison, and in certain cases sentence to the pillory, without the intervention of a jury,

was composed of all the members of the Privy Council and
of two of the judges, thus enabling the Sovereign to secure
the decision in cases in which he was personally affected
by a court in manifest dependence on himself. The same
thing may be said of the Court of High Commission, which
dealt with ecclesiastical offences and in which the judicial
authority was practically exercised by the Bishops and the
lawyers of the Ecclesiastical Courts, as the laymen named
in the commission seldom or never attended to their duties.
Again, the right exercised by Elizabeth of levying Impositions, or Customs-duties not voted by Parliament, was the
germ of an unparliamentary revenue which might make
it needless, except in times of great necessity, to consult
Parliament at all. It is true that Elizabeth exercised her
powers with extreme sagacity and moderation, and that the
nation, confident in her leadership, had not been ready to
take offence ; but it was certain, that if the time should
arrive when a ruler less trusted and less respected was on
the throne, there would be a strong disposition to lessen his
authority, especially if, as was the case at the opening of the
seventeenth century, the reasons for entrusting the Crown
with such extensive powers had ceased to exist.

This was precisely what happened during the twenty-two
years of the reign of James I. James was out of touch
with the national feeling, and though he was often wiser
in his aims than the House of Commons, he usually sought
to attain them in an unwise way. He was not tyrannical,
but his policy and his conduct struck no roots in the heart
of the nation ; and it soon became impossible to regard him
as in any sense a leader of the national action. At the same
time his financial difficulties, caused partly by an unavoidable growth of expenditure, but partly also by his lavish
generosity to his favourites, led him to press the real or
supposed rights of the Crown farther than Elizabeth had
cared to press them. Twice in his reign he raised a Benevolence, not indeed by positive order under the Great Seal,

but by invitation conveyed in letters from the Privy Council. The most important financial step taken by him, however, was the levy of largely increased Impositions. Elizabeth had, indeed, for special reasons, levied a few; and one of these, the Imposition on currants, was in 1607 the subject of a trial in the Court of Exchequer, known as Bates's case. Bates, a merchant who refused to pay the duty, on the ground that the King had no legal power to take it without a grant from Parliament, was declared to be in the wrong, and the Crown found itself, by the opinion of the Court which was constitutionally entrusted with the decision of such questions, entitled to raise, in addition to the Tonnage and Poundage—which, according to established precedent, had been voted to James for life by the first Parliament of his reign—as much revenue from exports and imports as the amount of the consumption of foreign articles would permit.

The claim of James to levy Impositions naturally raised opposition in the House of Commons, as it effected not merely the pockets of the members and their constituents, but the constitutional position of Parliament. According to the tradition of generations, the King ought in ordinary times 'to live of his own;' that is to say, to supply his needs from his hereditary revenue and from the Tonnage and Poundage which was intended to enable him to defend the realm by sea. In extraordinary times, when there was war or rebellion or any other demand for unusual expenditure, he might fairly expect Parliament to vote him subsidies, a form of direct taxation loosely resembling the modern Income Tax. In the early part of James's reign, however, the increasing necessities of the Crown seemed likely to set at naught this old theory, and subsidies were sometimes demanded and even granted when there was neither war nor rebellion. The frequent convocation of Parliament became a necessity for the Crown, and the House of Commons, in proportion as the Crown entered on unpopular courses, saw its opportunity of bringing the

Crown to act in accordance with its wishes by delaying or refusing a grant of subsidies. If however the King could substitute a certain revenue from Impositions levied by prerogative for an uncertain revenue from subsidies granted by Parliament, he would be relieved from the necessity of consulting Parliament except in really momentous crises.

The suspicion of danger which may have been entertained when Bates's case was adjudged in the Exchequer was converted into a certainty in 1608, when James ordered by letters patent the raising of new Impositions to the value of about £75,000, a sum which would increase in future years with the increasing trade of the country. When Parliament met in 1610 his right to do so was contested by the Commons, and a compromise was agreed to, by which James was to strike off about a third of the new duties as specially burdensome to the merchants, whilst the remainder, as matters then stood, about £50,000, was to be secured to him by an Act of Parliament in which words were to be inserted precluding him and his successors from ever again levying duties without Parliamentary consent. This compromise, however, was dependent on a larger bargain, known as the Great Contract, for the sale by the Crown in return of certain feudal rights, of which the principal was that of Wardship, for £200,000 a-year, and when the Great Contract failed, the compromise relating to the Impositions fell through as well. When the second Parliament of James I met in 1614, the Commons renewed their protests against the Impositions, but the Lords refused to discuss the question, and an early dissolution prevented any further steps from being taken.

This dispute on the subject of taxation affected the whole constitutional edifice. It raised the question which is at the bottom of all constitutional struggles, the question between the national will and the national law. Whatever may have been the value of the statutes and precedents quoted at the bar and on the bench in Bates's case, the judges were the only authorised exponents of the law, and the judges had decided that James's claim was legal. Against this there was nothing to allege but a resolution of the House of Commons, and a resolution of the House of Commons could not change the law. Only an Act of Parliament could do that, and in those days an Act of Parliament was not to be had without the real assent of King, Lords, and Commons. In this case, however, the assent of King and Lords was not to be had.

When the national will is strongly asserted, some way is certain to be found, in spite of all constitutional difficulties, to change the law. It is not to be supposed that any such assertion was likely to be made in 1610 or in 1614. Though the members of the House of Commons were dissatisfied, they were not as yet disaffected to the Crown, and even their dissatisfaction was not fully shared by the nation at large.

Nor were difficulties about religion likely, at this stage of our history, to incite to resistance. The Church of England during the Middle Ages had been to a great extent national, and when Henry VIII threw off the Papal jurisdiction she became entirely national. More than any other Church, indeed, she retained a connection with the past historical development of Catholic Christianity, and she claimed that in casting off the innovations of the Middle Ages she appealed to the Scriptures, and, in cases of doubt, to their interpretation by the Christian writers of the early centuries. Basing herself on this foundation, she retained the Episcopal office, which could be shown to have been in existence at least in very early times.

In theory a descendant of the Church of the first ages of Christianity, the Church of England cut off from Papal authority could not fail to be subjected to the influences of an age of religious change. On the one hand she was subjected to the Crown, because the nation was subjected to the Crown, and on the other hand her clergy and people were liable to be drawn this way and that by tides of opinion

flowing in from the perturbed Continent. To enter into
these matters in detail would be to write the religious
history of the England of the sixteenth century, and it is
enough to say that at the end of Elizabeth's reign, whilst
the Queen had succeeded in maintaining Episcopacy and
to a great extent the use of the Common Prayer Book as it
had been settled soon after her accession, the doctrine
taught and accepted by the vast majority of that part of the
clergy which was in any real sense of the word religious was
Calvinistic. Elizabeth was, however, slow to mark offences,
and though she had insisted on the complete use of the
Prayer Book and on conformity to the rubrics in important
places such as Cathedrals and College Chapels, she had
winked at refusals by the incumbents of country parishes
to wear the surplice and to carry out certain other cere-
monial rules. After the abortive Hampton Court Conference
in 1604 James resolved to enforce conformity, and a considerable number of the clergy were deprived of their
benefices for refusing to conform. These Puritans, as
they were called, found support in the House of Commons
on the ground that it would be well at a time when there
was a dearth of good preachers to retain the services of men
who were notoriously conscientious, and who were morally
and intellectually qualified for the fulfilment of their ministerial office. The position of the non-conforming Puritans
who appeared at Hampton Court and of their lay supporters
may at this time be easily defined. Both accepted the
Episcopal constitution of the Church and its relations with
the Crown. Both accepted the Prayer Book as a whole,
and the Calvinistic doctrine commonly taught in the pulpits.
On the other hand, whilst the laymen did not offer any
direct opposition to such ceremonies as the use of the
surplice, some of the clergy resigned their cures rather than
conform to them. Obviously the temper of the laity who
sympathised with the non-conforming clergy was still less
likely to lead to resistance than the temper roused in them

by the levy of the new Impositions. Yet, though internal peace was maintained, there was a rift between the Crown and the House of Commons, and tho rift was widened during the latter part of James's reign by difference of opinion on foreign politics. The proposed marriage of the Prince of Wales with a Spanish Infanta, and James's desire to settle the troubles on the Continent caused by the outbreak of the Thirty Years' War by means of the Spanish alliance, was received with disapprobation by all classes of Englishmen; and when, in the Parliament of 1621, the Commons petitioned the King to abandon the Spanish marriage, James denied the right of the House to treat of matters other than those on which he asked its advice. On this the Commons drew up a Protestation, claiming the right to discuss all matters relating to the affairs of the kingdom. James dissolved Parliament, and tore the Protestation out of the Journal Book.

In 1624 another Parliament met, which at first seemed likely to come to terms with the King; as after the failure of his negotiations with Spain he was about to take arms for the restoration of his son-in-law, the Elector Palatine. Differences of opinion, however, soon arose between James and the House of Commons as to the principles on which the war was to be conducted. An expedition sent out under Count Mansfeld ended in desperate failure. Under these circumstances James died in 1625. His successor, Charles I, was anxious to carry on war with Spain, but he was completely under the influence of the Duke of Buckingham, and all that went wrong was naturally attributed to Buckingham's mismanagement. Accordingly, the Commons in the first Parliament of Charles, which met in 1625, after showing their reluctance to grant supplies for the war, using Sir Nathaniel Rich as their mouthpiece in a last effort to find a compromise (No. 1, p. 1), proceeded to ask that the King should take the advice of counsellors in whom Parliament could confide. They did not indeed propose that he should dismiss Buckingham, but the granting of their request would have been a long step towards the establishment of a responsible ministry, and would have cut at the root of the Tudor system, under which the supremacy of the Crown was secured by the responsibility of ministers to itself alone. Charles, seeing the diminution of his authority which would result from the change, dissolved Parliament.

Charles's second Parliament met in 1626. An expedition to Cadiz had in the interval failed to accomplish anything, and there were reasons for believing that Buckingham was about to pick a quarrel with France in addition to the quarrel with Spain. All Buckingham's misdeeds were imputed to the most sordid motives, and the Commons had every inducement to believe the worst of his actions. Charges of crime in order to obtain the dismissal of a minister would commend themselves to a House which had no power to dismiss by simple resolution or petition, and Buckingham was therefore impeached as guilty, not of incompetence, but of high crimes and misdemeanours against the state (No. 3, p. 3). Charles, however, again interfered and dissolved his second Parliament as sharply as he had dissolved the first. Charles's failure in the same Parliament to keep under restraint the Earls of Arundel and Bristol (No. 4, p. 44), might have served as a warning to him that there were limits to the devotion even of the House of Lords.

In the autumn of 1626 Charles, finding his financial necessities pressing, and having failed to persuade his subjects to present him with a free gift (No. 5, p. 46), issued a commission for the levy of tonnage and poundage by prerogative (No. 6, p. 49), after which he proceeded to levy a forced loan (No. 7, p. 51). In 1627 he engaged in a war with France, and sent out a fleet and army under Buckingham to relieve the Huguenot stronghold of Rochelle which was being besieged by the King of France. This expedition, like the preceding one, ended in failure, and public opinion was even more

excited against Buckingham than before. In the meanwhile
the execution of the forced loan had been resisted, and Charles
had imprisoned leading personages who had refused payment.
Five of their number had applied for a writ of Habeas Corpus,
and the King's claim to imprison without showing cause,—
and thus by stating no issue which could go before a jury, to
prevent the imprisoned person from obtaining a trial—was
argued before the Court of King's Bench in what is known
as The Five Knights' Case (No. 8, p. 57). In the end the five
knights were remanded to prison, but the judges expressed
so much doubt as to the King's right permanently to imprison that Charles's authority in the matter was considerably shaken. The general result was that the judges treated
the King's power as something exceptional, to be employed
in special crises, and though they were willing to trust the
King to judge when such a crisis existed, they were unable
to regard arbitrary imprisonment as an ordinary instrument
of government.

Meanwhile, the soldiers who had returned from Rhé
were billeted in private houses in order that they might be
kept in readiness for a fresh expedition in the following
year, and were subjected to the discipline of Martial Law.
Complaints were soon heard of the oppressive nature of the
system. The Courts Martial too did not content themselves
with the punishment of soldiers, but also punished civilians
upon the complaint of soldiers.

II. *From the Meeting of the Third Parliament of Charles I to the Meeting of the Long Parliament.*

[1628–1640.]

When Charles's third Parliament met in 1628, it immediately occupied itself with these grievances. After a long
struggle, in which he refused to accept a Bill proposed by
Wentworth and brought in by Coke, with the object of pre-

venting the repetition of the conduct complained of without
passing judgment on the King's conduct in the past (No. 9,
p. 65), Charles consented to the Petition of Right (No. 10, p. 66),
which after declaring that the law had been broken, demanded
that the King should acknowledge the exaction of 'any gift,
loan, benevolence, tax, or such like charge, without common
consent by Act of Parliament,' all imprisonment without
cause shown, all billeting of soldiers in private houses, and
all exercise of Martial Law to be illegal (No. 10, p. 69).

The Petition of Right is memorable as the first statutory
restriction of the powers of the Crown since the accession of
the Tudor dynasty. Yet, though the principles laid down in
it had the widest possible bearing, its remedies were not
intended to apply to all questions which had arisen or might
arise between the Crown and the Parliament, but merely
to those which had arisen since Charles's accession. Parliament had waived, for the present at least, the consideration
of Buckingham's misconduct. It had also waived the consideration of the question of Impositions. That this was so
appears by a comparison of the language of the Petition of
Right with that of the Tonnage and Poundage Act of 1641
(No. 31, p. 159). The prohibition from taking without Parliamentary consent extends in the former to 'any gift, loan,
benevolence, tax, or such like charge,' in the latter to any
'subsidy, custom, impost, or charge whatsoever.' The
framers of the Petition of Right were the first lawyers of
the day, and it can hardly have been through inadvertence
that they omitted the decisive words necessary to include
Impositions if they had intended to do so. Nor was it
without significance that whilst the Houses in the preamble
to the Petition of Right refer to the imaginary statute *de
Tallagio non concedendo* as enacting that 'no tallage or aid
should be taken without consent,' they make no reference
to the clauses in the *Confirmatio Cartarum* which refer to the
duties upon merchandise.

The motives of the Commons in keeping silence on the

Impositions were probably twofold. In the first place, they probably wished to deal separately with the new grievances, because in dealing with them they would restrain the King's power to make war without Parliamentary consent. The refusal of Tonnage and Poundage would restrain his power to govern in time of peace. In the second place, they had a Tonnage and Poundage Bill before them. Such a Bill had been introduced into each of the preceding Parliaments, but in each case an early dissolution had hindered its consideration, and the long debates on the Petition of Right now made it impossible to proceed farther with it in the existing session. Yet, for three years the King had been collecting Tonnage and Poundage, just as he collected the Impositions, that is to say, as if he had no need of a Parliamentary grant. The Commons therefore proposed to save the right of Parliament by voting Tonnage and Poundage for a single year, and to discuss the matter at length the following session. When the King refused to accept this compromise they had some difficulty in choosing a counter-move. They were precluded from any argument from ancient statute and precedent, because the judges in Bates's case had laid down the law against them, and they therefore had recourse to the bold assertion that the Petition of Right had settled the question in their favour (No. 11, p. 70). Charles answered by proroguing Parliament, and took occasion in so doing to repudiate the doctrine which they had advanced (No. 12, p. 73).

Soon after the prorogation Buckingham was murdered, and it is possible that if no other question had been at issue between the Crown and the Commons than that of the Customs-duties the next session would have seen the end of the dispute. The Church question had, however, by this time reached a new stage. To the dispute about surplices had succeeded a dispute about doctrine and discipline. A school of theological students had arisen which rejected the authority of Calvin, and took up the principle advocated by Cranmer that the patristic writings afforded a key to the meaning of the Scriptures in doubtful points. In prose-cuting their studies they learnt to attach special value to the doctrine of sacramental grace, and to regard Episcopacy as a divine institution and not as a merely human arrangement; whilst, on the other hand, they based their convictions on historical study, thus setting their faces against the plea that truth was divinely revealed in the Scriptures alone, without the necessity of supplementing it by the con-clusions of human reason. In the *Ecclesiastical Polity* of the great Hooker these ideas were set forth with a large-ness of mind and a breadth of charity which made his work memorable as a landmark in the history of thought. It was the starting-point of a change which was to substitute reasonableness for dogmatism, and which was ultimately to blend with the political and philosophical ideas of the latter half of the seventeenth century in putting an end to in-tolerance and persecution. The followers of Hooker were at first the few who, in spite of their appeal to antiquity, were in their central convictions in advance of their age. To give such men their due is always hard for contemporaries, and it was especially hard at a time when the idea of an exclusive National Church had a firm hold on all minds. If there was anything likely to make it impossible, at least for the time, it would be an attempt to place them in positions of authority. Yet this was the very thing which Charles did. His trusted adviser in Church matters was Bishop Laud, and Laud, sharing Hooker's dislike of Calvinistic dogmatism, was fully penetrated with the conviction that he and his friends must either crush the Calvinists or be crushed by them, and that the only way to produce that unity in the Church which he desired to see was to be found in the authoritative enforcement of uniformity in the practices of the Church as laid down by law. Hence, both on the King's side and on that of his antagonists, political and religious considerations were closely connected. The Laudian clergy being in a minority exalted the Royal prerogative

from which they expected protection, and declared themselves in its favour even in such purely constitutional
questions as those relating to arbitrary taxation, whilst the
Calvinistic clergy and laity, feeling themselves to be in a
majority, exalted the authority of Parliament by which that
majority was represented.

One of the questions at issue was Calvin's doctrine of
predestination. The Calvinists held it to be one of the
fundamental tenets of Christianity and condemned those who
opposed it as Arminian heretics. Laud always asserted
that he was not an Arminian, as he considered the question
to be one beyond the reach of his faculties to resolve. It
was doubtless upon Laud's advice, though ostensibly upon
the advice of as many Bishops as could be got together
upon short notice, that Charles prefixed a Declaration on
the subject to a new edition of the Articles (No. 13, p. 75).
The Commons on their re-assembly for the session of 1629
took offence not merely at the Declaration itself, but at
the growth of ceremonialism amongst the clergy favoured
by the Court, and their feelings were doubtless expressed by
the resolutions drawn up by their sub-committee (No. 14,
p. 77), though in consequence of the early dissolution those
resolutions were never put to the vote in the House itself.
The quarrel about religion would certainly have embittered
the quarrel about Tonnage and Poundage, but the latter was
complicated by a fresh dispute about the liability of some
Customs-officers who had seized the goods of a member of
Parliament for refusal to pay unvoted Customs, to answer
their conduct before the House of Commons. The King
declared that his ministers were responsible only to himself,
and dissolved Parliament. Before the dissolution took place,
the Commons voted a Protestation (No. 15, p. 82), and a few
days later the King discussed the quarrel from his point of
view in a published Declaration (No. 16, p. 83). Eleven years
passed before a Parliament was again summoned.

During those eleven years the breach between the King

and his subjects grew constantly wider.   Not only Puritans
but ordinary Protestants were alienated by Laud's efforts to
enforce uniformity in the Church by insisting on obedience
to the law as interpreted by the Ecclesiastical Courts.   When
in 1633 Laud became Archbishop of Canterbury he was able
to act with greater authority.   The Declaration of Sports
(No. 17, p. 99) and the Act of the Privy Council on the
position of the Communion Table (No. 18, p. 103) may be
taken as specimens of the proceedings to which, under the
influence of the Archbishop, Charles lent his name.   For
these proceedings there was always some tolerable reason to
be given.   The real objection to them was that they took no
account of the religious feelings of the majority of religious
men in England.   In 1634 Laud undertook a metropolitical
visitation of the Province of Canterbury which lasted for
three years, and which imposed the new system upon every
parish in the Province, whilst Neile, the Archbishop of York,
took the same measures in the Northern Province.   The
authorisation of the circulation of books in which were set
forth doctrines hardly distinguishable from those of the
Roman Catholics, the intercourse of the King with the Papal
agents established at the Queen's Court, and the infliction
of cruel punishments, by order of the Star Chamber, upon
those who maligned the Bishops or assailed their jurisdiction,
spread far and wide the belief that a vast conspiracy to bring
about the submission of the Church of England to the Pope
was actually in existence.

Taken by itself, the dissatisfaction of thoughtful and
religious men would not have produced a Revolution.   It
is never possible, however, to set at naught the feelings of
thoughtful and religious men without taking steps which
rouse the ill-feeling of those who are neither thoughtful nor
religious.   After the dissolution of 1629 Charles had enforced
the payment of Tonnage and Poundage as well as of the
Impositions levied by his father, and with an increasing
trade and rising revenue was nearly in a position to make

both ends meet, so long as he did not incur any extraordinary expense. The effort to pay off the debts incurred in the late war and to obtain a surplus led to the introduction of unpopular monopolies granted to companies,—thus evading the Monopoly Act of 1624,—to the levying fines upon those who had neglected to take up their knighthood according to law, and to the imposition of fines on those who had encroached on the old boundaries of the forests. A more serious demand on the purses of the subjects was made by the imposition of Ship-money in 1634. The assertions made in the first writ (No. 19, p. 105) set forth so much of the King's objects in demanding the money as could be made public, and there can be no doubt that a fleet was absolutely needed for the defence of the country at a time when the French and Dutch navies had so preponderant a force.

The reasons why the imposition of Ship-money gave more offence than the levy of Tonnage and Poundage are easy to perceive. On the one hand direct taxation is always felt to be a greater annoyance than indirect, and on the other hand Ship-money was a new burden, whereas Tonnage and Poundage, and even the Impositions, had been levied for many years. The constitutional resistance rested on broader grounds. To levy direct taxation to meet extraordinary expenditure without recourse to Parliament was not only contrary to the Petition of Right, but was certain, if the system was allowed to establish itself, to enable the King to supply himself with all that he might need even in time of war without calling Parliament at all. As there could be no doubt that Charles's main ground in omitting to summon Parliament was his fear lest his ecclesiastical proceedings might be called in question, the dissatisfaction of those who resented his attack on their religion was reinforced by the dissatisfaction of those who resented his attack on the Constitution, and of the far greater number who resented his attack on their pockets.

On the King's side it was urged that Ship-money was not a tax at all, but an ancient payment in lieu of personal service in defence of the realm by sea, and also that the King was himself the sole judge of the existence of the danger which would require such exertions to be made. In 1637 Charles took the opinion of the judges on his case (No. 20, p. 108), and the whole question was thrashed out before the twelve judges in the Exchequer Chamber in the case of Hampden in 1637–38. The arguments on either side bristled with precedents and references to law books, but a fair idea of the broader grounds on which each party took its stand may be gathered from the extracts from the speech of Oliver St. John, who was one of Hampden's counsel (No. 21, p. 109), and from the argument of Sir Robert Berkeley (No. 22, p. 115). In reading St. John's speech, it must not be forgotten that he was precluded by his position as an advocate from adducing any considerations drawn from his suspicions of Charles's motives in levying Ship-money by prerogative rather than by Parliamentary authority.

Ultimately judgment was given for the King, only two of the judges dissenting on the main point at issue, though three others refrained from giving their support to the King on other grounds.

Whether, if England had been left to itself, any resistance would have ensued it is impossible to say. There were no signs of anything of the sort, and the whole organisation of the country being in the hands of the King, it would have been very difficult, unless the King chose to summon a Parliament, to obtain a nucleus for more than passive resistance. Passive resistance in the shape of a wide-spread refusal to pay Ship-money indeed existed, but however annoying may be the difficulties of a government exposed to general ill-will, they are not likely at once to endanger its existence. It is when dangers threaten it from abroad, and when it becomes necessary to rouse the national spirit

in its defence, that the weakness of an unpopular government stands clearly revealed.

This danger was already approaching.   In 1637 Charles
attempted to force a new liturgy and canons upon the
Scottish people, and in Scotland he had not the govern-
mental organisation on his side which he had in England.
The Bishops who had been set up by his father had far
less influence than the English Bishops, and the members
of the Privy Council which governed in his name, though
nominated by himself, were for the most part noblemen
whose position in the country was much stronger than
that of the English nobility, and who were actuated by
jealousy of the Scottish Bishops and by fear lest the King
should give wealth and power to the Bishops at the expense
of the nobility.   In consequence, resistance not only broke
out but organised itself ; and in 1638 a religious manifesto,
the Scottish National Covenant (No. 23, p. 124), was signed
by the greater part of the nation.   It attacked the church
system of Charles, though it nominally professed respect for
his authority and avoided all direct attack on Episcopacy.

All attempts at a compromise having failed, and an
Assembly which met at Glasgow in the end of 1638 having
continued to sit after Charles's High Commissioner, the
Marquis of Hamilton, had pronounced its dissolution, and
having then declared Episcopacy to be abolished, Charles
attempted in 1639 an invasion of Scotland.   He was unable,
however, to bring money enough together to support an
army, and he agreed in the Treaty of Berwick to terms
which involved a practical surrender of his claims to dictate
the religion of Scotland.   His subsequent attempt to con-
strue the Treaty to his own advantage led to the threat of a
new war, and on April 13, 1640, by the advice of Strafford,
the Lord Lieutenant of Ireland, who had come to England
in September, 1639, and had from that date become Charles's
principal counsellor, an English Parliament met at Westminster.

The Short Parliament, as it was called, was soon dissolved. It was ready to grant supplies if the King would
come to terms with the Scots, and this Charles refused to do.

A new war was the result. The Scots invaded England,
defeated a large part of the Royal Army at Newburn, and
occupied Northumberland and Durham. Charles had neither
an army nor a people behind his back, and he was forced to
treat with the invaders. The feelings of the English nation
were expressed in the Petition of the Twelve Peers for a New
Parliament, laid before the King on August 28, 1640 (No. 24,
p. 134). In addition to the piled-up grievances of the past
eleven years, was the new one that Charles was believed to
have purposed making himself master of England as well as
of Scotland by means of an Irish army led into England by
Strafford, and paid by subsidies granted by the Irish Parliament. So utterly powerless was Charles before the demands
of the Scots for compensation for the expenses of invading
England that, on September 7, he summoned a Great Council,
or an assembly of the House of Lords alone (No. 25, p. 136),
to meet at York to advise him and to guarantee a loan. On
November 7, the Long Parliament met at Westminster.

III. *From the meeting of the Long Parliament to the
outbreak of the Civil War.*

[1640–1642.]

For the first time in the reign of Charles I, a Parliament
met with an armed force behind it. Though the Scottish
army, which continued to occupy the northern counties
till August 1641, was not directly in its service, it depended
for its support upon the money voted by the English
Parliament, and would consequently have placed itself at
the disposition of Parliament if Charles had threatened
a dissolution. Charles was therefore no longer in a position
to refuse his assent to Bills of which he disapproved, and
the series of Constitutional Acts passed during the first

ten months of the existence of the Long Parliament (Nov. 1640–August 1641), bear witness to the direction taken by it in constitutional matters. The Triennial Act (No. 27, p. 144), enacting that Parliament was to meet at least once in three years, and appointing a machinery by which it might be brought together when that period had elapsed, if the Crown neglected to summon it, struck at Charles's late system of governing without summoning Parliament until it suited him to do so, but it did nothing to secure the attention of the King to the wishes of the Houses. Whilst measures were being prepared to give effect to the further changes necessary to diminish the King's authority, the attention of the Houses and of the country was fully occupied by the impeachment, which was ultimately turned into the attainder of the Earl of Strafford.

No great constitutional change can take place without giving dire offence to those at whose expense the change is made, and Parliament had therefore from the very beginning of its existence to take into account the extreme probability that Charles, if he should ever regain power, would attempt to set at naught all that it might do. Against this, they attempted to provide by striking at his ministers, especially at Strafford, whom they knew to have been, for some time, his chief adviser, and whom they regarded as the main supporter of his arbitrary government in the past, and also as the man who was likely from his ability and strength of will to be most dangerous to them in the future, in the event of an attempted reaction. They imagined that if he were condemned and executed no other minister would be found daring enough to carry out the orders of a King who was bent upon reducing Parliament to subjection. They therefore impeached him as a traitor, on the ground that his many arbitrary acts furnished evidence of a settled purpose to place the King above the law, and that such a purpose was tantamount to treason; because, whilst it was apparently directed to strengthening

the King, it in reality weakened him by depriving him
of the hearts of his subjects.

Whether it was justifiable or not to put Strafford to death
for actions which had never before been held to be treasonable, it is certain that the Commons, in imagining that
Strafford's death would end their troubles, under-estimated
the gravity of the situation. They imagined that the King,
in breaking through what they called the fundamental laws,
had been led astray by wicked counsel, and that they
might therefore fairly expect that when his counsellors were
punished or removed, he would readily acquiesce in changes
which would leave him all the legal power necessary for the
well-being of the State.

Such a view of the case was, however, far from being
accurate. As a matter of fact, the Constitutional arrangements bequeathed by the Tudors to the Stuarts had broken
down, and Charles could argue that he had but perpetuated
the leadership of the Tudors in the only way which the
ambition of the House of Commons left open to him, and
that therefore every attempt now made to subject him to
Parliament was a violation of those constitutional rights
which he ought to exercise for the good of the nation. It
is true that an ideally great man might have been en-
lightened by the failure of his projects, but Charles was
very far from being ideally great, and it was therefore
certain that he would regard the designs of the Commons as
ruinous to the well-being of the kingdom as well as to his own
authority. The circumstances of Strafford's trial increased
his irritation, and he had recourse to intrigues with the
English army which still remained on foot in Yorkshire,
hoping to engage it in his cause against the pretensions of
Parliament. It was against these intrigues that the Protestation (No. 28, p. 155) was directed. It was drawn up by
Pym, and was taken by every member of both Houses as
a token of their determination to resist any forcible inter-
ference with their proceedings. It was rapidly followed by

the King's assent, given under stress of mob violence, to the
Act for Strafford's attainder (No. 29, p. 156).

On the day on which the King's assent to Strafford's
death was given, he also consented to an Act against the
dissolution of the Long Parliament without its own consent
(No. 30, p. 158). It was the first Act which indicated the
new issues which had been opened by the manifest reluctance
of Charles to accept that diminution of his power on which
Parliament insisted. Taking into account the largeness of
the changes proposed, together with the character of the
King from whom power was to be abstracted, it is hardly
possible to avoid the conclusion that nothing short of a
change of Kings would meet the difficulties of the situation.
Only a King who had never known what it was to exercise
the old powers would feel himself at his ease under the new
restrictions.

However reasonable such a conclusion may be, it was not
only impossible, but undesirable, that it should be acted on
at once. Great as was both physically and morally the
injury inflicted on the country by the attempt of Parliament
to continue working with Charles, the nation had more to
gain from the effort to preserve the continuity of its traditions than it had to lose from the immediate evil results of
its mistake. If that generation of Englishmen was slow to
realise the truth in this matter, and suffered great calamities
in consequence, its very tenacity in holding firm to the
impossible solution of a compromise with Charles I, gave
better results even to itself than would have ensued if it
had been quick to discern the truth. A nation which easily
casts itself loose from the traditions of the past loses steadiness of purpose, and ultimately, wearied by excitement, falls
into the arms of despotism.

In spite, therefore, of the appearance of chaos in the
history of the years 1640–1649, the forces which directed
events are easily to be traced. During the first months of
the Long Parliament there is the resolution—whilst retaining

the Kingship—to transfer the general direction of government from the King to Parliament and more especially to the House of Commons, a resolution which at first seems capable of being carried out by the abolition of the institutions which had given an exceptional position to the Tudor and Stuart sovereigns.   Later on there is the gradual awakening of a part of the nation to the truth that it is impossible to carry out the new system in combination with Charles, and this leads to the putting forth by Parliament of a claim to sovereignty really incompatible with Kingship.   Even those, however, who are most ready to break with the past, strive hard to maintain political continuity by a succession of proposed compromises, not one of which is accepted by both parties.

The Tonnage and Poundage Act, which became law on June 22 (No. 31, p. 159), bears the impress of the first of these movements.   On the one hand, whilst it asserts the illegality of the levy of Customs-duties without a Parliamentary grant, it gives to Charles not merely the Tonnage and Poundage given to his father, but also 'such other sums of money as have been imposed upon any merchandise either outward or inward by pretext of any letters patent, commission under the Great Seal of England or Privy Seal, since the first year of his late Majesty King James, of blessed memory, and which were continued and paid at the beginning of this present Parliament' (p. 161).   In other words, it followed the precedent of the abortive Bill of 1610 (see p. xiv) by including the Impositions in the grant, and thus enabled the King 'to live of his own' in time of peace.   On the other hand, it shows how greatly Charles was distrusted by limiting the grant to less than two months, from May 25 to July 15 (p. 161).

The circumstances which caused this distrust are revealed in the Ten Propositions (No. 32, p. 163).   The English army was still under arms in Yorkshire, and though it was about to be disbanded, the King proposed to visit Scotland with the intention, as was then suspected, and is now known, of stirring up the Scots to assist him in England. At such a time it may well have seemed unwise to make the King financially independent, and subsequent events increasing the feeling, the Tonnage and Poundage Act was renewed for short periods only, till the outbreak of the Civil War put an end to any wish to supply the King.

In spite of the King's hope of bringing about a reaction with Scottish aid, he did not feel himself strong enough to refuse his assent to the Bills prepared for cutting off the powers acquired by the Tudors, and on July 5 he gave his consent to the Act for the Abolition of the Star Chamber (No. 34, p. 179) and to the Act for the Abolition of the High Commission (No. 35, p. 186). The work of branding with illegality the extraordinary financial means to which he had himself resorted was completed by the Act declaring the illegality of Ship-money (No. 36, p. 189), the Act for the Limitation of Forests (No. 37, p. 192), and the Act prohibiting the exaction of Knighthood Fines (No. 38, p. 196).

Thus far Parliament had been practically unanimous. The Constitution which had been virtually modified in 1629 to the profit of Monarchy, was legally modified in 1641 to the disadvantage of Monarchy. If there had been nothing more than constitutional questions at issue, it is highly probable that if the King had continued to intrigue with the object of redressing forcibly the balance in his favour, Parliament, backed by the active part of the nation, would have at last been almost unanimous in demanding a change of sovereigns. It is however seldom, if it is ever the case, that political movements are determined on such simple lines. Human action is influenced by many motives, and as the political current shifts and varies, ideas which have at one time hardly obtained recognition rise to the surface and become all important in the direction of events.

At the end of August, 1641, the political changes which had been unanimously adopted, and which, with the exception of the clauses in the Triennial Act for the automatic assembling of Parliament, were permanently accepted in 1660 by the Government of the Restoration, had been accomplished. Room was thereby made for the consideration of another class of changes on which considerable difference of opinion existed. Something must be done to settle the Church as well as the State, and excepting so far as the abolition of the High Commission was concerned, there was no such agreement about ecclesiastical as there had been about political reforms. It was indeed generally desired that the Church, like the State, should be regulated by Parliamentary law rather than by the Royal authority ; and that an end should be put to the alterations in the conduct of worship, which in Laud's eyes were but the restoration of legal order, whilst in the eyes of others they were unauthorised innovations. Further than this, agreement was not to be had. There were those who wished Episcopacy and the Common Prayer Book to be abolished, and there were others who wished them to be retained with some restraint of the authority of the Bishops, and with some more or less slight alteration of the forms of prayer.

These two tendencies had already made themselves felt: the first in the Root and Branch Petition (No. 26, p. 137), presented to the House of Commons on December 11, 1640, and in the so-called Root and Branch Bill for transferring Episcopal jurisdiction to Parliamentary Commissioners, which reached the committee stage in the House of Commons ; the second in the Bill on Church Reform (No. 33, p. 167), which was read twice in the House of Lords. Neither of these obtained the final sanction even of the House in which it had been introduced, and when in the beginning of September, whilst the King was away in Scotland, the Houses prepared for a short recess, the Resolutions of the Commons on Ecclesiastical Innovations (No. 39, p. 197) and the publication of an Order of the Lords on the Services of the Church (No. 40, p. 199) showed that there were divergent tendencies in the two Houses at least so far as Church matters were concerned.

The event which precipitated the division of parties was the Ulster Rebellion. The first indication that the majority of the Commons felt that, with a war in Ireland in prospect, it was necessary that harmony should exist between the Crown and Parliament is to be found in the Instructions to the Commons' Committee in Scotland sent up to the Lords on November 8 (No. 41, p. 199). The demand made in these Instructions was for the appointment of councillors and ministers approved by Parliament (p. 200). To grant such a wish would practically annihilate the independent action of the Crown, and the division of parties on ecclesiastical affairs now gave to the King a majority of the Lords and a large minority of the Commons upon whom he could rely. All those, in short, who wished to see considerable ecclesiastical changes made in the Puritan direction supported the authority of the House of Commons, whilst those who wished the changes to be few or none supported the authority of the King. When Charles returned to London on Nov. 25 his speech to the Recorder (No. 42, p. 201) showed that he was aware where his real strength lay, and his policy was completely in accordance with his conscience. On Dec. 1 a deputation of the Commons presented to him the Grand Remonstrance (No. 43, p. 202), which had been carried by a small majority before his return. After setting forth at length the details of the late misgovernment, the House asked for the employment of ministers in whom Parliament might confide (p. 231), and for the reference of Church reform to a synod of divines whose conclusions might be confirmed by Parliament (p. 229). As there was to be no toleration of Nonconformity, the plan of the framers of the Grand Remonstrance was to substitute the general enforcement of their own form of Church government and worship for that which had recently been enforced by the authority of the King and the Bishops. On December 10 Charles answered indirectly by a Proclamation on Religion (No. 44, p. 232), and directly on December 23 by his answer to the petition accompanying the Grand Remonstrance (No. 45, p. 233). The general outcome of the discussion was that the House of Commons wanted their will to prevail in all that was to be done, whilst the King was ready to hear what they had to say and to assent to just as much as he pleased.

If only an appeal to force could be averted, the majority of the Commons had the game in their own hands. They had but to refuse to continue the grant of Tonnage and Poundage to reduce Charles to bankruptcy. It was the consciousness that this was the case which filled the air with rumours of Royalist plots during the last fortnight of December, and which brought a mob of apprentices to support the Commons in Palace Yard, and a crowd of officers who had served in the now disbanded army of the North to support the King at Whitehall.

Such a tension of feeling could not last long, and the King was the first to move. On January 3, 1642, his Attorney-General impeached five leading members of the House of Commons, and one member of the House of Lords (No. 46, p. 236). On January 4, the King came in person to the House of Commons to seize the five members. The five took refuge in the city, which rose in their defence, and Charles, finding the forces of the city arrayed against him, left Westminster on January 10. On January 17, the Commons set forth a declaration telling the story from their point of view, and defending their own constitutional position (No. 47, p. 237).

Though the King absented himself from Westminster, negotiations between him and the Parliament still continued. On February 13 he gave his consent to the last two Acts which became law in his reign. The first was the Clerical Disabilities Act (No. 48, p. 241), by which the clergy were disabled from exercising temporal jurisdiction and the Bishops were deprived of their votes in the House of Lords, the other the Impressment Act (No. 49, p. 242), authorising the impressment of soldiers for the service of Ireland.   The fact that an army was being brought into existence for Ireland constituted a danger for whichever of the two parties failed to hold military command, and this last Act was soon followed by a claim put forward by Parliament to appoint the Lords Lieutenants of the Counties, who were at the head of the militia or civilian army which was, in time of peace, the only force at the disposal of the King.   As Charles, naturally enough, refused to give such power into the hands of those whom he regarded as his enemies, the Houses, on March 5, passed a Militia Ordinance to the effect which they desired (No. 50, p. 245).   An Ordinance was nothing more than a Bill which had been accepted by the two Houses but had not received the Royal assent, and for some months the Houses had claimed the right of acting on such Ordinances as if they had the force of law.

For the next few months a long and wordy controversy on the legality of this step arose, of which the King's Proclamation of May 27 (No. 52, p. 248), and the Declaration of the Houses of June 6 (No. 54, p. 254), may be accepted as specimens, whilst the Declaration of the Houses on Church Reform of April 8 (No. 51, p. 247) may be regarded as an attempt to minimise the difference between the two parties in ecclesiastical matters.

The Nineteen Propositions (No. 53, p. 249) have a wider scope.   They set forth as a whole the constitutional changes demanded by the prevailing party at Westminster.   They would simply have established government by persons appointed by Parliament in lieu of government by the King, and they may therefore be taken as definitely marking the acceptance by the majority of the House of Commons of the idea that the King's sovereignty must not merely be weakened but practically set aside (see p. xxxii). Against this proposed system were enlisted not only the feelings of Charles, but also those of every man who disliked the ecclesiastical or civil policy of the Houses. In other words, a question arose whether the unlimited power of the Houses would not be as despotically vexatious as had been the unlimited power of the King, and the solution of diminishing the sphere of government by enlarging the sphere of individual right did not as yet occur to either party.

Civil War was the natural result of such a condition of things. On June 12, Charles issued Commissions of Array (No. 55, p. 258) to summon the militia of the counties to his side, and on July 12, the Houses resolved, in addition to their claim to command the militia, to raise an army, and placed it under the command of the Earl of Essex (No. 56, p. 261). On August 22, the King raised his standard at Nottingham, and the Civil War began which was to decide, at least for a time, in whose hands was sovereignty in England.

IV. *From the outbreak of the Civil War to the execution of the King.*

[1642–1649.]

The effect of the Civil War is to be seen by comparing with the Nineteen Propositions (No. 53, p. 249), the Propositions presented to the King at Oxford on February 1, 1643 (No. 57, p. 262). So far as the constitutional proposals are concerned, the tendency of the latter document is to substitute indirect for direct action on the Crown. The following demands made in the Nineteen Propositions entirely disappear from the Oxford Propositions: namely, those for an oath to be taken by all Privy Councillors and Judges to maintain the Petition of Right and certain statutes to be named by Parliament (§ 11), for the dismissal of all Privy Councillors and Ministers of State except such as were approved by Parliament (§ 1); for the permanent rule that no Privy Councillor was to be appointed without the approbation of Parliament, and that no public act in which the Privy Council was to be consulted was to be recognised as proceeding from the King unless it was signed by the majority of the Council [1] (§ 2); for the restriction of appointments of the chief officers of State to those whose nominations were approved by Parliament (§ 3); for the placing of the education of the King's children (§ 4) and their marriage (§ 5) under the control of Parliament; as well as to the restriction of the right of Peers hereafter created to sit and vote in Parliament to those who were admitted with the consent of both Houses (§ 19). In lieu of all this, in the Oxford Propositions, Parliament defined more clearly the exemptions which it demanded should be added to the general pardon to be issued, especially declaring that Newcastle and Digby were to be excluded (§ 13), and that Bristol and Herbert of Raglan were to be incapacitated from office (§ 6), whilst they contented themselves with asking for the restoration of such Parliamentary Justices of the Peace as had been put out of office since April 1, 1642, and for the deprivation of office of such as were excepted against by Parliament (§ 9), as well as for the restitution to office of such members of either House as had been deprived since the beginning of the Long Parliament (§ 14).

To some extent, no doubt, these great concessions may be regarded as proceeding from a desire to conciliate Charles, and to make possible the peace which seemed more desirable after a brief experience of war than it had seemed before the commencement of hostilities. That there was no intention of conceding the substance of the dispute, appears from the fact that the claim put forward in the Nineteen Propositions to the command of the militia and forts (§§ 9, 15), is fully maintained in the Oxford Propositions (§ 7). The alterations made on the subject of the judges however require some consideration. In the Nineteen Propositions permanent provision was made for the submission of the nominations of the two Chief Justices and of the Chief Baron

[1] Thus anticipating the well-known clause in the Act of Settlement.

to the approbation of Parliament (§ 3), whilst the appointment of puisne judges was left as before in the hands of the King.   In the Oxford Propositions the names of twelve persons were recommended for judgeships, and of one person for the Mastership of the Rolls (§ 8), whilst no provision was made for the choice of their successors.

Taking these differences together, we seem to have arrived at a fresh stage in the constitutional ideas of the Long Parliament.   In August, 1641, it seemed enough to wrest from the King the special powers acquired by the Crown since the accession of the Tudors, trusting to the power of stopping supplies to give everything else that might be needed.   In June, 1642, it seemed necessary that Parliament should directly and permanently grasp the control over the military, administrative, and judicial powers of the Crown.   In February, 1643, it appears to have been thought that financial and military control would be sufficient, without assigning to Parliament any permanent direct influence over the judicial and administrative appointments. Is it possible that this change was owing to an increasing perception of the truth that with Charles's successor it might be easier to come to terms, and that the only important difficulty was to tide over the years whilst Charles I, bred up as he had been under the old system, was still upon the throne?

That Charles I should have consented, even to these modified constitutional proposals, was not to be expected; and it was the less likely that there should be any expression of feeling amongst his supporters in favour of their acceptance, as whilst the constitutional demands of Parliament had become less strict, its ecclesiastical demands had become more strict than in the preceding June.   The Nineteen Propositions had asked the King to consent to such a reformation of the Church government and liturgy as Parliament might advise (§ 8).   The Oxford Propositions demanded in addition the immediate abolition of Episcopacy.   The removal from the House of all the Episcopalian members, who were now fighting on the King's side, had probably combined with the desire of Parliament to gain the military assistance of the Scots to bring about this change.

When the negotiations at Oxford failed, and the prospects of success in the field grew more doubtful, the need for Scottish help grew more imperative. The terms of agreement between the two Parliaments were set forth in the Solemn League and Covenant (No. 58, p. 267). However helpful they may have been in bringing about the preponderance of the Parliamentary armies, they raised a fresh obstacle in the way of an understanding between the two English parties.

Everything therefore boded a continuance of the war, and the union of the armies of the Parliaments of England and Scotland rendered it necessary to establish some authority which would control the united armies. This was done by the two Ordinances of February 16 (No. 59, p. 271) and May 22, 1644 (No. 60, p. 273) appointing a Committee of both Kingdoms. Though this Committee was only to manage the war, it may be regarded as the first attempt to give practical shape to the idea of a government residing in a body of men acting under the control of Parliament.

The progress of the war in 1643 and 1644 resulted in sharpening the proposals presented to the King in November, 1644, and discussed at Uxbridge in the first months of 1645 (No. 61, p. 275). Not only did the demands for the exclusion from seats in the House of Lords of Peers afterwards created unless with the consent of Parliament, for the permanent submission of appointments of officers and judges to the approbation of Parliament, and for the education and marriage of the King's children being placed under Parliamentary control, which had been omitted from the Oxford Propositions, re-appear (§§ 19, 20, 21), but the necessity for Parliamentary approbation was to reach to all the judges instead of being confined to three as in the Nineteen Propositions, and there was added a new proposition asking that the right of declaring peace and war might only be exercised with the assent of Parliament (§ 23), and setting up a permanent body of Commissioners to act in combination with a similar body of Scottish Commissioners to control all military forces in both kingdoms with the most extensive powers (§ 17). Besides this, long lists were drawn up of the names of those Royalists who were to be subjected to divers penalties, and whole categories of unnamed persons were added, the expenses of the war being laid upon these Royalist delinquents (§ 14). As to religion in England, not only was it to be brought to the nearest possible uniformity with that of Scotland (§ 5), but the King himself was to swear and sign the Solemn League and Covenant (§ 2). Such demands can only have been made with the object of trampling upon the King's feelings as well as upon his political authority, and it would have been far more reasonable to ask his consent to an act of abdication than to such articles as these.

Charles's counter-demands of January 21, 1645 (No. 62, p. 286), are conceived in a far more reasonable spirit. They appeal to the King's legal rights, asking, in short, that the Constitution should be accepted as it had stood at the end of August, 1641, and as it was to stand at the Restoration in 1660, and that the Common Prayer Book should be preserved from 'scorn and violence,' and that a Bill should 'be framed for the ease of tender consciences.' If constitutional settlements could be judged as they stand upon paper without reference to the character of those who would have to work them, there could be no doubt that the King's offer afforded at least an admirable basis for negotiation. To return to a legal position, and to allow the Houses to trust to their exclusive control over the supplies to win piecemeal reforms would be to anticipate the political situation of the Restoration Government. It was the general distrust of the character of Charles which made this impossible, and which made his abdication or dethronement the only possible temporary solution. It was the instinctive feeling that this was the case, combined with a strong disinclination to acknowledge that it was so, which led the party then predominant in Parliament to fling at the King the insulting Propositions of Uxbridge: and this party was that—not of wild fanatics or dreamers—but of the steady Parliamentarians, whose voices were always raised in favour of peace.

If the negotiations at Uxbridge failed, as fail they must, there was nothing for it but to prepare for war. The army was remodelled, and the new model army better paid and disciplined than former armies had been must be put under commanders who would think first of military success only, without being hampered by political considerations. To effect this, the Self-denying Ordinance was passed on April 3, 1645 (No. 63, p. 287), and in order to weaken the King's power the Houses drew up a Negative Oath (No. 64, p. 289) to be taken by Royalists who wished to forsake the King and to live peaceably under the protection of Parliament.

The year 1645, the year of Naseby, was too fully occupied with military events to leave much time for constitutional reforms or proposals. On February 24, 1646, however, Wardship and all burdens connected with feudal tenures were abolished by order of the Houses (No. 65, p. 290), an immense boon to the gentry and nobility who formed the bulk of the members sitting in either House. On April 5, Parliament, hoping to win over some at least of the King's adherents, passed an Ordinance, authorising them to come under the protection of Parliament, on swearing what was known as the Negative Oath (No. 64, p. 289), engaging themselves to give no support to the King in future.

On July 4, 1646, when the war was practically at an end, and the King was in the hands of the Scots at Newcastle, Parliament, in combination with the Scottish Commissioners residing at Newcastle, despatched fresh propositions to Charles (No. 66, p. 290). The Propositions of Newcastle were framed on those of Uxbridge, and were to a great extent identical with them. The demands for a Presbyterian settle-

ment, for the King's taking the Covenant, for the appointment
of judges and officers, for the sweeping penalties on delinquents, remained pretty much as they had been.   The power
of the Commissioners was however considerably modified,
and the requests for subjecting peace and war as well as the
education of the King's children to the control of Parliament
disappeared entirely.   The militia was to be placed under
Parliamentary control for twenty years, a period which would
probably embrace the whole of Charles's remaining lifetime.

To these propositions Charles, on August 1, gave an
evasive answer (No. 67, p. 306); and on December 20 he gave
a second answer in a similar strain (No. 68, p. 308).

When in February, 1647, the King was removed from
the custody of the Scots at Newcastle to the custody of the
English Parliament at Holmby House, it seemed as if there
was no third course open to Parliament between the deposition of Charles and the acceptance of his terms.   Charles
had however been busy during the last months of his sojourn
at Newcastle in holding out hopes of concession on his part,
and especially of his granting Presbyterianism for three
years, in the expectation that he would, during that period,
be able to regain sufficient influence to obtain the restoration
of Episcopacy and the Prayer Book when it came to an end.
Parliament had now for some time been again split up into
two parties.   On the one side were the Presbyterians, who
were attempting to organise an Erastian Presbyterianism
in England, and whose principle was to substitute the pre-
dominance of Parliament in Church and State for that of
the King.   On the other side were the Independents, who
wished to introduce a large, if not a complete toleration,
and thus to liberate individual consciences from the control
both of Parliament and King.   As the Independents had
a great hold upon the army, the Presbyterians, who in the
beginning of 1647 commanded a majority in both Houses,
had strong reasons for falling back on the King.   The result
was a consultation between their leaders, who were joined

by one or two of the weaker Independents, such as the Earl of Northumberland, with the French ambassador Bellièvre, and the production on January 29 of a proposed answer which was to be sent through the Queen's hands to the King in order that, if he approved of it, he might return it to those who had drawn it up, on which they were ready to support the King's wish to come to London to enter into a personal negotiation with Parliament (No. 69, p. 309). On May 12, Charles sent to the Houses what was in form a third answer to the Propositions of Newcastle (No. 70, p. 311), but which was in reality intended to be a reply to the secret proposals of the Presbyterians, and which, in fact, accepted them with some not very important modifications.

The historical importance of these two documents can hardly be overrated. In them the alliance was struck between the King and the Presbyterian party which led to the Second Civil War in 1648 and ultimately to the Restoration in 1660. The Presbyterians, with a majority in Parliament at their disposal, gave up the attempt to coerce Charles which they had made in the Nineteen Propositions, and in the Propositions of Oxford, of Uxbridge, and Newcastle, and fell back on the principle of re-establishing his authority as it was in August, 1641, in return for the concession, scarcely more than nominal, of a three years' Presbyterianism.

The first step to the realisation of this scheme was an attempt on the part of the Presbyterians to get rid of the army, and when, chiefly through their mismanagement, the attempt failed, the army allied itself entirely with the Independents, carried off the King from Holmby House, and obtained the impeachment and suspension of the eleven leading Presbyterians in the House of Commons.

On August 1, the army came forward with its own plan for the settlement of the kingdom, the Heads of the Proposals which were drawn up by Ireton and amended by the Council of the Army after they had been informally submitted to the King (No. 71, p. 316).

The Heads of the Proposals were the most comprehensive attempt at a permanent settlement which had yet been devised. They did not, like the various propositions laid before Charles on former occasions, seek to establish a Parliamentary despotism upon the ruins of the despotism of the King. They proposed indeed to make the King's power subservient to that of the Parliament, but to lessen the power of Parliament by making it more amenable to the constituencies, and by restricting the powers of the State over the liberty of individuals.

The first object was mainly to be gained by providing for biennial Parliaments and for a redistribution of seats, which, by suppressing what in later times were known as rotten boroughs, would have made Parliament more representative (§ I, 1–5).

The second object was to be gained by the establishment of religious liberty, by depriving the Bishops of coercive jurisdiction, and by repealing all Acts imposing penalties upon attending or not attending on any special form of worship, or upon refusing to take the Covenant (§§ XI–XIII).

With the power of Parliament thus attenuated, it remained to be considered what were to be its relations with the Crown. Here the necessity of distinguishing between restrictions needed whilst the excitement of the Civil War was calming down, and restrictions permanently necessary, was not left out of sight. The militia was to be placed for ten years under the Parliament. After that it was to be commanded by the King, but not without the advice and control of Parliament (§ II, 1, 2). For seven years there was to be a Council of State, the members of which were to be at once agreed on, and this Council of State was to superintend the militia and to conduct foreign negotiations, the final decision in peace or war being reserved to Parliament (§ III, 4, 5, 6). No attempt was made to interfere with the King's choice of his officers, except that Royalists who had borne arms against the Parliament were to be excluded from office for five years, and from sitting in Parliament till after the end of the second biennial Parliament (§ II, 4). No Peers created after May 21, 1642, were to sit in Parliament without the consent of the Houses (§ V). Acts under the King's Great Seal since it had been carried off from Parliament were to be declared invalid, and those under the Parliament's Great Seal to be valid (§ VII).

Such were the principal proposals made in this noteworthy document. It is unnecessary to call attention to its vast superiority, from a constitutional point of view, to the Presbyterian plan of waiting upon events. Yet it was this very superiority which rendered it impossible to put it in execution. It contained too much that was new, too much in advance of the general intelligence of the times, to obtain that popular support without which the best Constitutions are but castles in the air; and even if this could have been got over, there was the fatal objection that it proceeded from an army. The Presbyterian plan was more suited to the slow and cautious progressiveness of human nature. It too, however, had for the present its root of failure in it, in that it was based on the calculation that Charles, if he were restored to power, would be amenable to Presbyterian pressure. He was already giving them hopes that he would be so. Before the end of July he had intimated to the Scots his readiness to make such concessions to them as would induce them to send an invading army to support the Presbyterians in England. The army, on its part, on August 6, took military possession of Westminster. Yet, even so, it found its hold upon Parliament uncertain, and instead of taking up the Heads of the Proposals, the Houses sent to the King a revised edition of the Propositions of Newcastle, differing only in a few unimportant particulars from the paper originally presented to Charles in 1646 by the Presbyterian Parliament and the Scots. In reply, the King, on September 9, despatched a letter expressing his preference for the army proposals (No. 72, p. 326). On

November 11, he fled from Hampton Court, where he had been under the custody of the army, to the Isle of Wight, where he was placed in virtual imprisonment in Carisbrooke Castle. On November 16 he wrote a letter to the Speaker of the House of Lords (No. 73, p. 328), offering to abandon the militia during his own life, but refusing to abolish Episcopacy, and proposing three years' Presbyterianism, to be followed by a system to be approved of by the King and the Houses, with full liberty to all those who should differ on conscientious grounds from that settlement, and consenting to consider the proposals of the army concerning elections and the succession of Parliaments. Parliament replied on December 14, by sending the Four Bills (No. 75, p. 335), which, together with the accompanying demands, were tantamount to a reiterated request for the acceptance of the Propositions of Newcastle.

On paper, at least, Charles had the advantage ; but on December 26, he concluded a secret engagement with the Scottish Commissioners (No. 76, p. 347), on the basis of the three years' Presbytery, but substituting for the full liberty for those who differed from the final settlement of the Church a clause providing that an effectual course was to be taken 'for suppressing the opinions and practices of Anti-Trinitarians, Anabaptists, Antinomians, Arminians,' &c. On this ground the Parliament of Scotland was to require the disbandment of all armies, and if that was denied, to assert 'the right which belongs to the Crown in the power of the militia, the Great Seal, bestowing of honours and offices of trust, choice of Privy Councillors, the right of the King's negative voice in Parliament,' &c. (p. 349). If this were denied, a Scottish army was to invade England with these objects, and also to endeavour that there might be 'a free and full Parliament in England, and that a speedy period be set to this present Parliament.' By additional articles (No. 77, p. 353), Charles engaged to certain personal conditions in favour of Scotsmen. The discrepancy between the terms offered to the Scots and those which he offered to the English Parliament offers a good illustration of the difficulty of coming to terms with Charles. The simple addition of the words 'the right of the King's negative voice in Parliament,' made the rest worthless. He would start with the understanding that Episcopacy was established by the law of the land, and would therefore hold its legal position as soon as the three Presbyterian years were over, except so far as it was modified by mutual agreement between Charles and the Houses. As, however, he was, according to the rules of the old Constitution and his present claim, entitled to reject any compromise which he disliked, he would find himself, when the three years were over, master of the situation.

Two days after the signature of the Engagement, Charles refused his consent to the Four Bills in a paper (No. 78, p. 353), to which the Houses replied on January 17, 1648, by the vote of No Addresses (No. 79, p. 356), breaking off all further negotiations with the King.

The secret engagement with the Scots produced the Second Civil War. The army returned exasperated, and after an attempt of the Parliament to come again to terms with the King in the Treaty of Newport, carried out Pride's Purge, and on January 8, 1649, obtained from the members who still remained sitting an Ordinance for the erection of a High Court of Justice for the trial of the King (No. 80, p. 357).

On January 15, 1649, whilst the King's fate was still in suspense, the Council of the Army set forth a document known as the Agreement of the People (No. 81, p. 359), a very much modified edition of the Agreement of the People offered by the Levellers in October, 1647 (No. 74, p. 333). It was a sketch of a written Constitution for a Republican Government based on the Heads of the Proposals, omitting everything that had reference to the King. The Heads of the Proposals had contemplated the retention of the Royal authority in some shape or another, and had been content to look for security to Acts of Parliament, because, though every Act was capable of being repealed, it could not be repealed without the consent both of the King and the Houses, and the Houses might be trusted to refuse their consent to the repeal of any Act which checked the despotism of the King; whilst the King could be trusted to refuse his consent to the repeal of any Act which checked the despotism of the Houses. With the disappearance of Royalty the situation was altered. The despotism of Parliament was the chief danger to be feared, and there was no possibility of averting this by Acts of the Parliament itself. Naturally, therefore, arose the idea of a written Constitution, which the Parliament itself would be incompetent to violate. According to the proposed scheme, the existing Parliament was to be dissolved on April 30, 1649. After this there was to be a biennial Parliament without a House of Lords, a redistribution of seats, and a rating franchise. For seven years all who had adhered to the King were to be deprived of their votes, and during the first and second Parliaments only those who had by contributions or by personal service assisted the Parliament, or who had refrained from abetting certain combinations against Parliament, were to be capable of being elected, whilst those who had actually supported the King in the war were to be excluded for fourteen years. Further, no official was to be elected. There was to be a Council for 'managing public affairs.' Further, six particulars were set down with which Parliament could not meddle, all laws made on those subjects having no binding force.

As to religion, there was to be a public profession of the Christian religion 'reformed to the greatest purity of doctrine,' and the clergy were to be maintained 'out of a public treasury,' but 'not by tithes.' This public religion was not to be 'Popery or Prelacy.' No one was to be compelled to conformity, but all religions which did not

create disturbances were to be tolerated. It was not, however, to be understood 'that this liberty shall necessarily
extend to Popery or Prelacy,' a clause the meaning of which
is not clear, but which was probably intended to leave the
question open to Parliament to decide. The Article on
Religion was, like the six reserved particulars, to be out of
the power of Parliament to modify or repeal.

The idea of reserving certain points from Parliamentary
action was one which was subsequently adopted in the
American Constitution, with this important difference, that
the American Constitution left a way open by which any
possible change could be effected by consulting the nation ;
whilst the Agreement of the People provided no way in
which any change in the reserved powers could be made at
all. In short, the founders of the American Constitution
understood that it was useless to attempt to bind a nation
in perpetuity, whilst the English Council of the Army either
did not understand it, or distrusted the nation too far to
make provision for what they knew must come in time.

It was this distrust of the nation—perfectly justified as
far as themselves and their projects were concerned—which
made it hopeless for the Council of the Army to build up
the edifice which they designed. It is well to note that the
document which to every sober student of Constitutional
History seems evidence that the scheme of the army was
a hopeless one, was published before the execution of the
King. That that execution made the difficulties in the way
of the establishment of a Republic greater than they had
been, it is impossible to deny ; but the main difficulties
would have existed even if the King had been deposed
instead of executed. There are two foundations upon which
government must rest if it is to be secure, traditional continuity derived from the force of habit, and national support
derived from the force of will. The Agreement of the People
swept the first aside, and only trusted the latter to a very
limited extent.

The King's execution was not long in following. On January 20 the charge against him was brought before the High Court of Justice (No. 82, p. 371). On the 21st, Charles delivered his reasons for declining the jurisdiction of the Court (No. 83, p. 374). Sentence of death was pronounced on the 27th (No. 84, p. 377). The death-warrant was signed on the 29th (No. 85, p. 380), and on the 30th Charles I was beheaded.

V. *The Commonwealth and Protectorate.*

[1649—1660.]

On February 13, 1649, the existing House of Commons, now claiming the powers and style of the entire Parliament, though sitting with sadly diminished numbers, appointed a Council of State (No. 86, p. 381), and on the 22nd drew up an Engagement to be taken by the Councillors to maintain and defend resolutions of Parliament for the establishment of a Commonwealth without King or House of Lords (No. 87, p. 384). It abolished the office of King on March 17 (No. 88, p. 384), and the House of Lords on March 19 (No. 89, p. 387). On May 19 it finally declared England to be a Commonwealth (No. 90, p. 388). On July 17, 1649, it passed a new Treason Law (No. 91, p. 388); and on January 2, 1650, directed an Engagement of Fidelity to the Commonwealth to be taken by all men of the age of eighteen (No. 92, p. 388). On September 27, 1650, it repealed all Acts and clauses of Acts imposing penalties for not coming to Church, but enacted instead that every one on the Lord's Day, and on days of public thanksgiving and humiliation, should be present somewhere 'in the practice of some religious duty' (No. 93, p. 391). So far the Parliament had gone in carrying out the Agreement of the People, but, as might be expected, it took no steps to limit its own powers, nor was it at all in a hurry to appoint a day for its own dissolution.

In the meanwhile, the only force which supported the new Commonwealth or could dictate to its representatives was that of the army. In 1649 a large part of the army under Cromwell had been engaged in the conquest of Ireland, and on August 12, 1652, an Act was passed for the settlement of Ireland on the principles which commended themselves to the conquerors (No. 94, p. 394). In 1650 Cromwell became Lord General, and in that year and in 1651 he conducted a war against the Scots, defeating them at Dunbar on September 3, 1650, and at Worcester on September 3, 1651. As soon as peace was restored, the leaders of the army became impatient for the fulfilment of the neglected demands of the Agreement of the People. On April 20, 1653, Cromwell dissolved the Parliament by force, and stated his reasons for doing so in a public Declaration (No. 95, p. 400). Instead, however, of summoning a Parliament either after the new scheme or after the old system, he allowed the Council of Officers, on advice from the Congregational ministers, to nominate an assembly, usually known by a nickname as the Barebones Parliament, to provide generally for the Commonwealth (No. 96, p. 405). In the end, the Assembly dissolved itself, surrendering authority to Cromwell as Lord Protector, who, on December 16, 1653, announced his intention of ruling according to a constitutional document prepared by a select body of officers, and known as the Instrument of Government (No. 97, p. 405).

The Instrument of Government was intended to suit a Constitutional Government carried on by a Protector and a single House. The Protector stepped into the place of the King, and there were clauses inserted to define and check the power of the Protector, which may fitly be compared with those of the Heads of the Proposals. The main difference lay in this, that the Heads of the Proposals were intended to check a King who, at least for some time to come, was to be regarded as hostile to the Parliament, whereas the Instrument of Government was drawn up with the sanction of the Protector, and therefore took it for granted that the Protector was not to be guarded against

as a possible enemy. His power however was to be limited
by Parliament, and still more by the Council.

Parliament was to be elected and to meet, not, as according
to the Agreement of the People, once in two, but once
in three years (§ 7), and to remain in session at least
five months (§ 8). It was to be elected in accordance
with a scheme for the redistribution of seats based on
that set forth in the Agreement of the People (§ 10),
the Protector and Council having leave to establish constituencies in Scotland and Ireland, which were now to
send members to the Parliament of Westminster. It was
the first attempt at a Parliamentary union between the
three countries, carried out at a time when such a union was
only possible because two of the countries had been con-
quered by one. Instead of the old freehold franchise, or
of the rating franchise of the Agreement of the People,
the franchise in the counties was to be given to the
possessors of real or personal estate to the value of £200
(§ 18). As nothing was said about the boroughs, the right
of election would remain in those who had it under the
Monarchy, that is to say, it would vary according to the
custom of each borough. This however was of less importance than it would have been in former years, as one
of the main features of the Instrument was an enormous
increase of the number of county members, and a proportional
decrease of the number of borough members. In those
boroughs in which the corporations elected, the feeling by
this time would be likely to be anti-Royalist. The dis-
qualification clauses were less stringently drawn than in the
Agreement of the People, but all who had abetted the King
in the war were to be deprived of their votes at the first
election and of the right of sitting in the first four Parliaments (§ 14). Those who had abetted the Rebellion in
Ireland, or were Roman Catholics, were permanently disqualified from sitting or voting.

The Council was named in the Instrument itself. When

vacancies occurred, Parliament was to give in six names, to be diminished to two by the Council, out of which one was to be selected by the Protector (§ 25). The chief officers of the State were to be chosen 'by the approbation of Parliament.'

The clauses relating to the power of Parliament in matters of finance seem to have been modelled on the old notion that 'the King was to live of his own' in ordinary times. A constant yearly revenue was to be raised for supporting an army of 30,000 men—now regarded as a permanent charge —and for a fleet sufficient to guard the seas, as well as £200,000 for the domestic administration. The total amount and the sources of the necessary taxation were to be settled by the Protector and Council; Parliament having no right to diminish it without the consent of the Protector (§ 27). With respect to war expenses, they were to be met by votes of Parliament, except that in the intervals of Parliament the Protector and Council might raise money to meet sudden emergencies from war till the Parliament could meet (§ 30), which the Protector and Council were bound to summon for an extraordinary session in such an emergency (§ 23).

As to legislation, a Bill passed by Parliament was to be presented before the Protector. If after twenty days he had not given his consent, or induced Parliament to withdraw the Bill, it became law unless it were contrary to the Instrument of Government (§ 24).

As to administration, 'the Chancellor, Keeper, or Commissioners of the Great Seal, the Treasurer, Admiral, Chief Governors of Ireland and Scotland, and the Chief Justices of both the Benches' were to be chosen by the approbation of Parliament (§ 34). All other appointments were in the hands of the Protector.

The functions of the Council were of considerable importance. In all important matters the Protector had to act by its advice, and when Parliament was not in session it was to join him in passing Ordinances which were to be obeyed until in the next session Parliament either confirmed them or disallowed them (§ 30). On the death of the Protector it was the Council which was to elect his successor (§ 32).

The articles on Liberty of Worship (§§ 36, 37) are almost verbally taken from the Agreement of the People, except that for the clause 'Nevertheless, it is not intended to be hereby provided that this liberty shall necessarily extend to Popery or Prelacy,' is substituted 'Provided this liberty be not extended to Popery or Prelacy, nor to such as, under the profession of Christ, hold forth and practise licentiousness.'

To obtain some sort of confirmation for this new Constitution, the returning Officer was to obtain from the electors by whom the members of Parliament were chosen a written acknowledgment 'that the persons elected shall not have power to alter the government as it is hereby settled in one single person and a Parliament' (§ 12).

The Instrument of Government suffered not only under the vice of ignoring the probable necessity of constitutional amendment in the future, as is shown by its silence on this head, combined with the elaborate provisions for a change in the amount of money set aside for fixed charges; but also under the vice of having no support either in traditional loyalty or in national sanction. If, however, we pass over these all-important faults, and discuss it from the purely constitutional point of view, it is impossible not to be struck with the ability of its framers, even if we pronounce their work to be not entirely satisfactory. It bears the stamp of an intention to steer a middle course between the despotism of a 'single person' and the despotism of a 'single House.' Parliament had supreme rights of legislation, and the Protector was not only sworn to administer the law, but every illegal act would come before the courts of law for condemnation. Parliament, too, had the right of disapproving the nominations to the principal ministerial offices, and of voting money for conducting operations in time of war. Where it fell short of the powers of modern Parliaments was in its inability to control administrative acts, and in its power-lessness to refuse supplies for the carrying on of the government in time of peace. A modern Parliament can exercise these powers with safety, because if it uses them foolishly a government can dissolve it and appeal to the nation, whereas Cromwell, who was but the head of a party in the minority, and whose real strength rested on the army, did not venture to appeal to the nation at large, or even to appeal too frequently to the constituencies who were to elect his Parliament.

The real constitutional safeguard was intended to be in the Council. Ultimately, after the death of the Councillors named in the Instrument, the Council would indirectly represent the Parliament, as no one would have a place on it whose name had not been one of six presented by Parliament. In the Council, the Protector would be in much the same position as a modern Prime Minister in his Cabinet, except that each member of the Council held his position for life, whereas a modern Prime Minister can obtain the resignation of any member of the Cabinet with whom he is in strong disagreement. On the other hand, the greater part of the members of a modern Cabinet are heads of executive departments, and thus have a certain independent position of their own. In some respects indeed, the relations between the Protector and the Council were more like those between an American President and the Senate in executive session, than those between an English Prime Minister and the Cabinet. The members of the American Senate are entirely independent of the President, as the members of the Council of the Protectorate were entirely independent of the Protector when once they had been chosen. On the other hand, the two bodies differed in a most important particular. The tendency of the American Senate, which is never officially brought into personal contact with the President, is to be antagonistic to the President. The tendency of the Council of State, which was in daily contact with the Protector, was to work with him instead of against him.

The chief points in which the Parliamentary constitutional scheme (No. 101, p. 427) differed from the Instrument of Government will be best seen if given in a tabulated form :—

Subject.	*Instrument of Government.*	*Parliamentary scheme.*
1. PROVISION FOR ALTERING THE CONSTITUTION.	None.	Cap. 2. By consent of Protector and Parliament.
2. ELECTION OF A FUTURE PROTECTOR.	Art. 32. By the Council.	Cap. 3. By the Council, except when Parliament is sitting, and then as Parliament may think fit.
8. ELECTION OF COUNCIL.	Art. 25. Parliament to nominate six, of which the Council is to choose two, of which the Protector is to choose one.	Cap. 39. To be nominated by the Protector, and approved by Parliament.
4. TENURE OF A COUNCILLOR'S OFFICE.	Art. 25. Removable for corruption and miscarriage by a Commission of seven members of Parliament, six members of the Council, and the Chancellor. In the intervals of Parliaments may be suspended by the Council with the consent of the Protector.	Cap. 40. Not to continue in office more than forty days after the meeting of Parliament, unless approved by Parliament.
5. REVENUE.	Art. 27. Protector and Council to raise enough to support 10,000 horse and 20,000 foot, and to have £200,000 annually for purposes of government. Extraordinary forces to be paid by consent of Parliament.	Cap. 18, 48. £400,000 to be permanently assigned to the Protector for military and naval expenses, £200,000 for purposes of government, and £700,000 a year till Dec. 25, 1659.

Subject.	*Instrument of Government.*	*Parliamentary scheme.*
6. PEACE AND WAR.	Art. 5. To be declared by Protector and Council.	Cap. 52. War to be declared with consent of Parliament. Cap. 53. Peace with consent of Parliament if sitting, or if not, with consent of Council, with such restrictions as may be imposed by Parliament.
7. CONTROL OF THE ARMY.	Art. 4. Protector to dispose of the Militia and forces during the session of Parliament by consent of Parliament, and, when Parliament is not sitting, to dispose of the Militia with the consent of the Council.	Cap. 45. The Present Protector to dispose of the forces during the session with consent of Parliament. Cap. 46. When Parliament is not in session, he is to dispose of the standing forces with the consent of the Council. Cap. 48. Those forces are during the life of the present Protector to be no more in number than shall be agreed on between the Protector and the Parliament. Cap. 47. After the death of the present Protector the standing forces are to be at the disposal of the Council till Parliament meets, and then to be disposed of as Parliament shall think fit. [N.B. The Militia is expressly excluded from these forces by the final proviso of the Bill, Cap. 59. See *Commonwealth and Protectorate*, iii. 245.
8. RELIGIOUS TOLERATION.	Art. 37. Toleration of worship to be given to all such as profess faith in God by Jesus Christ, if they do not use it to the	Cap. 42, 43. Toleration of worship for those who do not use it to civil injury of others, or the disturbance of the public

Subject.	Instrument of Government.	Parliamentary scheme.
8. RELIGIOUS TOLERATION (*continued*).	civil injury of others, and the disturbance of the public peace; but this liberty is not to be extended to Popery or Prelacy, or practice of licentiousness. Art. 38. All laws contrary to this liberty are null and void.	peace. Bills, however, shall become law without the Protector's consent which restrain damnable heresies. What are damnable heresies, however, are to be agreed on by Protector and Parliament. Bills are also to become law without the Protector's consent for restraining atheism, blasphemy, popery, prelacy, licentiousness, and profaneness. Also Bills against those who publicly maintain anything contrary to the fundamental principles of doctrines publicly professed. What those doctrines are, however, is to be agreed on by the Protector and Parliament.

It will now be understood on what grounds Cromwell dissolved the House. He objected especially to the limitation of the grant of £700,000 a year being terminable in 1659, as taking military finance, and with it the control of the army, out of the hands of the Protector after that date. After this he was obliged to carry on the government without it, supplying himself with the necessary funds by the vote of the Council, according to Article 27 of the Instrument of Government. Special expenses arising from the necessity of suppressing a Royalist conspiracy were met by the imposition of a tithe on Royalists, which had no constitutional sanction at all.

Amongst the temporary Ordinances issued by the Protector before the meeting of his first Parliament was one for the union of England and Scotland (No. 99, p. 422), followed by another permanent Ordinance in accordance with Article 10 of the Instrument of Government, for the distribution of seats in Scotland. In accordance with the same article, another Ordinance was issued for the distribution of seats in Ireland (No. 100, p. 425). Irish elections, however, were only a matter of interest to the English and Scottish colony, as all Roman Catholics and all persons who had supported the late Rebellion were permanently excluded from voting.

In 1656, the Protector called a second Parliament. By excluding from it about a hundred members whom he judged to be hostile to his government, he found himself on amicable terms with the new assembly. It presented to him a Humble Petition and Advice, asking that certain changes of the Constitution might be agreed to by mutual consent, and that he should assume the title of King. This title he rejected, and the Humble Petition and Advice was passed in an amended form on May 25, 1657 (No. 102, p. 427), and at once received the assent of the Protector. On June 26, it was modified in some details by the Additional Petition and Advice (No. 103, p. 459). Taking the two together, the result was to enlarge the power of Parliament and to diminish that of the Council. The Protector, in return, received the right of appointing his successor, and to name the life-members of 'the other House,' which was now to take the place of the House of Lords.

The Parliament gained the control over its own elections, and security that its members should not be arbitrarily excluded. For the complicated scheme of nomination to the Council, which was now to be called by the old name of the Privy Council, was to be substituted nomination by the Protector, with the consent of the Council, and the subsequent consent of Parliament. The members were only to be removable with the consent of Parliament. The principle of a permanent revenue sufficient to support the government in times of peace was accepted, but the mode in which it was to be raised was to be settled by Parliament and not by the Council.

In the matter of religious liberty, the general lines of the Instrument of Government were followed ; but certain opinions were named which must be held by all whose worship was to be tolerated (§ 11).

In accordance with the Petition and Advice (No. 102, § 5, p. 452), the Protector summoned certain persons to sit in the other House (No. 103, p. 463). A quarrel between the two Houses broke out, ostensibly on points of form, but in reality on a far deeper matter. The Humble Petition and Advice had not only given the Protector the right of naming the members of the other House, but had also declared that no future members nominated by himself or by any future Protector should be allowed to take their seats without the consent of the House (No. 102, § 5, p. 452). The result would be that, as Oliver had nominated Puritans only, no persons suspected of being opposed to Puritanism would be allowed to take their seats, and that consequently a Puritan barrier would be opposed to all anti-Puritan legislation by the representative House. Any attempt to weaken this barrier which had taken the place of the articles declared in the Instrument to be unalterable by Parliament roused Oliver's deepest indignation, and without delay he dissolved the Parliament in anger in 1658. After a period of disorder following Oliver's death in the same year, Charles II was restored to the Crown. Before he arrived he issued from Breda a Declaration of the principles on which he intended to govern (No. 105, p. 465). Those principles were set forth in four articles:—1. There was to be a general amnesty, except so far as Parliament might except certain persons. 2. There was to be a liberty for tender consciences according to such laws as Parliament should propose. 3. There was to be security given for property acquired during the late troublous times, in such a way as Parliament might determine. 4. Finally, full arrears were to be paid to the soldiers according to an Act of Parliament.

The Government of the Restoration accepted as its legal

basis the Acts passed by Charles I up to the end of August, 1641. Its principle however is to be found in the answer suggested to the King by the Parliamentary Presbyterians on January 29, 1647 (No. 69, p. 309). It was the policy of trusting to free discussion and the pressure of national opinion expressed in Parliament to decide disputed questions which then got the upper hand, so far as the Parliamentary Presbyterians were concerned, over the policy of imposing fixed conditions on the exercise of the Royal power. Such a policy necessarily brought the Cavaliers and the Parliamentary Presbyterians together, and it was to this union of the Cavaliers and the Parliamentary Presbyterians that the Restoration was due. The Cavaliers obtained the restoration of Monarchy and Episcopacy with the Book of Common Prayer. The Parliamentary Presbyterians obtained the dependence of the King and Bishops on Parliamentary action. Charles II was not what Charles I had been, nor were Juxon and Sheldon what Laud had been.

Charles II dated the Declaration of Breda in the twelfth year of his reign. In this there was, no doubt, much of the usual pretensions of dethroned Kings to regard all that passes in their absence as having no existence which demands recognition. Yet it was not with Charles II as it was with Louis XVIII, in the days of the Directory, the Consulate, and the Empire. Very few in France thought in those times that Louis XVIII ought to reign; whereas there is every reason to believe that the majority of political Englishmen during the Commonwealth and Protectorate thought that Charles II ought to be their King.

If then the Restoration was founded on the abandonment of the principles which were to be found alike in the Grand Remonstrance and in the Heads of the Proposals, are we to say, as has been said, that the whole Civil War was a mistake, and that the nation ought to have been guided in the autumn of 1641 by Hyde and Falkland, as it was to their principles that the Presbyterians returned in 1647, and the whole nation except a small minority returned in 1660? If constitutional forms were everything, it would hardly be possible to avoid this conclusion. As a matter of fact, however, great as is the importance of constitutional forms, the character of the governor and the governed is of far greater importance. The action of the Long Parliament up to August, 1641, effected necessary changes in the Constitution, but could not effect a change in the character of Charles I. Hence to the demand for the alteration of the Constitution was added, in addition to a call for ecclesiastical changes, a demand less universally felt, but felt by men of sufficient ability and strength of will to give effect to their resolutions, that Charles I must either bend or break. It was this part of the Revolution which was not accomplished till the deposition of Charles I, which unhappily took the form of his execution. After that there was nothing more to be done which could possibly have any permanent effect. Commonwealth and Protectorate were alike the creation of the army: and force, whilst it is able to remove obstacles from the natural development of a nation, is powerless permanently to block the way against it. The army could take care that a man like Charles I should not rule England, but the Agreement of the People, the Instrument of Government, and the Humble Petition and Advice were but academical studies, interesting as anticipating in many respects the constitutional and political development of England and of the United States of America, but utterly incapable of commending themselves to the conscience of contemporaries.

PART I

FROM THE ACCESSION OF CHARLES I TO THE MEETING OF THE THIRD PARLIAMENT OF HIS REIGN.

1. SPEECH OF SIR NATHANIEL RICH, PROPOSING TERMS ON WHICH THE HOUSE OF COMMONS MAY BE PREPARED TO GRANT SUPPLY.

[Aug. 6, 1625. Debates in the House of Commons in 1625 (Camden Soc.), Appendix, p. 139. See *Hist. of Engl.* v. 414.]

Some moved to give, and give presently, and some would not give at all, and some would give *sub modo*; and a fourth, to which he inclineth, is:

(1) That we should first move the King for his answer to our petition [1], for we can have no hope of a blessing so long as the execrable thing remaineth amongst us, and to have His Majesty's answer in Parliament, and after a parliamentary way.

(2) And there is a necessity that His Majesty should declare the enemy to give us satisfaction, and every one may contribute his reasons, which may do much good; but the proper design no man holdeth fit should be disclosed to us.

(3) And he wisheth that when His Majesty doth make a war, it may be debated and advised by his grave Council.

(4) And there is a necessity to look into the King's estate, how it may subsist of itself, which is an old parliamentary course, and hath always been used when as any great aid hath been required of the Commons.

[1] On religion.

(5) And also to crave His Majesty's answer to the impositions ; and, as for that objection that the time is not now fitting,
and that it will require a longer time than we may sit here, he
thinketh not so, for a committee might be named to digest into
heads, which might be presented unto His Majesty, and at this
time to capitulate with the King, being[1] that never had the
subject more cause to do it than we have now.

And is this without precedent ? No, and that in the best
time, even of that most renowned King, Edward III; for he
pretending to make a war, as now our King doth, he did desire
subsidies from his subjects, and they, before they would grant it,
did capitulate with him, and you shall find by the very Act
itself, which was in the twenty-second year of his reign, that
they did grant him a subsidy, and but one ; and that upon
condition, too, that if he did not go on with his war, the grant
should cease, and the same not to be levied.

2. Protestation of the Commons.

[Aug. 12, 1625.   Debates in the House of Commons in 1625 (Camden
Soc.), p. 125.   See *Hist. of Engl.* v. 431.]

We, the knights, citizens and burgesses of the Commons'
House of Parliament, being the representative body of the
whole Commons of this realm, abundantly comforted in His
Majesty's late gracious answer touching religion, and his
message for the care of our healths, do solemnly protest and
vow before God and the world, with one heart and voice, that
we are all resolved and do hereby declare that we will ever
continue most loyal and obedient subjects to our most gracious
sovereign Lord, King Charles; and that we will be ready in
a convenient time and in a parliamentary way freely and dutifully to do our utmost endeavours to discover and reform the
abuses and grievances of the realm and state; and in like sort
to afford all necessary supply to his most excellent Majesty
upon his present and all other his just occasions and designs;
most humbly beseeching our ever dear and dread sovereign in
his princely wisdom and goodness, to rest assured of the true
and hearty affections of his poor Commons, and to esteem the

---

[1] I.e. considering.

same (as we conceive it indeed) the greatest worldly reputation and security a just King can have, and to account all such as slanderers of the people's affections and enemies to the Commonwealth, that shall dare to say the contrary.

3. DOCUMENTS RELATING TO THE IMPEACHMENT OF THE DUKE OF BUCKINGHAM.

A. *The King's reply to the Address of the House of Commons.*

[March 15, 1626.   Brit. Mus. Add. MSS., 22,474, fol. 19.   See *Hist. of Engl.* vi. 78.]

Mr. Speaker: Here is much time spent in inquiring after grievances.   I would have that last, and more time bestowed in preventing and redressing them.   I thank you all for your kind offer of supply in general, but I desire you to descend to particulars and consider of your time and measure, for it concerneth yourselves who are like first to feel it if it be too short.

But some there are—I will not say all—that do make inquiry into the proceeding, not of any ordinary servant, but of one that is most near unto me.   It hath been said, 'What shall be done to the man whom the King delighteth to honour?'   But now it is the labour of some to seek what may be done against the man whom the King thinks fit to be honoured.

In a former time, when he was the instrument to break the treaties[1], you held him worthy of all that was conferred upon him by my father.   Since that time he hath done nothing but in prosecution of what was then resolved on; and hath engaged himself, his friends, and his estate for my service, and hath done his uttermost to set it forwards; and yet you question him.   And for some particulars wherewith he hath been pressed, however he hath made his answer, certain it is that I did command him to do what he hath done therein.   I would not have the House to question my servants, much less one that is so near me.   And therefore I hope to find justice at your hands to punish such as shall offend in that kind.

[1] I.e. the negotiations with Spain, in 1624.

B. *Speeches of the King and the Lord Keeper.*

[March 29, 1626. Rushworth, i. 221 seq. See *Hist of Engl.* vi. 82.]

His Majesty begins :—

My Lords and Gentlemen: I have called you hither to-day, I mean both Houses of Parliament, but it is for several and distinct reasons . . . And you, Gentlemen of the House of Commons . . . I must tell you that I am come here to show you your errors and, as I may term them, unparliamentary proceedings in this Parliament . . .

[The Lord Keeper] . . . First His Majesty would have you to understand, That there was never any King more loving to his people, or better affectioned to the right use of Parliaments, than His Majesty hath approved himself to be, not only by his long patience since the sitting down of this Parliament, but by those mild and calm directions which from time to time that House hath received by message and letter, and from his royal mouth; when the irregular humours of some particular persons wrought diversions and distractions there, to the disturbance of those great and weighty affairs, which the necessity of the times, the honour and safety of the King and Kingdom, called upon. And therefore His Majesty doth assure you, that when these great affairs are settled, and that His Majesty hath received satisfaction of his reasonable demands, he will as a just King hear and answer your just grievances, which in a dutiful way shall be presented unto him; and this His Majesty doth avow.

Next His Majesty would have you know of a surety, That as never any King was more loving to his people, nor better affectioned to the right use of Parliaments; so never King more jealous of his honor, nor more sensible of the neglect and contempt of his royal rights, which His Majesty will by no means suffer to be violated by any pretended colour of parliamentary liberty; wherein His Majesty doth not forget that the Parliament is his council, and therefore ought to have the liberty of a council; but His Majesty understands the difference betwixt council and controlling, and between liberty and the abuse of liberty. Concerning the Duke of Buckingham, His Majesty hath commanded me to tell you, That himself doth know better than any man living the sincerity of the Duke's proceedings; with what cautions of weight and discretion he hath been guided in his public employments from His Majesty and his blessed father; what enemies he hath procured at home and abroad; what peril of his person and hazard of his estate he ran into for the service of His Majesty, and his ever blessed father; and how forward he hath been in the service of this house many times since his return from Spain : and therefore His Majesty cannot believe that the aim is at the Duke of Buckingham, but findeth that these proceedings do directly wound the honour and judgment of himself and of his father. It is therefore His Majesty's express and final commandment, That you yield obedience unto those directions which you have formerly received, and cease this unparliamentary inquisition, and commit unto His Majesty's care, and wisdom, and justice, the future reformation of these things which you suppose to be otherwise than they should be. And His Majesty is resolved, that before the end of this session, he will set such a course both for the amending of anything that may be found amiss, and for the settling of his own estate, as he doubteth not but will give you ample satisfaction and comforts.

Next to this His Majesty takes notice, That you have suffered the greatest council of State to be censured and traduced in this house, by men whose years and education cannot attain to that depth : That foreign businesses have been entertained in this house, to the hindrance and disadvantage of His Majesty's negociations : That the same year, yea the first day of His Majesty's inauguration, you suffered his council, government and servants to be paralleled with the times of most exception : That your committees have presumed to examine the letters of Secretaries of State, nay his own, and sent a general warrant to his Signet Office not only to produce and shew the records, but their books and private notes made for His Majesty's service. This His Majesty holds as unsufferable, as it was in former times unusual.

Then His Majesty spake again :—

I must withall put you in mind a little of times past ; you may remember, that in the time of my blessed father, you did with your council and persuasion persuade both my father and me to break off the treaties. I confess I was your instrument for two reasons; one was, the fitness of the time; the other because I was seconded by so great and worthy a body, as the whole body of Parliament; then there was nobody in so great favour with you as this man whom you seem now to touch, but indeed, my father's government and mine. Now that you have all things according to your wishes, and that I am so far engaged, that you think there is no retreat; now you begin to set the dice, and make your own game; but I pray you be not deceived, it is not a parliamentary way, nor is it a way to deal with a King.

Mr. Cook told you, It was better to be eaten up by a foreign enemy, than to be destroyed at home; Indeed, I think it more honour for a King to be invaded, and almost destroyed by a foreign enemy, than to be despised by his own subjects.

Remember that Parliaments are altogether in my power for their calling, sitting and dissolution; therefore as I find the fruits of them good or evil, they are to continue or not to be; And remember, that if in this time, instead of mending your errors, by delay you persist in your errors, you make them greater and irreconcileable. Whereas on the other side, if you go on cheerfully to mend them, and look to the distressed state of Christendom, and the affairs of the Kingdom as it lyeth now by this great engagement; you will do yourselves honour, you shall encourage me to go on with Parliaments; and I hope all Christendom shall feel the good of it.

C. *Remonstrance of the House of Commons.*

[April 5, 1626. Rushworth, i. 243 seq. See *Hist. of Engl.* vi. p. 85 [1].]

Most Gracious Sovereign... Concerning your Majesty's servants and, namely, the Duke of Buckingham, we humbly beseech your Majesty to be informed by us your faithful Commons . . . that it hath been the ancient, constant and undoubted right and usage of Parliaments, to question and complain of all persons, of what degree soever, found grievous to the commonwealth, in abusing the power and trust committed to them by their sovereign . . . without which liberty in Parliament no private man, no servant to a King, perhaps no councillor, without exposing himself to

---

[1] The date there given of April 4 is incorrect.

the hazard of great enmity and prejudice, can be a means to
call great officers into question for their misdemeanours, but
the commonwealth might languish under their pressures without
redress: and whatsoever we shall do accordingly in this Parliament, we doubt not but it shall redound to the honour of the
Crown, and welfare of your subjects . . .

D. *The Commons' Declaration and Impeachment against the
Duke of Buckingham.*

[Presented to the House of Lords, May 10, 1626. Lords' Journals,
iii. 619. See *Hist. of Engl.* vi. 98–107.]

For the speedy redress of great evils and mischiefs, and of
the chief of these evils and mischiefs, which this kingdom
of England now grievously suffereth; and of late years hath
suffered, and to the honour and safety of our Sovereign Lord
the King, and of his crown and dignity, and to the good and
welfare of his people; the Commons in this present Parliament,
by the authority of our said Sovereign Lord the King assembled,
do, by this their bill, shew and declare against George, Duke,
Marquis and Earl of Buckingham, Earl of Coventry, Viscount
Villiers, Baron of Whaddon, Great Admiral of the kingdoms of
England and Ireland, and of the principality of Wales and of
the dominions and islands of the same, of the town of Calais
and of the marches of the same, and of Normandy, Gascony,
and Guienne, General Governor of the seas and ships of the
said Kingdoms, Lieutenant General, Admiral, Captain General
and Governor of His Majesty's Royal Fleet and Army, lately set
forth, Master of the Horse of our Sovereign Lord the King,
Lord Warden, Chancellor, and Admiral of the Cinque Ports
and of the members thereof, Constable of Dover Castle, Justice
in Eyre of all the forests and chases on this side of the river of
Trent, Constable of the Castle of Windsor, Gentleman of His
Majesty's Bedchamber, one of His Majesty's most Honourable
Privy Council in his realms both in England, Scotland and
Ireland, and Knight of the most Honourable Order of the
Garter; the misdemeanours, misprisions, offences, crimes, and
other matters, comprised in the articles hereafter following;

and him the said Duke do accuse and impeach of the said misdemeanours, misprisions, offences and crimes.

1. First, that whereas the great offices expressed in the said Duke's style and title have been the singular preferments of several persons eminent in wisdom and trust, and fully able for the weighty service and greatest employment of the State, whereby the said offices were both carefully and sufficiently executed, by several persons of such wisdom, trust, and ability; and others also that were employed by the royal progenitors of our Sovereign Lord the King, in places of less dignity, were much encouraged with the hopes of advancement; and whereas divers of the said places, severally of themselves, and necessarily, require the whole care, industry, and attendance of a most able person; he the said Duke, being young and inexperienced, hath of late years, with exorbitant ambition and for his own profit and advantage, procured and engrossed into his own hands the said several offices both to the danger of the State, the prejudice of that service which should have been performed in them, and to the great discouragement of others, that, by this procuring and engrossing of the said offices, are precluded from such hopes, as their virtues, abilities and public employments might otherwise have given them.

2. Whereas by the laws and statutes of this kingdom of England, if any person whatsoever give or pay any sum of money, fee or reward, directly or indirectly, for any office or offices, which in any wise touch or concern the administration of justice, or the keeping of any of the King's Majesty's towns, fortresses, or castles, being used, occupied or appointed as places of strength and defence, the same person is immediately, upon the same fee, money or reward, given or paid, to be adjudged a disabled person in the law to all intents and purposes, to have, occupy, and enjoy the said office or offices, for the which he so giveth or payeth any sum of money, fee or reward; he the said Duke did, in or about the month of January, in the sixteenth year of the late King James, of famous memory, give and pay unto the Right Honourable Charles then Earl of Nottingham, for the office of Great Admiral of England and Ireland, and the principality of Wales, and office of the General Governor of the seas and ships, to the intent that the said Duke

might obtain the said offices to his own use, the sum of three thousand pounds of lawful money of England; and did also about the same time, procure from the said King a further reward, for the surrender of the said office to the said Earl, of an annuity of a thousand pounds by the year, for and during the life of the said Earl; and, by the procurement of the said Duke the said King of famous memory, did by his letters patents, dated the 27th day of January, in the said year of his reign, under the Great Seal of England, grant to the said Earl the said annuity, which he the said Earl accordingly had and enjoyed during his life; and, by reason of the said sum of money so as aforesaid paid by the said Duke, and of his the said Duke's procurement of the said annuity, the said Earl of Nottingham did, in the same month, surrender unto the said late King of famous memory, his said offices, and his letters patents of them; and thereupon, and by reason of the premises, the said offices were obtained by the said Duke, for his life, from the said King of famous memory, by letters patents made to the said Duke of the same offices under the Great Seal of England, dated the 28th day of January, in the said sixteenth year of the said King of famous memory: And the said offices of Great Admiral and Governor, as aforesaid, are offices that highly touch and concern the administration and execution of justice, within the provision of the said laws and statutes of this realm; which notwithstanding, the said Duke hath unlawfully, ever since the first unlawful obtaining of the said grant of the said offices, retained in his hands, and exercised them against the laws and statutes aforesaid.

3. The said Duke did likewise, in and about the month of December, in the twenty-second year of the said late King James, of famous memory, give and pay unto the Right Honourable Edward late Lord Zouch, Lord Warden of the Cinque Ports, and of the members thereof, and Constable of the Castle of Dover, for the said offices, and for the surrender of the said offices of Lord Warden of the Cinque Ports and Constable of the said Castle of Dover to be made to the said late King, of famous memory, the sum of one thousand pounds of lawful money of England; and then also granted an annuity of five hundred pounds yearly to the said Lord Zouch, for the

life of the said Lord Zouch, to the intent that he the said Duke might thereby obtain the said offices to his own use; and for and by reason of the said sum of money so paid by the said Duke, and of the annuity so granted to the said Edward Lord Zouch the fourth day of December, in the year aforesaid, did surrender his said offices, and his letters patents of them, to the said late King; and thereupon, and by reason of the premises, he the said Duke obtained the said offices for his life from the late king, by his letters patents under the Great Seal of England, dated the sixth day of December, in the said twenty-second year. And the said office of the Lord Warden of the Cinque Ports, and of the members thereof, is an office that doth highly touch and concern administration of justice; and the said office of Constable of the Castle of Dover is an office that highly concerneth the keeping and defence of the town and port, and of the said Castle of Dover, which is and hath ever been, appointed a most eminent place of strength and defence of this kingdom; which notwithstanding, the said Duke hath unlawfully, ever since his first unlawful obtaining of the said offices, retained them in his hands, and executed them against the laws and statutes aforesaid.

4. Whereas the said Duke, by reason of his said offices of Great Admiral of the kingdoms of England and Ireland, and of the principality of Wales, and of Admiral of the Cinque Ports, and General Governor of the seas and ships of the said kingdoms, and by reason of the trust thereunto belonging, ought at all times since the said offices obtained, to have safely guarded, kept and preserved the said seas, and the dominion of them; and ought also, whensoever there wanted men, ships, munition or other strength whatsoever that might conduce to the better safe-guard of them, to have used, from time to time, his utmost endeavour, for the supply of such wants to the Right Honourable the Lords and others of the Privy Council, and by procuring such supply from his sovereign or otherwise; he the said Duke hath ever since the dissolution of the two treaties mentioned in the Act of Subsidy of the one and twentieth year of the late King, of famous memory, that is to say, the space of two years last past, neglected the just performance of his said office and duty; and broken the said trust therewith committed

unto him; and hath not, according to his said offices, during
the time aforesaid, safely kept the said seas, in so much that,
by reason of his neglect and default therein, not only the trade
and strength of this kingdom of England hath been, during the
said time, much decayed, but the same seas also have been, during
the same time, ignominiously infested by pirates and enemies, to
the loss both of very many ships and goods, and of many of the
subjects of our Sovereign Lord the King; and the dominion of the
said seas being the undoubted patrimony of the Kings of England,
is thereby also in most eminent danger to be utterly lost.

5. Whereas, about Michaelmas last year, a ship, called the
St. Peter of Newhaven [1] (whereof John Mallewe was master)
laden with divers goods, merchandises, monies, jewels and
commodities, to the value of forty thousand pounds or thereabouts, for the proper account of Monsieur de Villiers, the
then Governor of Newhaven, and other subjects of the French
king, being in perfect amity and league with our Sovereign
Lord the King, was taken at sea, by some of the ships of His
Majesty's late fleet, set forth under the command of the said
Duke, as well by direction from the said Duke as Great
Admiral of England as by the authority of the extraordinary
commission which he then had, for the command of the said
fleet; and was by them, together with the said goods and
lading, brought into the port of Plymouth, as a prize, amongst
many others, upon probabilities that the said ship or goods
belonged to the subjects of the King of Spain; and that divers
parcels of the said goods and loading were thence taken out of
the said ship of St. Peter's; that is to say sixteen barrels of
cochineal, eight bags of gold, three and twenty bags of silver,
two boxes of pearls and emeralds, a chain of gold, jewels,
monies, and commodities, to the value of twenty thousand
pounds or thereabouts; and by the said Duke were delivered
into the private custody of one Gabriel Marsh, servant to the
said Duke; and that the said ship with the residue of her
said goods and lading, was sent from thence up the river of
Thames; and there detained; whereupon there was an arrest
at Newhaven, in the kingdom of France, on the seventh day
of December last, of two English merchant ships trading

[1] I.e. Havre de Grâce.

thither, as was alledged in a certain petition by some English merchants trading into France, to the Lords and others of His Majesty's most honourable Privy Council. After which, that is to say, on the 28th day of the said month, His Majesty was pleased to order, with the advice of his Privy Council, that the said ship and goods belonging to the subjects of the French king, should be re-delivered to such as should re-claim them; and accordingly information was given unto His Majesty's Advocate, in the Chief Court of Admiralty, by the Right Honourable Sir John Coke, Knight, one of His Majesty's principal secretaries of state, for the freeing and discharging of the said ship and goods in the said Court of Admiralty. And afterwards, that is to say on the six and twentieth day of January last, it was decreed in the said Court, by the judge thereof, with the consent of the said advocate, that the said ship with whatsoever goods as seized or taken in her (except three hundred Mexico hides, sixteen sacks of ginger, one box of gilt beads, and five sacks of ginger more, mentioned in the said decree), should be clearly released from further detention, and delivered to the said master; and therefore a commission under seal was in that behalf duly sent out of the said Court unto Sir Allen Apsley, Sir John Wolstenholme, and others, for the due execution thereof: the said Duke, notwithstanding the said order, commission and decree, detained still to his own use the said gold, silver, pearls, emeralds, jewels, monies, and commodities, so taken out of the said ship as aforesaid; and for his own singular avail and covetise, on the sixth day of February last, having no information of any new proof, without any legal proceedings, by colour of his said office, unjustly caused the ship and goods to be again arrested and detained in public violation and contempt of the laws and statutes of this land, to the great disturbance of trade, and prejudice of the merchant.

6. Whereas the honour, wealth and strength of this realm of England is much increased by the traffic chiefly of such merchants as employ and build great warlike ships, a consideration that should move all Councillors of State, especially the Lord Admiral, to cherish and maintain such merchants; the said Duke, abusing the Lords of the Parliament in the twenty-

first year of the late King James, of famous memory, with pretence of serving the State, did oppress the East Indian merchants, and extorted from them ten thousand pounds, in the subtle and unlawful manner following:—About February, in the year aforesaid, he the said Duke, hearing some good success that those merchants had at Ormuz, in parts beyond the seas; by his agents, cunningly, in or about the month aforesaid, in the said year of the said King, endeavoured to draw from them some great sum of money; which their poverty and no gain by that success at Ormuz, made those merchants absolutely deny; whereupon he the said Duke, perceiving that the said merchants were then setting forth in the course of their trade, four ships and two pinnaces, laden with goods and merchandize of very great value, like to lose their voyage if they should not speedily depart; the said Duke, on the first day of March then following, in the said year of the said late King did move the Lords then assembled in the said Parliament, whether he should make stay of any ships which were in the ports (as being High Admiral he might); and namely those ships prepared for the East India voyage, which were of great burthen and well furnished; which motion being approved by their lordships, the Duke did stay those ships accordingly: But the fifth of March following, when the then deputy of that company, with other of those merchants, did make suit to the said Duke for the release of the said ships and pinnaces, he the said Duke said, he had not been the occasion of their staying; but that, having heard the motion with much earnestness in the Lords' House of Parliament, he could do no less than give the order they had done; and therefore he willed them to set down the reasons of their suit, which he would acquaint the house withall; yet in the mean time he gave them leave to let their said ships and pinnaces down as low as Tilbury. And the tenth of March following, an unusual joint action was, by his procurement, entered in the chief Court of Admiralty, in the name of the said late King, and of the Lord Admiral, against fifteen thousand pounds, taken piratically by some captains of the said merchant ships, and pretended to be in the hands of the East India Company; and thereupon the King's Advocate, in the name of advocate from the King and the said Lord Admiral, moved and obtained one attachment, which by the Sergeant of the said Court of Admiralty was served on the said merchants, in their court, the sixteenth day of March following : Whereupon the said merchants, though there was no cause for this their molestation by the Lord Admiral, yet the next day they were urged in the said Court of Admiralty to bring in the fifteen thousand pounds or go to prison; wherefore immediately the company of the said merchants did again send the deputy aforesaid and some others, to make new suit unto the said Duke, for the release of the said ships and pinnaces, who unjustly endeavouring to extort money from the said merchants protested that the ships should not go, except they compounded with him; and when they urged many more reasons for the release of the said ships and pinnaces, the answer of the said Duke was, that the then Parliament House must be first moved. The said merchants being in this perplexity in their consultation, the three and twentieth of that month, ever ready to give over that trade; yet, considering that they should lose more than was demanded, by unloading their ships, besides their voyage, they resolved to give the said Duke ten thousand pounds for his unjust demands; and he the said Duke by the undue means aforesaid, and under colour of his office and upon false pretence of rights, unjustly did exact and extort from them the said merchants, the said ten thousand pounds, and received the same about the twenty-eighth of April following the discharge of those ships; which were not released by him, till they the said merchants had yielded to give him the said Duke the said ten thousand pounds for the said release, and for the false pretence of rights made by the said Duke as aforesaid.

7. Whereas the ships of our Sovereign Lord the King and of his kingdoms aforesaid are the principal strength and defence of the said kingdoms and ought therefore to be always preserved, and safely kept, under the command, and for the service of our said Sovereign Lord the King, no less than any of the fortresses and castles of the said kingdoms; and whereas no subject of this realm ought to be dispossessed of any of his goods or chattels, without order of justice, or his own consent first duly had and obtained; the said Duke,

being Great Admiral of England, Governor General and keeper
of the said ships and seas, and thereof ought to have and
take especial and continual care and diligence how to preserve
the same; the said Duke, on or about the end of July last,
in the first year of our Sovereign Lord the King, did, under
the colour of the said office of Great Admiral of England,
and by indirect and subtle means and practices, procure one
of the principal ships of His Majesty's navy royal, called the
Vanguard, then under the command of Captain John Pen-
nington, and six other merchant ships of great burthen and
value, belonging to several persons inhabiting in London, the
natural subjects of His Majesty, to be conveyed over, with all
their ordnance, ammunition, tackle and apparel, into the ports
of the kingdom of France, to the end that being there, they
might be more easily put into the hands of the French king,
his ministers and subjects, and taken into their possession,
command and power; and accordingly the said Duke, by his
ministers and agents with menaces and other ill means and
practices, did there, without order of justice, and without
the consent of the said masters and owners unduly compel
and enforce the said masters and owners of the said six
merchant ships to deliver their said ships into the said possession, command and power of the said French king, his
ministers and subjects; and by reason of this compulsion, and
under the pretext of his power as aforesaid, and by his indirect
practices as aforesaid, the said ships aforesaid, as well the
said ship royal of His Majesty, as the others belonging to the
said merchants, were there delivered into the hands and command of the said French king his ministers and subjects,
without either sufficient security or assurance for re-delivery,
or other necessary condition in that behalf taken or propounded,
either by the said Duke himself, or otherwise by his direction,
contrary to the duty of the said offices of Great Admiral,
Governor General and keeper of the said ships and seas, and
to the faith and trust in that behalf reposed, and contrary
to the duty which he owed our Sovereign Lord the King in
his place of Privy Councillor, to the apparent weakening of
the naval strength of this kingdom, to the great loss and
prejudice of the said merchants, and against the liberty of

those subjects of our Sovereign Lord the King that are under the jurisdiction of the Admiralty.

8. The said Duke, contrary to the purpose of our Sovereign Lord the King and His Majesty's known zeal for the maintenance and advancement of the true religion established in the church of England, knowing the said ships were intended to be employed by the said French king against those of the same religion at Rochelle, and elsewhere in the kingdom of France, did procure the said ship royal, and compel as aforesaid the six other ships to be delivered unto the said French king's ministers and subjects as aforesaid, to the end that the said ships might be used and employed by the said French king, in his intended war against those of the said religion, in the said town of Rochelle, and elsewhere in the kingdom of France, and the said ships were, and have been since, so used and employed by the said French king, his subjects and ministers against them; and this the said Duke did as aforesaid, in great and most apparent prejudice of the said religion, contrary to the purpose and intention of our Sovereign Lord the King, and against his duty in that behalf, being a sworn councillor to His Majesty, and to the great scandal and dishonour of this nation; and notwithstanding the delivery of the said ships by his procurement and compulsion as aforesaid, to be employed as aforesaid, the said Duke in cunning and cautelous manner to mask his ill intentions, did at the parliament held at Oxon., in August last, before the committees of both Houses of the said Parliament intimate and declare, that the ships were not, nor should they be, so used and employed against those of the said religion, as aforesaid, in contempt of our Sovereign Lord the King, and in abuse of the said Houses of Parliament, and in violation of that truth which every man should profess.

9. Whereas the titles of honour of this kingdom of England were wont to be conferred as great rewards, upon such virtuous and industrious persons as had merited them by their faithful service; the said Duke by his importunate and subtle procurement, hath not only perverted that ancient and most honourable way, but also unduly for his own particular gain, he hath enforced some that were rich (though unwilling) to

purchase honour, as the Lord Robartes, Baron of Truro, who, by practice of the said Duke and his agents, was drawn up to London, in or about October, in the two and twentieth year of the reign of the late King James of famous memory, and there so threatened and dealt withall, that by reason thereof, he yielded to give, and accordingly did pay the sum of ten thousand pounds to the said Duke and to his use, for which said sum the said Duke, in the month of January, the two and twentieth year of the said late King, procured the title of Baron Robartes of Truro, to the said Lord Robartes; in which practice as the said Lord Robartes was much wronged in his particular, so the example thereof tendeth to the prejudice of the gentry and dishonour of the nobility of this kingdom.

10. Whereas no places of judicature, in the courts of justice of our Sovereign Lord the King, or other like preferments given by the Kings of this realm, ought to be procured by any subjects whatsoever, for any reward, bribe, or gift; he the said Duke in or about the month of December, in the eighteenth year of the reign of the late King James of famous memory, did procure of the said King the office of High Treasurer of England to the Lord Viscount Mandeville, now Earl of Manchester; which office at his procurement was given and granted accordingly to the Lord Viscount Mandeville; and as a reward for the said procurement of the same grant, he the said Duke, did then receive to his own use, of and from him the said Lord Viscount Mandeville, the sum of twenty thousand pounds, of lawful money of England. And also in or about the month of January in the sixteenth year of the said late King did procure of the said King of famous memory, the office of Master of the Wards and Liveries to and for Sir Lionel Cranfield, afterwards Earl of Middlesex, which office was upon the same procurement given and granted to the said Sir Lionel Cranfield; and as a reward for the same procurement, he the said Duke had to his own use or the use of some other person by him appointed, of the said Sir Lionel Cranfield, the sum of six thousand pounds of lawful money of England, contrary to the dignity of our Sovereign Lord the King, and against the duty which should have been performed by the said Duke unto him.

11. That he the said Duke hath within these ten years last past, procured divers titles of honour to his mother, brothers, kindred, and allies; as the title of Countess of Buckingham to his mother, whilst she was Sir Thomas Compton's wife; the title of Earl of Anglesea to his younger brother Christophei Villiers; the titles of Baron of Newnham Paddox, Viscount Feilding and the Earl of Denbigh to his sister's husband, Sir William Feilding; the title of Baron of Stoke, and Viscount Purbeck, to Sir John Villiers, elder brother of the said Duke, and divers more of the like kind to his kindred and allies; whereby the noble Barons of England, so well deserving in themselves and in their ancestors, have been much prejudiced, and the Crown disabled to reward extraordinary virtues in future times with honour; while the poor estate of those for whom such unnecessary advancement hath been procured is apparently likely to be more and more burdensome to the King; notwithstanding such annuities, pensions, and grants of lands annexed to the Crown, of great value, which the said Duke hath procured for those his kindred, to support their dignities.

12. He the said Duke not contented with the great advancement formerly received from the late King, of famous memory, by his procurement and practice, in the fourteenth year of the said King, for the support of the many places, honours, and dignities conferred on him, did obtain a grant of divers manors, parcel of the revenue of the Crown, and of the Duchy of Lancaster, to the yearly value of one thousand six hundred and ninety-seven pounds, two shillings, half-penny farthing of the old rent, with all woods, timber, trees, and advowsons; part whereof amounting to the sum of seven hundred forty seven pounds, thirteen shillings, and four pence, was rated at two and thirty thousand pounds, but in truth of a far greater value; and likewise, in the sixteenth year of the same King's reign, did procure divers other manors, annexed to the Crown, of the yearly value at the old rent of twelve hundred pounds or thereabouts, according as in a schedule hereunto annexed appeareth; in the warrant for passing of which lands he by his great favour, procured divers unusual clauses to be inserted; *videlicet*, that no perquisites of courts should be valued and that all bailiffs' fees should be reprised in the particulars upon which those

lands were rated; whereby a precedent hath been introduced, which all those that since that time have obtained any lands from the Crown have pursued to the damage of his late Majesty, and of our Sovereign Lord the King that now is, to an exceeding great value; and afterwards he surrendered to his said Majesty divers manors and lands, parcel of those lands formerly granted unto him to the value of seven hundred twenty three pounds, eighteen shillings, two pence half-penny per annum; in consideration of which surrender, he procured divers other lands of the said late King, to be sold and contracted for by his own servants and agents; and thereupon hath obtained grants of the same, to pass from his late Majesty to several persons of this Kingdom, and hath caused tallies to be strucken for the money, being the consideration mentioned in these grants in the receipt of the exchequer, as if such money had really come to his Majesty's coffers; whereas the said Duke (or some other by his appointment) hath indeed received the same sums, and expended them upon his own occasions; and, notwithstanding the great and inestimable gain by him made by the sale of offices, honours, and by other suits by him obtained from His Majesty and for the countenancing of divers projects and other courses burthensome to His Majesty's realms both of England and Ireland; the said Duke hath likewise, by his procurement and practice, received into his hands, and disbursed unto his own use, exceeding great sums, that were the monies of the late King, of famous memory, as appeareth also in the said schedule hereunto annexed; and the better to colour his doings in that behalf, hath obtained several privy seals from his late Majesty, and His Majesty that now is, warranting the payment of great sums to persons by him named, causing it to be recited in such privy seals, as if those sums were directed for secret services concerning the State, which were notwithstanding disposed of to his own use, and other privy seals by him procured for the discharge of those persons without accompt; and by the like fraud and practice, under colour of free gifts from His Majesty, he hath gotten into his hands great sums, which were intended by His Majesty be be disbursed for the preparing, furnishing and victualling of his royal navy; by which secret and colourable devices the constant and ordinary course of the exchequer hath been broken, there being no means by matter of record, to charge either treasurer or victualler of the navy with those sums which ought to have come to their hands, and to be accounted for to His Majesty; and such a confusion and mixture hath been made between the King's estate and the Duke's as cannot be cleared by the legal entries and records, which ought to be truly and faithfully made and kept, both for the safety of His Majesty's treasure and for the indemnity of his officers and subjects, whom it doth concern: and also in the sixteenth year of the said King, and in the twentieth year of the said King, did procure to himself several releases from the said King, of divers great sums of the money of the said King by him privately received; and which he procured that he might detain the same for the support of his places, honours, and dignities; and those things, and divers others of the like kind, as appeareth in the said schedule annexed, hath he done, to the exceeding diminution of the revenues of the Crown, and in deceit both of our Sovereign Lord the King that now is, and of the late King James of famous memory; and to the great detriment of the whole kingdom.

13. Whereas especial care and order hath been taken by the laws of this realm to restrain and prevent the unskilful administration of physic whereby the health and life of man may be much endangered ; and whereas most especially the royal persons of kings of this realm, in whom we their loyal subjects humbly challenge a great interest, are and always have been, esteemed by us so sacred, that nothing ought to be prepared for them, or administered unto them, in the way of physic or diet, in the times of their sickness, without the consent of some of their sworn physicians, apothecaries, or surgeons ; and the boldness of such (how near soever unto them in place and favour) who have forgotten their duty so far as to presume to offer any thing unto them beyond their experience, hath been always ranked in the number of high offences [1] and misdemeanours; and whereas the sworn physicians of our late Sovereign Lord King James of blessed memory, attending on His Majesty in the month of March, in the two and twentieth of his most gracious reign, in the times of his sickness, being an ague, did, in due

---

[1] 'Offenders,' in L. J.

and necessary care of and for the recovery of his health and preservation of his person, upon and after several mature consultations in that behalf had and holden, at several times in the same month, resolve and give directions, that nothing should be applied or given unto His Highness by way of physic or diet during his said sickness, but by and upon their general advice and consents, and after good deliberation thereof first had; more especially, by their like care, and upon like consultations, did justly resolve, and publicly give warning to and for all the gentlemen, and other servants and officers, of his said late Majesty's bed-chamber, that no meat or drink whatsoever should be given unto him within two or three hours before the usual time of and for the coming of his fit in the said ague, nor during the continuance thereof, nor afterwards untill his cold fit were past; the said Duke of Buckingham, being a sworn servant of his late Majesty, of and in His Majesty's said bed-chamber, contrary to his duty and the tender respect which he ought to have had of his most sacred person, and after the consultations, resolutions, directions, and warning aforesaid, did nevertheless, without any sufficient warrant in that behalf, unduly cause and procure certain plaisters and a certain drink or potion, to be provided for the use of his said Majesty, without the direction or privity of his said late Majesty's physicians, not prepared by any of His Majesty's sworn apothecaries or surgeons, but compounded of several ingredients to them unknown; notwithstanding the same plaister, or some plaister like thereunto, having been formerly administered unto his said Majesty, did procure such ill effects as that some of the said sworn physicians did altogether disallow thereof, and utterly refuse to meddle any further with his said Majesty until those plaisters were removed, as being prejudicial to the health of His Majesty; yet nevertheless the same plaister, as also a drink or potion, was provided by the said Duke, which he the said Duke by colour of some insufficient and slight pretences, did upon Monday the one and twentieth day of March in the two and twentieth year aforesaid, when His Majesty (by the judgment of his said physicians) was in the declination of his disease, cause and procure the said plaister to be applied to the breast and wrists of his said late Majesty; and then also at and in His Majesty's fit of the said ague, the same Monday, and at several times within two hours of the coming of the same fit, and before His Majesty's then cold fit was passed, did deliver and cause to be delivered several quantities of the said drink or potion to his late Majesty; who thereupon, at the same times, within the seasons in that behalf prohibited by His Majesty's physicians as aforesaid did, by the means and procurement of the said Duke, drink and take divers quantities of the said drink or potion applied and given unto and taken and received by his said Majesty as aforesaid, great distempers and divers ill symptoms appeared upon his said Majesty, insomuch that the said physicians, finding His Majesty the next morning much worse in the estate of his health, and holding a consultation thereabouts, did by joint consent, send unto the said Duke, praying him not to adventure to minister unto His Majesty any more physic, without their allowance and approbation, and his said Majesty himself, finding himself much diseased and affected with pain and sickness after his then fit, when, by the course of his disease, he expected intermission and ease, did attribute the cause of such his trouble unto the said plaister and drink, which the said Duke had so given and caused to be administered unto him.   Which said adventurous act, by a person obliged in duty and thankfulness, done to the person of so great a King, after so ill success of the like formerly administered, contrary to such directions as aforesaid, and accompanied with so unhappy an event, to the great grief and discomfort of all His Majesty's subjects in general, is an offence and misdemeanour of so high a nature, as may justly be called, and is by the said Commons deemed to be, an act of transcendent presumption and of dangerous consequence.

And the said Commons by protestation saving to themselves the liberty of exhibiting at any time hereafter any other accusation or impeachment against the said Duke, and also of replying to the answers that the said Duke shall make unto the said articles, or to any of them, and of offering further proof also of the premises, or any of them, as the case shall (according to the course of Parliament) require, do pray that the said Duke may be put to answer to all and every the premises; and that such proceeding, examination, trial, and judgment, may be upon every of them had and used, as is agreeable to law and justice.

E. *The humble answer and plea of George Duke of Buckingham,*
to the declaration and impeachment made against him before
your Lordships, by the Commons House of Parliament.

[Presented to the House of Lords, June 8, 1626. Lords' Journals, iii. 656.
See *Hist. of Engl.* vi. 116.]

The said Duke of Bucks being accused, and sought to be
impeached before your Lordships of the many misdemeanours,
misprisions, offences, and crimes, wherewith he is charged by
the Commons House of Parliament, and which are comprised in
the articles preferred against him, and were aggravated by those
whose service was used by that house in the delivery of them;
doth find in himself an unexpressible pressure of deep and hearty
sorrow, that so great and so worthy a body should hold him
suspected of those things that are objected against him;
whereas had that honourable house first known the very truth
of those particulars, whereof they had not there the means to
be rightly informed, he is well assured, in their own true
judgments, they would have forborne to have charged him
therewith. But the integrity of his own heart and conscience,
being the most able and most impartial witness, not accusing
him of the least thought of disloyalty to his sovereigns or to his
country, doth raise his spirits again to make his just defence
before your Lordships; of whose wisdom, justice, and honour,
he is so well assured, that he doth with confidence and yet with
all humbleness, submit himself and his cause to your examinations and judgments; before whom he shall, with all sincerity and
clearness, unfold and lay open the secrets of his actions and of his
heart; and, in his answer, shall not affirm the least substantial,
and as near as he can the least circumstantial point, which he
doth not believe he shall clearly prove before your Lordships.

The charge consisteth of thirteen several articles; whereunto
the Duke, saving to himself the usual benefit of not
being prejudiced by any words or want of form in his
answer, but that he might be admitted to make further
explanation and proof as there shall be occasion; and
saving to himself all privileges and rights belonging
to him as one of the peers of the realm; doth make
these several and distinct answers following, in the same
order they are laid down unto him :—

1. To the first which concerneth the plurality of offices which he holdeth, he answereth thus: That it is true he holdeth those several places and offices which are enumerated in the preamble of his charge; whereof only three are worthy the name of offices; *videlicet*, the Admiralty, the Wardenship of the Cinque Ports, and Mastership of the Horse. The others are rather titulary, and additions of honour. For these offices he humbly and freely acknowledgeth the bounty and goodness of His Most Gracious Majesty who is with God; who, when he had cast an eye of favour upon him, and had taken him into a more near place of service about his royal person, was more willing to multiply his graces and favours upon him than the Duke was forward to ask them; and for the most part, as many honourable persons, and his own most excellent Majesty above all others can best testify, did prevent the very desires of the Duke in asking.

And all these particular places he can and doth truly affirm, his late Majesty did bestow them of his own royal motion (except the Wardenship of the Cinque Ports only), and thereto also he gave his approbation and encouragement. And the Duke denieth that he obtained these places either to satisfy his exorbitant ambition or his own profit or advantage, as is objected against him; and he hopeth he shall give good satisfaction to the contrary, in his particular answers ensuing, touching the manner of his obtaining the places of Admiralty, and the Wardenship of the Cinque Ports; whereunto he humbly desireth to refer himself. And for the Mastership of the Horse to His Majesty, he saith it is a mere domestic office of attendance upon the King's person, whereby he receiveth some profit, yet but as a conveniency to render him more fit for his continual attendance. And in that place, the times compared, he hath retrenched the King's annual charge to a considerable value, as shall be made apparent. And for the number of places he holdeth, he saith that, if the Commonwealth doth not suffer thereby, he hopeth he may, without blame, receive and retain that which the liberal and bountiful hand of his master hath freely conferred upon him; and it is not without many precedents, both in ancient and modern times, that one man eminent in the esteem of his sovereign, hath at one time held as great and as many offices; but when it shall be discerned that he shall falsify or corruptly use those places or any of them, or that the public shall suffer thereby, he is so thankful for what he hath freely received, that, whensoever his gracious master shall require it, without disputing with his sovereign, he will readily lay down at his royal feet, not only his places and offices, but his whole fortunes and his life to do him service.

2. For his buying of the Admiral's place, the said Duke maketh this clear and true answer:—

That it is true, that in January, in the sixteenth year of his late Majesty's reign, his late Majesty by his letters patent under the great seal of England, granted unto the Duke the office of Admiralty, for his life, which grant, as he well knoweth it was made freely, and without any contract or bargain with the late Lord Admiral, or any other, and upon the voluntary surrender of that noble and well-deserving lord, so he is advised it will appear to be free from any defect in law, by reason of the statute of 5 Ed. VI, mentioned in this article of his charge, or of any other cause whatsoever. For he saith, that the true manner of his buying this office, and of all the passages thereof, which he is ready to make good by proof, was thus: That honourable lord, the Earl of Nottingham, then Lord Admiral, being grown so much in years, and finding that he was not then so able to perform that which appertained to his place, as in former times he had done to his great honour, and fearing lest His Majesty's service and commonwealth might suffer by his defeat, became an humble and earnest petitioner to his late Majesty, to admit him to surrender his office. His late Majesty was, at the first, unwilling unto it, out of his royal affection to his person, and true judgment of his worth. But the Earl renewed his petitions, and in some of them nominated the Duke to be his successor, without the Duke's privity or forethought of it. And about that time a gentleman of good place about the Navy, and of long experience, of himself came to the Duke, and earnestly moved him to undertake the place. The Duke apprehending the weight of the place, and considering his young years and want of experience to manage so great a charge, gave no ear unto it; but excused it, not for form, but really and ingenuously out of his apprehension of his then unfitness for it. This gentleman not thus satisfied, without the

Duke [1] applied himself to the late King, and moved His Majesty therein, and offered reasons for it, that the Duke was the fittest man at that time, and as the state of the Navy then stood, for that place; for he said it was then a time of peace; that the best service could be done for the present was to repair the navy and ships royal, which then were much in decay, and to retrench the king's charge, and to employ it effectually; and that before there was personal use of service otherwise, the Duke, being young and active might gain experience, and make himself as fit as any other; and that, in the mean time, none was so fit as himself, having the opportunity of His Majesty's favour, and nearness to his person, to procure a constant assignment and payment of monies for the navy, the want whereof was the greatest cause of the former defects.   These reasons persuaded his late Majesty, and upon His Majesty's own motion, persuaded the Duke to take the charge upon him.   And therefore the Earl, voluntarily, freely and willingly, and upon his own earnest and often suit, surrendered his place, without any precedent contract or promise whatsoever that might render the Duke in the least degree subject to the danger of the law (which was not then so much as once thought upon); and upon that surrender, the grant was made to the Duke.   But it is true, that His Majesty, out of his royal bounty, for recompence of the long and faithful service of the said Earl, and for an honourable memory of his deserts to him and the Crown of England, did grant him a pension of ten thousand pounds per annum, for his life; which in all ages hath been the royal way of princes, wherewith to reward ancient and well-deserving servants in their elder years, when, without their own faults, they are become less serviceable to the state.   And the Duke also, voluntarily and freely, and as an argument of his noble respect towards so honourable a predecessor, whom to his death he called father, whose estate, as he then understood, might well bear it, with his late Majesty's privity and approbation, did send him three thousand pounds in money; which he hopeth no person of worth and honour will esteem to be an act worthy of blame in him.   And when the Duke had thus obtained this place of

---

[1] I. e. 'without the Duke's acting in the matter.'

great trust, he was so careful of his duty that he would not
rely upon his own judgment or ability; but of himself humbly
besought his then Majesty to settle a Commission of fit and able
persons for the affairs of the Navy, by whose counsel and
assistance he might manage that weighty business with the
best advantage for His Majesty's service; which commission
was granted and still continueth; and without the advice of
those commissioners he had never done any thing of moment;
and by their advice and industry he hath thus husbanded the
King's money, and furthered the service; that whereas the
ordinary charge of the Navy was four and fifty thousand pounds
per annum, and yet the ships were very much decayed, and
their provisions neglected; the charge was reduced to thirty
thousand pounds per annum; and with that charge the ships
all repaired and made serviceable, and two new ships builded
yearly; and for the two last years, when there were no ships
built, the ordinary charge was reduced to twenty-one thousand
six hundred pounds per annum; and now he dare boldly affirm,
that His Majesty's Navy is in better state by much than ever
it was in any precedent time whatsoever.

3. For his buying the Wardenship of the Cinque Ports, he
    maketh this plain ingenuous and true answer:—

That in December, in the two and twentieth year of his
late Majesty's reign, he obtained the office of Lord Warden of
the Cinque Ports, and Constable of the Castle of Dover (being
one entire office) upon the surrender of the Lord Zouch, then
Lord Warden. The manner of obtaining whereof was thus:
The Lord Zouch being grown in years, and with his almost
continual lameness being grown less fit for that place, he discovered a willingness to leave it, and made several offers thereof
to the Duke of Richmond, and Richard, Earl of Dorset, deceased; but he was not willing to part with it without recompence; notice whereof coming to the Duke, by an offer from
the Lord Zouch, he, finding by experience how much and how
many ways both the King's service might and many times
did suffer, and how many inconveniences did arise to the
King's subjects, in their goods and ships and lives, by the inter-
mixture of the jurisdiction of the Admiralty and Wardenship
of the Cinque Ports, by the emulation, disaffection and con-

tention of their officers, as will clearly appear by these particulars, amongst many others that may be instanced.

(1) Where the Admiral's jurisdiction extends generally to all the narrow seas, the Warden of the Cinque Ports hath and exerciseth Admiral jurisdiction on all the sea coasts from Showe Beacon [1] in Essex, to the Red Noore [2] in Sussex; and within those limits there have been continual differences between the Lord Admiral and the Lord Warden, whether the Lord Warden's jurisdiction extends into the main sea, or only as far as the low water mark, and so much further into the sea as a man on horseback can reach with a lance; which occasioneth questions between those chief officers themselves.

(2) There are many and continual differences in executing warrants against offenders; the officers of the one refusing to obey or assist the authority of the other : whereby the offender, protected or countenanced by either, easily escapeth.

(3) Merchants and owners of goods questioned in the Admiralty are often enforced to sue in both courts, and often enforced, for their peace, to compound with both officers.

(4) The King's service is much hindered; for the usual rendezvous of the King's ships being at the Downs, and that being within the jurisdiction of the said Warden, the Lord Admiral or Captains of the King's ships have no power or warrant to press men from the shore, if the King's ships be in distress.

(5) When the King's ships or others be in danger on the Goodwins, or other places within view of the portsmen, they have refused to help with their boats lest the King's ships should command them on board; whereby many ships have perished, and much goods have been lost.

(6) When the warrants come to press a ship at road for the King's service, the officers take occasion to disobey the warrants, and prejudice the King's service; for if the warrant come from the Lord Warden they will pretend the ship to be out of their jurisdiction; if the warrant come from the Lord Admiral, they will pretend it to be within jurisdiction of the Cinque Ports; and so whilst the officers dispute the opportunity of the service is lost.

[1] Shoeburyness.

[2] Professor Burrows has suggested to me that this must be the ' Rooks of Nore ' to the east of Hastings.

(7) When the King's ships lye near the Ports, and the men come on shore, the officers refuse to assist the captains to reduce them to their ships without the Lord Warden's warrant.

(8) If the King's ships on the sudden have any need of pilots for the sands, coasts of Flanders or the like, wherein the portsmen are the best experienced, they will not serve without the Lord Warden's or his lieutenant's warrant, who perhaps are not near the place.

(9) When for great occasions for the service of the State, the Lord Admiral and the Lord Warden must both join their authority; if the officers for want of true understanding of their several limits and jurisdictions, mistake the warrants, the service which many times can brook no delay is lost, or not so effectually performed.

For these, and many other reasons of the like kind the Duke, not being led either with ambition or hope of profit, as hath been objected (for it could be no increase of honour unto him, having been honoured before with a greater place; nor for profit, for it hath not yielded him in a manner any profit at all, nor is like to yield him above three hundred pounds per annum at any time), but out of his desire to do the King and kingdom service, and prevent all differences and difficulties, which heretofore had, or hereafter might, hinder the same; he did entertain that motion: And doth confess, that not knowing, nor so much as thinking, of the said Act of Parliament before mentioned, he did agree to give the said Lord one thousand pounds in money, and five hundred pounds per annum, in respect of his surrender; he not being willing to leave his place without such consideration, nor the Duke willing to have it without his full satisfaction. And the occasion why the Duke of Buckingham gave that consideration to the Lord Zouch was, because the Duke of Richmond, in his life time, had first agreed to give the same consideration for it; and, if he had lived, he had had that place upon the same terms. And when the Lord Duke of Richmond was dead, his late Majesty directed the Duke of Buckingham to go through for that place; and, for the reasons aforementioned, to put both these offices together; and to give the same consideration to the said Lord which the Duke of Richmond should have given; and his late Majesty said, he would repay the money. And how far this act of his, in acquiring this office, accompanied with these circumstances, may be within the danger of the law, the King being privy to all the passages of it, and encouraging and directing of it, he humbly submitteth to judgment : And he humbly leaves it to your lordships' judgments, in what third way, an ancient servant to the Crown, by age and infirmity disabled to perform his service, can in an honourable course relinquish his place ; for if the King himself gave the reward, it may be said it is a charge to the Crown ; if the succeeding officer give the re-compence, it may be thus objected to be within the danger of the law : And howsoever it be, yet he hopeth it shall not be held in him a crime, when his intentions were just and honour-able, and for the furtherance of the King's service; neither is it without precedents, that, in former times of great employment, both these offices were put into one hand, by several grants.

4. To this article whereby the not guarding of the narrow seas, in these last two years, by the Duke, according to the trust and duty of an Admiral, is laid to his charge, whereof the consequence[s], supposed to have been merely through his default, are the ignominious infesting of the coast with pirates and enemies, the endangering of the dominion of those seas, the ex-treme loss of the merchants and decay of the trade and strength of the kingdom :—

The Duke maketh this answer, That he doubteth not but he shall make it appear, to the good satisfaction of your lordships, that, albeit there hath happened much loss to the King's subjects, within the said time of two years, by pirates and enemies, yet that hath not happened through the neglect of the Duke, or want of care or diligence in his place; for whereas, in former times, the ordinary guard for the narrow seas hath been but four ships, the Duke hath, since hostility began, and before, procured their number to be much increased; for since June 1624, there hath never been fewer than five of the King's ships, and ordinarily six, besides pinnaces, merchant ships and drumblers ; and all these well furnished and manned, sufficiently instructed and authorized for the service. He saith he hath, from time to time, upon all occasions, acquainted His Majesty and the Council Board therewith, and craved their advice, and used the assistance of the commissioners for the Navy in this service; and for the Dunkirkers, who have of late more infested these coasts than in former years, he saith there was that providence used for the repressing of them, that His Majesty's ships and the Hollanders joined together, the port of Dunkirk was blocked up, and so should have continued, had not a sudden storm dispersed them, which being the immediate hand of God, could not by any policy of man be prevented, at which time they took the opportunity to rove abroad; but it hath been so far from endangering the dominion of the narrow seas thereby as is suggested, that His Majesty's ships, or men of war, were never yet mastered or encountered by them, nor will they endure the sight of any of our ships; and when the Duke himself was in person, the Dunkirkers came into their harbours. But there is a necessity that, according to the fortune of wars, interchangeable losses will happen; yet hitherto, notwithstanding their more than wonted insolency, the loss of the enemy's part hath been as much if not more, than what hath happened unto us; and that loss which hath fallen hath chiefly come by this means, that the Dunkirkers' ships being of late years exercised in continual hostility with the Hollanders, are built as fit for flight as for fight, and so they pilfer upon our coasts, and creep to the shore, and escape from the King's ships; but to prevent that inconveniency for the time to come, there is already order taken for the building of some ships, which shall be of the like mould, light and quick of sail, to meet with the adverse part in their own way. And for the pirates of Sallee and those parts, he saith, it is but very lately that they found the way into our coasts; where by surprise, they might easily do hurt; but there hath been that provision taken by His Majesty, not without the care of the Duke, both by force and treaty to repress them for the time to come, as will give good satisfaction. All which he is assured will clearly appear upon proof.

5. To this article the Duke maketh this answer; that, about September last, this ship called St. Peter, amongst divers others, was seized on as lawful prize by His Majesty's ships and brought into Plimworth, as ships laden by the King of Spain. In the end of October or beginning of November, they were all brought

to the Tower of London. All of them were there unladen but the Peter; but the bulk of her goods were not stirred, because they were challenged by the subjects of the French King; and there did not then appear so much proof against her, and the goods in her, as against the rest. About the middle of November, allegations were generally put in against them all, in the Admiral Court, to justify the seizure; and all the pretendants were called in: Upon these proceedings, divers of the goods were condemned, and divers were released, in a legal course; and others of them were in suspense till full proof made. The eight and twentieth of December, complaint was made, on the behalf of some Frenchmen, at the Council board, concerning this ship and others; when the King by advice of his Council (His Majesty being present in person), did order that the ship of Newhaven, called the Peter, and the goods in her, and all such other goods of the other prizes as should be found to appertain to His Majesty's own subjects or to the subjects of his good brother the French King, or the States of the United Provinces, or any other princes or states in friendship or alliance with His Majesty, should be delivered: But this was not absolute, as was supposed by the charge; but was thus qualified, so as they were not fraudulently coloured; and it was referred to a judicial proceeding.

According to this great and honourable direction, the King's Advocate proceeded upon the general allegations formerly put in, the 26th of January; after, there was a sentence in the Admiralty, that the Peter should be discharged; and the King's Advocate not having then any knowledge of further proof, consented to it.

But this was not a definitive sentence, but a sentence inter-locutory, as it is termed in that court. Within four days after this ship prepared herself to be gone, and was falling down the river; then came new intelligence to the Lord Admiral by Mr. Lieutenant of the Tower, that all those ships were laden by the subjects of the King of Spain in Spain; that the Amirantazgo wafted them beyond the North Cape; that they were but coloured by Frenchmen; that there were witnesses ready to make good this new allegation; neither was it improbable to be so, for part of the goods in that ship have been confessed to be lawful prize[1]. This ship being now in falling down the river, and being a ship of the most value of all the rest, the Duke acquainted the King therewith, and by his commandment, made stay of the ship, lest otherwise it would be too late : which the Duke, in the duty of his place of Admiral, as he believeth, ought to have done without such commandment; and, if he had not done so, he might worthily have been blamed for his negligence ; and then he instantly sent for the Judge of the Admiralty, to be informed from him how far the sentence then already passed did bind, and whether it might stand with justice to make stay of her again, she being once discharged in such manner as before. The judge answered, as he was then advised, that it might justly be done, upon better proofs appearing ; yet discreetly, in a matter of that moment, he took time to give a resolute answer, that, in the interim, he might review the acts which had passed. The next day or very shortly after, the judge came again to the Duke, and upon advice, answered resolutely, that the ship and goods might justly be stayed, if the proofs fell out to be answerable to the information given ; whereof he said he could not judge till he had seen the depositions ; and, according to this resolution of the judge, did five other learned advocates, besides the King's Advocate, concur in opinion, being entreated by the Duke to advise thereof, so cautious was the Duke not to do an unjust act. Then he acquainted the King therewith ; and His Majesty commanded him to re-seize this ship, and to proceed judicially to the proofs, and the Duke often required the King's Advocate to hasten the examination of the witnesses; and many witnesses were produced and examined, in pursuance of this new information ; but the French merchants impatient of any delay complained again at the Council Board ; where it was ordered, not barely, that the ship and goods should be presently delivered upon security ; and upon security they had been then delivered if it had been given ; and security was once offered, but afterwards retracted ; and when all the witnesses produced were examined and published, the King's Advocate, having duly considered of them, forthwith acquainted

[1] ' Unlawful,' in L. J.

the Duke that the proofs came too short for the Peter; and thereupon the Duke gave order instantly for her final discharge, and she was discharged by order of the court accordingly. By which true narration of the fact, and all the proceedings, the Duke hopeth it will sufficiently appear, that he hath not done anything herein on his part which was not justifiable, and grounded upon deliberate and well advised counsels and warrants; but for the doing of this to his own lucre or advantage he utterly denieth it; for he saith that there was nothing removed out of the ship but some monies, and some small boxes of stones of very mean value, and other small portable things easy to be embezzled; and whatsoever was taken out of the ship was first publicly shewed to His Majesty himself, and then committed to the custody of Gabriel Marsh in the article mentioned, by inventory, then and still Marshal of the Admiralty, by him to be safely kept; whereof the money was employed for the King's immediate service and by his direction; and the rest was left in safe keeping, and are all since delivered and reimbursed to the owners or pretended owners, and not a penny profit thereof, or thereby, hath come to the Duke himself, as shall be made good by proof; and whereas the suggestion hath been made, that this accident was the cause of the embargo of the ships and goods of our merchants trading for France, he saith that it is utterly mistaken; for divers of their goods were embargoed before this happened; and, if, in truth the French had therein received that injury as either they pretended or is pretended for them, yet the embargoing of the goods of the English upon that occasion was utterly illegal and unwarrantable, for by the mutual articles between the two Kings they ought not to have righted themselves before legal complaint and a denial on our part, and then by way of reprisal and not by embargo, so that the Duke doth humbly leave it to the consideration of your Lordships, whether the harm which hath happened to our merchants hath not been more occasioned by the unseasonable justifying of the actions of the French, which animated them to increase their injuries, than by any act either by the Duke or any other.

    6. To this article which consisteth of two main points, the one of the extorting of ten thousand pounds unjustly

and without right from the East India Company; the other, admitting the Duke had a right as Lord Admiral, the compassing of it by undue ways, and abusing the Parliament to work his private ends :—

The Duke giveth this answer, wherein a plain narration of the fact, he hopeth, will clear the matters objected; and in this he shall lay down no more than will fully appear upon proof.

About the end of Michaelmas term 1623, the Duke had information given him, by a principal member of their own Company, that the Company had made a great advantage to themselves in the seas of East India, and other parts of Asia and Africa, by rich prizes gotten there forcibly from the Portugales and others; and a large part thereof was due to His Majesty, and [to] the Duke as Admiral by the law, for which neither of them had any satisfaction.

Whereupon directions were given for a legal prosecution in the Court of Admiralty, and to proceed in such manner as should be held fittest, by the advice of counsel.

In the months of December and January in that year, divers witnesses were examined in the Admiralty, according to the ordinary course of that court, to instruct and furnish an informative process in that behalf.

After this, the tenth of March 1623[1], an action was commenced in that court, in the joint names of His Majesty and the Admiral, grounded upon the former proceedings. This was prosecuted by the King's Advocate, and the demand at first was fifteen thousand pounds. The action being thus framed in both their names, by the advice of counsel, because it was doubtful in the judgment of the counsel, whether it did more properly belong to the one or to the other, or to both; and the form of entering that action being most usual in that court; on the 28th of April 1624 the judicial agreement and sentence thereupon passed in the Admiralty Court, wherein the Company's consent and their own offer plainly appeareth ; so that, for the first point of the right, it was very hard to conclude that the Duke has no right contrary to the Company's own consent, and the sentence of the court grounded upon their agreement, unless

[1] I. e. 162¾.

it shall fully appear that the Company was by strong hand
enforced thereto, and so the money extorted.

Therefore, to clear that scruple, that, as the matter of the
suit was just, or at least so probable, as the Company willingly
desired it for their peace, for the manner was just and honourable; your Lordships are humbly entreated to observe these
few true circumstances.   The suit in the Admiralty began
divers months before the first mention of it in Parliament;
and, some months before the beginning of that Parliament, it
was prosecuted in a legal course, and upon such grounds as be
yet maintained to be just.   The composition made by the
Company was not moved by the Duke; but his late Majesty
himself, on the behalf of himself and of the Duke, treated with
divers members of the Company about it, and the Duke himself
treated not at all with them.

The Company, without any compulsion at all, agreed to the
composition; not that they were willing to give so much if
they might have escaped for nothing, but they were willing to
give so much rather than to hazard the success of the suit.
And upon this composition concluded by His Majesty, the
Company desired and obtained a pardon for all that was objected
against them.   The motion in Parliament, about the story of
the Company's ships then ready prepared and furnished, was
not out of any respect the rather to draw them to give the
composition, but really out of an apprehension that there might
be need of their strength for the defence of the realm at home;
and, if so, then all private respects must give way to the public
interest.   These ships upon the importunity of the merchants,
and reasons given by them, were suffered nevertheless to fall
down to Tilbury, by his late Majesty's direction, to speed their
voyage the better, whilst they might be accommodated for this
voyage without prejudice to the public safety.   They were discharged when there was an accommodation propounded and
allowed; which was, that they should forthwith prepare other
ships for the home service, whilst they went on with their
voyage; which they accordingly did.

That the motion made in the Commons' House was without
the Duke's knowledge or privity; that when there was a rumour
that the Duke had drawn on the composition by staying of the

ships which were then gone, the Duke was so much offended thereat, that he would have had the formal communication to have broken off, and have proceeded in a legal course; and he sent to the Company to that purpose. But the Company gave him satisfaction that they had raised no such rumours, nor would nor could avow any such thing, and entreated him to rest satisfied with their public act to the contrary. That, after this, their ships being gone, themselves, careful of their future security, solicited the dispatch of the composition, consulted with counsel upon the instruments that passed about it, and were at the charge thereof; and the money was paid long after the sentence, and the sentence given after the ships were gone, and no security at all given for the money, but the sentence; and when this money was paid to the Duke, the whole sum (but two hundred pounds thereof only) was borrowed by the King, and employed by his own officers for the service of the Navy. If these things do upon proof appear to your Lordships, as he is assured they will, he humbly submitteth to your judgments, how far verbal affirmations, or informations extrajudicial, shall move your judgments, when judicial acts, and those which were acted and executed, do prove the contrary.

7. To this article, which is so mixed with actions of great princes, as that he dareth not in his duty publish every passage thereof, he cannot for the present make so particular an answer as he may, and hath, and will, do to the rest of his charge.

But he giveth this general answer, the truth whereof he humbly prayeth may rather appear to your Lordships by the proof than any discourse of his, which, in reason of state, will happily be conceived fit to be more privately handled.

That these ships were lent to the French King at first without the Duke's privity; that, when he knew it, he did that which belonged to an Admiral of England, and a true Englishman; and he doth deny that, by menace, or compulsion, or any other indirect or undue practice or means, by himself, or by any others, did deliver those ships, or any of them into the hands of the French, as is objected against him.

That the error which did happen, by what direction soever it were, was not in the intention any ways injurious, or dishonourable, or dangerous to this state or prejudicial to any private man interested in any of those ships; nor could have given any just offence at all, if those promises had been observed by others, which were professed and really performed by His Majesty and his subjects on their parts.

Since the Duke's answer delivered into the house, he hath himself openly declared to their Lordships, that for the better clearing of his honour and fidelity to the state in that part of his charge which is objected against him by this seventh article, he hath been an earnest and humble suitor to His Majesty, to give him leave, in his proof, to unfold the whole truth and secret of that great action; and hath obtained His Majesty's gracious leave therein; and accordingly doth intend to make such open and clear proof thereof, that he nothing doubteth but the same, when it shall appear, will not only clear him from blame, but be a testimony of his care and faithfulness in serving the state.

8. To this article, wherewith he is taxed to have practised for the employment of the ships against Rochelle, he answereth, that so far from practising, or consenting, that the said ships should so far be employed; that he shall make it clearly appear, that, when it was discovered that they would be employed against those of the religion, the protestation of the French being otherwise, and their pretence being that there was a peace concluded with those of the religion, and that the French King would use those ships against Genoa, which had been an action of no ill consequence to the affairs of Christendom; the Duke did by all fit and honourable means, endeavour to divert the course of their employment against Rochelle; and he doth truly and boldly affirm, that his endeavours under the royal care of his most excellent Majesty, hath been a great part of the means to preserve the town of Rochelle, as the proofs when they shall be produced will make appear; and when His Majesty did find that, beyond his intention and contrary to the faithful promises of the French they were so misemployed, he found himself bound in honour to intercede with the most Christian King, his good brother, for the peace of that town and of the religion, lest His Majesty's honour might otherwise suffer; which intercession His Majesty did sedulously and so successfully pursue that that town and the religion there will and do acknowledge the fruits thereof. And whereas it is

further objected against him, that when, in so unfaithful
a manner, he delivered the said ships into the power of a foreign
state, to the danger of the religion, and scandal and dishonour
of our nation, which he utterly denieth to be so; that to make
his ill intentions in cunning and cautelous manner he abused
the Parliament at Oxon, in affirming, before the committees of
both houses, that the said ships were not, nor should be, so
used or employed; he saith, under the favour of those who so
understood his words, that he did not then use those words
which are expressed in the charge to have been spoken by him;
but, there being then a jealousy of the mis-employing of those
ships, but the Duke having no knowledge thereof, the Duke
knowing well what the promises of the French were, but was
not then seasonable to be published; he, hoping that they would
not have varied from what was promised, did say, that the event
would show; which was no undertaking for them; but a declaration of that in general terms which should really be performed,
and which His Majesty had great cause to expect from them.

9. That the Duke did compel the Lord Robartes to buy his
title of honour, he utterly denieth; and he is very confident
that the Lord Robartes himself will not affirm it, or anything
tending that way; neither can he or any man else truly say so;
but the said Duke is able to prove that the Lord Robartes was
before willing to have given a much greater sum, but could not
then obtain it; and he did now obtain it by solicitation of his
own agents.

10. For the selling of places of judicature by the Duke, which
are specially instanced in the charge; he answereth, that he
received not, nor had a penny of these sums to his own use;
but the truth is, that the Lord Mandeville was made Lord
Treasurer by his late Majesty, without contracting for any
thing for it; but, after that he had the office conferred upon
him, his late Majesty moved him to lend him twenty thousand
pounds, upon promise of re-payment at the end of a year. The
Lord Mandeville yielded to it, so as he might have the Duke's
word that it should be re-paid unto him; accordingly the Duke
gave his word for it. The Lord Mandeville relied upon it, and
delivered the said sum to the hands of Mr. Porter, then the
Duke's servant, by the late King's appointment, to be disposed

as His Majesty should direct; and accordingly that very money was fully paid out to others; and the Duke neither had, of a penny thereof to his own use, as is suggested against him. And afterwards when the Lord Mandeville left that place, and his money was not repaid him, he urged the Duke upon his promise; whereupon the Duke, being jealous of his honour, and to keep his word, not having money to pay him, he assured lands of his own to the Lord Mandeville for his security.

But when the Duke was in Spain the Lord Mandeville obtained a promise from his late Majesty of some lands in fee farm, to such a value as he accepted of the same in satisfaction of the said money; which were afterwards passed unto him; and, at the Duke's return, the Lord Mandeville delivered back unto him the security of the Duke's lands which had been given unto him as aforesaid.

And for the six thousand pounds supposed to have been received by the Duke for procuring to the Earl of Middlesex the Mastership of the Wards, he utterly denieth it; but afterwards he heard that the Earl of Middlesex did disburse six thousand pounds about that time; and his late Majesty bestowed the same upon Sir Henry Mildmay, his servant, without the Duke's privity; and he had it and enjoyed it, and no penny of it came to the Duke, or to his use.

11. To this article the Duke answereth, that it is true that his late Majesty, out of his royal favour unto him, having honoured the Duke himself with many titles and dignities of his bounty, and as a great argument of his princely grace, did also think fit to honour those who were in equal degree of blood with him, and also to ennoble their mother, who was the stock that bare them. The title of Countess of Buckingham, bestowed upon the mother, was not without precedent; and she hath nothing from the Crown but a title of honour which dieth with her. The titles bestowed upon the Viscount Purbeck, the Duke's elder brother, were conferred upon him, who was a servant and of the bed-chamber to his now Majesty, then prince, by his Highness's means. The Earl of Anglesea was of his late Majesty's bed-chamber, and the honours and lands conferred on him was done when the Duke was in Spain. The Earl of Denbigh hath the honours mentioned in the charge;

but he hath not a foot of land which came from the Crown, or of the King's grant.

But if it were true that the Duke had procured honours for those that are so near and so dear unto him ; the Law of nature, and the King's royal favour, he hopeth, will plead for his excuse; and he rather believeth, he were to be condemned of all generous minds, if being in such favour with his master, he had minded only his own advancement, and had neglected those who were nearest unto him.

12. To this article he answereth this, that he doth humbly, and with all thankfulness, acknowledge the bountiful hand of his late Majesty unto him ; for which he oweth so much to the memory of that deceased King, and to the King's most Excellent Majesty that now is, and their posterity, that he shall willingly render back whatsoever he hath received, together with his life to do them service. But for the immense sums and values which are suggested to have been given unto him, he saith there are very great mistakings in the calculations, which are in the schedule in this article mentioned ; unto which the Duke will apply particular answers in another schedule, which shall express the truth in every particular as near as he can collect the same; to which he referreth himself; whereby it shall appear what a great disproportion there is between conjectures and certainties. And those gifts which he hath received, though he confesseth that they exceed his merit, yet they exceed not precedents of former times. But whatsoever it is that he hath, or hath had, he utterly denieth that he obtained the same or any part thereof by any undue solicitation or practice or did unduly obtain any release of any sums of money he received. But he having at several times, and upon several occasions, disposed of divers sums of the monies of his late Majesty, and of His Majesty that now is, by their private directions, he hath releases thereof for his discharge; which was honourable and gracious in their Majesties, who granted the same for their servant's indemnity, and he hopeth was not unfit for him to accept of, lest in future times he or his might be charged therewith, when they could not be able to give so clear an account thereof, as he hopeth he shall now be well able to do.

13. To this charge which is set forth with such an expression

of words as might argue an extraordinary guiltiness in the Duke, who by such intimate bonds of duty and thankfulness, was obliged to be tender of the life and health of his most dread and dear sovereign and master, he maketh this clear and true answer, that he did neither apply nor procure the plaister or posset drink, in the charge termed to be a potion, unto His Majesty, nor was present when the same was first taken or applied; but the truth is this, that His Majesty being sick of an ague, he took notice of the Duke's recovery of an ague not long before; and asked him how he recovered, and what he found did him most good. The Duke gave him a particular answer thereto; and that one who was the Earl of Warwick's physician had ministered a plaister and a posset drink unto him; and the chief thing that did him good was a vomit, which he wished the King had taken in the beginning of his sickness. The King was very desirous to have that plaister and posset drink sent for; but the Duke delayed it; whereupon the King impatiently asked whether it was sent for or not; and finding by the Duke's speeches that he had not sent for it, his late Majesty sent for John Baker, the Duke's servant, and with his own mouth commanded him to go for it. Whereupon the Duke besought His Majesty not to make use of it, but by the advice of his own physicians, nor until it should be first tried by James Palmer of his bed-chamber, who was then sick of an ague, and upon two children in the town, which the King said he would do. And in this resolution the Duke left His Majesty, and went to London; and in the mean time, in his absence, the plaister and posset drink was brought and applied by his late Majesty's own command. At the Duke's return, His Majesty was in taking the posset drink; and the King then commanded the Duke to give it to him, which he did in the presence of some of the King's physicians, they then no ways seeming to dislike it; the same drink being first taken by some of them, and divers of the King's bed-chamber; and he thinketh this was the second time the King took it.

Afterwards, when the King grew somewhat worse than before, the Duke heard a rumour as if this physic had done the King hurt, and that the Duke had ministered that physic unto him without advice. The Duke acquainted the King therewith. To whom the King, with much discontent, answered thus: 'They are worse than devils that say it;' so far from the truth it was, which now notwithstanding (as it seemeth) is taken up again by some, and with much confidence affirmed. And here the Duke humbly prayeth all your Lordships, not only to consider this truth of his answer; but also to commiserate the sad thoughts that this article hath revived in him. This being the plain, clear and evident truth of all those things which are contained and particularly expressed in his charge (the rest being in general require no answer); he being well assured that he hath herein affirmed nothing which he shall not make good by proof, in such way as your Lordships shall direct. He humbly referreth it to the judgment of your Lord-ships, how full of danger and prejudice it is to give too ready an ear and too easy a belief, unto reports or testimony without oath, which are not of weight enough to condemn any.

He humbly acknowledgeth how easy it was for him, in his young years and unexperienced to fall into thousands of errors, in those ten years wherein he had the honour to serve so great and so open-hearted a sovereign and master; but the fear of Almighty God, his sincerity to true religion established in the Church of England (though accompanied with many weaknesses and imperfections, which he is not ashamed humbly and heartily to confess), his awfulness not willing to offend so good and gracious a master, and his love and duty to his country, have restrained him, and preserved him (he hopeth) from running into heinous and high misdemeanours and crimes. But whatsoever, upon examination and mature deliberation, they shall appear to be, lest in anything unwittingly or unwillingly within the compass of so many years he shall have offended, he humbly prayeth your lordships, not only in those, but as to all the said misdemeanours, misprisions, offences and crimes, wherewith he standeth charged before your Lordships, to allow unto him the benefit of the free and general pardon, granted by his late Majesty in Parliament in the one and twentieth year of his reign, out of which he is not excepted; and of the gracious pardon of his now Majesty, granted to the said Duke, and vouchsafed in like manner at the time of his most happy inauguration and coronation; which said pardon under the Great Seal of England granted to the said Duke, bearing date the tenth day of February now last past, and here is shown forth to your Lordships, on which he doth humbly rely. And yet he hopeth your Lordships in your justice and honour, upon which with confidence he puts himself, will acquit him of and from those misdemeanours, offences, misprisions, and crimes, wherewith he hath been charged. And he hopeth and will daily pray, that for the future, he shall, by God's grace, so watch over his actions, both public and private, that he shall not give any just offence to any.

4. THE RESTRAINT OF THE EARLS OF ARUNDEL AND BRISTOL.

A. *Complaint of the House of Lords in Arundel's case.*

[March 14, 1626. Lords' Journals, iii. 526. See *Hist. of Engl.* vi. 91, 92.]

The Earl of Arundel being committed by the King to the Tower, sitting the Parliament, the House was moved, to take the same into their consideration, and so to proceed therein, as they might give no just offence to His Majesty, and yet preserve the privilege of Parliament.

The Lord Keeper thereupon signified to the House, that he was commanded to deliver this message from His Majesty unto their Lordships, viz. That the Earl of Arundel was restrained for a misdemeanour which was personal unto His Majesty, and lay in the proper knowledge of His Majesty, and had no relation to matters of Parliament.

B. *Petition of the Earl of Bristol.*

[March 30, 1626. Lords' Journals, iii. 544. See *Hist of Engl.* vi. 94.]

The petition of the Earl of Bristol, for his writ of summons, being referred to the Lords Committees for privileges, &c., the Earl of Hertford reported the same, on this manner, viz.

My Lords, whereas the Earl of Bristol hath preferred a petition unto this House, thereby signifying that his writ of summons is withheld from him . . . this petition being referred unto the Committee for privileges, and after diligent search, no precedent being found that any writ of summons hath been detained from any peer that is capable of sitting in the House of Parliament; and considering withal how far it may trench into the right of every member of this House, whether sitting by ancient right of inheritance or by patent, to have their writs detained; the Lords Committees are all of opinion, That it will be necessary for this House humbly to beseech His Majesty, that a writ of summons may be sent to this petitioner, and to such other Lords to whom no writ of summons hath been directed for this Parliament, excepting such as are made incapable to sit in Parliament by judgment of Parliament or any other legal judgment.

Whereupon the Duke of Buckingham signified unto the House, That upon the Earl of Bristol's petition, the King had sent him his writ of summons.

C. *Lord Keeper Coventry's Letter to the Earl of Bristol* [1].

[March 31, 1626.   Lords' Journals, iii. 563.]

My very good Lord, By His Majesty's commandment I herewith send unto your Lordship your writ of summons for the Parliament, but withal signify His Majesty's pleasure herein further; That, howsoever he gives way to the awarding of the writ, yet his meaning thereby is not to discharge any former direction for restraint of your Lordship's coming hither; but that you continue under the same restriction as you did before, so as your Lordship's personal attendance is to be forborne ...

THOMAS COVENTRY.

Dorset Court,
March 31, 1626.

---

[1] On April 17, Bristol, who had come to London and justified his action that the King's writ of summons was of greater weight than a letter from the Lord Keeper, accused Buckingham before the House of Lords. On the 21st, Charles accused him of high treason before the same House.

D. *The remonstrance and petition of the Peers on the restraint of the Earl of Arundel.*

[April 19, 1626.　Lords' Journals, iii. 564.　See *Hist. of Engl.* vi. 92.]

May it please your Majesty, we, the Peers of this your realm now assembled in Parliament, finding the Earl of Arundel absent from his place, that sometimes in this Parliament sat amongst us, his presence was therefore called for, but hereon a message was delivered unto us from your Majesty by the Lord Keeper, that the Earl of Arundel was restrained [&c., as above, p. 44].　This message occasioned us to enquire into the acts of our ancestors ... and after diligent search both of all stories, statutes and records that might inform us in this case, we find it to be an undoubted right and constant privilege of Parliament, that no Lord of Parliament, the Parliament sitting, or within the usual times of privilege of Parliament, is to be imprisoned or restrained without sentence or order of the House, unless it be for treason or felony, or for refusing to give surety for the peace ... wherefore we, your Majesty's loyal subjects and humble servants, the whole body of the Peers now in Parliament assembled, most humbly beseech your Majesty, that the Earl of Arundel, a member of this body, may presently be admitted, with your gracious favour, to come, sit, and serve your Majesty and the Commonwealth in the great affairs of this Parliament.　And we shall pray, &c.

This remonstrance and petition being read, it was generally approved of by the whole House, and agreed to be presented unto his Majesty by the whole House[1].

5. The King's Letter and Instructions for the Collection of a Free Gift.

[July 7, 1626.　S. P. Dom. xxxi. 30, 31.　See *Hist. of Engl.* vi. 125.]

Trusty and well beloved we greet you well.　It is not unknown unto you that in February last our high Court of Parliament was by us summoned and assembled to treat of the great and weighty affairs concerning the Church of England and the true religion therein established, and the defence and

---

[1] Arundel was at last released on June 5.

safety of the Kingdom ; and that they there continued together
until the 15th of June last, within which time many things
of good moment . . . were propounded and began to be handled;
and amongst other things, our Commons here assembled . . .
not for our own private use, but for the common safety of us
and our people, did, with one unanimous consent, agree [1] to
give unto us a supply of four entire subsidies and three fifteens,
and did, by order of that House, set down the days and times
for payment of the same; which their loving and free offer unto
us we did graciously accept and rely upon, and dispose of our
affairs accordingly, and afterwards with much patience, even
beyond the pressing necessity of our public affairs, continually
did expect the real performance thereof; and we are assured
the same had been performed accordingly, had not the disordered
passion of some members of that House, contrary to the good
inclination of the graver and wiser sort of them, so far misled
themselves and others, that they neither did nor would intend
that which concerned the public defence of the Kingdom, for
which they were specially called; wherefore, when no gracious
admonitions could stay them (though much against our heart)
we have dissolved that Parliament.

And the Parliament being now ended and yet the necessity
of a supply of money lying still upon us . . . and pressing us,
without which the common safety of us and our people cannot
be defended and maintained, but is in eminent and apparent
danger to be assailed and swallowed up by a vigilant and
powerful enemy, we have been enforced to cast all the ways
and means which honourably and justly we might take for
supply of these important affairs ; and many several courses
have been propounded and offered unto us : and although no
ordinary rules can prescribe a law to necessity, and the common
defence and safety and even the very subsistence of the whole
might justly warrant us, if out of our royal prerogative and
power we should take any way more extraordinary, or less
indifferent to any part thereof, yet we desiring nothing more
(next to the love and favour of Almighty God, by whose
gracious assistance we desire to govern ourselves and all our

[1] The agreement was merely by resolution. No bill having been
founded on it, it had no legal force.

actions) than the love of our people, which we esteem as our
greatest riches, we have made choice of that way which may
be most equal and acceptable to them.   And therefore we do
desire all our loving subjects, in a case of this unavoidable
necessity, to be a law unto themselves and lovingly, freely,
and voluntarily to perform that which by law, if it had passed
formally by an act, as was intended, they had been compellable
unto; and so in a timely way to provide not only for our but
for their own defence, and for the common safety of all our
friends and allies, and of our lives and honour; the performance
of which our request will not only give us an ample testimony
of the dutiful and good affections of our people in general,
but will give us just encouragement the more speedily to meet
in Parliament.

We therefore desire you forthwith to meet together and to
take such order as may best advance our service, and in our
name to desire and exhort our people according to such instructions as herewith we send unto you, that they would
not fail freely to give unto us a full supply answerable to the
necessity of our present occasions.   And these our Letters, &c.

Instructions to the Justices of Peace in the several Counties.

1. That speedily upon receipt of these Letters you assemble
together at some place convenient, and take them and the
matter thereby commended unto you, into your due considerations.

2. That when ye are thus assembled, ye call to mind the
resolution in the Parliament lately dissolved, to have given us
four subsidies, and three fifteens, and that the several days
of payment were ordered for the same; and therefore the sum
of money to have been raised thereby was in the judgment
of the Parliament but competent and the times of payment
convenient for the present and pressing occasions, and we are
confident that the same considerations will prevail with our
people.

3. That you let them know how much it will avail to our
affairs and to the affairs of our friends and allies, to assail
our enemies on their own coasts; and that we have begun
a preparation to that end but want monies to perfect the

same. And that whilst we are in these consultations, we are advertised from all parts, of powerful preparations made to assail us at home, or in Ireland, or both.

4. That you put them in mind that nothing invites an enemy more to invasion than an opinion that that part intended to be invaded is either secure, or distracted, and so unprovided for a resistance.

5. That therefore you, the Deputy Lieutenants, give present direction to have all the troops and bands of the county completed, mustered, trained, and so well furnished that they may be prepared to march unto the rendezvous at an hour's warning upon pain of death.

6. That ye conclude upon a constant way of propounding and pursuing this our supply in your several divisions, to the inhabitants of all the whole county.

7. That when you have first settled this work among yourselves, ye agree how to divide yourselves throughout the whole county into so many parts and divisions as ye in your judgments shall think fittest. . . .

8. [Collectors to be nominated by the justices.]

9. That ye assure them in our name and in our royal word, which we will not break with our people, that we will wholly employ all the monies which shall thus be given unto us, to the common defence of the kingdom and not to or for any other end whatsoever.

10. That together with the monies ye collect, ye send a perfect roll of the names of all those who do thus contribute, and of them who shall refuse, if any such be, that we may be thereby informed who are well affected to our service, and who are otherwise, and what monies are given unto us . . .

11. And lastly that all this be instantly performed, for that all delays will defeat and overthrow our greatest counsels and affairs.

6. Commission for raising Tonnage and Poundage with Impositions.

[July 26, 1626. Rymer's *Fœdera*, xviii. 737. See *Hist. of Engl.* vi. 125.]

Charles, by the grace of God [&c.], to our Lord Treasurer of England, now and for the time being, the Commissioners of our

Treasury for the time being, to our Chancellor and Under-
Treasurer of our Exchequer, now and for the time being, to our
Chief Baron and the rest of the Barons of our Exchequer [and
others], greeting.

Whereas the Lords and others of our Privy Council have
taken into their serious consideration the present state of our
revenue arising by customs subsidy and impost upon goods and
merchandise to be exported and imported out of and into this
our realm . . . and finding that it hath been constanly continued for many ages, and is now a principal part of the
revenue of our Crown, and is of necessity to be so continued
for the supportation thereof, which in the two last Parliaments
hath been thought upon, but could not be there settled by
authority of Parliament . . . by reason of the dissolution of
those Parliaments before those things which were there treated
of could be perfected, have therefore . . . specially ordered, that
all those duties upon goods and merchandizes, called by the
several names of customs subsidy and imposts, should be levied
. . . in such manner as the same were levied in the time of our
late dear father King James . . . and forasmuch as, through the
want of a parliamentary course to settle the payment of those
duties, many inconveniences may arise, which would tend to the
impairing of our revenue of that nature, if in convenient time
some settled course should not be taken for the prevention
thereof:—

Know ye therefore that we . . . by the advice of the Lords
and others of our Privy Council, do by these presents declare
our will and pleasure to be, that all those duties . . . shall be
levied in such manner as the same were levied at the time of
the decease of our said late father, and upon such accounts and
forms as now the same are collected, or hereafter shall be by us
appointed . . . all which our will and pleasure is shall continue
until such time as by Parliament (as in former times) it may
receive an absolute settling. And if any person whatsoever
shall refuse or neglect to pay the duties . . . aforesaid . . . then
our will and pleasure is, and we do further grant by these
presents unto the Lords and others of our Privy Council for the
time being, or unto the Lord Treasurer of England or Chancellor
of our Exchequer, now or for the time being, full power to

commit every such person to prison, who shall disobey this our order and declaration, there to continue until they . . . shall have conformed and submitted themselves unto due obedience concerning the premises . . .

Witness ourself at Westminster, the 26th day of July [1626].

Per breve a privato concilio.

7. The Commission and Instructions for raising the Forced Loan in Middlesex.

[Sept. 23, 1626. S. P. Dom. xxxv. 42, 43. See *Hist. of Engl.* vi. 144.]

Charles, by the grace of God [&c.], To our right trusty and right well beloved Counsellors George Lord Archbishop of Canterbury, Sir Thomas Coventry, Knight, Lord Keeper of our Great Seal of England, [and 40 others] greeting.

When the Imperial Crown of this realm descended first upon us, we found ourselves engaged in a war, undertaken and entered into by our late dear father of blessed memory, not willingly nor upon light or ill-grounded counsels, but by the many provocations of an ambitious enemy, and by the grave and deliberate counsels and persuasions of both the Houses of Parliament, upon promise of their continual assistance therein; and thereby not ourselves alone and our own people became thus engaged, but also our friends and allies, and amongst them and above all others our most dear uncle . . . the King of Denmark . . . whom in honour and in reason of State we may not desert, but by the advice of our Council are resolved to assist him presently with men and money, we evidently foreseeing that otherwise our common enemy will in an instant become master of all Germany, and consequently of all the ports and parts where the mass and bulk of our cloth is vented, and whence we must furnish ourselves of provision for our shipping, which how fatal it would be to us and our people may easily be discerned.

But when we came to enter into this great work, we found our treasures exhausted and our coffers empty, and our ordinary revenue hardly sufficient to support our ordinary charge, much less to undergo so great and extraordinary a burthen as a war will produce. Our affairs at home and abroad thus standing we, being willing to tread in the steps of our ancestors, with all the convenient speed we could, summoned a Parliament, but not finding that success therein which we had just cause to expect, we are enforced to this course we are now resolved upon; which was hastened the rather when our unavoidable necessities both at home and abroad multiplied upon us, when our enemies' great and mighty preparations both by sea and land threaten us daily, and when the late disaster[1] (the chance of war) which hath fallen upon our dearest uncle the King of Denmark, to the endangering of his royal person, the hazarding of his whole army, and the utter disheartening of all our party, do at once call upon us, and cry in our ears, that not our own honour alone, and the ancient renown of this nation (which is dear unto us), but the safety and very subsistence of ourself and people, the true religion of God, and the common cause of Christendom professing that true religion with us, are in apparent danger of suffering irreparably, unless not only a speedy but a present stop be made to so great a breach, which cannot endure so long a delay as the calling of a Parliament.

We therefore, in a case of this extremity, after diligent and deep enquiry into all the ways and means possible which are honourable and just in cases of such unavoidable necessity, have at last, by the advice of our whole Privy Council, resolved to require the aid of our good and loving subjects by lending unto us such a competent sum of money to be speedily collected to our use as may enable us to provide for their safeties and our own; to be repaid unto them as soon as we shall be any ways enabled thereunto, upon showing forth of the acquittance of the collector testifying the receipt thereof. And these sums we are confident will readily and cheerfully be lent unto us by our loving subjects, when they shall be truly informed from us of what importance and of what necessity that is which we now require of them, and when they shall be assured by us, which we faithfully promise and undertake on the royal word of a King, (which we will be jealous not to break with our people), that not a penny of those monies which thus we borrow of them shall be bestowed or expended but upon those public and general services only, wherein every of them and the whole body of the

[1] The battle of Lutter, August 17, 1626.

kingdom, their wives, children and posterity, have their personal
and common interest.

Know ye therefore that we, reposing special trust and confidence in your fidelities ... appoint you to be our Commissioners,
... and command you ... that, all other occasions set apart, you
or any three or more of you ... do with all speed, after the
receipt of this our Commission, . . . call before you all such
persons within our county of Middlesex[1] and the liberties thereof
as by our instructions (which we shall send unto you herewith)
are appointed; and that ye acquaint them with this our will
and pleasure, and see it ... performed accordingly ... And we
authorise you or any two or more of you to minister an oath to
such persons and in such cases as by our said instructions are
directed.

... per ipsum regem [dated 23 Sept. 1626].

[Endorsed] A Commission to the Lords and others of His
Majesty's Privy Council and others, concerning the loan of
monies to His Majesty within the county of Middlesex.

*Instructions which our Commissioners for the loan of money
are exactly and effectually to observe and follow.*

First, with all speed, after the receipt of this our Commission, ye shall assemble yourselves together; ye shall determine in what manner ye shall proceed to the execution of this
our Commission in the several parts and divisions of the whole
county; and before your departing ... you shall yourselves for
a good example to others lend unto us those several sums of
money which are hereby required of you to be lent, testified
by the writing of your names with your own hands: that when
you shall in our name require others to lend, they shall discern
your own forwardness, and that you do not move others to
that which you forbear to do yourselves; the Lords and others
of our Privy Council, attending our person, having already done
the same by the subscription of every of their names. And
before your parting you shall cause those of that one hundred
to appear before you, and proceed with them, according to these
our Commission and instructions.

---

[1] A similar Commission for London, containing 100 names, dated Feb. 5.
1628, is printed in Rymer, xviii. 835-8.

2. And because we would expedite this service, and ease you of importunity, and leave no way to the partial information of others, in the under or over valuation of men's estates (which is often subject to much error), we have thought this to be the most indifferent and equal way of conjecturing at every man's ability to lend, by taking those rates for our guide, at which they were assessed in the book of the last subsidy, and to require the loan of so much money only, as the entire rate and value comes unto at which they are rated and set there: as namely he that is set at one hundred pounds in lands, to lend us a hundred pounds in money, and so after that rate for a more or less sum. And he that is set at a hundred pounds in goods to lend us a hundred marks [1]: and he that is set at ten pounds goods, to lend us twenty nobles [2]: and so pro rata, for a greater or lesser sum. And where there are bearers or contributors they shall assist the subsidy-men.

3. When you have agreed amongst yourselves of the several days and places of your sitting . . . you shall send your warrants under your hands, or the hands of two of you at the least, to the high constable, petty constables, and other officers of those several divisions, personally to warn all such persons who were assessed for the last subsidy, or to leave such warrant in writing at their dwelling-houses, that they fail not to give you meeting at the times and places appointed by you and that those officers to whom your warrants are directed fail not to give an account to you of their service therein.

4. That at every of those meetings, when there is a convenient number assembled, you use all possible endeavours, to cause every of them willingly and cheerfully to lend those sums unto us, opening unto them the necessity and unavoidableness of this course . . . and assuring them that this course . . . shall not be drawn into example or precedent.

5. That if you shall meet with any objections . . . that you use all diligence for removing them . . . And if any shall object or whisper, that if this way of raising money take place, then no Parliament shall hereafter be called, that you satisfy such, that the suddenness and importance of the occasions are such, as cannot possibly admit of that delay which the summoning

[1] A mark is 6s. 8d.   [2] A noble is 3s. 2d.

assembly and resolutions of a Parliament do necessarily draw
with it ; . . . but that we are fully purposed to call a Parliament
as soon as fitly we may, and as oft as the Commonwealth and
State occasions shall require the same . . .

6. That ye appoint the days of payment of the sums of
money to be lent unto us to be within fourteen days, and persuade such as shall be able to pay it, to pay it at one entire
payment . . . But to such as ye in your discretions shall think
it more convenient, ye may accept of one half at the fourteen
days, and the other half to be paid before the twentieth day of
December now next ensuing.

7. That you treat apart with every one of those which are to
lend unto us, and not in the presence or hearing of any others,
unless you see cause to the contrary in your discretions.   And
as every one giveth consent, that you cause him or her to set
his or her name and mark to a book, roll, or list, to be made by
you, testifying their assent, with a mark or distinction of the
times of payment accorded unto.   And if ye shall find any who
either shall deny to lend us, or shall make delays or excuses,
let them know they do thereby incur our high displeasure;
and if they persist in their obstinacy notwithstanding that,
then ye shall examine such persons upon oath, whether he hath
been dealt withal . . . to refuse to lend, or to make excuse for
his not lending : who hath so dealt with him, and what speeches
or persuasions he or they have used, tending to that purpose.
And ye shall also charge every such person in our name, upon
his allegiance, not to disclose to any other what his answer
was; and ye shall enjoin him in like manner to be forth-
coming and ready to attend us or our Council when he shall
be sent for, to answer his contempt and neglect of us in this
case.

8. You shall show your own affections and zeal to this business and to our service by your effectual treating with all men
freely to run this course, and in using your powers, favours and
credits, which every [one] of you have in the country . . . to
advance this business, that it may come off cheerfully and soundly.
And that ye yourselves by any means discover not any coldness
or unwillingness to the service, whereby any other to their discouragement may gather that you have no heart to the work

although for form's sake you must take it upon you, being employed therein; . . .

9. That in your treating with your neighbours about this business, you show your own discretions and affections, by making choice of such to begin with, who are likely to give the best examples, and when you have a competent number of the hands to the roll or list of the lenders, that ye show the same to others, as they come before you, to lead them to lend in the like manner.

10. You shall observe and discover by all good ways and means, whether any, publicly or underhand, be workers or persuaders of others' dissent or dislike from this course, . . . and as much as ye may, ye shall hinder all discourses about it. And ye shall certify our Privy Council, in writing, of the names, qualities and dwelling places of all such refractory persons, with all speed, and specially if ye shall discover any combination or confederacy against these our proceedings.

11. Ye shall let all to know whom it may concern, that we are well pleased upon lending of these sums required, to remit all that which by letters in our name was desired upon the late benevolence or free gift. And if any have already paid to our use any such sum, that the sum be accepted for so much as in part of this loan, and if it exceed the sum desired to be lent, that the surplus shall be repaid to them without fee or charge.

12. Likewise, if since the last Parliament any have received privy seals, our pleasure [is] that if they have not already paid in any monies thereupon, that they agreeing to the loan of the sum required be excused of the payment of the privy seals. And if they have already paid . . . any such sum of money upon these privy seals, [allowance is to be made as in preceding clause].

13. If ye either know or find any able person not set in the last subsidy, that ye deal with every such inhabitant after the same manner and according to the same proportion as is held with other sufficient men according to your best judgments and discretions, and insert their names and sums in the said book, roll, or list, among the others of them. But ye are not to admit of any suit to be made, or any reasons to be given for the abating of any such sums, the time and the instant occasions

not now admitting any such dispute, which would but disturb and protract the service.

14. [appointment of collectors.]

15. [directions to collectors.]

16. And if any of the Commissioners shall be absent from the execution of this service (which we hope will not be), that the rest of you the Commissioners certify their names who shall make such default, as also the names of all such who upon these summons do not come and attend you.

17. And we do hereby explain and declare that the charge given by the said Commission, or by these our instructions, . . . be not intended to any of our Privy Council, for that they are daily employed otherwise in our service, nor to any peer of this realm not resident in the county where he is named a Commissioner, nor to any other that by our special directions is otherwise employed in our service.

And these our instructions we require and command you . . . to keep secret to yourselves, and not impart or disclose the same to any others [1].

8. THE CASE OF THE FIVE KNIGHTS, BEFORE THE COURT OF KING'S BENCH.

[Nov. 15-28, 1627.   State Trials, iii. 114-139.   See *Hist. of Engl.* vi. 213.]

A.   *Return of the Warden of the Fleet to the Writ of Habeas Corpus* [2].

Responsio Johannis Liloe, guardiani Prisonae de le Fleet.

Ego Johannes Liloe [&c.] serenissimo domino regi apud Westminster.   Post receptionem hujus brevis quod in hac schedula est mentionatum, certifico quod Walterus Erle miles, in eodem brevi nominatus, detentus est in prisona de le Fleet sub custodia mea praedicta, per speciale mandatum domini regis mihi significatum per warrantum dominorum duorum et aliorum de privato concilio perhonorabilissimo dicti domini regis, cujus quidem tenor sequitur in haec verba:

[1] An abstract of these instructions is given in Rushworth, i. 418, 419, under ten heads only.

[2] The writ is in the ordinary form.

Whereas Sir Walter Erle, Knight, was heretofore committed to your custody, these are to will and require you still to detain him, letting you know that both his first commitment and this direction for the continuance of him in prison were and are by His Majesty's special commandment. From Whitehall, 7 Novembris 1627. Thomas Coventry C.S., Henry Manchester, Thomas Suffolk, Bridgwater, Kelly, R Dunelm., Thomas Edmunds, John Coke, Marlborough, Pembroke, Salisbury, Totnes, Grandison, Gulielm. Bath and Wells, Robert Naunton, Richard Weston, Humphry May.

To the Guardian of the Fleet or his deputy.

Et haec est causa detentionis praedicti Walteri Earl sub custodia mea in prisona praedicta. Attamen corpus ejusdem Walteri coram domino rege ad diem et locum praedictum, post receptionem brevis praedicti paratum habeo prout istud breve in se exiget et requiret.

B. *Serjeant Bramston's Argument.*

May it please your Lordship, I shall humbly move upon this return in the behalf of Sir John Heveningham, with whom I am of Counsel—it is his petition—that he may be bailed from his imprisonment ... The exception that I take to this return is as well to the matter and substance of the return, as to the manner and legal form thereof ... For the matter and substance of the return, it is not good, because there ought to be a cause of that imprisonment. This writ [of Habeas Corpus] is the means, and the only means, that the subject hath in this and such-like case to obtain his liberty ... and the end of this writ is to return the cause of the imprisonment, that it may be examined in this Court, whether the parties ought to be discharged or not. But that cannot be done upon this return, for the cause of the imprisonment of this gentleman at first is so far from appearing particularly by it, that there is no cause at all expressed in it ... If the law be that upon this return this gentleman should be re-manded—I will not dispute whether or no a man may be imprisoned before he be convicted according to the law—but, if this return shall be good, then his imprisonment shall not continue on for a time, but for ever; and the subjects of this kingdom may be restrained of their liberties perpetually, and by law there can be no remedy for the subject; and therefore this return cannot stand with the laws of the realm or that of Magna Carta, nor with the statute of 28 Edw. 3, c. 3; for if a man be not bailable upon this return, they cannot have the benefit of these two laws, which are the inheritance of the subject. . . .

Mr. Selden's Argument.

My Lords, I am of counsel with Sir Edmund Hampden. . . . I shall humbly move you that this gentleman may also be bailed; for under favour, my Lord, there is no cause in the return why he should be any farther imprisoned and restrained of his liberty. . . . Now, my Lord, I will speak a word or two to the matter of the return; and that is touching the imprisonment, 'per speciale mandatum domini regis,' by the Lords of the Council, without any cause expressed. . . . I think that by the constant and settled laws of this kingdom, without which we have nothing, no man can be justly imprisoned by either of them, without a cause of the commitment expressed in the return. . . . The statute of Magna Carta, cap. 29—that statute if it were fully executed as it ought to be, every man would enjoy his liberty better than he doth . . . out of the very body of this Act of Parliament, besides the explanation of other statutes, it appears, 'Nullus liber homo capiatur vel imprisonetur nisi per legem terrae.' . . . My Lords, I know these words, 'legem terrae,' do leave the question where it was, if the interpretation of the statute were not. But I think, under your Lordships' favour, there it must be intended, by 'due course of law,' to be either by presentment or by indictment. My Lords, if the meaning of these words, 'per legem terrae,' were but, as we use to say, 'according to the law'—which leaves the matter very uncertain; and [if] 'per speciale mandatum &c.' be within the meaning of these words 'according to the law,' then this Act had done nothing.

C. *Attorney-General Heath's Argument.*

May it please your Lordship, against this return the counsel of the gentlemen have . . . divided their objections into two main points, the one the form, the other the matter. . . .

Touching the matter of the return, the main point thereof, it is but a single question and I hope, my Lord, of no great difficulty; and that is, whether they be replevisable[1], or not replevisable. It appears that the commitment is not in a legal and ordinary way, but that it is ' per speciale mandatum domini regis': which implies, not only the fact done, but so extraordinarily done, that it is notorious to be His Majesty's immediate act and will it should be so: [and the question is] whether in this case they should be bailable or not in this Court. ... The King cannot command your Lordship, or any other Court of Justice, to proceed otherwise than according to the laws of this kingdom, for it is part of your Lordship's oath, to judge according to the law of the kingdom. But, my Lord, there is a great difference between those legal commands and that *absoluta potestas* that a sovereign hath, by which a king commands. But when I call it *absoluta potestas*, I do not mean that it is such a power as that a king may do what he pleaseth, for he hath rules to govern himself by, as well as your Lordships, who are subordinate judges under him. The difference is, the king is the head of the same fountain of justice, which your Lordship administers to all his subjects. All justice is derived from him, and what he doth, he doth not as a private person, but as the head of the commonwealth, as *justiciarius regni*, yea, the very essence of justice under God upon earth is in him. And shall we generally, not as subjects only, but as lawyers, who govern themselves by the rules of the law, not submit to his command, but make enquiries whether they be lawful, and say that the King doth not this or that in course of justice?

If your Lordship, sitting here, shall proceed according to justice, who calleth your actions in question? except there are some errors in the proceeding, and then you are subject to a writ of error. But who shall call in question the actions or the justice of the king, who is not to give any account of them? as in this our case, that he commits a subject, and shows no cause for it. The King commits and often shows no cause; for it is sometimes generally, 'per speciale mandatum domini regis': sometimes 'pro certis causis ipsum dominum regem

[1] I.e. bailable.

moventibus.' But if the King do this, shall it not be good?
It is all one when the commitment is ' per speciale mandatum
[&c.],' and when it is 'pro certis causis [&c.]' . . . And, my
Lord, unless the return doth open to you the secrets of the
commitment, your Lordship cannot judge whether the party
ought by law to be remanded or delivered, and therefore, if the
King allow and give warrant to those that make the return
that they shall express the cause of the commitment—as many
times he doth, either for suspicion of felony, or making money,
or the like— . . . this Court in its jurisdiction were proper to
try these criminal causes, and your Lordship doth proceed in
them, although the commitment be 'per speciale mandatum
domini regis' . . . But if there be no cause expressed, this
Court hath always used to remand them : for it hath been used,
and it is to be intended a matter of State, and that it is not
ripe nor timely for it to appear.

My Lord, the main fundamental ground of argument upon
this case begins with Magna Carta . . . No freeman can be imprisoned but by 'legale judicium parium suorum vel per legem
terrae.' But will they have it understood that no man should
be committed, but first he shall be indicted or presented?
I think that no learned man will offer that ; for certainly there
is no justice of peace in a county, nor constable within a town,
but he doth otherwise, and might commit before an indictment
can be drawn or a presentment made. What then is meant by
these words, ' per legem terrae ' ? If any man shall say, this
doth not warrant that the King may, for reasons moving him,
commit a man and not be answerable for it, neither to the party
nor (under your Lordship's favour) unto any court of justice, but
to the High Court of Heaven, I do deny it and will prove it by
our statutes.

[Stat. 25 Edw. III, cap. 4 ; 28 Edw. III, cap. 3 ; and other
Statutes, recited and examined.].

And now, my Lord, we are where we were, to find out the
true meaning of Magna Carta—for there is the foundation of
[our] case; all this that hath been said concerneth other
things, and is nothing to the thing in question. There is not

a word either of the commitment of the King, or commandment of the Council, in all the statutes and records. . . .

The next thing I shall offer to your Lordships is this . . . it is the resolution of all the judges, which was given in the 34th of Queen Elizabeth. It fell out upon an unhappy occasion, which was thus. The judges they complained that sheriffs and other officers could not execute the process of the law as they ought, for that the parties on whom such process should be executed, were sent away by some of the Queen's Council, that they could not be found. The judges hereupon petitioned the Lord Chancellor, that he would be a suitor to Her Majesty that nothing be done hereafter. And thereupon the judges were desired to show in what cases men that were committed were not bailable, whether upon the commitment of the Queen or any other. The judges make answer, that if a man shall be committed by the Queen, by her command, or by the Privy Council, he is not bailable. If your Lordship ask me what authority I have for this, I can only say I have it out of the book of the Lord Anderson, written with his own hand [1] . . . This, my Lord, was the resolution of all the judges and [the] barons of the Exchequer, and not [2] [of] some great one.

Now I will apply myself to that which has been enforced by the counsel on the other side, which was the reason, that the subject hath interest in this case. My Lord, I do acknowledge it, but I must say that the sovereign hath great interest in it too. And sure I am that the first stone of sovereignty was no sooner laid, but this power was given to the sovereign. If you ask me whether it be unlimited—My Lord, I say it is not the question now in hand; but the common law, which hath long flourished under the government of our King and his progenitors, kings of this realm, hath ever had that reverent respect of the sovereign, as that it hath concluded the King can do no wrong. . . . But the King commits a subject, and expresseth no cause of the commitment. What then? shall it be thought that there is no cause why he should be committed. Nay, my Lord, the course of all times hath been, to say there is no cause expressed, and therefore the matter is not ripe; and thereupon the courts of judicature have ever rested satisfied

[1] See *Hist. of Engl.* 1603–1642, vi. 244.   [2] Printed text, 'by.'

therewith: they would not search into it. My Lords, there be *arcana Dei, et arcana imperii*. . . . There may as much hazard come to the commonwealth in many other things with which the King is trusted, as in this particular there can accrue to the subject. . . . It may be divers men do suffer wrongfully in prison, but therefore shall all prisoners be delivered? That were a great mischief. . . . The King may pardon all traitors and felons; and if he should do it, may not the subjects say, If the King do this, the bad will overcome the good? But shall any say, The King cannot do this? No: we may only say, He will not do this.

. . . I shall conclude what I shall say in this case—to answer the fear rather than the just ground of them that say this may be a cause of great danger—with the words of Bracton [lib. i, cap. 8]. Speaking of a writ for wrong done by the King to the subject touching land, he hath these words: 'Si autem ab eo petatur (cum breve non currat contra ipsum), locus erit supplicationi, quod factum suum corrigat et emendet; quod quidem si non fecerit, satis sufficit ei ad poenam, quod Dominum expectet ultorem. Nemo quidem de factis suis praesumat disputare, multo fortius contra factum suum venire.' . . . And therefore I pray your Lordship, that these gentlemen may be remitted, and left to go the right way for their delivery, which is by a petition to the King. Whether it be a petition of right or of grace I know not; it must be, I am sure, to the King, from whom I do personally understand that these gentlemen did never yet present any petition to him that came to his knowledge.

### D.	*Lord Chief Justice Hyde's Judgment.*

. . . The exceptions which have been taken to this return were two; the one for the form, the other for the substance. . . . In our case the cause of the detention is sufficiently answered, which is the demand of the writ, and therefore we resolve that the form of this return is good.

The next thing is the main point in law, whether the substance or matter of the return be good or no: wherein the substance is this—he [the Warden] doth certify that they are detained in prison by the special command of the King; and whether this be good in law or no, that is the question. . . . [After examination of precedents] Then the precedents are all against you every one of them, and what shall guide our judgments, since there is nothing alleged in this case but precedents? That, if no cause of the commitment be expressed, it is to be presumed to be for matter of state, which we cannot take notice of; you see we find none, no, not one, that hath been delivered by bail in the like cases, but by the hand of the King or his direction. . . . We have looked upon that precedent that was mentioned by Mr. Attorney—the resolution of all the judges of England in 34 Eliz. . . . The question now is, whether we may deliver these gentlemen or not . . . and this resolution of all the judges teacheth us; and what can we do but walk in the steps of our forefathers? . . . If in justice we ought to deliver you, we would do it; but upon these grounds and these records, and the precedents and resolutions, we cannot deliver you, but you must be remanded.

PART II

9. NOTES OF A BILL BROUGHT IN BY SIR EDWARD COKE TO
SECURE THE LIBERTIES OF THE SUBJECT.

[April 29, 1628. Harl. MSS. 1771, fol. 123. See *Hist. of Engl.* vi. 264-5.]

*An Act for the better securing of every freeman touching
the propriety of his goods and liberty of his person.*

Whereas it is enacted and declared by Magna Carta that no
freeman is to be convicted, destroyed, &c., and whereas by
a statute made in E. 7, called *de tallagio non concedendo*; and
whereas by the Parliament, 5 E. 3, and 29 E. 3, &c.; and
whereas by the said great Charter was confirmed, and that the
other laws, &c.

Be it enacted that Magna Carta and these Acts be put in
due execution and that all allegements, awards, and rules given
or to be given to the contrary shall be void; and whereas by the
common law and statute it appeareth that no freeman ought to
be committed [1] by command of the King, &c.; and if any freeman be so committed and the same returned upon a *habeas
corpus*, he ought to be delivered or bailed, and whereas by the
common law and statutes every freeman hath a propriety of his

---

[1] 'convicted' in MS.

goods and estate as no tax, tallage, &c., nor any soldier can be
billeted in his house, &c.

Be it enacted that no tax, tallage, or loan shall be levied &c.,
by the King or any minister by Act of Parliament, and that
none be compelled to receive any soldiers into his house against
his will.

10. The Petition of Right.

[June 7, 1628.   3 Car. I, cap. 1.   Statutes of the Realm, v. 23.   See
Hist. of Engl. vi. 274–309.]

*The Petition exhibited to His Majesty by the Lords Spiritual
and Temporal, and Commons in this present Parliament
assembled, concerning divers Rights and Liberties of the
Subjects, with the King's Majesty's Royal Answer thereunto in full Parliament.*

To the King's Most Excellent Majesty.

Humbly show unto our Sovereign Lord the King, the Lords
Spiritual and Temporal, and Commons in Parliament assembled,
that whereas it is declared and enacted by a statute made
in the time of the reign of King Edward the First, commonly called *Statutum de Tallagio non concedendo*[1], that no
tallage or aid shall be laid or levied by the King or his heirs
in this realm, without the goodwill and assent of the Archbishops, Bishops, Earls, Barons, Knights, Burgesses, and other
the freemen of the commonalty of this realm : and by authority
of Parliament holden in the five and twentieth year of the
reign of King Edward the Third[2], it is declared and enacted,
that from thenceforth no person shall be compelled to make
any loans to the King against his will, because such loans were
against reason and the franchise of the land ; and by other laws
of this realm it is provided, that none should be charged by
any charge or imposition, called a Benevolence, or by such like
charge[3], by which the statutes before-mentioned, and other
the good laws and statutes of this realm, your subjects have

[1] This is now held not to have been a statute.   See Stubbs, *Const. Hist.*
(ed. 1875), ii. 143, *Select Charters*, p. 87.
[2] I have failed to discover this statute.
[3] In 1484, 1 Ric. III. c. 2

inherited this freedom, that they should not be compelled to contribute to any tax, tallage, aid, or other like charge, not set by common consent in Parliament:

Yet nevertheless, of late divers commissions directed to sundry Commissioners in several counties with instructions have issued, by means whereof your people have been in divers places assembled, and required to lend certain sums of money unto your Majesty, and many of them upon their refusal so to do, have had an oath administered unto them, not warrantable by the laws or statutes of this realm, and have been constrained to become bound to make appearance and give attendance before your Privy Council, and in other places, and others of them have been therefore imprisoned, confined, and sundry other ways molested and disquieted: and divers other charges have been laid and levied upon your people in several counties, by Lords Lieutenants, Deputy Lieutenants, Commissioners for Musters, Justices of Peace and others, by command or direction from your Majesty or your Privy Council, against the laws and free customs of this realm:

And where also by the statute called, 'The Great Charter of the Liberties of England [1],' it is declared and enacted, that no freeman may be taken or imprisoned or be disseised of his freeholds or liberties, or his free customs, or be outlawed or exiled; or in any manner destroyed, but by the lawful judgment of his peers, or by the law of the land:

And in the eight and twentieth year of the reign of King Edward the Third [2], it was declared and enacted by authority of Parliament, that no man of what estate or condition that he be, should be put out of his lands or tenements, nor taken, nor imprisoned, nor disherited, nor put to death, without being brought to answer by due process of law:

Nevertheless, against the tenor of the said statutes [3], and other the good laws and statutes of your realm, to that end provided, divers of your subjects have of late been imprisoned without any cause showed, and when for their deliverance they were brought before your Justices, by your Majesty's writs of Habeas Corpus, there to undergo and receive as the Court

[1] 9 Hen. III. 29.   [2] 28 Ed. III. 3.
[3] 37 Ed. III. 18; 38 Ed. III. 9; 42 Ed. III. 3; 17 Ric. II. 6.

should order, and their keepers commanded to certify the causes of their detainer; no cause was certified, but that they were detained by your Majesty's special command, signified by the Lords of your Privy Council, and yet were returned back to several prisons, without being charged with anything to which they might make answer according to the law:

And whereas of late great companies of soldiers and mariners have been dispersed into divers counties of the realm, and the inhabitants against their wills have been compelled to receive them into their houses, and there to suffer them to sojourn, against the laws and customs of this realm, and to the great grievance and vexation of the people:

And whereas also by authority of Parliament, in the 25th year of the reign of King Edward the Third[1], it is declared and enacted, that no man shall be forejudged of life or limb against the form of the Great Charter, and the law of the land: and by the said Great Charter and other the laws and statutes of this your realm[2], no man ought to be adjudged to death; but by the laws established in this your realm, either by the customs of the same realm or by Acts of Parliament: and whereas no offender of what kind soever is exempted from the proceedings to be used, and punishments to be inflicted by the laws and statutes of this your realm: nevertheless of late divers commissions under your Majesty's Great Seal have issued forth, by which certain persons have been assigned and appointed Commissioners with power and authority to proceed within the land, according to the justice of martial law against such soldiers and mariners, or other dissolute persons joining with them, as should commit any murder, robbery, felony, mutiny, or other outrage or misdemeanour whatsoever, and by such summary course and order, as is agreeable to martial law, and is used in armies in time of war, to proceed to the trial and condemnation of such offenders, and them to cause to be executed and put to death, according to the law martial:

By pretext whereof, some of your Majesty's subjects have been by some of the said Commissioners put to death, when and where, if by the laws and statutes of the land they had

[1] 25 Ed. III. 9.   [2] 9 Hen. III. 29; 25 Ed. III. 4; 28 Ed. III. 3.

deserved death, by the same laws and statutes also they might, and by no other ought to have been, adjudged and executed:

And also sundry grievous offenders by colour thereof, claiming an exemption, have escaped the punishments due to them by the laws and statutes of this your realm, by reason that divers of your officers and ministers of justice have unjustly refused, or forborne to proceed against such offenders according to the same laws and statutes, upon pretence that the said offenders were punishable only by martial law, and by authority of such commissions as aforesaid, which commissions, and all other of like nature, are wholly and directly contrary to the said laws and statutes of this your realm:

They do therefore humbly pray your Most Excellent Majesty, that no man hereafter be compelled to make or yield any gift, loan, benevolence, tax, or such like charge, without common consent by Act of Parliament; and that none be called to make answer, or take such oath, or to give attendance, or be confined, or otherwise molested or disquieted concerning the same, or for refusal thereof; and that no freeman, in any such manner as is before-mentioned, be imprisoned or detained; and that your Majesty will be pleased to remove the said soldiers and mariners, and that your people may not be so burdened in time to come; and that the foresaid commissions for proceeding by martial law, may be revoked and annulled; and that hereafter no commissions of like nature may issue forth to any person or persons whatsoever, to be executed as aforesaid, lest by colour of them any of your Majesty's subjects be destroyed or put to death, contrary to the laws and franchise of the land.

All which they most humbly pray of your Most Excellent Majesty, as their rights and liberties according to the laws and statutes of this realm: and that your Majesty would also vouchsafe to declare, that the awards, doings, and proceedings to the prejudice of your people, in any of the premises, shall not be drawn hereafter into consequence or example: and that your Majesty would be also graciously pleased, for the further comfort and safety of your people, to declare your royal will and pleasure, that in the things aforesaid all your officers and ministers shall serve you, according to the laws and statutes of this realm, as they tender the honour of your Majesty, and the prosperity of this kingdom.

[Which Petition being read the 2nd of June 1628, the King's answer was thus delivered unto it.

The King willeth that right be done according to the laws and customs of the realm; and that the statutes be put in due execution, that his subjects may have no cause to complain of any wrong or oppressions, contrary to their just rights and liberties, to the preservation whereof he holds himself as well obliged as of his prerogative.

On June 7 the answer was given in the accustomed form, *Soit droit fait comme il est désiré.*]

11. The Remonstrance against Tonnage and Poundage.

[June 25, 1628. Rushworth, i. 628. See *Hist. of Engl.* vi. 323.]

Most Gracious Sovereign, your Majesty's most loyal and dutiful subjects, the Commons in this present Parliament assembled, being in nothing more careful than of the honour and prosperity of your Majesty, and the kingdom, which they know do much depend upon that happy union and relation betwixt your Majesty and your people, do with much sorrow apprehend, that by reason of the incertainty of their continuance together, the unexpected interruptions which have been cast upon them, and the shortness of time in which your Majesty hath determined to end this Session, they cannot bring to maturity and perfection divers businesses of weight, which they have taken into their consideration and resolution, as most important for the common good: amongst other things they have taken into especial care the preparing of a Bill for the granting of your Majesty such a subsidy of Tonnage and Poundage, as might uphold your profit and revenue in as ample a manner as their just care and respect of trade (wherein not only the prosperity, but even the life of the kingdom doth consist) would permit: but being a work which will require much time, and preparation by conference with your Majesty's officers, and with the merchants, not only of London, but of other remote parts, they find it not possible to be accomplished at this time: where-

fore considering it will be much more prejudicial to the right
of the subject, if your Majesty should continue to receive the
same without authority of law, after the determination of a
Session, than if there had been a recess by adjournment only,
in which case that intended grant would have related to the
first day of the Parliament; and assuring themselves that your
Majesty is resolved to observe that your royal answer, which
you have lately made to the Petition of Right of both Houses of
Parliament; yet doubting lest your Majesty may be misinformed
concerning this particular case, as if you might continue to take
those subsidies of Tonnage and Poundage, and other impositions
upon merchants, without breaking that answer, they are forced
by that duty which they owe to your Majesty, and to those whom
they represent, to declare, that there ought not any imposition
to be laid upon the goods of merchants, exported or imported,
without common consent by Act of Parliament, which is the
right and inheritance of your subjects, founded not only upon
the most ancient and original constitution of this kingdom, but
often confirmed and declared in divers statute laws.

And for the better manifestation thereof, may it please
your Majesty to understand, that although your royal predecessors the Kings of this realm have often had such subsidies,
and impositions granted unto them, upon divers occasions,
especially for the guarding of the seas, and safeguard of
merchants; yet the subjects have been ever careful to use
such cautions, and limitations in those grants, as might
prevent any claim to be made, that such subsidies do proceed
from duty, and not from the free gift of the subjects: and
that they have heretofore used to limit a time in such grants,
and for the most part but short, as for a year or two, and
if it were continued longer, they have sometimes directed a
certain space of cessation, or intermission, that so the right
of the subject might be more evident. At other times it
hath been granted upon occasion of war, for a certain
number of years, with proviso, that if the war were ended in
the meantime, then the grant should cease; and of course it
hath been sequestered into the hands of some subjects to be
employed for the guarding of the seas. And it is acknowledged by the ordinary answers of your Majesty's predecessors

in their assent to the Bills of subsidies of Tonnage and
Poundage, that it is of the nature of other subsidies, proceeding from the goodwill of the subject. Very few of your
predecessors had it for life, until the reign of Henry VII[1],
who was so far from conceiving he had any right thereunto,
that although he granted commissions for collecting certain
duties and customs due by law, yet he made no commissions
for receiving the subsidy of Tonnage and Poundage, until
the same was granted unto him in Parliament. Since his
time all the Kings and Queens of this realm have had the
like grants for life by the free love and goodwill of the
subjects. And whensoever the people have been grieved by
laying any impositions or other charges upon their goods
and merchandises, without authority of law (which hath
been very seldom), yet upon complaint in Parliament they
have been forthwith relieved; saving in the time of your
royal father, who having through ill counsel raised the rates
and charges upon merchandises to that height at which they
now are, yet he was pleased so far forth to yield to the complaint of his people, as to offer that if the value of those
impositions which he had set might be made good unto him,
he would bind himself and his heirs by Act of Parliament
never to lay any other; which offer the Commons at that
time, in regard of the great burden, did not think fit to yield
unto. Nevertheless, your loyal Commons in this Parliament,
out of their especial zeal to your service, and especial regard
of your pressing occasions, have taken into their consideration, so to frame a grant of subsidy of Tonnage or Poundage
to your Majesty, that both you might have been the better
enabled for the defence of your realm, and your subjects, by
being secure from all undue charges, be the more encouraged
cheerfully to proceed in their course of trade; by the increase
whereof your Majesty's profit, and likewise the strength of the
kingdom would be very much augmented.

But not now being able to accomplish this their desire,
there is no course left unto them, without manifest breach

[1] Tonnage and Poundage was granted for life to Edward IV in 1464
(3 & 4 Ed. IV), *Rot. Parl.* v. 508. It was also granted in 1483 to
Richard III for life (1 Ric. III), *ib.* vi. 238.

of their duty, both to your Majesty and their country, save
only to make this humble declaration, 'That the receiving
of Tonnage and Poundage, and other impositions not granted
by Parliament, is a breach of the fundamental liberties of
this kingdom, and contrary to your Majesty's royal answer
to the said Petition of Right.' And therefore they do most
humbly beseech your Majesty to forbear any further receiving of the same, and not to take it in ill part from those of
your Majesty's loving subjects, who shall refuse to make payment
of any such charges, without warrant of law demanded.

And as by this forbearance, your Most Excellent Majesty
shall manifest unto the world your royal justice in the observation of your laws : so they doubt not, but hereafter, at the
time appointed for their coming again, they shall have occasion
to express their great desire to advance your Majesty's honour
and profit.

12. The King's Speech at the Prorogation of Parliament at the end of the Session of 1628.

[June 26, 1628.   *Lords' Journals*, iii. 879.   See *Hist. of Engl.* vi. 324.]

It may seem strange, that I come so suddenly to end this
Session ; wherefore before I give my assent to the Bills, I will
tell you the cause, though I must avow, that I owe an account
of my actions to none but to God alone.   It is known to every
one, that a while ago the House of Commons gave me a Remonstrance [1], how acceptable every man may judge ; and for
the merit of it, I will not call that in question, for I am sure no
wise man can justify it.

Now since I am certainly informed, that a second Remonstrance [2] is preparing for me to take away my profit of Tonnage
and Poundage, one of the chief maintenances of my Crown,
by alleging I have given away my right thereof by my answer
to your Petition ; this is so prejudicial unto me, that I am
forced to end this Session some few hours before I meant it,

---

[1] A general remonstrance on the misgovernment of the kingdom, in
which Buckingham was named as the author of abuses, had been presented
to the King on June 17.
[2] See No. 11.

being willing not to receive any more Remonstrances, to which
I must give a harsh answer.

And since I see that even the House of Commons begins
already to make false constructions of what I granted in your
Petition, lest it might be worse interpreted in the country,
I will now make a declaration concerning the true meaning
thereof:

The profession of both Houses, in time of hammering this
Petition, was no ways to intrench upon my Prerogative, saying,
they had neither intention nor power to hurt it. Therefore it must needs be conceived that I have granted no new,
but only confirmed the ancient liberties of my subjects: yet
to show the clearness of my intentions, that I neither repent,
nor mean to recede from anything I have promised you, I do
here declare, that those things which have been done, whereby
men had some cause to suspect the liberties of the subjects
to be trenched upon,—which indeed was the first and true
ground of the Petition,—shall not hereafter be drawn into
example for your prejudice; and in time to come, on the word
of a king, you shall not have the like cause to complain.

But as for Tonnage and Poundage, it is a thing I cannot
want, and was never intended by you to ask, nor meant—
I am sure—by me to grant.

To conclude, I command you all that are here to take
notice of what I have spoken at this time, to be the true
intent and meaning of what I granted you in your Petition;
but especially, you my Lords the Judges, for to you only
under me belongs the interpretation of laws; for none of the
House of Commons, joint or separate, (what new doctrine
soever may be raised) have any power either to make or
declare a law without my consent[1].

[1] The last clause of this paragraph is corrected from *Parl. Hist.* ii. 434

13. THE KING'S DECLARATION PREFIXED TO THE ARTICLES OF RELIGION.

[November, 1628. Commonly printed with the Book of Common Prayer. See *Hist. of Engl.* vii. 20.]

Being by God's ordinance, according to our just title, Defender of the Faith, and Supreme Governor of the Church, within these our dominions, we hold it most agreeable to this our kingly office, and our own religious zeal, to conserve and maintain the Church committed to our charge, in the unity of true religion, and in the bond of peace; and not to suffer unnecessary disputations, altercations, or questions to be raised, which may nourish faction both in the Church and Commonwealth. We have therefore, upon mature deliberation, and with the advice of so many of our Bishops as might conveniently be called together, thought fit to make this declaration following:

That the Articles of the Church of England (which have been allowed and authorised heretofore, and which our clergy generally have subscribed unto) do contain the true doctrine of the Church of England agreeable to God's Word: which we do therefore ratify and confirm, requiring all our loving subjects to continue in the uniform profession thereof, and prohibiting the least difference from the said Articles; which to that end we command to be new printed, and this our declaration to be published therewith:

That we are supreme Governor of the Church of England: and that if any difference arise about the external policy, concerning the injunctions, canons, and other constitutions whatsoever thereto belonging, the Clergy in their Convocation is to order and settle them, having first obtained leave under our broad seal so to do: and we approving their said ordinances and constitutions; providing that none be made contrary to the laws and customs of the land.

That out of our princely care that the churchmen may do the work which is proper unto them, the Bishops and Clergy, from time to time in Convocation, upon their humble desire, shall have license under our broad seal to deliberate of, and to do all such things as, being made plain by them, and assented unto by us, shall concern the settled continuance of the doctrine and discipline of the Church of England now established; from which we will not endure any varying or departing in the least degree.

That for the present, though some differences have been ill raised, yet we take comfort in this, that all clergymen within our realm have always most willingly subscribed to the Articles established; which is an argument to us, that they all agree in the true, usual, literal meaning of the said Articles; and that even in those curious points, in which the present differences lie, men of all sorts take the Articles of the Church of England to be for them; which is an argument again, that none of them intend any desertion of the Articles established.

That therefore in these both curious and unhappy differences, which have for so many hundred years, in different times and places, exercised the Church of Christ, we will, that all further curious search be laid aside, and these disputes shut up in God's promises, as they be generally set forth to us in the holy scriptures, and the general meaning of the Articles of the Church of England according to them. And that no man hereafter shall either print, or preach, to draw the Article aside any way, but shall submit to it in the plain and full meaning thereof: and shall not put his own sense or comment to be the meaning of the Article, but shall take it in the literal and grammatical sense.

That if any public Reader in either of our Universities, or any Head or Master of a College, or any other person respectively in either of them, shall affix any new sense to any Article, or shall publicly read, determine, or hold any public disputation, or suffer any such to be held either way, in either the Universities or Colleges respectively; or if any divine in the Universities shall preach or print any thing either way, other than is already established in Convocation with our royal assent; he, or they the offenders, shall be liable to our displeasure, and the Church's censure in our commission ecclesiastical, as well as any other: and we will see there shall be due execution upon them.

14. RESOLUTIONS ON RELIGION DRAWN BY A SUB-COMMITTEE OF THE HOUSE OF COMMONS.

[February 24, 1628–9. Cobbett's Parliamentary History, ii. col. 483.
See *Hist. of Engl.* vii. 65.]

Heads of Articles to be insisted on, and agreed upon, at a Sub-Committee for Religion.

I. That we call to mind, how that, in the last Session of this Parliament, we presented to His Majesty an humble declaration of the great danger threatened to this Church and State, by divers courses and practices tending to the change and innovation of religion.

II. That what we then feared, we do now sensibly feel; and therefore have just cause to renew our former complaints herein.

III. That, yet nevertheless, we do, with all thankfulness, acknowledge the great blessing we have received from Almighty God, in setting a king over us, of whose constancy in the profession and practice of the true religion here established, we rest full assured; as likewise of his most pious zeal and careful endeavour for the maintenance and propagation thereof; being so far from having the least doubt of His Majesty's remissness therein, that we, next under God, ascribe unto his own princely wisdom and goodness, that our holy religion hath yet any countenance at all amongst us.

IV. And for that the pious intention and endeavours, even of the best and wisest princes, are often frustrated through the unfaithfulness and carelessness of their ministers; and that we find a great unhappiness to have befallen His Majesty this way; we think, that being now assembled in Parliament to advise of the weighty and important affairs concerning Church and State; we cannot do a work more acceptable than, in the first place, according to the dignity of the matter, and necessity of the present occasions, faithfully and freely to make known, what we conceive may conduce to the preservation of God's religion, in great peril now to be lost; and, therewithal, the safety and tranquillity of His Majesty and his kingdoms now threatened with certain dangers. For the clearer proceedings

therein, we shall declare, 1. What those dangers and inconveniences are. 2. Whence they arise. 3. In some sort, how
they may be redressed.

The dangers may appear partly from the consideration of
the state of religion abroad; and partly from the condition
thereof within His Majesty's own dominions, and especially
within this kingdom of England.

From abroad we make these observations: 1. By the mighty
and prevalent party, by which true religion is actually opposed,
and the contrary maintained. 2. Their combined counsels,
forces, attempts, and practices, together with a most diligent
pursuit of their designs, aiming at the subversion of all the
Protestant Churches in Christendom. 3. The weak resistance
that is made against them. 4. Their victorious and successful
enterprises, whereby the Churches of Germany, France, and
other places, are in a great part already ruined, and the rest
in the most weak and miserable condition.

In His Majesty's own dominions, these: 1. In Scotland, the
stirs lately raised and insolences committed by the Popish party,
have already not a little disquieted that famous Church; of
which, with comfort we take notice, His Majesty hath expressed
himself exceeding sensible; and hath accordingly given most
royal and prudent directions therein. 2. Ireland is now almost
wholly overspread with Popery, swarming with friars, priests,
and Jesuits, and other superstitious persons of all sorts; whose
practice is daily to seduce His Majesty's subjects from their
allegiance, and to cause them to adhere to his enemies. That
even in the city of Dublin, in the view of the State, where not
many years since, as we have been credibly informed, there
were few or none that refused to come to church, there are
lately restored and erected for friars, Jesuits, and idolatrous
mass-priests, thirteen houses, being more in number than the
parish churches within that city; besides many more likewise
erected in the best parts of the kingdom; and the people,
almost wholly, revolted from our religion, to the open exercise
of Popish superstition. The danger from hence is further
increased, by reason of the intercourse which the subjects, of all
sorts, in that kingdom, have into Spain, and the Archduchess's
country; and that, of late, divers principal persons being

Papists are trusted with the command of soldiers; and great numbers of the Irish are acquainted with the exercise of arms and martial discipline; which, heretofore, hath not been permitted, even in times of greatest security.   3. Lastly, here in England we observe an extraordinary growth of Popery, insomuch that in some counties, where in Queen Elizabeth's time there were few or none known Recusants, now there are above 2000, and all the rest generally apt to revolt.   A bold and open allowance of their religion, by frequent and public resort to mass, in multitudes, without control, and that even to the Queen's Court; to the great scandal of His Majesty's government.   Their extraordinary insolence; for instance, the late erecting of a College of Jesuits in Clerkenwell, and the strange proceedings thereupon used in favour of them. The subtle and pernicious spreading of the Arminian faction; whereby they have kindled such a fire of division in the very bowels of the State, as if not speedily extinguished, it is of itself sufficient to ruin our religion; by dividing us from the Reformed Churches abroad, and separating amongst ourselves at home, by casting doubts upon the religion professed and established; which, if faulty or questionable in three or four Articles, will be rendered suspicious to unstable minds, in all the rest, and incline them to Popery, to which those tenets, in their own nature, do prepare the way: so that if our religion be suppressed and destroyed abroad, disturbed in Scotland, lost in Ireland, undermined and almost outdared in England, it is manifest that our danger is very great and imminent.

The causes of which danger here, amongst divers others, we conceive to be chiefly these instanced in :   1. The suspension or negligence in execution of the laws against Popery.   2. The late proceedings against the College of Jesuits[1].   3. Divers letters sent by Sir Robert Heath, His Majesty's Attorney, into the country, for stay of proceedings against Recusants. 4. The publishing and defending points of Popery in sermons and books, without punishment;   instance Bishop Montague's three books, viz. 'The Gag[2],' 'Invocation of Saints[3],' and his

[1] *Hist. of Engl.* vi. 238.
[2] *A gag for the new gospel!   No! a new gag for an old goose.*   1624.
[3] *Immediate address unto God alone ... enlarged to a just treatise of invocation of saints.*   1624.

'Appeal[1];' also Dr. Cosin's 'Horary[2]' and the Bishop of Gloucester's Sermons[3].   5. The bold and unwarranted introducing,
practising, and defending of sundry new ceremonies, and laying
of injunctions upon men by governors of the Church and others,
without authority, in conformity to the Church of Rome; as, for
example, in some places erecting of altars, in others changing
the usual and prescribed manner of placing the communion
table, and setting it at the upper end of the chancel, north and
south, in imitation of the High Altar; by which they, also,
call it, and adorn it with candlesticks, which, by the injunctions,
10 Eliz., were to be taken away; and do also make obeisance
by bowing thereunto, commanding men to stand up at *Gloria
Patri*; bringing men to question and trouble for not obeying
that command for which there is no authority; enjoining that
no woman be churched without a veil; setting up of pictures,
lights, and images in churches; praying towards the east, crossing *ad omnem motum et gestum.*   6. The false and counterfeit
conformity of Papists, whereby they do not only evade the law,
but obtain places of trust and authority: instance Mr. Browne
of Oxford, and his treatise written to that purpose; the Bishop
of Gloucester; and the now Bishop of Durham.   7. The
suppressing and restraint of the orthodox doctrine, contained
in the Articles of Religion, confirmed in Parliament, 13 Eliz.,
according to the sense which hath been received publicly, and
taught as the doctrine of the Church of England in those
points, wherein the Arminians differ from us and other the
Reformed Churches; wherein the essence of our Articles, in
those controverted points, is known and proved.   8. The
publishing of books, and preaching of sermons, contrary to the
former orthodox doctrine, and suppressing books written in
defence thereof: instance Bishop Montague's 'Gag' and
'Appeal,' Mr. Jackson's 'Book of the Essence and Attributes of
God,' Dr. White's two sermons preached at Court, one upon the
5th of November, the other on Christmas Day last: and for
orthodox books suppressed, instance in all that have been

---

[1] *Appello Caesarem*, 1625.

[2] *A collection of private devotions* ... called the Hours of Prayer, 1627.

[3] Probably the *Fall of Man*, by Godfrey Goodman, published in 1616.
He was now Bishop of Gloucester. A new edition was issued in 1629
against his wish.

written against Bishop Montague and Cosin, yea even Bishop Carleton's book. 9. That these persons who have published and maintained such Papistical, Arminian, and superstitious opinions and practices, who are known to be unsound in religion, are countenanced, favoured, and preferred: instance, Mr. Montague made Bishop of Chichester; also the late Bishop of Carlisle [1], since his last Arminian sermon preached at Court, advanced to the bishopric of Norwich; a known Arminian [2] made Bishop of Ely; the Bishop of Oxford [3], a long-suspected Papist, advanced to the bishopric of Durham; Mr. Cosin, advanced to dignity and a great living; Dr. Wren, made Dean of Windsor, and one of the High Commission Court. 10. That some prelates near the King, having gotten the chief administration of ecclesiastical affairs under His Majesty, discountenance and hinder the preferment of those that are orthodox, and favour such as are contrary: instance, the Bishops of Winchester [4] and London [5], in divers particulars.

The points wherein the Arminians differ from us and other the Reformed Churches, in the sense of the Articles confirmed in Parliament, 13 Eliz., may be known and proved in these controverted points, viz.: 1. By the Common Prayer, established in Parliament. 2. By the book of Homilies, confirmed by the acts of religion. 3. By the Catechism concerning the points printed in the Bible, and read in churches, and divers other impressions published by authority. 4. Bishop Jewel's works, commanded to be kept in all churches, that every parish may have one of them. 5. The public determination of divinity professors, published by authority. 6. The public determination of divines in both the Universities. 7. The Resolution of the Archbishop of Canterbury and other rev. bishops and divines assembled at Lambeth, for this very purpose, to declare their opinions concerning those points, anno 1595, unto which the Archbishop of York and all his province did likewise agree. 8. The Articles of Ireland, though framed by the Convocation there, yet allowed by the Clergy and State here. 9. The suffrage of the British divines, sent by King James, to the Synod of Dort. 10. The uniform consent of our writers published by

---

[1] Francis White.　　　[2] John Buckeridge.　　　[3] John Howson.
[4] Richard Neile.　　　[5] William Laud.

authority. 11. The censures, recantations, punishments, and submissions, made, enjoined, and inflicted upon those that taught contrary thereunto, as Barrow and Barrett in Cambridge, and Bridges in Oxford.

The remedy of which abuses we conceive may be these: 1. Due execution of laws against Papists. 2. Exemplary punishments to be inflicted upon teachers, publishers, and maintainers of Popish opinions, and practising of superstitious ceremonies, and some stricter laws in that case to be provided. 3. The orthodox doctrine of our Church, in these now controverted points by the Arminian sect, may be established and freely taught; according as it hath been hitherto generally received, without any alteration or innovation; and severe punishment, by the same laws to be provided against such as shall, either by word or writing, publish anything contrary thereunto. 4. That the said books of Bishop Montague and Cosin may be burned. 5. That such as have been authors, or abettors, of those Popish and Arminian innovations in doctrine, may be condignly punished. 6. That some good order may be taken for licensing books hereafter. 7. That His Majesty would be graciously pleased to confer bishoprics, and other ecclesiastical preferments, with advice of his Privy Council, upon learned, pious, and orthodox men. 8. That bishops and clergymen being well chosen, may reside upon their charge, and with diligence and fidelity perform their several duties, and that accordingly they may be countenanced and preferred. 9. That some course may, in this Parliament, be considered of, for providing competent means to maintain a godly, able minister in every parish church of this kingdom. 10. That His Majesty would be graciously pleased to make a special choice of such persons, for the execution of his ecclesiastical commissions, as are approved for integrity of life and soundness of doctrine.

15. PROTESTATION OF THE HOUSE OF COMMONS.

[March 2, 1628–9. Rushworth, i. 660. See *Hist. of Engl.* vii. **75.**]

1. Whosoever shall bring in innovation of religion, or by favour or countenance seek to extend or introduce Popery

or Arminianism, or other opinion disagreeing from the true
and orthodox Church, shall be reputed a capital enemy to
this Kingdom and Commonwealth.

2. Whosoever shall counsel or advise the taking and levying
of the subsidies of Tonnage and Poundage, not being granted
by Parliament, or shall be an actor or instrument therein,
shall be likewise reputed an innovator in the Government, and
a capital enemy to the Kingdom and Commonwealth.

3. If any merchant or person whatsoever shall voluntarily
yield, or pay the said subsidies of Tonnage and Poundage, not
being granted by Parliament, he shall likewise be reputed a
betrayer of the liberties of England, and an enemy to the same[1].

16. THE KING'S DECLARATION SHOWING THE CAUSES OF THE LATE DISSOLUTION.

[March 10, 162⅞. Rushworth, i. App. 1. See *Hist. of Engl.* vii. 78.]

Howsoever princes are not bound to give account of their
actions, but to God alone; yet for the satisfaction of the
minds and affections of our loving subjects, we have thought
good to set down thus much by way of declaration, that we
may appear to the world in the truth and sincerity of our
actions, and not in those colours in which we know some
turbulent and ill-affected spirits (to mask and disguise their
wicked intentions, dangerous to the State) would represent
us to the public view.

We assembled our Parliament the seventeenth day of March,
in the third year of our reign, for the safety of religion, for
securing our kingdoms and subjects at home, and our friends
and allies abroad; and therefore at the first sitting down of
it we declared the miserable afflicted estate of those of the
reformed religion, in Germany, France, and other parts of
Christendom; the distressed extremities of our dearest uncle,
the King of Denmark[2], chased out of a great part of his
dominions; the strength of that party which was united against

---

[1] This protestation was recited by Holles after the Speaker had been held
down in his chair, as the King was approaching to break open the door of
the House of Commons.

[2] Christian IV.

us; that (besides the Pope, and the House of Austria, and their ancient confederates) the French King professed the rooting out of the Protestant Religion; that, of the Princes and States on our party, some were overrun, others diverted, and some disabled to give assistance : for which, and other important motives, we propounded a speedy supply of treasure, answerable to the necessity of the cause.

These things in the beginning were well resented by the House of Commons, and with much alacrity and readiness they agreed to grant a liberal aid : but before it was brought to any perfection, they were diverted by a multitude of questions raised amongst them touching their liberties and privileges, and by other long disputes, that the Bill did not pass in a long time; and by that delay our affairs were put into a far worse case than at the first, our foreign actions then in hand being thereby disgraced and ruined for want of timely help.

In this, as we are not willing to derogate from the merit and good intentions of those wise and moderate men of that House, (to whose forwardness we attribute it, that it was propounded and resolved so soon): so we must needs say, that the delay of passing it, when it was resolved, occasioned by causeless jealousies, stirred up by men of another temper, did much lessen both the reputation and reality of that supply: and their spirit, infused into many of the Commissioners and Assessors in the country, hath returned up the subsidies in such a scanty proportion, as is infinitely short, not only of our great occasions, but of the precedents of former subsidies, and of the intentions of all well-affected men in that House.

In those large disputes, as we permitted many of our high prerogatives to be debated, which in the best times of our predecessors had never been questioned without punishment or sharp reproof, so we did endeavour to have shortened those debates, for winning of time, which would have much advantaged our great affairs both at home and abroad. And therefore both by speeches and messages we did often declare our gracious and clear resolution to maintain, not only the Parliament, but all our people, in their ancient and just liberties without either violation or diminution; and in the end, for their full satisfaction and security, did by an answer, framed in the form by themselves desired, to their Parliamentary Petition[1], confirm their ancient and just liberties and rights, which we resolve with all constancy and justice to maintain.

This Parliament, howsoever, besides the settling our necessary supply and their own liberties, they wasted much time in such proceedings, blasting our government, as we are unwilling to remember, yet we suffered them to sit, until themselves desired us to appoint a time for recess, not naming either adjournment or prorogation.

Whereupon, by advice of our Council, we resolved to prorogue and make a Session; and to that end prefixed a day, by which they might (as was meet in so long a sitting) finish some profitable and good laws; and withal, gave order for a gracious pardon to all our subjects; which, according to the use of former Parliaments, passed the Higher House, and was sent down to the Commons. All which being graciously intended by us, was ill-entertained by some disaffected persons of that House, who by their artifices in a short time raised so much heat and distemper in the House,—for no other visible cause but because we had declared our resolution to prorogue, as our Council advised, and not to adjourn, as some of that House (after our resolution declared, and not before) did manifest themselves to affect,—that seldom hath greater passion been seen in that House, upon the greatest occasions. And some glances in the House, but upon open rumours abroad, were spread, that by the answer to the Petition we had given away, not only our impositions upon goods exported and imported, but the Tonnage and Poundage—whereas in the debate and hammering of that Petition, there was no speech or mention in either House concerning those impositions, but concerning taxes and other charges, within the land; much less was there any thought thereby to debar us of Tonnage and Poundage, which both before and after the Answer to that Petition the House of Commons, in all their

[1] i. e. The Petition of Right.

speeches and treaties, did profess they were willing to grant; and at the same time many other misinterpretations were raised of that Petition and Answer, by men not well distinguishing between well-ordered liberty and licentiousness; as if by our answer to that Petition we had let loose the reins of our government: and in this distemper, the House of Commons laying aside the Pardon (a thing never done in any former Parliament) and other business, fit to have been concluded that Session, some of them went about to frame and contrive a Remonstrance against our receiving of Tonnage and Poundage, which was so far proceeded in the night before the prefixed time for concluding the Session, and so hastened by the contrivers thereof, that they meant to have put it to the vote of the House the next morning, before we should prorogue the Session: and therefore finding our gracious favours in that Session, afforded to our people, so ill-requited, and such sinister strains made upon our answer to that Petition, to the diminution of our profit, and (which was more) to the danger of our government: we resolved to prevent the finishing of that Remonstrance, and other dangerous intentions of some ill-affected persons, by ending the Session the next morning, some few hours sooner than was expected, and by our own mouth to declare to both Houses the cause thereof; and for hindering the spreading of those sinister interpretations of that Petition and Answer, to give some necessary directions for settling and quieting our government until another meeting; which we performed accordingly the six and twentieth of June last.

The Session thus ended, and the Parliament risen, that intended Remonstrance gave us occasion to look into the business of Tonnage and Poundage: and therefore, though our necessities pleaded strongly for us, yet we were not apt to strain that point too far, but resolved to guide ourself by the practice of former ages, and examples of our most noble predecessors; thinking those counsels best warranted, which the wisdom of former ages, concurring with the present occasions did approve; and therefore gave order for a diligent search of records: upon which it was found, that although in the Parliament holden in the first year of the reign of King

Edward the Fourth, the subsidy of Tonnage and Poundage was not granted unto that King, but was first granted unto him by Parliament in the third year of his reign; yet the same was accounted and answered to that King, from the first day of his reign, all the first and second years of his reign, and until it was granted by Parliament: and that in the succeeding times of King Richard the Third, King Henry the Seventh, King Henry the Eighth, King Edward the Sixth, Queen Mary, and Queen Elizabeth, the subsidy of Tonnage and Poundage was not only enjoyed by every of those Kings and Queens, from the death of each of them deceasing, until it was granted by Parliament unto the successor; but in all those times (being for the most part peaceable, and not burdened with like charges and necessities, as these modern times) the Parliament did most readily and cheerfully, in the beginning of every of those reigns, grant the same, as a thing most necessary for the guarding of the seas, safety and defence of the realm, and supportation of the royal dignity: and in the time of our royal father of blessed memory, he enjoyed the same a full year, wanting very few days, before his Parliament began; and above a year before the Act of Parliament for the grant of it was passed: and yet when the Parliament was assembled, it was granted without difficulty. And in our own time we quietly received the same three years and more, expecting with patience, in several Parliaments, the like grant thereof, as had been made to so many of our predecessors; the House of Commons still professing that multitude of other businesses, and not want of willingness on their part, had caused the settling thereof to be so long deferred: and therefore, finding so much reason and necessity for the receiving of the ordinary duties in the Custom House, to concur with the practice of such a succession of Kings and Queens, famous for wisdom, justice, and government; and nothing to the contrary, but that intended Remonstrance, hatched out of the passionate brains of a few particular persons; we thought it was so far from the wisdom and duty of a House of Parliament, as we could not think that any moderate and discreet man (upon composed thoughts, setting aside passion and distemper) could be against receiving of Tonnage and Poundage;

especially since we do, and still must, pursue those ends, and undergo that charge, for which it was first granted to the Crown; it having been so long and constantly continued to our predecessors, as that in four several Acts of Parliament for the granting thereof to King Edward the Sixth, Queen Mary, Queen Elizabeth, and our blessed father, it is in express terms mentioned, to have been had and enjoyed by the several Kings, named in those acts, time out of mind, by authority of Parliament: and therefore upon these reasons we held it agreeable to our kingly honour, and necessary for the safety and good of our kingdom, to continue the receipt thereof, as so many of our predecessors had done. Wherefore when a few merchants (being at first but one or two), fomented, as it is well known, by those evil spirits, that would have hatched that undutiful Remonstrance, began to oppose the payment of our accustomed duties in the Custom House, we gave order to the officers of our customs to go on, notwithstanding that opposition, in the receiving of the usual duties; and caused those that refused to be warned to attend at the Council Board, that by the wisdom and authority of our Council they might be reduced to obedience and duty; where some of them, without reverence or respect to the honour and dignity of that presence, behaved themselves with such boldness and insolency of speech, as was not to be endured by a far meaner assembly, much less to be countenanced by a House of Parliament, against the body of our Privy Council.

And as in this we did what in reason and honour was fit for the present, so our thoughts were daily intentive upon the reassembling of our Parliament, with full intention on our part to take away all ill understanding between us and our people, whose love as we desired to continue and preserve, so we used our best endeavours to prepare and facilitate the way to it; and to this end, having taken a strict and exact survey of our government, both in the Church and Commonwealth, and what things were most fit and necessary to be reformed: we found in the first place that much exception had been taken at a book entitled *Appello Caesarem*, or an *Appeal to Caesar*, and published in the year 1625 by Richard Montague, then Bachelor of Divinity, and now

Bishop of Chichester; and because it did open the way to
those schisms and divisions which have since ensued in the
Church, we did, for remedy and redress thereof, and for the
satisfaction of the consciences of our good people, not only
by our public proclamation, call in that book, which ministered matter of offence, but to prevent the like danger for
hereafter, reprinted the Articles of Religion, established in
the time of Queen Elizabeth of famous memory, and by a
declaration before those Articles[1], we did tie and restrain all
opinions to the sense of those Articles, that nothing might
be left for private fancies and innovations. For we call God
to record, before whom we stand, that it is, and always hath
been, our heart's desire to be found worthy of that title, which
we account the most glorious in all our Crown, Defender of
the Faith. Neither shall we ever give way to the authorising
of anything, whereby any innovation may steal or creep into
the Church, but to preserve that unity of doctrine and discipline, established in the time of Queen Elizabeth, whereby the
Church of England hath stood and flourished ever since.

And as we were careful to make up all breaches and rents
in religion at home, so did we, by our proclamation and
commandment, for the execution of laws against Priests and
Popish Recusants, fortify all ways and approaches against
that foreign enemy; which, if it have not succeeded according
to our intention, we must lay the fault where it is, in the
subordinate officers and ministers in the country, by whose
remissness Jesuits and Priests escape without apprehension,
and Recusants, from those convictions and penalties which
the law and our commandment would have inflicted on them:
for we do profess, that, as it is our duty, so it shall be our
care, to command and direct well; but it is the part of
others to perform the ministerial office, and when we have
done our office we shall account ourself, and all charitable
men will account us innocent, both to God and men; and
those that are negligent we will esteem as culpable both to
God and us, and therefore will expect that hereafter they give
us a better account.

And, as we have been careful for the settling of religion and

[1] See p. 75.

quieting the Church, so were we not unmindful of the preservation of the just and ancient liberties of our subjects, which we
secured to them by our gracious answer to the Petition in Parliament, having not since that time done any act whereby to
infringe them : but our care is, and hereafter shall be, to keep
them entire and inviolable, as we would do our own right and
sovereignty, having for that purpose enrolled the Petition and
Answer in our Courts of Justice.

Next to the care of religion and of our subjects' rights, we
did our best for the provident and well-ordering of that aid
and supply, which was granted us the last Session, whereof
no part hath been wastefully spent, nor put to any other use,
than those for which it was desired and granted, as upon
payment of our fleet and army ; wherein our care hath been
such as we chose rather to discontent our dearest friends and
allies, and our nearest servants, than to leave our soldiers
and mariners unsatisfied, whereby any vexation or disquiet
might arise to our people. We have also, with part of those
monies, begun to supply our magazines and stores of munition,
and to put our navy into a constant form and order. Our
fleet likewise is fitting, and almost in a readiness, whereby
the narrow seas may be guarded, commerce maintained, and
our kingdom secured from all foreign attempts. These acts
of ours might have made this impression in all good minds,
that we were careful to direct our counsels, and dispose our
actions, as might most conduce to the maintenance of religion,
honour of our government, and safety of our people. But
with mischievous men once ill-affected, *seu bene seu male facta
premunt*; and whatsoever once seemed amiss is ever remembered, but good endeavours are never regarded.

Now all these things that were the chief complaints the
last Session, being by our princely care so seriously reformed,
the Parliament reassembled the twentieth of January last.
We expected, according to the candour and sincerity of our
own thoughts, that men would have framed themselves for
the effecting of a right understanding between us and our
people; but some few malevolent persons, like empirics and
lewd artists, did strive to make new work, and to have some
disease on foot, to keep themselves in request, and to be

employed and entertained in the cure. And yet to manifest
how much offences have been diminished, the committees for
grievances, committees for Courts of Justice, and committees
for trade, have, since the sitting down of the Parliament,
received few complaints, and those such as they themselves
have not thought to be of that moment or importance, with
which our ears should be acquainted.

No sooner therefore was the Parliament set down but these
ill-affected men began to sow and disperse their jealousies,
by casting out some glances and doubtful speeches, as if the
subject had not been so clearly and well dealt with, touching
the liberties, and touching the Petition answered the last
Parliament. This being a plausible theme, thought on for
an ill purpose, easily took hold on the minds of many that
knew not the practice. And thereupon the second day of
the Parliament, a committee was appointed to search whether
the Petition and our Answer thereunto were enrolled in the
Parliament roll, and in the Courts at Westminster, and in
what manner the same was done. And a day also was then
appointed, on which the House, being resolved into a committee, should take into consideration those things wherein
the liberty of the subject had been invaded, against the
Petition of Right. This, though it produced no other effect
of moment or importance, yet was sufficient to raise a jealousy
against our proceedings, in such as were not well acquainted
with the sincerity and clearness of them. There followed
another of no less skill; for although our proceeding before
the Parliament, about matters of religion, might have satisfied
any moderate men of our zealous care thereof (as we are sure
it did the most), yet, as bad stomachs turn the best things
into their own nature for want of good digestion, so those
distempered persons have done the like of our good intents
by a bad and sinister interpretation; for, when they did
observe that many honest and religious minds in that House
did complain of those dangers that did threaten the Church,
they likewise took the same word in their mouth, and their
cry likewise was *Templum Domini, Templum Domini*, when
the true care of the Church never came into their hearts;
and what the one did out of zeal unto religion, the other

took up as a plausible theme to deprave our government, as
if we, our clergy and council, were either senseless or careless
of religion; and this wicked practice hath been to make us seem
to walk before our people as if we halted before God.

Having by these artifices made a jealous impression in the
hearts of many, and a day being appointed to treat of the
grant of Tonnage and Poundage, at the time prefixed, all
express great willingness to grant it. But a new strain is
found out, that it could not be done without great peril to
the right of the subject, unless we should disclaim any right
therein, but by grant in Parliament, and should cause all
those goods to be restored, which, upon commandment from
us or our Council, were staid by our officer until those duties
were paid, and consequently should put ourselves out of the
possession of the Tonnage and Poundage before they were
granted; for else, it was pretended, the subject stood not in
fit case to grant it. A fancy and cavil raised of purpose to
trouble the business; it being evident that all the Kings
before-named did receive that duty, and were in actual
possession of it before, and at the very time, when it was
granted to them by Parliament. And although we, to remove
all difficulties, did from our own mouth, in those clear and
open terms that might have satisfied any moderate and well-
disposed minds, declare that it was our meaning, by the gift
of our people, to enjoy it, and that we did not challenge it
of right, but took it *de bene esse*, showing thereby not the
right but the necessity by which we were to take it (wherein
we descended, for their satisfaction, so far beneath ourself,
as we are confident never any of our predecessors did the
like, nor was the like ever required or expected from them).
Yet for all this, the Bill of Tonnage and Poundage was laid
aside, upon pretence they must first clear the right of the
subject therein; under colour whereof, they entertain the
complaints, not only of John Rolle, a member of their House,
but also of Richard Chambers, John Fowkes, and Bartholomew
Gilman, against the officers of our customs, for detaining
their goods upon refusal to pay the ordinary duty, accustomed
to be paid for the same. And upon these complaints they
send for the officers of the customs, enforcing them to attend

day after day by the space of a month together; they cause them to produce their letters patents under our Great Seal, and the warrants made by our Privy Council for levying of those duties. They examine the officers upon what questions they please, thereby to entrap them for doing our service and commandments. In these and other their proceedings, because we would not give the least show of interruption, we endured long with much patience both these and sundry other strange and exorbitant encroachments and usurpations, such as were never before attempted in that House.

We are not ignorant how much that House hath of late years endeavoured to extend their privileges, by setting up general committees for religion, for Courts of Justice, for trade, and the like; a course never heard of until of late: so as, where in former times the Knights and Burgesses were wont to communicate to the House such business as they brought from their countries; now there are so many chairs erected, to make inquiry upon all sorts of men, where complaints of all sorts are entertained, to the unsufferable disturbance and scandal of justice and government, which, having been tolerated awhile by our father and ourself, hath daily grown to more and more height; insomuch that young lawyers sitting there take upon them to decry the opinions of the Judges; and some have not doubted to maintain that the resolutions of that House must bind the Judges, a thing never heard of in ages past: but in this last assembly of Parliament they have taken on them much more than ever before.

They sent messengers to examine our Attorney-General (who is an officer of trust and secrecy) touching the execution of some commandments of ours, of which, without our leave first obtained, he was not to give account to any but ourself. They sent a captious and directory message to the Lord Treasurer, Chancellor, and Barons of the Exchequer, touching some judicial proceedings of theirs in our Court of Exchequer.

They sent messengers to examine upon sundry questions, our two Chief Justices and three other of our Judges, touching their judicial proceedings at the Gaol Delivery at Newgate, of which they are not accountable to the House of Commons.

And whereas suits were commenced in our Court of Star Chamber, against Richard Chambers, John Fowkes, Bartholomew Gilman, and Richard Phillips, by our Attorney-General, for great misdemeanours; they resolved that they were to have privilege of Parliament against us for their persons, for no other cause but because they had petitions depending in that House; and (which is more strange) they resolved that a signification should be made from that House, by a letter to issue under the hand of their Speaker unto the Lord Keeper of our Great Seal, that no attachments should be granted out against the said Chambers, Fowkes, Gilman, or Phillips, during their said privilege of Parliament. Whereas it is far above the power of that House to give direction to any of our Courts at Westminster to stop attachments against any man, though never so strongly privileged; the breach of privilege being not in the Court that grants, but in the party or minister that puts in execution such attachments. And therefore, if any such letter had come to the Lord Keeper, as it did not, he should have highly offended us if he had obeyed it. Nay, they went so far as they spared not the honour of our Council Board, but examined their proceedings in the case of our customers, interrogating what this or that man of our Council said in direction of them in the business committed to their charge. And when one of the members of that House, speaking of our counsellors said we had wicked counsel; and another said that the Council and Judges sought to trample under feet the liberty of the subject; and a third traduced our Court of Star Chamber for the sentence given against Savage, they passed without check or censure by the House. By which may appear, how far the members of that House have of late swoln beyond the rules of moderation and the modesty of former times; and this under pretence of privilege and freedom of speech, whereby they take liberty to declare against all authority of Council and Courts at their pleasure.

They sent for our Sheriff of London to examine him in a cause whereof they had no jurisdiction; their true and ancient jurisdiction extending only to their own members, and to the conservation of their privileges, and not to the censure of foreign persons and causes, which have no relation to their privileges, the same being but a late innovation. And yet upon an enforced strain of a contempt, for not answering to their satisfaction, they commit him to the Tower of London, using that outward pretext for a cause of committing him, the true and inward cause being, for that he had showed himself dutiful to us and our commandments in the matter concerning our customs.

In these innovations (which we will never permit again) they pretended indeed our service, but their drift was to break, by this means, through all respects and ligaments of government, and to erect an universal over-swaying power to themselves, which belongs only to us, and not to them.

Lastly, in their proceedings against our customers, they went about to censure them as delinquents, and to punish them for staying some goods of some factious merchants in our store-house, for not paying those duties which themselves had formerly paid, and which the customers, without interruption, had received of all other merchants many years before, and to which they were authorised both by our Great Seal and by several directions and commandments from us and our Privy Council.

To give some colour to their proceeding herein, they went about to create a new privilege (which we will never admit), that a Parliament-man hath privilege for his goods against the King; the consequence whereof would be, that he may not be constrained to pay any duties to the King during the time of privilege of Parliament. It is true, they would have this case to have been between the merchants and our farmers of our customs, and have severed them from our interest and commandment, thereby the rather to make them liable to the censure and punishment of that House. But on the other side, we holding it both unjust and dishonourable to withdraw ourself from our officers in anything they did by our commandment, or to disavow anything that we had enjoined to be done; upon Monday, the twenty-third of February, sent a message unto them by Secretary Coke[1], thanking them for the respect they had showed in severing the interest of our farmers from

---

[1] Sir John Coke.

our own interest and commandment. Nevertheless we were bound in honour to acknowledge a truth, that what was done by them was done by our express commandment and direction; and if, for doing thereof, our farmers should suffer, it would highly concern us in honour. Which message was no sooner delivered unto them, but in a tumultuous and discontented manner they called Adjourn, Adjourn; and thereupon, without any cause given on our part, in a very unusual manner, adjourned unto the Wednesday following.

On which day, by the uniform wisdom of our Privy Council, we caused both Houses to be adjourned until the second day of March, hoping that in the meantime a better and more right understanding might be begotten between us and the members of that House, whereby the Parliament might come to a happy issue.

But understanding by good advertisement that their discontent did not in that time digest and pass away, we resolved to make a second adjournment until the tenth of March, which was done, as well to take time to ourself to think of some means to accommodate those difficulties, as to give them time to advise better; and accordingly we gave commandment for a second adjournment in both Houses, and for cessation of all business till the day appointed, which was very dutifully obeyed in the Higher House, no man contradicting or questioning it. But when the same commandment was delivered in the House of Commons by their Speaker, it was straightway contradicted; and although the Speaker declared unto them it was an absolute right and power in us to adjourn as well as to prorogue or dissolve, and declared and read unto them divers precedents of that House to warrant the same; yet our commandment was most contemptuously disobeyed, and some rising up to speak said they had business to do before the House should be adjourned[1].

Whilst the Duke of Buckingham lived he was entitled to all the distempers and ill events of former Parliaments, and

---

[1] Note by Rushworth: 'Here are the passages concerning the members' deportment in the House, mentioned in this Declaration, which we forbear to repeat, in regard the same are at large expressed in the Information in the *Star Chamber*, before mentioned.'

therefore much endeavour was used to demolish him, as the only wall of separation between us and our people. But now he is dead, no alteration was found amongst those envenomed spirits which troubled then the blessed harmony between us and our subjects, and continue still to trouble it. For now under the pretence of public care of the Commonwealth they suggest new and causeless fears, which in their own hearts they know to be false; and devise new engines of mischief, so to cast a blindness upon the good affections of our people, that they may not see the truth and largeness of our heart towards them. So that now it is manifest, the Duke was not alone the mark these men shot at, but was only as a near minister of ours, taken up, on the by, and in their passage to their more secret designs; which were only to cast our affairs into a desperate condition to abate the powers of our Crown, and to bring our government into obloquy, that in the end all things may be overwhelmed with anarchy and confusion.

We do not impute these disasters to the whole House of Commons, knowing that there were amongst them many religious, grave, and well-minded men; but the sincerer and better part of the House was overborne by the practices and clamours of the other, who, careless of their duties, and taking advantage of the times and our necessities, have enforced us to break off this meeting; which, had it been answered with like duty on their parts as it was invited and begun with love on ours, might have proved happy and glorious both to us and this whole nation.

We have thus declared the manifold causes we had to dissolve this Parliament, whereby all the world may see how much they have forgotten their former engagements at the entry into the war, themselves being persuaders to it; promising to make us feared by our enemies and esteemed by our friends, and how they turned the necessities grown by that war to enforce us to yield to conditions incompatible with monarchy.

And now that our people may discern that these provocations of evil men (whose punishments we reserve to a due time) have not changed our good intentions to our subjects, we do here profess to maintain the true religion and doctrine

established in the Church of England, without admitting or
conniving at any backsliding either to Popery or schism.
We do also declare that we will maintain the ancient and
just rights and liberties of our subjects, with so much constancy and justice that they shall have cause to acknowledge
that under our government and gracious protection they live
in a more happy and free estate than any subjects in the
Christian world.   Yet let no man hereby take the boldness
to abuse that liberty, turning it to licentiousness; nor mis-
interpret the Petition by perverting it to a lawless liberty,
wantonly or frowardly, under that or any other colour, to
resist lawful and necessary authority.   For as we will maintain our subjects in their just liberties, so we do and will
expect that they yield as much submission and duty to our
royal prerogatives, and as ready obedience to our authority
and commandments, as hath been promised to the greatest
of our predecessors.

   And for our ministers, we will not that they be terrified
by those harsh proceedings that have been strained against
some of them.   For, as we will not command anything unjust
or dishonourable, but shall use our authority and prerogatives
for the good of our people; so we will expect that our ministers
obey us, and they shall assure themselves we will protect them.

   As for our merchants, we let them know we shall always
endeavour to cherish and enlarge the trade of such as be
dutiful, without burthening them beyond what is fitting;
but the duty of five in the hundred for guarding of the seas,
and defence of the realm, to which we hold ourselves still
obliged (and which duty hath continued without interruption
so many succession of ages), we hold no good or dutiful subject will deny it, being so necessary for the good of the whole
kingdom : and if any factious merchant will affront us in
a thing so reasonable, and wherein we require no more, nor
in no other manner, than so many of our predecessors have
done, and have been dutifully obeyed, let them not deceive
themselves, but be assured that we shall find honourable and
just means to support our estate, vindicate our sovereignty,
and preserve the authority which God hath put into our
hands.

And now having laid down the truth and clearness of our proceedings, all wise and discreet men may easily judge of those rumours and jealous fears that are maliciously and wickedly bruited abroad; and may discern, by examination of their own hearts, whether (in respect of the free passage of the Gospel, indifferent and equal administration of justice, freedom from oppression, and the great peace and quietness which every man enjoyeth under his own vine and fig-tree) the happiness of this nation can be paralleled by any of our neighbour countries; and if not, then to acknowledge their own blessedness, and for the same be thankful to God, the author of all goodness.

17. THE DECLARATION OF SPORTS [1].

[October 18, 1633.   See *Hist. of Engl.* vii. 318–324.]

Our dear father of blessed memory, in his return from Scotland, coming through Lancashire, found that his subjects were debarred from lawful recreations upon Sundays after evening prayers ended, and upon Holy-days; and he prudently considered that, if these times were taken from them, the meaner sort who labour hard all the week should have no recreations at all to refresh their spirits: and after his return, he further saw that his loyal subjects in all other parts of his kingdom did suffer in the same kind, though perhaps not in the same degree: and did therefore in his princely wisdom publish a Declaration to all his loving subjects concerning lawful sports to be used at such times, which was printed and published by his royal commandment in the year 1618, in the tenor which hereafter followeth :

Whereas upon our return the last year out of Scotland, we did publish our pleasure touching the recreations of our people in those parts under our hand; for some causes us thereunto moving, we have thought good to command these our directions then given in Lancashire, with a few words thereunto added,

---

[1] The full title is, 'The King's Majesty's declaration to his subjects concerning lawful sports to be used.   Imprinted at Lond. by Robert Barker, Printer to the King's most excellent Majesty : and by the Assigns of Robert Bill, M.DC.XXXIII.'

and most appliable to these parts of our realms, to be published to all our subjects.

Whereas we did justly in our progress through Lancashire rebuke some Puritans and precise people, and took order that the like unlawful carriage should not be used by any of them hereafter, in the prohibiting and unlawful punishing of our good people for using their lawful recreations and honest exercises upon Sundays, and other Holy-days, after the afternoon sermon or service, we now find that two sorts of people wherewith that country is much infected, we mean Papists and Puritans, have maliciously traduced and calumniated those our just and honourable proceedings : and therefore, lest our reputation might upon the one side (though innocently) have some aspersion laid upon it, and that upon the other part our good people in that country be misled by the mistaking and misinterpretation of our meaning, we have therefore thought good hereby to clear and make our pleasure to be manifested to all our good people in those parts.

It is true that at our first entry to this Crown and kingdom we were informed, and that too truly, that our county of Lancashire abounded more in Popish Recusants than any county of England, and thus hath still continued since, to our great regret, with little amendment, save that, now of late, in our last riding through our said country, we find both by the report of the Judges, and of the Bishop of that Diocese, that there is some amendment now daily beginning, which is no small contentment to us.

The report of this growing amendment amongst them made us the more sorry, when with our own ears we heard the general complaint of our people, that they were barred from all lawful recreations and exercise upon the Sunday's afternoon, after the ending of all divine service, which cannot but produce two evils: the one the hindering of the conversion of many, whom their priests will take occasion hereby to vex, persuading them that no honest mirth or recreation is lawful or tolerable in our religion, which cannot but breed a great discontentment in our people's hearts, especially of such as are peradventure upon the point of turning: the other inconvenience is, that this prohibition barreth the common and meaner sort of

people from using such exercises as may make their bodies
more able for war, when His Majesty or his successors shall
have occasion to use them ; and in place thereof sets up filthy
tippling and drunkenness, and breeds a number of idle and
discontented speeches in their ale-houses.   For when shall the
common people have leave to exercise, if not upon the Sundays
and Holy-days, seeing they must apply their labour and win
their living in all working-days?

Our express pleasure therefore is, that the laws of our
kingdom and canons of the Church be as well observed in
that county, as in all other places of this our kingdom: and
on the other part, that no lawful recreation shall be barred to
our good people, which shall not tend to the breach of our
aforesaid laws and canons of our Church: which to express
more particularly, our pleasure is, that the Bishop, and all other
inferior churchmen and churchwardens, shall for their parts be
careful and diligent, both to instruct the ignorant, and convince and reform them that are misled in religion, presenting
them that will not conform themselves, but obstinately stand
out, to our Judges and Justices: whom we likewise command
to put the law in due execution against them.

Our pleasure likewise is, that the Bishop of that Diocese
take the like strait order with all the Puritans and Pre-
cisians within the same, either constraining them to conform
themselves or to leave the county, according to the laws of our
kingdom and canons of our Church, and so to strike equally
on both hands against the contemners of our authority and
adversaries of our Church ; and as for our good people's lawful
recreation, our pleasure likewise is, that after the end of divine
service our good people be not disturbed, letted or discouraged
from any lawful recreation, such as dancing, either men or
women ; archery for men, leaping, vaulting, or any other such
harmless recreation, nor from having of May-games, Whitsun-
ales, and Morris-dances; and the setting up of May-poles and
other sports therewith used: so as the same be had in due
and convenient time, without impediment or neglect of divine
service: and that women shall have leave to carry rushes to
the church for the decorating of it, according to their old
custom ; but withal we do here account still as prohibited all

unlawful games to be used upon Sundays only, as bear and bull-baitings, interludes and at all times in the meaner sort of people by law prohibited, bowling [1].

And likewise we bar from this benefit and liberty all such known Recusants, either men or women, as will abstain from coming to church or divine service, being therefore unworthy of any lawful recreation after the said service, that will not first come to the church and serve God: prohibiting in like sort the said recreations to any that, though conform in religion, are not present in the church at the service of God, before their going to the said recreations. Our pleasure likewise is, that they to whom it belongeth in office, shall present and sharply punish all such, as in abuse of this our liberty, will use these exercises before the end of all divine services for that day: and we likewise straightly command that every person shall resort to his own parish church to hear divine service, and each parish by itself to use the said recreation after divine service: prohibiting likewise any offensive weapons to be carried or used in the said times of recreation: and our pleasure is, that this our Declaration shall be published by order from the Bishop of the Diocese, through all the parish churches, and that both our Judges of our circuit and our Justices of our Peace be informed thereof.

> Given at our Manor of Greenwich the four and twentieth
> day of May, in the sixteenth year of our Reign, of
> England, France and Ireland; and of Scotland the one
> and fiftieth.

Now out of a like pious care for the service of God, and for suppressing of any humours that oppose truth, and for the ease, comfort and recreation of our well-deserving people, His Majesty doth ratify and publish this our blessed father's Declaration: the rather, because of late in some counties of our kingdom, we find that under pretence of taking away abuses, there hath been a general forbidding, not only of ordinary meetings, but of the Feasts of the Dedication of the Churches, commonly called Wakes. Now our express will and pleasure is, that these Feasts, with others, shall be observed, and that

[1] See 33 Henry VIII. c. ix. § 11.

our Justices of the Peace, in their several divisions, shall look to it, both that all disorders there may be prevented or punished, and that all neighbourhood and freedom, with manlike and lawful exercises be used: and we further command all Justices of Assize in their several circuits to see that no man do trouble or molest any of our loyal and dutiful people, in or for their lawful recreations, having first done their duty to God, and continuing in obedience to us and our laws: and for this we command all our Judges, Justices of Peace, as well within liberties as without, Mayors, Bailiffs, Constables, and other officers, to take notice of, and to see observed, as they tender our displeasure.   And we further will that publication of this our command be made by order from the Bishops, through all the parish churches of their several dioceses respectively.

> Given at our Palace of Westminster, the eighteenth day of October, in the ninth year of our Reign.

> God save the King

18. ACT OF THE PRIVY COUNCIL ON THE POSITION OF THE COMMUNION TABLE AT ST. GREGORY'S.

[November 3, 1633.   Prynne's *Canterbury's Doome*, 88.   See *Hist. of Engl.* vii. 310.]

At Whitehall, the third day of November, 1633.
Present, the King's Most Excellent Majesty.
Lord Archbishop of Canterbury [William Laud],
Lord Keeper [Sir Thomas Coventry],
Lord Archbishop of York [Richard Neile],
Lord Treasurer [Earl of Portland],
Lord Privy Seal [Earl of Manchester],
Lord Duke of Lennox,
Lord Chamberlain [of the Household, Earl of Pembroke and Montgomery],
Earl of Bridgwater,
Earl of Carlisle,
Lord Cottington,
Master Treasurer [of the Household, Sir Thomas Edmondes],

Master Comptroller [of the Household, Sir Henry Vane],
Lord High Chamberlain [Earl of Lindsey],
Earl Marshal [Earl of Arundel],
Master Secretary Coke,
Master Secretary Windebanke.

This day was debated before His Majesty sitting in Council, the question and difference which grew about the removing of the communion table in St. Gregory's church, near the cathedral church of St. Paul, from the middle of the chancel to the upper end, and there placed altar-wise, in such manner as it standeth in the said cathedral and mother church (as also in all other cathedrals and in His Majesty's own chapel), and as it is consonant to the practice of approved antiquity: which removal and placing of it in that sort was done by order from the Dean and Chapter of St. Paul's who are ordinaries thereof, as was avowed before His Majesty by Doctor King and Doctor Montfort, two of the prebends there; yet some few of the parishioners, being but five in number, did complain of this act by appeal to the Court of Arches, pretending that the Book of Common Prayer and the 82nd Canon do give permission to place the communion table where it may stand with the most fitness and convenience. Now His Majesty having heard a particular relation made by the counsel of both parties of all the carriage and proceedings in this cause, was pleased to declare his dislike of all innovation and receding from ancient constitutions, grounded upon just and warrantable reasons, especially in matters concerning ecclesiastical order and government, knowing how easily men are drawn to affect novelties, and how soon weak judgments in such cases may be overtaken and abused. And he was also pleased to observe, that if these few parishioners might have their wills, the difference thereby from the foresaid cathedral mother church, by which all other churches depending thereon ought to be guided, would be the more notorious, and give more subject of discourse and disputes that might be spared, by reason of St. Gregory's standing close to the wall thereof. And likewise for so much as concerns the liberty given by the said communion book or canon, for placing the communion table in any church or chapel with most convenience; that liberty is not so to be understood, as if it were ever left to the discretion of the parish, much less to the particular fancy of any humorous person, but to the judgment of the ordinary to whose place and function it doth properly belong to give direction in that point, both for the thing itself, and for the time, when and how long, as he may find cause. Upon which consideration His Majesty declared himself, that he well approved and confirmed the act of the said ordinary, and also gave command that if those few parishioners before mentioned do proceed in their said appeal, then the Dean of the Arches [1] (who was then attending at the hearing of the cause) shall confirm the said order of the aforesaid Dean and Chapter.

19. Specimen of the First Writ of Ship-money.

[October 20, 1634. Rushworth, ii. 257. See *Hist. of Engl.* vii. 356, 369.]

Carolus Rex, &c.

To the Mayor, commonalty, and citizens of our city of London, and to the sheriffs of the same city, and good men in the said city and in the liberties, and members of the same, greeting: Because we are given to understand that certain thieves, pirates, and robbers of the sea, as well Turks, enemies of the Christian name, as others, being gathered together, wickedly taking by force and spoiling the ships, and goods, and merchandises, not only of our subjects, but also the subjects of our friends in the sea, which hath been accustomed anciently to be defended by the English nation, and the same, at their pleasure, have carried away, delivering the men in the same into miserable captivity: and forasmuch as we see them daily preparing all manner of shipping farther to molest our merchants, and to grieve the kingdom, unless remedy be not sooner applied, and their endeavours be not more manly met withal; also the dangers considered which, on every side, in these times of war do hang over our heads, that it behoveth us and our subjects to hasten the defence of the sea and kingdom with all expedition or

[1] Sir Henry Marten.

speed that we can; we willing by the help of God chiefly
to provide for the defence of the kingdom, safeguard of the sea,
security of our subjects, safe conduct of ships and merchandises
to our kingdom of England coming, and from the same
kingdom to foreign parts passing; forasmuch as we, and our
progenitors, Kings of England, have been always heretofore
masters of the aforesaid sea, and it would be very irksome unto
us if that princely honour in our times should be lost or in any
thing diminished.   And although that charge of defence which
concerneth all men ought to be supported by all, as by the
laws and customs of the kingdom of England hath been accustomed to be done: notwithstanding we considering that you
constituted in the sea-coasts, to whom by sea as well great
dangers are imminent, and who by the same do get more plentiful
gains for the defence of the sea, and conservation of our princely
honour in that behalf, according to the duty of your allegiance
against such attempts, are chiefly bound to set to your helping
hand; we command firmly, enjoining you the aforesaid Mayor,
commonalty and citizens, and sheriffs of the said city, and the
good men in the same city and in the liberties, and members of
the same, in the faith and allegiance wherein you are bound
unto us, and as you do love us and our honour, and under the
forfeiture of all which you can forfeit to us, that you cause
to be prepared and brought to the port of Portsmouth, before
the first day of March now next ensuing, one ship of war of
the burden of nine hundred tons, with three hundred and fifty
men at the least, as well expert masters, as very able and skilful
mariners; one other ship of war of the burden of eight hundred
tons, with two hundred and sixty men at the least, as well
skilful masters, as very able and expert mariners: four other
ships of war, every of them of the burden of five hundred tons,
and every of them with two hundred men at the least, as well
expert masters, as very able and skilful mariners: and one
other ship of war of the burden of three hundred tons, with
a hundred and fifty men, as well expert masters, as very able
and skilful mariners: and also every of the said ships with
ordnance, as well greater as lesser, gunpowder, and spears and
weapons, and other necessary arms sufficient for war, and with
double tackling, and with victuals, until the said first of March,

competent for so many men ; and from that time, for twenty-six
weeks, at your charges, as well in victuals as men's wages, and
other things necessary for war, during that time, upon defence
of the sea in our service, in command of the admiral of the
sea, to whom we shall commit the custody of the sea, before
the aforesaid first day of March, and as he, on our behalf, shall
command them to continue ; so that they may be there the same
day, at the farthest, to go from thence with our ships, and the
ships of other faithful subjects, for the safeguard of the sea, and
defence of you and yours, and repulse and vanquishing of whomsoever busying themselves to molest or trouble upon the sea our
merchants, and other subjects, and faithful people coming into
our dominions for cause of merchandise, or from thence returning
to their own countries. Also we have assigned you, the aforesaid
Mayor and Aldermen of the city aforesaid, or any thirteen, or
more of you, within thirteen days after the receipt of this writ,
to assess all men in the said city, and in the liberties, and
members of the same, and the landholders in the same, not
having a ship, or any part of the aforesaid ships, nor serving
in the same, to contribute to the expenses, about the necessary
provision of the premises ; and to assess and lay upon the
aforesaid city, with the liberties and members thereof, viz.
upon every of them according to their estate and substances,
and the portion assessed upon them ; and to nominate and
appoint collectors in this behalf. Also we have assigned
you, the aforesaid Mayor, and also the Sheriffs of the city
aforesaid, to levy the portions so as aforesaid assessed upon
the aforesaid men and landholders, and every of them in the
aforesaid city, with the liberties and members of the same, by
distress and other due means ; and to commit to prison all those
whom you shall find rebellious and contrary in the premises,
there to remain until we shall give further order for their
delivery. And moreover we command you, that about the
premises you diligently attend, and do, and execute those things
with effect, upon peril that shall fall thereon : but we will not,
that under colour of our aforesaid command, more should be
levied of the said men than shall suffice for the necessary
expenses of the premises ; or that any who have levied money
for contribution to raise the aforesaid charges, should by him

detain the same, or any part thereof; or should presume, by any manner of colour, to appropriate the same to other uses; willing, that if more than may be sufficient shall be collected, the same may be paid out among the contributors, for the rate of the part to them belonging.

>Witness myself, at Westminster the twentieth day of October, in the tenth year of our reign[1].

20. The King's Case laid before the Judges, with their Answer[2].

[February 7, 1637. Rushworth, ii. 355. See *Hist. of Engl.* viii. 207.]

Carolus Rex.

When the good and safety of the kingdom in general is concerned, and the whole kingdom in danger, whether may not the King, by writ under the Great Seal of England, command all the subjects of our kingdom at their charge to provide and furnish such a number of ships, with men, victuals, and munition, and for such time as we shall think fit for the defence and safeguard of the kingdom from such danger and peril, and by law compel the doing thereof, in case of refusal or refractoriness: and whether in such a case is not the King the sole judge both of the danger, and when and how the same is to be prevented and avoided?

May it please your Most Excellent Majesty,

We have, according to your Majesty's command, every man by himself, and all of us together, taken into serious consideration the case and question signed by your Majesty, and inclosed

---

[1] In 1635 the writs were extended to the inland counties.

[2] An earlier opinion had been given by the Judges at Finch's instance in November, 1635 (Rushworth, iii. App. 249), to the following effect :—
' I am of opinion that, as when the benefit doth more particularly redound to the ports or maritime parts, as in case of piracy or depredations upon the seas, that the charge hath been, and may be lawfully imposed upon them according to precedents of former times ; so when the good and safety of the kingdom in general is concerned, and the whole kingdom in danger (of which His Majesty is the only judge), then the charge of the defence ought to be borne by all the realm in general. This I hold agreeably both to law and reason.'

in your royal letter; and we are of opinion, that when the good
and safety of the kingdom in general is concerned, and the
kingdom in danger, your Majesty may, by writ under the Great
Seal of England, command all your subjects of this your
kingdom, at their charge to provide and furnish such a number
of ships, with men, victuals, and munition, and for such time
as your Majesty shall think fit for the defence and safeguard
of this kingdom from such danger and peril: and that by law
your Majesty may compel the doing thereof in case of refusal,
or refractoriness: and we are also of opinion, that in such case
your Majesty is the sole judge both of the danger, and when
and how the same is to be prevented and avoided.

John Bramston,	George Croke,
John Finch,	Thomas Trevor,
Humphry Davenport,	George Vernon,
John Denham,	Francis Crawley,
Richard Hutton,	Robert Berkeley,
William Jones,	Richard Weston.

21. EXTRACTS FROM THE SPEECH OF OLIVER ST. JOHN IN THE SHIP-MONEY CASE.

[November, 1637.   Rushworth, ii. 481.   See *Hist. of Engl.* viii. 271.]

.   .   .   .

My Lords, by the law the King is *Pater familiae*, who by the
law of economics is not only to keep peace at home, but to
protect his wife and children and whole families from injuries
from abroad.

It is his vigilance and watchfulness that discovers who are
our friends and foes, and that after such discovery first warns
us of them, for he only hath power to make war and peace.

Neither hath the law only intrusted the care of the defence
to His Majesty, but it hath likewise, secondly, put the *arma-
tam potestatem* and means of defence wholly in his hands; for
when the enemy is by him discovered and declared, it is not
in the power of the subject to order the way and means of
defence, either by sea or by land, according as they shall think
fit; for no man without commission or special license from His

Majesty, can set forth any ships to sea for that purpose; neither can any man, without such commission or license, unless upon sudden coming of enemies, erect a fort, castle, or bulwark, though upon his own ground; neither, but upon some such emergent cause, is it lawful for any subject, without special commission, to arm or draw together any troops or companies of soldiers, or to make any general collections of money of any of His Majesty's subjects, though with their consent.

Neither, in the third place, is His Majesty armed only with this primitive prerogative power of *generalissimo*, and commander-in-chief, that none can advance towards the enemy until he gives the signal, nor in other manner than according to his direction; but likewise with all other powers requisite for the full execution of all things incident to so high a place, as well in times of eminent danger as of actual war. The sheriff of each county, who is but His Majesty's minister, he hath the *Posse Comitatus*; and therefore it must needs follow, that the *Posse Regni* is in himself.

My Lords, not to burn daylight longer, it must needs be granted that in this business of defence the *suprema potestas* is inherent in His Majesty, as part of his crown and kingly dignity.

So that as the care and provision of the law of England extends in the first place to foreign defence, and secondly lays the burden upon all, and for ought I have to say against it, it maketh the quantity of each man's estate the rule whereby this burden is to be equally apportioned upon each person; so likewise hath it in the third place made His Majesty the sole judge of dangers from foreigners, and when and how the same are to be prevented, and to come nearer, hath given him power by writ under the Great Seal of England, to command the inhabitants of each county to provide shipping for the defence of the kingdom, and may by law compel the doing thereof.

So that, my Lords, as I still conceive the question will not be *de persona*, in whom the *suprema potestas* of giving the authorities or powers to the sheriff, which are mentioned in this writ, doth lie, for that it is in the King; but the question is only *de modo*, by what medium or method this supreme power, which is in His Majesty, doth infuse and let out itself into this particular; and whether or no in this cause such of them have been used, as have rightly accommodated, and applied this power unto this writ in the intended way of defence for the law of England, for the applying of that supreme power, which it hath settled in His Majesty, to the particular causes and occasions that fall out, hath set down methods and known rules, which are necessary to be observed.

In His Majesty there is a two-fold power, *voluntas*, or *potestas interna*, or *naturalis*; *externa*, or *legalis*, which by all the Judges of England, 2 R. 3. fo. 11, is expressed *per voluntatem Regis in camera*, and *voluntatem Regis per legem*.

My Lords, the forms and rules of law are not observed; this supreme power not working *per media*, it remains still in himself as *voluntas Regis interna*, and operates not to the good and relief of the subject that standeth in need.

To instance,

His Majesty is the fountain of bounty; but a grant of lands without Letters Patent transfers no estate out of the King to the patentee, nor by Letters Patents, but by such words as the law hath prescribed.

His Majesty is the fountain of justice; and though all justice which is done within the realm flows from this fountain, yet it must run in certain and known channels: an assize in the King's Bench, or an appeal of death in the Common Pleas, are *coram non judice*, though the writ be His Majesty's command; and so of the several jurisdictions of each Court, the justice whereby all felons and traitors are put to death, proceeds from His Majesty; but if a writ of execution of a traitor or felon be awarded by His Majesty, without appeal or indictment preceding, an appeal of death will lie by the heir against the executioner. If the process be legal, and in a right Court, yet I conceive that His Majesty alone, without assistance of the Judges of the Court, cannot give judgment. I know that King John, H. 3, and other Kings, have sat on the King's Bench, and in the Exchequer; but for ought appears they were assisted by their Judges. This I ground upon the Book Case of 2 R. 3. fo. 10 & 11.

Where the party is to make fine and ransom at the King's will and pleasure, this fine, by the opinion of the Judges of

England, must be set by the Judges before whom the party was convicted, and cannot be set by the King: the words of the book are thus: *In terminis, et non per Regem per se in camera sua nec aliter coram se nisi per justitiarios suos; et haec est voluntas Regis, scilicet per justitiarios suos et per legem suam* to do it.

And as without the assistance of his Judges, who are his settled counsel at law, His Majesty applies not the law and justice in many cases unto his subjects; so likewise in other cases: neither is this sufficient to do it without the assistance of his great Council in Parliament; if an erroneous judgment was given before the Statute of 27 Eliz. in the King's Bench, the King could not relieve his grieved subjects any way but by Writ of Error in Parliament; neither can he out of Parliament alter the old laws, nor make new, or make any naturalizations or legitimations, nor do some other things; and yet is the Parliament His Majesty's Court too, as well as other his Courts of Justice. It is His Majesty that gives life and being to that, for he only summons, continues, and dissolves it, and he by his *le volt* enlivens all the actions of it; and after the dissolution of it, by supporting his Courts of Justice, he keeps them still alive, by putting them in execution: and although in the Writ of Wast, and some other writs, it is called *Commune Concilium Regni*: in respect that the whole kingdom is representatively there; and secondly, that the whole kingdom have access thither in all things that concern them, other Courts affording relief but in special causes; and thirdly, in respect that the whole kingdom is interested in, and receive benefit by the laws and things there passed; yet it is *Concilium Regni* no otherwise than the Common Law is *Lex Terrae*, that is *per modum Regis* whose it is; if I may so term it in a great part, even in point of interest, as he is the head of the Commonwealth, and whose it is wholly in trust for the good of the whole body of the realm; for he alone is trusted with the execution of it.

· · · · · · · · ·

The second thing which I observe is this, by the cases before cited it appears, that without the assistance in Parliament, His Majesty cannot in many cases communicate either his justice or power unto his subjects.

· · · · · · · · ·

My Lords, I have now done with the stating of the question :
the things whereupon I shall spend all the rest of my time are
these five.

1. Admitting that the ordinary means before-mentioned had
been all used, and that they had not been sufficient, whether in
this case His Majesty, without consent in Parliament, may,
in this case of extraordinary defence, alter the property of the
subject's goods for the doing thereof.

2. In the next place I shall endeavour to answer to some
objections which may be made to the contrary.

3. In the third place, for qualifying of this I shall admit,
that in some cases the property of the subject's goods, for
the defence of the realm, may be altered without consent in
Parliament; and I shall show what they be in particular, and
compare them and the present occasion together.

4. In the fourth place, because of some precedents of the
matter of fact, and likewise legal authorities that may seem to
prove a legality in this particular of shipping for the defence at
sea, whatever it be in the general; I shall therefore endeavour
an answer to such of them as I have met withal.

And shall conclude in the last place with the authorities in
point.

For the first, that to the altering of the property of the
subject's goods, though for the defence of the realm, that a
parliamentary assistance is necessary.

In this it must be granted in the first place, that the law
ties no man, and much less the King, to impossibilities.

And secondly, that the kingdom must be defended.

As therefore the law hath put this great trust upon His
Majesty; so when the supplies, which by the ways before
mentioned it hath put into his hands, are spent, therein it
hath provided other ways for a new supply, which is the first
thing that I shall present to your Lordships, and this is the
aids and subsidies in Parliament.

That amongst the *ardua Regni negotia*, for which Parliaments are called, this of the defence is not only one of them,
but even the chief, is cleared by this, that of all the rest none
is named particularly in the summons, but only this; for all the
summons to Parliament show the cause of the calling of them to

be *pro quibusdam arduis negotiis nos et defensionem Regni nostri Angliae et Ecclesiae Anglicanae concernentibus*. And in conclusion, the party summoned is commanded to be there *sicut honorem nostrum, et salvationem, et defensionem Regni et Ecclesiae diligit.*

And in all the ancient summons of Parliament, when aid was demanded, the particular cause of defence and against what enemy in special was mentioned.

.   .   .   .

My Lords, the Parliament, as it is best qualified and fitted to make this supply for some of each rank, and that through all the parts of the kingdom being there met, His Majesty having declared the danger, they best knowing the estates of all men within the realm, are fittest, by comparing the danger and men's estates together, to proportion the aid accordingly.

And secondly, as they are fittest for the preservation of that fundamental propriety which the subject hath in his lands and goods, because each subject's vote is included in whatsoever is there done; so that it cannot be done otherwise, I shall endeavour to prove to your Lordships both by reason and authority.

My first reason is this, that the Parliament by the law is appointed as the ordinary means for supply upon extraordinary occasions, when the ordinary supplies will not do it: if this in the writ therefore may, without resorting to that, be used, the same argument will hold as before in resorting to the extraordinary, by [exclusion ?] of the ordinary, and the same inconvenience follow.

My second reason is taken from the actions of former Kings in this of the defence.

The aids demanded by them, and granted in Parliament, even for this purpose of the defence, and that in times of imminent danger, are so frequent, that I will spare the citing of any of them: it is rare in a subject, and more in a prince, to ask and take that of gift, which he may and ought to have of right, and that without so much as a *salvo*, or declaration of his right.

.   .   .   .

My Lords, it appears not by anything in the writ, that any war at all was proclaimed against any State, or that if any

His Majesty's subjects had taken away the goods of any prince's subjects in Christendom, but that the party might have recovered them before your Lordships in any His Majesty's Courts; so that the case in the first place is, whether in times of peace His Majesty may, without consent in Parliament, alter the property of the subject's goods for the defence of the realm.

Secondly, the time that will serve the turn for the bringing in of the supplies and means of the defence, appears to your Lordships judicially by the writ, that is seven months within four days; for the writ went out Aug. 4, and commands the ship to be at Portsmouth, the place of the rendezvous, the first of March following; and thereby it appears that the necessity in respect of the time was not such, but that a parliamentary consent might in that time have been endeavoured for the effecting of the supply.

·   ·   ·   ·   ·   ·   ·   ·   ·

22. Extracts from the Argument of Sir Robert Berkeley, Justice of the King's Bench.

[1638. State Trials, iii. col. 1090. See *Hist. of Engl.* viii. 278.]

For my clear delivery and expression of myself, I divide all that I shall say into these four heads. (1) I will state the case and will settle the proper question of it, as the pleadings are. (The true stating and settling of a case conduceth much to the right answer of it.) (2) I will consider the policy and fundamental rules of the Common Law, applicable unto that which upon stating the case shall appear to be the proper question. (3) I will consider the Acts of Parliament, the answer to petitions in Parliament, and the several Magna Chartas of the liberties of England, which concern the King's proceeding in this case. (4) I will answer the material objections, which have been made on the other side.

Upon my first general head. I hope that none doth imagine, that it either is or can be drawn by consequence, to be any part of the question in this case, whether the King may at all times, and upon all occasions, impose charges upon his subjects in general, without common consent in Parliament? If that were made the question, it is questionless that he may not. The people of the kingdom are subjects, not slaves, freemen, not villains, to be taxed *de alto et basso*.

Though the King of England hath a monarchical power, and hath *jura summae majestatis*, and hath an absolute trust settled in his crown and person, for government of his subjects; yet his government is to be *secundum leges regni*. It is one of the questions in the *juramentum regis*, at his coronation (see the old Magna Charta, fol. 164); *Concedis justas leges et consuetudines regni esse tuendas?* And the king is to answer, *Concedo*. By those laws the subjects are not tenants at the king's will, of what they have. They have in their lands *Feodum simplex*, which by Littleton's description is, *haereditas legitima, vel pura*. They have in their goods a property, a peculiar interest, a *meum et tuum*. They have a birthright in the laws of the kingdom. No new laws can be put upon them; none of their laws can be altered or abrogated without common consent in Parliament.

Thus much I speak to avoid misapprehensions and misreports upon that which I shall say in this case; not as if there were cause of saying so much upon anything challenged on the King's side. We have in print His Majesty's own most gracious Declaration, that it is his maxim, that the people's liberties strengthen the King's prerogative, and that the King's prerogative is to defend the people's liberties.

Secondly, though Mr. Hampden's counsel have spent all their powder in citing a multitude of records, beginning with one in King John's time, and so downwards, to prove that the King's ministers have paid, that the barons have been by writs commanded sometimes to pay, sometimes to make allowances, out of the King's moneys or dues,—in cases of foreign auxiliary, and voluntary wars: in cases of particular or ordinary defence of the realm, as upon rebellion of subjects, or inroads by enemies, into parts, marches, or maritime; such enemies I mean, as are not greatly formidable, as are apt to run away when they hear of any force coming against them: in cases of setting forth ships, for scouring the seas from petty pirates, so that merchants may have safe passage: in cases where victuals, or other pro-

visions, were taken from particular persons, by way of purvey-
ance, for soldiers, or for the King's army : in cases of borrowing
of money by the King's officers for war, or ordinary or extraordinary defence : in cases of taking money or goods against
the owner's consent, by warrant for the King's use, for war, or
other manner of defence : in cases where particular men's ships,
horses, or armour, were lost in the wars : in cases where private
men's houses were used in the King's service : lastly, in cases of
general and extraordinary defence, where the King had sufficient
aids for that purpose granted to him in Parliament.   Although
I confess it be true, that the King in all these cited cases must
pay of his own, without imposing upon the subject; yet I say
that those cases come not close to our case : for every of those
cases hath a manifest, particular, and just reason ; but none of
these reasons are applicable to the case now in question, as is
easy to demonstrate, if a man would enter into every of these
particulars; which I forbear, for saving of time.   And these
records being taken away, the multitude of vouchers on
Mr. Hampden's side will be greatly abated.

Thirdly, the case of the ancient tribute called Danegelt, of
which Mr. Hampden's counsel hath spoken, though it come
nearer than any of the former mentioned cases, yet it much
differs from the charge imposed in our case.

. . . .

Fourthly, I affirm, with some clearness, under favour, that
the charge now demanded is not within the ancient acceptation
or signification of the words, aids, mises, prizes, taxes, or talliages,
which it is to be agreed cannot be exacted by the King, without consent in Parliament.   Neither is it within the compass
of the word subsidy, which may not be levied, but upon grant
of it in Parliament.   Aids, if you take the word in a general
sense, they were of two kinds : (1) Such as were aids and
services too, as *pur faire fitz chevalier, pur file marier.*   That
kind of aid, common persons, who had seigniories, had right
unto, as well as the King.   No colour of comprehending this
kind of aids, within the word, aids, pertinent to this question.
(2) To the second kind of aids, were sums of money from the
subject to the King, by way of help, *ad agenda*[1] *regis*; as for

------

[1] Corrected from Stowe MSS. 187/2.

making of castles, building of bridges, helps for voluntary or
auxiliary wars, or for the King to do his pleasure with, and the
like . . . . . Mises were presentations in kind of a benevolence,
upon a King's first coming to his crown; such are yielded at
this day in Wales to a Prince of Wales. Prises are taking of
part of the subject's goods from them to the King's use without
pay; hence prisage of wines at this day.

. . . .

Fifthly, it cannot be said that the present case is to be
stated so, as unless the charge commanded be obeyed, an
assured infallible ruin and subversion of this kingdom will
happen, and that instantly. In such a case, *quid non* is lawful; and happy he who by doing any exploit can save the ship
from sinking, the body from falling.

Sixthly, it is to be observed that the principal command
in the Shipping-Writ is not to levy money, it is to provide
a ship; which ship being to be provided at the charge of a
multitude, in regard the thing cannot be done any manner
of way, but by the means of that which is *mensura rerum*,
namely, money, therefore the instructions in the Shipping-
Writ are not only apt, but necessary; that an assessment
be made, whereby proportionable sums of money may be
collected for the provision of the thing commanded. And
thereupon it may be said, that the sum assessed upon every
one, and in our case upon Mr. Hampden, is not a debt *vi
termini*, but is rather a duty to be performed as a means
conducing to the principal end. The refusal of performance
of which duty is a refusal to obey the principal thing commanded, *qui negat medium, destruit finem*. And the principal
thing commanded, being of a kind concerning the commonwealth, the King, who is the head, the sovereign of the
commonwealth, and who hath, as incident to his regal office,
power of coercion, is by law to exercise such his power of
coercion, to inforce such as refuse to join with others in performance of that which is commanded for the commonwealth.
And this being the true state and way of the proceedings in the
present case, it is apparent, that, though the *Scire Facias* against
Mr. Hampden be in the King's name, yet it is not to have
execution as for the King's money, or as for a debt due to

the King from Mr. Hampden.   But as is manifest, if the whole
contexture of the Writ of *Scire Facias* be observed, it is nothing
else but to bring on a declaratory payment.   That Mr. Hampden
ought *onerari* to the payment of the 20s. assessed upon him.   So
that with his 20s., together with the other money of Buckinghamshire men, assessed also upon every of them particularly,
the ship commanded from the county of Buckingham may be
provided.

Seventhly and lastly, having declared of what nature our case
is not, I come now to tell you what the state of it is.   The true
state of our question must be made out of the whole record or
pleading of the case, the matter of fact wherein the defendant
hath confessed (as I noted in the beginning).   In the writ of
Aug. 11 Car. and in the Writ of *Mittimus*, there are causes
expressed of the issuing of the writ of Aug. 11, of the Shipping-
Writ; those causes are several, but not to be severed, all of
them are to be laid together into the balance.

1. *Piratae congregati*, upon the English seas.   2. *Piratae
navigium indies preparantes, ad mercatores ulterius molestandos,
et ad regnum gravandum.*   3. *Pericula* are *undique regno
Angliae, in his guerrinis temporibus.*   4. Those *pericula* do *im-
minere regno, nisi citius remedium ponatur*; where the word
citius is a comparative word, relative to slow ways of remedy,
amongst which Parliaments is one.   5. *Regi et subditis con-
venit, omni qua poterint festinatione accelerare, ad regni defensionem, maris tuitionem, et securitatem subditorum.*

Out of all those positions it appears that there is in the
case real and manifest peril; not *panicus terror*, fear without
cause; *tempora* are *de facto guerrina*, there is *de facto navium
congregatio*.

Again, we must observe, that in this case: 1. The command
is, *ad proficiscendum cum navibus regis*.   So the King himself
is to join with the subject in the common defence.   Here is not
a *quod tibi fieri non vis*.   Here is rather a *contributio* than
a *tributio*.   2. The ships and arms to be provided are to continue the subject's own in property.   The King doth not assume
the property of them to himself; he only commands them to be
made and used for the common defence.   This appears by the
words *ad proficiscendum cum navibus nostris*.   So the writ

sets a distinction between *naves nostrae* (that is, the King's) and the ships to be provided. See the like of this, m. 28 and 29 Ed. 1, *Communia*, with the King's Remembrancer, for galleys commanded upon the like occasion; and P. 5, E. 2, and P. 13, E. 2, with the King's Remembrancer, *inter brevia directa baronibus*. 3. The subjects are commanded, in this case, to be at the expenses, *tam in victualibus, quam hominum salariis ad guerram necessariis*. This I shall prove clearly anon, to be consonant to law, and warranted by many precedents in the like cases. 4. All the counties of the kingdom, that is, all the kingdom in general, is charged, not any spared; the clergy, the King himself, are to join in the provisions. 5. The final end and scope of all this preparation is *defensio regni, tuitio maris, retentio dominii maris, securitas subditorum, salus reipublicae*.

.   .   .   .

Now whether to set the commonwealth free and in safety from this peril of ruin and destruction, the King may not, of his own royal authority, and without common assent in Parliament, impose a charge upon his subjects in general to provide such shipping as is necessary in his royal judgment, to join with His Majesty's own ships to attend them for such time as His Majesty in his royal wisdom shall think fit, and also to enjoin them to be themselves at the expenses, *tam in victualibus quam hominum salariis et aliis ad guerram necessariis ?*

I would be loth to irritate any differing in opinion from me with provoking or odious terms; but I cannot more fully express myself (and so I desire it may be taken as an expression, and not as a comparison) than in saying, that it is a dangerous tenet, a kind of judaizing opinion, to hold that the weal public must be exposed to peril of utter ruin and subversion, rather than such a charge as this, which may secure the commonwealth, may be imposed by the King upon the subject, without common consent in Parliament. So that the security of the commonwealth, for the very subsistence of it, must stay and expect until a Parliament provide for it; in which interim of time, it is possible, nay, apparently probable, yea, in a manner to be presumed, that all may be, yea, will be brought to a final period of destruction and desolation.

All know that the Jews were so strict, that they would not use means for defence of themselves and their country upon their Sabbath. Their enemies took the advantage, and ruined their state.

The Second General Head.—I now come to my second general head, wherein I proposed to consider of the fundamental policy, and maxims, and rules of law, for the government of this realm, and of the reasons of law pertinent to our case, which are very many. I will briefly and severally point at those which make impression on me. 1. It is plain that as originally, even before the Romans' time, the frame of this kingdom was a monarchical state, so for divers hundreds of years past, upon the Romans' desertion of it, and after the heptarchy ended, it was, and continued, and still continueth monarchical. And our gracious sovereign is a monarch, and the rights of free monarchy appertain unto him; and yet still with this, that he must *leges ad consuetudines regni servare, et praecipue leges et consuetudines et libertates a glorioso rege Edwardo* (that is, Edward the Confessor) *clero populoque concessas*; as appears in the old *Magn. Chart.* fol. 164, tit. *juramentum regis quando coronatur*.

2. Where Mr. Holborne[1] supposed a fundamental policy in the creation of the frame of this kingdom, that in case the monarch of England should be inclined to exact from his subjects at his pleasure, he should be restrained, for that he could have nothing from them, but upon a common consent in Parliament.

He is utterly mistaken herein. I agree the Parliament to be a most ancient and supreme court, where the King and Peers, as judges, are in person, and the whole body of the Commons representatively. There Peers and Commons may, in a fitting way, *parler lour ment*, and show the estate of every part of the kingdom; and amongst other things, make known their grievances (if there be any) to their sovereign, and humbly petition him for redress.

But the former fancied policy I utterly deny. The law knows no such king-yoking policy. The law is of itself an old and trusty servant of the King's; it is his instrument or

[1] One of Hampden's counsel.

means which he useth to govern his people by. I never
read nor heard that *lex* was *Rex*; but it is common and most
true that *Rex* is *lex*, for he is *lex loquens*, a living, a speaking,
an acting law : and because the King is *lex loquens*, therefore
it is said that *Rex censetur habere omnia jura in scrinio
pectoris sui.*

There are two maxims of the law of England, which plainly
disprove Mr. Holborne's supposed policy. The first is, ' That
the King is a person trusted with the state of the commonwealth.' The second of these maxims is, ' That the King cannot
do wrong.' Upon these two maxims the *jura summae majestatis*
are grounded, with which none but the King himself (not his
high court of Parliament without leave) hath to meddle, as,
namely, war and peace, value of coin, Parliament at pleasure,
power to dispense with penal laws, and divers others; amongst
which I range these also, of regal power to command provision
(in case of necessity) of means from the subjects, to be adjoined
to the King's own means for the defence of the commonwealth,
for the preservation of the *salus reipublicae.* Otherwise I do
not understand how the King's Majesty may be said to have
the majestical right and power of a free monarch.

It is agreed that the King is, by his regal office, bound
to defend his people against foreign enemies; our books are
so, Fitzherbert, *Natura brevium*, fol. 118, *Est a intendre que
le roy doit de droit ; saver et defendre son realme com' vers le
meere, com' vers enemies. Juramentum Regis*, cited before,
*servabis ecclesiae Dei, clero, et populo, pacem ex integro secun-
dum vires tuas*; if *ex integro*, then against all disturbers of
the general peace amongst them, most chiefly, in my judgment, against dangerous foreigners.

Bracton and Glanvill, in the front of their books, published that the King must have arms as well as laws ; arms
and strength against foreign enemies, laws for doing justice
at home. Certainly if he must have these two necessaries,
he must be enabled with means for them, and that of himself,
not dependent *ex aliorum arbitrio*; for it is *regula juris,
lex est, quando quis aliquid alicui concedit, concedit et id sine
quo res ipsa esse non potest.*

3. Though I have gone already very high, I shall go yet to

a higher contemplation of the fundamental policy of our laws:
which is this, that the King of mere right ought to have, and
the people of mere duty are bound to yield unto the King,
supply for the defence of the kingdom. And when the Parliament itself doth grant supply in that case, it is not merely a
benevolence of the people, but therein they do an act of justice
and duty to the King. I know the most solemn form of Parliament, and of the humble expression of the Commons, of their
hearty affection and goodwill to their King, in tendering to him
their bills of subsidies or fifteenths.

. . . .

4. I confess, that by the fundamental law of England, the
Parliament is *commune concilium regis et regni*, that it is the
greatest, the most honourable and supreme court in the kingdom;
that no man ought to think any dishonourable thing of it : yet
give me leave to say that it is but a *concilium*; to say so is no
dishonour to it : the King may call it, prorogue it, dissolve it,
at his pleasure; and whatsoever the King doth therein, is
always to be taken for just and necessary. We must consider
that it is a great body, moves slowly; sudden despatches cannot
be expected in it. Besides, though the Parliament cannot err,
parliament-men may *de facto*; every particular member of the
House hath his free voice; some of them may chance to make
scruples, where there is no cause; it is possible some of them
may have sinister ends; these things breed delays, so they may
disturbances.—I would to God the late woeful experience of
this kingdom had not verified these speculations. Yea, there
have been, in former times, censures of Parliaments themselves :
the Good Parliament, *temp.* Ed. 3, *parliamentum indoctorum*,
temp. Hen. 4, and in the same King's time, if we believe my
Lord Coke, 11, fo. 113, Brangwit, *id est*, the White-Crow
Act. These matters are considerable in such cases as ours is.
Wherein apparently *Mora trahit periculum*, and to follow the
rule, *Festina lente*, is most dangerous.

5. The point of *retentio dominii maris* (which is in the case)
is not of an ordinary consideration; for, besides the ancient
inheritance and right which the crown of England hath in it, it
is obvious to every judgment, that in the continuance or not
continuance of it to the crown, not only the *bene esse*, but even

the *esse* itself of the commonwealth doth consist; and therefore it behoveth the subjects *accelerare* to the tuition of it: slowness is an argument of stupidity, or want of that sensibleness of the diminution of that right which every subject ought of right, and hath a concerning reason, to propose to himself.

23. THE SCOTTISH NATIONAL COVENANT.

[February 27, 1638. Rushworth, ii. 734. See *Hist. of Engl.* viii. 329.]

The confession of faith of the Kirk of Scotland, subscribed at first by the King's Majesty and his household in the year of God 1580; thereafter by persons of all ranks in the year 1581, by ordinance of the lords of the secret council, and acts of the general assembly; subscribed again by all sorts of persons in the year 1590, by a new ordinance of council, at the desire of the general assembly; with a general band for the maintenance of the true religion, and the King's person, and now subscribed in the year 1638, by us noblemen, barons, gentlemen, burgesses, ministers, and commons under subscribing; together with our resolution and promises for the causes after specified, to maintain the said true religion, and the King's Majesty, according to the confession aforesaid, and Acts of Parliament; the tenure whereof here followeth.

We all, and every one of us underwritten, do protest, that after long and due examination of our own consciences in matters of true and false religion, we are now thoroughly resolved of the truth, by the word and spirit of God; and therefore we believe with our hearts, confess with our mouths, subscribe with our hands, and constantly affirm before God and the whole world, that this only is the true Christian faith and religion, pleasing God, and bringing salvation to man, which now is by the mercy of God revealed to the world by the preaching of the blessed evangel, and received, believed, and defended by many and sundry notable kirks and realms, but chiefly by the Kirk of Scotland, the King's Majesty, and three estates of this realm, as God's eternal truth and only ground of our salvation; as more particularly is expressed in the confession of our faith, established and publicly confirmed by sundry Acts of Parliament; and now of a long time hath been openly professed by the King's Majesty, and whole body of this realm, both in burgh and land. To the which confession and form of religion we willingly agree in our consciences in all points, as unto God's undoubted truth and verity, grounded only upon His written Word; and therefore we abhor and detest all contrary religion and doctrine, but chiefly all kind of papistry in general and particular heads, even as they are now damned and confuted by the Word of God and Kirk of Scotland. But in special we detest and refuse the usurped authority of that Roman Antichrist upon the Scriptures of God, upon the Kirk, the civil magistrate, and consciences of men; all his tyrannous laws made upon indifferent things against our Christian liberty; his erroneous doctrine against the sufficiency of the written Word, the perfection of the law, the office of Christ and His blessed evangel; his corrupted doctrine concerning original sin, our natural inability and rebellion to God's law, our justification by faith only, our imperfect sanctification and obedience to the law, the nature, number, and use of the holy sacraments; his five bastard sacraments, with all his rites, ceremonies, and false doctrine, added to the ministration of the true sacraments, without the Word of God; his cruel judgments against infants departing without the sacrament; his absolute necessity of baptism; his blasphemous opinion of transubstantiation or real presence of Christ's body in the elements, and receiving of the same by the wicked, or bodies of men; his dispensations, with solemn oaths, perjuries, and degrees of marriage, forbidden in the Word; his cruelty against the innocent divorced; his devilish mass; his blasphemous priesthood; his profane sacrifice for the sins of the dead and the quick; his canonization of men, calling upon angels or saints departed, worshipping of imagery, relics, and crosses; dedicating of kirks, altars, days, vows to creatures; his purgatory, prayers for the dead, praying or speaking in a strange language; with his processions and blasphemous litany, and multitude of advocates or mediators; his manifold orders, auricular confession; his desperate and uncertain repentance; his general and doubtsome faith; his satisfactions of men for their sins; his justification by works, *opus operatum*, works of supererogation, merits, pardons, peregrinations and stations; his holy water, baptizing of bells, conjuring of spirits, crossing, saning, anointing, conjuring, hallowing of God's good creatures, with the superstitious opinion joined therewith; his worldly monarchy and wicked hierarchy; his three solemn vows, with all his shavelings of sundry sorts; his erroneous and bloody decrees made at Trent, with all the subscribers and approvers of that cruel and bloody band conjured against the Kirk of God. And finally, we detest all his vain allegories, rites, signs, and traditions, brought in the Kirk without or against the Word of God, and doctrine of this true reformed Kirk. To which we join ourselves willingly, in doctrine, religion, faith, discipline, and life of the holy sacraments, as lively members of the same, in Christ our head, promising and swearing, by the great name of the Lord our God, that we shall continue in the obedience of the doctrine and discipline of this Kirk, and shall defend the same according to our vocation and power all the days of our lives, under the pains contained in the law, and danger both of body and soul in the day of God's fearful judgment. And seeing that many are stirred up by Satan and that Roman Antichrist, to promise, swear, subscribe, and for a time use the holy sacraments in the Kirk, deceitfully against their own consciences, minding thereby, first under the external cloak of religion, to corrupt and subvert secretly God's true religion within the Kirk; and afterwards, when time may serve, to become open enemies and persecutors of the same, under vain hope of the Pope's dispensation, devised against the Word of God, to his great confusion, and their double condemnation in the day of the Lord Jesus.

We therefore, willing to take away all suspicion of hypocrisy, and of such double dealing with God and His Kirk, protest and call the Searcher of all hearts for witness, that our minds and hearts do fully agree with this our confession, promise, oath, and subscription: so that we are not moved for any worldly respect, but are persuaded only in our consciences, through the knowledge and love of God's true religion printed in our hearts by the Holy Spirit, as we shall answer to Him in the day when the secrets of all hearts shall be disclosed. And because we

perceive that the quietness and stability of our religion and
Kirk doth depend upon the safety and good behaviour of the
King's Majesty, as upon a comfortable instrument of God's
mercy granted to this country for the maintenance of His Kirk,
and ministration of justice among us, we protest and promise
with our hearts under the same oath, hand-writ, and pains,
that we shall defend his person and authority with our goods,
bodies, and lives, in the defence of Christ His evangel, liberties
of our country, ministration of justice, and punishment of
iniquity, against all enemies within this realm or without, as
we desire our God to be a strong and merciful defender to us in
the day of our death, and coming of our Lord Jesus Christ;
to Whom, with the Father and the Holy Spirit, be all honour
and glory eternally.

Like as many Acts of Parliament not only in general do
abrogate, annul, and rescind all laws, statutes, acts, constitutions, canons civil or municipal, with all other ordinances
and practick penalties whatsoever, made in prejudice of the true
religion, and professors thereof, or of the true Kirk discipline,
jurisdiction, and freedom thereof; or in favours of idolatry and
superstition; or of the papistical kirk (as Act 3. Act 31. Parl. 1.
Act 23. Parl. 11. Act 114. Parl. 12, of K. James VI), that
papistry and superstition may be utterly suppressed, according
to the intention of the Acts of Parliament reported in Act 5.
Parl. 20. K. James VI. And to that end they ordained all
papists and priests to be punished by manifold civil and ecclesiastical pains, as adversaries to God's true religion preached,
and by law established within this realm (Act. 24. Parl. 11.
K. James VI) as common enemies to all Christian government
(Act 18. Parl. 16. K. James VI), as rebellers and gainstanders
of our Sovereign Lord's authority (Act 47. Parl. 3. K. James
VI), and as idolaters (Act 104. Parl. 7. K. James VI), but also
in particular (by and attour the confession of faith) do abolish
and condemn the Pope's authority and jurisdiction out of this
land, and ordains the maintainers thereof to be punished (Act 2.
Parl. 1. Act. 51. Parl. 3. Act 106. Parl. 7. Act 114. Parl. 12. of
K. James VI); do condemn the Pope's erroneous doctrine, or
any other erroneous doctrine repugnant to any of the Articles
of the true and Christian religion publicly preached, and by

law established in this realm; and ordains the spreaders or makers of books or libels, or letters or writs of that nature, to be punished (Act 46. Parl. 3. Act 106. Parl. 7. Act 24. Parl. 11. K. James VI); do condemn all baptism conform to the Pope's kirk, and the idolatry of the Mass; and ordains all sayers, wilful hearers, and concealers of the Mass, the maintainers and resetters of the Priests, Jesuits, trafficking Papists, to be punished without exception or restriction (Act 5. Parl. 1. Act 120. Parl. 12. Act 164. Parl. 13. Act 193. Parl. 14. Act. 1. Parl. 19. Act 5. Parl. 20 K. James VI); do condemn all erroneous books and writs containing erroneous doctrine against the religion presently professed, or containing superstitious rights and ceremonies papistical, whereby the people are greatly abused; and ordains the home-bringers of them to be punished (Act 25. Parl. 11. K. James VI); do condemn the monuments and dregs of bygone idolatry, as going to crosses, observing the festival days of saints, and such other superstitious and papistical rites, to the dishonour of God, contempt of true religion, and fostering of great errors among the people, and ordains the users of them to be punished for the second fault as idolaters (Act 104. Parl. 7. K. James VI).

Like as many Acts of Parliament are conceived for maintenance of God's true and Christian religion, and the purity thereof in doctrine and sacraments of the true Church of God, the liberty and freedom thereof in her national synodal assemblies, presbyteries, sessions, policy, discipline, and jurisdiction thereof, as that purity of religion and liberty of the Church was used, professed, exercised, preached, and confessed according to the reformation of religion in this realm. (As for instance: Act 99. Parl. 7. Act 23. Parl 11. Act 114. Parl. 12. Act 160. Parl. 13. K. James VI, ratified by Act 4. K. Charles.) So that Act 6. Parl. 1. and Act 68. Parl. 6. of K. James VI, in the year of God 1579, declares the ministers of the blessed evangel, whom God of His mercy had raised up or hereafter should raise, agreeing with them that then lived in doctrine and administration of the sacraments, and the people that professed Christ, as He was then offered in the evangel, and doth communicate with the holy sacraments (as in the reformed Kirks of this realm they were presently administered) according to the confession of faith to be the true and holy Kirk of Christ Jesus within this realm, and discerns and declares all and sundry, who either gainsays the word of the evangel, received and approved as the heads of the confession of faith, professed in Parliament in the year of God 1560, specified also in the first Parliament of K. James VI, and ratified in this present Parliament, more particularly do specify; or that refuses the administration of the holy sacraments as they were then ministrated, to be no members of the said Kirk within this realm and true religion presently professed, so long as they keep themselves so divided from the society of Christ's body. And the subsequent Act 69. Parl. 6. K. James VI, declares that there is no other face of Kirk, nor other face of religion than was presently at that time by the favour of God established within this realm, which therefore is ever styled God's true religion, Christ's true religion, the true and Christian religion, and a perfect religion, which by manifold Acts of Parliament all within this realm are bound to profess to subscribe the Articles thereof, the confession of faith, to recant all doctrine and errors repugnant to any of the said Articles (Act 4 and 9. Parl. 1. Act 45. 46. 47. Parl. 3. Act 71. Parl. 6. Act 106. Parl. 7. Act 24. Parl. 11. Act 123. Parl. 12. Act 194 and 197. Parl. 14 of K. James VI). And all magistrates, sheriffs, &c., on the one part, are ordained to search, apprehend, and punish all contraveners (for instance, Act 5. Parl. 1. Act 104. Parl. 7. Act2 5. Parl. 11. K. James VI). And that, notwithstanding of the King's Majesty's licences on the contrary, which are discharged and declared to be of no force, in so far as they tend in any ways to the prejudice and hindrance of the execution of the Acts of Parliament against Papists and adversaries of the true religion (Act 106. Parl. 7. K. James VI). On the other part, in Act 47. Parl. 3. K. James VI, it is declared and ordained, seeing the cause of God's true religion and His Highness's authority are so joined as the hurt of the one is common to both; and that none shall be reputed as loyal and faithful subjects to our Sovereign Lord or his authority, but be punishable as rebellers and gainstanders of the same, who shall not give their confession and make profession of the said true religion; and that they, who after defection shall give the confession of their faith of new, they shall promise to continue therein in time coming, to maintain our Sovereign Lord's authority, and at the uttermost of their power to fortify, assist, and maintain the true preachers and professors of Christ's religion, against whatsoever enemies and gainstanders of the same; and namely, against all such of whatsoever nation, estate, or degree they be of, that have joined or bound themselves, or have assisted or assists to set forward and execute the cruel decrees of Trent, contrary to the preachers and true professors of the Word of God, which is repeated word by word in the Articles of Pacification at Perth, the 23rd of Feb., 1572, approved by Parliament the last of April 1573, ratified in Parliament 1578, and related Act 123. Parl. 12. of K. James VI, with this addition, that they are bound to resist all treasonable uproars and hostilities raised against the true religion, the King's Majesty and the true professors.

Like as all lieges are bound to maintain the King's Majesty's royal person and authority, the authority of Parliaments, without which neither any laws or lawful judicatories can be established (Act 130. Act 131. Parl. 8. K. James VI), and the subjects' liberties, who ought only to live and be governed by the King's laws, the common laws of this realm allanerly (Act 48. Parl. 3. K. James I, Act 79. Parl. 6. K. James VI, repeated in Act 131. Parl. 8. K. James VI), which if they be innovated or prejudged the commission anent the union of the two kingdoms of Scotland and England, which is the sole Act of 17 Parl. James VI, declares such confusion would ensue as this realm could be no more a free monarchy; because by the fundamental laws, ancient privileges, offices, and liberties of this kingdom, not only the princely authority of His Majesty's royal descent hath been these many ages maintained, also the people's security of their lands, livings, rights, offices, liberties and dignities preserved. And therefore for the preservation of the said true religion, laws and liberties of this kingdom, it is statute by Act 8. Parl. 1. repeated in Act 99. Parl. 7. ratified in Act 23. Parl. 11 and 14. Act of K. James VI and 4 Act of K. Charles, that all Kings and Princes at their coronation and reception of their princely authority, shall make their faithful promise by their solemn oath in the presence of the Eternal God, that during the whole

time of their lives they shall serve the same Eternal God to the
utmost of their power, according as He hath required in His
most Holy Word, contained in the Old and New Testaments,
and according to the same Word shall maintain the true religion
of Christ Jesus, the preaching of His Holy Word, the due and
right ministration of the sacraments now received and preached
within this realm (according to the confession of faith immediately preceding) ; and shall abolish and gainstand all false
religion contrary to the same ; and shall rule the people committed to their charge according to the will and commandment
of God revealed in His foresaid Word, and according to the
lowable laws and constitutions received in this realm, no ways
repugnant to the said will of the Eternal God ; and shall procure to the utmost of their power, to the Kirk of God, and whole
Christian people, true and perfect peace in all time coming ;
and that they shall be careful to root out of their Empire all
heretics and enemies to the true worship of God, who shall be
convicted by the true Kirk of God of the aforesaid crimes.
Which was also observed by His Majesty at his Coronation in
Edinburgh, 1633, as may be seen in the Order of the Coronation.

In obedience to the commands of God, conform to the practice of the godly in former times, and according to the laudable
example of our worthy and religious progenitors, and of many
yet living amongst us, which was warranted also by act of
council, commanding a general band to be made and subscribed
by His Majesty's subjects of all ranks for two causes : one was,
for defending the true religion, as it was then reformed, and is
expressed in the confession of faith above written, and a former
large confession established by sundry acts of lawful general
assemblies and of Parliament, unto which it hath relation, set
down in public catechisms, and which had been for many years
with a blessing from heaven preached and professed in this Kirk
and kingdom, as God's undoubted truth grounded only upon
His written Word.   The other cause was for maintaining the
King's Majesty, his person and estate ; the true worship of God
and the King's authority being so straitly joined, as that they
had the same friends and common enemies, and did stand and
fall together.   And finally, being convinced in our minds, and
confessing with our mouths, that the present and succeeding

generations in this land are bound to keep the aforesaid national
oath and subscription inviolable :—

We noblemen, barons, gentlemen, burgesses, ministers, and
commons under subscribing, considering divers times before, and
especially at this time, the danger of the true reformed religion,
of the King's honour, and of the public peace of the kingdom,
by the manifold innovations and evils generally contained and
particularly mentioned in our late supplications, complaints,
and protestations, do hereby profess, and before God, His angels
and the world, solemnly declare, that with our whole hearts we
agree and resolve all the days of our life constantly to adhere
unto and to defend the aforesaid true religion, and forbearing
the practice of all novations already introduced in the matters
of the worship of God, or approbation of the corruptions of the
public government of the Kirk, or civil places and power of
kirkmen, till they be tried and allowed in free assemblies and
in Parliaments, to labour by all means lawful to recover the
purity and liberty of the Gospel as it was established and professed before the aforesaid novations ; and because, after due
examination, we plainly perceive and undoubtedly believe that
the innovations and evils contained in our supplications, complaints, and protestations have no warrant of the Word of God,
are contrary to the articles of the aforesaid confessions, to the
intention and meaning of the blessed reformers of religion in
this land, to the above-written Acts of Parliament, and do
sensibly tend to the re-establishing of the popish religion and
tyranny, and to the subversion and ruin of the true reformed
religion, and of our liberties, laws and estates ; we also declare
that the aforesaid confessions are to be interpreted, and ought
to be understood of the aforesaid novations and evils, no less
than if every one of them had been expressed in the aforesaid
confessions ; and that we are obliged to detest and abhor them,
amongst other particular heads of papistry abjured therein ;
and therefore from the knowledge and conscience of our duty
to God, to our King and country, without any worldly respect
or inducement so far as human infirmity will suffer, wishing
a further measure of the grace of God for this effect, we promise
and swear by the great name of the Lord our God. to continue
in the profession and obedience of the aforesaid religion ; that

we shall defend the same, and resist all these contrary errors
and corruptions according to our vocation, and to the utmost
of that power that God hath put into our hands, all the days of
our life. And in like manner, with the same heart we declare
before God and men, that we have no intention or desire to
attempt anything that may turn to the dishonour of God or the
diminution of the King's greatness and authority; but on
the contrary we promise and swear that we shall to the utmost
of our power, with our means and lives, stand to the defence
of our dread Sovereign the King's Majesty, his person and
authority, in the defence and preservation of the aforesaid true
religion, liberties and laws of the kingdom; as also to the
mutual defence and assistance every one of us of another, in the
same cause of maintaining the true religion and His Majesty's
authority, with our best counsels, our bodies, means and whole
power, against all sorts of persons whatsoever; so that whatsoever shall be done to the least of us for that cause shall be
taken as done to us all in general, and to every one of us in
particular; and that we shall neither directly or indirectly suffer
ourselves to be divided or withdrawn by whatsoever suggestion,
combination, allurement or terror from this blessed and loyal
conjunction; nor shall cast in any let or impediment that may
stay or hinder any such resolution as by common consent shall
be found to conduce for so good ends; but on the contrary
shall by all lawful means labour to further and promote the
same; and if any such dangerous and divisive motion be made
to us by word or writ, we and every one of us shall either
suppress it or (if need be) shall incontinently make the same
known, that it may be timously obviated. Neither do we fear
the foul aspersions of rebellion, combination or what else our
adversaries from their craft and malice would put upon us,
seeing what we do is so well warranted, and ariseth from an
unfeigned desire to maintain the true worship of God, the
majesty of our King, and the peace of the kingdom, for the
common happiness of ourselves and posterity. And because
we cannot look for a blessing from God upon our proceedings,
except with our profession and subscription, we join such a life
and conversation as beseemeth Christians who have renewed
their covenant with God; we therefore faithfully promise, for

ourselves, our followers, and all other under us, both in public,
in our particular families and personal carriage, to endeavour
to keep ourselves within the bounds of Christian liberty, and to
be good examples to others of all godliness, soberness and
righteousness, and of every duty we owe to God and man;
and that this our union and conjunction may be observed without
violation we call the living God, the searcher of our hearts to
witness, who knoweth this to be our sincere desire and unfeigned
resolution, as we shall answer to Jesus Christ in the great day,
and under the pain of God's everlasting wrath, and of infamy,
and of loss of all honour and respect in this world; most humbly
beseeching the Lord to strengthen us by His Holy Spirit for
this end, and to bless our desires and proceedings with a happy
success, that religion and righteousness may flourish in the land,
to the glory of God, the honour of our King, and peace and
comfort of us all.

In witness whereof we have subscribed with our hands all
the premises, &c.

24. Petition of Twelve Peers for the summoning of a new Parliament.

[August 28, 1640.   State Papers, Charles I, Domestic, cccclxv. 16.
See *Hist. of Engl.* ix. 199.]

To the King's Most Excellent Majesty.

The humble Petition of your Majesty's most loyal and obedient
subjects, whose names are here underwritten in behalf of
themselves and divers others.

Most Gracious Sovereign,

The sense of that duty and service which we owe to your
Sacred Majesty, and our earnest affection to the good and
welfare of this your realm of England, have moved us in all
humility to beseech your Royal Majesty to give us leave to offer
unto your princely wisdom the apprehension which we and
other your faithful subjects have conceived of the great distempers and dangers now threatening the Church and State
and your Royal person, and the fittest means by which they
may be removed and prevented.

The evils and dangers whereof your Majesty may be pleased to take notice are these:

That your Majesty's sacred person is exposed to hazard and danger in the present expedition against the Scottish army, and by occasion of this war your revenue is much wasted, your subjects burdened with coat-and-conduct-money, billeting of soldiers, and other military charges, and divers rapines and disorders committed in several parts in this your realm, by the soldiers raised for that service, and your whole kingdom become full of fear and discontents.

The sundry innovations in matters of religion, the oath and canons lately imposed upon the clergy and other your Majesty's subjects.

The great increase of Popery, and employing of Popish Recusants, and others ill-affected to the religion by law established in places of power and trust, especially in commanding of men and arms both in the field and in sundry counties of this your realm, whereas by the laws they are not permitted to have arms in their own houses.

The great mischiefs which may fall upon this kingdom if the intentions which have been credibly reported, of bringing in Irish and foreign forces, shall take effect.

The urging of ship-money, and prosecution of some sheriffs in the Star Chamber for not levying of it.

The heavy charges of merchandise to the discouragement of trade, the multitude of monopolies, and other patents, whereby the commodities and manufactures of the kingdom are much burthened, to the great and universal grievance of your people.

The great grief of your subjects by the long intermission of Parliaments, in the late and former dissolving of such as have been called, without the hoped effects which otherwise they might have procured.

For remedy whereof, and prevention of the dangers that may ensue to your royal person and to the whole state, they do in all humility and faithfulness beseech your most Excellent Majesty that you would be pleased to summon a Parliament within some short and convenient time, whereby the causes of these and other great grievances which your people lie under may be taken away, and the authors and counsellors of them may be there brought to such legal trial and condign punishment as the nature of the several offences shall require, and that the present war may be composed by your Majesty's wisdom without bloodshed, in such manner as may conduce to the honour and safety of your Majesty's person, the comforts of your people, and the uniting of both of your realms against the common enemies of the reformed religion. And your Majesty's petitioners shall ever pray, &c.

Rutland.	Bolingbroke.
Fra. Bedford.	Mulgrave.
W. Hertford.	W. Say and Sele.
Rob. Essex.	Rob. Brooke.
Exeter.	E. Mandeville [1].
Warwick.	Ed. Howard (of Escrick) [2].

25. THE KING'S WRIT SUMMONING THE GREAT COUNCIL.

[September 7, 1640. Rushworth, iii. 1257. See *Hist. of Engl.* ix. 201.]

Rex Reverendissimo in Christo Patri ac fideli consiliario nostro Willielmo eadem gratia Cantuar. Archiepiscopo, totius Angliae primati et Metropolitano salutem. Quia super quibusdam arduis et urgentissimis negotiis nos et Regni nostri statum Coronaeque nostrae Jura specialiter concernentibus vobiscum et cum aliis Praelatis, Magnatibus et Proceribus ipsius Regni apud civitatem nostram Ebor. die Jovis, 24 die instantis mensis Septembris colloquium habere volumus et tractatum, vobis in fide et dilectione quibus nobis tenemini firmiter injungimus et mandamus, quod cessante excusatione quacunque, dictis die et loco personaliter intersitis nobiscum et cum Praelatis, Magnatibus et Proceribus praedictis super dictis negotiis tractaturi vestrumque consilium impensuri, et hoc sicut nos et honorem nostrum ac tranquillitatem regni nostri juriumque nostrorum praedictorum diligitis, nullatenus omittatis. Teste etc. 7 Sept.

[1] Baron Kimbolton in his own right.

[2] The signatures as here given are no doubt the correct ones, as the copy on which they appear has a note on it in Nicholas's hand. Other copies with a different set of signatures were in circulation, one of which, containing several errors, appears in Rushworth. As the signatures are scattered about the paper, I have placed them in order of precedence.

PART III

26. The Root and Branch Petition.

[December 11, 1640.   Rushworth, iv. 93.   See *Hist. of Eng.* ix. 247.]

To the Right Honourable the Commons House of
Parliament.

*The humble Petition of many of His Majesty's subjects in
and about the City of London, and several Counties of
the Kingdom,*

Sheweth,

That whereas the government of archbishops and lord bishops,
deans and archdeacons, &c., with their courts and ministrations
in them, have proved prejudicial and very dangerous both to
the Church and Commonwealth, they themselves having formerly
held that they have their jurisdiction or authority of human
authority, till of these later times, being further pressed about
the unlawfulness, that they have claimed their calling immediately from the Lord Jesus Christ, which is against the laws
of this kingdom, and derogatory to His Majesty and his state
royal.   And whereas the said government is found by woeful
experience to be a main cause and occasion of many foul evils,
pressures and grievances of a very high nature unto His Majesty's
subjects in their own consciences, liberties and estates, as in
a schedule of particulars hereunto annexed may in part appear :

We therefore most humbly pray, and beseech this honourable

assembly, the premises considered, that the said government, with all its dependencies, roots and branches, may be abolished, and all laws in their behalf made void, and the government according to God's Word may be rightly placed amongst us : and we your humble suppliants, as in duty we are bound, will daily pray for His Majesty's long and happy reign over us, and for the prosperous success of this high and honourable Court of Parliament.

A Particular of the manifold evils, pressures, and grievances caused, practised and occasioned by the Prelates and their dependents.

1. The subjecting and enthralling all ministers under them and their authority, and so by degrees exempting them from the temporal power ; whence follows,

2. The faint-heartedness of ministers to preach the truth of God, lest they should displease the prelates; as namely, the doctrine of predestination, of free grace, of perseverance, of original sin remaining after baptism, of the sabbath, the doctrine against universal grace, election for faith foreseen, free-will against antichrist, non-residents, human inventions in God's worship; all which are generally withheld from the people's knowledge, because not relishing to the bishops.

3. The encouragement of ministers to despise the temporal magistracy, the nobles and gentry of the land ; to abuse the subjects, and live contentiously with their neighbours, knowing that they, being the bishops' creatures, shall be supported.

4. The restraint of many godly and able men from the ministry, and thrusting out of many congregations their faithful, diligent, and powerful ministers, who lived peaceably with them, and did them good, only because they cannot in conscience submit unto and maintain the bishops' needless devices ; nay, sometimes for no other cause but for their zeal in preaching, or great auditories.

5. The suppressing of that godly design set on foot by certain saints, and sugared with many great gifts by sundry well-affected persons for the buying of impropriations, and placing of able ministers in them, maintaining of lectures, and founding of free schools, which the prelates could not endure,

lest it should darken their glories, and draw the ministers from their dependence upon them.

6. The great increase of idle, lewd and dissolute, ignorant and erroneous men in the ministry, which swarm like the locusts of Egypt over the whole kingdom; and will they but wear a canonical coat, a surplice, a hood, bow at the name of Jesus, and be zealous of superstitious ceremonies, they may live as they list, confront whom they please, preach and vent what errors they will, and neglect preaching at their pleasures without control.

7. The discouragement of many from bringing up their children in learning; the many schisms, errors, and strange opinions which are in the Church; great corruptions which are in the Universities; the gross and lamentable ignorance almost everywhere among the people; the want of preaching ministers in very many places both of England and Wales; the loathing of the ministry, and the general defection to all manner of profaneness.

8. The swarming of lascivious, idle, and unprofitable books and pamphlets, play-books and ballads; as namely, Ovid's 'Fits of Love,' 'The Parliament of Women,' which came out at the dissolving of the last Parliament; Barns's 'Poems,' Parker's 'Ballads,' in disgrace of religion, to the increase of all vice, and withdrawing of people from reading, studying, and hearing the Word of God, and other good books.

9. The hindering of godly books to be printed, the blotting out or perverting those which they suffer, all or most of that which strikes either at Popery or Arminianism; the adding of what or where pleaseth them, and the restraint of reprinting books formerly licensed, without relicensing.

10. The publishing and venting of Popish, Arminian, and other dangerous books and tenets; as namely, 'That the Church of Rome is a true Church, and in the worst times never erred in fundamentals;' 'that the subjects have no propriety in their estates, but that the King may take from them what he pleaseth;' 'that all is the King's, and that he is bound by no law;' and many other, from the former whereof hath sprung,

11. The growth of Popery and increase of Papists, Priests and Jesuits in sundry places, but especially about London since

the Reformation; the frequent venting of crucifixes and Popish pictures both engraven and printed, and the placing of such in Bibles.

12. The multitude of monopolies and patents, drawing with them innumerable perjuries; the large increase of customs and impositions upon commodities, the ship-money, and many other great burthens upon the Commonwealth, under which all groan.

13. Moreover, the offices and jurisdictions of archbishops, lord bishops, deans, archdeacons, being the same way of Church government, which is in the Romish Church, and which was in England in the time of Popery, little change thereof being made (except only the head from whence it was derived), the same arguments supporting the Pope which do uphold the prelates, and overthrowing the prelates, which do pull down the Pope; and other Reformed Churches, having upon their rejection of the Pope cast the prelates out also as members of the beast. Hence it is that the prelates here in England, by themselves or their disciples, plead and maintain that the Pope is not Antichrist, and that the Church of Rome is a true Church, hath not erred in fundamental points, and that salvation is attainable in that religion, and therefore have restrained to pray for the conversion of our Sovereign Lady the Queen.   Hence also hath come,

14. The great conformity and likeness both continued and increased of our Church to the Church of Rome, in vestures, postures, ceremonies and administrations, namely as the bishops' rochets and the lawn-sleeves, the four-cornered cap, the cope and surplice, the tippet, the hood, and the canonical coat; the pulpits, clothed, especially now of late, with the Jesuits' badge upon them every way.

15. The standing up at *Gloria Patri* and at the reading of the Gospel, praying towards the East, the bowing at the name of Jesus, the bowing to the altar towards the East, cross in baptism, the kneeling at the Communion.

16. The turning of the Communion-table altar-wise, setting images, crucifixes, and conceits over them, and tapers and books upon them, and bowing or adoring to or before them; the reading of the second service at the altar, and forcing people to come up thither to receive, or else denying the sacrament to

them; terming the altar to be the mercy-seat, or the place of God Almighty in the church, which is a plain device to usher in the Mass.

17. The christening and consecrating of churches and chapels, the consecrating fonts, tables, pulpits, chalices, churchyards, and many other things, and putting holiness in them; yea, reconsecrating upon pretended pollution, as though everything were unclean without their consecrating; and for want of this sundry churches have been interdicted, and kept from use as polluted.

18. The Liturgy for the most part is framed out of the Romish Breviary, Rituals, Mass-book, also the Book of Ordination for archbishops and ministers framed out of the Roman Pontifical.

19. The multitude of canons formerly made, wherein among other things excommunication, *ipso facto*, is denounced for speaking of a word against the devices abovesaid, or subscription thereunto, though no law enjoined a restraint from the ministry without subscription, and appeal is denied to any that should refuse subscription or unlawful conformity, though he be never so much wronged by the inferior judges. Also the canons made in the late Sacred Synod, as they call it, wherein are many strange and dangerous devices to undermine the Gospel and the subjects' liberties, to propagate Popery, to spoil God's people, ensnare ministers, and other students, and so to draw all into an absolute subjection and thraldom to them and their government, spoiling both the King and the Parliament of their power.

20. The countenancing plurality of benefices, prohibiting of marriages without their licence, at certain times almost half the year, and licensing of marriages without banns asking.

21. Profanation of the Lord's Day, pleading for it, and enjoining ministers to read a Declaration set forth (as it is thought) by their procurement for tolerating of sports upon that day, suspending and depriving many godly ministers for not reading the same only out of conscience, because it was against the law of God so to do, and no law of the land to enjoin it.

22. The pressing of the strict observation of the saints'

days, whereby great sums of money are drawn out of men's
purses for working on them; a very high burthen on most
people, who getting their living on their daily employments,
must either omit them, and be idle, or part with their money,
whereby many poor families are undone, or brought behind-
hand; yet many churchwardens are sued, or threatened to be
sued by their troublesome ministers, as perjured persons, for not
presenting their parishioners who failed in observing holy-days.

23. The great increase and frequency of whoredoms and
adulteries, occasioned by the prelates' corrupt administration of
justice in such cases, who taking upon them the punishment of
it, do turn all into monies for the filling of their purses;
and lest their officers should defraud them of their gain, they
have in their late canon, instead of remedying these vices,
decreed that the commutation of penance shall not be without
the bishops' privity.

24. The general abuse of that great ordinance of excommunication, which God hath left in His Church as the last
and greatest punishment which the Church can inflict upon
obstinate and great offenders; and the prelates and their officers,
who of right have nothing to do with it, do daily excommunicate
men, either for doing that which is lawful, or for vain, idle, and
trivial matters, as working, or opening a shop on a holy-day,
for not appearing at every beck upon their summons, not paying
a fee, or the like; yea, they have made it, as they do all other
things, a hook or instrument wherewith to empty men's purses,
and to advance their own greatness; and so that sacred ordinance of God, by their perverting of it, becomes contemptible to
all men, and is seldom or never used against notorious offenders,
who for the most part are their favourites.

25. Yea further, the pride and ambition of the prelates being
boundless, unwilling to be subject either to man or laws, they
claim their office and jurisdiction to be *Jure Divino*, exercise
ecclesiastical authority in their own names and rights, and
under their own seals, and take upon them temporal dignities,
places and offices in the Commonwealth, that they may sway
both swords.

26. Whence follows the taking Commissions in their own
Courts and Consistories, and where else they sit in matters

determinable of right at Common Law, the putting of ministers upon parishes, without the patron's and people's consent.

27. The imposing of oaths of various and trivial articles yearly upon churchwardens and sidesmen, which they cannot take without perjury, unless they fall at jars continually with their ministers and neighbours, and wholly neglect their own calling.

28. The exercising of the oath *ex officio*, and other proceedings by way of inquisition, reaching even to men's thoughts, the apprehending and detaining of men by pursuivants, the frequent suspending and depriving of ministers, fining and imprisoning of all sorts of people, breaking up of men's houses and studies, taking away men's books, letters, and other writings, seizing upon their estates, removing them from their callings, separating between them and their wives against both their wills, the rejecting of prohibitions with threatenings, and the doing of many other outrages, to the utter infringing the laws of the realm and the subjects' liberties, and ruining of them and their families; and of later time the judges of the land are so awed with the power and greatness of the prelates, and other ways promoted, that neither prohibition, *Habeas Corpus*, nor any other lawful remedy can be had, or take place, for the distressed subjects in most cases; only Papists, Jesuits, Priests, and such others as propagate Popery or Arminianism, are countenanced, spared, and have much liberty; and from hence followed amongst others these dangerous consequences.

1. The general hope and expectation of the Romish party, that their superstitious religion will ere long be fully planted in this kingdom again, and so they are encouraged to persist therein, and to practise the same openly in divers places, to the high dishonour of God, and contrary to the laws of the realm.

2. The discouragement and destruction of all good subjects, of whom are multitudes, both clothiers, merchants and others, who being deprived of their ministers, and overburthened with these pressures, have departed the kingdom to Holland, and other parts, and have drawn with them a great manufacture of cloth and trading out of the land into other places where they reside, whereby wool, the great staple of the kingdom, is become

of small value, and vends not; trading is decayed, many poor people want work, seamen lose employment, and the whole land is much impoverished, to the great dishonour of this kingdom and blemishment to the government thereof.

3. The present wars and commotions happened between His Majesty and his subjects of Scotland, wherein His Majesty and all his kingdoms are endangered, and suffer greatly, and are like to become a prey to the common enemy in case the wars go on, which we exceedingly fear will not only go on, but also increase to an utter ruin of all, unless the prelates with their dependences be removed out of England, and also they and their practices, who, as we under your Honour's favours, do verily believe and conceive have occasioned the quarrel.

All which we humbly refer to the consideration of this Honourable Assembly, desiring the Lord of heaven to direct you in the right way to redress all these evils.

27. The Triennial Act.

[February 15, 164⅟. 16 Car. I. cap. 1. Statutes of the Realm, v. 54. See *Hist. of Engl.* ix. 253, 262, 290.]

An Act for the preventing of inconveniences happening by the long intermission of Parliaments.

I. Whereas by the laws and statutes of this realm the Parliament ought to be holden at least once every year for the redress of grievances, but the appointment of the time and place for the holding thereof hath always belonged, as it ought, to His Majesty and his royal progenitors : and whereas it is by experience found that the not holding of Parliaments accordingly hath produced sundry and great mischiefs and inconveniences to the King's Majesty, the Church and Commonwealth; for the prevention of the like mischiefs and inconveniences in time to come :

II. Be it enacted by the King's Most Excellent Majesty, with the consent of the Lord's spiritual and temporal, and the Commons in this present Parliament assembled, that the said laws and statutes be from henceforth duly kept and observed ; and your Majesty's loyal and obedient subjects, in this present

Parliament now assembled, do humbly pray that it be enacted :
and be it enacted accordingly, by the authority of this present
Parliament, that in case there be not a Parliament summoned
by writ under the Great Seal of England, and assembled and
held before the 10th of September, which shall be in the third
year next after the last day of the last meeting and sitting
in this present Parliament, the beginning of the first year to
be accounted from the said last day of the last meeting and
sitting in Parliament ; and so from time to time, and in all
times hereafter, if there shall not be a Parliament assembled
and held before the 10th day of September, which shall be in
the third year next after the last day of the last meeting and
sitting in Parliament before the time assembled and held ; the
beginning of the first year to be accounted from the said last
day of the last meeting and sitting in Parliament ; that then
in every such case as aforesaid, the Parliament shall assemble
and be held in the usual place at Westminster, in such manner,
and by such means only, as is hereafter in this present Act
declared and enacted, and not otherwise, on the second Monday,
which shall be in the month of November, then next ensuing.
And in case this present Parliament now assembled and held,
or any other Parliament which shall at any time hereafter be
assembled and held by writ under the Great Seal of England,
or in case any Parliament shall be assembled and held by
authority of this present Act ; and such Parliaments, or any
of them, shall be prorogued, or adjourned, or continued by
prorogation or adjournment, until the 10th day of September,
which shall be in the third year next after the last day of the
last meeting and sitting in Parliament, to be accounted as
aforesaid ; that then in every such case, every such Parliament
so prorogued or adjourned, or so continued by prorogation or
adjournment, as aforesaid, shall from the said 10th day of
September be thenceforth clearly and absolutely dissolved, and
the Lord Chancellor of England, the Lord Keeper of the Great
Seal of England, and every Commissioner and Commissioners,
for the keeping of the Great Seal of England, for the time being,
shall within six days after the said 10th day of September,
in every such third year as aforesaid, in due form of law
and without any further warrant or direction from His Majesty,

his heirs or successors, seal, issue forth, and send abroad several and respective writs to the several and respective peers of this realm, commanding every such peer that he personally be at the Parliament to be held at Westminster on the second Monday which shall be in November next following the said 10th day of September, then and there to treat concerning the high and urgent affairs concerning His Majesty, the state and defence of the kingdom and Church of England; and shall also seal and issue forth, and send abroad several and respective writs to the several and respective sheriffs of the several and respective counties, cities and boroughs of England and Wales, and to the Constable of the Castle of Dover, Lord Warden of the Cinque Ports, or his lieutenant for the time being, and to the Mayor and Bailiffs of Berwick upon Tweed, and to all and every other officers and persons to whom writs have used to be directed, for the electing of the knights, citizens, barons and burgesses of and for the said Counties, Cities, Cinque Ports and Boroughs of England and Wales respectively, in the accustomed form, to appear and serve in the Parliament to be held at Westminster on the said second Monday, which shall be in November aforesaid; which said peers, after the said writs received, and which said knights, citizens, barons and burgesses chosen by virtue of the said writs, shall then and there appear and serve in Parliament accordingly. And the said Lord Chancellor, Lord Keeper, Commissioner and Commissioners aforesaid, shall respectively take a solemn oath upon the Holy Evangelists for the due issuing of writs, according to the tenor of this Act, *in haec verba,*—

'You shall swear that you shall truly and faithfully issue forth, and send abroad all writs of summons to Parliament for both Houses, at such time, and in such manner, as is expressed and enjoined by an Act of Parliament, entitled, "An Act for the preventing of inconveniences happening by the long intermission of Parliaments."'

Which oath is forthwith to be taken by the present Lord Keeper, and to be administered by the Clerk of the Crown to every Lord Chancellor, Lord Keeper, Commissioner and Commissioners aforesaid; and that none of the said officers respectively shall henceforth execute any the said offices before they have taken the said oath. And if the said Lord Chancellor, Lord Keeper, or any of the said Commissioners shall fail, or forbear so to issue out the said writs, according to the true meaning of this Act, then he or they respectively shall, beside the incurring of the grievous sin of perjury, be disabled, and become, by virtue of this Act, incapable, *ipso facto*, to bear his and their said offices respectively ; and be further liable to such punishments as shall be inflicted upon him or them by the next, or any other ensuing Parliament. And in case the said Lord Chancellor, Lord Keeper, Commissioner or Commissioners aforesaid, shall not issue forth the said writs as aforesaid : or in case that the Parliament do not assemble and be held at the time and place before appointed, then the Parliament shall assemble and be held in the usual place at Westminster, in such manner, and by such means only, as is hereafter in this present Act declared and enacted, and not otherwise, on the third Monday which shall be in the month of January then next ensuing. And the peers of this realm shall by virtue of this Act be enabled, and are enjoined to meet in the Old Palace of Westminster, in the usual place there, on the third Monday in the said month of November : and they or any twelve or more of them, then and there assembled, shall on or before the last Monday of November next following the tenth day of September aforesaid, by virtue of this Act, without other warrant, issue out writs in the usual form, in the name of the King's Majesty, his heirs or successors, attested under the hands and seals of twelve or more of the said peers, to the several and respective sheriffs of the several and respective counties, cities, and boroughs of England and Wales; and to the Constable of the Castle of Dover, Lord Warden of the Cinque Ports, or his lieutenant for the time being, and to the Mayor and Bailiffs of Berwick upon Tweed ; and to all and every other the said officers and persons to whom writs have been used to be directed, for the electing of the knights, citizens, barons and burgesses, of and for the said Counties, Cities, Cinque Ports and Boroughs, to be and appear at the Parliament at Westminster aforesaid, to be held on the third Monday in January then next following : all and every which writs the Clerks of the Petty Bag, and

other clerks, to whom the writing of the writs for summons
to the Parliament doth and shall belong, or whom the said
Lords, or twelve or more of them shall appoint, shall at the
command of the said Lords so assembled, or of any twelve
or more of them, make and prepare ready for the signature
of the said Lords, or any twelve or more of them, under pain of
the loss of their places and offices, and of such other punishment as in the next, or any other ensuing Parliament, shall
be inflicted on him or them : and it is enacted that the said
writs so issued shall be of the same power and force to all
intents and purposes, as the writs or summons to Parliament
under the Great Seal of England have ever been or ought to be.
And all the messengers of the Chamber or others who shall be
appointed by the said Lords, or any twelve or more, are hereby
required faithfully and speedily to deliver the said writs to every
person and persons, sheriffs, officers, and others, to whom the
same shall be directed : which if the said messengers or any of
them shall fail to perform, they shall forfeit their respective
places, and incur such other pains and punishments as by that
or any other ensuing Parliament shall be imposed on them.

III. And it is also further enacted, that all and every the
peers of this realm shall make their appearance, and shall
assemble on the said third Monday in January, in such manner,
and to such effect, and with such power, as if they had received
every of them writs of summons to Parliament under the
Great Seal of England, in the usual and accustomed manner.
And in case the said Lords, or twelve or more of them, shall
fail to issue forth such writs, or that the said writs do not come
to the said several Counties, Cities, Cinque Ports and Boroughs,
so that an election be not thereupon made ; and in case there be
not a Parliament assembled and held before the 23rd day
of the said month of January, and so from time to time, and
in all times hereafter, if there shall not be a Parliament assembled and held before the said 23rd day of January, then in every
such case as aforesaid the Parliament shall assemble, and be
held in the usual place at Westminster, in such manner, and
by such means only, as is hereafter in this present Act declared
and enacted, and not otherwise, on the second Tuesday which
shall be in the month of March next after the said 23rd day

of January; at which Parliament the peers of this realm shall make their appearance, and shall assemble at the time and place aforesaid, and shall each of them be liable unto such pains and censures for his and their not appearing and serving then and there in Parliament, as if he or they had been summoned by writ under the Great Seal of England, and had not appeared and served; and to such further pains and censures, as by the rest of the peers in Parliament assembled they shall be adjudged unto.

IV. And for the better assembling of the knights, citizens, barons, and burgesses to the said Parliament, as aforesaid, it is further enacted, that the several and respective sheriffs of the several and respective Counties, Cities and Boroughs of England and Wales, and the Chancellors, Masters and Scholars of both and every of the Universities, and the Mayor and Bailiffs of the borough of Berwick upon Tweed, shall at the several courts and places to be held and appointed for their respective Counties, Universities, Cities and Boroughs, next after the said 23rd day of January, cause such knight and knights, citizen and citizens, burgess and burgesses of their said Counties, Universities, Cities and Boroughs respectively, to be chosen by such persons, and in such manner, as if several and respective writs of summons to Parliament, under the Great Seal of England, had issued, and been awarded. And in case any of the several Sheriffs, or the Chancellors, Masters and Scholars of either of the Universities, or the Mayor and Bailiffs of Berwick respectively, do not before ten of the clock in the forenoon of the same day wherein the several and respective courts and places shall be held or appointed for their several and respective Counties, Universities, Cities and Boroughs as aforesaid, begin and proceed on according to the meaning of this law, in causing elections to be made of such knight and knights, citizen and citizens, burgess and burgesses, of their said Counties, Universities, Cities and Boroughs as aforesaid, then the freeholders of each County, and the Masters and Scholars of every the Universities, and the citizens and others having voices in such election respectively, in each University, City and Borough, that shall be assembled at the said courts or places to be held, or appointed, as aforesaid, shall forthwith, without further warrant or direction, proceed to the election of such knight or knights, citizen or citizens, burgess or burgesses aforesaid, in such manner as is usual in cases of writs of summons issued and awarded.

V. And it is further enacted that the several and respective sheriffs of their several and respective counties, and the Constables of the Castle of Dover, and Lord Warden of the Cinque Ports, or his lieutenant for the time being respectively, shall after the said 23rd day of January, and before the 8th day of February then immediately next ensuing, award and send forth their precepts to the several and respective cities and boroughs within their several counties, and likewise unto the said Cinque Ports respectively, commanding them respectively to make choice of such citizen and citizens, barons, burgess and burgesses, to serve in the said Parliament, at the time and place aforesaid: which said Cities, Cinque Ports and Boroughs respectively, shall before the last day of the said month of February make election of such citizen and citizens, barons, burgess and burgesses, as if writs for summoning of a Parliament, under the Great Seal of England, has issued and been awarded. And in case no such precept shall come unto the said Cities, Cinque Ports and Boroughs respectively, by the time herein limited: or in case any precept shall come, and no election be made thereupon, before the said last day of February, that then the several citizens, burgesses, and other persons that ought to elect and send citizens, barons, and burgesses to the Parliament, shall on the first Tuesday in March then next ensuing the said last day of February make choice of such citizen and citizens, barons, burgess and burgesses, as if a writ of summons under the Great Seal of England had issued and been awarded, and precepts thereupon issued, to such Cities, Cinque Ports and Boroughs: which knights, citizens, barons and burgesses so chosen shall appear and serve in Parliament at the time and place aforesaid, and shall each of them be liable unto such pains and censures for his and their not appearing and serving then and there in Parliament, as if he or they had been elected and chosen by virtue of a writ under the Great Seal of England, and shall be likewise subject unto such further pains and censures for his and their not appearing and serving then and there

in Parliament, as if he or they had been elected and chosen
by virtue of a writ under the Great Seal of England, and
shall be likewise subject to such further pains and censures
as by the rest of the knights, citizens and burgesses assembled
in the Commons House of Parliament, he or they shall be
adjudged unto.   And the sheriffs and other officers and persons
to whom it appertaineth shall make returns, and accept and
receive the returns of such elections in like manner as if writs
of summons had issued, and been executed, as hath been used
and accustomed: and in default of the sheriffs and other officers
respectively, in not accepting or making return of such elections,
it shall and may be lawful to and for the several freeholders,
and other persons that have elected, to make returns of the
knights, citizens, barons and burgesses by them elected, which
shall be as good and effectual to all intents and purposes as
if the sheriff or other officers had received a writ of summons
for a Parliament, and had made such returns: and that such
elections, precepts and returns shall be had and made at such
times, by such persons, and in such manner, as before in this
Act is expressed and declared, according to the true intent and
meaning of this law; any writ, proclamation, edict, act, restraint,
inhibition, order or warrant to the contrary in any wise notwithstanding.   And in case any person or persons shall be so
hardy to advise, frame, contrive, serve or put in execution any
such writs, proclamation, edict, act, restraint, inhibition, order
or warrant thereupon, then he or they so offending shall incur
and sustain the pains, penalties and forfeitures limited, ordained
and provided in and by the Statute of Provision and Premunire
made in the 16th year of King Richard the Second, and shall
from thenceforth be disabled, during his life, to sue and implead
any person in any action real or personal, or to make any gift,
grant, conveyance, or other disposition of any his lands, tenements, hereditaments, goods or chattels which he hath to his
own use, either by act executed in his lifetime, or by his last
will, or otherwise, or to take any gift, conveyance, or legacy
to his own use: and if any Sheriff, Constable of the Castle of
Dover, or Lord Warden of the Cinque Ports, shall not perform
his duty enjoined by this Act, then he shall lose and forfeit
the sum of £1000, and every County, City, Cinque Port and

Borough that shall not make election of their knights, citizens, barons and burgesses, respectively, shall incur the penalties following (that is to say) every County the sum of £1000, and every City, which is no County, £200, and every Cinque Port and Borough the sum of £100 ; all and every of which several forfeitures, and all other forfeitures in this Act mentioned, shall and may be recovered in any of the King's Courts of Record at Westminster, without naming the Christian name and surname of the said Mayor for the time being, by action of debt, bill, plaint or information, wherein no essoine, protection, wager of law, aid, prayer, privilege, injunction, or order of restraint, shall be in any wise prayed, granted or allowed, nor any more than one imparlance : and if any person after notice given that the action depending is grounded and prosecuted upon or by virtue of this Statute shall cause or procure any such action to be stayed or delayed before judgment by colour or means of any order, warrant, power or authority, save only of the court wherein such action as aforesaid shall be brought or depending, or after judgment had upon such action, shall cause or procure the execution of, or upon any such judgment, to be stayed or delayed by colour or means of any order, warrant, power or authority, save only by writ of error or attaint, that then the said persons so offending shall incur and sustain all and every the pains, penalties and forfeitures, limited, ordained and provided in and by the said Statute of Provision and Premunire, made in the 16th of King Richard the Second. And if any Lord Mayor of London shall at any time hereafter commence or prefer any such suit, action or information, and shall happen to die or be removed out of his office before recovery and execution had, that yet not such action, suit or information, sued, commenced or preferred, shall by such displacing or death be abated, discontinued or ended, but that it shall and may be lawful to and for the Lord Mayor of the City of London next succeeding in that office and place, to prosecute, pursue and follow all and every such action, bill, plaint or information for the causes aforesaid, so hanging and depending in such manner and form, and to all intents and purposes, as that Lord Mayor might have done, which first commenced or preferred the same. The fifth part of all and every the forfeitures in this

Act mentioned, shall go and be, to, and for the use and behoof of the City of London, and the other four parts and residue to be employed and disposed to, and for such only uses, intents and purposes as by the knights, citizens and burgesses in Parliament assembled, shall be declared, directed and appointed.

Provided that in case the freeholders of any County and inhabitants, or other persons having or claiming power to make election of any knights, citizens, barons or burgesses, shall proceed to making of election of their knights, citizens, barons and burgesses, which election shall afterwards fall out to be adjudged or declared void in law by the House of Commons, by reason of equality of voices or misdemeanour of any person whatsoever, then the said County, City, Cinque Port or Borough shall not incur the penalties in this law, so as an election *de facto* be made.

VI. And it is further enacted, that no Parliament henceforth to be assembled shall be dissolved or prorogued within fifty days at least after the time appointed for the meeting thereof, unless it be by assent of His Majesty, his heirs or successors, and of both Houses in Parliament assembled; and that neither the House of Peers nor the House of Commons shall be adjourned within fifty days at least after the meeting thereof, unless it be by the free consent of every the said Houses respectively.

VII. And be it further enacted and declared by authority of this present Parliament, that the Peers to be assembled at any Parliament by virtue of this Act, shall and may from time to time, at any time during such their assembly in Parliament, choose and declare such person to be Speaker for the said Peers as they shall think fit. And likewise that the said knights, citizens and burgesses to be assembled at any Parliament by virtue of this Act, shall and may from time to time, at any time during such their assembly in Parliament, choose and declare one of themselves to be Speaker for the said knights, citizens and burgesses of the House of Commons assembled in the said Parliament as they shall think fit; which said Speakers, and every of them, as well for the said Peers as for the said House of Commons respectively, shall, by virtue of this Act, be perfect and complete Speakers for the said Houses respectively, and shall have as full and large power, jurisdiction and privileges, to all intents and purposes, as any Speaker or Speakers of either of the said Houses respectively, heretofore have had or enjoyed.

VIII. And it is further enacted and declared, that all Parliaments hereafter to be assembled by authority of this Act and every member thereof shall have and enjoy all rights, privileges, jurisdictions and immunities, as any Parliament summoned by writ under the Great Seal of England, or any member thereof might or ought to have; and all and every the members that shall be elected and chosen to serve in any Parliament hereafter to be assembled by authority of this Act as aforesaid, shall assemble and meet in the Commons House of Parliament, and shall enter into the same, and have voices in such Parliament before and without the taking of the several oaths of supremacy and allegiance, or either of them, any law or statute to the contrary thereof in any wise notwithstanding.

IX. Provided always, that if the King's Majesty, his heirs or successors, shall at any time during any Parliament hereafter to be assembled by authority of this Act as aforesaid, award or direct any commission or commissions unto any person or persons whatsoever, thereby giving power and authority to him or them to take and receive the oath of supremacy and allegiance, of all or any the members of the Commons House of Parliament, and any the members of that House being duly required thereunto, shall refuse or neglect to take and pronounce the same, that from thenceforth such person so refusing or neglecting shall be deemed no member of that House, nor shall have any voice therein, and shall suffer such pains and penalties as if he had presumed to sit in the same House without election, return or authority.

X. And it is likewise provided and enacted, that this Statute shall be publicly read yearly at every General Sessions of the Peace, to be held next after the Epiphany, and every Assizes then next ensuing by the Clerk of the Peace and Clerk of the Assizes for the time being respectively. And if they or either of them shall neglect or fail to do the same accordingly, then such party so neglecting or failing shall forfeit the sum of one hundred pounds.

XI. And it is lastly provided and enacted, that His Majesty's royal assent to this Bill shall not thereby determine this present

Session of Parliament [1], and that all statutes and Acts of Parliament which are to have continuance unto the end of this present Session, shall be of full force after His Majesty's assent, until this present Session be fully ended and determined ; and if this present Session shall determine by dissolution of this present Parliament, then all the Acts and statutes aforesaid shall be continued until the end of the first Session of the next Parliament.

28. THE PROTESTATION.

[May 3, 1641.   Rushworth, viii. 735.   See *Hist. of Engl.* ix. 353.]

We the knights, citizens and burgesses of the Commons House in Parliament, finding to the grief of our hearts that the designs of the Priests and Jesuits, and other adherents to the See of Rome, have of late been more boldly and frequently put in practice than formerly, to the undermining and danger of the true reformed Protestant religion in His Majesty's dominions established ; and finding also that there hath been, and having just cause to suspect there still are, even during the sittings in Parliament, endeavours to subvert the fundamental laws of England and Ireland, and to introduce the exercise of an arbitrary and tyrannical government by most pernicious and wicked counsels, practices, plots and conspiracies; and that the long intermission and unhappier breach of Parliaments hath occasioned many illegal taxations, whereby the subjects have been prosecuted and grieved ; and that divers innovations and superstitions have been brought into the Church, multitudes driven out of His Majesty's dominions, jealousies raised and fomented between the King and his people ; a Popish army levied in Ireland, and two armies [2] brought into the bowels of this kingdom, to the hazard of His Majesty's royal person, the consumption of the revenue of the crown and the treasure of this realm.   And lastly, finding

[1] It was at that time the custom that the royal assent was given to Bills at the end of the Session, and it was consequently argued that the assent put an end to the Session.

[2] The Scottish army and the English army opposed to it.

the great cause of jealousy, that endeavours have been, and are used, to bring the English army into a misunderstanding of this Parliament, thereby to incline that army by force to bring to pass those wicked counsels; have therefore thought good to join ourselves in a Declaration of our united affections and resolutions and to make this ensuing Protestation:—

I, A. B., do, in the presence of God, promise, vow and protest to maintain and defend, as far as lawfully I may with my life, power and estate, the true reformed Protestant religion expressed in the doctrine of the Church of England, against all Popery and popish innovation within this realm, contrary to the said doctrine, and according to the duty of my allegiance, I will maintain and defend His Majesty's royal person and estate, as also the power and privilege of Parliaments, the lawful rights and liberties of the subjects, and every person that shall make this Protestation in whatsoever he shall do, in the lawful pursuance of the same; and to my power, as far as lawfully I may, I will oppose, and by all good ways and means endeavour to bring to condign punishment all such as shall by force, practice, counsels, plots, conspiracies or otherwise do anything to the contrary in this present Protestation contained: and further, that I shall in all just and honourable ways endeavour to preserve the union and peace betwixt the three kingdoms of England, Scotland and Ireland, and neither for hope, fear or any other respects, shall relinquish this promise, vow and protestation.

29. THE ACT FOR THE ATTAINDER OF THE EARL OF STRAFFORD.

[May 10, 1641. Statutes of the Realm, v. 177. See *Hist. of Engl.* ix. 329–366.]

Whereas the knights, citizens and burgesses of the House of Commons in this present Parliament assembled, have, in the name of themselves and of all the Commons of England, impeached Thomas Earl of Strafford of high treason, for endeavouring to subvert the ancient and fundamental laws and government of His Majesty's realms of England and Ireland, and to introduce an arbitrary and tyrannical government against law in the said kingdoms, and for exercising a tyrannous and exorbitant power above and against the laws of the said kingdoms, over the liberties, estates and lives of His Majesty's subjects; and likewise for having by his own authority commanded the laying and sessing of soldiers upon His Majesty's subjects in Ireland, against their consents, to compel them to obey his unlawful summons and orders, made upon paper petitions in causes between party and party, which accordingly was executed upon divers of His Majesty's subjects in a warlike manner within the said realm of Ireland; and in so doing did levy war against the King's Majesty and his liege-people in that kingdom; and also for that he, upon the unhappy dissolution of the last Parliament, did slander the House of Commons to His Majesty; and did counsel and advise His Majesty that he was loose and absolved from rules of government; and that he had an army in Ireland which he might employ to reduce this kingdom, for which he deserves to undergo the pains and forfeitures of high treason. And the said Earl hath also been an incendiary of the wars between the two kingdoms of England and Scotland, all which offences hath been sufficiently proved against the said Earl upon his impeachment.

Be it therefore enacted by the King's Most Excellent Majesty, and by the Lords and Commons in this present Parliament assembled, and by authority of the same, that the said Earl of Strafford, for the heinous crimes and offences aforesaid, stand and be adjudged and attainted of high treason, and shall suffer such pains of death, and incur the forfeitures of his goods and chattels, lands, tenements and hereditaments of any estate of freehold or inheritance in the said kingdoms of England and Ireland, which the said Earl or any other to his use, or in trust for him, have or had, the day of the first sitting of this Parliament, or at any time since.

Provided[1] that no judge or judges, justice or justices whatsoever, shall adjudge or interpret any act or thing to be treason, nor hear or determine any treason nor in any other

---

[1] Note by Rushworth: 'This proviso hath occasioned the common discourse and opinion that this judgment against the Earl was enacted never to be drawn into precedent in Parliament, whereas it expressly respects only judges in inferior courts.'

manner than he or they should or ought to have done before
the making of this Act, and as if this Act had never been had
nor made; saving always unto all and singular persons, bodies,
politic and corporate, their heirs and successors, others than
the said Earl and his heirs, and such as claim from, by, or
under him, all such right, title and interest of, in, and to all
and singular such of the lands, tenements and hereditaments,
as he, they, or any of them had before the first day of this
present Parliament, anything herein contained to the contrary
notwithstanding.

Provided that the passing of this present Act, or His
Majesty's assent thereunto, shall not be any determination of
this present Sessions of Parliament; but that this present
Sessions of Parliament, and all Bills and matters whatsoever
depending in Parliament, and not fully enacted or determined,
and all statutes and Acts of Parliament which have their
continuance until the end of this present Sessions of Parliament, shall remain, continue, and be in full force, as if this
Act had not been.

30. THE ACT AGAINST DISSOLVING THE LONG PARLIAMENT WITHOUT ITS OWN CONSENT.

[May 10, 1641.   17 Car. I. cap. 7.   Statutes of the Realm, v. 103.
See *Hist. of Engl.* ix. 359, 367.]

*An Act to prevent inconveniences which may happen by the
untimely adjourning, proroguing, or dissolving this present
Parliament.*

Whereas great sums of money must of necessity be speedily
advanced and provided for the relief of His Majesty's army
and people in the northern parts of this realm, and for preventing the imminent danger it is in, and for supply of other
His Majesty's present and urgent occasions, which cannot be
so timely effected as is requisite without credit for raising the
said monies; which credit cannot be obtained until such
obstacles be first removed as are occasioned by fears, jealousies
and apprehensions of divers His Majesty's loyal subjects, that

this present Parliament may be adjourned, prorogued, or dissolved, before justice shall be duly executed upon delinquents, public grievances redressed, a firm peace between the two nations of England and Scotland concluded, and before sufficient provision be made for the re-payment of the said monies so to be raised; all which the Commons in this present Parliament assembled, having duly considered, do therefore most humbly beseech your Majesty that it may be declared and enacted.

And be it declared and enacted by the King, our Sovereign Lord, with the assent of the Lords and Commons in this present Parliament assembled, and by the authority of the same, that this present Parliament now assembled shall not be dissolved unless it be by Act of Parliament to be passed for that purpose; nor shall be, at any time or times, during the continuance thereof, prorogued or adjourned, unless it be by Act of Parliament to be likewise passed for that purpose; and that the House of Peers shall not at any time or times during this present Parliament be adjourned, unless it be by themselves or by their own order; and in like manner, that the House of Commons shall not, at any time or times, during this present Parliament, be adjourned, unless it be by themselves or by their own order; and that all and every thing or things whatsoever done, or to be done for the adjournment, proroguing, or dissolving of this present Parliament, contrary to this Act, shall be utterly void and of none effect.

31. THE TONNAGE AND POUNDAGE ACT.

[June 22, 1641.   17 Car. I. cap. 8.   Statutes of the Realm, v. 104.
See *Hist. of Engl.* ix. 400.]

A subsidy granted to the King, of tonnage, poundage, and other sums of money payable upon merchandise exported and imported.

1. Whereas upon examination in this present Parliament of divers of the farmers, customers, and collectors of the customs upon merchandise, and likewise upon their own confession, it appeared that they have taken divers great sums of money of

His Majesty's subjects, and likewise of merchants aliens for goods imported and exported by the names of a subsidy of tonnage and poundage, and by colour of divers other impositions laid upon merchandise, which have been taken and received against the laws of the realm, in regard the said sums of money and impositions were not granted by common consent in Parliament, and for so doing have deserved condign punishment. Be it therefore declared and enacted by the King's Most Excellent Majesty and the Lords and Commons in this present Parliament assembled : and it is hereby declared and enacted, That it is and hath been the ancient right of the subjects of this realm, that no subsidy, custom, impost, or other charge whatsoever ought or may be laid or imposed upon any merchandise exported or imported by subjects, denizens, or aliens without common consent in Parliament : yet nevertheless the Commons before whom those examinations were taken, taking into their consideration the great peril that might ensue to this realm by the not guarding of the seas, and the other inconveniences which might follow in case the said sums of money should upon the sudden be forborne to be paid by and with the advice and consent of the Lords in this present Parliament assembled, and by the authority of the same, do give and grant to our supreme liege Lord and Sovereign one subsidy called tonnage, that is to say, of every tun of wine that is or shall come into this realm or any His Majesty's dominions by way of merchandise the sum of three shillings, and so after that rate, and of every tun of sweet wines, as well malmsey as other, that is or shall come into this realm by any merchant alien three shillings, and so after the rate over and above the three shillings above mentioned, and of every awme of Rhenish wine that is or shall so come in twelve pence; and also one other subsidy called poundage, that is to say, of all manner of goods and merchandise of every merchant, denizen and alien carried or to be carried out of this realm, or any His Majesty's dominions, or to be brought into the same by way of merchandise, of the value of every twenty shillings of the same goods and merchandise twelve pence, and so after the rate; and of every twenty shillings value of tin and pewter vessel carried out of this realm by every or any merchant alien, twelve pence over and above the

twelve pence aforesaid, except and foreprized out of this grant
of subsidy of poundage all manner of woollen cloth made or
wrought, or which shall be made or wrought within this realm
of England and by every or any merchant denizen, and not
born alien, carried or to be carried out of this realm ; and all
manner of wools, woolfells, hides, and backs of leather, that is
or shall be carried out of this realm ; and all wines not before
limited to pay subsidy or tonnage, and all manner of fresh fish
and bestial coming or that shall come into this realm.

II. And further the said Commons by the advice, assent,
and authority aforesaid, do give and grant unto our said liege
Lord, our Sovereign for the causes aforesaid, one other subsidy,
that is to say, of every merchant born denizen of and for every
sack of wool thirty-three shillings four pence, and of and for
every two hundred and forty woolfells thirty-three shillings
four pence, and of and for every last of hides and backs three
pounds six shillings eight pence, and so after the same rate
for every less or greater quantity for any the same merchandise
more or less ; and of every merchant stranger not born denizen,
of and for every sack of wool three pounds six shillings eight
pence ; and of and for every two hundred forty woolfells three
pounds six shillings eight pence, and for every last of hides
and backs three pounds thirteen shillings four pence, and so
of all the said wools, woolfells, hides and backs, and of every
of them after the rate, and such other sums of money as have
been imposed upon any merchandise either outward or inward
by pretext of any letters patents, commission under the Great
Seal of England or Privy Seal, since the first year of the reign
of his late Majesty King James of blessed memory, and which
were continued and paid at the beginning of this present
Parliament; to have, take, enjoy, and perceive the subsidies
aforesaid, and other the fore-mentioned sums and every of them,
and every part and parcel of them to our said liege Lord and
Sovereign from the five and twentieth of May, one thousand six
hundred forty-one, to the fifteenth of July next ensuing.

III. And be it further enacted by the authority aforesaid:
that the said subsidy of tonnage, poundage, wools, and other
sums of money shall be taken and employed during the time
aforesaid to and for the intents and purposes, and upon and

under such provisions, clauses, and limitations as are contained
in one Act made in the Parliament held in the first year of the
reign of his said late Majesty King James of blessed memory,
entitled An Act for the granting of a Subsidy to the King, of
Tonnage, Poundage, Wools, &c.

IV. And it is hereby declared that the sums of money hereby
granted upon merchandise are not the rates intended to be continued, but the same to be hereafter in this present Parliament
altered in such manner as shall be thought fit.

V. Provided that no penalty or forfeiture contained in this
present Act or in the said Act made in the first year of King
James do or shall ensue to any person or persons, unless they
refuse to compound for any merchandise or goods imported
or exported after notice given of this act, penalty, and forfeiture by proclamation, where the said goods are or ought to
be entered.

VI. And it is further enacted that any customer or comptroller, or any other officer or person that after the determination of this grant shall take or receive or cause to be taken
or received the said subsidy, sums of money or any other
imposition upon merchandise whatsoever exported or imported
(except the same by grant in Parliament be due, or by such
grant shall become due or have been continually paid from the
end of the reign of the late King Edward the Third until
the beginning of the reign of the late Queen Mary), shall
incur and sustain the pains, penalties, and forfeitures ordained
and provided by the Statute of Provision and Premunire made
in the sixteenth year of King Richard the Second, and shall
also from thenceforth be disabled during his life to sue or
implead any person in any action real, mixed or personal, or in
any court whatsoever.

VII. Provided always that this Act shall not extend to any
imposition or charge upon any sort of tobacco of English plantations, but that the said tobaccos shall be charged only with
the payment of two pence in the pound and no more.

32. THE TEN PROPOSITIONS.

[June 24, 1641. Rushworth, iv. 298. See *Hist. of Engl.* ix. 401.]

A large conference with the Lords, concerning several particulars
about disbanding the army, the Capuchins, &c.

I. The first head, concerning the disbanding of the armies ; and under this there are several particulars.

1. That five regiments, according to the former order of both Houses, be first disbanded.

2. That the Commissioners for Scotland be entreated to retire some part of their army.

3. That their lordships will join with us in a petition to His Majesty, to declare his pleasure concerning the disbanding of the five regiments, for which there is present money provided, and of the rest of the army as soon as money is ready.

4. And to declare if any be refractory, and contemn His Majesty's authority, that he will use it for the punishment of them.

5. And that the Lord General[1] go down to his charge of the army, and begin his journey on Saturday next ; and that the Master of the Ordnance go then down also to take care of his charge of artillery.

II. The second head is concerning His Majesty's journey to Scotland.

That His Majesty will be pleased to allow a convenient time before his journey into Scotland ; that both armies be first disbanded, and some of the business of importance, concerning the peace of the kingdom depending in Parliament, may be dispatched before his going : this is seconded with divers reasons.

1. The safety of His Majesty's person.

2. Preventing the jealousies of his subjects.

3. Suppressing of the hopes of persons ill-affected, that may have designs upon the army to disturb the peace of the kingdom.

---

[1] The Earl of Holland.

4. Great advantage to the King's affairs, and contentment to his people.

5. That some of the Bills now depending in Parliament, whereof divers are sent up already to the Lords, and some proceeding in this House, may receive his royal assent before he go to Scotland; and that we may have time to pass the Bill of Tonnage to His Majesty for supporting of the royal estate, and to settle His Majesty's revenues for the best advantage of his service; and for these reasons to allow some time before he go into the North.

III. The third head, concerning His Majesty's Council and Ministers of State.

1. Both Houses to make suit to His Majesty to remove from him all such counsellors as I am commanded to describe; viz. such as have been active for the time past in furthering those courses contrary to religion, liberty, good government of the kingdom, and as have lately interested themselves in those Councils, to stir up division between him and his people.

2. As we desire removal of those that are evil, so to take into his Council for managing of the great affairs of this kingdom such officers and counsellors as his people and Parliament may have just cause to confide in. This is all concerning the third head.

IV. The fourth head, touching the Queen's Most Excellent Majesty, which containeth divers particulars.

1. That His Majesty be pleased, by advice of his Parliament, to persuade the Queen to accept some of the nobility, and others of trust, into Her Majesty's service, into such places as are now in her disposal.

2. That no Jesuit, nor any in orders, what countrymen soever, whether French or Italian, be received into Her Majesty's service; nor any Priests of His Majesty's dominion, English Scottish, or Irish; and that they be restrained from coming to the Court.

3. That the College of Capuchins at Somerset House may be dissolved and sent out of the kingdom. These two which I last mentioned concerning the Queen, Priests, Jesuits, and Capuchins, I am commanded to deliver you some particulars for.

(1) Public danger and scandal of this kingdom, and peace of the kingdom.

(2) The disaffection of some of those wicked conspirators is expressed in two letters; which letters were here read openly.

(3) A particular letter of Father Phillips here also read.

(4) Because of the Priests, Jesuits, and the College, there are divers great quantities of gold transported frequently.

(5) Particular touching the Queen is upon special occasions of His Majesty's absence, that their lordships will be pleased to join with us to advise the King that some of the nobility, and others of quality, with competent guards, may be appointed to attend the Queen's person, against all designs of papists, and of ill-affected persons, and of restraining resort thither in his absence.

V. The fifth head concerns the King's children, that some persons of public trust, and well-affected in religion, may be placed about the Prince, who may take care of his education, and of the rest of his children, especially in matters of religion and liberty.

VI. The sixth head concerneth such as shall come into the kingdom with titles of being the Pope's nuncio, that it may be declared that if any man come into this kingdom with instructions from the Pope of Rome, it be a case of high treason; and that he be out of the King's protection and out of the protection of the law; and I am to inform your lordships, that there is notice given upon very good grounds, that Count Rossetti[1] doth yet continue in the kingdom and yet resorts unto the Court.

VII. The seventh head is concerning the security and peace of the kingdom.

1. That there may be good lord-lieutenants, and deputy-lieutenants; and such as may be faithful and trusty, and careful of the peace of the kingdom.

2. That the trained bands be furnished with arms and powder, and bullets, and exercised and made fit for service; and that a special oath may be prepared, by consent of both

---

[1] The Pope's agent at the Queen's Court.

Houses, authorised by law; and to be taken by the lord-lieutenants and deputy-lieutenants, captains, and other officers, such an oath as may be fit to secure us in these times of danger.

3. That the Cinque Ports and all the ports of the kingdom may be put into good hands; and a list of those in whose charge they now are may be presented in Parliament, and special care taken for the reparation and provision of those ports.

4. That my Lord Admiral[1] may inform the Parliament in what case His Majesty's navy is, which is to be provided for out of tonnage and poundage for the security and peace of the kingdom.

VIII. The eighth head, that His Majesty be pleased to give directions to his learned council to prepare a general pardon in such a large manner as may be for the relief of His Majesty's subjects.

IX. The ninth head doth concern a committee of both Houses, that their lordships would appoint a number of their members to join together, with a proportionable number of this House, who from time to time may confer upon some particular causes, as shall be most effectual for the common good.

X. The tenth and last head, that His Majesty be moved that he would be pleased to be very sparing in sending for Papists to Court; and that if any should come without being sent for, that the laws be severely put in execution against them; and that the English ladies that are recusants, be removed from Court; and that His Majesty be moved to give his assent, that the persons of the most active Papists, either Lords or Commons, may be so restrained as may be most necessary for the safety of the kingdom; and that no pensions be allowed to such recusants as are held dangerous to the state.

---

[1] The Earl of Northumberland.

33. Bill on Church Reform read twice in the House of Lords [1].

[House of Lords' MSS. First reading July 1, second reading July 3, 1641 [2]. See Fuller, *Church History*, ed. Brewer, vi. 188; *Hist. of Engl.* ix. 409.]

An Act for the better regulating of Archbishops, Bishops, Deans, Deans and Chapters, Canons and Prebends, and the better ordering of their revenues, and for the better governing of the Courts Ecclesiastical and the Ministers thereof, and the proceeding therein.

Whereas the preaching of God's Holy Word hath of late years been much neglected in several places, and to the end that Archbishops and Bishops may from henceforth give good examples to others in Holy Orders, by doing their duties in their own persons for the better instruction of the people committed to their charge, His Majesty, out of his abundant goodness and religious care of the souls of his people, is graciously pleased that it be enacted, and by the authority of this present Parliament be it enacted, that every Archbishop and Bishop, being under the age of seventy years, and not being hindered by sickness and being within his diocese, shall from henceforth, from and after the first day of January now next ensuing, upon every Lord's Day throughout the year, preach in some one Cathedral Church, Parish Church or public Chapel, upon pain to forfeit the sum of five pounds for every default therein, to the use of the poor of the same parish where the said Archbishop or Bishop shall then be,

[1] Indorsed 'The Bishops' Bill. Hodie 1[d] vice lecta est Billa, 1° Julii, 1641. 2[d] vice lecta est 3° Julii, 1641. Committed to the whole House.'

[2] Fuller says that the bishops and divines, directed by the lords ' to consult together for correction of what was amiss' in the Church 'and to settle peace,' of which John Williams, Bishop of Lincoln, was chairman, considered four subjects :—Innovations in doctrine ; innovations in discipline; the Common Prayer; and regulation of government. Their proposal on the latter head, he says, 'was not brought in, because the Bishop of Lincoln had undertaken the draft thereof, but not finished it.' Fuller seems to have been mistaken, as the Bill here given was certainly brought into the House of Lords, and can hardly be other than that proposed by Williams.

where he make such default, and of the poor of the four
parishes thereunto next adjoining, the same to be levied of
the goods of every such offender by distress and sale thereof,
and rendering the overplus to the owner thereof, by warrant
of any one Justice of the Peace next or near adjoining to the
place where such offence shall be committed, to be directed
to the constable, churchwardens and overseers of the poor
of the said several parishes and every of them. And to the
intent that the said Archbishops, Bishops and all other persons now or at any time hereafter being in Holy Orders,
may not be hindered to discharge their duties in the office of
the Ministry by intermeddling with secular affairs: be it
therefore enacted by the authority aforesaid, that no Archbishop, Bishop, Parson, Vicar or other person whatsoever, that
hath received or at any time hereafter shall receive any degree
in Holy Orders with cure of souls, shall at any time from and
after the said first day of January have any suffrage or vote,
or use or execute any power or authority in the Court usually
called the Star-Chamber, nor shall have any suffrage or voice,
or use or execute any judicial power or authority in any
other temporal Court whatsoever; nor shall be any Justice
of Peace, nor use nor execute the office of a Justice of the
Peace by virtue or colour of any statute, commission, charter
or otherwise within the kingdom of England or dominion of
Wales; nor shall have or enjoy any judicial room or place
in any of the said Courts, nor shall execute any commission
that shall issue from any standing temporal Court whatsoever;
nor shall be of the Privy Council of His Majesty, his heirs
or successors, but shall be wholly disabled and incapable to
have, receive, use or execute any of the said offices, places,
powers and authorities aforesaid. And be it further enacted
by the authority aforesaid, that all acts from and after the
said first day of January which shall be done or executed
by any Archbishop, Bishop, Parson, Vicar or other person
whatsoever in Holy Orders, and all and every suffrage, vote
and voice to be given or delivered by them or any of them,
contrary to the purport and true meaning of this present
Act, shall be utterly void in law to all intents, constructions
and purposes; and be it further enacted by the authority

aforesaid, that if any Archbishop, Bishop, Parson, Vicar or
other person whatsoever in Holy Orders from or after the
said first day of January, shall give his or their votes, suffrage or voice, or shall do or execute anything prohibited or
forbidden by this Act, contrary to the true intent and meaning thereof, shall for the first offence forfeit and lose so much
money as shall amount unto the full and true value of one
whole year's profit and benefit of all his and their spiritual
and ecclesiastical livings, benefices, dignities and promotions
whatsoever, the same to be recovered in any of His Majesty's
Courts of Record by action of debt, bill, plaint or information by him or them that will sue for the same, in which
suit no essoine, protection, wager of law, aid, prayer, privilege, injunction or order of restraint, nor any more than one
imparlance shall be in anywise prayed, granted, admitted or
allowed, the one moiety whereof to be unto our Sovereign
Lord the King, his heirs and successors, and the other
moiety to him or them that will sue for the same. And
if any Archbishop, Bishop, Parson, Vicar or other person
whatsoever, once convict of any offence concerning the
premises or against whom any such recovery shall be had as
aforesaid, shall therein offend again or shall thereafter do
anything contrary to the true intent and meaning of this law,
and shall be thereof duly convicted by indictment, information
or any other lawful ways or means, then such party shall
from and after such conviction, forfeit and lose, and be incapable to hold all and every the spiritual and ecclesiastical
livings, benefices, dignities and promotions which he shall
then have, and be from thenceforth utterly disabled to have,
receive, take or enjoy any the same spiritual or ecclesiastical
livings, benefices, dignities or promotions whatsoever ; and
that all the spiritual and ecclesiastical livings, benefices,
dignities and promotions which he shall have at the time of
such conviction[1], shall be to all intents, constructions and
purposes utterly void. Provided always, and be it enacted
by the authority aforesaid, that no lapse shall incur against
the patron or such person as ought to present unto, collate
or dispose of all or any such spiritual or ecclesiastical bene-

---

[1] Convention in MS.

fices, livings, dignities or promotions until six months after notice given by the Ordinary of the Diocese within which such spiritual or ecclesiastical living, benefice, dignity or promotion shall be, unto the patron or other person that ought to present thereunto, or collate or dispose thereof. And be it likewise further provided and enacted, that this Act, or any clause or thing therein contained, shall not extend unto the exercise of any jurisdiction, power or authority within either of the two Universities or the liberties thereof, nor unto any person or persons being or who hereafter shall be in Holy Orders, and who is or hereafter shall be a Duke, Marquis, Earl, Viscount, Baron or Peer of this kingdom by descent, nor unto the exercise of any the power of a Justice of Peace at any time heretofore given by any Act of Parliament to the Dean of Westminster within the liberties of Westminster, at Saint Martin's Le Grand in London.

And to the end that Archbishops and Bishops within their several dioceses may have such assistance as may hereafter tend and be for the better execution of their said offices and places, be it therefore enacted by the authority aforesaid, that within every shire or county of each several diocese within the kingdom of England and dominion of Wales there be nominated, in such manner as is hereafter expressed, twelve ministers being in Holy Orders, and being fit both in respect of their life and doctrine, to be assistants to every such Archbishop and Bishop, together with the Dean and Chapter of each several diocese, in conferring of Holy Orders and in the exercise and administration of ecclesiastical jurisdiction, and for such other purposes as be hereafter declared; and that none of the said Archbishops or Bishops at any time from henceforth shall confer any Holy Orders upon any person or persons without the presence and approbation of four of the said assistants at the least; and that none of the said Archbishops or Bishops, or any Dean, Archdeacon, Chancellor, Commissary, Official, Surrogate or other person having or exercising any ecclesiastical jurisdiction within any of the dioceses aforesaid, or within any places of peculiar or exempt jurisdiction whatsoever, shall pronounce any sentence of degradation, deprivation or suspension against any minister

or other person in Holy Orders, or any sentence of excommunication or absolution of or against any person whatsoever,
or shall proceed to the final sentence of any cause whatsoever
depending in any of their several Courts, or to the sentence
or taxation of costs or charges of suit, or to the making of
any request or instance to any ordinary or superior Judge to
hear or determine any cause depending before them without
the presence and approbation of two or, at the least, of one of
the said assistants next dwelling; and that the said assistants
shall from time to time be nominated or chosen in manner
following, that is to say: before the said first day of January
four of them by the King's Majesty, his heirs or successors,
under the sign manual; four other of them by the order of
the Lords in Parliament assembled, and the other four by the
order of the House of Commons in Parliament assembled;
and upon the death or removal of any of the said assistants
out of any of the shires or counties in the several dioceses
aforesaid respectively, such other person or persons shall be
named in their stead and to supply their rooms, as by His
Majesty, his heirs or successors, shall be nominated and appointed in like manner as is aforesaid, which said assistants
and every of them respectively, shall from time to time
hereafter give their personal attendance in and for the due
execution of the trust by this Act in them reposed, at each
public Ordination within each several diocese, and at such
other times when any such sentence, or any such taxation
of costs, or any such act for request or instance shall be
made as is aforesaid, upon sufficient notice to be given or
left at their several dwelling-houses by the known apparitor
of any such Archbishop or Bishop by the space of fourteen
days next before any meeting shall be had for any of the
purposes aforesaid; and if any such assistant, having such
notice as is aforesaid, shall fail to appear at the place so intimated unto him as is aforesaid, that then the said assistant
for every such default shall forfeit £10, to be levied by distress
and sale of the goods of every such offender (rendering to
every such offender the overplus) to the use of the poor of
the parish where such assistant shall be then dwelling, by
warrant from any Justice of the Peace next or nigh adjoining

to the said parish, to be directed to the constable, churchwarden or overseer of the same parish or any of them, unless
the said offender shall have such reasonable excuse for his
said default as shall be allowed by the said Archbishop or by
the Bishop of the same diocese and the said then other
assistants respectively, or the greater number of them, within three months next after any such default.   And be it also
enacted by the authority aforesaid, that all sentences and
other of the acts of Courts aforesaid, which at any time
hereafter shall be sped, pronounced, declared or made in any
other manner than is by this present Act appointed, shall
be utterly void to all intents and purposes; and that all and
every Archbishop, Bishop and other the ecclesiastical Judges
aforesaid, which shall speed, pronounce, declare or make
any of the said sentences or acts of Court, or which shall
confer any Holy Orders otherwise than as by this Act is
limited and appointed, shall *ipso facto* be suspended from the
exercise of their said respective places, offices and functions
by the space of one whole year next ensuing every such
offence, and shall forfeit for every such offence the sum of
£100, to be recovered by bill, action, plaint or information
by any person that shall sue for the same in any of His
Majesty's Courts of Record, in which no wager of law, essoine,
protection, privilege, injunction or order of restraint, nor any
more than one imparlance shall be admitted or allowed, the
one moiety of the said forfeiture to be to such person or
persons as will sue for the same, and the other to be employed
to and for the relief of the poor of the parish where the said
offence shall be committed.

And that from henceforth such persons may be preferred
to be Archbishops and Bishops which shall be of the best
integrity of life, soundness of doctrine and fitness for government, be it therefore enacted by authority of this present
Parliament, that upon every avoidance of any of the Archbishops or Bishops aforesaid at any time hereafter to be made,
the Dean and Chapter of each several diocese respectively, and
the said assistants of all the shires and counties within the
said diocese, so to be named as is aforesaid, or the greater
number of the said Dean, Chapter and assistants then living

within twenty days next after every such avoidance, shall,
by a writing under their hands and seals, recommend and
present to His Majesty, his heirs or successors, the names
of three persons in Holy Orders within the same or any other
of the said dioceses, whom in their judgments they shall hold
fit and worthy for so great a function; and that thereupon
His Majesty, his heirs or successors, shall and may be pleased
by his or their Letters Patents, under the Great Seal of
England, to nominate one of the said three persons to be
Archbishop or Bishop of the see so respectively being void;
and if the same be a Bishopric which shall be so void, that
then the nomination by His Majesty, his heirs or successors,
to be as aforesaid made, shall be made to the Archbishop of
the Province within which the see of the said Bishopric shall
happen to be; and if it shall be an Archbishopric which
shall be so void, that then every such nomination shall be
made to the other Archbishop or, in his vacancy, to four
such Bishops within this realm of England as shall be
thereunto appointed by His Majesty, his heirs or successors;
and that with all convenient speed, after every such nomination to be made as is aforesaid, the said Archbishop or
four Bishops, to whom the same shall be made as is aforesaid,
shall invest and consecrate the said person so nominated to
the said Archbishopric or Bishopric so being void; and that
every person hereafter being so nominated as aforesaid to any
Archbishopric or Bishopric, and so invested and consecrated
and receiving their temporalities out of the hands of His
Majesty, his heirs or successors, and taking their oath and
making their homage as in such case is now accustomed,
shall and may from thenceforth be installed and have and
take their restitution out of the hands of His Majesty, his
heirs or successors, of all the possessions, rents and profits
belonging to the said Archbishopric or Bishopric whereunto
they shall be so nominated as is aforesaid, and shall be from
thenceforth enabled fully and to all intents and purposes to
do, execute and perform all and every thing and things in
the present Act expressed and declared to be done by every
such Archbishop and Bishop respectively, and in such manner
as in and by this present Act is expressed, limited and

appointed, and also to do all such other thing or things as any Archbishop or Bishop of the same see might lawfully do before the making of this present Act; and if the said Dean, Chapter and assistants shall defer or delay such their nomination and presentment of the names of the said three persons longer than by the space of twenty days next after the avoidance of any such Archbishopric or Bishopric as is aforesaid, that then upon every such default the King's Majesty, his heirs and successors, at their liberty and pleasure, shall and may nominate and present any such person as they shall think fit, as if this present Act had not been made, anything herein to the contrary thereof notwithstanding. And for every such default the said Dean and Chapter and assistants, or such of them as shall be in such default as is aforesaid, shall forfeit the sum of £100 to be recovered by bill, action, plaint or information by any person that will sue for the same in any of His Majesty's said Courts of Record, in which no wager of law, essoine, protection, privilege, injunction or other order of restraint, nor any more than one imparlance shall be admitted or allowed, the one moiety of the said forfeiture to be to such person or persons as will sue for the same, and the other to be employed to and for the use of such Commissioners as shall be hereafter nominated by this present Act for the buying in of impropriations.

And to the intent the revenues of Deans and Chapters and of all Cathedrals and Collegiate Churches may be better employed for the good of the Church and advancement of religion, and that the Deans, Canons, Prebendaries and Residentiaries may not themselves live idly during the time of their residencies, but spend their times for the instructing of the people, well ordering of the Church, and good example of other Ministers; be it further enacted, that all Deans and Chapters, and Residentiaries and Prebendaries in Cathedral or Collegiate Churches, that hold any living or livings with cure of souls, shall so dispose of their time of residency in the said Cathedral or Collegiate Churches, as that they shall not severally and respectively spend more time in their said residence than sixty days in one year, all local statutes of the said Churches to the contrary notwithstanding;

and that they shall likewise preach or provide to be preached
two sermons upon every Lord's Day, the one in the forenoon
and the other in the afternoon, and one upon every Holy
Day, and one Lecture upon every Wednesday, for which they
shall pay to the Lecturer one hundred marks per annum at
the least, in every one of the said Cathedral and Collegiate
Churches, upon pain and penalty of £100 to the King upon
every default, and to be suspended from the profit of their
places for one whole year, and the profit of that year to be
employed to raise a stock for the poor of that city or town,
where such Cathedral or Collegiate Church is situate.   And
further, that when any Archbishop, Bishop, Dean, Dean and
Chapter, or any other Dignitary or Prebendary of any
Cathedral or Collegiate Church, Master, Fellows and Scholars
of any College in either University or elsewhere in the
kingdom of England, shall take a fine or sum of money
for the renovation or letting of any lease belonging to any
of their several corps or the communalty of their Church or
College, or shall increase the rent upon any such lease, they
shall lay aside one-fourth part of that fine or sum of money,
and of that increase of yearly rent, for the buying in of impropriations of parsonages or vicarages or portions of tithes
now made lay fees, all such sums of money to be delivered
into the hands of so many able Commissioners as shall from
time to time be nominated by the orders of both Houses of
Parliament, in every shire or county of England and Wales,
for the collecting and receiving of the said money, and for the
purchasing and bringing in of such impropriations, when the
money shall arise to a sufficient sum for such an employment,
and that such fine shall not be agreed or concluded of between
the lessors and lessees, or any other on their behalf, without the
approbation of three of the said Commissioners under their
hands in writing.

And be it further enacted, that every impropriation or
parsonage or vicarage or portion of tithes now impropriate,
shall by due course of law, upon the purchases thereof, be
made disappropriate and annexed to the Church, and made
presentative for ever, without any license of mortmain to be
obtained for the same; and that the said Commissioners shall

present a Clerk for the first time: the Archbishop, Bishop, Dean, Dean and Chapter (wherein these Dignities and Prebendaries are endowed), as also the Master, Fellows and Scholars of the said Colleges from whom those sums of money are received respectively, shall ever after the first time severally and respectively present or nominate such Clerks as shall have and receive the benefit thereof. And it is further provided and enacted, that of the sum remaining of any fine or sum of money received by or from any of these persons, bodies or corporations before mentioned, for any lease or increase of rent upon any impropriate rectory belonging to any of the said Archbishops, Bishops, Deans, Deans and Chapters, Dignities, Prebendaries, Masters, Fellows and Scholars of any of the said former Colleges, one-tenth part of the remaining fine shall be duly paid unto the Vicar or Curate (where no vicarage is endowed) that dischargeth the cure of the said impropriation, until the same shall be reunited and annexed to the Church, and be employed for the use and benefit of that minister who shall officiate the cure; and if any of the said Archbishops, Bishops, Deans, Deans and Chapters, Dignities, Prebendaries, Masters, Fellows and Scholars of any of the said Colleges, or any of them shall defraud or fail to pay unto the said Commissioners, or the said Vicars respectively, the said several apportioned fines and sums of money, the same being lawfully demanded at the two usual feasts of the year, the one of St. Michael the Archangel and the other of the Annunciation of Our Lady, all persons and corporations so offending shall forfeit unto the said Commissioners and Vicars respectively three times the value of that fine or sum of money so detained or not justly and duly paid, the same to be recovered by the Commissioners and Vicars respectively in any Court of Law or Equity.

Be it likewise enacted, that every Residentiary or Canon of any Cathedral or Collegiate Church, that hath a living with cure of souls, shall pay unto his Curate that preacheth and officiates that cure at or upon that living for his hire or his wages (over and besides his ordinary entertainment for the other part of the year), a proportion of the moiety of the value of that benefice, be it more or less, for that time of the year wherein

such Prebendary, Residentiary or Canon liveth at the Cathedral
Church, and is non-resident from his parsonage or vicarage;
and that every Parson or Vicar that hath two or more livings
with cure of souls, shall maintain upon that living on which he
doth reside, an able minister and preacher, that shall preach
twice every Lord's Day, and shall pay unto him for his entertainment a full moiety of the profits of the said benefice for the
time he doth not reside thereon, first-fruits, tenths and subsidies
being first deducted.

And for the better regulating of Ecclesiastical Courts, which
are now an extreme grievance and vexation to the common
people of England, be it enacted, that no citation shall at any
time hereafter issue forth against any of the King's subjects,
without the articles and libel be first left in Court ready to be
showed and delivered to the party cited, under pain of suspension
ab officio et beneficio in both the Judge and Registrar; and that
no cause hereafter be proceeded in against any of the King's
subjects *ex officio mero*, but both the Judge and Registrar shall
be liable to pay the costs and double damages to the party
so proceeded against, in case the cause be not confessed or
proved against him; and further, that none of the King's subjects hereafter be put to accuse themselves by or upon their
own oaths in any criminal cause whatsoever in any of the said
Courts Ecclesiastical, unless it be voluntarily taken by them
to clear themselves from a fame, thereby to satisfy the Church
or Congregation; and that the defendant being cited, shall
answer within twenty days after the day assigned for his
appearance, and the agent and defendant shall examine all their
witnesses in that cause, which they mean to produce upon the
articles, libel and interrogatories, or other proofs and evidences,
within four months then next following, or else the defendant to
be dismissed and have costs paid unto him, her or them, for
their unjust vexation. And to avoid that dilatory and vexatious
course yet in use, it is further enacted, that no exceptions be
admitted against witnesses, but either for some matters appearing of record in one of the King's Courts, or for some matters
proved against or confessed by the party produced in some
Ecclesiastical Court before that time, whereby it shall appear
that such witness is a party interested in the cause, or a person

to whose testimony credit is not to be given; and that causes in this Court may come to a speedier end than heretofore, be it further enacted, that if any cause be protracted so that it be not ended within one twelve-month after the first beginning of the suit, then at the end of the year the defendant shall be dismissed with his costs, to be paid, the one half by the plaintiff, and the other by the Judge and the Proctor for the agent or plaintiff in that Court, unless they shall show unto the Bishop of the diocese, with the attestation of one or more of the assistants, that the defendant did wilfully hinder the same, in which case the Bishop, with two or more assistants, shall order according to reason and justice.

And to avoid the excessive number of Proctors and Apparitors in Courts Ecclesiastical, be it further enacted, that the Bishops and six of the assistants shall name the number and also the choice of the Proctors and Apparitors in their several dioceses respectively, that are to plead and serve in all the several Ecclesiastical Courts within this kingdom, and that no Judge, Proctor or Registrar shall suffer any suitor, plaintiff or defendant, to go upon trust for their fees in any cause of instance, under pain of suspension from their places for one year for every time so offending; and that the Proctor shall have no fee allowed him at the taxation but for those days only wherein he doth plead or defend actually, and not for desiring continuance of days; and whereas there are now, by reason of unnecessary appeals, four or five instances or processes in all or most causes and proceedings ecclesiastical, to the great vexation and undoing of the plaintiff and defendant, and the apparent wrong and scandal of all inferior judicatories, Bishops, and ecclesiastical jurisdiction, be it enacted, that from henceforth there shall lie from the first ecclesiastical Judge in the cause, be he Dean, Archdeacon, Prebendary, Official, Commissary, Chancellor, or of any other title whatsoever, assisted as is before required, but two appeals only, one to the Bishop of the diocese, who shall not hear the same otherwise than accompanied with six of the said assistants at the least, so to be nominated as aforesaid, and then from the Bishop so assisted to the King's Majesty's delegates only and immediately, amongst the which the Archbishops of Canterbury and of York, with respect to the causes arising from their several provinces, shall be always in every Commission, and of the quorum *in ferenda sententia*, in all causes wherein the appeal lieth not from their own sentence, and all other appeals from the several dioceses to the Arches or audience to be from henceforth utterly abolished as an intolerable vexation to the subject—and altogether un-necessary; which Courts of Arches and audience are by virtue of this Act utterly suppressed and made void as concerning appeals from inferior Courts; and the Lord Keeper for the time being is hereby required to be very careful what persons he doth nominate for Judges delegates in this high and supreme Court in causes ecclesiastical, which care hath hitherto been much neglected.

Lastly, because the Church of England hath now lived under no certain ecclesiastical laws, but in an interim only, from the 25th of Henry VIII to this present, by reason that the persons for the purging of the ecclesiastical laws and the squaring of them to the common laws of the realm have not as yet met together, be it enacted by the authority aforesaid, that sixteen persons, to be named, six by the King's Majesty, five by the House of Lords, and five by the House of Commons respectively, understanding in both the laws, do presently meet, and taking the form begun by Doctor Haddon into their consideration, reduce by their general assent, or by the assent of the major part of them, all the canon laws of use and practice within this kingdom into as short a body and digest in the English tongue as well can be, so as they may be understood as well by the Bishops, Deans, Archdeacons, and Prebendaries, as also by the rest of the King's liege people, and may be more ascertained in matter and form, and receive the allowance of the King and the Parliament.

34. THE ACT FOR THE ABOLITION OF THE COURT OF STAR CHAMBER.

[July 5, 1641.   Statutes of the Realm, v. 110.   17 Car. I. cap. 10.   See *Hist. of Engl.* ix. 404.]

An Act for the Regulating the Privy Council and for taking away the Court commonly called the Star Chamber.

I. Whereas by the Great Charter many times confirmed in Parliament, it is enacted that no freeman shall be taken or imprisoned, or disseized of his freehold or liberties or free customs, or be outlawed or exiled or otherwise destroyed, and that the King will not pass upon him or condemn him but by lawful judgment of his Peers or by the law of the land; and by another statute made in the fifth year of the reign of King Edward the Third [1], it is enacted that no man shall be attached by any accusation nor forejudged of life or limb, nor his lands, tenements, goods nor chattels seized into the King's hands against the form of the Great Charter and the law of the land [2]: and by another statute made in the five-and-twentieth year of the reign of the same King Edward the Third [3], it is accorded, assented and established that none shall be taken by petition or suggestion made to the King or to his Council, unless it be by indictment or presentment of good and lawful people of the same neighbourhood where such deeds be done, in due manner or by process made by writ original at the common law, and that none be put out of his franchise or freehold unless he be duly brought in to answer and forejudged of the same by the course of the law, and if anything be done against the same, it shall be redressed and holden for none: and by another statute made in the eight-and-twentieth year of the reign of the same King Edward the Third [4], it is amongst other things enacted that no man of what estate or condition soever he be shall be put out of his lands or tenements, nor taken nor imprisoned nor disinherited without being brought in to answer by due process of law: and by another statute made in the two-and-fortieth year of the reign of the said King Edward the Third [5], it is enacted that no man be put to answer without presentment before Justices or matter of record, or by due process and writ original according to the old law of the land, and if anything be done to the contrary, it shall be void in law and holden for error: and by another statute made in the six-and-thirtieth year of the same King Edward the Third [6], it is amongst other things enacted, that all pleas which shall be pleaded in any Courts before any of the King's Justices, or in his other places or before any of his other ministers, or in

---

[1] 5 E. III. c. 9.
[2] Magna Carta, 9 H. III. c. 29.
[3] 25 E. III. st. 5. c. 4.
[4] 28 E. III. c. 3.
[5] 42 E. III. c. 3.
[6] 36 E. III. c. 15.

the Courts and places of any other Lords within the realm,
shall be entered and enrolled in Latin : and whereas by the
statute made in the third year of King Henry the Seventh[1],
power is given to the Chancellor, the Lord Treasurer of England
for the time being, and the Keeper of the King's Privy Seal,
or two of them calling unto them a Bishop and a Temporal Lord
of the King's most honourable Council, and the two Chief
Justices of the King's Bench and Common Pleas for the time
being, or other two Justices in their absence, to proceed as in
that Act is expressed for the punishment of some particular
offences therein mentioned : and by the statute made in the one-
and-twentieth year of King Henry the Eighth[2], the President
of the Council is associated to join with the Lord Chancellor
and other Judges in the said statute of the third of Henry the
Seventh mentioned : but the said Judges have not kept themselves to the points limited by the said statute, but have undertaken to punish where no law doth warrant, and to make
decrees for things having no such authority, and to inflict
heavier punishments than by any law is warranted ; and forasmuch as all matters examinable or determinable before the
said Judges, or in the Court commonly called the Star Chamber,
may have their proper remedy and redress, and their due
punishment and correction by the common law of the land, and
in the ordinary course of justice elsewhere, and forasmuch as
the reasons and motives inducing the erection and continuance
of that Court do now cease, and the proceedings, censures and
decrees of that Court have by experience been found to be an
intolerable burden to the subjects, and the means to introduce
an arbitrary power and government : and forasmuch as the
Council Table hath of late times assumed unto itself a power
to intermeddle in civil causes and matters only of private
interest between party and party, and have adventured to
determine of the estates and liberties of the subject contrary
to the law of the land and the rights and privileges of the
subject, by which great and manifold mischiefs and inconveniences have arisen and happened, and much uncertainty
by means of such proceedings hath been conceived concerning

[1] 3 H. VII. c. 1. § 1.   [2] 21 H. VIII. c. 20.

men's rights and estates: for settling whereof and preventing the like in time to come, be it ordained and enacted by the authority of this present Parliament, that the said Court commonly called the Star Chamber, and all jurisdiction, power and authority belonging unto or exercised in the same Court, or by any of the Judges, Officers or Ministers thereof be, from the first day of August in the year of our Lord God one thousand six hundred forty and one, clearly and absolutely dissolved, taken away, and determined; and that from the said first day of August neither the Lord Chancellor or Keeper of the Great Seal of England, the Lord Treasurer of England, the Keeper of the King's Privy Seal, or President of the Council, nor any Bishop, Temporal Lord, Privy Councillor, or Judge, or Justice whatsoever, shall have any power or authority to hear, examine or determine any matter or thing whatsoever in the said Court commonly called the Star Chamber, or to make, pronounce or deliver any judgment, sentence, order or decree, or to do any judicial or ministerial act in the said Court: and that all and every Act and Acts of Parliament, and all and every article, clause, and sentence in them and every of them, by which any jurisdiction, power or authority is given, limited or appointed unto the said Court, commonly called the Star Chamber, or unto all or any the Judges, Officers or Ministers thereof, or for any proceedings to be had or made in the said Court, or for any matter or thing to be drawn into question, examined or determined, there shall, for so much as concerneth the said Court of Star Chamber, and the power and authority thereby given unto it be, from the said first day of August, repealed and absolutely revoked and made void.

II. And be it likewise enacted, that the like jurisdiction now used and exercised in the Court before the President and Council in the Marches of Wales; and also in the Court before the President and Council established in the northern parts; and also in the Court commonly called the Court of the Duchy of Lancaster, held before the Chancellor and Council of the Court; and also in the Court of Exchequer of the County Palatine of Chester, held before the Chamberlain and Council of that Court; the like jurisdiction being exercised there, shall, from the said first day of August one thousand six

hundred forty and one, be also repealed and absolutely revoked
and made void, any law, prescription, custom or usage; or the
said statute made in the third year of King Henry the Seventh;
or the statute made the one-and-twentieth of Henry the Eighth;
or any Act or Acts of Parliament heretofore had or made to
the contrary thereof in any wise notwithstanding; and that
from henceforth no court, council, or place of judicature shall
be erected, ordained, constituted, or appointed within this realm
of England or dominion of Wales, which shall have, use or exercise the same or the like jurisdiction, as is or hath been used,
practised or exercised in the said Court of Star Chamber.

III. Be it likewise declared and enacted by authority of this
present Parliament, that neither His Majesty nor his Privy Council have or ought to have any jurisdiction, power or authority
by English bill, petition, articles, libel, or any other arbitrary
way whatsoever, to examine or draw into question, determine
or dispose of the lands, tenements, hereditaments, goods or
chattels of any the subjects of this kingdom, but that the same
ought to be tried and determined in the ordinary Courts of
Justice and by the ordinary course of the law.

IV. And be it further provided and enacted, that if any
Lord Chancellor or Keeper of the Great Seal of England,
Lord Treasurer, Keeper of the King's Privy Seal, President
of the Council, Bishop, Temporal Lord, Privy Councillor, Judge,
or Justice whatsoever, shall offend or do anything contrary to
the purport, true intent and meaning of this law; then he or
they shall for such offence forfeit the sum of £500 of lawful
money of England unto any party grieved, his executors or
administrators, who shall really prosecute for the same, and first
obtain judgment thereupon to be recorded in any Court of
Record at Westminster by action of debt, bill, plaint or information, wherein no essoine[1], protection, wager of law, aid,
prayer, privilege, injunction or order of restraint shall be in any
wise prayed, granted or allowed, nor any more than one imparlance; and if any person against whom any such judgment or
recovery shall be had as aforesaid, shall after such judgment
or recovery offend again in the same, then he or they for such
offence shall forfeit the sum of £1000 of lawful money of England

[1] Allegation of absence from lawful reasons.

unto any party grieved, his executors or administrators, who shall really prosecute for the same, and first obtain judgment thereupon to be recorded in any Court of Record at Westminster by action of debt, bill, plaint or information, in which no essoine, protection, wager of law, aid, prayer, privilege, injunction or order of restraint shall be in any wise prayed, granted or allowed, nor any more than one imparlance. And if any person against whom any such judgment or recovery shall be had as aforesaid, shall after such judgment or recovery offend again in the same kind, and shall be thereof duly convicted by indictment, information or any other lawful way or means, that such person so convicted shall be from thenceforth disabled and become by virtue of this Act incapable *ipso facto* to bear his and their said office and offices respectively, and shall be likewise disabled to make any gift, grant, conveyance or other disposition of any his lands, tenements, hereditaments, goods or chattels, or to take any benefit of any gift, conveyance or legacy to his own use.

V. And every person so offending shall likewise forfeit and lose unto the party grieved, by anything done contrary to the true intent and meaning of this law, his treble damages which he shall sustain and be put unto by means or occasion of any such act or thing done, the same to be recovered in any of His Majesty's Courts of Record at Westminster by action of debt, bill, plaint or information, wherein no essoine, protection, wager of law, aid, prayer, privilege, injunction or order of restraint, shall be in any wise prayed, granted or allowed, nor any more than one imparlance.

VI. And be it also provided and enacted, that if any person shall hereafter be committed, restrained of his liberty or suffer imprisonment [by the order or decree of any such Court of Star Chamber or other Court aforesaid, now or at any time hereafter having or pretending to have the same or like jurisdiction, power or authority to commit or imprison as aforesaid, or by the command or warrant of the King's Majesty, his heirs or successors, in their own person or by the command or warrant of the Council Board or of any of the Lords or others of His Majesty's Privy Council[1]], that

---

[1] Annexed to the original Act in a separate schedule.

in every such case every person so committed, restrained
of his liberty, or suffering imprisonment, upon demand or
motion made by his counsel or other employed by him for
that purpose unto the Judges of the Court of King's Bench
or Common Pleas in open Court, shall, without delay upon
any pretence whatsoever, for the ordinary fees usually paid
for the same, have forthwith granted unto him a Writ of
Habeas Corpus to be directed generally unto all and every
sheriff's gaoler, minister, officer or other person in whose
custody the party committed or restrained shall be, and the
sheriff's gaoler, minister, officer or other person in whose
custody the party so committed or restrained shall be, shall
at the return of writ and according to the command thereof,
upon due and convenient notice thereof given unto him [at
the charge of the party who requireth or procureth such
writ, and upon security by his own bond given to pay the
charge of carrying back the prisoner if he shall be remanded
by the Court to which he shall be brought, as in like cases
hath been used, such charges of bringing up and carrying
back the prisoner to be always ordered by the Court if any
difference shall arise thereabout[1]], bring or cause to be brought
the body of the said party so committed or restrained unto and
before the Judges or Justices of the said Court from whence
the same writ shall issue in open Court, and shall then likewise certify the true cause of such his detenior or imprisonment, and thereupon the Court, within three court days after
such return made and delivered in open Court, shall proceed
to examine and determine whether the cause of such commitment appearing upon the said return be just and legal or
not, and shall thereupon do what to justice shall appertain,
either by delivering, bailing or remanding the prisoner.
And if anything shall be otherwise wilfully done or omitted
to be done by any Judge, Justice, officer or other person
aforementioned, contrary to the direction and true meaning
hereof, that then such person so offending shall forfeit to
the party grieved his treble damages, to be recovered by such
means and in such manner as is formerly in this Act limited and
appointed for the like penalty to be sued for and recovered.

[1] Annexed to the original Act in a separate schedule.

VII. Provided always and be it enacted, that this Act and the several clauses therein contained shall be taken and expounded to extend only to the Court of Star Chamber, and to the said Courts holden before the President and Council in the Marches of Wales, and before the President and Council in the northern parts, and also to the Court commonly called the Court of the Duchy of Lancaster, holden before the Chancellor and Council of that Court, and also in the Court of Exchequer of the County Palatine of Chester, held before the Chamberlain and Council of that Court, and to all Courts of like jurisdiction to be hereafter erected, ordained, constituted or appointed as aforesaid, and to the warrants and directions of the Council Board, and to the commitments, restraints, and imprisonments of any person or persons made, commanded or awarded by the King's Majesty, his heirs or successors, in their own person or by the Lords and others of the Privy Council and every one of them.

VIII. And lastly, provided and be it enacted, that no person or persons shall be sued, impleaded, molested or troubled for any offence against this present Act, unless the party supposed to have so offended shall be sued or impleaded for the same within two years at the most after such time wherein the said offence shall be committed.

35. THE ACT FOR THE ABOLITION OF THE COURT OF HIGH COMMISSION.

[July 5, 1641. 17 Car. I. cap. 11. Statutes of the Realm, v. 112. See *Hist. of Engl.* ix. 404.]

An Act for the repeal of a branch of a Statute primo Elizabethae, concerning Commissioners for causes ecclesiastical.

I. Whereas in the Parliament holden in the first year of the reign of the late Queen Elizabeth, late Queen of England, there was an Act made and established, entitled 'An Act restoring to the Crown the ancient jurisdiction over the State ecclesiastical and spiritual,' and abolishing all foreign power repugnant to the same: in which Act, amongst other things,

there is contained one clause, branch, article or sentence whereby it was enacted to this effect : namely, that the said late
Queen's Highness, her heirs and successors, Kings or Queens
of this realm, should have full power and authority by virtue of
that Act, by Letters Patents under the Great Seal of England,
to assign, name and authorise when and as often as Her Highness, her heirs or successors, should think meet and convenient,
and for such and so long time as should please Her Highness,
her heirs or successors, such person or persons being natural
born subjects to Her Highness, her heirs or successors, as Her
Majesty, her heirs or successors, should think meet to exercise,
use, occupy and execute under Her Highness, her heirs and
successors, all manner of jurisdictions, privileges, and pre-
eminence in any wise touching or concerning any spiritual or
ecclesiastical jurisdiction within these her realms of England and
Ireland, or any other Her Highness's dominions and countries,
and to visit, reform, redress, order, correct and amend all such
errors, heresies, schisms, abuses, offences, contempts and enormi-
ties whatsoever, which by any manner spiritual or ecclesiastical
power, authority or jurisdiction can or may lawfully be reformed, ordered, redressed, corrected, restrained, or amended,
to the pleasure of Almighty God, the increase of virtue and
the conservation of the peace and unity of this realm.
And that such person or persons so to be named, assigned,
authorised and appointed by Her Highness, her heirs or
successors, after the said Letters Patents to him or them made
and delivered as aforesaid, should have full power and
authority by virtue of that Act and of the said Letters Patents
under Her Highness, her heirs or successors, to exercise, use
and execute all the premises, according to the tenor and
effect of the said Letters Patents, any matter or cause to the
contrary in any wise notwithstanding; and whereas by
colour of some words in the foresaid branch of the said Act,
whereby Commissioners are authorised to execute their
commission according to the tenor and effect of the King's
Letters Patents, and by Letters Patents grounded thereupon,
the said Commissioners have, to the great and insufferable
wrong and oppression of the King's subjects, used to fine and
imprison them, and to exercise other authority not belonging

to ecclesiastical jurisdiction restored by that Act, and divers
other great mischiefs and inconveniences have also ensued
to the King's subjects by occasion of the said branch and
commissions issued thereupon, and the executions thereof:
therefore for the repressing and preventing of the foresaid
abuses, mischiefs and inconveniences in time to come, be it
enacted by the King's Most Excellent Majesty and the Lords
and Commons in this present Parliament assembled, and by
the authority of the same, that the foresaid branch, clause,
article or sentence contained in the said Act, and every word,
matter and thing contained in that branch, clause, article or
sentence shall from henceforth be repealed, annulled, revoked,
annihilated and utterly made void for ever, anything in the
said Act to the contrary in any wise notwithstanding.

II. And be it also enacted by the authority aforesaid, that
no Archbishop, Bishop, nor Vicar General, nor any Chancellor,
Official, nor Commissary of any Archbishop, Bishop or Vicar
General, nor any Ordinary whatsoever, nor any other spiritual
or ecclesiastical Judge, Officer or Minister of Justice, nor any
other person or persons whatsoever exercising spiritual or
ecclesiastical power, authority or jurisdiction by any grant,
licence or commission of the King's Majesty, his heirs or
successors, or by any power or authority derived from the
King, his heirs or successors, or otherwise, shall from and
after the first day of August, which shall be in the year of
our Lord God one thousand six hundred forty and one,
award, impose or inflict any pain, penalty, fine, amercement,
imprisonment or other corporal punishment upon any of
the King's subjects for any contempt, misdemeanour, crime,
offence, matter or thing whatsoever belonging to spiritual or
ecclesiastical cognizance or jurisdiction, or shall *ex officio*, or
at the instance or promotion of any other person whatsoever,
urge, enforce, tender, give or minister unto any churchwarden,
sidesman or other person whatsoever any corporal oath, whereby
he or she shall or may be charged or obliged to make any
presentment of any crime or offence, or to confess or to accuse
him or herself of any crime, offence, delinquency or misdemeanour, or any neglect or thing whereby, or by reason
whereof, he or she shall or may be liable or exposed to any

censure, pain, penalty or punishment whatsoever, upon pain
and penalty that every person who shall offend contrary to this
statute shall forfeit and pay treble damages to every person
thereby grieved, and the sum of £100 to him or them who
shall demand and sue for the same ; which said treble damages
and sum of £100 shall and may be demanded and recovered
by action of debt, bill or plaint in any Court of Record
wherein no privilege, essoine, protection or wager of law shall
be admitted or allowed to the defendant.

III. And be it further enacted, that every person who shall
be once convicted of any act or offence prohibited by this
statute, shall for such act or offence be from and after such
conviction utterly disabled to be or continue in any office or
employment in any Court of Justice whatsoever, or to exercise
or execute any power, authority or jurisdiction by force of
any Commission or Letters Patents of the King, his heirs or
successors.

IV. And be it further enacted, that from and after the said
first day of August, no new Court shall be erected, ordained
or appointed within this realm of England or dominion of
Wales, which shall or may have the like power, jurisdiction
or authority as the said High Commission Court now hath
or pretendeth to have ; but that all and every such Letters
Patents, Commissions and Grants made or to be made by His
Majesty, his heirs or successors, and all powers and authorities
granted or pretended or mentioned to be granted thereby, and
all acts, sentences and decrees, to be made by virtue or colour
thereof shall be utterly void and of none effect.

36. ACT DECLARING THE ILLEGALITY OF SHIP-MONEY.

[August 7, 1641.   17 Car. I. cap. 14.   Statutes of the Realm, v. 116.
See *Hist. of Engl.* ix. 415.]

*An Act for the declaring unlawful and void the late proceedings
touching Ship-money, and for the vacating of all records
and process concerning the same.*

I. Whereas divers writs of late time issued under the Great
Seal of England, commonly called Ship-writs, for the charging

of the Ports, Towns, Cities, Boroughs, and Counties of this
realm respectively, to provide and furnish certain ships for
His Majesty's service; and whereas upon the execution of the
same writs and returns of certioraries thereupon made, and
the sending the same by *Mittimus* into the Court of Exchequer,
process hath been thence made against sundry persons pretended to be charged by way of contribution for the making
up of certain sums assessed for the providing of the said ships;
and in especial in Easter Term in the thirteenth year of the
reign of our Sovereign Lord the King that now is, a Writ
of *Scire facias* was awarded out of the Court of Exchequer to
the then Sheriff of Buckinghamshire against John Hampden,
Esquire, to appear and show cause why he should not be
charged with a certain sum so assessed upon him: upon
whose appearance and demurrer to the proceedings therein
the Barons of the Exchequer adjourned the same case into the
Exchequer Chamber, where it was solemnly argued divers days;
and at length it was there agreed by the greater part of all
the Justices of the Courts of King's Bench and Common Pleas,
and of the Barons of the Exchequer there assembled, that the
said John Hampden should be charged with the said sum so as
aforesaid assessed on him; the main grounds and reasons of
the said Justices and Barons which so agreed being, that when
the good and safety of the kingdom in general is concerned,
and the whole kingdom in danger, the King might by writ
under the Great Seal of England command all the subjects of
this his kingdom at their charge to provide and furnish such
number of ships with men, victuals and munition, and for
such time as the King should think fit for the defence and
safeguard of the kingdom from such danger and peril, and
that by law the King might compel the doing thereof in case
of refusal or refractoriness, and that the King is the sole
judge both of the danger, and when and how the same is to
be prevented and avoided; according to which grounds and
reasons all the Justices of the said Courts of King's Bench
and Common Pleas, and the said Barons of the Exchequer,
having been formerly consulted with by His Majesty's command, had set their hands to an extrajudicial opinion expressed to the same purpose, which opinion with their names

thereunto was also by His Majesty's command enrolled in the Courts of Chancery, King's Bench, Common Pleas and Exchequer, and likewise entered among the remembrances of the Court of Star Chamber, and according to the said agreement of the said Justices and Barons, judgment was given by the Barons of the Exchequer that the said John Hampden should be charged with the said sum so assessed on him : and, whereas some other actions and process depend, and have depended in the said Court of Exchequer and in some other Courts, against other persons for the like kind of charge grounded upon the said writs commonly called Ship-writs; all which writs and proceedings as aforesaid were utterly against the law of the land: be it therefore declared and enacted by the King's Most Excellent Majesty and the Lords and the Commons in this present Parliament assembled, and by the authority of the same, that the said charge imposed upon the subject for the providing and furnishing of ships commonly called Ship-money, and the said extrajudicial opinion of the said Justices and Barons and the said writs, and every of them, and the said agreement or opinion of the greater part of the said Justices and Barons, and the said judgment given against the said John Hampden, were and are contrary to and against the laws and statutes of this realm, the right of property, the liberty of the subjects, former resolutions in Parliament, and the Petition of Right made in the third year of the reign of His Majesty that now is.

II. And it is further declared and enacted by the authority aforesaid, that all and every the particulars prayed or desired in the said Petition of Right shall from henceforth be put in execution accordingly, and shall be firmly and strictly holden and observed as in the same Petition they are prayed and expressed ; and that all and every the records and remembrances of all and every the judgment, enrolments, entry, and proceedings as aforesaid, and all and every the proceedings whatsoever, upon or by pretext or colour of any of the said writs commonly called Ship-writs, and all and every the dependents on any of them, shall be deemed and adjudged, to all intents, constructions and purposes, to be utterly void and disannulled ; and that all and every the said judgment, enrolments, entries, proceedings and dependents of what kind soever, shall be vacated and cancelled in such manner and form as records use to be that are vacated.

37. ACT FOR THE LIMITATION OF FORESTS.

[August 7, 1641.   17 Car. I. cap. 16.   Statutes of the Realm, v. 119.
See *Hist. of Engl.* ix. 415.]

An Act for the certainty of forests, and of the meers[1]*, meets*[2]*,
limits and bounds of the forests.*

I. Whereas by Act of Parliament made in the first year of the reign of the late King Edward the Third[3], it is ordained that the old perambulation of the forest in the time of King Edward the First should be thenceforth holden in like form as it was then ridden and bounded, and in such places where it was not bounden, the King would that it should be bounden by good men and lawful: and whereas for many ages past certain meets, meers, limits and bounds of the forests, have been commonly known and observed in the several Counties, wherein the said forests lie: and whereas of late divers presentments have been made and some judgments given whereby the meets, meers, limits and bounds of some of the said forests have been variously extended or pretended to extend beyond some of the meets, meers, limits and bounds so commonly known and formerly observed, to the great grievance and vexation of many persons having lands adjoining to the said meets, meers, limits and bounds so commonly known and formerly observed: and whereas of late time some endeavours or pretences have been to set on foot forests in some parts of this realm and the dominion of Wales, where in truth none have been or ought to be, or at least have not been used of long time: for remedy thereof, may it please your Most Excellent Majesty that it be declared and enacted by authority of Parliament; and be it declared and enacted by the King's Most Excellent Majesty

---

[1] Borders.   [2] Measurements.
[3] 1 E. III. st. 2. c. 1.

and the Lords and Commons in this present Parliament
assembled, and by the authority of the same, that from henceforth the meets, meers, limits and bounds of all and every the
forests respectively, shall be to all intents and purposes taken,
adjudged and deemed to extend no further respectively than the
meets, meers, limits and bounds which in the several Counties
respectively wherein the said forests do lie were commonly
known, reputed, used or taken to be the meets, meers, limits
and bounds of the said forests respectively in the twentieth
year of the reign of our late Sovereign Lord King James, and
not beyond in any wise any perambulation, or perambulations,
presentments, extents, surveys, judgments, records, decrees, or
other matter or thing whatsoever to the contrary notwithstanding: and that all and every the presentments since the
said twentieth year made, and all and every other presentment
and presentments, and all and every judgment and award upon
or by reason or pretext of any such present or presentments,
and all and every perambulation, and perambulations, surveys,
extents, and other act and acts at any time heretofore had or
made, by which the meets, meers, limits or bounds of the said
forest, or any of them, are or are pretended to be further extended
than as aforesaid; and also all and every presentment of any
other person or persons at any Justice seat, Swainemote, or
Court of Attachments, for or by reason or by colour of any
act or acts whatsoever done or committed in any place without
or beyond the said meets, meers, limits or bounds respectively,
so commonly known, reputed, used, or taken as aforesaid, and
all and every fine and fines, and amercement and amercements,
upon by reason or colour of any such presentment or presentments, shall from henceforth be adjudged, deemed, and taken
to be utterly void and of no force or effect; any law, statute,
record or pretence whatsoever to the contrary notwithstanding.

II. And be it further enacted by the authority aforesaid,
that no place or places within this realm of England or dominion
of Wales, where no such Justice seat, Swainemote, or Court of
Attachment have been held or kept, or where no Verderers
have been chosen, or regard made within the space of sixty
years next before the first year of His Majesty's reign that
now is, shall be at any time hereafter judged, deemed, or taken

to be forest, or within the bounds or meets of the forest; but the same shall be from henceforth for ever hereafter disafforested, and freed, and exempted from the forest laws; any Justice seat, Swainemote, or Court of Attachment held or kept within or for any such place or places at any time or times since the beginning of His Majesty's said reign, or any presentment, enquiry, act, or thing heretofore made, or hereafter to be made or done to the contrary notwithstanding.

III. Provided also, and be it further enacted by the authority aforesaid, that for the better putting into certainty all and every the meets, meers, bounds and limits of all and every the forests as aforesaid, the Lord Chancellor or Lord Keeper of the Great Seal of England for the time being shall, by virtue of this Act, upon request of any of the Peers of this kingdom, or of the Knights and Burgesses of the Parliament or any of them, grant several commissions under the Great Seal of England to Commissioners to be nominated respectively by the said Peers, Knights and Burgesses, or any of them, to enquire of and find out by inquests of good and lawful men upon oath, and by the oaths of witnesses to be produced at the said inquests, and by all other lawful means, all and every the meers, meets, bounds and limits of the forests respectively, which were commonly known to be their meers, meets, bounds and limits respectively in the said twentieth year of the reign of our late Sovereign Lord King James; and to return the inquests so taken into the Court of Chancery, and that all and every the Sheriffs and Bailiffs of and in every County wherein any such inquests shall be so to be taken; and all and every the Verderers, Foresters, Rangers, and other officers of the forest respectively, where any such officers be, shall be assistant and attendant to the executions of the said commissions, according as by virtue of the said commissions respectively they shall be commanded; and where no such officers are or where such officers be, if they or any of them shall refuse or neglect such assistance and attendance as aforesaid, then the said Commissioners shall and may proceed without them in the execution of the said commissions.

IV. And be it further enacted by the authority aforesaid, that the forests whereof the meets, meers, limits and bounds shall be so returned and certified by virtue of any the said commissions as aforesaid, from thenceforth shall not extend, nor be extended, nor be deemed, adjudged, or taken to extend any further in any wise than the meets, meers, limits and bounds that shall be so returned and certified; and that all the places and territories that shall be without the meets, meers, limits and bounds so returned and certified, shall be and are hereby declared to be from thenceforth free to all intents and purposes as if the same had never been forest, or so reputed; any Act or Acts, matter or thing whatsoever to the contrary thereof notwithstanding.

V. Provided, and be it further enacted by the authority aforesaid, that all and every the grounds, territories or places which have been or are disafforested or mentioned to be disafforested in or by any Letters Patents, Charters, or otherwise since the said twentieth year of the reign of our said late Sovereign Lord King James, shall be excluded and left out of the meets, meers, limits and bounds of the forests which are to be enquired of, returned and certified by virtue of the said commissions, or any of them respectively, and shall be, and hereby are declared and enacted to be utterly disafforested, free, and exempt to all intents and purposes as if the same had never been at all forest, or so reputed; any thing in this present Act contained, or any other Act, matter or thing whatsoever to the contrary in any wise notwithstanding.

VI. Provided nevertheless and be it enacted that the tenants, owners, and occupiers, and every of them, of lands and tenements, which shall be excluded and left out of the meets, meers, limits or bounds of the forests to be returned and certified by virtue of any the said commissions, shall or may use and enjoy such common and other profits and easements within the forests as anciently or accustomarily they have used and enjoyed; anything in this present Act contained, or any Act or Ordinance made in the three-and-thirtieth year of King Edward the First, or any custom or law of the forest, or any other matter or thing to the contrary thereof notwithstanding.

38. ACT PROHIBITING THE EXACTION OF KNIGHTHOOD FINES.

[August 10, 1641. 17 Car. I. cap. 20. Statutes of the Realm, v. 131.
See *Hist. of Engl.* ix. 417.

*An Act for the prevention of vexatious proceedings touching
the Order of Knighthood.*

Whereas upon pretext of an ancient custom or usage of this realm of England, that men of full age being not Knights, and being seized of lands or rents of the yearly value of forty pounds or more (especially if their seizen had so continued by the space of three years next past), might be compelled by the King's writ to receive, or take upon them the Order of Knighthood, or else to make fine for the discharge or respite of the same, several writs, about the beginning of His Majesty's reign issued out of the Court of Chancery for proclamations to be made in every County to that purpose, and for certifying the names of all such persons, and for summoning them personally to appear in the King's presence, before a certain day, to be there ready to receive the said Order or Dignity: upon return of which writs, and transmitting the same with their returns into the Court of Exchequer, and upon other writs for further inquiry of the names of such persons issuing out of the said Court of Exchequer, process by *distringas* was thence made against a very great number of persons, many of which were altogether unfit, in regard either of estate or quality, to receive the said Order or Dignity, and very many were put to grievous fines and other vexations for the same, although in truth it were not sufficiently known how, or in what sort, or where they, or any of them, should, or might have addressed themselves for receiving the said Order or Dignity, and for saving themselves thereby from the said fines, process and vexations: and whereas it is most apparent that all and every such proceeding, in regard of the matter therein pretended, is altogether useless and unreasonable: may it therefore please your Most Excellent Majesty that it be by authority of Parliament declared and enacted; and be it declared and enacted by the King's Most Excellent Majesty, and the Lords

and Commons in this Parliament assembled, and by the
authority of the same, that from henceforth no person or
persons of what condition, quality, estate or degree soever,
shall at any time be distrained or otherwise compelled by any
writ or process of the Court of Chancery or Court of Exchequer,
or otherwise by any means whatsoever, to receive or take
upon him or them respectively the Order or Dignity of Knighthood, nor shall suffer or undergo any fine, trouble or molestation
whatsoever by reason or colour of his or their having not
received or not taken upon him or them the said Order or
Dignity; and that all and every writ or process whatsoever,
and all and every proceeding which shall hereafter be had
or made contrary to the intent of this Act, shall be deemed
and adjudged to be utterly void; and that all and every
process, proceeding, and charge now depending by reason or
colour of the said pretended custom or writs aforesaid, or of
any the dependents thereof, shall from henceforth cease, and
stand, lie and remain discharged and utterly void, any former
law or custom, or any pretence of any former law or custom
or any other matter whatsoever to the contrary in any wise
notwithstanding.

39. Resolutions of the House of Commons on Ecclesiastical Innovations.

[September 1, 1641.   Journals of the House of Commons, ii. 279.   See
Hist. of Engl. x. 14.]

Whereas divers innovations in or about the worship of God
have been lately practised in this kingdom, by enjoining some
things and prohibiting others, without warrant of law, to the
great grievance and discontent of His Majesty's subjects; for
the suppression of such innovations, and for preservation of the
public peace, it is this day ordered by the Commons in Parliament assembled :

That the churchwardens of every parish church and chapel
respectively, do forthwith remove the communion table from
the east end of the church, chapel, or chancel into some
other convenient place; and that they take away the rails,

and level the chancels as heretofore they were before the late innovations :

That all crucifixes, scandalous pictures of any one or more persons of the Trinity, and all images of the Virgin Mary, shall be taken away and abolished ; and that all tapers, candlesticks and basins be removed from the communion table :

That all corporal bowing at the name of Jesus, or towards the east end of the church, chapel, or chancel, or towards the communion table be henceforth forborne :

That the orders aforesaid be observed in all the several cathedral churches of this kingdom, and all the collegiate churches or chapels in the two Universities, or any other part of the kingdom ; and in the Temple Church, and the chapels of the other Inns of Court, by the Deans of the said cathedral churches, by the Vice-Chancellors of the said Universities, and by the heads and governors of the several colleges and halls aforesaid ; and by the benchers and readers in the said Inns of Court respectively :

That the Lord's Day shall be duly observed and sanctified ; all dancing or other sports, either before or after divine service, be forborne and restrained ; and that the preaching of God's Word be permitted in the afternoon in the several churches and chapels of this kingdom ; and that ministers and preachers be encouraged thereunto :

That the Vice-Chancellors of the Universities, heads and governors of colleges, all parsons, vicars, churchwardens, &c. make certificates of the performance of these orders : and if the same shall not be observed in any of the places aforementioned, upon complaint thereof made to the two next Justices of Peace, Mayor, or head officers of cities, or towns corporate ; it is ordered, that the said Justices, Mayor, or other head officer respectively, shall examine the truth of all such complaints, and certify by whose default the same are committed : all which certificates are to be delivered in Parliament before the thirteenth of October next.

40. Order of the House of Lords on the Services of the Church.

[September 9, 1641. Imprinted at London by Robert Barker, printer to the King's Most Excellent Majesty, and by the Assigns of John Bill. See *Hist. of Engl.* x. 16.]

Die Sabbati 16 Januarii, 1640[1].

It is this day ordered by the Lords spiritual and temporal in the High Court of Parliament assembled, that the divine service be performed as it is appointed by the Acts of Parliament of this realm; and that all such as shall disturb that wholesome order, shall be severely punished according to the law; and the parsons, vicars, and curates in the several parishes, shall forbear to introduce any rites or ceremonies that may give offence, otherwise than those which are established by the laws of the land.

Die Jovis 9 Septemb., 1641.

It is this day voted by the Lords in Parliament, that the order abovesaid shall be printed and published.

41. Extract from the Instructions to the Committee in Scotland, proposed by the House of Commons.

[November 8, 1641[2]. Journals of the House of Lords, iv. 431. See *Hist. of Engl.* x. 55–57.]

. . . .

7. Lastly[3], you shall represent to His Most Excellent Majesty this our humble and faithful declaration: that we cannot without much grief remember the great miseries, burdens, and distempers, which have for divers years afflicted all his kingdoms and dominions, and brought them to the last point of ruin and destruction; all which have issued from the cunning, false and malicious practices of some of those who have been admitted into very near places of counsel and

[1] I. e. 1641.
[2] Presented to the Lords on November 9.
[3] The preceding instructions relate to the preparations for the Irish war.

authority about him, who have been favourers of Popery, superstition and innovation, subverters of religion, honour and justice, factors for promoting the designs of foreign princes and states, to the great and apparent danger of his royal person, crown and dignity, and of all his people; authors of false scandals and jealousies betwixt His Majesty and his loving subjects, enemies to the peace, union and confidence betwixt him and his Parliament, which is the surest foundation of prosperity and greatness to His Majesty, and of comfort and hope to them; that, by their counsels and endeavours, those great sums which have been lately drawn from the people have been either consumed unprofitably, or in the maintenance of such designs as have been mischievous and destructive to the State; and whilst we have been labouring to support His Majesty to purge out the corruptions and restore the decays both of the Church and State, others of their faction and party have been contriving by violence to suppress the liberty of Parliament, and endanger the safety of those who have opposed such wicked and pernicious courses.

8. That we have just cause of belief that those conspiracies and commotions in Ireland are but the effects of the same counsels; and if persons of such aims and conditions shall still continue in credit, authority and employment, the great aids which we shall be enforced to draw from his people for subduing the rebellion in Ireland, will be applied to the fomenting and cherishing of it there, and encouraging some such-like attempt by the Papists and ill-affected subjects in England, and in the end, to the subversion of religion and destruction of his loyal subjects in both kingdoms; and do therefore most humbly beseech His Majesty to change those counsels, from which such ill courses have proceeded, and which have caused so many miseries and dangers to himself and all his dominions; and that he will be graciously pleased to employ such counsellors and ministers as shall be approved by his Parliament, who are his greatest and most faithful Council, that so his people may with courage and confidence undergo the charge and hazard of this war, and, by their bounty and faithful endeavours (with God's favour and blessing) restore to His Majesty and this kingdom that honour, peace,

safety and prosperity which they have enjoyed in former times.

And, if herein His Majesty shall not vouchsafe to condescend to our humble supplication, although we shall always continue with reverence and faithfulness to his person and his crown, to perform those duties of service and obedience to which, by the laws of God and this kingdom, we are obliged, yet we shall be forced, in discharge of the trust which we owe to the State, and to those whom we represent, to resolve upon some such way of defending Ireland from the rebels as may concur to the securing of ourselves from such mischievous counsels and designs as have lately been, and still are in practice and agitation against us, as we have just cause to believe; and to commend those aids and contributions which this great necessity shall require, to the custody and disposing of such persons of honour and fidelity as we have cause to confide in.

42. The King's Speech to the Recorder of the City of London.

[November 25, 1641. Rushworth, iv. 430. See *Hist. of Engl.* x. 84.]

Mr. Recorder,

I must desire you, because my voice cannot reach to all those that I desire should hear me, to give most hearty thanks to all the good citizens of London, for their hearty expressions of their love to me this day; and, indeed, I cannot sufficiently express the contentment I have received therein, for now I see that all these tumults and disorders have only risen from the meaner sort of people, and that the affections of the better, and main part of the City, have ever been loyal and affectionate to my person and government.

And likewise it comforts me to see, that all those mis-reports that have been made of me in my absence, have not the least power to do me prejudice in your opinions, as may be easily seen by this day's expression of joy.

And now I think it fit for me to assure you, that I am returned with as hearty and kind affections to my people in general, and to this City in particular, as can be desired by loving subjects : the first I shall express by governing you all according to the laws of this kingdom, and in maintaining and protecting the true Protestant religion, according as it hath been established in my two famous predecessors' times, Queen Elizabeth and my father ; and this I will do, if need be, to the hazard of my life and all that is dear to me.

As for the City in particular, I shall study by all means their prosperity ; and I assure you, I will singly grant those few reasonable demands you have now made unto me, in the name of the City ; and likewise, I shall study to re-establish that flourishing trade which now is in some disorder amongst you, which I doubt not to effect with the good assistance of the Parliament.

One thing I have thought of, as a particular affection to you, which is, to give back unto you freely that part of Londonderry which heretofore was evicted from you. This, I confess, as that kingdom is now, is no great gift, but I hope to recover it first, and then to give it to you whole and entirely; and for the legal part of this I command you, Mr. Recorder, to wait upon me to see it punctually performed.

I will end as I begun, to desire you, Mr. Recorder, to give all the City thanks in better expressions than I can make, though I must tell you it will be far short of that real contentment I find in my heart, for this real and seasonable demonstration of their affections to me.

43. The Grand Remonstrance, with the Petition Accompanying it.

[Presented to the King, December 1, 1641.   Rushworth, iv. 437.   See *Hist. of Engl.* x. 59–64, 71–79, 88.]

The Petition of the House of Commons, which accompanied the Remonstrance of the state of the kingdom, when it was presented to His Majesty at Hampton Court, December 1, 1641.

Most Gracious Sovereign,

Your Majesty's most humble and faithful subjects the Commons in this present Parliament assembled, do with much thankfulness and joy acknowledge the great mercy and favour of God, in giving your Majesty a safe and peaceable return out of Scotland into your kingdom of England, where the pressing dangers and distempers of the State have caused us with much earnestness to desire the comfort of your gracious presence, and likewise the unity and justice of your royal authority, to give more life and power to the dutiful and loyal counsels and endeavours of your Parliament, for the prevention of that eminent ruin and destruction wherein your kingdoms of England and Scotland are threatened. The duty which we owe to your Majesty and our country, cannot but make us very sensible and apprehensive, that the multiplicity, sharpness and malignity of those evils under which we have now many years suffered, are fomented and cherished by a corrupt and ill-affected party, who amongst other their mischievous devices for the alteration of religion and government, have sought by many false scandals and imputations, cunningly insinuated and dispersed amongst the people, to blemish and disgrace our proceedings in this Parliament, and to get themselves a party and faction amongst your subjects, for the better strengthening themselves in their wicked courses, and hindering those provisions and remedies which might, by the wisdom of your Majesty and counsel of your Parliament, be opposed against them.

For preventing whereof, and the better information of your Majesty, your Peers and all other your loyal subjects, we have been necessitated to make a declaration of the state of the kingdom, both before and since the assembly of this Parliament, unto this time, which we do humbly present to your Majesty, without the least intention to lay any blemish upon your royal person, but only to represent how your royal authority and trust have been abused, to the great prejudice and danger of your Majesty, and of all your good subjects.

And because we have reason to believe that those malignant parties, whose proceedings evidently appear to be mainly for the advantage and increase of Popery, is composed, set up, and acted by the subtile practice of the Jesuits and other engineers and factors for Rome, and to the great danger of this kingdom, and most grievous affliction of your loyal subjects, have so far prevailed as to corrupt divers of your Bishops and others in prime places of the Church, and also to bring divers of these instruments to be of your Privy Council, and other employments of trust and nearness about your Majesty, the Prince, and the rest of your royal children.

And by this means have had such an operation in your counsel and the most important affairs and proceedings of your government, that a most dangerous division and chargeable preparation for war betwixt your kingdoms of England and Scotland, the increase of jealousies betwixt your Majesty and your most obedient subjects, the violent distraction and interruption of this Parliament, the insurrection of the Papists in your kingdom of Ireland, and bloody massacre of your people, have been not only endeavoured and attempted, but in a great measure compassed and effected.

For preventing the final accomplishment whereof, your poor subjects are enforced to engage their persons and estates to the maintaining of a very expensive and dangerous war, notwithstanding they have already since the beginning of this Parliament undergone the charge of £150,000 sterling, or thereabouts, for the necessary support and supply of your Majesty in these present and perilous designs. And because all our most faithful endeavours and engagements will be ineffectual for the peace, safety and preservation of your Majesty and your people, if some present, real and effectual course be not taken for suppressing this wicked and malignant party:—

We, your most humble and obedient subjects, do with all faithfulness and humility beseech your Majesty,—

1. That you will be graciously pleased to concur with the humble desires of your people in a parliamentary way, for the preserving the peace and safety of the kingdom from the malicious designs of the Popish party:—

For depriving the Bishops of their votes in Parliament, and abridging their immoderate power usurped over the Clergy, and other your good subjects, which they have perniciously abused to the hazard of religion, and great prejudice and oppression to the laws of the kingdom, and just liberty of your people·—

For the taking away such oppressions in religion, Church

government and discipline, as have been brought in and
fomented by them :—

For uniting all such your loyal subjects together as join in
the same fundamental truths against the Papists, by removing
some oppressive and unnecessary ceremonies by which divers
weak consciences have been scrupled, and seem to be divided
from the rest, and for the due execution of those good laws which
have been made for securing the liberty of your subjects.

2. That your Majesty will likewise be pleased to remove
from your council all such as persist to favour and promote
any of those pressures and corruptions wherewith your people
have been grieved; and that for the future your Majesty will
vouchsafe to employ such persons in your great and public
affairs, and to take such to be near you in places of trust,
as your Parliament may have cause to confide in; that in
your princely goodness to your people you will reject and
refuse all mediation and solicitation to the contrary, how
powerful and near soever.

3. That you will be pleased to forbear to alienate any of
the forfeited and escheated lands in Ireland which shall
accrue to your Crown by reason of this rebellion, that out of
them the Crown may be the better supported, and some satisfaction made to your subjects of this kingdom for the great expenses
they are like to undergo [in] this war.

Which humble desires of ours being graciously fulfilled
by your Majesty, we will, by the blessing and favour of God,
most cheerfully undergo the hazard and expenses of this war, and
apply ourselves to such other courses and counsels as may
support your real estate with honour and plenty at home, with
power and reputation abroad, and by our loyal affections,
obedience and service, lay a sure and lasting foundation of
the greatness and prosperity of your Majesty, and your royal
posterity in future times.

The Grand Remonstrance.

The Commons in this present Parliament assembled, having
with much earnestness and faithfulness of affection and zeal
to the public good of this kingdom, and His Majesty's honour

and service, for the space of twelve months wrestled with great dangers and fears, the pressing miseries and calamities, the various distempers and disorders which had not only assaulted, but even overwhelmed and extinguished the liberty, peace and prosperity of this kingdom, the comfort and hopes of all His Majesty's good subjects, and exceedingly weakened and undermined the foundation and strength of his own royal throne, do yet find an abounding malignity and opposition in those parties and factions who have been the cause of those evils, and do still labour to cast aspersions upon that which hath been done, and to raise many difficulties for the hindrance of that which remains yet undone, and to foment jealousies between the King and Parliament, that so they may deprive him and his people of the fruit of his own gracious intentions, and their humble desires of procuring the public peace, safety and happiness of this realm.

For the preventing of those miserable effects which such malicious endeavours may produce, we have thought good to declare the root and the growth of these mischievous designs : the maturity and ripeness to which they have attained before the beginning of the Parliament : the effectual means which have been used for the extirpation of those dangerous evils, and the progress which hath therein been made by His Majesty's goodness and the wisdom of the Parliament : the ways of obstruction and opposition by which that progress hath been interrupted : the courses to be taken for the removing those obstacles, and for the accomplishing of our most dutiful and faithful intentions and endeavours of restoring and establishing the ancient honour, greatness and security of this Crown and nation.

The root of all this mischief we find to be a malignant and pernicious design of subverting the fundamental laws and principles of government, upon which the religion and justice of this kingdom are firmly established. The actors and promoters hereof have been :

1. The Jesuited Papists, who hate the laws, as the obstacles of that change and subversion of religion which they so much long for.

2. The Bishops, and the corrupt part of the Clergy, who cherish formality and superstition as the natural effects and

more probable supports of their own ecclesiastical tyranny and usurpation.

3. Such Councillors and Courtiers as for private ends have engaged themselves to further the interests of some foreign princes or states to the prejudice of His Majesty and the State at home.

The common principles by which they moulded and governed all their particular counsels and actions were these:

First, to maintain continual differences and discontents between the King and the people, upon questions of prerogative and liberty, that so they might have the advantage of siding with him, and under the notions of men addicted to his service, gain to themselves and their parties the places of greatest trust and power in the kingdom.

A second, to suppress the purity and power of religion and such persons as were best affected to it, as being contrary to their own ends, and the greatest impediment to that change which they thought to introduce.

A third, to conjoin those parties of the kingdom which were most propitious to their own ends, and to divide those who were most opposite, which consisted in many particular observations.

To cherish the Arminian part in those points wherein they agree with the Papists, to multiply and enlarge the difference between the common Protestants and those whom they call Puritans, to introduce and countenance such opinions and ceremonies as are fittest for accommodation with Popery, to increase and maintain ignorance, looseness and profaneness in the people; that of those three parties, Papists, Arminians and Libertines, they might compose a body fit to act such counsels and resolutions as were most conducible to their own ends.

A fourth, to disaffect the King to Parliaments by slander and false imputations, and by putting him upon other ways of supply, which in show and appearance were fuller of advantage than the ordinary course of subsidies, though in truth they brought more loss than gain both to the King and people, and have caused the great distractions under which we both suffer.

As in all compounded bodies the operations are qualified according to the predominant element, so in this mixed party, the Jesuited counsels, being most active and prevailing, may easily be discovered to have had the greatest sway in all their determinations, and if they be not prevented, are likely to devour the rest, or to turn them into their own nature.

In the beginning of His Majesty's reign the party began to revive and flourish again, having been somewhat damped by the breach with Spain in the last year of King James, and by His Majesty's marriage with France; the interests and counsels of that State being not so contrary to the good of religion and the prosperity of this kingdom as those of Spain; and the Papists of England, having been ever more addicted to Spain than France, yet they still retained a purpose and resolution to weaken the Protestant parties in all parts, and even in France, whereby to make way for the change of religion which they intended at home.

1. The first effect and evidence of their recovery and strength was the dissolution of the Parliament at Oxford, after there had been given two subsidies to His Majesty, and before they received relief in any one grievance many other more miserable effects followed.

2. The loss of the Rochel fleet, by the help of our shipping, set forth and delivered over to the French in opposition to the advice of Parliament, which left that town without defence by sea, and made way, not only to the loss of that important place, but likewise to the loss of all the strength and security of the Protestant religion in France.

3. The diverting of His Majesty's course of wars from the West Indies, which was the most facile and hopeful way for this kingdom to prevail against the Spaniard, to an expenseful and successless attempt upon Cadiz, which was so ordered as if it had rather been intended to make us weary of war than to prosper in it.

4. The precipitate breach with France, by taking their ships to a great value without making recompense to the English, whose goods were thereupon imbarred and confiscated in that kingdom.

5. The peace with Spain without consent of Parliament, contrary to the promise of King James to both Houses, whereby the Palatine's cause was deserted and left to chargeable and

hopeless treaties, which for the most part were managed by those who might justly be suspected to be no friends to that cause.

6. The charging of the kingdom with billeted soldiers in all parts of it, and the concomitant design of German horse, that the land might either submit with fear or be enforced with rigour to such arbitrary contributions as should be required of them.

7. The dissolving of the Parliament in the second year of His Majesty's reign, after a declaration of their intent to grant five subsidies.

8. The exacting of the like proportion of five subsidies, after the Parliament dissolved, by commission of loan, and divers gentlemen and others imprisoned for not yielding to pay that loan, whereby many of them contracted such sicknesses as cost them their lives.

9. Great sums of money required and raised by privy seals.

10. An unjust and pernicious attempt to extort great payments from the subject by way of excise, and a commission issued under the seal to that purpose.

11. The Petition of Right, which was granted in full Parliament, blasted, with an illegal declaration to make it destructive to itself, to the power of Parliament, to the liberty of the subject, and to that purpose printed with it, and the Petition made of no use but to show the bold and presumptuous injustice of such ministers as durst break the laws and suppress the liberties of the kingdom, after they had been so solemnly and evidently declared.

12. Another Parliament dissolved 4 Car., the privilege of Parliament broken, by imprisoning divers members of the House, detaining them close prisoners for many months together, without the liberty of using books, pen, ink or paper; denying them all the comforts of life, all means of preservation of health, not permitting their wives to come unto them even in the time of their sickness.

13. And for the completing of that cruelty, after years spent in such miserable durance, depriving them of the necessary means of spiritual consolation, not suffering them to go abroad to enjoy God's ordinances in God's House, or God's ministers to

come to them to minister comfort to them in their private chambers.

14. And to keep them still in this oppressed condition, not admitting them to be bailed according to law, yet vexing them with informations in inferior courts[1], sentencing and fining some of them for matters done in Parliament; and extorting the payments of those fines from them, enforcing others to put in security of good behaviour before they could be released.

15. The imprisonment of the rest, which refused to be bound, still continued, which might have been perpetual if necessity had not the last year brought another Parliament to relieve them, of whom one died[2] by the cruelty and harshness of his imprisonment, which would admit of no relaxation, notwithstanding the imminent danger of his life did sufficiently appear by the declaration of his physician, and his release, or at least his refreshment, was sought by many humble petitions, and his blood still cries either for vengeance or repentance of those Ministers of State, who have at once obstructed the course both of His Majesty's justice and mercy.

16. Upon the dissolution of both these Parliaments, untrue and scandalous declarations were published to asperse their proceedings, and some of their members unjustly; to make them odious, and colour the violence which was used against them; proclamations set out to the same purpose; and to the great dejecting of the hearts of the people, forbidding them even to speak of Parliaments.

17. After the breach of the Parliament in the fourth of His Majesty, injustice, oppression and violence broke in upon us without any restraint or moderation, and yet the first project was the great sums exacted through the whole kingdom for default of knighthood, which seemed to have some colour and shadow of a law, yet if it be rightly examined by that obsolete law which was pretended for it, it will be found to be against all the rules of justice, both in respect of the persons charged, the proportion of the fines demanded, and the absurd and unreasonable manner of their proceedings.

18. Tonnage and Poundage hath been received without colour

---

[1] I. e. inferior to Parliament.   [2] Sir John Eliot.

or pretence of law; many other heavy impositions continued against law, and some so unreasonable that the sum of the charge exceeds the value of the goods.

19. The Book of Rates[1] lately enhanced to a high proportion, and such merchants that would not submit to their illegal and unreasonable payments, were vexed and oppressed above measure; and the ordinary course of justice, the common birthright of the subject of England, wholly obstructed unto them.

20. And although all this was taken upon pretence of guarding the seas, yet a new unheard-of tax of ship-money was devised, and upon the same pretence, by both which there was charged upon the subject near £700,000 some years, and yet the merchants have been left so naked to the violence of the Turkish pirates, that many great ships of value and thousands of His Majesty's subjects have been taken by them, and do still remain in miserable slavery.

21. The enlargements of forests, contrary to *Carta de Foresta*, and the composition thereupon.

22. The exactions of coat and conduct money and divers other military charges.

23. The taking away the arms of trained bands of divers counties.

24. The desperate design of engrossing all the gunpowder into one hand, keeping it in the Tower of London, and setting so high a rate upon it that the poorer sort were not able to buy it, nor could any have it without licence, thereby to leave the several parts of the kingdom destitute of their necessary defence, and by selling so dear that which was sold to make an unlawful advantage of it, to the great charge and detriment of the subject.

25. The general destruction of the King's timber, especially that in the Forest of Deane, sold to Papists, which was the best store-house of this kingdom for the maintenance of our shipping.

---

[1] The Book of Rates was issued from time to time by the King to state the value of goods according to the current prices of the day. This was necessary because Poundage was laid on goods by the £1 value, not on their weight or measure. Most writers confuse this Book of Rates with the setting of impositions by patent, which was a very different thing.

26. The taking away of men's right, under the colour of the King's title to land, between high and low water marks.

27. The monopolies of soap, salt, wine, leather, sea-coal, and in a manner of all things of most common and necessary use.

28. The restraint of the liberties of the subjects in their habitation, trades and other interests.

29. Their vexation and oppression by purveyors, clerks of the market and saltpetre men.

30. The sale of pretended nuisances, as building in and about London.

31. Conversion of arable into pasture, continuance of pasture, under the name of depopulation, have driven many millions out of the subjects' purses, without any considerable profit to His Majesty.

32. Large quantities of common and several grounds hath been taken from the subject by colour of the Statute of Improvement, and by abuse of the Commission of Sewers, without their consent, and against it.

33. And not only private interest, but also public faith, have been broken in seizing of the money and bullion in the mint, and the whole kingdom like to be robbed at once in that abominable project of brass money.

34. Great numbers of His Majesty's subjects for refusing those unlawful charges, have been vexed with long and expensive suits, some fined and censured, others committed to long and hard imprisonments and confinements, to the loss of health in many, of life in some, and others have had their houses broken up, their goods seized, some have been restrained from their lawful callings.

35. Ships have been interrupted in their voyages, surprised at sea in a hostile manner by projectors, as by a common enemy.

36. Merchants prohibited to unlade their goods in such ports as were for their own advantage, and forced to bring them to those places which were much for the advantage of the monopolisers and projectors.

37. The Court of Star Chamber hath abounded in extravagant censures, not only for the maintenance and improvement of monopolies and their unlawful taxes, but for divers other causes where there hath been no offence, or very small;

whereby His Majesty's subjects have been oppressed by grievous fines, imprisonments, stigmatisings, mutilations, whippings, pillories, gags, confinements, banishments; after so rigid a manner as hath not only deprived men of the society of their friends, exercise of their professions, comfort of books, use of paper or ink, but even violated that near union which God hath established between men and their wives, by forced and constrained separation, whereby they have been bereaved of the comfort and conversation one of another for many years together, without hope of relief, if God had not by His overruling providence given some interruption to the prevailing power, and counsel of those who were the authors and promoters of such peremptory and heady courses.

38. Judges have been put out of their places for refusing to do against their oaths and consciences; others have been so awed that they durst not do their duties, and the better to hold a rod over them, the clause *Quam diu se bene gesserit* was left out of their patents, and a new clause *Durante bene placito* inserted.

39. Lawyers have been checked for being faithful to their clients; solicitors and attorneys have been threatened, and some punished, for following lawful suits. And by this means all the approaches to justice were interrupted and forecluded.

40. New oaths have been forced upon the subject against law.

41. New judicatories erected without law. The Council Table have by their orders offered to bind the subjects in their freeholds, estates, suits and actions.

42. The pretended Court of the Earl Marshal was arbitrary and illegal in its being and proceedings.

43. The Chancery, Exchequer Chamber, Court of Wards, and other English Courts, have been grievous in exceeding their jurisdiction.

44. The estate of many families weakened, and some ruined by excessive fines, exacted from them for compositions of wardships.

45. All leases of above a hundred years made to draw on wardship contrary to law.

46. Undue proceedings used in the finding of offices to make the jury find for the King.

47. The Common Law Courts, feeling all men more inclined to seek justice there, where it may be fitted to their own desire, are known frequently to forsake the rules of the Common Law, and straying beyond their bounds, under pretence of equity, to do injustice.

48. Titles of honour, judicial places, serjeantships at law, and other offices have been sold for great sums of money, whereby the common justice of the kingdom hath been much endangered, not only by opening a way of employment in places of great trust, and advantage to men of weak parts, but also by giving occasion to bribery, extortion, partiality, it seldom happening that places ill-gotten are well used.

49. Commissions have been granted for examining the excess of fees, and when great exactions have been discovered, compositions have been made with delinquents, not only for the time past, but likewise for immunity and security in offending for the time to come, which under colour of remedy hath but confirmed and increased the grievance to the subject.

50. The usual course of pricking Sheriffs not observed, but many times Sheriffs made in an extraordinary way, sometimes as a punishment and charge unto them; sometimes such were pricked out as would be instruments to execute whatsoever they would have to be done.

51. The Bishops and the rest of the Clergy did triumph in the suspensions, excommunications, deprivations, and degradations of divers painful, learned and pious ministers, in the vexation and grievous oppression of great numbers of His Majesty's good subjects.

52. The High Commission grew to such excess of sharpness and severity as was not much less than the Romish Inquisition, and yet in many cases by the Archbishop's power was made much more heavy, being assisted and strengthened by authority of the Council Table.

53. The Bishops and their Courts were as eager in the country; although their jurisdiction could not reach so high in rigour and extremity of punishment, yet were they no less grievous in respect of the generality and multiplicity of vexations, which lighting upon the meaner sort of tradesmen and artificers did impoverish many thousands.

54. And so afflict and trouble others, that great numbers to avoid their miseries departed out of the kingdom, some into New England and other parts of America, others into Holland,

55. Where they have transported their manufactures of cloth, which is not only a loss by diminishing the present stock of the kingdom, but a great mischief by impairing and endangering the loss of that particular trade of clothing, which hath been a plentiful fountain of wealth and honour to this nation.

56. Those were fittest for ecclesiastical preferment, and soonest obtained it, who were most officious in promoting superstition, most virulent in railing against godliness and honesty.

57. The most public and solemn sermons before His Majesty were either to advance prerogative above law, and decry the property of the subject, or full of such kind of invectives.

58. Whereby they might make those odious who sought to maintain the religion, laws and liberties of the kingdom, and such men were sure to be weeded out of the commission of the peace, and out of all other employments of power in the government of the country.

59. Many noble personages were councillors in name, but the power and authority remained in a few of such as were most addicted to this party, whose resolutions and determinations were brought to the table for countenance and execution, and not for debate and deliberation, and no man could offer to oppose them without disgrace and hazard to himself.

60. Nay, all those that did not wholly concur and actively contribute to the furtherance of their designs, though otherwise persons of never so great honour and abilities, were so far from being employed in any place of trust and power, that they were neglected, discountenanced, and upon all occasions injured and oppressed.

61. This faction was grown to that height and entireness of power, that now they began to think of finishing their work, which consisted of these three parts.

62. I. The government must be set free from all restraint of laws concerning our persons and estates.

63. II. There must be a conjunction between Papists and Protestants in doctrine, discipline and ceremonies; only it must not yet be called Popery.

64. III. The Puritans, under which name they include all those that desire to preserve the laws and liberties of the kingdom, and to maintain religion in the power of it, must be either rooted out of the kingdom with force, or driven out with fear.

65. For the effecting of this it was thought necessary to reduce Scotland to such Popish superstitions and innovations as might make them apt to join with England in that great change which was intended.

66. Whereupon new canons and a new liturgy were pressed upon them, and when they refused to admit of them, an army was raised to force them to it, towards which the Clergy and the Papists were very forward in their contribution.

67. The Scots likewise raised an army for their defence.

68. And when both armies were come together, and ready for a bloody encounter, His Majesty's own gracious disposition, and the counsel of the English nobility and dutiful submission of the Scots, did so far prevail against the evil counsel of others, that a pacification was made, and His Majesty returned with peace and much honour to London.

69. The unexpected reconciliation was most acceptable to all the kingdom, except to the malignant party; whereof the Archbishop and the Earl of Strafford being heads, they and their faction began to inveigh against the peace, and to aggravate the proceedings of the states, which so incensed His Majesty, that he forthwith prepared again for war.

70. And such was their confidence, that having corrupted and distempered the whole frame and government of the kingdom, they did now hope to corrupt that which was the only means to restore all to a right frame and temper again.

71. To which end they persuaded His Majesty to call a Parliament, not to seek counsel and advice of them, but to draw countenance and supply from them, and to engage the whole kingdom in their quarrel.

72. And in the meantime continued all their unjust levies of money, resolving either to make the Parliament pliant

to their will, and to establish mischief by a law, or else to break it, and with more colour to go on by violence to take what they could not obtain by consent. The ground alleged for the justification of this war was this,

73. That the undutiful demands of the Parliaments in Scotland was a sufficient reason for His Majesty to take arms against them, without hearing the reason of those demands, and thereupon a new army was prepared against them, their ships were seized in all ports both of England and Ireland, and at sea, their petitions rejected, their commissioners refused audience.

74. This whole kingdom most miserably distempered with levies of men and money, and imprisonments of those who denied to submit to those levies.

75. The Earl of Strafford passed into Ireland, caused the Parliament there to declare against the Scots, to give four subsidies towards that war, and to engage themselves, their lives and fortunes, for the prosecution of it, and gave directions for an army of eight thousand foot and one thousand horse to be levied there, which were for the most part Papists.

76. The Parliament met upon the 13th of April, 1640. The Earl of Strafford and Archbishop of Canterbury, with their party, so prevailed with His Majesty, that the House of Commons was pressed to yield a supply for maintenance of the war with Scotland, before they had provided any relief for the great and pressing grievances of the people, which being against the fundamental privilege and proceeding of Parliament, was yet in humble respect to His Majesty, so far admitted as that they agreed to take the matter of supply into consideration, and two several days it was debated.

77. Twelve subsidies were demanded for the release of ship-money alone, a third day was appointed for conclusion, when the heads of that party began to fear the people might close with the King, in satisfying his desires of money; but that withal they were like to blast their malicious designs against Scotland, finding them very much indisposed to give any countenance to that war.

78. Thereupon they wickedly advised the King to break off the Parliament and to return to the ways of confusion, in

which their own evil intentions were most likely to prosper
and succeed.

79. After the Parliament ended the 5th of May, 1640,
this party grew so bold as to counsel the King to supply
himself out of his subjects' estates by his own power, at his
own will, without their consent.

80. The very next day some members of both Houses had
their studies and cabinets, yea, their pockets searched: another
of them not long after was committed close prisoner for not
delivering some petitions which he received by authority of
that House.

81. And if harsher courses were intended (as was reported) it is very probable that the sickness of the Earl of
Strafford, and the tumultuous rising in Southwark and about
Lambeth were the causes that such violent intentions were
not brought into execution.

82. A false and scandalous Declaration against the House
of Commons was published in His Majesty's name, which yet
wrought little effect with the people, but only to manifest
the impudence of those who were authors of it.

83. A forced loan of money was attempted in the City of
London.

84. The Lord Mayor and Aldermen in their several wards,
enjoined to bring in a list of the names of such persons as
they judged fit to lend, and of the sums they should lend. And
such Aldermen as refused to do so were committed to prison.

85. The Archbishop and the other Bishops and Clergy
continued the Convocation, and by a new commission turned
it into a provincial Synod, in which, by an unheard-of presumption, they made canons that contain in them many
matters contrary to the King's prerogative, to the fundamental
laws and statutes of the realm, to the right of Parliaments, to
the property and liberty of the subject, and matters tending
to sedition and of dangerous consequence, thereby establishing
their own usurpations, justifying their altar-worship, and those
other superstitious innovations which they formerly introduced
without warrant of law.

86. They imposed a new oath upon divers of His Majesty's
subjects, both ecclesiastical and lay, for maintenance of their

own tyranny, and laid a great tax on the Clergy, for supply of His Majesty, and generally they showed themselves very affectionate to the war with Scotland, which was by some of them styled *Bellum Episcopale*, and a prayer composed and enjoined to be read in all churches, calling the Scots rebels, to put the two nations in blood and make them irreconcileable.

87. All those pretended canons and constitutions were armed with the several censures of suspension, excommunication, deprivation, by which they would have thrust out all the good ministers, and most of the well-affected people of the kingdom, and left an easy passage to their own design of reconciliation with Rome.

88. The Popish party enjoyed such exemptions from penal laws as amounted to a toleration, besides many other encouragements and Court favours.

89. They had a Secretary of State, Sir Francis Windebanck, a powerful agent for speeding all their desires.

90. A Pope's Nuncio residing here, to act and govern them according to such influences as he received from Rome, and to intercede for them with the most powerful concurrence of the foreign Princes of that religion.

91. By his authority the Papists of all sorts, nobility, gentry, and clergy, were convocated after the manner of a Parliament.

92. New jurisdictions were erected of Romish Archbishops, taxes levied, another state moulded within this state, independent in government, contrary in interest and affection, secretly corrupting the ignorant or negligent professors of our religion, and closely uniting and combining themselves against such as were found in this posture, waiting for an opportunity by force to destroy those whom they could not hope to seduce.

93. For the effecting whereof they were strengthened with arms and munitions, encouraged by superstitious prayers, enjoined by the Nuncio to be weekly made for the prosperity of some great design.

94. And such power had they at Court, that secretly a commission was issued out, or intended to be issued to some great men of that profession, for the levying of soldiers, and

to command and employ them according to private instructions, which we doubt were framed for the advantage of those who were the contrivers of them.

95. His Majesty's treasure was consumed, his revenue anticipated.

96. His servants and officers compelled to lend great sums of money.

97. Multitudes were called to the Council Table, who were tired with long attendances there for refusing illegal payments.

98. The prisons were filled with their commitments; many of the Sheriffs summoned into the Star Chamber, and some imprisoned for not being quick enough in levying the ship-money; the people languished under grief and fear, no visible hope being left but in desperation.

99. The nobility began to weary of their silence and patience, and sensible of the duty and trust which belongs to them: and thereupon some of the most ancient of them did petition His Majesty at such a time, when evil counsels were so strong, that they had occasion to expect more hazard to themselves, than redress of those public evils for which they interceded.

100. Whilst the kingdom was in this agitation and dis-temper, the Scots, restrained in their trades, impoverished by the loss of many of their ships, bereaved of all possibility of satisfying His Majesty by any naked supplication, entered with a powerful army into the kingdom, and without any hostile act or spoil in the country they passed, more than forcing a passage over the Tyne at Newburn, near Newcastle, possessed themselves of Newcastle, and had a fair opportunity to press on further upon the King's army.

101. But duty and reverence to His Majesty, and brotherly love to the English nation, made them stay there, whereby the King had leisure to entertain better counsels.

102. Wherein God so blessed and directed him that he summoned the Great Council of Peers to meet at York upon the 24th of September, and there declared a Parliament to begin the 3rd of November then following.

103. The Scots, the first day of the Great Council, pre-sented an humble Petition to His Majesty, whereupon the Treaty was appointed at Ripon.

104. A present cessation of arms agreed upon, and the full conclusion of all differences referred to the wisdom and care of the Parliament.

105. As our first meeting, all oppositions seemed to vanish, the mischiefs were so evident which those evil counsellors produced, that no man durst stand up to defend them: yet the work itself afforded difficulty enough.

106. The multiplied evils and corruption of fifteen years, strengthened by custom and authority, and the concurrent interest of many powerful delinquents, were now to be brought to judgment and reformation.

107. The King's household was to be provided for:—they had brought him to that want, that he could not supply his ordinary and necessary expenses without the assistance of his people.

108. Two armies were to be paid, which amounted very near to eighty thousand pounds a month.

109. The people were to be tenderly charged, having been formerly exhausted with many burdensome projects.

110. The difficulties seemed to be insuperable, which by the Divine Providence we have overcome. The contrarieties incompatible, which yet in a great measure we have reconciled.

111. Six subsidies have been granted and a Bill of poll-money, which if it be duly levied, may equal six subsidies more, in all £600,000.

112. Besides we have contracted a debt to the Scots of £220,000, yet God hath so blessed the endeavours of this Parliament, that the kingdom is a great gainer by all these charges.

113. The ship-money is abolished, which cost the kingdom about £200,000 a year.

114. The coat and conduct-money, and other military charges are taken away, which in many countries amounted to little less than the ship-money.

115. The monopolies are all suppressed, whereof some few did prejudice the subject, above £1,000,000 yearly.

116. The soap £100,000.

117. The wine £300,000.

118. The leather must needs exceed both, and salt could be no less than that.

119. Besides the inferior monopolies, which, if they could be exactly computed, would make up a great sum.

120. That which is more beneficial than all this is, that the root of these evils is taken away, which was the arbitrary power pretended to be in His Majesty of taxing the subject, or charging their estates without consent in Parliament, which is now declared to be against law by the judgment of both Houses, and likewise by an Act of Parliament.

121. Another step of great advantage is this, the living grievances, the evil counsellors and actors of these mischiefs have been so quelled.

122. By the justice done upon the Earl of Strafford, the flight of the Lord Finch and Secretary Windebanck,

123. The accusation and imprisonment of the Archbishop of Canterbury, of Judge Berkeley; and

124. The impeachment of divers other Bishops and Judges, that it is like not only to be an ease to the present times, but a preservation to the future.

125. The discontinuance of Parliaments is prevented by the Bill for a triennial Parliament, and the abrupt dissolution of this Parliament by another Bill, by which it is provided it shall not be dissolved or adjourned without the consent of both Houses.

126. Which two laws well considered may be thought more advantageous than all the former, because they secure a full operation of the present remedy, and afford a perpetual spring of remedies for the future.

127. The Star Chamber.

128. The High Commission.

129. The Courts of the President and Council in the North were so many forges of misery, oppression and violence, and are all taken away, whereby men are more secured in their persons, liberties and estates, than they could be by any law or example for the regulation of those Courts or terror of the Judges.

130. The immoderate power of the Council Table, and the excessive abuse of that power is so ordered and restrained, that we may well hope that no such things as were frequently done by them, to the prejudice of the public liberty,

will appear in future times but only in stories, to give us and our posterity more occasion to praise God for His Majesty's goodness, and the faithful endeavours of this Parliament.

131. The canons and power of canon-making are blasted by the votes of both Houses.

132. The exorbitant power of Bishops and their courts are much abated, by some provisions in the Bill against the High Commission Court, the authors of the many innovations in doctrine and ceremonies.

133. The ministers that have been scandalous in their lives, have been so terrified in just complaints and accusations, that we may well hope they will be more modest for the time to come; either inwardly convicted by the sight of their own folly, or outwardly restrained by the fear of punishment.

134. The forests are by a good law reduced to their right bounds.

135. The encroachments and oppressions of the Stannary Courts, the extortions of the clerk of the market.

136. And the compulsion of the subject to receive the Order of Knighthood against his will, paying of fines for not receiving it, and the vexatious proceedings thereupon for levying of those fines, are by other beneficial laws reformed and prevented.

137. Many excellent laws and provisions are in preparation for removing the inordinate power, vexation and usurpation of Bishops, for reforming the pride and idleness of many of the clergy, for easing the people of unnecessary ceremonies in religion, for censuring and removing unworthy and unprofitable ministers, and for maintaining godly and diligent preachers through the kingdom.

138. Other things of main importance for the good of this kingdom are in proposition, though little could hitherto be done in regard of the many other more pressing businesses, which yet before the end of this Session we hope may receive some progress and perfection.

139. The establishing and ordering the King's revenue, that so the abuse of officers and superfluity of expenses may be cut off, and the necessary disbursements for His Majesty's honour, the defence and government of the kingdom, may be more certainly provided for.

140. The regulating of courts of justice, and abridging both the delays and charges of law-suits.

141. The settling of some good courses for preventing the exportation of gold and silver, and the inequality of exchanges between us and other nations, for the advancing of native commodities, increase of our manufactures, and well balancing of trade, whereby the stock of the kingdom may be increased, or at least kept from impairing, as through neglect hereof it hath done for many years last past.

142. Improving the herring-fishing upon our coasts, which will be of mighty use in the employment of the poor, and a plentiful nursery of mariners for enabling the kingdom in any great action.

143. The oppositions, obstructions and the difficulties wherewith we have been encountered, and which still lie in our way with some strength and much obstinacy, are these; the malignant party whom we have formerly described to be the actors and promotors of all our misery, they have taken heart again.

144. They have been able to prefer some of their own factors and agents to degrees of honour, to places of trust and employment, even during the Parliament.

145. They have endeavoured to work in His Majesty ill impressions and opinions of our proceedings, as if we had altogether done our own work, and not his; and had obtained from him many things very prejudicial to the Crown, both in respect of prerogative and profit.

146. To wipe out this slander we think good only to say thus much: that all that we have done is for His Majesty, his greatness, honour and support, when we yield to give £25,000 a month for the relief of the Northern Counties; this was given to the King, for he was bound to protect his subjects.

147. They were His Majesty's evil counsellors, and their ill instruments that were actors in those grievances which brought in the Scots.

148. And if His Majesty please to force those who were the authors of this war to make satisfaction, as he might justly and easily do, it seems very reasonable that the people might well be excused from taking upon them this burden, being altogether innocent and free from being any cause of it.

149. When we undertook the charge of the army, which cost above £50,000 a month, was not this given to the King? Was it not His Majesty's army? Were not all the commanders under contract with His Majesty, at higher rates and greater wages than ordinary?

150. And have we not taken upon us to discharge all the brotherly assistance of £300,000, which we gave the Scots? Was it not toward repair of those damages and losses which they received from the King's ships and from his ministers?

151. These three particulars amount to above £1,100,000.

152. Besides, His Majesty hath received by impositions upon merchandise at least £400,000.

153. So that His Majesty hath had out of the subjects' purse since the Parliament began, £1,500,000, and yet these men can be so impudent as to tell His Majesty that we have done nothing for him.

154. As to the second branch of this slander, we acknowledge with much thankfulness that His Majesty hath passed more good Bills to the advantage of the subjects than have been in many ages.

155. But withal we cannot forget that these venomous councils did manifest themselves in some endeavours to hinder these good acts.

156. And for both Houses of Parliament we may with truth and modesty say thus much: that we have ever been careful not to desire anything that should weaken the Crown either in just profit or useful power.

157. The triennial Parliament for the matter of it, doth not extend to so much as by law we ought to have required (there being two statutes still in force for a Parliament to be once a year), and for the manner of it, it is in the King's power that it shall never take effect, if he by a timely summons shall prevent any other way of assembling.

158. In the Bill for continuance of this present Parliament, there seems to be some restraint of the royal power in dissolving of Parliaments, not to take it out of the Crown, but to suspend the execution of it for this time and occasion only: which was so necessary for the King's own security and the public peace, that without it we could not have undertaken

any of these great charges, but must have left both the armies to disorder and confusion, and the whole kingdom to blood and rapine.

159. The Star Chamber was much more fruitful in oppression than in profit, the great fines being for the most part given away, and the rest stalled [1] at long times.

160. The fines of the High Commission were in themselves unjust, and seldom or never came into the King's purse. These four Bills are particularly and more specially instanced.

161. In the rest there will not be found so much as a shadow of prejudice to the Crown.

162. They have sought to diminish our reputation with the people, and to bring them out of love with Parliaments.

163. The aspersions which they have attempted this way have been such as these:

164. That we have spent much time and done little, especially in those grievances which concern religion.

165. That the Parliament is a burden to the kingdom by the abundance of protections which hinder justice and trade; and by many subsidies granted much more heavy than any formerly endured.

166. To which there is a ready answer; if the time spent in this Parliament be considered in relation backward to the long growth and deep root of those grievances, which we have removed, to the powerful supports of those delinquents, which we have pursued, to the great necessities and other charges of the commonwealth for which we have provided.

167. Or if it be considered in relation forward to many advantages, which not only the present but future ages are like to reap by the good laws and other proceedings in this Parliament, we doubt not but it will be thought by all indifferent judgments, that our time hath been much better employed than in a far greater proportion of time in many former Parliaments put together; and the charges which have been laid upon the subject, and the other inconveniences which they have borne, will seem very light in respect of the benefit they have and may receive.

168. And for the matter of protections, the Parliament is

---

[1] I.e. ordered to be paid by instalments.

so sensible of it that therein they intended to give them whatsoever ease may stand with honour and justice, and are in a way of passing a Bill to give them satisfaction.

169. They have sought by many subtle practices to cause jealousies and divisions betwixt us and our brethren of Scotland, by slandering their proceedings and intentions towards us, and by secret endeavours to instigate and incense them and us one against another.

170. They have had such a party of Bishops and Popish lords in the House of Peers, as hath caused much opposition and delay in the prosecution of delinquents, hindered the proceedings of divers good Bills passed in the Commons' House, concerning the reformation of sundry great abuses and corruptions both in Church and State.

171. They have laboured to seduce and corrupt some of the Commons' House to draw them into conspiracies and combinations against the liberty of the Parliament.

172. And by their instruments and agents they have attempted to disaffect and discontent His Majesty's army, and to engage it for the maintenance of their wicked and traitorous designs; the keeping up of Bishops in votes and functions, and by force to compel the Parliament to order, limit and dispose their proceedings in such manner as might best concur with the intentions of this dangerous and potent faction.

173. And when one mischievous design and attempt of theirs to bring on the army against the Parliament and the City of London hath been discovered and prevented;

174. They presently undertook another of the same damnable nature, with this addition to it, to endeavour to make the Scottish army neutral, whilst the English army, which they had laboured to corrupt and envenom against us by their false and slanderous suggestions, should execute their malice to the subversion of our religion and the dissolution of our government.

175. Thus they have been continually practising to disturb the peace, and plotting the destruction even of all the King's dominions; and have employed their emissaries and agents in them, all for the promoting their devilish designs, which the vigilancy of those who were well affected hath still dis-

covered and defeated before they were ripe for execution in England and Scotland.

176. Only in Ireland, which was farther off, they have had time and opportunity to mould and prepare their work, and had brought it to that perfection that they had possessed themselves of that whole kingdom, totally subverted the government of it, routed out religion, and destroyed all the Protestants whom the conscience of their duty to God, their King and country, would not have permitted to join with them, if by God's wonderful providence their main enterprise upon the city and castle of Dublin had not been detected and prevented upon the very eve before it should have been executed.

177. Notwithstanding they have in other parts of that kingdom broken out into open rebellion, surprising towns and castles, committed murders, rapes and other villainies, and shaken off all bonds of obedience to His Majesty and the laws of the realm.

178. And in general have kindled such a fire, as nothing but God's infinite blessing upon the wisdom and endeavours of this State will be able to quench it.

179. And certainly had not God in His great mercy unto this land discovered and confounded their former designs, we had been the prologue to this tragedy in Ireland, and had by this been made the lamentable spectacle of misery and confusion.

180. And now what hope have we but in God, when as the only means of our subsistence and power of reformation is under Him in the Parliament ?

181. But what can we the Commons, without the conjunction of the House of Lords, and what conjunction can we expect there, when the Bishops and recusant lords are so numerous and prevalent that they are able to cross and interrupt our best endeavours for reformation, and by that means give advantage to this malignant party to traduce our proceedings ?

182. They infuse into the people that we mean to abolish all Church government, and leave every man to his own fancy for the service and worship of God, absolving him of that obedience which he owes under God unto His Majesty, whom we know to be entrusted with the ecclesiastical law

as well as with the temporal, to regulate all the members of the Church of England, by such rules of order and discipline as are established by Parliament, which is his great council, in all affairs both in Church and State.

183. We confess our intention is, and our endeavours have been, to reduce within bounds that exorbitant power which the prelates have assumed unto themselves, so contrary both to the Word of God and to the laws of the land, to which end we passed the Bill for the removing them from their temporal power and employments, that so the better they might with meekness apply themselves to the discharge of their functions, which Bill themselves opposed, and were the principal instruments of crossing it.

184. And we do here declare that it is far from our purpose or desire to let loose the golden reins of discipline and government in the Church, to leave private persons or particular congregations to take up what form of Divine Service they please, for we hold it requisite that there should be throughout the whole realm a conformity to that order which the laws enjoin according to the Word of God. And we desire to unburden the consciences of men of needless and superstitious ceremonies, suppress innovations, and take away the monuments of idolatry.

185. And the better to effect the intended reformation, we desire there may be a general synod of the most grave, pious, learned and judicious divines of this island; assisted with some from foreign parts, professing the same religion with us, who may consider of all things necessary for the peace and good government of the Church, and represent the results of their consultations unto the Parliament, to be there allowed of and confirmed, and receive the stamp of authority, thereby to find passage and obedience throughout the kingdom.

186. They have maliciously charged us that we intend to destroy and discourage learning, whereas it is our chiefest care and desire to advance it, and to provide a competent maintenance for conscionable and preaching ministers throughout the kingdom, which will be a great encouragement to scholars, and a certain means whereby the want, meanness and ignorance, to which a great part of the clergy is now subject, will be prevented.

187. And we intended likewise to reform and purge the fountains of learning, the two Universities, that the streams flowing from thence may be clear and pure, and an honour and comfort to the whole land.

188. They have strained to blast our proceedings in Parliament, by wresting the interpretations of our orders from their genuine intention.

189. They tell the people that our meddling with the power of episcopacy hath caused sectaries and conventicles, when idolatrous and Popish ceremonies, introduced into the Church by the command of the Bishops, have not only debarred the people from thence, but expelled them from the kingdom.

190. Thus with Elijah[1], we are called by this malignant party the troublers of the State, and still, while we endeavour to reform their abuses, they make us the authors of those mischiefs we study to prevent.

191. For the perfecting of the work begun, and removing all future impediments, we conceive these courses will be very effectual, seeing the religion of the Papists hath such principles as do certainly tend to the destruction and extirpation of all Protestants, when they shall have opportunity to effect it.

192. It is necessary in the first place to keep them in such condition as that they may not be able to do us any hurt, and for avoiding of such connivance and favour as hath heretofore been shown unto them.

193. That His Majesty be pleased to grant a standing Commission to some choice men named in Parliament, who may take notice of their increase, their counsels and proceedings, and use all due means by execution of the laws to prevent all mischievous designs against the peace and safety of this kingdom.

194. Thus some good course be taken to discover the counterfeit and false conformity of Papists to the Church, by colour whereof persons very much disaffected to the true religion have been admitted into place of greatest authority and trust in the kingdom.

195. For the better preservation of the laws and liberties

---

[1] *Eliab* in Rushworth.

of the kingdom, that all illegal grievances and exactions be presented and punished at the sessions and assizes.

196. And that Judges and Justices be very careful to give this in charge to the grand jury, and both the Sheriff and Justices to be sworn to the due execution of the Petition of Right and other laws.

197. That His Majesty be humbly petitioned by both Houses to employ such councillors, ambassadors and other ministers, in managing his business at home and abroad as the Parliament may have cause to confide in, without which we cannot give His Majesty such supplies for support of his own estate, nor such assistance to the Protestant party beyond the sea, as is desired.

198. It may often fall out that the Commons may have just cause to take exceptions at some men for being councillors, and yet not charge those men with crimes, for there be grounds of diffidence which lie not in proof.

199. There are others, which though they may be proved, yet are not legally criminal.

200. To be a known favourer of Papists, or to have been very forward in defending or countenancing some great offenders questioned in Parliament ; or to speak contemptuously of either Houses of Parliament or Parliamentary proceedings.

201. Or such as are factors or agents for any foreign prince of another religion ; such are justly suspected to get councillors' places, or any other of trust concerning public employment for money ; for all these and divers others we may have great reason to be earnest with His Majesty, not to put his great affairs into such hands, though we may be unwilling to proceed against them in any legal way of charge or impeachment.

202. That all Councillors of State may be sworn to observe those laws which concern the subject in his liberty, that they may likewise take an oath not to receive or give reward or pension from any foreign prince, but such as they shall within some reasonable time discover to the Lords of His Majesty's Council.

203. And although they should wickedly forswear themselves, yet it may herein do good to make them known to

be false and perjured to those who employ them, and thereby bring them into as little credit with them as with us.

204. That His Majesty may have cause to be in love with good counsel and good men, by showing him in an humble and dutiful manner how full of advantage it would be to himself, to see his own estate settled in a plentiful condition to support his honour; to see his people united in ways of duty to him, and endeavours of the public good; to see happiness, wealth, peace and safety derived to his own kingdom, and procured to his allies by the influence of his own power and government.

44. THE KING'S PROCLAMATION ON RELIGION.

[December 10, 1641. Rushworth, iv. 456. See *Hist. of Engl.* x. 98.]

By the King.

A proclamation for obedience to the laws, ordained for the establishing of the true religion in this kingdom of England.

His Majesty considering it is a duty most beseeming, and that most obligeth sovereign authority in a Christian King to be careful (above all other things) of preserving and advancing the honour and service of Almighty God, and the peace and tranquillity of the Church, to which end His Majesty with his Parliament hath it under consideration, how all just scruples may be removed, and being in the meantime sensible that the present division, separation and disorder about the worship and service of God, as it is established by the laws and statutes of this kingdom in the Church of England, tendeth to great distraction and confusion, and may endanger the subversion of the very essence and substance of true religion; hath resolved for the preservation of unity and peace (which is most necessary at this time for the Church of England), require obedience to the laws and statutes ordained for the establishing of the true religion in this kingdom, whereby the honour of God may be advanced, to the great comfort and happiness both of His Majesty and his good subjects.

His Majesty doth therefore charge and command, that Divine Service be performed in this his kingdom of England

and dominion of Wales, as is appointed by the laws and statutes established in this realm; and that obedience be given by all his subjects, ecclesiastical and temporal, to the said laws and statutes concerning the same. And that all Judges, officers and ministers, ecclesiastical and temporal, according to justice and their respective duties, do put the said Acts of Parliament in due execution against all wilful contemners and disturbers of Divine Service contrary to the said laws and statutes.

His Majesty doth further command that no parsons, vicars or curates in their several parishes shall presume to introduce any rite or ceremonies other than those which are established by the laws and statutes of the land.

Dated the tenth day of December, in the
seventeenth year of His Majesty's reign.

45. The King's Answer to the Petition accompanying the Grand Remonstrance.

[December 23, 1641. Rushworth, iv. 452. See *Hist. of Engl.* x. 108.]

We having received from you, soon after our return out of Scotland, a long petition consisting of many desires of great moment, together with a declaration of a very unusual nature annexed thereunto, we had taken some time to consider of it, as befitted us in a matter of that consequence, being confident that your own reason and regard to us, as well as our express intimation by our comptroller[1], to that purpose, would have restrained you from the publishing of it till such time as you should have received our answer to it; but, much against our expectation, finding the contrary, that the said declaration is already abroad in print, by directions from your House as appears by the printed copy, we must let you know that we are very sensible of the disrespect. Notwithstanding, it is our intention that no failing on your part shall make us fail in ours of giving all due satisfaction to the desires of our people in a parliamentary way; and therefore we send you this answer to your petition, reserving ourself in point of the declaration

[1] Sir Thomas Jermyn. See Journals of the House of Commons, ii. 330.

which we think unparliamentary, and shall take a course to do that which we shall think fit in prudence and honour.

To the petition, we say that although there are divers things in the preamble of it which we are so far from admitting that we profess we cannot at all understand them, as of 'a wicked and malignant party prevalent in the government'; of 'some of that party admitted to our Privy Council and to other employments of trust, and nearest to us and our children'; of 'endeavours to sow among the people false scandals and imputations, to blemish and disgrace the proceedings of the Parliament'; all, or any of them, did we know of, we should be as ready to remedy and punish as you to complain of, so that the prayers of your petition are grounded upon such premises as we must in no wise admit; yet, notwithstanding, we are pleased to give this answer to you.

To the first, concerning religion, consisting of several branches, we say that, for preserving the peace and safety of this kingdom from the design of the Popish party, we have, and will still, concur with all the just desires of our people in a parliamentary way: that, for the depriving of the Bishops of their votes in Parliament, we would have you consider that their right is grounded upon the fundamental law of the kingdom and constitution of Parliament. This we would have you consider; but since you desire our concurrence herein in a parliamentary way, we will give no further answer at this time.

As for the abridging of the inordinate power of the clergy, we conceive that the taking away of the High Commission Court hath well moderated that; but if there continue any usurpations or excesses in their jurisdictions, we therein neither have nor will protect them.

Unto that clause which concerneth corruptions (as you style them) in religion, in Church government, and in discipline, and the removing of such unnecessary ceremonies as weak consciences might check at: that for any illegal innovations which may have crept in, we shall willingly concur in the removal of them: that, if our Parliament shall advise us to call a national synod, which may duly examine such ceremonies as give just cause of offence to any, we shall take it into consideration, and apply ourself to give due satisfaction therein; but we are very sorry to hear, in such general terms, corruption in religion objected, since we are persuaded in our consciences that no Church can be found upon the earth that professeth the true religion with more purity of doctrine than the Church of England doth, nor where the government and discipline are jointly more beautified and free from superstition, than as they are here established by law, which, by the grace of God, we will with constancy maintain (while we live) in their purity and glory, not only against all invasions of Popery, but also from the irreverence of those many schismatics and separatists, wherewith of late this kingdom and this city abounds, to the great dishonour and hazard both of Church and State, for the suppression of whom we require your timely aid and active assistance.

To the second prayer of the petition, concerning the removal and choice of councillors, we know not any of our Council to whom the character set forth in the petition can belong: that by those whom we had exposed to trial, we have already given you sufficient testimony that there is no man so near unto us in place or affection, whom we will not leave to the justice of the law, if you shall bring a particular charge and sufficient proofs against him; and of this we do again assure you, but in the meantime we wish you to forbear such general aspersions as may reflect upon all our Council, since you name none in particular.

That for the choice of our councillors and ministers of state, it were to debar us that natural liberty all freemen have; and as it is the undoubted right of the Crown of England to call such persons to our secret counsels, to public employment and our particular service as we shall think fit, so we are, and ever shall be, very careful to make election of such persons in those places of trust as shall have given good testimonies of their abilities and integrity, and against whom there can be no just cause of exception whereon reasonably to ground a diffidence; and to choices of this nature, we assure you that the mediation of the nearest unto us hath always concurred.

To the third prayer of your petition concerning Ireland,

we understand your desire of not alienating the forfeited lands thereof, to proceed from much care and love, and likewise that it may be a resolution very fit for us to take; but whether it be seasonable to declare resolutions of that nature before the events of a war be seen, that we much doubt of. Howsoever, we cannot but thank you for this care, and your cheerful engagement for the suppression of that rebellion; upon the speedy effecting whereof, the glory of God in the Protestant profession, the safety of the British there, our honour, and that of the nation, so much depends; all the interests of this kingdom being so involved in that business, we cannot but quicken your affections therein, and shall desire you to frame your counsels, to give such expedition to the work as the nature thereof and the pressures in point of time require; and whereof you are put in mind by the daily insolence and increase of those rebels.

For conclusion, your promise to apply yourselves to such courses as may support our royal estate with honour and plenty at home, and with power and reputation abroad, is that which we have ever promised ourself, both from your loyalties and affections, and also for what we have already done, and shall daily go adding unto, for the comfort and happiness of our people.

46. The Impeachment of one member of the House of Lords, and of five members of the House of Commons.

[January 3, 1642.   Journals of the House of Lords, iv. 501.   See *Hist. of Engl.* x. 130.]

Articles of high treason and other high misdemeanours against the Lord Kimbolton, Mr. Denzil Holles, Sir Arthur Haslerigg, Mr. John Pym, Mr. John Hampden and Mr. William Strode.

1. That they have traitorously endeavoured to subvert the fundamental laws and government of the kingdom of England, to deprive the King of his regal power, and to place in subjects an arbitrary and tyrannical power over the lives, liberties and estates of His Majesty's liege people.

2. That they have traitorously endeavoured, by many foul aspersions upon His Majesty and his government, to alienate the affections of his people, and to make His Majesty odious unto them.

3. That they have endeavoured to draw His Majesty's late army to disobedience to His Majesty's commands, and to side with them in their traitorous designs.

4. That they have traitorously invited and encouraged a foreign power to invade His Majesty's kingdom of England.

5. That they have traitorously endeavoured to subvert the rights and the very being of Parliaments.

6. That for the completing of their traitorous designs they have endeavoured (as far as in them lay) by force and terror to compel the Parliament to join with them in their traitorous designs, and to that end have actually raised and countenanced tumults against the King and Parliament.

7. And that they have traitorously conspired to levy, and actually have levied, war against the King.

47. A Declaration of the House of Commons touching a late breach of their Privileges.

[January 17, 164½. Rushworth, iv. 484. See Journals of the House of Commons, ii. 373, 383.]

Whereas the chambers, studies and trunks of Mr. Denzil Holles, Sir Arthur Haslerigg, Mr John Pym, Mr. John Hampden and Mr. William Strode, Esquires, members of the House of Commons, upon Monday the third of this instant January, by colour of His Majesty's warrant, have been sealed up by Sir William Killigrew and Sir William Fleming and others, which is not only against the privilege of Parliament, but the common liberty of every subject; which said members afterwards the same day were under the like colour, by Serjeant Francis, one of His Majesty's serjeants-at-arms, contrary to all former precedents, demanded of the Speaker, sitting in the House of Commons, to be delivered unto him, that he might arrest them of high treason; and whereas afterwards, the next day His Majesty in his royal person came to the said House, attended with a great multitude of men, armed in warlike manner with halberds, swords and pistols. who came up to the very door of the House, and placed themselves there, and in other places and passages near to the said House, to the great terror and disturbance of the members then sitting, and according to their duty, in a peaceable and orderly manner, treating of the great affairs of England and Ireland ; and His Majesty, having placed himself in the Speaker's chair, demanded of them the persons of the said members to be delivered unto him, which is a high breach of the rights and privileges of Parliament, and inconsistent with the liberties and freedom thereof; and whereas afterwards His Majesty did issue forth several warrants to divers officers, under his own hand, for the apprehension of the persons of the said members, which by law he cannot do ; there being not all this time any legal charge or accusation, or due process of law issued against them, nor any pretence of charge made known to that House, all which are against the fundamental liberties of the subject and the rights of Parliament; whereupon we are necessitated according to our duty to declare, and we do hereby declare, that any person that shall arrest Mr. Holles, Sir Arthur Haslerigg, Mr. Pym, Mr. Hampden and Mr. Strode, or any of them, or any other members of Parliament by pretence or colour of any warrant issuing out from the King only, is guilty of the breach of liberties of the subject and of the privileges of Parliament, and a public enemy to the commonwealth ; and that the arresting of the said members or any of them, or of any other member of Parliament, by any warrant whatsoever without a legal proceeding against them, and without consent of that House, whereof such person is a member, is against the liberty of the subject, and a breach of privilege of Parliament ; and the person which shall arrest any of these persons, or any other members of the Parliament, is declared a public enemy of the commonwealth. Notwithstanding all which we think fit farther to declare, that we are so far from any endeavour to protect any of our members that shall be in due manner prosecuted according to the laws of the kingdom and the rights and privileges of Parliament for treason or any other misdemeanour, that none shall be more ready and willing than we ourselves to bring them to a speedy and due trial; being sensible that it equally imports us, as well to see justice done against them that are criminal as to defend the just rights and liberties of the subjects and Parliament of England.

And whereas, upon several examinations taken the 7th day of this instant January, before the committee appointed by the House of Commons to sit in London, it did fully appear that many soldiers, Papists and others, to the number of about five hundred, came with His Majesty on Tuesday last to the said House of Commons, armed with swords, pistols and other weapons, and divers of them pressed to the door of the said House, thrust away the door-keepers, and placed themselves between the said door and the ordinary attendants of His Majesty, holding up their swords, and some holding up their pistols ready cocked near the said door and saying, 'I am a good marksman; I can hit right, I warrant you,' and they not suffering the said door according to the custom of Parliament to be shut, but said they would have the door open, and if any opposition were against them, they made no question but they should make their party good, and that they would maintain their party; and when several members of the House of Commons were coming into the House, their attendants desiring that room might be made for them, some of the said soldiers answered, 'A pox of God confound them,' and others said, 'A pox take the House of Commons, let them come and be hanged, what ado is here with the House of Commons?' And some of the said soldiers did likewise violently assault, and by force disarm some of the attendants and servants of the members of the House of Commons waiting in the room next the said House, and upon the King's return out of the said House, many of them by wicked oaths and otherwise, expressed much discontent that some members of the said House for whom they came were not there, and others of them said, 'When comes the word?' And no word being given, at His Majesty's coming out they cried, 'A lane, a lane'; afterwards some of them being demanded what they thought the said company intended to have done, answered that, questionless, in the posture they were set, if the word had been given, they should have fallen upon the House of Commons and have cut all their throats. Upon all which we are of opinion, that it is sufficiently proved that the coming of the said soldiers, Papists and others, with His Majesty to the House of Commons on Tuesday last, being the 4th of this instant January, in the manner aforesaid, was to take away some of the members of the said House; and if they should have found opposition or denial, then to have fallen upon the said House in an hostile manner. And we do hereby declare, that the same was a traitorous design against the King and Parliament. And whereas the said Mr. Holles, Sir Arthur Haslerigg, Mr. Pym, Mr. Hampden, and Mr. Strode, upon report of the coming of the said soldiers, Papists and others, in the warlike and hostile manner aforesaid did, with the approbation of the House, absent themselves from the service of the House, for avoiding the great and many inconveniences which otherwise apparently [1] might have happened; since which time a printed paper, in the form of a Proclamation, bearing date the 6th day of this instant January hath issued out, for the apprehending and imprisoning of them, therein suggesting, that through the conscience of their own guilt they were absent and fled, not willing to submit themselves to justice; we do further declare, that the said printed paper is false, scandalous and illegal; and that, notwithstanding the said printed paper, or any warrant issued out, or any other matter yet appearing against them or any of them, they may and ought to attend the service of the said House of Commons and the several Committees now on foot; and that it is lawful for all persons whatsoever to lodge, harbour or converse with them or any of them; and whosoever shall be questioned for the same, shall be under the protection and privilege of Parliament.

And we do further declare, that the publishing of several articles purporting a form of a charge of high treason against Lord Kimbolton, one of the members of the Lords' House, and against the said Mr. Holles, Sir Arthur Haslerigg, Mr. Pym, Mr. Hampden and Mr. Strode, by Sir William Killigrew, Sir William Fleming and others of the Inns of Court, and elsewhere in the King's name, was a high breach of the

[1] I. e. evidently.

privilege of Parliament, a great scandal to His Majesty and
his government, a seditious act manifestly tending to the subversion of the peace of the kingdom, and an injury and dishonour to the said members, there being no legal charge or
accusation against them.

That the privileges of Parliament and the liberties of the
subjects so violated and broken, cannot be fully and sufficiently vindicated unless His Majesty will be graciously pleased
to discover the names of those persons who advised His
Majesty to issue out warrants for the sealing of the chambers
and studies of the said members, to send a serjeant-at-arms to
demand the said members, to issue out several warrants under
His Majesty's own hand to apprehend the said members, His
Majesty's coming thither in his own royal person, the publishing of the said articles and printed paper, in the form of
a Proclamation, against the said members in such manner as
is before declared, to the end that such persons may receive
condign punishment.

And this House doth further declare, that all such persons
as have given any counsel, or endeavoured to set or maintain
division or dislike between the King and Parliament, or have
listed their names or otherwise entered into any combination
or agreement to the aiding or assisting to any such counsel or
endeavour, or have persuaded any other so to do, or that shall
do any the things above mentioned ; and that shall not forthwith discover the same to either House of Parliament, or the
Speaker of either of the said Houses respectively, and disclaim
it, are declared public enemies of the State and peace of this
kingdom, and shall be enquired of and proceeded against accordingly.

48. The Clerical Disabilities Act.

[February 13, 1641½.   17 Car. I, cap. 27.   Statutes of the Realm, v. 138.
See *Hist. of Engl.* x. 165.]

*An Act for disenabling all persons in Holy Orders to
exercise any temporal jurisdiction or authority.*

1. Whereas Bishops and other persons in Holy Orders
ought not to be entangled with secular jurisdiction, the office-

of the ministry being of such great importance that it will take up the whole man; and for that it is found by long experience that their intermeddling with secular jurisdictions hath occasioned great mischiefs and scandal both to Church and State; His Majesty, out of his religious care of the Church, and souls of his people, is graciously pleased that it be enacted, and by authority of this present Parliament be it enacted, that no Archbishop or Bishop or other person that now is or hereafter shall be in Holy Orders, shall at any time after the 15th day of February, in the Year of Our Lord one thousand six hundred forty-one[1], have any seat or place, suffrage, or voice, or use, or execute any power or authority in the Parliaments of this realm, nor shall be of the Privy Council of His Majesty, his heirs or successors, or Justice of the Peace of *oyer* and *terminer* or gaol delivery, or execute any temporal authority by virtue of any commission, but shall be wholly disabled and be incapable to have, receive, use or execute any of the said offices, places, powers, authorities and things aforesaid.

2. And be it further enacted by the authority aforesaid, that all acts from and after the said 15th day of February, which shall be done or executed by any Archbishop or Bishop, or other person whatsoever in Holy Orders, and all and every suffrage or voice given or delivered by them or any of them, or other thing done by them or any of them contrary to the purport and true meaning of this present Act, shall be utterly void to all intents, constructions and purposes.

49. THE IMPRESSMENT ACT.

[February 13, 1641½.   17 Car. I, cap. 28.   Statutes of the Realm, v. 138.
See *Hist. of Engl.* x. 166.]

An Act for the better raising and levying of soldiers for the present defence of the kingdoms of England and Ireland.

I. Forasmuch as great commotions and rebellions have been lately raised and stirred up in His Majesty's kingdom of Ireland by the wicked plots and conspiracies of divers of His

[1] I.e. 1641½.

Majesty's subjects there (being traitorously affected), to the great endangering not only of the said kingdom, but also of this kingdom of England, unless a speedy course be taken for the preventing thereof, and for the raising and pressing of men for those services: and whereas by the laws of this realm none of His Majesty's subjects ought to be impressed or compelled to go out of his county to serve as a soldier in the wars, except in case of necessity of the sudden coming in of strange enemies into the kingdom, or except they be otherwise bound by tenure of their lands or possessions; therefore in respect of the great and urgent necessity of providing a present supply of men for the preventing of these great and imminent dangers, and for the speedy suppressing of the said heinous and dangerous rebellions, be it enacted by authority of this present Parliament, that the Justices of the Peace of every county and riding within this realm, or any three or more of them, as also the Mayor or other head officer or officers of every city or town corporate within this realm having Justices of the Peace, together with any two or more Justices of the Peace of the same city or town corporate respectively, or in default of such Justices, then with two or more Justices of the Peace of the county wherein the said city or town is, shall and may at any time or times between the 1st of December one thousand six hundred forty and one and the 1st of November, which shall be in the year of Our Lord God one thousand six hundred forty-two, within their several limits and jurisdictions raise, levy and impress so many men for soldiers, gunners and chirurgeons, as shall be appointed by order of the King's Majesty, his heirs or successors, and both Houses of Parliament, for the said services, and to command all and every the high constables, other constables, and inferior officers of and within every such county, riding, city or town corporate, or the liberties thereof respectively, by warrant under the hands and seals of such Justices of the Peace, Mayor, or other head officer or officers, as are authorised by this Act as aforesaid, to bring before them any such person or persons as shall be fit and necessary for the said services, which said persons so to be impressed as aforesaid, and every of them shall have such imprest money, and such allowance for coat and conduct unto the place of their rendezvous, as likewise such wages and entertainment from the time of their first entering into pay during their continuance in the said services, and such other necessary charges and allowances shall be made touching the said press : the said money and other charges and allowances to be paid by such persons and in such manner as by order of His Majesty, his heirs and successors, and of both Houses of Parliament, shall be appointed; and if any person or persons shall wilfully refuse to be impressed for the said services, that then it shall and may be lawful to and for the said persons so authorised as aforesaid to the said press, to commit such offender to prison, there to remain without bail or mainprize by the space of six months, and until he shall pay the sum of £10 to the Treasurers for the maimed soldiers of the same county, city or town corporate, where any such Treasurers are to be employed for and towards the relief and maintenance of such soldiers, gunners and chirurgeons, as shall happen to be maimed in the said services, or if none such shall happen to be, then for the relief of other the maimed soldiers of the said county, city or town corporate respectively; and in default of payment of the said sum, then the said person offending to remain in prison by the space of one whole year over and above the said six months, without bail or mainprize.

II. Provided always that this Act shall not extend to the pressing of any clergyman, or any scholars or students or privileged persons of either of the Universities, Inns of Court or Chancery, or any of the trained bands of this realm, or to the pressing of any other person who was rated towards the payment of the last subsidies, or that shall be rated or taxed towards the payment of any subsidies hereafter to be granted before the time of such impressing, or to the eldest son of any person who is or shall be before the time of such impressing rated in the subsidy-book at £3 lands or £5 goods, or to any person of the rank or degree of an esquire or upwards, or to the son of any such person of the said rank or degree, or of the widow of any such person, or to any person under the age of eighteen or above the age of threescore years, or to any mariners, seamen or fishermen.

III. Provided also, and be it enacted, that no money or

other reward shall be taken, or other corrupt practice used in or for the pressing, changing or releasing of any person impressed, or to be impressed by force of this Act, by any person hereby authorised in that behalf or their agents, under pain of forfeiture of £20 by every person so offending for every such offence, to be paid and employed to the Treasurers of the maimed soldiers in manner and to the uses aforesaid.

IV. Provided also, and be it enacted, that this present Act shall not extend to the impressing of any of the menial servants of the members or assistants or officers of the Lords' House of Parliament, or to the menial servants of the members or officers of the House of Commons, or of any of the inhabitants of the Isle of Wight, or of the Isle of Anglesey, or of any of the Cinque Ports, or members thereof.

50. THE MILITIA ORDINANCE.

[March 5, 164½. Journals of the House of Lords, iv. 587. See *Hist. of Engl.* x. 167, 171 [1].]

An Ordinance of the Lords and Commons in Parliament, for the safety and defence of the kingdom of England and dominion of Wales.

Whereas there hath been of late a most dangerous and desperate design upon the House of Commons, which we have just cause to believe to be an effect of the bloody counsels of Papists and other ill-affected persons, who have already raised a rebellion in the kingdom of Ireland ; and by reason of many discoveries we cannot but fear they will proceed not only to stir up the like rebellion and insurrections in this kingdom of England, but also to back them with forces from abroad.

For the safety therefore of His Majesty's person, the Parliament and kingdom in this time of imminent danger :

---

[1] A very similar Ordinance was sent up to the Lords on Feb. 15 and accepted by them on the 16th (Journals of the House of Lords, iv. 587). It was sent to the King, and his answer having been voted to be a denial, the Lords returned the Ordinance to the Commons in a slightly altered form. It was finally adopted by both Houses on March 5.

It is ordained by[1] the Lords and Commons now in Parliament assembled, that Henry Earl of Holland shall be Lieutenant of the County of Berks, Oliver Earl of Bolingbroke shall be Lieutenant of the County of Bedford, &c.

.   .   .   .

And shall severally and respectively have power to assemble and call together all and singular His Majesty's subjects, within the said several and respective counties and places, as well within liberties as without, that are meet and fit for the wars, and them to train and exercise and put in readiness, and them after their abilities and faculties well and sufficiently from time to time to cause to be arrayed and weaponed, and to take the muster of them in places most[2] fit for that purpose ; and the aforesaid Henry Earl of Holland, Oliver Earl of Bolingbroke, &c., shall severally and respectively have power within the several and respective counties and places aforesaid, to nominate and appoint such persons of quality as to them shall seem meet to be their Deputy Lieutenants, to be approved of by both Houses of Parliament:

And that any one or more of the said deputies so assigned and approved of in the absence or by the command of the said Henry Earl of Holland, Oliver Earl of Bolingbroke, &c., shall have power and authority to do and execute within the said several and respective counties and places to them assigned as aforesaid, all such powers and authorities before in this present Ordinance contained ; and the aforesaid Henry Earl of Holland, Oliver Earl of Bolingbroke, &c., shall have power to make colonels, captains and other officers, and to remove out of their places, and make others from time to time, as they shall think fit for that purpose; and the said Henry Earl of Holland, Oliver Earl of Bolingbroke, &c., their deputy or deputies in their absence or by their command, shall have power to lead, conduct and employ the persons aforesaid arrayed and weaponed, for the suppression of all rebellions, insurrections and invasions that may happen within the several and respective counties and places ; and shall have power and

[1] 'by the King's Most Excellent Majesty,' is here inserted in the Ordinance of February 16.
[2] 'most' is omitted in the Ordinance of February 16.

authority to lead, conduct and employ the persons aforesaid arrayed and weaponed, as well within their said several and respective counties and places, as within any other part of this realm of England or dominion of Wales, for the suppression of all rebellions, insurrections and invasions that may happen, according as they from time to time shall receive directions from [1] the Lords and Commons assembled in Parliament.

And be it further ordained, that Sir John Gayre, Sir Jacob Garret, Knights, &c., citizens of London, or any six or more of them, shall have such power and authority within the City of London as any of the Lieutenants before named are authorised to have by this Ordinance, within the said several and respective counties (the nomination and appointment of Deputy Lieutenants only excepted). And it is further ordained, that such persons as shall not obey in any of the premises, shall answer their neglect and contempt to the Lords and Commons in a Parliamentary way, and not otherwise nor elsewhere, and that every the powers granted as aforesaid shall continue until it shall be otherwise ordered or declared by both Houses of Parliament and no longer.

51. The Declaration of the Houses on Church Reform.

[April 8, 1642. Journals of the House of Lords, iv. 706. See *Hist. of Engl.* x. 186.]

The Lords and Commons so declare, that they intend a due and necessary reformation of the government and liturgy of the Church, and to take away nothing in the one or the other but what shall be evil and justly offensive, or at least, unnecessary and burdensome ; and, for the better effecting thereof, speedily to have consultation with godly and learned divines ; and because this will never of itself attain the end sought therein, they will therefore use their utmost endeavour to establish learned and preaching ministers, with a good and sufficient maintenance, throughout the whole kingdom, wherein

---

[1] 'by His Majesty's authority, signified unto them by' stands in the Ordinance of February 16 in the place of 'from.'

many dark corners are miserably destitute of the means of salvation, and many poor ministers want necessary provision.

52. The King's Proclamation condemning the Militia Ordinance.

[May 27, 1642.   Journals of the House of Lords, v. 111.   See *Hist. of Engl.* x. 202.]

By the King.

A Proclamation, forbidding all His Majesty's subjects belonging to the trained bands or militia of this kingdom to rise, march, muster or exercise, by virtue of any Order or Ordinance of one or both Houses of Parliament, without consent or warrant from His Majesty, upon pain of punishment according to the laws.

Whereas, by the statute made in the seventh year of King Edward the First [1], the Prelates, Earls, Barons and Commonalty of the realm affirmed in Parliament, that to the King it belongeth, and his part it is by his royal seigniory straightly to defend wearing of armour and all other force against the peace, at all times when it shall please him, and to punish them which do the contrary according to the laws and usages of the realm; and hereunto all subjects are bound to aid the King as their sovereign lord, at all seasons when need shall be; and whereas we understand that, expressly contrary to the said statute and other good laws of this our kingdom, under colour and pretence of an Ordinance of Parliament, without our consent, or any commission or warrant from us, the trained bands and militia of this kingdom have been lately, and are intended to be put in arms, and drawn into companies in a warlike manner, whereby the peace and quiet of our subjects is, or may be, disturbed; we being desirous, by all gracious and fair admonitions, to prevent that some malignant persons in this our kingdom do not by degrees seduce our good subjects from their due obedience to us and the laws of this our kingdom, subtilely endeavouring, by a general combustion or confusion, to hide their mis-

[1] This is not printed amongst the Statutes of the Realm. See No. 54.

chievous designs and intentions against the peace of this our
kingdom, and under a specious pretence of putting our
trained bands into a posture, draw and engage our good
subjects in a warlike opposition against us, as our town of
Hull is already by the treason of Sir John Hotham, who at
first pretended to put a garrison into the same only for
security and service.

We do therefore, by this our Proclamation, expressly charge
and command all our sheriffs, and all colonels, lieutenant-
colonels, sergeant-majors, captains, officers and soldiers, belonging to the trained bands of this our kingdom, and likewise all high and petty constables, and other our officers and
subjects whatsoever, upon their allegiance, and as they tender
the peace of this our kingdom, not to muster, levy, raise or
march, or to summon or warn, upon any warrant, order or
ordinance from one or both of our Houses of Parliament
(whereunto we have not, or shall not, give our express consent), any of our trained bands or other forces, to rise, muster,
march or exercise, without express warrant under our hand
or warrant from our sheriff of the county, grounded upon a
particular writ to that purpose under our Great Seal; and in
case any of our trained bands shall rise or gather together
contrary to this our command, we shall then call them in due
time to a strict account, and proceed legally against them, as
violators of the laws and disturbers of the peace of this kingdom.

Given at our Court at York

the 27th day of May, 1642.

53. THE NINETEEN PROPOSITIONS SENT BY THE TWO HOUSES
OF PARLIAMENT TO THE KING AT YORK.

[June 1[1], 1642.   Journals of the House of Lords, v. 97.   See *Hist.
of Engl.* x. 196.]

Your Majesty's most humble and faithful subjects, the
Lords and Commons in Parliament, having nothing in their

---

[1] Rushworth (iv. 772) gives the date of June 2, but see Lords' Journals,
v. 100. In my History I have followed Rushworth's date. The propositions
may not have been actually despatched till that day. At all events June 1
is the date of their final acceptance by the Houses.

thoughts and desires more precious and of higher esteem (next to the honour and immediate service of God) than the just and faithful performance of their duty to your Majesty and this kingdom : and being very sensible of the great distractions and distempers, and of the imminent dangers and calamities which those distractions and distempers are like to bring upon your Majesty and your subjects ; all which have proceeded from the subtile insinuations, mischievous practices and evil counsels of men disaffected to God's true religion, your Majesty's honour and safety, and the public peace and prosperity of your people, after a serious observation of the causes of those mischiefs, do in all humility and sincerity present to your Majesty their most dutiful petition and advice, that out of your princely wisdom for the establishing your own honour and safety, and gracious tenderness of the welfare and security of your subjects and dominions, you will be pleased to grant and accept these their humble desires and propositions, as the most necessary effectual means, through God's blessing, of removing those jealousies and differences which have unhappily fallen betwixt you and your people, and procuring both your Majesty and them a constant course of honour, peace, and happiness.

The Nineteen Propositions.

1. That the Lords and others of your Majesty's Privy Council, and such great officers and Ministers of State, either at home or beyond the seas, may be put from your Privy Council, and from those offices and employments, excepting such as shall be approved of by both Houses of Parliament ; and that the persons put into the places and employments of those that are removed may be approved of by both Houses of Parliament ; and that the Privy Councillors shall take an oath for the due execution of their places, in such form as shall be agreed upon by both Houses of Parliament.

2. That the great affairs of the kingdom may not be concluded or transacted by the advice of private men, or by any unknown or unsworn councillors, but that such matters as concern the public, and are proper for the High Court

of Parliament, which is your Majesty's great and supreme council, may be debated, resolved and transacted only in Parliament, and not elsewhere: and such as shall presume to do anything to the contrary shall be reserved to the censure and judgment of Parliament: and such other matters of state as are proper for your Majesty's Privy Council shall be debated and concluded by such of the nobility and others as shall from time to time be chosen for that place, by approbation of both Houses of Parliament: and that no public act concerning the affairs of the kingdom, which are proper for your Privy Council, may be esteemed of any validity, as proceeding from the royal authority, unless it be done by the advice and consent of the major part of your Council, attested under their hands: and that your Council may be limited to a certain number, not exceeding five and twenty, nor under fifteen: and if any councillor's place happen to be void in the interval of Parliament, it shall not be supplied without the assent of the major part of the Council, which choice shall be confirmed at the next sitting of Parliament, or else to be void.

3. That the Lord High Steward of England, Lord High Constable, Lord Chancellor, or Lord Keeper of the Great Seal, Lord Treasurer, Lord Privy Seal, Earl Marshall, Lord Admiral, Warden of the Cinque Ports, Chief Governor of Ireland, Chancellor of the Exchequer, Master of the Wards, Secretaries of State, two Chief Justices and Chief Baron, may always be chosen with the approbation of both Houses of Parliament; and in the intervals of Parliament, by assent of the major part of the Council, in such manner as is before expressed in the choice of councillors.

4. That he, or they unto whom the government and education of the King's children shall be committed, shall be approved of by both Houses of Parliament; and in the intervals of Parliament, by the assent of the major part of the Council, in such manner as is before expressed in the choice of councillors; and that all such servants as are now about them, against whom both Houses shall have any just exceptions, shall be removed.

5. That no marriage shall be concluded or treated for any

of the King's children, with any foreign prince, or other person whatsoever, abroad or at home, without the consent of Parliament, under the penalty of a premunire, upon such as shall conclude or treat of any marriage as aforesaid; and that the said penalty shall not be pardoned or dispensed with but by the consent of both Houses of Parliament.

6. That the laws in force against Jesuits, priests, and Popish recusants, be strictly put in execution, without any toleration or dispensation to the contrary; and that some more effectual course may be enacted, by authority of Parliament, to disable them from making any disturbance in the State, or eluding the law by trusts or otherwise.

7. That the votes of Popish lords in the House of Peers may be taken away, so long as they continue Papists: and that your Majesty will consent to such a Bill as shall be drawn for the education of the children of Papists by Protestants in the Protestant religion.

8. That your Majesty will be pleased to consent that such a reformation be made of the Church government and liturgy, as both Houses of Parliament shall advise; wherein they intend to have consultations with divines, as is expressed in their declaration to that purpose; and that your Majesty will contribute your best assistance to them, for the raising of a sufficient maintenance for preaching ministers throughout the kingdom; and that your Majesty will be pleased to give your consent to laws for the taking away of innovations and superstition, and of pluralities, and against scandalous ministers.

9. That your Majesty will be pleased to rest satisfied with that course that the Lords and Commons have appointed for ordering of the militia, until the same shall be further settled by a Bill; and that your Majesty will recall your Declarations and Proclamations against the Ordinance made by the Lords and Commons concerning it.

10. That such members of either House of Parliament as have, during the present Parliament, been put out of any place and office, may either be restored to that place and office, or otherwise have satisfaction for the same, upon the petition of that House whereof he or they are members.

11. That all Privy Councillors and Judges may take an oath, the form whereof to be agreed on and settled by Act of Parliament, for the maintaining of the Petition of Right and of certain statutes made by the Parliament, which shall be mentioned by both Houses of Parliament: and that an enquiry of all the breaches and violations of those laws may be given in charge by the Justices of the King's Bench every Term, and by the Judges of Assize in their circuits, and Justices of the Peace at the sessions, to be presented and punished according to law.

12. That all the Judges, and all the officers placed by approbation of both Houses of Parliament, may hold their places *quam diu bene se gesserint.*

13. That the justice of Parliament may pass upon all delinquents, whether they be within the kingdom or fled out of it; and that all persons cited by either House of Parliament may appear and abide the censure of Parliament.

14. That the general pardon offered by your Majesty may be granted, with such exceptions as shall be advised by both Houses of Parliament.

15. That the forts and castles of this kingdom may be put under the command and custody of such persons as your Majesty shall appoint, with the approbation of your Parliament: and in the intervals of Parliament, with approbation of the major part of the Council, in such manner as is before expressed in the choice of councillors.

16. That the extraordinary guards and military forces now attending your Majesty, may be removed and discharged; and that for the future you will raise no such guards or extraordinary forces, but according to the law, in case of actual rebellion or invasion.

17. That your Majesty will be pleased to enter into a more strict alliance with the States of the United Provinces, and other neighbouring princes and states of the Protestant religion, for the defence and maintenance thereof, against all designs and attempts of the Pope and his adherents to subvert and suppress it; whereby your Majesty will obtain a great access of strength and reputation, and your subjects be much encouraged and enabled, in a Parliamentary way, for your aid

and assistance, in restoring your royal sister and her princely issue to those dignities and dominions which belong unto them, and relieving the other Protestant princes who have suffered in the same cause.

18. That your Majesty will be pleased, by Act of Parliament, to clear the Lord Kimbolton and the five members of the House of Commons, in such manner that future Parliaments may be secured from the consequence of that evil precedent.

19. That your Majesty will be graciously pleased to pass a Bill for restraining peers made hereafter, from sitting or voting in Parliament, unless they be admitted thereunto with the consent of both Houses of Parliament.

And these our humble desires being granted by your Majesty, we shall forthwith apply ourselves to regulate your present revenue in such sort as may be for your best advantage; and likewise to settle such an ordinary and constant increase of it, as shall be sufficient to support your royal dignity in honour and plenty, beyond the proportion of any former grants of the subjects of this kingdom to your Majesty's royal predecessors. We shall likewise put the town of Hull into such hands as your Majesty shall appoint, with the consent and approbation of Parliament, and deliver up a just account of all the magazine, and cheerfully employ the uttermost of our power and endeavours in the real expression and performance of our most dutiful and loyal affections, to the preserving and maintaining the royal honour, greatness and safety of your Majesty and your posterity.

54. DECLARATION OF THE HOUSES IN DEFENCE OF THE MILITIA ORDINANCE.

[June 6, 1642. Journals of the House of Lords, v. 112. See *Hist. of Engl.* x. 200.]

A Declaration of the Lords and Commons in Parliament concerning His Majesty's Proclamation[1], *the 27th of May*, 1642.

The Lords and Commons, having perused His Majesty's Proclamation forbidding all His Majesty's subjects belonging

[1] No. 52.

to the trained bands or militia of this kingdom, to rise, march, muster or exercise, by virtue of any Order or Ordinance of one or both Houses of Parliament, without consent or warrant from His Majesty, upon pain of punishment according to the laws:

Do thereupon declare, that neither the statute of the seventh of Edward the First, therein vouched, nor any other law of this kingdom, doth restrain or make void the Ordinance agreed upon by both Houses of Parliament, for the ordering and disposing the militia of the kingdom in this time of extreme and imminent danger, nor expose His Majesty's subjects to any punishment for obeying the same, notwithstanding that His Majesty hath refused to give his consent to that Ordinance, but ought to be obeyed by the fundamental laws of this kingdom.

The declaration of 7 Edward I, quoted in His Majesty's Proclamation, runneth thus:

The King to the Justices of his Bench sendeth greeting: Whereas of late, before certain persons deputed to treat upon sundry debates had between us and certain great men of our realm, amongst other things it was accorded, that in our next Parliament, after provision shall be made by us, and the common assent of Prelates, Earls and Barons, that in all Parliaments, treaties and other assemblies, which should be made in the realm of England for ever, that every man shall come, without all force and armour, well and peaceably, to the honour of us and our realm; and now, in our next Parliament at Westminster, after the said treaties, the Prelates, Earls, Barons and the Commonalty of our realm, there assembled to take advice of this business, have said, that to us belongeth, and our part is, through our royal seigniory, straightly to defend force of armour, and all other force against our peace at all times when it shall please us, and to punish them which shall do contrary according to our laws and usages of our realm.

And hereunto they are bound to aid us, as their sovereign lord, at all seasons when need shall be; we command you, that you cause these things to be read before you in the said Bench and there to be enrolled.

Given at Westminster the 30th day of October.

The occasion of this Declaration was for the restraint of armed men from coming to the Parliament to disturb the peace of it, and is very improperly alleged for the maintenance of such levies as are now raised against the Parliament, the title of the statute being thus, ' To all Parliaments and treaties every man shall come without force and arms'; so the question is not whether it belong to the King or no to restrain such force, but, if the King shall refuse to discharge that duty and trust, whether there is not a power in the two Houses to provide for the safety of the Parliament and peace of the kingdom, which is the end for which the Ordinance concerning the militia was made, and, being agreeable to the scope and purposes of the law, cannot in reason be adjudged to be contrary to it; for, although the law do affirm it to be in the King, yet it doth not exclude those in whom the law hath placed a power for that purpose, as in the courts of justice, the sheriffs and other officers and ministers of those courts; and as their power is derived from the King by his patent, yet cannot it be restrained by His Majesty's command, by his Great Seal or otherwise; much less can the power of Parliament be concluded by His Majesty's command, because the authority thereof is of a higher and more eminent nature than any of these courts.

It is acknowledged that the King is the fountain of justice and protection, but the acts of justice and protection are not exercised in his own person, nor depend upon his pleasure, but by his courts and by his ministers, who must do their duty therein, though the King in his own person should forbid them; and therefore, if judgments should be given by them against the King's will and personal command, yet are they the King's judgments.

The High Court of Parliament is not only a court of judicature, enabled by the laws to adjudge and determine the rights and liberties of the kingdom, against such patents and grants of His Majesty as are prejudicial thereunto, although strengthened both by his personal command and by his Proclamation under the Great Seal; but it is likewise a council, to provide for the necessities, prevent the imminent dangers, and preserve the public peace and safety of the kingdom, and to declare the King's pleasure in those things as are requisite thereunto; and what they do herein hath the stamp of the royal authority, although His Majesty, seduced by evil counsel, do in his own person oppose or interrupt the same; for the King's supreme and royal pleasure is exercised and declared in this High Court of law and council, after a more eminent and obligatory manner than it can be by personal act or resolution of his own.

Seeing therefore the Lords and Commons, which are His Majesty's great and high council, have ordained, that for the present and necessary defence of the realm, the trained bands and militia of this kingdom should be ordered according to that Ordinance, and that the town of Hull should be committed to the custody of Sir John Hotham, to be preserved from the attempts of Papists and other malignant persons, who thereby might put the kingdom into a combustion, which is so far from being a force against the King's peace that it is necessary for the keeping and securing thereof, and for that end alone is intended; and all His Majesty's loving subjects, as well by that law as by other laws, are bound to be obedient thereunto; and what they do therein is (according to that law) to be interpreted to be done in aid of the King, in discharge of that trust which he is tied to perform; and it is so far from being liable to punishment, that, if they should refuse to do it, or be persuaded by any commission or command of His Majesty to do the contrary, they might justly be punished for the same, according to the laws and usages of the realm; for the King, by his sovereignty, is not enabled to destroy his people, but to protect and defend them; and the High Court of Parliament, and all other His Majesty's officers and ministers, ought to be subservient to that power and authority which the law hath placed in His Majesty to that purpose, though he himself, in his own person, should neglect the same.

Wherefore the Lords and Commons do declare the said Proclamation to be void in law, and of none effect; for that, by the constitution and policy of this kingdom, the King by his Proclamation cannot declare the law contrary to the judgment and resolution of any of the inferior courts of justice, much less against the High Court of Parliament; for if it were admitted that the King, by his Proclamation, may declare a law, thereby his Proclamations will in effect become laws, which would turn to the subverting of the law of the land, and the rights and liberties of the subjects.

And the Lords and Commons do require and command all constables, petty constables, and all other His Majesty's officers and subjects whatsoever, to muster, levy, raise, march and exercise, or to summon or warn any, upon warrants from the Lieutenants, Deputy Lieutenants, Captains, or other officers of the trained bands, and all others, according to the said Ordinance of both Houses, and shall not presume to muster, levy, raise, march or exercise, by virtue of any commission or other authority whatsoever, as they will answer the contrary at their perils; and in their so doing, they do further declare that they shall be protected by the power and authority of both Houses of Parliament; and that whatsoever shall oppose, question or hinder them in the execution of the said Ordinance, shall be proceeded against as violators of the laws and disturbers of the peace of the kingdom.

55. THE KING'S LETTER SENT WITH THE COMMISSIONS OF ARRAY TO LEICESTERSHIRE.

[June 12, 1642.   Rushworth, iv. 657.   See *Hist. of Engl.* x. 202.]

Charles R.

Right trusty and right well-beloved cousins, and right trusty and well-beloved, we greet you well.   Whereas it hath been declared by the votes of both Houses of Parliament the 15th day of March last, that the kingdom hath of late, and still is in so evident and imminent danger, both from enemies abroad and a Popish discontented party at home, that there is an urgent and inevitable necessity of putting our subjects into a posture of defence for the safeguard both of our person and people; and that sithence divers inhabitants of divers counties have addressed their petitions to that purpose: and whereas a small number of both Houses (after it had been rejected by the Lords in a full House, and without our royal assent, or the opinion of the Judges concerning the legality of it)

have attempted by way of Ordinance, to put in execution the
militia of the kingdom, and to dispossess many of our ancient
nobility of the command and trust reposed in them by us, and
have nominated divers others who have no interest, nor live
near to some of the counties to which they are nominated for
the Lieutenancy, whereby they cannot be properly serviceable
to the counties wherewith they are entrusted, nor our people
receive that content and security which we desire they should.
To submit to the execution of which power by the way of
Ordinance, without it were reduced into a law by Act of Parliament established by our royal assent, were to reduce and
expose our subjects to a mere arbitrary government, which by
God's grace we shall never permit.

We, therefore, considering that by the laws of the realm it
belongeth to us to order and govern the militia of the kingdom,
have thereupon by our Proclamation of the 27th of May last,
prohibited all manner of persons whatsoever upon their allegiance
to muster, levy or summon upon any warrant, order or ordinance
from one or both Houses of Parliament, whereunto we have
not, or shall not give our express consent to any of the trained
bands, or other officers without express warrant under our
hands, or warrant from our Sheriff of the county, grounded
upon a particular writ to that purpose under our Great Seal;
and considering that in ancient time the militia of the kingdom
was ever disposed of by the Commissions of Array, and that
by a particular statute upon record in the Tower, made in
the fifth year of Henry the Fourth[1], by full consent of the
Prelates, Earls, Barons and Commons, and at their suit, and
by the advice and opinion of the Judges then had, such Commissions were mitigated in respect of some clauses perilous
to the Commissioners, and approved of for the time to come.
And by the subsequent records it appeareth that all our royal
predecessors have continually exercised that power by such
Commissions, till of late time they have been discontinued
by the grants of particular Commissions of Lieutenancy, little
differing in substance from the said Commissions of Array,
against which the Houses it seems have taken some exception;

---

[1] Rolls of Parliament, iii. 526.

and though we are no way satisfied of the illegality of them, our counsel being never heard in the defence thereof, yet being willing to avoid all exceptions at present, we have thought fit to refer it to that ancient legal way of disposing the power of the militia by Commissions of Array for defence of us, our kingdom and our county; authorizing you, or any three or more of you, to array and train our people, and to apportion and assess such persons as have estates and are not able to bear arms, to find arms for other men in a reasonable and moderate proportion; and to conduct them so arrayed, as well to the coasts as to other places, for the opposition and destruction of our enemies in case of danger, as to your discretions, or any three or more of you, shall seem meet, whereof you Henry Earl of Huntingdon, and in your absence William Earl of Devonshire, or Henry Hastings, Esq., to be one; and being both confident in a great measure both of the loyal affections of our people, and very tender to bring any unnecessary burden or charge on them by augmenting the number of the trained bands, we do for the present only require that you do forthwith cause to be mustered and trained all the ancient trained bands and freehold bands of the county, carefully seeing that they be supplied with able and sufficient persons, and completely armed; unless you find that there be just cause, and that it shall be with the good liking of the inhabitants for their own better security, to make any increase of their number; and over such bands to appoint and set such colonels, captains and officers as you shall think most fit for the discharge of that service, being such persons as have considerable interest in the county, and not strangers; and in case of any opposition, you are to raise the power of the county to suppress it, and to commit all such persons as are found rebellious herein into the custody of our Sheriff, whose care and assistance we especially require: and that he shall from time to time issue forth such warrants for the assembling of our people at such times and places as by you shall be agreed on, according to the trust reposed in him by our said Commission: and we have authorized you our Commissioners, or any three of you after such array made, from time to time to train and take musters of our said bands, and to provide beacons and other necessaries, for the better exercising of our people, and discovery of sudden invasions and commotions.   Of all which your proceedings herein we expect a plenary and speedy account, according to the trust reposed in you, and authority given you by our Commission on that behalf.

> Given at our Court at York the 12th day of June, in
> the 18th year of our reign, 1642.

56.   The Votes of the Houses for raising an Army.

[July 12, 1642.   Rushworth, iv. 755.   See *Hist. of Engl.* x. 211.]

Die Martis 12 Julii, 1642.

Resolved upon the question, that an army shall be forthwith raised for the safety of the King's person, defence of both Houses of Parliament, and of those who have obeyed their orders and commands, and preserving of the true religion, the laws, liberty and peace of the kingdom.

Resolved upon the question, that the Earl of Essex shall be general.

Resolved upon the question, that this House doth declare, that in this cause, for the safety of the King's person, defence of both Houses of Parliament, and of those who have obeyed their orders and commands, and preserving of the true religion, the laws, liberty and peace of the kingdom, they will live and die with the Earl of Essex, whom they have nominated general in this cause.

Resolved upon the question, that a petition shall be framed, to move His Majesty to a good accord with his Parliament to prevent a civil war.

PART IV

FROM THE OUTBREAK OF THE CIVIL WAR TO THE EXECUTION OF THE KING.

57. THE PROPOSITIONS PRESENTED TO THE KING AT THE TREATY OF OXFORD.

[February 1, 164⅔. Rushworth, v. 165. See *Great Civil War*, i. 89.]

The humble desires and propositions of the Lords and Commons in Parliament assembled, tendered to His Majesty, Feb., 1642.

We your Majesty's most humble and faithful subjects, the Lords and Commons in Parliament assembled, having in our thoughts the glory of God, your Majesty's honour and the prosperity of your people, and being most grievously afflicted with the pressing miseries and calamities which have over-whelmed your two kingdoms of England and Ireland since your Majesty hath, by the persuasion of evil counsellors, withdrawn yourself from the Parliament, raised an army against it, and by force thereof protected delinquents from the justice of it, constraining us to take arms for the defence of our religion, laws, liberties, privileges of Parliament, and for the sitting of the Parliament in safety, which fears and dangers are continued and increased by the raising, drawing together, and arming of great numbers of Papists, under the command of the Earl of Newcastle, likewise by making Lord Herbert of Raglan, and other known papists, commanders of great forces, whereby many grievous oppressions, rapines and cruelties have been, and are daily exercised upon the persons and estates of your people, much innocent blood hath been spilt, and the Papists have attained means of attempting and hopes of effecting their mischievous design of rooting out the reformed religion, and destroying the professors thereof :—in the tender sense and compassion of these evils, under which your people and kingdom lie (according to the duty which we owe to God, your Majesty, and the kingdom, for which we are intrusted), do most earnestly desire that an end may be put to these great distempers and distractions, for the preventing of that desolation which doth threaten all your Majesty's dominions. And as we have rendered, and still are ready to render unto your Majesty that subjection, obedience and service which we owe unto you, so we most humbly beseech your Majesty to remove the cause of this war, and to vouchsafe us that peace and protection which we and our ancestors have formerly enjoyed under your Majesty, and your royal predecessors, and graciously to accept and grant these most humble desires and propositions.

I. That your Majesty will be pleased to disband your armies, as we likewise shall be ready to disband all those forces which we have raised; and that you will be pleased to return to your Parliament.

II. That you will leave delinquents to a legal trial and judgment of Parliament.

III. That the Papists not only be disbanded, but disarmed according to law.

IV. That your Majesty will be pleased to give your royal assent unto the Bill for taking away superstitious innovations: to the Bill for the utter abolishing and taking away of all Archbishops, Bishops, their Chancellors and Commissaries, Deans, Sub-deans, Deans and Chapters, Archdeacons, Canons and Prebendaries, and all Chanters, Chancellors, Treasurers, Sub-treasurers, Succentors and Sacrists, and all Vicars Choral and Choristers, old Vicars and new Vicars of any Cathedral or Collegiate Church, and all other their under officers out of the Church of England: to the Bill against scandalous ministers: to the Bill against pluralities: and to the Bill for consultation to be had with godly, religious, and learned divines: that your Majesty will be pleased to promise to pass such other good Bills for settling of Church government, as upon consultation with the assembly of the said divines shall be resolved on by both Houses of Parliament, and by them be presented to your Majesty.

V. That your Majesty, having expressed in your answer to the Nineteen Propositions of both Houses of Parliament, a hearty affection and intention for the rooting out of Popery out of this kingdom; and that if both the Houses of Parliament can yet find a more effectual course to disable Jesuits, priests, and Popish recusants from disturbing the State or deluding the laws, that you would willingly give your consent unto it; that you would be graciously pleased, for the better discovery and speedier conviction of recusants, that an oath may be established by Act of Parliament to be administered in such manner as by both Houses shall be agreed on; wherein they shall abjure and renounce the Pope's supremacy, the doctrine of transubstantiation, purgatory, worshipping of the consecrated host, crucifixes and images; and the refusing the said oath, being tendered in such manner as shall be appointed by Act of Parliament, shall be a sufficient conviction in law of recusancy. And that your Majesty will be graciously pleased to give your royal assent unto a Bill for the education of the children of Papists, by Protestants in the Protestant religion: that for the more effectual execution of the laws against the Popish recusants, your Majesty would be pleased to consent to a Bill for the true levying of the penalties against them, and that the same penalty may be levied and disposed of in such manner as both Houses of Parliament shall agree on, so as your Majesty be at no loss: and likewise to a Bill whereby the practice of Papists against the State may be prevented, and the laws against them duly executed.

VI. That the Earl of Bristol may be removed from your Majesty's counsels, and that both he and the Lord Herbert, eldest son to the Earl of Worcester[1], may likewise be restrained from coming within the verge of the Court, and that they may not bear any office, or have any employments concerning the State or commonwealth.

---

[1] I.e. Lord Herbert of Raglan, afterwards created, by warrant only, Earl of Glamorgan.

VII. That your Majesty will be graciously pleased by Act of Parliament to settle the militia both by sea and land, and for the forts and ports of the kingdom, in such a manner as shall be agreed on by both Houses.

VIII. That your Majesty will be pleased by your Letters Patent to make Sir John Brampston Chief Justice of your Court of King's Bench, William Lenthall, Esq., the now Speaker of the Commons' House, Master of the Rolls, and to continue the Lord Chief Justice Bankes Chief Justice of the Court of Common Pleas, and likewise to make Mr. Serjeant Wilde Chief Baron of your Court of Exchequer. And that Mr. Justice Bacon may be continued, and Mr. Serjeant Rolle and Mr. Serjeant Atkins made Justices of the King's Bench. That Mr. Justice Reeves and Mr. Justice Foster may be continued, and Mr. Serjeant Pheasant made one of your Justices of your Court of Common Pleas; that Mr. Serjeant Creswell, Mr. Samuel Browne, and Mr. John Puleston, may be Barons of the Exchequer; and that all these, and all the Judges of the same Courts, for the time to come, may hold their places by Letters Patent under the Great Seal, *Quam diu se bene gesserint*, and that the several persons not before named, that do hold any of these places before mentioned, may be removed.

IX. That all such persons as have been put out of the Commissions of Peace, or *oyer* and *terminer*, or from being *custodes rotulorum*, since the first day of April 1642 (other than such as were put out by desire of both, or either of the Houses of Parliament), may again be put into those commissions and offices; and that such persons may be put out of those commissions and offices, as shall be excepted against by both Houses of Parliament.

X. That your Majesty will be pleased to pass the Bill now presented to your Majesty to vindicate and secure the privileges of Parliament from the ill consequence of the late precedent in the charge and proceeding against the Lord Kimbolton, now Earl of Manchester, and the five members of the House of Commons.

XI. That your Majesty's royal assent may be given unto such Acts as shall be advised by both Houses of Parliament, for the satisfying and paying the debts and damages wherein the two Houses of Parliament have engaged the public faith of the kingdom.

XII. That your Majesty will be pleased, according to a gracious answer heretofore received from you, to enter into a more strict alliance with the States of the United Provinces, and other neighbouring princes and States of the Protestant religion, for the defence and maintenance thereof against all designs and attempts of the Popish and Jesuitical faction, to subvert and suppress it, whereby your subjects may hope to be free from the mischiefs which this kingdom hath endured through the power which some of that party have had in your counsels, and will be much encouraged in a parliamentary way for your aid and assistance in restoring your royal sister and the prince elector to those dignities and dominions which belong unto them, and relieving the other distressed Protestant princes who have suffered in the same cause.

XIII. That in the general pardon which your Majesty hath been pleased to offer to your subjects, all offences and misdemeanours committed before the 10th of January, 1641 [1], which have been, or shall be questioned or proceeded against in Parliament, upon complaint in the House of Commons before the 10th of January, 1643 [2], shall be excepted; which offences and misdemeanours shall nevertheless be taken and adjudged to be fully discharged against all other inferior Courts. That likewise there shall be an exception of offences committed by any person or persons, which hath or have had any hand or practice in the rebellion of Ireland, which hath or have given any counsel, assistance or encouragement to the rebels there for the maintenance of that rebellion, as likewise an exception of William, Earl of Newcastle, and George, Lord Digby.

XIV. That your Majesty will be pleased to restore such members of either House of Parliament to their several places of services and employment, out of which they have been put since the beginning of this Parliament; that they may receive satisfaction and reparation for those places, and for the profits

---

[1] I.e. 164$\frac{1}{2}$.

[2] I.e. the following Jan. 10, 164$\frac{2}{3}$.

which they have lost by such removals, upon the petition of
both Houses of Parliament ; and that all others may be
restored to their offices and employments, who have been put
out of the same upon any displeasure conceived against them
for any assistance given to both Houses of Parliament, or
obeying their commands, or forbearing to leave their attendance
upon the Parliament without licence, or for any other occasion
arising from these unhappy differences between your Majesty
and both Houses of Parliament, upon the like petition of both
Houses.

These things being granted and performed, as it hath always
been our hearty prayer, so shall we be enabled to make it our
hopeful endeavour that your Majesty and your people may
enjoy the blessings of peace, truth and justice ; the royalty
and greatness of your throne may be supported by the loyal
and bountiful affections of your people ; their liberties and
privileges maintained by your Majesty's protection and justice ;
and this public honour and happiness of your Majesty and
all your dominions communicated to other Churches and States
of your alliance, and derived to your royal posterity and the
future generations in this kingdom for ever.

58. THE SOLEMN LEAGUE AND COVENANT.

[Taken by the House of Commons, September 25, 1643. Rushworth,
v. 478. See *Great Civil War*, i. 229–236.]

*A solemn league and covenant for Reformation and Defence of
Religion, the honour and happiness of the King, and the
peace and safety of the three kingdoms of England, Scotland
and Ireland.*

We noblemen, barons, knights, gentlemen, citizens, burgesses, ministers of the Gospel, and commons of all sorts
in the kingdoms of England, Scotland and Ireland, by the
providence of God living under one King, and being of one
reformed religion ; having before our eyes the glory of God,
and the advancement of the kingdom of our Lord and
Saviour Jesus Christ, the honour and happiness of the King's
Majesty and his posterity, and the true public liberty, safety
and peace of the kingdoms, wherein every one's private

condition is included; and calling to mind the treacherous and bloody plots, conspiracies, attempts and practices of the enemies of God against the true religion and professors thereof in all places, especially in these three kingdoms, ever since the reformation of religion; and how much their rage, power and presumption are of late, and at this time increased and exercised, whereof the deplorable estate of the Church and kingdom of Ireland, the distressed estate of the Church and kingdom of England, and the dangerous estate of the Church and kingdom of Scotland, are present and public testimonies: we have (now at last) after other means of supplication, remonstrance, protestations and sufferings, for the preservation of ourselves and our religion from utter ruin and destruction, according to the commendable practice of these kingdoms in former times, and the example of God's people in other nations, after mature deliberation, resolved and determined to enter into a mutual and solemn league and covenant, wherein we all subscribe, and each one of us for himself, with our hands lifted up to the most high God, do swear,

I.

That we shall sincerely, really and constantly, through the grace of God, endeavour in our several places and callings, the preservation of the reformed religion in the Church of Scotland, in doctrine, worship, discipline and government, against our common enemies; the reformation of religion in the kingdoms of England and Ireland, in doctrine, worship, discipline and government, according to the Word of God, and the example of the best reformed Churches; and we shall endeavour to bring the Churches of God in the three kingdoms to the nearest conjunction and uniformity in religion, confession of faith, form of Church government, directory for worship and catechising, that we, and our posterity after us, may, as brethren, live in faith and love, and the Lord may delight to dwell in the midst of us.

II.

That we shall in like manner, without respect of persons, endeavour the extirpation of Popery, prelacy (that is, Church

government by Archbishops, Bishops, their Chancellors and
Commissaries, Deans, Deans and Chapters, Archdeacons, and
all other ecclesiastical officers depending on that hierarchy),
superstition, heresy, schism, profaneness, and whatsoever shall
be found to be contrary to sound doctrine and the power of
godliness, lest we partake in other men's sins, and thereby be in
danger to receive of their plagues; and that the Lord may
be one, and His name one in the three kingdoms.

III.

We shall with the same sincerity, reality and constancy, in
our several vocations, endeavour with our estates and lives
mutually to preserve the rights and privileges of the Parliaments,
and the liberties of the kingdoms, and to preserve and defend
the King's Majesty's person and authority, in the preservation
and defence of the true religion and liberties of the kingdoms,
that the world may bear witness with our consciences of our
loyalty, and that we have no thoughts or intentions to diminish
His Majesty's just power and greatness.

IV.

We shall also with all faithfulness endeavour the discovery
of all such as have been or shall be incendiaries, malignants
or evil instruments, by hindering the reformation of religion,
dividing the King from his people, or one of the kingdoms
from another, or making any faction or parties amongst the
people, contrary to the league and covenant, that they may be
brought to public trial and receive condign punishment, as the
degree of their offences shall require or deserve, or the supreme
judicatories of both kingdoms respectively, or others having
power from them for that effect, shall judge convenient.

V.

And whereas the happiness of a blessed peace between these
kingdoms, denied in former times to our progenitors, is by the
good providence of God granted to us, and hath been lately
concluded and settled by both Parliaments: we shall each one
of us, according to our places and interest, endeavour that they

may remain conjoined in a firm peace and union to all posterity, and that justice may be done upon the wilful opposers thereof, in manner expressed in the precedent articles.

VI.

We shall also, according to our places and callings, in this common cause of religion, liberty and peace of the kingdom, assist and defend all those that enter into this league and covenant, in the maintaining and pursuing thereof; and shall not suffer ourselves, directly or indirectly, by whatsoever combination, persuasion or terror, to be divided and withdrawn from this blessed union and conjunction, whether to make defection to the contrary part, or give ourselves to a detestable indifferency or neutrality in this cause, which so much concerneth the glory of God, the good of the kingdoms, and the honour of the King; but shall all the days of our lives zealously and constantly continue therein, against all opposition, and promote the same according to our power, against all lets and impediments whatsoever; and what we are not able ourselves to suppress or overcome we shall reveal and make known, that it may be timely prevented or removed: all which we shall do as in the sight of God.

And because these kingdoms are guilty of many sins and provocations against God, and His Son Jesus Christ, as is too manifest by our present distresses and dangers, the fruits thereof: we profess and declare, before God and the world, our unfeigned desire to be humbled for our own sins, and for the sins of these kingdoms; especially that we have not as we ought valued the inestimable benefit of the Gospel; that we have not laboured for the purity and power thereof; and that we have not endeavoured to receive Christ in our hearts, nor to walk worthy of Him in our lives, which are the causes of other sins and transgressions so much abounding amongst us; and our true and unfeigned purpose, desire and endeavour, for ourselves and all others under our power and charge, both in public and in private, in all duties we owe to God and man, to amend our lives, and each one to go before another in the example of a real reformation, that the Lord may turn away His wrath and heavy indignation, and establish these Churches and kingdoms in truth and peace. And this covenant we make in the presence of Almighty God, the Searcher of all hearts, with a true intention to perform the same, as we shall answer at that Great Day when the secrets of all hearts shall be disclosed: most humbly beseeching the Lord to strengthen us by His Holy Spirit for this end, and to bless our desires and proceedings with such success as may be a deliverance and safety to His people, and encouragement to the Christian Churches groaning under or in danger of the yoke of Antichristian tyranny, to join in the same or like association and covenant, to the glory of God, the enlargement of the kingdom of Jesus Christ, and the peace and tranquillity of Christian kingdoms and commonwealths.

59. The Ordinance appointing the First Committee of both Kingdoms.

[February 16, 164¾. Journals of the House of Lords, vi. 430. See *Great Civil War*, i. 306.]

An Ordinance for the appointing a Committee of both Houses of Parliament, to join with the Committees and Commissioners of Scotland, for the better managing the affairs of both nations in the common cause, according to the ends expressed in the late covenant and treaty between the two nations of England and Scotland.

Whereas, by the covenant and treaty ratified and established between the two kingdoms, both nations are engaged in one common cause against the enemies of their religion and liberties, and, by the late entrance of the Scottish forces into this kingdom in pursuance hereof, are firmly united in a joint posture of arms for their own necessary defence, and for the attaining of the ends expressed in the covenant and treaty.

And whereas both kingdoms have thought it necessary that they should be joined in their counsels as well as in their forces, and, in pursuance thereof, the Convention of the Estates

of Scotland have appointed Committees, residing in Scotland
and in the Scottish Army, and have sent some of the
said Committees[1] as Commissioners for the purposes aforesaid, to repair unto and to reside near the Parliament, who,
since their arrival, have presented their commission and powers,
with their earnest desire that the Parliament would lay down
some speedy and constant way of communicating the desires
and joining the counsels of both kingdoms, in pursuance of
the covenant, treaty and common interest of His Majesty's
dominions.

In consideration hereof, the Lords and Commons do nominate,
ordain and appoint Algernon Earl of Northumberland, Robert
Earl of Essex (Lord General), Robert Earl of Warwick (Lord
Admiral), Edward Earl of Manchester, William Viscount Say
and Sele, Philip Lord Wharton, John Lord Robarts, William
Pierpoint, Sir Henry Vane (senior), Sir Philip Stapleton, Sir
William Waller, Sir Gilbert Gerrard, Sir William Armyne,
Sir Arthur Haslerigg, Sir Henry Vane (junior), John Crewe,
Robert Wallop, Oliver St. John (Solicitor-General), Oliver
Cromwell, Samuel Browne and John Glynn (Recorder), or
any six of them, whereof one Lord and two Commoners, to
treat with the Committees and Commissioners appointed by our
brethren of Scotland, in such things as shall by them be propounded from and in the name of the kingdom of Scotland, for
the ends aforesaid; as likewise to propound to the Committees
and Commissioners of Scotland whatever they shall receive in
charge from both Houses, and, from time to time, to advise
and consult concerning the same, and report the results to
both Houses.

And further power and authority is hereby given to them,
or any six of them, whereof one Lord and two Commoners
as a joint Committee with the Committee and Commissioners
of Scotland, to advise, consult, order and direct, concerning the
carrying on and managing of the war for the best advantage
of the three kingdoms, and the keeping a good intelligence
between the three kingdoms, their forces, committees and
counsels; and likewise with power to hold good correspondence
and intelligence with foreign States; and further to advise and

---

[1] As we should now say, 'members of the Committee.'

consult of all things in pursuance of the ends in the late covenant and treaty.

Provided always, that nothing in this Ordinance shall authorise the Committee hereby appointed to advise, treat or consult concerning any cessation of arms or making peace, without express directions from both Houses of Parliament.

And lastly, the said Committee are to observe such orders and directions as they, from time to time, shall receive from both Houses of Parliament; provided also, that this Ordinance shall continue for three months and no longer.

60. The Ordinance appointing the Second Committee of both Kingdoms.

[May 22, 1644.   Journals of the House of Commons, iii. 504.
See *Great Civil War*, i. 343.]

An Ordinance for the appointing a Committee of both Houses, to join with the Committees and Commissioners of Scotland, for the better managing of the affairs of both nations, in the common cause, according to the ends expressed in the last covenant and treaty between the two nations of England and Scotland.

Whereas by the covenant and treaty ratified and established between the two kingdoms, both nations are engaged in one common cause against the enemies of the religion and liberties; and by the late entrance of the Scottish forces into this kingdom, in pursuance hereof, are firmly united in a joint posture of arms for their own necessary defence, and for maintaining of the ends expressed in the covenant; and forasmuch as nothing can be more advantageous and conducible to the purpose aforesaid than that the conduct of the affairs of both kingdoms, in prosecution of the ends before mentioned, be managed by the joint advice and direction of both nations or their Committees authorised in that behalf; that is, not only the counsels, resolutions and forces of both kingdoms may be to the utmost improved to the common good, and a right intelligence and firmer unity held and preserved between and within themselves, but also a good correspondency may be set on foot and maintained abroad with other States in a joint way, to countermine the wicked confederacies and designs of the Popish and Antichristian faction in all parts against the true Protestant reformed religion, and the welfare of His Majesty's three kingdoms: and whereas the Convention of the Estates of Scotland have appointed Committees residing in Scotland and in the Scottish army, and have sent some of the said Committees as Commissioners for the purposes aforesaid, to repair unto and reside near the two Houses, whereof some are already in the city: in consideration hereof the Lords and Commons assembled in Parliament, do nominate, ordain and appoint Algernon Earl of Northumberland, Robert Earl of Essex (Lord General), Robert Earl of Warwick (Lord Admiral), Edward Earl of Manchester, William Viscount Say and Sele, Philip Lord Wharton, John Lord Robarts, William Pierpoint, Sir Henry Vane (senior), Sir Philip Stapilton, Sir William Waller, Sir Gilbert Gerard, Sir William Armyn, Sir Arthur Haslilrig, Sir Henry Vane (junior), John Crew, Robert Wallop, Oliver St. John (Solicitor-General), Oliver Cromwell, Samuel Browne, John Glyn (Recorder), or any three of them (whereof a member of each House to be present), to treat with the Committees and Commissioners appointed by our brethren of Scotland, in such things as shall by them be propounded from and in the name of the kingdom of Scotland for the ends aforesaid: and, from time to time, to advise and consult with them concerning the same: and do further give power unto the members of both Houses above-named, and unto John Earl of Loudoun (Lord High Chancellor of Scotland), John Lord Maitland, Sir Archibald Johnston of Warriston, and Mr. Robert Barclay, or any seven of them (whereof a member of each House is to be present), as a Committee to order and direct whatsoever doth or may concern the managing of the war, keeping good intelligence between the forces of the three kingdoms, and whatsoever may concern the peace of His Majesty's dominions, and all other things in pursuance of the ends expressed in the said Covenant and Treaty: and the Committee of both Houses are to observe such orders as they shall, from time to time, receive from both Houses.

61. THE PROPOSITIONS OF THE HOUSES PRESENTED TO THE
   KING AT OXFORD, AND SUBSEQUENTLY DISCUSSED AT
   THE TREATY OF UXBRIDGE.

[Presented to the King, November 24[1], 1644.   Journals of the House
of Lords, vii. 54.   See *Great Civil War*, ii. 76, 85, 124.

1. That by Act of Parliament in each kingdom respectively,
all oaths, declarations and proclamations against both or either
of the Houses of Parliament of England, and the late Convention of Estates in Scotland, or Committees flowing from
the Parliament or Convention in Scotland, or their Ordinances
and proceedings, or against any for adhering unto them; and
all indictments, outlawries and attainders against any for the
said causes, be declared null, suppressed and forbidden; and
that this be publicly intimated in all parish churches within
His Majesty's dominions, and all other places needful.

2. That His Majesty, according to the laudable example
of his royal father of happy memory, may be pleased to swear
and sign the late solemn League and Covenant; and that an
Act of Parliament be passed in both kingdoms respectively, for
enjoining the taking thereof by all the subjects of the three
kingdoms, and the Ordinances concerning the manner of taking
the same in both kingdoms be confirmed by Acts of Parliament
respectively, with such penalties as, by mutual advice of both
kingdoms, shall be agreed upon.

3. That the Bill be passed for the utter abolishing and
taking away of all Archbishops, Bishops, their Chancellors
and Commissaries, Deans and Sub-Deans, Deans and Chapters,
Archdeacons, Canons and Prebendaries, and all Chanters,
Chancellors, Treasurers, Sub-Treasurers, Succentors and Sacrists,
and all Vicars Choral and Choristers, old Vicars and new
Vicars of any Cathedral or Collegiate Church; and all other
their under officers out of the Church of England and dominion
of Wales, and out of the Church of Ireland, with such alterations concerning the estates of Prelates, as shall agree with
the articles of the late Treaty of the date at Edinburgh,
29 of November, 1643, and joint Declaration of both kingdoms.

[1] See Journals of the House of Lords, vii. 82.

4. That the Ordinance concerning the calling and sitting of the Assembly of Divines be confirmed by Act of Parliament.

5. The reformation of religion, according to the Covenant, be settled by Act of Parliament, in such manner as both Houses shall agree upon after consultation had with the Assembly of Divines; and for as much as both kingdoms are mutually obliged, by the same Covenant, to endeavour the nearest conjunction and uniformity in matters of religion, that such unity and uniformity in religion, according to the Covenant, as after consultation had with the Divines of both kingdoms, now assembled, shall be jointly agreed upon by both Houses of the Parliament of England, and by the Church and kingdom of Scotland, be confirmed by Acts of Parliament of both kingdoms respectively.

6. That for the more effectual disabling Jesuits, Priests, Papists and Popish recusants from disturbing the State and deluding the laws, and for the better discovering and speedy conviction of recusants, an oath be established by Act of Parliament, to be administered by them, wherein they shall abjure and renounce the Pope's supremacy, the doctrine of transubstantiation, purgatory, worshipping of the consecrated host, crucifixes and images, and all other Popish superstitions and errors: and refusing the said oath, being tendered in such manner as shall be appointed by the said Act, to be sufficient conviction in law of recusancy.

7. An Act of Parliament for education of the children of Papists by Protestants, in the Protestant religion.

8. An Act for the true levying of the penalties against them, which penalties to be levied and disposed in such manner as both Houses shall agree on, wherein to be provided that His Majesty shall have no loss.

9. That an Act be passed in Parliament, whereby the practices of Papists against the State may be prevented, and the laws against them duly executed, and a stricter course taken to prevent the saying or hearing of Mass in the Court or any other part of this kingdom.

10. The like for the kingdom of Scotland, concerning the four last preceding propositions, in such manner as the Estates of Parliament there shall think fit.

11. That the King do give his royal assent,

To an Act for the due observation of the Lord's Day;

And to the Bill for the suppression of innovations in churches and chapels, in and about the worship of God, and for the better advancement of the preaching of God's Holy Word in all parts of this kingdom;

And to the Bill against the enjoying of pluralities of benefices by spiritual persons, and non-residency;

And to an Act to be framed and agreed upon by both Houses of Parliament, for the reforming and regulating of both Universities, of the Colleges of Westminster, Winchester and Eton;

And to an Act in like manner to be agreed upon for the suppressing of interludes and stage plays: this Act to be perpetual;

And to an Act for the taking the accounts of the kingdom;

And to an Act to be made for relief of sick and maimed soldiers, and of poor widows and children of soldiers;

And to such Act or Acts for raising of moneys for the payment and satisfying of the public debts and damages of the kingdom, and other public uses as shall hereafter be agreed on by both Houses of Parliament;

And to an Act or Acts of Parliament for taking away the Court of Wards and Liveries, and all Wardships, Liveries, *primer seisins*, and *ouster les mains*, and all other charges incident or arising for or by reason of Wardship, Livery, *primer seisin* or *ouster les mains*;

And for the taking away of all tenures by homage, and all fines, licences, seizures and pardons for alienation, and all other charges incident thereunto, and for turning of all tenures by knight service, either of His Majesty or others, or by knight service or socage *in capite* of His Majesty, into free and common socage: and that His Majesty will please to accept, in recompense thereof, £100,000 *per annum*;

And give assurance of his consenting in the Parliament of Scotland to an Act ratifying the Acts of Convention of the Estates of Scotland, called by the Council and Conservatory of Peace and the Commissioners for common burdens, and assembled the 22nd day of June, 1643, and several times continued since in such manner, and with such additions and other Acts as the Estates convened in this present Parliament shall think convenient[1].

12. That an Act be passed in the Parliaments of both kingdoms respectively for confirmation of the treaties passed betwixt the two kingdoms, viz. the large treaty[2], the late treaty for the coming of the Scots army into England and the settling of the garrison of Berwick of the 29th of November, 1643; the treaty concerning Ireland of the 6th of August, 1642; with all other ordinances and proceedings passed betwixt the two kingdoms in pursuance of the said treaties.

13[3]. That an Act of Parliament be passed to make void the cessation of Ireland, and all treaties with the rebels without consent of both Houses of Parliament, and to settle the prosecution of the war in Ireland in both Houses of Parliament, to be managed by the joint advice of both kingdoms, and the King to assist and to do no act to discountenance or molest them therein.

14. That an Act be passed in the Parliaments of both kingdoms respectively for establishing the joint declaration of both kingdoms, bearing date the 30th of January, 1643, in England, and 1644 in Scotland, with the qualifications ensuing:—

5. That the persons who shall expect no pardon be only these following: Rupert and Maurice, Count Palatines of the Rhine, James Earl of Derby, John Earl of Bristol, William Earl of Newcastle, Francis Lord Cottington, John Lord Paulet, George Lord Digby, Edward Lord Lyttelton, William Laud, Archbishop of Canterbury, Matthew Wren, Bishop of Ely, Sir Robert Heath, Knight, Doctor Bramhall, Bishop of Derry, Sir John Byron, Knight, Sir William Widdrington, Colonel George Goring, Henry Jermyn, Esq., Sir Ralph Hopton, Sir Francis Doddington, Mr. Endymion Porter, Sir George Radcliffe, Sir Marmaduke Langdale, Sir John Hotham, Captain John Hotham his son, Sir Henry Vaughan, Sir Francis Winde-bank, Sir Richard Grenvile, Mr. Edward Hyde, Sir John

[1] Articles 12 and 13 with the preamble of 14 are misplaced by Rushworth.
[2] I.e. the treaty of 1641.
[3] The figure is omitted in the Journals.

Marley, Sir Nicholas Cole, Sir Thomas Riddell, junior, Colonel
Ward, Sir John Strangways, Sir John Culpepper, Sir Richard
Lloyd, John Bodvile, Esq., Mr. David Jenkins, Sir George
Strode, Sir Alexander Carew, Marquis of Huntly, Earl of
Montrose, Earl of Nithsdale, Earl of Traquair, Earl of Carn-
wath, Viscount of Aboyne, Lord Ogilvy, Lord Reay, Lord
Harris, Ludovic Lindsay, sometime Earl of Crawford, Patrick
Ruthven, sometime Earl of Forth, James King, sometime Lord
Eythin, Irvine younger of Drum, Gordon younger of Gight,
Leslie of Auchintoul, Sir Robert Spottiswood of Dunipace,
Colonel John Cochrane, Mr. John Maxwell, sometime pretended
Bishop of Ross, Mr. Walter Balcanquhal, and all such others,
as being processed by the Estates for treason, shall be con-
demned before the Act of oblivion be passed.

ii. All Papists and Popish recusants who have been, now are,
or shall be actually in arms, or voluntarily assisting against the
Parliaments or Estates of either kingdom.

iii. All persons who have had any hand in the plotting,
designing or assisting the rebellion in Ireland.

iv. That Humphrey Bennet, Esq., Sir Edward Ford, Sir
John Penruddock, Sir George Vaughan, Sir John Weld, Sir
Robert Lee, Sir John Pate, John Acland, Edmund Windham,
Esquires, Sir John Fizherbert, Sir Edward Laurence, Sir
Ralph Dutton, Henry Lingen, Esq., Sir William Russell of
Worcestershire, Thomas Lee of Adlington, Esq., Sir John
Girlington, Sir Paul Neale, Sir William Thorold, Sir Edward
Hussey, Sir Tho. Liddell, senior, Sir Philip Musgrave, Sir
John Digby of Nottingham, Sir Henry Fletcher, Sir Richard
Minshull, Lawrence Halstead, John Denham, Esquires, Sir
Edmund Fortescue, Peter St. Hill, Esq., Sir Thomas Tildesley,
Sir Henry Griffith, Michael Wharton, Esq., Sir Henry Spiller,
Sir George Benion, Sir Edward Nicholas, Sir Edward Walgrave,
Sir Edward Bishop, Sir Robert Ouseley, Sir John Mandy,
Lord Cholmley, Sir Thomas Aston, Sir Lewis Dives, Sir Peter
Osborne, Samuel Thornton, Esq., Sir John Lucas, John Blaney,
Esq., Sir Thomas Chedle, Sir Nicholas Kemish, and Hugh
Lloyd, Esq., and all such of the Scottish nation as have
concurred in the votes at Oxford against the kingdom of
Scotland and their proceedings, or have sworn or subscribed

the Declaration against the Convention and Covenant; and all such as have assisted the rebellion in the North, or the invasion in the South of the said kingdom of Scotland, or the late invasion made there by the Irish and their adherents; and that the members of either House of Parliament, who have not only deserted the Parliament, but have also been voted by both kingdoms traitors, may be removed from His Majesty's counsels, and be restrained from coming within the verge of the Court; and that they may not without the advice and consent of both kingdoms, bear any office or have any employment concerning the State or Commonwealth; and also, that the members of either House of Parliament who have deserted the Parliament and adhered to the enemies thereof, and not rendered themselves before the last of October, 1644, may be removed from His Majesty's counsels, and be restrained from coming within the verge of the Court, and that they may not, without the advice and consent of both Houses of Parliament, bear any office or have any employment concerning the State or Commonwealth; and in case any of them shall offend therein, to be guilty of high treason, and incapable of any pardon by His Majesty, and their estates to be disposed as both Houses of Parliament in England, or the Estates of the Parliament in Scotland respectively, shall think fit.

v. That by Act of Parliament all Judges and officers towards the law common or civil, who have deserted the Parliament and adhered to the enemies thereof, be made incapable of any place of judicature or office, towards the law common or civil: and that all Serjeants, Counsellors and Attorneys, Doctors, Advocates and Proctors of the law common or civil, who have deserted the Parliament and adhered to the enemies thereof, be made incapable of any practice in the law common or civil, either in public or in private: and that they, and likewise all Bishops, Clergymen, and other ecclesiastical persons, who have deserted the Parliament and adhered to the enemies thereof, shall not be capable of any preferment or employment, either in Church or Commonwealth, without the advice and consent of both Houses of Parliament.

vi. The persons of all others to be free of all personal censure, notwithstanding any act or thing done in or concerning this war, they taking the Covenant.

vii. The estates of those persons, excepted in the first three preceding qualifications, to pay public debts and damages.

viii. A third part in full value of the estates of the persons made incapable of any employment as aforesaid, to be employed for the payment of the public debts and damages, according to the Declaration.

ix. And likewise a tenth part of the estates of all other delinquents within the joint Declarations; and in case the estates and proportions aforementioned shall not suffice for the payment of the public engagement, whereunto they are only to be employed, that then a new proportion may be appointed by the joint advice of both kingdoms, providing it exceed not the one moiety of the estates of the persons made incapable as aforesaid, and that it exceed not a sixth part of the estate of the other delinquents.

x. That the persons and estates of all common soldiers, and others of the kingdom of England, who in lands or goods be not worth £200 sterling; and the persons and estates of all common soldiers, and others of the kingdom of Scotland, who in lands or goods be not worth £100 sterling, be at liberty and discharged.

xi. That an Act be passed whereby the debts of the kingdom, and the persons of delinquents, and the value of their estates may be known; and which Act shall appoint in what manner the confiscations and proportions before mentioned may be levied and applied to the discharge of the said engagements.

15. That by Act of Parliament the subjects of the kingdom of England may be appointed to be armed, trained and disciplined in such manner as both Houses shall think fit, the like for the kingdom of Scotland, in such manner as the Estates of Parliament there shall think fit.

16. That an Act of Parliament be passed for the settling of the admiralty and forces at sea, and for the raising of such moneys for maintenance of the said forces and of the navy, as both Houses of Parliament shall think fit; the like for the

kingdom of Scotland, in such manner as the Estates of Parliament there shall think fit.

17. An Act for the settling of all forces both by sea and land, in Commissioners to be nominated by both Houses of Parliament, of persons of known integrity, and such as both kingdoms may confide in for their faithfulness to religion and peace of the kingdoms   of the House of Peers, and   of the House of Commons, who shall be removed or altered from time to time as both Houses shall think fit; and when any shall die, others to be nominated in their places by the said Houses; which Commissioners shall have power,

(i) To suppress any forces raised without authority of both Houses of Parliament, or in the intervals of Parliaments, without consent of the said Commissioners, to the disturbance of the public peace of the kingdoms, and to suppress any foreign forces that shall invade this kingdom; and that it shall be high treason in any who shall levy any force without such authority or consent, to the disturbance of the public peace of the kingdoms, any commission under the Great Seal or warrant to the contrary notwithstanding, and they to be incapable of any pardon from His Majesty, and their estates to be disposed of as both Houses of Parliament shall think fit.

(ii) To preserve the peace now to be settled, and to prevent all disturbance of the public peace that may arise by occasion of the late troubles: so for the kingdom of Scotland.

(iii) To have power to send part of themselves, so as they exceed not a third part or be not under the number of   to reside in the kingdom of Scotland, to assist and vote as single persons with the Commissioners of Scotland in those matters wherein the kingdom of Scotland is only concerned: so for the kingdom of Scotland.

(iv) That the Commissioners of both kingdoms may meet as a joint Committee, as they shall see cause, or send part of themselves as aforesaid, to do as followeth:

(i) To preserve the peace between the kingdoms and the King, and every one of them.

(ii) To prevent the violation of the Articles of Peace, as aforesaid, or any troubles arising in the kingdoms by breach of the said articles, and to hear and determine all differences that may occasion the same according to the Treaty, and to do further according as they shall respectively receive instructions from both Houses of Parliament of England, or the Estates of the Parliament in Scotland, and in the intervals of Parliaments from the Commissioners for the preservation of the public peace

(iii) To raise and join the forces of both kingdoms to resist all foreign invasion, and to suppress any forces raised within any of the kingdoms, to the disturbance of the public peace of the kingdoms, by any authority under the Great Seal, or other warrant whatsoever, without consent of both Houses of Parliament in England, and the Estates of the Parliament in Scotland, or the said Commissioners of that kingdom whereof they are subjects; and that in those cases of joint concernment to both kingdoms, the Commissioners to be directed to be all there, or such part as aforesaid, to act and direct as joint Commissioners of both kingdoms.

(iv) To order the war of Ireland according to the Ordinance of the 11th of April, and to order the militia to conserve the peace of the kingdom of Ireland.

18. That His Majesty give his assent to what the two kingdoms shall agree upon, in prosecution of the articles of the large Treaty, which are not yet finished.

19. That by Act of Parliament all Peers made since the day that Edward Lord Lyttelton, then Lord Keeper of the Great Seal, deserted the Parliament, and that the said Great Seal was surreptitiously conveyed away from the Parliament, being the 21st day of May, 1642, and who shall be hereafter made, shall not sit or vote in the Parliament of England, without consent of both Houses of Parliament; and that all honour and title conferred on any without consent of both Houses of Parliament since the 20th day of May, 1642, being the day that both Houses declared that the King, seduced by evil counsel, intended to raise war against the Parliament, be declared null and void. The like for the kingdom of Scotland, those being excepted whose patents were passed the Great Seal before the 4th of June, 1644.

20. That by Act of Parliament the Deputy or Chief Governor, or other Governors of Ireland, be nominated by both Houses of

Parliament, or in the intervals of Parliament by the Commissioners, to continue during the pleasure of the said Houses, or
in the intervals of Parliament during the pleasure of the
aforementioned Commissioners, to be approved or disallowed
by both Houses at their next sitting. And that the Chancellor
or Lord Keeper, Lord Treasurer, Commissioners of the Great
Seal or Treasury, Lord Warden of the Cinque Ports, Chancellors
of the Exchequer and Duchy, Secretary of State, Judges of
both Benches, and of the Exchequer of the kingdoms of England
and Ireland, be nominated by both Houses of Parliament, to
continue *quam diu se bene gesserint*, and in the intervals of
Parliament by the aforementioned Commissioners, to be approved
or disallowed by both Houses at their next sitting; the like for
the kingdom of Scotland, adding the Justice General, and in
such manner as the Estates in Parliament there shall think fit.

21. That by Act of Parliament the education of your Majesty's
children, and the children of your heirs and successors, be in
the true Protestant religion, and that their tutors and governors
be of known integrity, and be chosen by the Parliaments of
both kingdoms, or in the intervals of Parliaments, by the
aforenamed Commissioners, to be approved or disallowed by
both Parliaments at their next sitting. And that if they be
male, they be married to such only as are of the true Protestant
religion, if they be females, they may not be married but with
the advice and consent of both Parliaments, or in the intervals
of Parliament, of their Commissioners.

22. That your Majesty will give your royal assent to such
ways and means as the Parliaments of both kingdoms shall
think fitting for the uniting of the Protestant princes, and for
the entire restitution and re-establishment of Charles Lodowick,
Prince Elector Palatine, his heirs and successors, to his electoral
dignity, rights and dominions, provided that this extend not to
Prince Rupert or Prince Maurice, or the children of either of
them, who have been the instruments of so much bloodshed and
mischief against both kingdoms.

23. That by Act of Parliament the concluding of peace or war
with foreign Princes and States, be with advice and consent of
both Parliaments, or in the intervals of Parliaments, by their
Commissioners.

24. That an Act of Oblivion be passed in the Parliaments of both kingdoms respectively, relative to the qualifications in the propositions aforesaid, concerning the joint Declaration of both kingdoms, with the exception of all murderers, thieves, and other offenders not having relation to the war.

25. That the members of both Houses of Parliament, or others, who have during this Parliament been put out of any place or office, pension or benefit, for adhering to the Parliament, may either be restored thereunto or otherwise have recompense for the same, upon the humble desire of both Houses of Parliament. The like for the kingdom of Scotland.

26. That the armies may be disbanded at such time and in such manner as shall be agreed upon by the Parliaments of both kingdoms, or such as shall be authorised by them to that effect.

27. That an Act be passed for the granting and confirming of the charters, customs, liberties and franchises of the City of London, notwithstanding any *nonuser, misuser,* or *abuser.* That the militia of the City of London may be in the ordering and government of the Lord Mayor, Aldermen, and Commons in Common Council assembled, or such as they shall from time to time appoint, whereof the Lord Mayor and Sheriffs for the time being to be there. And that the militia of the parishes without London, and the liberties within the weekly bills of mortality, may be under command of the Lord Mayor, Aldermen, and Commons in Common Council of the said City, to be ordered in such manner as shall be agreed on and appointed by both Houses of Parliament.

That the Tower of London may be in the government of the City of London, and the chief officer and governor thereof from time to time be nominated and removable by the Common Council.

That the citizens or forces of London shall not be drawn out of the City into any other parts of the kingdom without their own consent, and that the drawing of their forces into other parts of the kingdom in these distracted times may not be drawn into example for the future.

And for prevention of inconveniences, which may happen by the long intermission of Common Councils, it is desired that there be an Act that all Bye-laws and Ordinances already made or hereafter to be made by the Lord Mayor, Aldermen, and Commons in Common Council assembled, touching the calling, continuing, directing and regulating of the same, shall be as effectual in law to all intents and purposes, as if the same were particularly enacted by the authority of Parliament. And that the Lord Mayor, Aldermen, and Commons in Common Council may add to or repeal the said Ordinances from time to time as they shall see cause.

That such other propositions as shall be made for the City for their further safety, welfare and government, and shall be approved of by both Houses of Parliament, may be granted and confirmed by Act of Parliament.

62. The King's Propositions to be discussed at Uxbridge.

[January 21, 1645. Rushworth, v. 858.]

1. That His Majesty's own revenue, magazines, towns, forts and ships, which have been taken or kept from him by force, be forthwith restored unto him.

2. That whatsoever hath been done or published contrary to the known laws of the land, or derogatory to His Majesty's legal and known power and rights, be renounced and recalled; that no seed may remain for the like to spring out of for the future.

3. That whatsoever illegal power hath been claimed or exercised by or over his subjects, as imprisoning or putting to death their persons without law, stopping their *Habeas Corpuses*, and imposing upon their estates without Act of Parliament, &c., either by both or either House, or any Committee of both or either, or by any persons appointed by any of them, be disclaimed, and all such persons so committed forthwith discharged.

4. That as His Majesty hath always professed his readiness to that purpose, so he will most cheerfully consent to any good Acts to be made for the suppression of Popery, and for the firmer settling of the Protestant religion established by law; as also that a good Bill may be framed for the better preserving of the Book of Common Prayer from scorn and violence; and

that another Bill may be framed for the ease of tender
consciences, in such particulars as shall be agreed upon.   For
all which His Majesty conceives the best expedient to be, that
a National Synod be legally called with all convenient speed.

5. That all such persons, as upon the Treaty shall be excepted
and agreed upon on either side out of the general pardon, shall
be tried *per pares*, according to the usual course and known
law of the land, and that it be left to that either to acquit or
condemn them.

6. And to the intent this Treaty may not suffer interruption
by any intervening accidents, that a cessation of arms and free
trade for all His Majesty's subjects may be agreed upon with all
possible speed.

> Given at the Court at Oxford, the twenty-first day of
> January, 1644.

63. THE SELF-DENYING ORDINANCE.

[April 3, 1645.   Rushworth, vi. 16.   See *Great Civil War*, ii. 188–191.]

*An Ordinance of the Lords and Commons assembled in Parlia-
ment, for the discharging of the Members of both Houses
from all offices, both military and civil.*

Be it ordained by the Lords and Commons assembled in
Parliament, that all and every of the members of either House
of Parliament shall be, and by authority of this Ordinance are
discharged at the end of forty days after the passing of this
Ordinance [1], of and from all and every office or command
military or civil, granted or conferred by both or either of the
said Houses of this present Parliament, or by any authority
derived from both or either of them since the 20th day of
November, 1640.

And be it further ordained, that all other governors and
commanders of an island, town, castle or fort, and all other
colonels and officers inferior to colonels in the several armies,

---

[1] In the first Ordinance sent up by the Commons on December 19, 1644,
and thrown out by the Lords on January 13, 164⅘, members of either
Houses were absolutely disqualified from serving.

not being members of either of the Houses of Parliament, shall, according to their respective commissions, continue in their several places and commands, wherein they were employed and intrusted the 20th day of March, 1644, as if this Ordinance had not been made. And that the vice-admiral, rear-admiral, and all other captains and other inferior officers in the fleet, shall, according to their several and respective commissions, continue in their several places and commands, wherein they were employed and intrusted the said 20th day of March, as if this Ordinance had not been made.

Provided always, and it is further ordained and declared, that during this war, the benefit of all offices, being neither military nor judicial, hereafter to be granted, or any way to be appointed to any person or persons by both or either House of Parliament, or by authority derived from thence, shall go and inure to such public uses as both Houses of Parliament shall appoint. And the grantees and persons executing all such offices shall be accountable to the Parliament for all the profits and perquisites thereof, and shall have no profit out of any such office, other than a competent salary for the execution of the same, in such manner as both Houses of Parliament shall order and ordain.

Provided that this Ordinance shall not extend to take away the power and authority of any Lieutenancy or Deputy-Lieutenancy in the several counties, cities or places, or of any *Custos Rotulorum*, or of any commission for Justices of Peace, or sewers, or any commission of *Oyer* and *Terminer*, or gaol-delivery.

Provided always, and it is hereby declared, that those members of either House who had offices by grant from His Majesty before this Parliament, and were by His Majesty displaced sitting this Parliament, and have since by authority of both Houses been restored, shall not by this Ordinance be discharged from their said offices or profits thereof, but shall enjoy the same; anything in this Ordinance to the contrary thereof notwithstanding.

64. THE NEGATIVE OATH.

[April 5, 1645. Rushworth, vi. 141.]

An Ordinance of the Lords and Commons assembled in Parlia-
ment, for enabling the Commissioners of the Great Seal, and
the other Committees in their several Counties, to tender an
Oath to all such persons of what degree or quality soever,
that shall come in to the protection of the Parliament.

Be it ordained by the Lords and Commons in Parliament
assembled, that all and every person of what degree or quality
soever, that hath lived or shall live within the King's quarters,
or been aiding, assisting or adhering unto the forces raised
against the Parliament, and hath or shall come to inhabit or
reside under the power and protection of the Parliament, shall
swear upon the holy evangelist in manner following:

'I, A. B., do swear from my heart that I will not directly or
indirectly adhere unto or willingly assist the King in this war,
or in this cause against the Parliament, nor any forces raised
without the consent of the two Houses of Parliament in this
cause or war. And I do likewise swear that my coming and
submitting myself under the power and protection of the
Parliament, is without any manner of design whatsoever, to
the prejudice of the proceedings of the two Houses of this
present Parliament, and without the direction, privity or advice
of the King, or any of his Council or officers, other than what
I have now made known. So help me God, and the contents of
this Book.'

And be it further ordained by the authority aforesaid, that
the Commissioners for keeping of the Great Seal of England
for the time being, shall have power, and are hereby authorised
to tender and administer the said oath unto any peer, or wife
or widow of any peer, so coming to inhabit as abovesaid.

And it shall be lawful to and for the Committee of the House
of Commons for examinations, the Committee for the militia in
London, and all Committees of Parliament in the several counties
and cities of the kingdom, to tender and administer the said
oath unto every other person so coming to inhabit as abovesaid:
and if any person (not being a member of, or assistant unto

either of the Houses of the Parliament) shall refuse or neglect to take the said oath so duly tendered unto him or her as above-said, the said Commissioners and Committees respectively shall and may commit the same person to some prison, there to remain without bail or mainprize until he shall conform thereunto.

65. ORDER OF THE TWO HOUSES FOR TAKING AWAY THE COURT OF WARDS.

[February 24, 164⅚.   Lords' Journals, viii. 183.]

That the Court of Wards and Liveries, and all wardships, liveries, *primer seisins* and *ouster les mains*, and all other charges incident or arising for or by reason of wardships, livery, *primer seisin* or *ouster les mains*, be from this day taken away; and that all tenures by homage, and all fines, licences, seizures, pardons for alienation, and all other charges incident thereunto, be likewise taken away; and that all tenures by knight service, either of His Majesty or others, or by knight service, or socage *in capite* of His Majesty, be turned into free and common socage.

66. THE PROPOSITIONS OF THE HOUSES SENT TO THE KING AT NEWCASTLE.

[Sent to the King, July 13, 1646.   Rushworth, vi. 309.   See *Great Civil War*, iii. 127.]

May it please your Majesty,

We the Lords and Commons assembled in the Parliament of England, in the name and on the behalf of the kingdom of England and Ireland, and the Commissioners of the Parliament of Scotland, in the name and on the behalf of the kingdom of Scotland, do humbly present unto your Majesty the humble desires and propositions for a safe and well-grounded peace, agreed upon by the Parliaments of both kingdoms respectively, unto which we do pray your Majesty's assent; and that they, and all such Bills as shall be tendered to your Majesty in pursuance of them, or any of them, may be established and

enacted for Statutes and Acts of Parliament, by your Majesty's
royal assent, in the Parliament of both kingdoms respectively.

1. Whereas both Houses of the Parliament of England have
been necessitated to undertake a war in their just and lawful
defence, and afterwards both kingdoms of England and Scotland joined in solemn League and Covenant were engaged to
prosecute the same ;

That by Act of Parliament in each kingdom respectively, all
oaths, declarations and proclamations heretofore had, or hereafter
to be had, against both or either of the Houses of Parliament
of England, the Parliaments of the kingdom of Scotland, and
the late Convention of Estates in Scotland, or the Committees
flowing from the Parliament or Convention in Scotland, or their
ordinances and proceedings, or against any for adhering unto
them, or for doing or executing any office, place or charge, by
any authority derived from them; and all judgments, indictments, outlawries, attainders and inquisitions in any the said
causes; and all grants thereupon had or made, or to be made
or had, be declared null, suppressed and forbidden : and that
this be publicly intimated in all parish churches within His
Majesty's dominions, and all other places needful.

2. That His Majesty, according to the laudable example of
his royal father of happy memory, may be pleased to swear and
sign the late solemn League and Covenant; and that an Act
of Parliament be passed in both kingdoms respectively, for
enjoining the taking thereof by all the subjects of the three
kingdoms; and the Ordinances concerning the manner of
taking the same in both kingdoms be confirmed by Acts of
Parliament respectively, with such penalties as, by mutual
advice of both kingdoms, shall be agreed upon.

3. That a Bill be passed for the utter abolishing and
taking away of all Archbishops, Bishops, their Chancellors
and Commissaries, Deans and Sub-deans, Deans and Chapters,
Archdeacons, Canons and Prebendaries, and all Chaunters,
Chancellors, Treasurers, Sub-treasurers, Succentors and Sacrists,
and all Vicars Choral and Choristers, old Vicars and new Vicars
of any Cathedral or Collegiate Church, and all other under
officers, out of the Church of England and dominion of Wales,
and out of the Church of Ireland, with such alterations con-

cerning the estates of Prelates, as shall agree with the articles of the late Treaty of the date at Edinburgh, November 29, 1643, and joint Declaration of both kingdoms.

4. That the Ordinances concerning the calling and sitting of the Assembly of Divines be confirmed by Act of Parliament.

5. That reformation of religion, according to the Covenant, be settled by Act of Parliament, in such manner as both Houses have agreed, or shall agree upon, after consultation had with the Assembly of Divines.

6. Forasmuch as both kingdoms are mutually obliged by the same Covenant, to endeavour the nearest conjunction and uniformity in matters of religion, according to the Covenant, as after consultation had with the Divines of both kingdoms assembled, is or shall be jointly agreed upon by both Houses of Parliament of England, and by the Church and kingdom of Scotland, be confirmed by Acts of Parliament of both kingdoms respectively.

7. That for the more effectual disabling Jesuits, Priests, Papists and Popish recusants from disturbing the State and deluding the laws, and for the better discovering and speedy conviction of recusants, an oath be established by Act of Parliament, to be administered to them, wherein they shall abjure and renounce the Pope's supremacy, the doctrine of transubstantiation, purgatory, worshipping of the consecrated host, crucifixes and images, and all other Popish superstitions and errors; and refusing the said oath, being tendered in such manner as shall be appointed by the said Act, to be a sufficient conviction of recusancy.

8. An Act of Parliament for education of the children of Papists by Protestants in the Protestant religion.

9. An Act for the true levying of the penalties against them, which penalties to be levied and disposed in such manner as both Houses shall agree on, wherein to be provided that His Majesty shall have no loss.

10. That an Act be passed in Parliament, whereby the practices of Papists against the State may be prevented, and the laws against them duly executed, and a stricter course taken to prevent the saying or hearing of Mass in the Court or any other part of this kingdom.

11. The like for the kingdom of Scotland, concerning the four last preceding propositions, in such manner as the Estates of the Parliament there shall think fit.

12. That the King do give his royal assent to an Act for the due observance of the Lord's Day;

And to the Bill for the suppression of innovations in churches and chapels, in and about the worship of God, &c.;

And for the better advancement of the preaching of God's Holy Word in all parts of this kingdom;

And to the Bill against the enjoying of pluralities of benefices by spiritual persons, and non-residency;

And to an Act to be framed and agreed upon by both Houses of Parliament, for the reforming and regulating of both Universities, of the Colleges of Westminster, Winchester and Eton;

And to such Act or Acts for raising of monies for the payment and satisfaction of the public debts and damages of the kingdom, and other public uses, as shall hereafter be agreed on by both Houses of Parliament: and that if the King doth not give his assent thereunto, then it being done by both Houses of Parliament, the same shall be as valid to all intents and purposes, as if the royal assent had been given thereunto.

The like for the kingdom of Scotland.

And that His Majesty give assurance of his consenting in the Parliament of Scotland to an Act acknowledging and ratifying the Acts of the Convention of Estates of Scotland, called by the Council and Conservers of the Peace and the Commissioners for the common burdens, and assembled the 22nd of June, 1643, and several times continued since, and of the Parliament of that kingdom since convened.

13. That the Lords and Commons in the Parliament of England assembled, shall during the space of twenty years, from the 1st of July, 1646, arm, train and discipline, or cause to be armed, trained and disciplined, all the forces of the kingdoms of England and Ireland and dominion of Wales, the Isles of Guernsey and Jersey, and the town of Berwick upon Tweed, already raised both for sea and land service; and shall arm, train and discipline, or cause to be raised, levied, armed, trained and disciplined, any other forces for land and sea service, in

the kingdoms, dominions, and places aforesaid, as in their judgments they shall from time to time, during the said space of twenty years, think fit and appoint : and that neither the King, his heirs or successors, nor any other but such as shall act by the authority or approbation of the said Lords and Commons, shall during the said space of twenty years exercise any of the powers aforesaid.

And the like for the kingdom of Scotland, if the Estates of the Parliament there shall think fit.

That money be raised and levied for the maintenance and use of the said forces for land service, and of the navy and forces for sea service, in such sort and by such ways and means as the said Lords and Commons shall from time to time, during the said space of twenty years, think fit and appoint, and not otherwise.   That all the said forces, both for land and sea service, so raised or levied, or to be raised or levied, and also the admiralty and navy, shall from time to time, during the said space of twenty years, be employed, managed, ordered and disposed by the said Lords and Commons, in such sort and by such ways and means as they shall think fit and appoint, and not otherwise.   And the said Lords and Commons, during the said space of twenty years, shall have power,

(i) To suppress all forces raised or to be raised, without authority and consent of the said Lords and Commons, to the disturbance of the public peace of the kingdoms of England and Ireland and dominion of Wales, the Isles of Guernsey and Jersey, and the town of Berwick upon Tweed, or any of them.

(ii) To suppress any foreign forces who shall invade or endeavour to invade the kingdoms of England and Ireland, dominion of Wales, the Isles of Guernsey and Jersey, and the town of Berwick upon Tweed, or any of them.

(iii) To conjoin such forces of the kingdom of England with the forces of the kingdom of Scotland, as the said Lords and Commons shall from time to time, during the said space of twenty years, judge fit and necessary ; to resist all foreign invasions, and to suppress any forces raised or to be raised against or within either of the said kingdoms, to the disturbance of the public peace of the said kingdoms, or any of them, by any authority under the Great Seal, or any warrant

whatsoever, without consent of the said Lords and Commons of
the Parliament of England, and the Parliament or the Estates
of the Parliament of Scotland respectively. And that no forces
of either kingdom shall go into or continue in the other kingdom, without the advice and desire of the said Lords and
Commons of the Parliament of England, and the Parliament
of the kingdom of Scotland, or such as shall be by them
appointed for that purpose: and that after the expiration of
the said twenty years, neither the King, his heirs or successors,
or any person or persons, by colour or pretence of any commission, power, deputation or authority, to be derived from
the King, his heirs or successors, or any of them, shall raise,
arm, train, discipline, employ, order, manage, disband or dispose
of any of the forces by sea or land, of the kingdoms of England
and Ireland, the dominion of Wales, Isles of Guernsey and
Jersey, and the town of Berwick upon Tweed: nor exercise
any of the said powers or authorities in the precedent articles
mentioned and expressed to be during the said space of twenty
years, in the said Lords and Commons: nor do any act or thing
concerning the execution of the said powers or authorities,
or any of them, without the consent of the said Lords and
Commons first had and obtained. That after the expiration
of the said twenty years, in all cases wherein the Lords and
Commons shall declare the safety of the kingdom to be concerned,
and shall thereupon pass any Bill or Bills for the raising, arming,
disciplining, employing, managing, ordering or disposing of the
forces by sea or land, of the kingdoms of England and Ireland,
the dominion of Wales, Isles of Guernsey and Jersey, and the
town of Berwick upon Tweed, or of any part of the said forces,
or concerning the admiralty and navy, or concerning the levying
of monies for the raising, maintenance or use of the said forces
for land service, or of the navy and forces for sea service, or
of any part of them: and if that the royal assent to such Bill
or Bills shall not be given in the House of Peers within such
time after the passing thereof by both Houses of Parliament,
as the said Houses shall judge fit and convenient, that then
such Bill or Bills so passed by the said Lords and Commons
as aforesaid, and to which the royal assent shall not be given
as is herein before expressed, shall nevertheless after declaration

of the said Lords and Commons made in that behalf, have the force and strength of an Act or Acts of Parliament, and shall be as valid to all intents and purposes as if the royal assent had been given thereunto.

Provided, that nothing herein before contained shall extend to the taking away of the ordinary legal power of Sheriffs, Justices of Peace, Mayors, Bailiffs, Coroners, Constables, Headboroughs, or other officers of justice, not being military officers, concerning the administration of justice; so as neither the said Sheriffs, Justices of the Peace, Mayors, Bailiffs, Coroners, Constables, Headboroughs, and other officers, nor any of them, do levy, conduct, employ or command any forces whatsoever, by colour or pretence of any commission of array, or extraordinary command from His Majesty, his heirs or successors, without the consent of the said Lords and Commons.

And if any persons shall be gathered and assembled together in warlike manner or otherwise, to the number of thirty persons, and shall not forthwith disband themselves, being required thereto by the said Lords and Commons, or command from them or any of them, especially authorised for that purpose, then such person or persons not so disbanding themselves, shall be guilty and incur the pains of high treason, being first declared guilty of such offence by the said Lords and Commons; any commission under the Great Seal, or other warrant to the contrary notwithstanding: and he or they that shall offend herein, to be incapable of any pardon from His Majesty, his heirs or successors, and their estates shall be disposed as the said Lords and Commons shall think fit, and not otherwise.

Provided, that the City of London shall have and enjoy all their rights, liberties and franchises, customs and usages, in the raising and employing the forces of that City for the defence thereof, in full and ample manner, to all intents and purposes, as they have or might have used or enjoyed the same at any time before the making of the said Act or proposition; to the end that City may be fully assured it is not the intention of the Parliament to take from them any privileges or immunities in raising or disposing of their forces which they have or might have used or enjoyed heretofore.

The like for the kingdom of Scotland, if the Estates of the Parliament there shall think fit.

14. That by Act of Parliament all Peers made since the day that Edward Lord Lyttelton, then Lord Keeper of the Great Seal, deserted the Parliament, and that the said Great Seal was surreptitiously conveyed away from the Parliament, being the 21st day of May, 1642, and who shall be hereafter made, shall not sit or vote in the Parliament of England, without consent of both Houses of Parliament; and that all honour and title conferred on any without consent of both Houses of Parliament since the 20th of May, 1642, being the day that both Houses declared that the King, seduced by evil counsel, intended to raise war against the Parliament, be null and void.

The like for the kingdom of Scotland, those being excepted whose patents were passed the Great Seal before the 14th of June, 1644.

15. That an Act be passed in the Parliaments of both Houses respectively, for confirmation of the Treaties passed between the two kingdoms; viz. the large Treaty, the late Treaty for the coming of the Scots army into England, and the settling of the garrison of Berwick, of the 29th of November, 1643, and the Treaty between Ireland of the 6th of August, 1642, for the bringing of 10,000 Scots into the province of Ulster in Ireland; with all other Ordinances and proceedings passed between the two kingdoms, and whereunto they are obliged by the aforesaid Treaties.

And that Algernon Earl of Northumberland, John Earl of Rutland, Philip Earl of Pembroke and Montgomery, Robert Earl of Essex, Theophilus Earl of Lincoln, James Earl of Suffolk, Robert Earl of Warwick, Edward Earl of Manchester, Henry Earl of Stamford, Francis Lord Dacres, Philip Lord Wharton, Francis Lord Willoughby, Dudley Lord North, John Lord Hunsdon, William Lord Gray, Edward Lord Howard of Escrick, Thomas Lord Bruce, Ferdinando Lord Fairfax, Mr. Nathaniel Fiennes, Sir William Armin, Sir Philip Stapleton, Sir Henry Vane, senior, Mr. William Pierpoint, Sir Edward Aiscough, Sir William Strickland, Sir Arthur Haslerig, Sir John Fenwick, Sir William Brereton, Sir Thomas Widdrington, Mr. John Toll, Mr. Gilbert Millington, Sir William Constable, Sir John

Wray, Sir Henry Vane, junior, Mr. Henry Darley, Oliver
St. John, Esq., His Majesty's Solicitor-General, Sir Denzil Hollis,
Mr. Alexander Rigby, Mr. Cornelius Holland, Mr. Samuel
Vassal, Mr. Peregrine Pelham, John Glyn, Esq., Recorder of
London, Mr. Henry Martin, Mr. Alderman Hoyle, Mr. John
Blackiston, Mr. Serjeant Wilde, Mr. Richard Barrois, Sir Anthony
Irby, Mr. Ashhurst, Mr. Billingham, and Mr. Tolson, Members
of both Houses of the Parliament of England, shall be the Com-
missioners for the kingdom of England, for conservation of the
peace between the two kingdoms; to act according to the powers
in that behalf expressed in the articles of the large Treaty,
and not otherwise.

That His Majesty give his assent to what the two kingdoms
shall agree upon, in prosecution of the articles of the large
Treaty, which are not yet finished.

16. That an Act be passed in the Parliaments of both
kingdoms respectively, for establishing the joint Declaration
of both kingdoms bearing date the 30th of January, 1643, in
England, and 1644 in Scotland; with the qualifications ensuing:

1st Qualification. That the persons who shall expect no
pardon be only these following : Rupert and Maurice, Counts
Palatine of the Rhine, James Earl of Derby, John Earl of
Bristol, William Earl of Newcastle, Francis Lord Cottington,
George Lord Digby, Matthew Wren, Bishop of Ely, Sir Robert
Heath, Knt., Dr. Bramhall, Bishop of Derry, Sir William Wid-
drington, Col. George Goring, Henry Jermyn, Esq., Sir Ralph
Hopton, Sir John Byron, Sir Francis Doddington, Sir Francis
Strangways, Mr. Endymion Porter, Sir George Radcliffe, Sir
Marmaduke Langdale, Henry Vaughan, Esq., now called Sir
Henry Vaughan, Sir Francis Windebank, Sir Richard Grenvile,
Mr. Edward Hyde, now called Sir Edward Hyde, Sir John
Marley, Sir Nicholas Cole, Sir Thomas Riddell, junior, Sir John
Culpepper, Mr. Richard Lloyd, now called Sir Richard Lloyd,
Mr. David Jenkins, Sir George Strode, George Carteret, Esq.,
now called Sir George Carteret, Sir Charles Dallison, Knt.,
Richard Lane, Esq., now called Sir Richard Lane, Sir Edward
Nicholas, John Ashburnham, Esq., Sir Edward Herbert, Knt.,
Attorney-General, Earl of Traquair, Lord Harris, Lord Reay,
George Gordon, sometime Marquis of Huntly, James Graham,

sometime Earl of Montrose, Robert Maxwell, late Earl of Nithsdale, Robert Dalyel, sometime Earl of Carnwath, James Gordon,
sometime Viscount of Aboyne, Ludovic Lindsay, sometime Earl
of Crawford, James Ogilvy, sometime Earl of Airlie, James
Ogilvy, sometime Lord Ogilvy, Patrick Ruthven, sometime Earl
of Forth, James King, sometime Lord Eythin, Alaster Mac-
donald, Irvine the younger of Drum, Gordon the younger of
Gight, Leslie of Auchintoul, Col. John Cochrane, Graham of
Gorthie, Mr. John Maxwell, sometime pretended Bishop of Ross,
and all such others as being processed by the Estates for treason,
shall be condemned before the Act of Oblivion be passed.

2nd Qualification.   All Papists and Popish recusants who
have been, now are, or shall be actually in arms, or volun-
tarily assisting against the Parliament or Estates of either
kingdom ; and by name the Marquis of Winton, Earl of
Worcester, Edward Lord Herbert of Raglan, son to the Earl
of Worcester, Lord Brudenell, Caryl Mollineux, Esq., Lord
Arundel of Wardour, Sir Francis Howard, Sir John Wintour,
Sir Charles Smith, Sir John Preston, Sir Basil Brooke, Lord
Audley, Earl of Castlehaven, in the kingdom of Ireland, William
Sheldon, of Beely, Esq., Sir Henry Bedingfield.

3rd Qualification.   All persons who have had any hand in
the plotting, designing or assisting the rebellion of Ireland,
except such persons who have only assisted the said rebellion,
have rendered themselves, or come in to the Parliament of
England.

4th Qualification.   That Humphrey Bennet, Esq., Sir
Edward Ford, Sir John Penruddock, Sir George Vaughan,
Sir John Weld, Sir Robert Lee, Sir John Pate, John Acland,
Edmund Windham, Esq., Sir John Fitzherbert, Sir Edward
Lawrence, Sir Ralph Dutton, Henry Lingen, Esq., Sir William
Russell of Worcestershire, Thomas Lee of Adlington, Esq., Sir
John Girlington, Sir Paul Neale, Sir William Thorold, Sir
Edward Hussey, Sir Thomas Liddell, senior, Sir Philip Mus-
grave, Sir John Digby of Nottinghamshire, Sir Henry Fletcher,
Sir Richard Minshull, Lawrence Halstead, John Denham, Esq.,
Sir Edmund Fortescue, Peter St. Hill, Esq., Sir Thomas Til-
desley, Sir Henry Griffith, Michael Wharton, Esq., Sir Henry
Spiller, Mr. George Benion, now called Sir George Benion,

Sir Edward Walgrave, Sir Robert Ouseley, Sir John Mandy, Lord Cholmley, Sir Thomas Acton, Sir Lewis Dives, Sir Peter Osborne, Samuel Thornton, Esq., Sir John Lucas, John Blaney, Esq., Sir Thomas Chedle, Sir Nicholas Kemish, Hugh Lloyd, Esq., Sir Nicholas Crispe, Sir Peter Ricaut.

And all such of the Scottish nation as have concurred in the votes at Oxford, against the kingdom of Scotland and their proceedings, or have sworn or subscribed the Declaration against the Convention and Covenant; and all such as have assisted the rebellion in the North, or the invasion in the South of the said kingdom of Scotland, or the late invasion made there by the Irish, and their adherents, be removed from His Majesty's counsels, and be restrained from coming within the verge of the Court; and that they may not without the advice and consent of both Houses of the Parliament of England, or the Estates in the Parliament of Scotland respectively, bear any office, or have any employment concerning the State or Commonwealth: and in case any of them should offend therein, to be guilty of high treason, and incapable of any pardon from His Majesty, and their estates to be disposed of as both Houses of the Parliament of England, or the Estates of the Parliament in Scotland respectively shall think fit: and that one full third part upon full value of the estates of the persons aforesaid, made incapable of employment as aforesaid, be employed for the payment of the public debts and damages, according to the Declaration.

1st Branch. That the late members, or any who pretended themselves late members of either House of Parliament, who have not only deserted the Parliament, but have also sat in the unlawful assembly at Oxford, called or pretended by some to be a Parliament, and voted both kingdoms traitors, and have not voluntarily rendered themselves before the last of October, 1644, be removed from His Majesty's counsels, and be restrained from coming within the verge of the Court; and that they may not, without advice and consent of both kingdoms, bear any office or have any employment concerning the State or Commonwealth. And in case any of them shall offend therein, to be guilty of high treason, and be incapable of any pardon by His Majesty; and their estates to be disposed as both Houses of

Parliament in England, or the Estates of the Parliament of Scotland respectively shall think fit.

2nd Branch.   That the late members, or any who pretended themselves members of either House of Parliament, who have sat in the unlawful assembly at Oxford, called or pretended by some to be a Parliament, and have not voluntarily rendered themselves before the last of October, 1644, be removed from His Majesty's counsels, and restrained from coming within the verge of the Court; and that they may not, without the advice and consent of both Houses of Parliament, bear any office or have any employment concerning the State or Commonwealth. And in case any of them shall offend therein, to be guilty of high treason, and incapable of any pardon from His Majesty, and their estates to be disposed of as both Houses of the Parliament of England shall think fit.

3rd Branch.   That the late members, or any who pretended themselves members of either House of Parliament, who have deserted the Parliament, and adhered to the enemies thereof, and have not rendered themselves before the last of October, 1644, be removed from His Majesty's counsels, and be restrained from coming within the verge of the Court; and that they may not, without the advice and consent of both Houses of Parliament, bear any office or have any employment concerning the State or Commonwealth.   And in case any of them shall offend therein, to be guilty of high treason, and incapable of any pardon from His Majesty, and their estates to be disposed as both Houses of Parliament in England shall think fit.

5th Qualification.   That all Judges and officers towards the law, common or civil, who have deserted the Parliament and adhered to the enemies thereof, be incapable of any place of judicature, or office towards the law, common or civil: and that all serjeants, councillors, and attorneys, doctors, advocates, and proctors of the law, common or civil, either in public or private, shall not be capable of any preferment or employment in the Commonwealth, without the advice and consent of both Houses of Parliament: and that no Bishop or Clergyman, no Master or Fellow of any College or Hall in either of the Universities, or elsewhere, or any Master of school or hospital, or any ecclesiastical person, who hath deserted the Parliament and adhered to the enemies thereof, shall hold or enjoy, or be capable of any preferment or employment in Church or Commonwealth. But all their said several preferments, places and promotions, shall be utterly void, as if they were naturally dead : nor shall they otherwise use their function of the ministry, without advice and consent of both Houses of Parliament : provided, that no lapse shall incur by this vacancy until six months past after notice thereof.

6th Qualification. That all persons who have been actually in arms against the Parliament, or have counselled or voluntarily assisted the enemies thereof, are disabled to be Sheriffs, Justices of the Peace, Mayors, or other Head Officers of any City or Corporation, Commissioners of *Oyer* and *Terminer*, or to sit and serve as members or assistants in either of the Houses of Parliament, or to have any military employments in this kingdom, without the consent of both Houses of Parliament.

7th Qualification. The persons of all others to be free of all personal censure, notwithstanding any act or thing done in or concerning this war, they taking the Covenant.

8th Qualification. The estates of those persons excepted in the first three precedent qualifications, and the estates of Edward Lord Lyttelton and of William Laud, late Archbishop of Canterbury, to pay public debts and damages.

9th Qualification. 1st Branch : that two full parts in three to be divided of all the estates of the members of either House of Parliament, who have not only deserted the Parliament, but have also voted both kingdoms traitors, and have not rendered themselves before the 1st of December, 1645, shall be taken and employed for the payment of the public debts and damages of the kingdom.

2nd Branch : that two full parts in three to be divided of the estates of such late members of either House of Parliament as sat in the unlawful assembly at Oxford, and shall not have rendered themselves before the 1st of December, 1645, shall be taken and employed for the payment of the public debts and damages of the kingdom.

3rd Branch : that one full moiety of the estates of such persons, late members of either of the Houses of Parliament, who have deserted the Parliament, and adhered to the enemies thereof, and shall not have rendered themselves before the 1st of December, 1645, shall be taken and employed for the payment of public debts and damages of the kingdom.

10th Qualification.   That a full third part of the value of the estates of all Judges and officers towards the law, common or civil, and of all serjeants, councillors and attorneys, doctors, advocates and proctors of the law, common or civil; and of all Bishops, Clergymen, Masters and Fellows of any College or Hall in either of the Universities, or elsewhere; and of all Masters of hospitals, and of ecclesiastical persons, who have deserted the Parliament and adhered to the enemies thereof, and have not rendered themselves before the 1st of December, 1645, shall be taken and employed for the payment of public debts and damages of the kingdom.

That a full sixth part of the value of the estates of the persons excepted in the sixth qualification, concerning such as have been actually in arms against the Parliament, or have counselled or voluntarily assisted the enemies thereof, and are disabled according to the said qualification, to be taken and employed for the payment of the public debts and damages of the kingdom.

11th Qualification.   That the persons and estates of all common soldiers and others of the kingdom of England, who in lands or goods be not worth £200 sterling, and the persons and estates of all common soldiers and others of the kingdom of Scotland, who in his lands or goods be not worth £100 sterling, be at liberty and discharged.

1st Branch.   This proposition to stand as to the English, and as to the Scots likewise, if the Parliament of Scotland or their Commissioners shall think fit.

2nd Branch.   That the 1st of May last is now the day limited for the persons to come in, that are comprised within the former qualification.

That an Act be passed, whereby the debts of the kingdom and the persons of delinquents, and the value of their estates may be known: and which Act shall appoint in what manner the confiscations and proportions before mentioned may be levied and applied to the discharge of the said engagements.

The like for the kingdom of Scotland, if the Estates of the

Parliament, or such as shall have power from them, shall think fit.

17. That an Act of Parliament be passed to declare and make void the cessation of Ireland, and all Treaties and conclusions of peace, or any articles thereupon with the rebels, without consent of both Houses of Parliament: and to settle the prosecution of the wars of Ireland, as both Houses of the Parliament of England have agreed, or shall agree upon, after consultation had with the Assembly of Divines here.

That the Deputy or Chief Governor, or other Governors of Ireland, and the Presidents of the several provinces of that kingdom, be nominated by both the Houses of the Parliament of England; or in the intervals of Parliament, by such Committees of both Houses of Parliament as both Houses of the Parliament of England shall nominate and appoint for that purpose: and that the Chancellor or Lord Keeper, Lord Treasurer, Commissioners of the Great Seal or Treasury, Lord Warden of the Cinque Ports, Chancellor of the Exchequer and Duchy, Secretaries of State, Master of the Rolls, Judges of both Benches, and Barons of the Exchequer, of the kingdoms of England and Ireland, and the Vice-Treasurer and Treasurer at War, of the kingdom of Ireland, be nominated by both Houses of the Parliament of England, to continue *quam diu se bene gesserint*; and in the intervals of Parliament by the afore-mentioned Committee, to be approved or disallowed by both Houses at their next sitting.

The like for the kingdom of Scotland, concerning the nomination of the Lords of the Privy Council, Lords of Session and Exchequer, Offices of State and Justice-General, in such manner as the Estates of Parliament there shall think fit.

18. That the militia of the City of London, and liberties thereof, may be in the ordering and government of the Lord Mayor, Aldermen, and Commons in Council assembled, or such as they shall from time to time appoint (whereof the Lord Mayor and Sheriffs for the time being to be three), to be employed and directed from time to time, in such manner as shall be agreed on and appointed by both Houses of Parliament.

That no citizen of the City of London, nor any of the forces of the said City, should be drawn forth or compelled to go

out of the said City, or liberties thereof, for military service, without their own free consent.

That an Act be passed for granting and confirming of the charters, customs, liberties and franchises of the City of London, notwithstanding any *nonuser, misuser,* or *abuser*.

That the Tower of London may be in the government of the City of London, and the chief officer and governor thereof, from time to time, be nominated and removable by the Common Council : and for prevention of inconveniences which may happen by the long intermission of Common Councils, it is desired that there may be an Act that all by-laws and ordinances already made, or hereafter to be made by the Lord Mayor, Aldermen, and Commons in Common Council assembled, touching the calling, continuing, directing and regulating the said Common Councils, be as effectual in law to all intents and purposes, as if the same were particularly enacted by the authority of Parliament. And that the Lord Mayor, Aldermen, and Commons in Common Council may add to or repeal the said Ordinances from time to time, as they shall see cause.

That such other propositions as shall be made for the City, for their further safety, welfare and government, and shall be approved of by both Houses of Parliament, may be granted and confirmed by Act of Parliament.

19. That all grants, commissions, presentations, writs, processes, proceedings, and other things passed under the Great Seal of England, in the custody of the Lords and others Commissioners appointed by both Houses of Parliament for the custody thereof, and by Act of Parliament with the royal assent, shall be declared and enacted to be of like force and effect to all intents and purposes, as the same or like grants, commissions, presentations, writs, processes, proceedings, and other things under any Great Seal of England in any time heretofore were or have been : and that for time to come, the said Great Seal, now remaining in custody of the said Commissioners, continue and be used for the Great Seal of England : and that all grants, commissions and presentations, writs, processes, proceedings, and other things whatsoever, passed under or by authority of any other Great Seal since the 22nd day of May, anno dom. 1642, or hereafter to be

passed, be invalid, and of no effect to all intents and purposes; except such writs, process and commissions, as being passed under any other Great Seal than the said Great Seal in the custody of the Commissioners aforesaid, on or after the said 22nd of May, and before the 28th day of November, anno dom. 1643, were afterwards proceeded upon, returned into, or put in use in any of the King's Courts at Westminster; and except the grant to Mr. Justice Bacon to be one of the Justices of the King's Bench; and except all acts and proceedings by virtue of any such commissions of gaol-delivery, assize, and *Nisi Prius* or *Oyer* and *Terminer*, passed under any Great Seal than the Seal aforesaid, in the custody of the said Commissioners, before the 1st of October, 1642.

And that all grants of offices, lands, tenements or hereditaments, made or passed under the Great Seal of Ireland, unto any person or persons, bodies politic or corporate, since the cessation made in Ireland the 15th day of September, 1643, shall be null and void: and that all honours and titles conferred upon any person or persons in the said kingdom of Ireland, since the said cessation, shall be null and void.

67. The King's first answer to the Propositions presented at Newcastle.

[August 1, 1646. Journals of the House of Lords, viii. 460. See *Great Civil War*, iii. 133.]

Charles R.

The propositions tendered to His Majesty by the Commissioners from the Lords and Commons assembled in the Parliament of England at Westminster, and the Commissioners of the Parliament of Scotland (to which the Houses of Parliament have taken twice so many months for deliberation, as they have assigned days for His Majesty's answer), do import so great alterations in government both in the Church and kingdom, as it is very difficult to return a particular and positive answer, before a full debate, wherein these propositions, and the necessary explanations, true sense and reasons thereof, be rightly weighed and understood; and that His Majesty

(upon a full view of the whole propositions) may know what is left, as well as what is taken away and changed: in all which he finds (upon discourse with the said Commissioners) that they are so bound up from any capacity either to give reasons for the demands they bring, or to give ear to such desires as His Majesty is to propound, as it is impossible for him to give such a present judgment of, and answer to these propositions, whereby he can answer to God that a safe and well-grounded peace will ensue (which is evident to all the world can never be, unless the just power of the Crown, as well as the freedom and propriety of the subject, with the just liberty and privileges of Parliament, be likewise settled): to which end His Majesty desires and proposeth to come to London, or any of his houses thereabouts, upon the public faith and security of the two Houses of his Parliament, and the Scots Commissioners, that he shall be there with freedom, honour and safety; where by his personal presence he may not only raise a mutual confidence between him and his people, but also have these doubts cleared, and these difficulties explained unto him, which he now conceives to be destructive to his just regal power, if he should give a full consent to these propositions as they now stand: as likewise, that he may make known to them such his reasonable demands, as he is most assured will be very much conducible to that peace which all good men desire and pray for, by the settling of religion, the just privileges of Parliament, with the freedom and propriety of the subject: and His Majesty assures them, that as he can never condescend unto what is absolutely destructive to that just power which, by the laws of God and the land, he is born unto; so he will cheerfully grant and give his assent unto all such Bills (at the desires of his two Houses), or reasonable demands for Scotland, which shall be really for the good and peace of his people, not having regard to his own particular (much less of anybody's else) in respect of the happiness of these kingdoms. Wherefore His Majesty conjures them as Christians, as subjects, and as men who desire to leave a good name behind them, that they will so receive and make use of this answer, that all issues of blood may be stopped, and these unhappy distractions peaceably settled.

At Newcastle, the 1st of August, 1646.

Charles R.

Upon assurance of a happy agreement, His Majesty will immediately send for the Prince his son, absolutely answering for his perfect obedience.

68. THE KING'S SECOND ANSWER TO THE PROPOSITIONS PRESENTED AT NEWCASTLE.

[December 20, 1646. Journals of the House of Lords, viii. 627. See *Great Civil War*, iii. 183.]

Charles R.

His Majesty's thoughts being always sincerely bent to the peace of his kingdoms, was and will be ever desirous to take all ways which might the most clearly make appear the candour of his intentions to his people : and to this end could find no better way than to propose a personal free debate with his two Houses of Parliament upon all the present differences ; yet finding, very much against his expectations, that this offer was laid aside, His Majesty bent all his thoughts to make his intentions fully known, by a particular answer to the propositions delivered to him in the name of both kingdoms, 24th July last : but the more he endeavoured it, he more plainly saw that any answer he could make would be subject to misinformations and misconstructions, which upon his own paraphrases and explanations he is most confident will give so good satisfaction, as would doubtless cause a happy and lasting peace. Lest therefore that good intentions may produce ill effects, His Majesty again proposes and desires to come to London, or any of his houses thereabouts, upon the public faith and security of his two Houses of Parliament and the Scots Commissioners, that he shall be there with honour, freedom and safety : where, by his personal presence, he may not only raise a mutual confidence between him and his people, but also have those doubts cleared and those difficulties explained to him, without which he cannot, but with the aforesaid mischievous inconveniences, give a particular answer to the Propositions : and with which he doubts not but so to manifest his real intentions for the settling of religion, the just privileges of Parliament, with the freedom and propriety of the subject, that it shall not be in the power of wicked and malicious men to hinder the establishing of that firm peace which all honest men desire : assuring them that as he will make no other demands but such as he believes confidently to be just, and much conducing to the tranquillity of the people : so he will be most willing to condescend unto them in whatsoever shall be really for their good and happiness : not doubting likewise but you will also have a due regard to maintain the just power of the Crown, according to your many protestations and professions : for certainly except King and people have reciprocal care each of other, neither can be happy.

To conclude, 'tis your King who desires to be heard, the which if refused to a subject by a King, he would be thought a tyrant for it, and for that end which all men profess to desire. Wherefore His Majesty conjures you, as you desire to show yourselves really what you profess, even as you are good Christians and subjects, that you will accept this his offer, which he is confident God will so bless, that it will be the readiest means by which these kingdoms may again become a comfort to their friends, and a terror to their enemies.

Newcastle, the 20th of December, 1646.

69. Suggested answer to the Propositions drawn up for the King by the leading Presbyterians and a small number of the Independents, and forwarded by the French Ambassador to Cardinal Mazarin to be laid before Queen Henrietta Maria.

[January 29, February 8, 164⁷⁄₈.   Archives des Affaires Étrangères, Angleterre, lv. fol. 185. See *Great Civil War*, iii. 213.]

Mémoire envoyé par M. de Bellievre au Cardinal Mazarin [1].

Les sincères intentions du Roy n'ayant pas esté bien entendues par les responses que sa Maté vous a fait cydevant, elle juge à propos de vous faire connoistre quelle estoit lors sa pensée, semblable à la résolution en laquelle elle est aujourd'huy, elle estimoit, lorsque vous ayant fait sçavoir en termes généraux

[1] This document is only known to exist in the French form.

qu'elle vouloit establir la religion et les justes privilèges des
Parlements avec la seureté de ses sujets, aux desirs desquels
elle prétendoit s'accommoder, et faire toutes les choses qui
seroient véritablement pour leur bien et leur advantage, vous
deviez estre satisfait.

Mais pour vous le faire entendre plus particulièrement, elle
vous dit qu'elle est preste de confirmer pour trois ans le Gou-
vernement Presbytérial puisqu'il a esté pour ce temps estably
par les deux maisons: que sa Maté veut approuver ce qui a esté
fait par le grand sçeau jusqu'à ce jour, depuis que les deux
maisons s'en sont servy: qu'elle est aussy en volonté de mettre
le pouvoir de la milice tant par terre que par mer entre les
mains de telles personnes que les deux maisons nommeront, leur
donnant pouvoir de changer les dites personnes à leur volonté,
et d'en substituer d'autres en leurs places; et ce pour l'espace
de dix années, s'il est jugé qu'il faille tant de temps pour assurer
la confirmation de la paix et l'accomplissement des choses qui
auront esté agréées.

Sa Maté donnera pareillement pleine satisfaction touchant
la conduite de la guerre en Irlande et touchant l'establissement
de la religion en la manière qu'elle sera establie en Angleterre,
et sa Maté consentira de tout son cœur à l'acte qui sera fait
pour la confirmation des privilèges et des coustumes de la
ville de Londres: elle se portera d'autant plus volontiers à
accorder ce qui est cy dessus, qu'elle ne doute point que vous
voudrez avoir la considération que vous devez pour maintenir
le juste pouvoir de sa couronne, que ses amis ne seront point
en peyne pour l'avoir suivy, et qu'il sera pourveu par un acte
d'amnistie et pardon général passé dans le Parlement, à ce que
toutes les semences de trouble et de mescontentement soyent
entièrement assoupies.

Comme aussy que les expediens seront pris que l'on jugera
les plus propres pour l'acquit des debtes publiques et de celles
de sa Maté; le Roy faisant voir quelle est son intention touchant
les choses les plus importantes de celles qui sont contenues
dans les Propositions, vous pouvez juger que ce qu'il a demandé
à estre ouy, ainsy qu'il le demande encore présentement; et
que pour cet effect il puisse venir à Londres, ou en l'une de ses
maisons qui en sont proches, sur la foy et l'asseurance publique

que vous luy donnerez, qu'il y demeurera avec honneur, seureté et liberté.

Ce n'est que pour y pouvoir plus promptement et avec plus de facilité que d'un autre lieu prendre et donner des esclaircissements, faire et recevoir les Propositions qui peuvent faire naistre une confiance réciproque entre sa Maté et ses sujets et contribuer à establir et maintenir une bonne paix tant desirée par les gens de bien[1].

70. The King's third answer to the Propositions presented at Newcastle.

[May 12, 1647. Journals of the House of Lords, ix. 193. See *Great Civil War*, iii. 252.]

Charles R.

As the daily expectation of the coming of the Propositions[2] hath made His Majesty this long time to forbear the giving of his answer unto them, so the appearance of their sending being now no more, for any thing he can hear, than it was at his first coming hither[3], notwithstanding that the Earl of Lauderdale hath been at London these ten days[4] (whose not coming was said to be the only stop), hath caused His Majesty thus to anticipate their coming unto him; and yet, considering his condition, that his servants are denied access to him, all but very few, and those by appointment, not his own election, and that it is a declared crime for any but the Commissioners, or such who are particularly permitted by them, to converse with His Majesty; or that any letters should be given to or received from him; may he not truly say that he is not in case fit to make confessions or give answers, since he is not master of those ordinary actions which are the undoubted rights of every free-born man, how mean soever his birth be. And certainly he would still be silent on this subject until his

---

[1] 'Le mémoire cy joint est ce que les Presbytériens qui veulent un Roy et se veulent bien passer du Covenant, et quelques personnes de qualité de party contraire, jugent que le Roy de la G. B. doit envoyer à ce Parlement arrivant à Homby.' Bellievre to Mazarin, Jan. 29–Feb. 8, 1647. Arch. des Aff. Etr. Angl. lv. p. 177.

[2] The Houses had for some time been engaged in amending the Propositions sent to Newcastle, but had been interrupted by their quarrel with the army.

[3] I e. Holmby House. [4] As a Scottish Commissioner.

condition were much mended (did he not prefer such a right understanding between him and his Parliament of both kingdoms, which may make a firm and lasting peace in all his dominions, before any particular of his own or any earthly blessing), and therefore His Majesty hath diligently employed his utmost endeavours (for divers months past) so to inform his understanding and satisfy his conscience, that he might be able to give such answers to the Propositions as would be most agreeable to his Parliaments; but he ingenuously proposes that, notwithstanding all the pains that he hath taken thereon, the nature of some of them appears such unto him, that (without disclaiming that reason which God hath given him to judge by for the good of him and his people, and without putting the greatest violence upon his own conscience) he cannot give his consent to all of them; yet His Majesty (that it may appear to all the world how desirous he is to give full satisfaction) hath thought fit hereby to express his readiness to grant what he may, and his willingness to receive from them, and that personally, if his two Houses at Westminster shall approve thereof, such further information in the rest, as may but convince his judgment and satisfy those doubts which are not yet clear to him; desiring them also to consider that, if His Majesty intended to wind himself out of these troubles by indirect means, were it not most easy for him now readily to consent to whatsoever hath or shall be proposed unto him, and afterwards choose his time to break all, alleging that forced concessions are not to be kept:—surely he might, and not yet incur a hard censure from any indifferent men. But maxims of this kind are not the guides of His Majesty's actions; for he freely and clearly avows that he holds it unlawful for any man, and most base in a King, to recede from his promises for having been obtained by force or under restraint.

Wherefore His Majesty, not only rejecting those arts which he esteems unworthy of him, but even passing by that which he might well insist upon as a point of honour, in respect of his present condition, thus answers the first Proposition:

That, upon His Majesty's coming to London, he will heartily join in all that shall concern the honour of his two kingdoms or the Assembly of States of Scotland, or of the Commissioners or Deputies of either kingdoms, particularly in those things which are desired in that Proposition; upon confidence that all of them respectively with the same tenderness will look upon those things which concern His Majesty's honour.

In answer to all the Propositions concerning religion, His Majesty proposeth that he will confirm the Presbyterial government, the Assembly of Divines at Westminster, and the Directory, for three years (being the time set down by the two Houses), so that His Majesty and his household be not hindered from using that form of God's service which they have formerly; and also that a free consultation and debate be had with the Divines at Westminster (twenty of His Majesty's nomination being added unto them), whereby it may be determined by His Majesty and the two Houses, how the Church shall be governed after the said three years, or sooner if differences may be agreed.

Touching the Covenant, His Majesty is not therein yet satisfied, and desires to respite his particular answer thereunto until his coming to London: because, it being a matter of conscience, he cannot give a resolution therein till he may be assisted with the advice of some of his own chaplains (which hath hitherto been denied him), and such other divines as shall be most proper to inform him therein; and then he will make clearly appear both his zeal to the Protestant profession and the union of these two kingdoms, which he conceives to be the main drift of the Covenant.

To the seventh and eighth Propositions, His Majesty will consent.

To the ninth, His Majesty doubts not but to give good satisfaction, when he shall be particularly informed how the said penalties shall be levied and disposed of.

To the tenth, His Majesty's answer is, that he hath been always ready to prevent the practices of Papists; and therefore is content to pass an Act of Parliament for that purpose, and also that the laws against them be duly executed.

His Majesty will give his consent to the Act for the due observation of the Lord's Day, for the suppression of innovations, and those concerning the preaching of God's Word, and touching non-residence and pluralities.

And His Majesty will be willing to pass such Act or Acts
as shall be requisite to raise moneys for the payment and
satisfying of all public debts: expecting also that his will be
therein concluded.

As to the Proposition touching the militia: though His
Majesty cannot consent unto it *in terminis* as it is proposed
(because thereby, he conceives, he wholly parts with the power
of the sword intrusted to him by God and the laws of the
land for the protection and government of his people, thereby
at once divesting himself, and disinheriting his posterity of
that right and prerogative of the Crown which is absolutely
necessary to the kingly office, and so weakening monarchy in
this kingdom that little more than the name and shadow of
it will remain), yet, if it be only security for the preservation
of the peace of this kingdom after these unhappy troubles, and
the due performance of all the agreements which are now to
be concluded, which is desired (which His Majesty always
understood to be the case, and hopes that herein he is not
mistaken), His Majesty will give abundant satisfaction; to
which end he is willing to consent, by Act of Parliament, that
the whole power of the militia, both by sea and land, for the
space of ten years, be in such persons as the two Houses of
Parliament shall nominate (giving them power, during the
said term, to change the said persons, and to substitute others
in their places at pleasure), and afterwards to return to the
proper channel again, as it was in the times of Queen Elizabeth
and King James of blessed memory. And now His Majesty
conjures his two Houses of Parliament, as they are Englishmen
and lovers of peace, by the duty they owe to His Majesty their
King, and by the bowels of compassion they have to their
fellow-subjects, that they will accept of this His Majesty's offer,
whereby the joyful news of peace may be restored to this
languishing kingdom. His Majesty will grant the like to the
kingdom of Scotland, if it be desired; and he will agree to all
things that are propounded touching the conserving of peace
between the two kingdoms.

Touching Ireland, other things being agreed, His Majesty
will give satisfaction therein.

As to the mutual declarations proposed to be established in

both kingdoms by Act of Parliament, and the qualifications, modifications and branches, which follow in the Propositions, His Majesty only professes that he doth not sufficiently understand, nor is able to reconcile many things contained in them; but this he well knows, that a general act of oblivion is the best bond of peace, and that after intestine trouble, the wisdom of this and other kingdoms hath usually and happily, in all ages, granted general pardons, whereby the numerous discontentments of many persons and families otherwise exposed to ruin might not become fuel to new disorders, or seed of future troubles. His Majesty therefore desires that his two Houses of Parliament would seriously descend into these considerations, and likewise tenderly look upon his condition herein, and the perpetual dishonour that must cleave to him, if he should thus abandon so many persons of condition and fortune that have engaged themselves with and for him out of a sense of duty; and propounds, as a very acceptable testimony of their affection to him, that a general act of oblivion and full pardon be forthwith passed by Act of Parliament.

Touching the new Great Seal, His Majesty is very willing to confirm both it and all acts done by virtue thereof until this present time; so that it be not thereby pressed to make void those acts of his done by virtue of his Great Seal, which in honour and justice he is obliged to maintain; and that the future government thereof may be in His Majesty, according to the due course of law.

Concerning the officers mentioned in the 17th Article, His Majesty, when he shall come to Westminster, will gratify his Parliament all that possibly he may, without destroying the relations which are necessary to the Crown.

His Majesty will willingly consent to the Act for the confirmation of the privileges and customs of the City of London, and all that is mentioned in the Propositions for their particular advantage.

And now that His Majesty hath thus far endeavoured to comply with the desires of his two Houses of Parliament, to the end that this agreement may be firm and lasting, without the least force or question of restraint to blemish the same, His Majesty earnestly desires presently to be admitted to his

Parliament at Westminster, with that honour which is due to their Sovereign, there solemnly to confirm the same, and legally to pass the Acts before mentioned; and to give and receive as well satisfaction in all the remaining particulars, as likewise such other pledges of mutual love, trust and confidence, as shall most concern the good and prosperity of him and his people, upon which happy agreement His Majesty will despatch his directions to the Prince his son, to return immediately to him, and will undertake for his ready obedience thereunto.

71. THE HEADS OF THE PROPOSALS OFFERED BY THE ARMY.

[August 1, 1647. Rushworth, vii. 731. See *Great Civil War*, iii. 329–333, 340–343.]

The Heads of the Proposals agreed upon by his Excellency Sir Thomas Fairfax and the Council of the Army, to be tendered to the Commissioners of Parliament residing with the Army, and with them to be treated on by the Commissioners of the Army : containing the particulars of their desires in pursuance of their former declarations and papers, in order to the clearing and securing of the rights and liberties of the kingdom, and the settling a just and lasting peace. To which are added some further particular desires (for the removing and redressing of divers pressing grievances), being also comprised in or necessary pursuance of their former representations and papers appointed to be treated upon.

I. That (things hereafter proposed, being provided for by this Parliament) a certain period may (by Act of Parliament) be set for the ending of this Parliament (such period to be put within a year at most), and in the same Act provision to be made for the succession and constitution of Parliaments in future, as followeth :

1. That Parliaments may biennially be called and meet at a certain day, with such provision for the certainty thereof, as in the late Act was made for triennial Parliaments ; and

what further or other provision shall be found needful by the Parliament to reduce it to more certainty; and upon the passing of this, the said Act for triennial Parliaments to be repealed.

2. Each biennial Parliament to sit 120 days certain (unless adjourned or dissolved sooner by their own consent), afterwards to be adjournable or dissolvable by the King, and no Parliament to sit past 240 days from their first meeting, or some other limited number of days now to be agreed on; upon the expiration whereof each Parliament to dissolve of course, if not otherwise dissolved sooner.

3. The King, upon advice of the Council of State, in the intervals between biennial Parliaments, to call a Parliament extraordinary, provided it meet above 70 days before the next biennial day, and be dissolved at least 60 days before the same; so as the course of biennial elections may never be interrupted.

4. That this Parliament and each succeeding biennial Parliament, at or before adjournment or dissolution thereof, may appoint Committees to continue during the interval for such purposes as are in any of these Proposals referred to such Committees.

5. That the elections of the Commons for succeeding Parliaments may be distributed to all counties, or other parts or divisions of the kingdom, according to some rule of equality or proportion, so as all counties may have a number of Parliament members allowed to their choice, proportionable to the respective rates they bear in the common charges and burdens of the kingdom, according to some other rule of equality or proportion, to render the House of Commons (as near as may be) an equal representative of the whole; and in order thereunto, that a present consideration be had to take off the elections of burgesses for poor decayed or inconsiderable towns, and to give some present addition to the number of Parliament members for great counties that have now less than their due proportion, to bring all (at present), as near as may be, to such a rule of proportion as aforesaid.

6. That effectual provision be made for future freedom of elections, and certainty of due returns.

7. That the House of Commons alone have the power from

time to time to set down further orders and rules for the ends expressed in the two last preceding articles, so as to reduce the elections of members for that House to more and more perfection of equality in the distribution, freedom in the election, order in the proceeding thereto, and certainty in the returns, with orders and rules (in that case) to be in laws.

8. That there be a liberty for entering dissents in the House of Commons, with provision that no member be censurable for ought said or voted in the House further than to exclusion from that trust; and that only by the judgment of the House itself.

9. That the judicial power, or power of final judgment in the Lords and Commons (and their power of exposition and application of law, without further appeal), may be cleared; and that no officer of justice, minister of state, or other person adjudged by them, may be capable of protection or pardon from the King without their advice or consent.

10. That the right and liberty of the Commons of England may be cleared and vindicated as to a due exemption from any judgment, trial or other proceeding against them by the House of Peers, without the concurring judgment of the House of Commons: as also from any other judgment, sentence or proceeding against them, other than by their equals, or according to the law of the land.

11. The same Act to provide that grand jurymen may be chosen by and for several parts or divisions of each county respectively, in some equal way (and not to remain as now, at the discretion of an Under-Sheriff to be put on or off), and that such grand jurymen for their respective counties, may at each Assize present the name of persons to be made Justices of the Peace from time to time, as the county hath need for any to be added to the Commission, and at the Summer Assize to present the names of three persons, out of whom the King may prick one to be Sheriff for the next year.

II. For the future security of Parliament and the militia in general, in order thereunto, that it be provided by Act of Parliament:

1. That the power of the militia by sea and land, during the space of ten years next ensuing, shall be ordered and

disposed by the Lords and Commons assembled, and to be assembled in the Parliament or Parliaments of England, by such persons as they shall nominate and appoint for that purpose from time to time during the said space.

2. That the said power shall not be ordered, disposed or exercised by the King's Majesty that now is, or by any person or persons by any authority derived from him, during the said space, or at any time hereafter by His said Majesty, without the advice and consent of the said Lords and Commons, or of such Committees or Council in the intervals of Parliament as they shall appoint.

3. That during the same space of ten years the said Lords and Commons may by Bill or Ordinance raise and dispose of what moneys and for what forces they shall from time to time find necessary; as also for payment of the public debts and damages, and for all other the public uses of the kingdom.

4. And to the end the temporary security intended by the three particulars last precedent may be the better assured, it may therefore be provided,

That no subjects that have been in hostility against the Parliament in the late war, shall be capable of bearing any office of power or public trust in the Commonwealth during the space of five years, without the consent of Parliament or of the Council of State; or to sit as members or assistants of either House of Parliament, until the second biennial Parliament be passed.

III. For the present form of disposing the militia in order to the peace and safety of this kingdom and the service of Ireland:

1. That there be Commissioners for the Admiralty, with the Vice-Admiral and Rear-Admiral, now to be agreed on, with power for the forming, regulating, appointing of officers and providing for the Navy, and for ordering the same to, and in the ordinary service of the Kingdom; and that there be a sufficient provision and establishment for pay and maintenance thereof.

2. That there be a General for command of the land forces that are to be in pay both in England, Ireland and Wales, both for field and garrison.

3. That there be Commissioners in the several counties for the standing militia of the respective counties (consisting of

trained bands and auxiliaries not in pay), with power for the proportioning, forming, regulating, training and disciplining of them.

4. That there be a Council of State, with power to superintend and direct the several and particular powers of the militia last mentioned, for the peace and safety of this kingdom, and of Ireland.

5. That the same Council may have power as the King's Privy Council, for and in all foreign negotiations; provided that the making of war or peace with any other kingdom or state shall not be without the advice and consent of Parliament.

6. That the said power of the Council of State be put into the hands of trusty and able persons now to be agreed on, and the same persons to continue in that power (*si bene se gesserint*) for the certain term not exceeding seven years.

7. That there be a sufficient establishment now provided for the salary forces both in England and Ireland, the establishment to continue until two months after the meeting of the first biennial Parliament.

IV. That an Act be passed for disposing the great offices for ten years by the Lords and Commons in Parliament; or by such Committees as they shall appoint for that purpose in the intervals (with submission to the approbation of the next Parliament), and after ten years they to nominate three, and the King out of that number to appoint one for the succession upon any vacancy.

V. That an Act be passed for restraining of any Peers made since the 21st day of May, 1642, or to be hereafter made, from having any power to sit or vote in Parliament without consent of both Houses.

VI. That an Act be passed for recalling and making void all declarations and other proceedings against the Parliament, or against any that have acted by or under their authority in the late war, or in relation to it; and that the Ordinances for indemnity may be confirmed.

VII. That an Act be passed for making void all grants, &c. under the Great Seal, that was conveyed away from the Parliament, since the time that it was so conveyed away (except as in the Parliament's propositions), and for making those valid that have been or shall be passed under the Great Seal, made by the authority of both Houses of Parliament.

VIII. That an Act be passed for confirmation of the Treaties between the two kingdoms of England and Scotland, and for appointing conservators of the peace between them.

IX. That the Ordinance for taking away the Court of Wards and Liveries be confirmed by Act of Parliament; provided His Majesty's revenue be not damnified therein, nor those that last held offices in the same left without reparation some other way.

X. An Act to declare void the cessation of Ireland, &c., and to leave the prosecution of that war to the Lords and Commons in the Parliament of England.

XI. An Act to be passed to take away all coercive power, authority, and jurisdiction of Bishops and all other Ecclesiastical Officers whatsoever, extending to any civil penalties upon any: and to repeal all laws whereby the civil magistracy hath been, or is bound, upon any ecclesiastical censure to proceed (*ex officio*) unto any civil penalties against any persons so censured.

XII. That there be a repeal of all Acts or clauses in any Act enjoining the use of the Book of Common Prayer, and imposing any penalties for neglect thereof; as also of all Acts or clauses of any Act, imposing any penalty for not coming to church, or for meetings elsewhere for prayer or other religious duties, exercises or ordinances, and some other provision to be made for discovering of Papists and Popish recusants, and for disabling of them, and of all Jesuits or priests from disturbing the State.

XIII. That the taking of the Covenant be not enforced upon any, nor any penalties imposed on the refusers, whereby men might be restrained to take it against their judgments or consciences; but all Orders and Ordinances tending to that purpose to be repealed.

XIV. That (the things here before proposed being provided, for settling and securing the rights, liberties, peace and safety of the kingdom) His Majesty's person, his Queen, and royal issue, may be restored to a condition of safety, honour and freedom in this nation, without diminution to their personal rights, or further limitation to the exercise of the regal power than according to the particulars foregoing

XV. For the matter of composition:

1. That a less number out of the persons excepted in the two first qualifications (not exceeding five for the English) being nominated particularly by the Parliament, who (together with the persons in the Irish Rebellion, included in the third qualification) may be reserved to the further judgment of the Parliament as they shall find cause, all other excepted persons may be remitted from the exception, and admitted to composition.

2. That the rates of all future compositions may be lessened and limited, not to exceed the several proportions hereafter expressed respectively. That is to say,

(1) For all persons formerly excepted, not above a third part.

(2) For the late members of Parliament under the first branch of the fourth qualification in the Propositions, a fourth part.

(3) For other members of Parliament in the second and third branches of the same qualification, a sixth part.

(4) For the persons nominated in the said fourth qualification, and those included in the tenth qualification, an eighth part.

(5) For all others included in the sixth qualification, a tenth part: and that real debts either upon record, or proved by witnesses, be considered and abated in the valuation of their estates in all the cases aforesaid.

3. That those who shall hereafter come to compound, may not have the Covenant put upon them as a condition without which they may not compound, but in case they shall not willingly take it, they may pass their compositions without it.

4. That the persons and estates of all English not worth £200 in land or goods, be at liberty and discharged: and that the King's menial servants that never took up arms, but only attended his person according to their offices, may be freed from composition, or to pay (at most) but the proportion of one year's revenue, or a twentieth part.

5. That in order to the making and perfecting of composi-

tions at the rates aforesaid, the rents, revenues, and other duties and profits of all sequestered estates whatsoever (except the estates of such persons who shall be continued under exception as before), be from henceforth suspended and detained in the hands of the respective tenants, occupants and others from whom they are due, for the space of six months following.

6. That the faith of the army, or other forces of the Parliament given in articles upon surrenders to any of the King's party, may be fully made good; and where any breach thereof shall appear to have been made, full reparation and satisfaction may be given to the parties injured, and the persons offending (being found out) may be compelled thereto.

XVI. That there may be a general Act of Oblivion to extend unto all (except the persons to be continued in exception as before), to absolve from all trespasses, misdemeanours, &c. done in prosecution of the war; and from all trouble or prejudice for or concerning the same (after their compositions past), and to restore them to all privileges, &c. belonging to other subjects, provided as in the fourth particular under the second general head aforegoing concerning security.

And whereas there have been of late strong endeavours and practices of a factious and desperate party to embroil this kingdom in a new war, and for that purpose to induce the King, the Queen, and the Prince to declare for the said party, and also to excite and stir up all those of the King's late party to appear and engage for the same, which attempts and designs, many of the King's party (out of their desires to avoid further misery to the kingdom) have contributed their endeavours to prevent (as for divers of them we have had particular assurance): we do therefore desire, that such of the King's party who shall appear to have expressed, and shall hereafter express, that way their good affections to the peace and welfare of the kingdom, and to hinder the embroiling of the same in a new war, may be freed and exempted from compositions, or to pay but one year's revenue, or a twentieth part.

These particulars aforegoing are the heads of such Proposals as we have agreed on to tender in order to the settling of the peace of this kingdom, leaving the terms of peace for the kingdom of Scotland to stand as in the late Propositions of both kingdoms, until that kingdom shall agree to any alteration.

Next to the Proposals aforesaid for the present settling of a peace, we shall desire that no time may be lost by the Parliament for despatch of other things tending to the welfare, ease and just satisfaction of the kingdom, and in special manner:

I. That the just and necessary liberty of the people to represent their grievances and desires by way of petition, may be cleared and vindicated, according to the fifth head in the late representation or Declaration of the army sent from St. Albans [1].

II. That (in pursuance of the same head in the said Declaration) the common grievances of this people may be speedily considered of, and effectually redressed, and in particular,

1. That the excise may be taken off from such commodities, whereon the poor people of the land do ordinarily live, and a certain time to be limited for taking off the whole.

2. That the oppressions and encroachments of forest laws may be prevented for the future.

3. All monopolies (old or new) and restraints to the freedom of trade to be taken off.

4. That a course may be taken, and Commissioners appointed to remedy and rectify the inequality of rates lying upon several counties, and several parts of each county in respect of others, and to settle the proportion of land rates to more equality throughout the kingdom; in order to which we shall offer some further particulars, which we hope may be useful.

5. The present unequal troublesome and contentious way of ministers' maintenance by tithes to be considered of, and some remedy applied.

6. That the rules and course of law, and the officers of it, may be so reduced and reformed, as that all suits and questions of right may be more clear and certain in the issues,

---

[1] Rushworth, vii. 569.

and not so tedious nor chargeable in the proceedings as now; in order to which we shall offer some further particulars hereafter.

7. That prisoners for debt or other creditors (who have estates to discharge them) may not by embracing imprisonment, or any other ways, have advantage to defraud their creditors, but that the estates of all men may be some way made liable to their debts (as well as tradesmen are by commissions of bankrupt), whether they be imprisoned for it or not; and that such prisoners for debt, who have not wherewith to pay, or at least do yield up what they have to their creditors, may be freed from imprisonment or some way provided for, so as neither they nor their families may perish by imprisonment.

8. Some provision to be made, that none may be compelled by penalty or otherwise to answer unto questions tending to the accusing of themselves or their nearest relations in criminal causes; and no man's life to be taken away under two witnesses.

9. That consideration may be had of all Statutes, and the laws or customs of Corporations, imposing any oaths either to repeal, or else to qualify and provide against the same, so far as they may extend or be construed to the molestation or ensnaring of religious and peaceable people, merely for nonconformity in religion.

III. That according to the sixth head in the Declaration of the army, the large power given to Committees or Deputy-Lieutenants during the late times of war and distraction, may be speedily taken into consideration to be recalled and made void, and that such powers of that nature as shall appear necessary to be continued, may be put into a regulated way, and left to as little arbitrariness as the statute and necessity of the things (wherein they are conversant) will bear.

IV. That (according to the seventh head in the said Declaration) an effectual course may be taken that the kingdom may be righted, and satisfied in point of accompts for the vast sums that have been levied.

V. That provision may be made for payment of arrears to the army, and the rest of the soldiers of the kingdom who have concurred with the army in the late desires and proceedings thereof; and in the next place for payment of the

public debts and damages of the kingdom; and that to be
performed, first to such persons whose debt or damages
(upon the public account) are great, and their estates small,
so as they are thereby reduced to a difficulty of subsistence:
in order to all which, and to the fourth particular last proceeding, we shall speedily offer some further particulars (in
the nature of rules), which we hope will be of good use
towards public satisfaction.

August 1, 1647.

> Signed by the appointment of his Excellency Sir
> Thomas Fairfax and the Council of War.
>
> J. RUSHWORTH.

72. THE KING'S ANSWER TO THE PROPOSITIONS OF PARLIAMENT.

[Despatched by the King September 9, 1647.   Rushworth, vii. 810.
See *Great Civil War*, iii. 361, 366.]

Charles Rex.

His Majesty cannot choose but be passionately sensible (as
he believes all his good subjects are) of the late great distractions, and still languishing and unsettled state of this
kingdom; and he calls God to witness, and is willing to give
testimony to all the world, of his readiness to contribute his
utmost endeavours for restoring it to a happy and flourishing
condition.

His Majesty having perused the Propositions now brought to
him, finds them the same in effect which were offered to him at
Newcastle: to some of which, as he could not then consent
without violation of his conscience and honour, so neither can
he agree to others now, conceiving them in many respects more
disagreeable to the present condition of affairs than when they
were formerly presented to him, as being destructive to the
main principal interests of the army, and of all those whose
affections concur with them: and His Majesty having seen the
Proposals of the army to the Commissioners from his two Houses
residing with them, and with them to be treated on in order to
the clearing and securing the right and liberties of the kingdom,

and the settling a just and lasting peace, to which Proposals, as he conceives his two Houses not to be strangers, so he believes they will think with him, that they much more conduce to the satisfaction of all interests, and may be a fitter foundation for a lasting peace, than the Propositions which at this time are tendered to him.

He therefore propounds (as the best way in his judgment in order to peace) that his two Houses would instantly take into consideration those Proposals, upon which there may be a personal treaty with His Majesty, and upon such other Propositions as His Majesty shall make, hoping that the said Proposals may be so moderated in the said treaty as to render them the more capable of His Majesty's full concessions, wherein he resolves to give full satisfaction unto his people for whatsoever shall concern the settling of the Protestant profession, with liberty to tender consciences, and the securing of the laws, liberties and properties of all his subjects, and the just privileges of Parliament for the future; and likewise by his present deportment in this treaty, he will make the world clearly judge of his intentions in the matter of future government: in which treaty His Majesty will be pleased (if it be thought fit) that Commissioners from the army (whose the Proposals are) may likewise be admitted.

His Majesty therefore conjures his two Houses of Parliament by the duty they owe to God and His Majesty their King, and by the bowels of compassion they have to their fellow subjects, both for relief of their present sufferings, and to prevent future miseries, that they will forthwith accept His Majesty's offer, whereby the joyful news of peace may be restored to this distressed kingdom.

And for what concerns the kingdom of Scotland mentioned in the Propositions, His Majesty will very willingly treat upon those particulars with Scotch Commissioners, and doubts not but to give a reasonable satisfaction to that His Majesty's kingdom.

73. Letter of Charles I to the Speaker of the House of Lords.

[Received by the House of Lords, November 17, 1647. Parliamentary History, iii. 799. See Masson's *Life of Milton*, iii. 577. See *Great Civil War*, iv. 24.]

Charles Rex.

His Majesty is confident, that before this time, his two Houses of Parliament have received the message which he left behind him at Hampton Court the 11th of this month; by which they will have understood the reasons which enforced him to go from thence; as likewise his constant endeavours for the settling of a safe and well-grounded peace wheresoever he should be; and being now in a place where he conceives himself to be at much more freedom and security than formerly, he thinks it necessary, not only for making good of his own professions, but also for the speedy procuring of a peace in these languishing and distressed kingdoms, at this time to offer such grounds to his two Houses for that effect, which upon due examination of all interest may best conduce thereunto.

And because religion is the best and chiefest foundation of peace, His Majesty will begin with that particular.

That for the abolishing Archbishops, Bishops, &c. His Majesty clearly professeth that he cannot give his consent thereunto, both in relation as he is a Christian and a King; for the first he avows, that he is satisfied in his judgment that this order was placed in the Church by the Apostles themselves, and ever since their time hath continued in all Christian Churches throughout the world, until this last century of years; and in this Church in all times of change and reformation it hath been upheld by the wisdom of his ancestors, as the great preserver of doctrine, discipline and order in the service of God. As a King at his coronation, he hath not only taken a solemn oath to maintain this order, but His Majesty and his predecessors in their confirmations of the Great Charter, have inseparably woven the right of the Church into the liberty of the subjects; and yet he is willing it be provided, that the particular Bishops perform their several duties of their callings, both by their personal residence and frequent preaching in their dioceses, as also that they exercise no act of jurisdiction or ordination, with-

out the consent of their Presbyters, and will consent that their
powers in all things be so limited, that they be not grievous to
the tender consciences of others.   He sees no reason why he
alone, and those of his judgment, should be pressed to a violation of theirs : nor can His Majesty consent to the alienation
of Church lands, because it cannot be denied to be a sin of the
highest sacrilege; as also that it subverts the intentions of
so many pious donors, who have laid a heavy curse upon all
such profane violations, which His Majesty is very unwilling to
undergo; and besides the matter of consequence, His Majesty
believes it to be a prejudice to the public good, many of his
subjects having the benefit of renewing leases at much easier
rates than if those possessions were in the hands of private
men; not omitting the discouragement it will be to all learning
and industry, when such eminent rewards shall be taken away,
which now lie open to the children of meanest persons.   Yet
His Majesty, considering the great present distempers concerning
Church discipline, and that the Presbyterian government is now
in practice, His Majesty, to eschew confusion as much as may
be, and for the satisfaction of his two Houses, is content that
the same government be legally permitted to stand in the same
condition it now is for three years ; provided that His Majesty
and those of his judgment, or any other who cannot in conscience submit thereunto, be not obliged to comply with the
Presbyterian government, but have free practice of their own
profession, without receiving any prejudice thereby; and that
a free consultation and debate be had with the divines of Westminster (twenty of His Majesty's nomination being added unto
them); whereby it may be determined by His Majesty and the
two Houses, how the Church government after the said time
shall be settled (or sooner, if differences may be agreed), as is
most agreeable to the Word of God, with full liberty to all
those who shall differ upon conscientious grounds from that
settlement; always provided, that nothing aforesaid be understood to tolerate those of the Popish profession, nor exempting
any Popish recusant from the penalties of the laws ; or to tolerate
the public profession of Atheism or blasphemy, contrary to the
doctrine of the Apostles', Nicene and Athanasian Creeds, they
having been received by, and had in reverence of all the Christian

Churches, and more particularly by this of England, ever since the Reformation.

Next the militia being that right, which is inseparably and undoubtedly inherent to the Crown by the laws of this nation, and that which former Parliaments, as likewise this, have acknowledged so to be, His Majesty cannot so much wrong that trust, which the laws of God and this land hath annexed to the Crown, for the protection and security of his people, as to divest himself and successors of the power of the sword; yet to give an infallible evidence of his desire to secure the performance of such agreements as shall be made in order to a peace, His Majesty will consent to an Act of Parliament, that the whole power of the militia, both by sea and land, for and during his whole reign, shall be ordered and disposed by the two Houses of Parliament, or by such persons as they shall appoint, with powers limited for suppressing of forces within this kingdom to the disturbance of the public peace, and against foreign invasion; and that they shall have power during his said reign to raise monies for the purpose aforesaid; and that neither His Majesty that now is, or any other by any authority derived only from him, shall execute any of the said powers during His Majesty's said reign, but such as shall act by the consent and approbation of the two Houses of Parliament: nevertheless His Majesty intends that all patents, commissions, and other acts concerning the militia, be made and acted as formerly; and that after His Majesty's reign, all the power of the militia shall return entirely to the Crown, as it was in the times of Queen Elizabeth and King James of blessed memory.

After this head of the militia, the consideration of the arrears due to the army is not improper to follow; for the payment whereof, and the ease of his people, His Majesty is willing to concur in any thing that can be done without the violation of his conscience and honour.

Wherefore if his two Houses shall consent to remit unto him such benefit out of sequestrations from Michaelmas last, and out of compositions that shall be made before the concluding of the peace, and the arrears of such as have been already made, the assistance of the clergy, and the arrears of such rents of his own revenue as his two Houses shall not have received before the concluding of the peace, His Majesty will undertake within the space of eighteen months the payment of £400,000 for the satisfaction of the army; and if those means shall not be sufficient, His Majesty intends to give way for the sale of forest lands for that purpose. This being the public debt which in His Majesty's judgment is first to be satisfied: and for other public debts already contracted upon Church lands or any other engagements, His Majesty will give his consent to such Act or Acts for raising of monies for payment thereof, as both Houses hereafter shall agree upon, so as they be equally laid; whereby his people, already too heavily burdened by these late distempers, may have no more pressures upon them than this absolute necessity requires.

And for the further securing all fears, His Majesty will consent that an Act of Parliament be passed for the disposing of the great offices of State, and naming of Privy Councillors for the whole term of his reign, by the two Houses of Parliament, their patents and commissions being taken from His Majesty, and after to return to the Crown, as is expressed in the articles of the militia. For the Court of Wards and Liveries, His Majesty very well knows the consequence of taking that away, by turning of all tenures into common socage, as well in point of revenue to the Crown, as in the protection of many of his subjects being infants; nevertheless, if the continuance thereof seem grievous to his subjects, rather than he will fail on his part in giving satisfaction, he will consent to an Act for taking of it away, so as a full recompense be settled upon His Majesty and his successors in perpetuity; and that the arrears now due be reserved unto him towards the payment of the arrears of the army.

And that the memory of these late distractions may be wholly wiped away, His Majesty will consent to an Act of Parliament for the suppressing and making null all Oaths, Declarations and Proclamations against both or either House of Parliament, and of all indictments and other proceedings against any persons for adhering unto them; and His Majesty proposeth, as the best expedient to take away all seed of future differences, that there be an Act of Oblivion to extend to all his subjects.

As for Ireland, the cessation therein long since determined; but for the future, all other things being fully agreed, His Majesty will give full satisfaction to His Houses concerning that kingdom.

And although His Majesty cannot consent in honour and justice to avoid all his own grants and acts passed under his Great Seal since the 22nd of May 1642, or to the confirming of all the grants and acts passed under that made by the two Houses, yet His Majesty is confident, that upon perusal of particulars, he shall give full satisfaction to his two Houses to what may be reasonably desired in that particular.

And now His Majesty conceives, that by these his offers, which he is ready to make good upon the settlement of a peace, he hath clearly manifested his intentions to give full security and satisfaction to all interests, for what can justly be desired in order to the future happiness of his people, and for the perfecting of these concessions, as also for such other things as may be proposed by the two Houses; and for such just and reasonable demands as His Majesty shall find necessary to propose on his part, he earnestly desires a personal treaty at London with his two Houses, in honour, freedom and safety; it being, in his judgment, the most proper, and indeed only means to a firm and settled peace, and impossible without it to reconcile former, or avoid future misunderstandings.

All these being by treaty perfected, His Majesty believes his two Houses will think it reasonable that the Proposals of the army concerning the succession of Parliaments, and their due elections, should be taken into consideration.

As for what concerns the kingdom of Scotland, His Majesty will very readily apply himself to give all reasonable satisfaction, when the desires of the two Houses of Parliament on their behalf, or of the Commissioners of that kingdom, or of both joined together, shall be made known unto him.

> For the Speaker of the Lords' House *pro tempore*, to be communicated to the Lords and Commons in the Parliament of England, at Westminster, and the Commissioners of the Parliament of Scotland.
>
> CHARLES REX.

74. The Agreement of the People, as presented to the Council of the Army.

[An agreement of the People for a firm and present peace, &c., E. 412, 21. October 28, 1647.   See *Great Civil War*, iii. 383–394.]

An Agreement of the People for a firm and present peace upon grounds of common right.

Having by our late labours and hazards made it appear to the world at how high a rate we value our just freedom, and God having so far owned our cause as to deliver the enemies thereof into our hands, we do now hold ourselves bound in mutual duty to each other to take the best care we can for the future to avoid both the danger of returning into a slavish condition and the chargeable remedy of another war ; for, as it cannot be imagined that so many of our countrymen would have opposed us in this quarrel if they had understood their own good, so may we safely promise to ourselves that, when our common rights and liberties shall be cleared, their endeavours will be disappointed that seek to make themselves our masters. Since, therefore, our former oppressions and scarce-yet-ended troubles have been occasioned, either by want of frequent national meetings in Council, or by rendering those meetings ineffectual, we are fully agreed and resolved to provide that hereafter our representatives be neither left to an uncertainty for the time nor made useless to the ends for which they are intended.   In order whereunto we declare :—

That the people of England, being at this day very un-equally distributed by Counties, Cities, and Boroughs for the election of their deputies in Parliament, ought to be more indifferently proportioned according to the number of the inhabitants ; the circumstances whereof for number, place, and manner are to be set down before the end of this present Parliament.

II.

That, to prevent the many inconveniences apparently arising from the long continuance of the same persons in authority, this present Parliament be dissolved upon the last day of September which shall be in the year of our Lord 1648

III.

That the people do, of course, choose themselves a Parliament once in two years, viz. upon the first Thursday in every 2d March [1], after the manner as shall be prescribed before the end of this Parliament, to begin to sit upon the first Thursday in April following, at Westminster or such other place as shall be appointed from time to time by the preceding Representatives, and to continue till the last day of September then next ensuing, and no longer.

IV.

That the power of this, and all future Representatives of this Nation, is inferior only to theirs who choose them, and doth extend, without the consent or concurrence of any other person or persons, to the enacting, altering, and repealing of laws, to the erecting and abolishing of offices and courts, to the appointing, removing, and calling to account magistrates and officers of all degrees, to the making war and peace, to the treating with foreign States, and, generally, to whatsoever is not expressly or impliedly reserved by the represented to themselves :

Which are as followeth.

1. That matters of religion and the ways of God's worship are not at all entrusted by us to any human power, because therein we cannot remit or exceed a tittle of what our consciences dictate to be the mind of God without wilful sin : nevertheless the public way of instructing the nation (so it be not compulsive) is referred to their discretion.

2. That the matter of impresting and constraining any of us to serve in the wars is against our freedom ; and therefore we do not allow it in our Representatives ; the rather, because money (the sinews of war), being always at their disposal, they can never want numbers of men apt enough to engage in any just cause.

3. That after the dissolution of this present Parliament, no person be at any time questioned for anything said or done

---

[1] I. e. in March in every other year.

in reference to the late public differences, otherwise than in execution of the judgments of the present Representatives or House of Commons.

4. That in all laws made or to be made every person may be bound alike, and that no tenure, estate, charter, degree, birth, or place do confer any exemption from the ordinary course of legal proceedings whereunto others are subjected.

5. That as the laws ought to be equal, so they must be good, and not evidently destructive to the safety and well-being of the people.

These things we declare to be our native rights, and therefore are agreed and resolved to maintain them with our utmost possibilities against all opposition whatsoever; being compelled thereunto not only by the examples of our ancestors, whose blood was often spent in vain for the recovery of their freedoms, suffering themselves through fraudulent accommodations to be still deluded of the fruit of their victories, but also by our own woeful experience, who, having long expected and dearly earned the establishment of these certain rules of government, are yet made to depend for the settlement of our peace and freedom upon him that intended our bondage and brought a cruel war upon us.

75. The Four Bills, with the Propositions Accompanying Them.

[Passed the House of Lords December 14, 1647. Old Parliamentary History, vi. 405. See *Great Civil War*, iv. 31, 36.]

The Four Bills sent to the King in the Isle of Wight to be passed, together with the Propositions sent unto him at the same time, which, upon the passing of those Bills, were to be treated upon.

The Lords and Commons assembled in Parliament have commanded us to present to your Majesty these Four Bills, which have passed the two Houses of Parliament.

I. *Soit baillé aux Seigneurs,*
A ceste Bille les Seigneurs sont assentuz.

An Act concerning the raising, settling and maintaining forces, by sea and land, within the kingdoms of England

and Ireland and dominion of Wales, the isles of Guernsey and
Jersey, and the town of Berwick-upon-Tweed.

Be it enacted by the King's Majesty, and by the Lords and
Commons assembled in Parliament, and by the authority of
the same, that the Lords and Commons in the Parliament of
England now assembled or hereafter to be assembled, shall,
during the space of twenty years, from the 1st of November,
1647, arm, train and discipline, or cause to be armed, trained
and disciplined, all the forces of the kingdoms of England and
Ireland and the dominion of Wales, the isles of Guernsey and
Jersey, and the town of Berwick-upon-Tweed, already raised
both for sea and land service; and shall appoint all commanders
and officers for the said forces; and shall from time to time,
during the said space of twenty years, raise, levy, arm, train
and discipline, or cause to be raised, levied, armed, trained and
disciplined any other forces for land and sea service, in the kingdoms, dominions and places aforesaid, as in their judgments they
shall, from time to time, during the said space of twenty years,
think fit and appoint; and shall, from time to time, appoint all
commanders and officers for the said forces, or remove them as
they shall see cause; and shall likewise nominate, appoint, place
or displace, as they shall see cause, all commanders and officers
within the several garrisons, forts and places of strength, as
shall be within the kingdoms of England, Ireland and dominion
of Wales, the isles of Guernsey and Jersey, and the town of
Berwick-upon-Tweed; and that neither the King, his heirs or
successors, nor any other but such as shall act by the authority
or approbation of the said Lords and Commons, shall, during
the said space of twenty years, exercise any of the powers aforesaid.

And be it further enacted, by the authority aforesaid, that
monies be raised and levied for the maintenance and use of
the said forces for land service, and of the navy and forces
for sea service, in such sort and by such ways and means,
as the said Lords and Commons shall, from time to time,
during the said space of twenty years, think fit and appoint,
and not otherwise; and that the said forces both for land and
sea service, so raised or levied, or to be raised or levied;
and also the Admiralty or navy shall, from time to time,

during the said space of twenty years, be employed, managed, ordered, disposed or disbanded by the said Lords or Commons, in such sort, and by such ways and means, as they shall think fit and appoint, and not otherwise.

And be it further enacted, by the authority aforesaid, that the said Lords and Commons, during the said space of twenty years, shall have power in such sort, and by such ways and means as they shall think fit and appoint, to suppress all forces raised without authority and consent of the said Lords and Commons, to the disturbance of the public peace of the kingdoms of England and Ireland and dominion of Wales, and the isles of Guernsey and Jersey, and the town of Berwick-upon-Tweed, or any of them ; and also to suppress any foreign forces who shall invade, or endeavour to invade, the kingdoms of England and Ireland and dominion of Wales, and the isles of Guernsey and Jersey, and the town of Berwick-upon-Tweed, or any of them ; and likewise to conjoin such forces of the kingdom of England with the forces of the kingdom of Scotland, as the said Lords and Commons shall, from time to time, during the said space of twenty years, judge fit and necessary to resist all foreign invasions, and to suppress any forces raised, or to be raised, against or within either of the said kingdoms, to the disturbance of the public peace of the said kingdoms, or any of them, by any authority under the Great Seal, or other warrant whatsoever, without consent of the said Lords and Commons of the Parliament of England and the Parliament or the Estates of the Parliament of Scotland respectively : and that no forces of either kingdoms shall go into or continue in the other kingdom without the advice and desire of the said Lords and Commons of the Parliament of England, and the Parliament of Scotland, or such as shall be by them respectively appointed for that purpose.

And be it enacted by the authority aforesaid, that after the expiration of the said twenty years, neither the King, his heirs or successors, or any person or persons, by colour or pretence of any commission, power, deputation or authority to be derived from the King, his heirs or successors, or any of them, shall raise, arm, train, discipline, employ, order, manage, disband or dispose of any of the forces, by sea and land, of the kingdoms of England and Ireland, the dominion of Wales, the isles of Guernsey and Jersey, and the town of Berwick-upon-Tweed, or any of them : nor exercise any of the said powers or authorities before mentioned and expressed to be, during the said space of twenty years, in the said Lords and Commons : nor do any act or thing concerning the execution of the said powers or authorities, or any of them, without the consent of the said Lords and Commons first had and obtained.

And be it further also enacted, that after the expiration of the said twenty years, in all cases wherein the said Lords and Commons shall declare the safety of the kingdom to be concerned, and shall thereupon pass any Bill or Bills for the raising, arming, training, disciplining, employing, managing, ordering or disposing of the forces by sea or land, of the kingdoms of England and Ireland, the dominion of Wales, the isles of Guernsey and Jersey, and the town of Berwick-upon-Tweed, or any part of the said forces, or concerning the said Admiralty or navy, or concerning the levying of monies for the raising, maintenance, or use of the said forces for land service, or of the navy and forces for sea service, or any part of them, and if that the royal assent to such Bill or Bills shall not be given in the House of Peers, within such time after the passing thereof by both Houses of Parliament as the said Houses shall judge fit and convenient, that then such Bill or Bills so passed by the said Lords and Commons as aforesaid, and to which the royal assent shall not be given as is herein before expressed, shall nevertheless, after Declaration of the said Lords and Commons made in that behalf, have the force and strength of an Act or Acts of Parliament ; and shall be valid, to all intents and purposes, as if the royal assent had been given thereunto.

Provided always, and be it further enacted, by the authority aforesaid, that nothing hereinbefore contained shall extend to the taking away of the ordinary legal power of Sheriffs, Justices of Peace, Mayors, Bailiffs, Coroners, Constables, Headboroughs or other officers of justice, not being military officers, concerning the administration of justice ; so as neither the said Sheriffs, Justices of the Peace, Mayors, Bailiffs, Coroners, Constables, Headboroughs, and other officers, or any of them, do levy, conduct, employ, or command any forces whatsoever, by colour or pretence of any Commission of Array, or extraordinary command from His Majesty, his heirs or successors, without the consent of the said Lords and Commons; and that if any persons shall be gathered and assembled together in warlike manner, or otherwise, to the number of thirty persons, and shall not forthwith separate and disperse themselves, being required thereto by the said Lords and Commons, or command from them, or any of them especially authorised for that purpose, then such person and persons, not so separating and dispersing themselves, shall be guilty, and incur the pains of high treason; being first declared guilty of such offence by the said Lords and Commons, any Commission under the Great Seal, or other warrant to the contrary notwithstanding; and he or they that shall offend herein, shall be incapable of any pardon from His Majesty, his heirs and successors, and their estates shall be disposed as the said Lords and Commons shall think fit, and not otherwise.

Provided also further, that the City of London shall have and enjoy all their rights, liberties, franchises, customs and usages in the raising and employing the forces of that City for the defence thereof, in as full and ample manner, to all intents and purposes, as they have, or might have, used or enjoyed the same at any time before the sitting of this present Parliament.

II. *Soit baillé aux Seigneurs,*
A ceste Bille les Seigneurs sont assentuz.

An Act for justifying the proceedings of Parliament in the late war, and for declaring all Oaths, Declarations, Proclamations and other proceedings against it to be void.

Whereas the Lords and Commons assembled in Parliament have been necessitated to make and prosecute a war in their just and lawful defence; and thereupon Oaths, Declarations and Proclamations have been made against them, and their Ordinances and proceedings, and against others for adhering unto them, and for executing offices, places and charges by authority derived from them; and judgments, indictments, outlawries, attainders and inquisitions for the causes aforesaid have been had and made against some of the members of the Houses of Parliament, and other His Majesty's good subjects, and grants have been made of their lands and goods :

Be it therefore declared, and hereby enacted, by the King's Majesty, and by the Lords and Commons assembled in Parliament, and by authority of the same, that all Oaths, Declarations, and Proclamations heretofore had or made against both or either of the Houses of Parliament, or any of the members of either of them, for the causes aforesaid, or against their Ordinances or proceedings, or against any for adhering unto them, or for doing or executing any office, place or charge, by any authority derived from the said Houses, or either of them, and all judgments, indictments, outlawries, attainders, inquisitions and grants thereupon made, and all other proceedings for any the causes aforesaid, had, made, done or executed, or to be had, made, done or executed, whether the same be done by the King or any Judges, Justices, Sheriffs, Ministers, or any others, are void and of no effect, and are contrary to and against the laws of this realm.

And be it further enacted, and hereby declared, by the authority aforesaid, that all Judges, Justices of the Peace, Mayors, Sheriffs, Constables, and other Officers and Ministers shall take notice hereof; and are hereby prohibited and discharged, in all time to come, from awarding any writ, process or summons, and from pronouncing or executing any judgment, sentence or decree, or any way proceeding against or molesting any of the said members of the two Houses of Parliament, or against any of the subjects of this kingdom, for any of the causes aforesaid.

III.   *Soit baillé aux Seigneurs,*
A ceste Bille les Seigneurs sont assentuz.

An Act concerning Peers lately made and hereafter to be made.

Be it enacted, by the King's Majesty and by the Lords and Commons assembled in Parliament, that all honour and title of peerage conferred on any since the 20th day of May, 1642 (being the day that Edward Lord Lyttelton, then Lord-Keeper of the Great Seal, deserted the Parliament, and that the said Great Seal was surreptitiously conveyed away from the

Parliament), be and is hereby made and declared null and void.

Be it further enacted, and it is hereby enacted, by the authority aforesaid, that no person that shall hereafter be made a Peer, or his heirs, shall sit or vote in the Parliament of England without consent of both Houses of Parliament.

IV.   *Soit baillé aux Seigneurs,*
A ceste Bille les Seigneurs sont assentuz.

An Act concerning the adjournments of both Houses of Parliament.

Be it declared and enacted, by the King's Majesty and by the Lords and Commons assembled in Parliament, and by the authority of the same, that when and as often as the Lords and Commons assembled in this present Parliament shall judge it necessary to adjourn both Houses of the present Parliament to any other place of the kingdom of England than where they now sit, or from any place adjourn the same again to the place where they now sit, or to any other place within the kingdom of England, then such their adjournment and adjournments to such place, and for such time as they shall appoint, shall at all times, and from time to time, be valid and good, any Act, Statute or usage to the contrary notwithstanding.

Provided always, and be it enacted by the authority aforesaid, that no adjournment or adjournments to be had or made, by reason or colour of this Act, shall be deemed, adjudged or taken to make, end or determine any Session of this present Parliament.

And they have also commanded us to present to your Majesty these ensuing Propositions :—

1. That an Act or Acts of Parliament be passed, that all grants, commissions, presentations, &c. (This Proposition is the same with the nineteenth Proposition presented to the King at Newcastle. See p. [305[1]].)

2. That an Act or Acts of Parliament be passed, that the King do give his royal assent to such Act or Acts, for raising monies, &c. (This is the same with the sixth clause of the twelfth Proposition, at Newcastle, p. [293].)

---

[1] The references in square brackets are inserted in place of those in the Parliamentary History.

3. That the King do give his consent, that the members of both Houses of Parliament, or others who have adhered to the Parliament, and have been put out by the King of any place or office, pension or benefit, be restored thereunto.

4. That an Act or Acts of Parliament be passed, to declare and make void the cessation of Ireland, &c. (The same as the seventeenth Proposition, p. [304].)

5. That an Act or Acts of Parliament be passed for indemnity, agreeable to the two Ordinances of both Houses already passed for that purpose.

6. That His Majesty be desired to give his assent to an Act or Acts of Parliament, for the taking away the Court of Wards and Liveries, and of all wardships, liveries, *primer seisins* and *ouster les mains;* and of all other charges incident unto, or arising for, or by reason of any wardships, liveries, *primer seisins* or *ouster les mains;* and of all tenures by homage, fines, licences, seizures and pardons for alienation; and of all other charges incident or belonging thereunto, or for or by reason thereof, from the 24th of February, 1645 [1], and that all tenures by knight service, grand sergeanty, petty sergeanty, or socage *in capite,* either of His Majesty, or of any other person or persons, may be, from the time aforesaid, turned into free and common socage, and that the sum of £50,000 per annum be granted to the King by way of recompense.

7. That an Act or Acts of Parliament shall be passed, declaring the King's approbation of the making the Treaties between the kingdoms of England and Scotland, &c. [2].

8. That the arrears of pay due to the army and others the soldiery of this kingdom, who have faithfully served the Parliament in this war, shall be secured and paid unto them out of the remaining part of the lands and revenues of Archbishops and Bishops, belonging to their archbishoprics or bishoprics, after such engagements satisfied as are already charged there-

---

[1] i.e. 1645⅚. See No. 65.

[2] The same as the fifteenth, p. 297, except that there it is styled an 'Act for Confirmation of the Treaties,' &c., and these words are omitted in the new Proposition, with (all other Ordinances and proceedings passed between the two kingdoms, and whereunto they are obliged by the aforesaid Treaties). There are also some alterations in the names of the Commissioners.

upon by an Ordinance of both Houses of Parliament, and out of two-thirds in three to be divided of all the forfeitures of lands ; and all the fines of the persons mentioned or comprehended in the three first qualifications of the Proposition concerning delinquents ; and also out of all forest lands within the kingdom of England and dominion of Wales, provision being made upon the disafforestation thereof, for the relief of the inhabitants within the same, and all other the subjects of this realm, who have right of common, or any other right in the said forests ; and that the King do give his consent to such Act or Acts as shall be presented to him by both Houses of Parliament, for the sale or disposing of the said lands and fines for the purpose aforesaid.

9. That an Act or Acts of Parliament be passed, for the utter abolishing and taking away of all Archbishops, Bishops, &c. (The same as the third Proposition, p. [291].)

10. That the several Ordinances, the one entitled ' An Ordinance of Parliament for abolishing of Archbishops and Bishops within the kingdom of England and dominion of Wales ; and for settling of their lands and possessions upon trustees for the use of the Commonwealth' ; the other entitled 'An Ordinance of the Lords and Commons assembled in Parliament for appointing the sale of Bishops' lands for the use of the Commonwealth,' be confirmed by Act of Parliament.

11. That the King do give his consent to such Act or Acts of Parliament as shall be tendered to him by both Houses of Parliament, for the sale of the lands of Deans and Sub-Deans, Deans and Chapters, Archdeacons, Canons and Prebendaries, and all Chantors, Chancellors, Treasurers, Sub-Treasurers, Succentors and Sacrists, and all Vicars Choral and Choristers, old Vicars and new Vicars of any Cathedral or Collegiate Church, and for the disposal thereof, as both Houses shall think fit.

12. That the persons expressed and contained in the three first qualifications following be proceeded with and their estates disposed of as both Houses of Parliament shall think fit to appoint ; and that their persons shall not be capable of pardon by His Majesty without consent of both Houses of Parliament ; the Houses hereby declaring, that they will not proceed as to the taking away of life of any in the first qualification to above the number of seven persons.

First qualification.

Rupert and Maurice, Counts Palatine of the Rhine, &c.

The second, third and fourth qualifications, and the three branches of the fourth, the same as on pp. [299–301]. The fifth, sixth and seventh qualifications, the same as at pp. [301–2]. The eighth qualification, and the three branches thereof, are the same as the ninth at Newcastle, p. [302], the eighth of those being now dropped. The ninth qualification the same as the tenth. The tenth qualification the same as the eleventh, p. [303], except the omission of what regards Scotland, and the following addition :

Provided that all and every the delinquents, which by or according to the several and respective Ordinances or Orders made by both or either the Houses of Parliament, on or before the 24th day of April, 1647, are to be admitted to make their fines and compositions under the rate and proportions of the qualifications aforesaid, shall, according to the said Ordinances and Orders respectively, be thereunto admitted, and further also, that no person or persons whatsoever (except such Papists as having been in arms or voluntarily assisted against the Parliament, having by concealing their quality procured their admission to composition) which have already compounded, or shall hereafter compound, and be thereunto admitted by both Houses of Parliament, at any of the rates and propositions aforesaid, or under respectively, shall be put to any other fine than that they have or shall respectively so compound for ; except for such estates, or such part of their estates, and for such values thereof respectively, as have been or shall be concealed or omitted in the particulars whereupon they compound ; and that all and every of them shall have thereupon their pardons in such manner and form as is agreed by both Houses of Parliament.

13. That an Act or Acts be passed, whereby the debts of the kingdom, and the persons of delinquents, and the value of their estates may be known, &c.

(This is the second paragraph of the second branch of the eleventh qualification at p. [303].)

14. That the King be desired to give his consent to such

Act or Acts of Parliament as shall be presented unto him for the settling of the Presbyterian government and directory in England and Ireland, according to such Ordinances as have already, since the sitting of this Parliament, passed both Houses, and are herewithal sent; which Act or Acts are to stand in force to the end of the next Session of Parliament after the end of this present Session.

That no persons whatsoever shall be liable to any question or penalty for nonconformity to the form of government and Divine Service appointed in the said Ordinances; and that all such persons as shall not conform to the said form of government and Divine Service, shall have liberty to meet for the service and worship of God, and for the exercise of religious duties and ordinances, in any fit and convenient places, so as nothing be done by them to the disturbance of the peace of the kingdom : that all tithes or other maintenance appertaining to any church or chapel, which do now belong to the Ministers of such churches or chapels, shall be applied to the use and benefit of such Ministers as do conform to the government settled in the said Ordinances, and to none other, unless it be by the consent of the present Incumbent.

That nothing in this provision shall extend to any toleration of the Popish religion, nor to exempt any Popish recusants from any penalties imposed upon them for the exercise of the same.

That this indulgence shall not extend to tolerate the printing, publishing or preaching of any thing contrary to the principles of the Christian religion, as they are contained in the first, second, third, fourth, fifth, sixth, seventh, ninth, tenth, eleventh, twelfth, thirteenth, fourteenth and fifteenth Articles of the Church of England, according to the true sense and meaning of them, and as they have been cleared and vindicated by the Assembly of Divines, now sitting at Westminster ; nor of any thing contrary to those points of faith, for the ignorance whereof men are to be kept from the Sacrament of the Lord's Supper, as they are contained in the rules and directions for that purpose, passed both Houses the 20th of October, 1645.

That it be also provided, that this indulgence shall not extend to exempt any person or persons from any penalty by law imposed, or to be imposed, upon them for absenting themselves upon the Lord's Day from hearing the Word of God, unless they can show reasonable cause of their absence, or that they were present elsewhere to hear the Word of God preached or expounded unto them, so as the said preaching or expounding be not by any Minister sequestered and not restored.

That this indulgence shall not extend to tolerate the use of the Book of Common Prayer in any place whatsoever.

That liberty shall be given to all Ministers of the Gospel, though they cannot conform to the present Government in all things, being not under sequestration, nor sequesterable, to preach any lecture or lectures, in any church or chapel, where they shall be desired by the inhabitants thereof; provided that it be not at such hours as the Minister of the said parish doth ordinarily preach himself, and shall receive such means and maintenance as doth, or shall, thereunto appertain.

15. That an Act or Acts of Parliament be passed, that the Deputy or Chief Governor, or other Governors of Ireland, &c.

(This Proposition is the same as the third[1] clause of the seventeenth presented at Newcastle, p. [304].)

(The sixteenth, seventeenth, eighteenth and nineteenth Articles, for the more effectual disabling of Jesuits and Papists from disturbing the State and eluding the laws; for the education of the children of Papists in the Protestant religion, &c., are the same as the seventh, eighth, ninth and tenth Propositions, at p. [292], but are now extended to Ireland.)

(The twentieth, twenty-first, twenty-second and twenty-third Articles relate to the observation of the Sabbath, innovations in worship, preaching, pluralities, non-residence; and are the same as the first four clauses of the twelfth Proposition, p. [293]. After which follows this instruction to the Commissioners of both Houses.)

They have also commanded us to desire that your Majesty will give your royal assent to these Bills, by your Letters Patent under the Great Seal of England, and signed by your hand, and declared and notified to the Lords and Commons assembled together in the House of Peers, according to the law declared in that behalf; it appearing unto them, upon

[1] ? Second.

mature deliberation, that it stands not with the safety and security of the kingdom and Parliament, to have your Majesty's assent at this time given otherwise. They desire, therefore, that your Majesty be pleased to grant your warrant for the draught of a Bill for such your Letters Patent, to be presented to your Majesty; and then a warrant to Edward Earl of Manchester and William Lenthall, Esq., Speaker of the House of Commons, who have now the custody of the Great Seal of England, to put the same to such your Majesty's Letters Patent signed as aforesaid, thereby authorising Algernon Earl of Northumberland, Henry Earl of Kent, John Earl of Rutland, Philip Earl of Pembroke, William Earl of Salisbury, Robert Earl of Warwick, and Edmund Earl of Mulgrave, or any three of them, to give your Majesty's royal assent unto the said Bills, according to the law in that behalf declared; and for the other particulars contained in the aforementioned Propositions, the two Houses of Parliament will, after such your Majesty's assent given to the said Bills, send their Committee of both Houses to treat with your Majesty in the Isle of Wight thereupon.

76. The Engagement between the King and the Scots.

[December 26, 1647. Clarendon MSS. 2685, 2686. See *Great Civil War*, iv. 39.]

Charles R.

His Majesty giving belief to the professions of those who have entered into the League and Covenant, and that their intentions are real for preservation of His Majesty's person and authority according to their allegiance, and no ways to diminish his just power and greatness, His Majesty, so soon as he can with freedom, honour and safety be present in a free Parliament, is content to confirm the said League and Covenant by Act of Parliament in both kingdoms, for security of all who have taken or shall take the said Covenant, provided that none who is unwilling shall be constrained to take it. His Majesty will likewise confirm by Act of Parliament in England, Presbyterial government, the directory for worship, and Assembly of Divines at Westminster for three years, so that

His Majesty and his household be not hindered from using that form of Divine Service he hath formerly practised; and that a free debate and consultation be had with the Divines at Westminster, twenty of His Majesty's nomination being added unto them, and with such as shall be sent from the Church of Scotland, whereby it may be determined by His Majesty and the two Houses how the Church government, after the said three years, shall be fully established as is most agreeable to the Word of God: that an effectual course shall be taken by Act of Parliament, and all other ways needful or expedient, for suppressing the opinions and practices of Anti-Trinitarians, Anabaptists, Antinomians, Arminians, Familists, Brownists, Separatists, Independents, Libertines, and Seekers, and generally for suppressing all blasphemy, heresy, schism, and all such scandalous doctrines and practices as are contrary to the light of nature, or to the known principles of Christianity, whether concerning faith, worship or conversation, or to the power of Godliness, or which may be destructive to order and government, or to the peace of the Church and kingdom; that in the next Session of Parliament after that the kingdom of Scotland shall declare for His Majesty in pursuance of this Agreement, he shall in person or by commission confirm the League and Covenant according to the first Article. Concerning the Acts passed in the last triennial Parliament of his kingdom of Scotland, and the Committees appointed by the same, His Majesty is content then also to give assurance by Act of Parliament that neither he nor his successors shall quarrel, call in question, or command the contrary of any of them, nor question any for giving obedience to the same; and whereas after the return of the Scottish army to Scotland, the Houses of Parliament of England did resolve and appoint the army under command of Sir Thomas Fairfax to disband, and they having entered into an engagement to the contrary, His Majesty was carried away from Holdenby against his will by a party of the said army, and detained in their power until he was forced to fly from amongst them to the Isle of Wight; and since that time His Majesty and the Commissioners of the kingdom of Scotland have earnestly pressed that His Majesty might come to London in safety, honour and freedom for a personal treaty

with the two Houses and the Commissioners of the Parliament
of Scotland, which hath not been granted : and whereas the
said army hath in a violent manner forced away divers members
of both Houses from the discharge of their trust, and possessed
themselves of the City of London and all the strengths and
garrisons of the kingdom, and, through the power and influence
of the said army and their adherents, Propositions and Bills
have been sent to His Majesty without the advice and consent
of the kingdom of Scotland, contrary to the Treaty between
the kingdoms, which are destructive to religion, His Majesty's
just rights, the privileges of Parliament, and liberty of the
subject, from which Propositions and Bills the said Scots Commissioners have dissented in the name of the kingdom of
Scotland ; and, forasmuch as His Majesty is willing to give
satisfaction concerning the settling of religion and other matter
in difference, as is expressed in this Agreement, the kingdom of
Scotland doth oblige and engage themselves first in a peaceable
way and manner to endeavour that His Majesty may come to
London in safety, honour and freedom for a personal treaty
with the Houses of Parliament and the Commissioners of
Scotland upon such Propositions as shall be mutually agreed
on between the kingdoms, and such Propositions as His Majesty
shall think fit to make; and that for this end all armies may
be disbanded, and in case this shall not be granted, that
Declarations shall be emitted by the kingdom of Scotland in
pursuance of this Agreement, against the unjust proceedings
of the two Houses of Parliament towards His Majesty and
the kingdom of Scotland, wherein they shall assert the right
which belongs to the Crown in the power of the militia, the
Great Seal, bestowing of honours and offices of trust, choice
of Privy Councillors, the right of the King's negative voice
in Parliament; and that the Queen's Majesty, the Prince, and
the rest of the royal issue, ought to remain where His Majesty
shall think fit, in either of the kingdoms, with safety, honour
and freedom ; and upon the issuing of the said Declarations,
that an army shall be sent from Scotland into England, for
preservation and establishment of religion, for defence of His
Majesty's person and authority, and restoring him to his govern
ment, to the just rights of the Crown and his full revenues,

for defence of the privileges of Parliament and liberties of the
subject, for making a firm union between the kingdoms, under
His Majesty and his posterity, and settling a lasting peace;
in pursuance whereof the kingdom of Scotland will endeavour
that there may be a free and full Parliament in England, and
that His Majesty may be with them in honour, safety and freedom, and that a speedy period be set to this present Parliament,
and that the said army shall be upon the march before the said
peaceable message and Declaration be delivered to the House;
and it is further agreed that all such in the kingdoms of
England or Ireland, as shall join with the kingdom of Scotland in pursuance of this Agreement, shall be protected by
His Majesty in their persons and estates; and that all such
His Majesty's subjects of England and Ireland as shall join with
him in pursuance of this Agreement may come to the Scotch
army and join with them, or else put themselves into other
bodies in England and Wales for prosecution of the same
ends as the King's Majesty shall judge most convenient, and
under such Commanders or Generals of the English nation as
His Majesty shall think fit, and that all such shall be protected
by the kingdom of Scotland and their army in their persons
and estates, and where any injury or wrong is done to them
therein, that they shall be careful to see them fully repaired so
far as is in their power to do, and likewise, where any injury
or wrong is done to those that join with the kingdom of Scotland, His Majesty shall be careful for their full reparation;
that His Majesty or any by his authority or knowledge shall
not make nor admit of any cessation, pacification, nor agreement for peace whatsoever, nor of any Treaty, Propositions,
Bills, or any other ways for that end, with the Houses of
Parliament or any army or party in England and Ireland,
without the advice and consent of the kingdom of Scotland;
nor any having their authority shall either make or admit of
any of these any manner of way with any whatsoever without
His Majesty's advice and consent; that, upon the settling of
a peace, there be an Act of Oblivion to be agreed on by His
Majesty and both his Parliaments of both kingdoms; that
His Majesty, the Prince, or both shall come into Scotland
upon the invitation of that kingdom and their declaration that

they shall be in safety, freedom and honour, when possibly they
can come with safety and conveniency; and that His Majesty
shall contribute his utmost endeavours both at home and abroad
for assisting the kingdom of Scotland in carrying on this war by
sea and land, and for their supply by monies, arms, ammunition,
and all other things requisite, as also for guarding the coasts
of Scotland with ships, and protecting all Scottish merchants
in the free exercise of trade and commerce with other nations;
and His Majesty is very willing and doth authorise the Scots
army to possess themselves of Berwick, Carlisle, Newcastle-
upon-Tyne, Tynemouth, and Hartlepool, for to be places of
retreat and magazine, and, when the peace of the kingdom is
settled, the kingdom of Scotland shall remove their forces, and
deliver back again the said towns and castles; that, according
to the large Treaty, payment may be made of the remainder
of the Brotherly Assistance which yet rests unpaid; and likewise of the £200,000 due upon the late Treaty made with the
Houses of Parliament for the return of the Scots army, as also
that payment shall be made to the kingdom of Scotland for the
charge and expense of their army in this future war, together
with due recompense for the losses which they shall sustain
therein: that due satisfaction, according to the Treaty on that
behalf between the kingdoms, shall be made to the Scottish
army in Ireland, out of the land of that kingdom or otherwise;
that His Majesty, according to the intention of his father, shall
endeavour a complete union of the kingdoms, so as they may
be one under His Majesty and his posterity; and, if that cannot
be speedily effected, that all liberties, privileges, concerning
commerce, traffic, and manufactories peculiar to the subjects of
either nation, shall be common to the subjects of both kingdoms
without distinction; and that there be a communication of
mutual capacity of all other privileges of the subject in the two
kingdoms; that a competent number of ships shall be yearly
assigned and appointed out of His Majesty's navy, which shall
attend the coast of Scotland for a guard and freedom of trade
to his subjects of that nation; that His Majesty doth declare
that his successors as well as himself are obliged to the per-
formances of the Articles and conditions of this Agreement;
that His Majesty shall not be obliged to the performance of the

aforesaid Articles until the kingdom of Scotland shall declare for him in pursuance of this Agreement, and that the whole Articles and conditions aforesaid shall be finished, perfected and performed before the return of the Scots army; and that when they return into Scotland at the same time, *simul et semel*, all arms be disbanded in England.

Carisbrook, the 26th of December.

Charles Rex.

We do declare and oblige ourselves *in verbo principis*, that the kingdom of Scotland engaging to perform the written Articles, we shall perform our part therein as is above expressed in the said Articles.

At Carisbrook Castle, the 26th of December. Charles R. [his little seal [1].]

We, whose names are underwritten, do hereby engage ourselves upon our honour, faith and conscience, and all that is dearest to honest men, to endeavour to the utmost of our powers that the kingdom of Scotland shall engage to perform the within written conditions in so far as relates to them, His Majesty engaging to perform his part of the aforesaid Articles; and we are most confident that the kingdom of Scotland will do the same; and we are most willing, upon the perfecting of the said Agreement, to hazard our lives and fortunes in pursuance thereof. By the clause of confirming Presbyterian government by Act of Parliament, His Majesty hath declared to us that he is neither obliged to desire the settling of Presbyterian government, nor to present a Bill for that effect; and we likewise understand that no person whatsoever suffer in his estate or corporal punishment for not submitting to Presbyterian government, His Majesty understanding that this shall not extend to those that are mentioned in the clause against toleration.

This was declared in the presence of Lord Loudoun, Lord Lauderdale, Lord Lanerick, and the King took them as witnesses and not assentors, December 27.

Loudoun, Lauderdale, Lanerick.

---

[1] The words in brackets are evidently the work of the copyist. What follows is taken from No. 2685, in Clarendon's hand.

77. Additional Articles of the Engagement.

[December 26, 1647. The Lauderdale Papers, Camden Society, i. 2.
See *Great Civil War*, iv. 41.]

Charles Rex.

His Majesty, out of the natural affection he bears to his
ancient and native kingdom, and to demonstrate how sensible
he is of their affection expressed to him in the time of his
extremity, and how heartily desirous he is to put marks of
his grace and favour upon his subjects of that nation which may
remain to all posterity, doth declare that he is resolved:—

That Scottish men equally with English be employed by
His Majesty and his successors, in foreign negotiations and
treaties in all time coming;

That a considerable and competent number of Scotsmen[1] be
upon His Majesty's Council, and his successors' in England,
and so reciprocally the same number of Englishmen upon His
Majesty's Council in Scotland. That Scottish men according
to the number and proportion [of a third part in number and
quality be employed[2]] in places of trust and offices about His
Majesty's person, the Queen's Majesty, the Prince and the rest
of the royal issue, and their families in all time coming.

That His Majesty and the Prince, or at least one of them,
shall reside in Scotland frequently as their occasions can permit
—whereby their subjects of that kingdom may be known unto
them[3].

78. The King's reply to the Four Bills and the
accompanying Propositions.

[December 28, 1647. Old Parliamentary History, xvi. 483. See *Great
Civil War*, iv. 41.]

For the Speaker of the Lords' House *pro tempore*, to be
communicated to the Lords and Commons in the Parliament

---

[1] This originally stood: 'That Scottish men at least to the number of
the third part.'

[2] The words in brackets are inserted in the margin in Charles's hand,
instead of 'aforesaid,' &c.

[3] This additional Agreement was sealed with Charles's signet. It was
originally dated Carisbrook, 26 Dec. 1647, but the date is scratched out.

of Westminster, and the Commissioners of the Parliament of Scotland.

Charles Rex.

The necessity of complying with all engaged interests in these great distempers, for a perfect settlement of peace, His Majesty finds to be none of the least difficulties he hath met with since the time of his afflictions; which is too visible, when at the same time that the two Houses of the English Parliament do present to His Majesty several Bills and Propositions for his consent, the Commissioners for Scotland do openly protest against them: so that were there nothing in the case but the consideration of that difference, His Majesty cannot imagine how to give such an answer to what is now proposed, as thereby to promise himself his great end, a perfect peace.

And when His Majesty further considers how impossible it is, in the condition he now stands, to fulfil the desires of his two Houses, since the only ancient and known ways of passing laws are either by His Majesty's personal assent in the House of Peers, or by commission under his Great Seal of England, he cannot but wonder at such failings in the manner of address which is now made unto him; unless his two Houses intend that His Majesty shall allow of a Great Seal made without his authority, before there be any consideration had thereupon in a Treaty, which as it may hereafter hazard the security itself, so for the present it seems very unreasonable to His Majesty. And although His Majesty is willing to believe that the intention of very many in both Houses in sending these Bills before a treaty was only to obtain a trust from him, and not to take any advantage by passing them, to force other things from him, which are either against his conscience or honour; yet His Majesty believes it clear to all understandings, that these Bills contain, as they are now penned, not only the divesting himself of all sovereignty, and that without possibility of recovering it, either to him or his successors, except by

Lauderdale told Burnet of its existence. Hyde wrote on the back of his copy of the Engagement (Clar. MSS. 2685), that these terms occur in a copy in the possession of Lord Culpepper which he saw, but of which he was not allowed to take a copy. He also states that they did not occur in the copy in the hands of Prince Rupert.

repeal of these Bills, but also the making his concessions guilty
of the greatest pressures that can be made upon the subject; as
in other particulars, so by giving an arbitrary and unlimited power
to the two Houses for ever, to raise and levy forces for land
and sea service, on what persons, without distinction or quality,
and to what numbers, they please : and likewise, for the payment of them, to levy what monies, in such sort, and by such
ways and means, and consequently upon the estates of whatsoever
persons they shall think fit and appoint, which is utterly
inconsistent with the liberty and prosperity of the subject, and
His Majesty's trust in protecting them. So that, if the major
part of both Houses shall think it necessary to put the rest of
the Propositions into Bills, His Majesty leaves all the world to
judge how unsafe it would be for him to consent thereunto; and
if not, what a strange condition, after the passing of these four
Bills, His Majesty and all his subjects would be cast into.

And here His Majesty thinks it not unfit to wish his two
Houses to consider well the manner of their proceeding; that
when His Majesty desires a personal treaty with them for the
settling of a peace, they in manner propose the very subject
matter of the most essential parts thereof to be first granted,
a thing which will be hardly credible to posterity. Wherefore
His Majesty declares, that neither the desire of being freed from
this tedious and irksome condition of life His Majesty hath so
long suffered, nor the apprehension of what may befall him, in
case his two Houses shall not afford him a personal treaty, shall
make him change his resolution of not consenting to any Act till
the whole peace be concluded.

Yet then he intends not only to give just and reasonable
satisfaction in the particulars presented to him, but also to
make good all other concessions mentioned in his message of
the 17th of November last[1], which he thought would have
produced better effects than what he finds in the Bills and
Propositions now presented unto him.

And yet His Majesty cannot give over, but now again
earnestly presseth for a personal treaty (so passionately is he
affected with the advantages which peace will bring to His

Majesty and all his subjects), of which he will not at all despair, there being no other visible way to obtain a well-grounded peace: however, His Majesty is very much at ease within himself, for having fulfilled the offices both of a Christian and of a King; and will patiently wait the good pleasure of Almighty God to incline the hearts of his two Houses to consider their King, and to compassionate their fellow subjects' miseries.

Given at Carisbrook Castle in the Isle of Wight,

December 28, 1647.

79. THE VOTE OF NO ADDRESSES.

[January 17, 164⅞. Old Parliamentary History, xvi. 489. See *Great
Civil War*, iv. 50-53.]

The Lords and Commons assembled in Parliament, after many addresses to His Majesty for the preventing and ending of this unnatural war raised by him against his Parliament and kingdom, having lately sent Four Bills to His Majesty which did contain only matter of safety and security to the Parliament and kingdom, referring the composure of all other differences to a personal treaty with His Majesty; and having received an absolute negative, do hold themselves obliged to use their utmost endeavours speedily to settle the present government in such a way as may bring the greatest security to this kingdom in the enjoyment of the laws and liberties thereof; and in order thereunto, and that the House may receive no delays nor interruptions in so great and necessary a work, they have taken these resolutions, and passed these votes, viz.:

1. That the Lords and Commons do declare that they will make no further addresses or applications to the King.

2. That no application or addresses be made to the King by any person whatsoever, without the leave of both Houses.

3. That the person or persons that shall make breach of this order shall incur the penalties of high treason.

4. That the two Houses declare they will receive no more any message from the King; and do enjoin that no person whatsoever do presume to receive or bring any message from the King to both or either of the Houses of Parliament, or to any other person.

80. THE ACT[1] ERECTING A HIGH COURT OF JUSTICE FOR THE KING'S TRIAL.

[Passed the Commons January 6, 164⅞. Old Parliamentary History, xviii. 489. See *Great Civil War*, iv. 288–291.]

Whereas it is notorious that Charles Stuart, the now King of England, not content with the many encroachments which his predecessors had made upon the people in their rights and freedom, hath had a wicked design totally to subvert the ancient and fundamental laws and liberties of this nation, and in their place to introduce an arbitrary and tyrannical government, and that besides all other evil ways and means to bring his design to pass, he hath prosecuted it with fire and sword, levied and maintained a civil war in the land, against the Parliament and kingdom; whereby this country hath been miserably wasted, the public treasure exhausted, trade decayed, thousands of people murdered, and infinite other mischiefs committed; for all which high and treasonable offences the said Charles Stuart might long since have justly been brought to exemplary and condign punishment: whereas also the Parliament, well hoping that the restraint and imprisonment of his person, after it had pleased God to deliver him into their hands, would have quieted the distempers of the kingdom, did forbear to proceed judicially against him, but found, by sad experience, that such their remissness served only to encourage him and his accomplices in the continuance of their evil practices, and in raising new commotions, rebellions and invasions: for prevention therefore of the like or greater inconveniences, and to the end no Chief Officer or Magistrate whatsoever may hereafter presume, traitorously and maliciously, to imagine or contrive the enslaving or destroying of the English nation, and to expect impunity for so doing; be it enacted and ordained by the [Lords] and Commons in Parliament assembled, and it is hereby enacted and ordained by the authority thereof, that the Earls of Kent, Nottingham, Pembroke, Denbigh and Mulgrave, the Lord Grey of Wark, Lord Chief Justice Rolle of the King's Bench, Lord

---

[1] From henceforth the Commons gave the name of 'Act' to an Ordinance which had passed their House only.

Chief Justice St. John of the Common Pleas, and Lord Chief
Baron Wylde, the Lord Fairfax, Lieutenant-General Cromwell,
&c. [in all about 150], shall be and are hereby appointed and
required to be Commissioners and Judges for the hearing, trying
and judging of the said Charles Stuart; and the said Commissioners, or any twenty or more of them, shall be, and are
hereby authorised and constituted an High Court of Justice, to
meet and sit at such convenient times and place as by the said
Commissioners, or the major part, or twenty or more of them,
under their hands and seals, shall be appointed and notified
by proclamation in the Great Hall or Palace-Yard of Westminster; and to adjourn from time to time, and from place to
place, as the said High Court, or the major part thereof, at
meeting shall hold fit; and to take order for the charging of
him, the said Charles Stuart, with the crimes and treasons
above mentioned, and for receiving his personal answer thereunto, and for examination of witnesses upon oath (which the
Court hath hereby authority to administer) or otherwise, and
taking any other evidence concerning the same; and thereupon,
or in default of such answer, to proceed to final sentence according
to justice and the merit of the cause; and such final sentence to
execute, or cause to be executed, speedily and impartially.

And the said Court is hereby authorised and required to
choose and appoint all such officers, attendants and other circumstances as they, or the major part of them, shall in any sort
judge necessary or useful for the orderly and good managing
of the premises; and Thomas Lord Fairfax the General, and
all officers and soldiers under his command, and all officers of
justice, and other well-affected persons, are hereby authorised
and required to be aiding and assisting unto the said Court in
the due execution of the trust hereby committed unto them;
provided that this Act, and the authority hereby granted, do
continue in force for the space of one month from the date of
the making thereof, and no longer.

81. THE AGREEMENT OF THE PEOPLE.

[January 15 [1], 164⁸⁄₉. Old Parliamentary History, xviii. 519. See *Great Civil War*, iv. 295.]

An Agreement of the People of England, and the places there-with incorporated, for a secure and present peace, upon grounds of common right, freedom and safety.

Having, by our late labours and hazards, made it appear to the world at how high a rate we value our just freedom, and God having so far owned our cause as to deliver the enemies thereof into our hands, we do now hold ourselves bound, in mutual duty to each other, to take the best care we can for the future, to avoid both the danger of returning into a slavish condition and the chargeable remedy of another war: for as it cannot be imagined that so many of our countrymen would have opposed us in this quarrel if they had understood their own good, so may we hopefully promise to ourselves, that when our common rights and liberties shall be cleared, their endeavours will be disappointed that seek to make themselves our masters. Since therefore our former oppressions and not-yet-ended troubles have been occasioned either by want of frequent national meetings in council, or by the undue or unequal constitution thereof, or by rendering those meetings ineffectual, we are fully agreed and resolved, God willing, to provide, that hereafter our Representatives be neither left to an uncertainty for times nor be unequally constituted, nor made useless to the ends for which they are intended. In order whereunto we declare and agree,

First, that, to prevent the many inconveniences apparently arising from the long continuance of the same persons in supreme authority, this present Parliament end and dissolve upon, or before, the last day of April, 1649.

Secondly, that the people of England (being at this day very

---

[1] For the Agreement of the People as originally drawn up in October, 1647, see No. 74. It is here printed with the subsequent modifications, as presented to the House of Commons on January 20. The petition which accompanied it (Old Parl. Hist. xviii. 516) was dated January 15, and that may therefore be taken as the date when the Agreement received the final approbation of the Council of the Officers.

unequally distributed by counties, cities, and boroughs, for the election of their Representatives) be indifferently proportioned; and, to this end, that the Representative of the whole nation shall consist of 400 persons, or not above; and in each county, and the places thereto subjoined, there shall be chosen, to make up the said Representative at all times, the several numbers here mentioned, viz.

KENT, with the Boroughs, Towns, and Parishes therein, except such
   as are hereunder particularly named 10
   Canterbury, with the Suburbs adjoining and Liberties thereof . . 2
   Rochester, with the Parishes of Chatham and Stroud . . . 1
   The Cinque Ports in Kent and Sussex, viz. Dover, Romney, Hythe,
   Sandwich, Hastings, with the Towns of Rye and Winchelsea . 3

SUSSEX, with the Boroughs, Towns, and Parishes therein, except
   Chichester 8
   Chichester, with the Suburbs and Liberties thereof 1

SOUTHAMPTON COUNTY, with the Boroughs, Towns, and Parishes
   therein, except such as are hereunder named . . . 8
   Winchester, with the Suburbs and Liberties thereof . . . 1
   Southampton Town and the County thereof 1

DORSETSHIRE, with the Boroughs, Towns, and Parishes therein, except
   Dorchester 7
   Dorchester 1

DEVONSHIRE, with the Boroughs, Towns, and Parishes therein, except
   such as are hereunder particularly named 12
   Exeter 2
   Plymouth 2
   Barnstaple 1

CORNWALL, with the Boroughs, Towns, and Parishes therein . . 8

SOMERSETSHIRE, with the Boroughs, Towns, and Parishes therein,
   except such as are hereunder named 8
   Bristol 3
   Taunton-Dean 1

WILTSHIRE, with the Boroughs, Towns, and Parishes therein, except
   Salisbury 7
   Salisbury 1

BERKSHIRE, with the Boroughs, Towns, and Parishes therein, except
   Reading 5
   Reading 1

SURREY, with the Boroughs, Towns, and Parishes therein, except
   Southwark 5
   Southwark 2

MIDDLESEX, with the Boroughs, Towns, and Parishes therein, except
   such as are hereunder named 4
   London 8
   Westminster and the Duchy 2

HERTFORDSHIRE, with the Boroughs, Towns, and Parishes therein . 6

BUCKINGHAMSHIRE, with the Boroughs, Towns, and Parishes therein . 6

OXFORDSHIRE, with the Boroughs, Towns, and Parishes therein, except
such as are hereunder named 4
   Oxford City 2
   Oxford University 2

GLOUCESTERSHIRE, with the Boroughs, Towns, and Parishes therein,
except Gloucester 7
   Gloucester 2

HEREFORDSHIRE, with the Boroughs, Towns, and Parishes therein,
except Hereford 4
   Hereford 1

WORCESTERSHIRE, with the Boroughs, Towns, and Parishes therein,
except Worcester 4
   Worcester 2

WARWICKSHIRE, with the Boroughs, Towns, and Parishes therein,
except Coventry 5
   Coventry 2

NORTHAMPTONSHIRE, with the Boroughs, Towns, and Parishes therein,
except Northampton 5
   Northampton 1

BEDFORDSHIRE, with the Boroughs, Towns, and Parishes therein . 4

CAMBRIDGESHIRE, with the Boroughs, Towns, and Parishes therein,
except such as are hereunder particularly named . . . 4
   Cambridge University 2
   Cambridge Town 2

ESSEX, with the Boroughs, Towns, and Parishes therein, except
Colchester 11
   Colchester 2

SUFFOLK, with the Boroughs, Towns, and Parishes therein, except
such as are hereafter named 10
   Ipswich 2
   St. Edmund's Bury 1

NORFOLK, with the Boroughs, Towns, and Parishes therein, except
such as are hereunder named 9
   Norwich 3
   Lynn 1
   Yarmouth 1

LINCOLNSHIRE, with the Boroughs, Towns, and Parishes therein,
except the City of Lincoln and the Town of Boston . . . 11
   Lincoln 1
   Boston 1

RUTLANDSHIRE, with the Boroughs, Towns, and Parishes therein . 1

HUNTINGDONSHIRE, with the Boroughs, Towns, and Parishes therein . 3

LEICESTERSHIRE, with the Boroughs, Towns, and Parishes therein,
except Leicester 5
   Leicester 1

NOTTINGHAMSHIRE, with the Boroughs, Towns, and Parishes therein, except Nottingham 4
Nottingham 1

DERBYSHIRE, with the Boroughs, Towns, and Parishes therein, except Derby 5
Derby 1

STAFFORDSHIRE, with the City of Lichfield, the Boroughs, Towns, and Parishes therein 6

SHROPSHIRE, with the Boroughs, Towns, and Parishes therein, except Shrewsbury 6
Shrewsbury 1

CHESHIRE, with the Boroughs, Towns, and Parishes therein, except Chester 5
Chester 2

LANCASHIRE, with the Boroughs, Towns, and Parishes therein, except Manchester 6
Manchester and the Parish 1

YORKSHIRE, with the Boroughs, Towns, and Parishes therein, except such as are hereafter named 15
York City and the County thereof 3
Kingston upon Hull and the County thereof 1
Leeds Town and Parish 1

DURHAM COUNTY PALATINE, with the Boroughs, Towns, and Parishes therein, except Durham and Gateside 3
Durham City 1

NORTHUMBERLAND, with the Boroughs, Towns, and Parishes therein, except such as are hereunder named 3
Newcastle upon Tyne and the County thereof, with Gateside . 2
Berwick 1

CUMBERLAND, with the Boroughs, Towns, and Parishes therein . . 3

WESTMORELAND, with the Boroughs, Towns, and Parishes therein . 2

WALES.

ANGLESEA, with the Parishes therein 2

BRECKNOCK, with the Boroughs and Parishes therein . . . 3

CARDIGAN, with the Boroughs and Parishes therein . . . 3

CARMARTHEN, with the Boroughs and Parishes therein . . . 3

CARNARVON, with the Boroughs and Parishes therein . . . 2

DENBIGH, with the Boroughs and Parishes therein . . . 2

FLINT, with the Boroughs and Parishes therein 1

MONMOUTH, with the Boroughs and Parishes therein . . . 4

GLAMORGAN, with the Boroughs and Parishes therein . . . 4

MERIONETH, with the Boroughs and Parishes therein .   .   .   2

MONTGOMERY, with the Boroughs and Parishes therein   .   .   . 3

RADNOR, with the Boroughs and Parishes therein   2

PEMBROKE, with the Boroughs, Towns, and Parishes therein   .   . 4

Provided, that the first or second Representative may, if they see cause, assign the remainder of the 400 representers, not hereby assigned, or so many of them as they shall see cause for, unto such counties as shall appear in this present distribution to have less than their due proportion. Provided also, that where any city or borough, to which one representer or more is assigned, shall be found in a due proportion not competent alone to elect a representer, or the number of representers assigned thereto, it is left to future Representatives to assign such a number of parishes or villages near adjoining to such city or borough, to be joined therewith in the elections, or may make the same proportionable.

Thirdly. That the people do, of course, choose themselves a Representative once in two years, and shall meet for that purpose upon the first Thursday in every second May, by eleven in the morning; and the Representatives so chosen to meet upon the second Thursday in the June following, at the usual place in Westminster, or such other place as, by the foregoing Representative, or the Council of State in the interval, shall be, from time to time, appointed and published to the people, at the least twenty days before the time of election: and to continue their sessions there, or elsewhere, until the second Thursday in December following, unless they shall adjourn or dissolve themselves sooner; but not to continue longer. The election of the first Representative to be on the first Thursday in May, 1649; and that, and all future elections, to be according to the rules prescribed for the same purpose in this Agreement, viz. 1. That the electors in every division shall be natives or denizens of England; not persons receiving alms, but such as are assessed ordinarily towards the relief of the poor; no servants to, and receiving wages from, any particular person; and in all elections, except for the Universities, they shall be men of twenty-one years of age, or upwards, and housekeepers, dwelling within the division for which the election is : provided, that (until the end of seven years next ensuing the time herein limited for the end of this present Parliament) no person shall be admitted to, or have any hand or voice in, such elections, who hath adhered unto or assisted the King against the Parliament in any of the late wars or insurrections; or who shall make or join in, or abet, any forcible opposition against this Agreement. 2. That such persons, and such only, may be elected to be of the Representative, who, by the rule aforesaid, are to have voice in elections in one place or other. Provided, that of those none shall be eligible for the first or second Representative, who have not voluntarily assisted the Parliament against the King, either in person before the 14th of June, 1645, or else in money, plate, horse, or arms, lent upon the Propositions, before the end of May, 1643; or who have joined in, or abetted, the treasonable engagement in London, in 1647; or who declared or engaged themselves for a cessation of arms with the Scots that invaded this nation the last summer; or for compliance with the actors in any insurrections of the same summer; or with the Prince of Wales, or his accomplices, in the revolted fleet. Provided also, that such persons as, by the rules in the preceding Article, are not capable of electing until the end of seven years, shall not be capable to be elected until the end of fourteen years next ensuing. And we desire and recommend it to all men, that, in all times, the persons to be chosen for this great trust may be men of courage, fearing God and hating covetousness ; and that our Representatives would make the best provisions for that end. 3. That whoever, by the rules in the two preceding Articles, are incapable of electing, or to be elected, shall presume to vote in, or be present at, such election for the first or second Representative ; or, being elected, shall presume to sit or vote in either of the said Representatives, shall incur the pain of confiscation of the moiety of his estate, to the use of the public, in case he have any visible estate to the value of £50, and if he has not such an estate, then shall incur the pain of imprisonment for three months. And if any person shall forcibly oppose, molest or hinder the people, capable of electing as aforesaid, in their quiet and free election of representers, for the first

Representative, then each person so offending shall incur the penalty of confiscation of his whole estate, both real and personal; and, if he has not an estate to the value of £50, shall suffer imprisonment during one whole year without bail or mainprize. Provided, that the offender in each such case be convicted within three months next after the committing of his offence, and the first Representative is to make further provision for the avoiding of these evils in future elections. 4. That to the end all officers of state may be certainly account-able, and no faction made to maintain corrupt interests, no member of a Council of State, nor any officer of any salary-forces in army or garrison, nor any treasurer or receiver of public money, shall, while such, be elected to be of a Repre-sentative: and in case any such election shall be, the same to be void. And in case any lawyer shall be chosen into any Representative or Council of State, then he shall be incapable of practice as a lawyer during that trust. 5. For the more convenient election of Representatives, each county, wherein more than three representers are to be chosen, with the town corporate and cities, if there be any, lying within the compass thereof, to which no representers are herein assigned, shall be divided by a due proportion into so many, and such parts, as each part may elect two, and no part above three representers. For the setting forth of which divisions, and the ascertaining of other circumstances hereafter expressed, so as to make the elections less subject to confusion or mistake, in order to the next Representative, Thomas Lord Grey of Groby, Sir John Danvers, Sir Henry Holcroft, knights; Moses Wall, gentle-man; Samuel Moyer, John Langley, Wm. Hawkins, Abraham Babington, Daniel Taylor, Mark Hilsley, Rd. Price, and Col. John White, citizens of London, or any five or more of them, are intrusted to nominate and appoint, under their hands and seals, three or more fit persons in each county, and in each city and borough, to which one representer or more is assigned. to be as Commissioners for the ends aforesaid, in the respective counties, cities and boroughs; and, by like writing under their hands and seals, shall certify into the Parliament Records, before the 11th of February next, the names of the Commissioners so appointed for the respective counties, cities

and boroughs, which Commissioners, or any three or more of
them, for the respective counties, cities and boroughs, shall
before the end of February next, by writing under their hands
and seals, appoint two fit and faithful persons, or more, in
each hundred, lathe or wapentake, within the respective
counties, and in each ward within the City of London, to take
care for the orderly taking of all voluntary subscriptions to
this Agreement, by fit persons to be employed for that purpose
in every parish; who are to return the subscription so taken to
the persons that employed them, keeping a transcript thereof
to themselves; and those persons, keeping like transcripts, to
return the original subscriptions to the respective Commissioners by whom they were appointed, at, or before, the 14th
day of April next, to be registered and kept in the chief
court within the respective cities and boroughs. And the
said Commissioners, or any three or more of them, for the
several counties, cities and boroughs, respectively, shall, where
more than three representers are to be chosen, divide such
counties, as also the City of London, into so many, and such
parts as are aforementioned, and shall set forth the bounds
of such divisions; and shall, in every county, city and borough,
where any representers are to be chosen, and in every such
division as aforesaid within the City of London, and within
the several counties so divided, respectively, appoint one place
certain wherein the people shall meet for the choice of the
representers; and some one fit person, or more, inhabiting
within each borough, city, county or division, respectively, to
be present at the time and place of election, in the nature of
Sheriffs, to regulate the elections; and by poll, or otherwise,
clearly to distinguish and judge thereof, and to make return
of the person or persons elected, as is hereafter expressed; and
shall likewise, in writing under their hands and seals, make
certificates of the several divisions, with the bounds thereof,
by them set forth, and of the certain places of meeting, and
persons, in the nature of Sheriff, appointed in them respectively
as aforesaid; and cause such certificates to be returned into
the Parliament Records before the end of April next; and
before that time shall also cause the same to be published in
every parish within the counties, cities and boroughs re-

spectively; and shall in every such parish likewise nominate and appoint, by warrant under their hands and seals, one trusty person, or more, inhabiting therein, to make a true list of all the persons within their respective parishes, who, according to the rules aforegoing, are to have voice in the elections; and expressing who amongst them are, by the same rules, capable of being elected; and such list, with the said warrant, to bring in and return, at the time and place of election, unto the person appointed in the nature of Sheriff, as aforesaid, for that borough, city, county or division respectively; which person so appointed as Sheriff, being present at the time and place of election; or, in case of his absence, by the space of one hour after the time limited for the peoples' meeting, then any person present that is eligible, as aforesaid, whom the people then and there assembled shall choose for that end, shall receive and keep the said lists and admit the persons therein contained, or so many of them as are present, unto a free vote in the said election; and, having first caused this Agreement to be publicly read in the audience of the people, shall proceed unto, and regulate and keep peace and order in the elections; and, by poll or otherwise, openly distinguish and judge of the same; and thereof, by certificate or writing under the hands and seals of himself, and six or more of the electors, nominating the person or persons duly elected, shall make a true return into the Parliament Records within twenty-one days after the election, under pain for default thereof, or, for making any false return, to forfeit £100 to the public use; and also cause indentures to be made, and unchangeably sealed and delivered, between himself and six or more of the said electors, on the one part, and the persons, or each person, elected severally, on the other part, expressing their election of him as a representer of them according to this Agreement, and his acceptance of that trust, and his promise accordingly to perform the same with faithfulness, to the best of his understanding and ability, for the glory of God and good of the people. This course is to hold for the first Representative, which is to provide for the ascertaining of these circumstances in order to future Representatives.

Fourthly. That 150 members at least be always present

in each sitting of the Representative, at the passing of any
law or doing of any act whereby the people are to be bound;
saving, that the number of sixty may make a House for
debates or resolutions that are preparatory thereunto.

Fifthly.   That the Representative shall, within twenty
days after their first meeting, appoint a Council of State for
the managing of public affairs, until the tenth day after the
meeting of the next Representative, unless that next Representative think fit to put an end to that trust sooner.   And
the same Council to act and proceed therein, according to such
instructions and limitations as the Representative shall give,
and not otherwise.

Sixthly.   That in each interval between biennial Representatives, the Council of State, in case of imminent danger or
extreme necessity, may summon a Representative to be forthwith chosen, and to meet; so as the Session thereof continue
not above eighty days; and so as it dissolve at least fifty
days before the appointed time for the next biennial Representative; and upon the fiftieth day so preceding it shall
dissolve of course, if not otherwise dissolved sooner.

Seventhly.   That no member of any Representative be
made either receiver, treasurer, or other officer, during that
employment, saving to be a member of the Council of State.

Eighthly.   That the Representatives have, and shall be
understood to have, the supreme trust in order to the preservation and government of the whole; and that their power
extend, without the consent or concurrence of any other person
or persons, to the erecting and abolishing of Courts of Justice
and public offices, and to the enacting, altering, repealing and
declaring of laws, and the highest and final judgment, concerning
all natural or civil things, but not concerning things spiritual or
evangelical.   Provided that, even in things natural and civil,
these six particulars next following are, and shall be, understood to be excepted and reserved from our Representatives,
viz. 1. We do not empower them to impress or constrain any
person to serve in foreign war, either by sea or land, nor for
any military service within the kingdom; save that they may
take order for the forming, training, and exercising of the
people in a military way, to be in readiness for resisting of

foreign invasions, suppressing of sudden insurrections, or for assisting in execution of the laws; and may take order for the employing and conducting of them for those ends; provided, that, even in such cases, none be compellable to go out of the county he lives in, if he procure another to serve in his room. 2. That, after the time herein limited for the commencement of the first Representative, none of the people may be at any time questioned for any thing said or done in relation to the late wars or public differences, otherwise than in execution or pursuance of the determinations of the present House of Commons, against such as have adhered to the King, or his interest, against the people; and saving that accomptants for public moneys received, shall remain accountable for the same. 3. That no securities given, or to be given, by the public faith of the nation, nor any engagements of the public faith for satisfaction of debts and damages, shall be made void or invalid by the next or any future Representatives; except to such creditors as have, or shall have, justly forfeited the same: and saving, that the next Representative may confirm or make null, in part or in whole, all gifts of lands, moneys, offices, or otherwise, made by the present Parliament to any member or attendant of either House. 4. That, in any laws hereafter to be made, no person, by virtue of any tenure, grant, charter, patent, degree or birth, shall be privileged from subjection thereto, or from being bound thereby, as well as others. 5. That the Representative may not give judgment upon any man's person or estate, where no law hath before provided; save only in calling to account and punishing public officers for abusing or failing in their trust. 6. That no Representative may in any wise render up, or give, or take away, any of the foundations of common right, liberty, and safety contained in this Agreement, nor level men's estates, destroy property, or make all things common; and that, in all matters of such fundamental concernment, there shall be a liberty to particular members of the said Representatives to enter their dissents from the major vote.

Ninthly. Concerning religion, we agree as followeth:— 1. It is intended that the Christian Religion be held forth and recommended as the public profession in this nation,

which we desire may, by the grace of God, be reformed to
the greatest purity in doctrine, worship and discipline, according to the Word of God ; the instructing the people thereunto
in a public way, so it be not compulsive; as also the maintaining of able teachers for that end, and for the confutation or
discovering of heresy, error, and whatsoever is contrary to sound
doctrine, is allowed to be provided for by our Representatives ;
the maintenance of which teachers may be out of a public
treasury, and, we desire, not by tithes : provided, that Popery
or Prelacy be not held forth as the public way or profession
in this nation.   2. That, to the public profession so held forth,
none be compelled by penalties or otherwise; but only may
be endeavoured to be won by sound doctrine, and the example
of a good conversation.   3. That such as profess faith in God
by Jesus Christ, however differing in judgment from the doctrine, worship or discipline publicly held forth, as aforesaid,
shall not be restrained from, but shall be protected in, the
profession of their faith and exercise of religion, according
to their consciences, in any place except such as shall be set
apart for the public worship; where we provide not for them,
unless they have leave, so as they abuse not this liberty to the
civil injury of others, or to actual disturbance of the public
peace on their parts.   Nevertheless, it is not intended to be
hereby provided, that this liberty shall necessarily extend to
Popery or Prelacy.   4. That all laws, ordinances, statutes, and
clauses in any law, statute, or ordinance to the contrary of the
liberty herein provided for, in the two particulars next preceding
concerning religion, be, and are hereby, repealed and made void.

Tenthly.   It is agreed, that whosoever shall, by force of
arms, resist the orders of the next or any future Representative
(except in case where such Representative shall evidently
render up, or give, or take away the foundations of common
right, liberty, and safety, contained in this Agreement), he
shall forthwith, after his or their such resistance, lose the
benefit and protection of the laws, and shall be punishable with
death, as an enemy and traitor to the nation.   Of the things
expressed in this Agreement : the certain ending of this Parliament, as in the first Article; the equal or proportionable
distribution of the number of the representers to be elected,

as in the second; the certainty of the people's meeting to elect
for Representatives biennial, and their freedom in elections;
with the certainty of meeting, sitting and ending of Representatives so elected, which are provided for in the third
Article; as also the qualifications of persons to elect or be
elected, as in the first and second particulars under the third
Article; also the certainty of a number for passing a law or
preparatory debates, provided for in the fourth Article; the
matter of the fifth Article, concerning the Council of State,
and of the sixth, concerning the calling, sitting and ending of
Representatives extraordinary; also the power of Representatives
to be, as in the eighth Article, and limited, as in the six
reserves next following the same : likewise the second and third
Particulars under the ninth Article concerning religion, and
the whole matter of the tenth Article ; all these we do account
and declare to be fundamental to our common right, liberty,
and safety: and therefore do both agree thereunto, and resolve
to maintain the same, as God shall enable us.   The rest of the
matters in this Agreement we account to be useful and good
for the public ; and the particular circumstances of numbers,
times, and places, expressed in the several Articles, we account
not fundamental; but we find them necessary to be here
determined, for the making the Agreement certain and prac-
ticable, and do hold these most convenient that are here set
down ; and therefore do positively agree thereunto.   By the
appointment of his Excellency the Lord-General and his General
Council of Officers.

JOHN RUSHWORTH, Sec.

82. THE CHARGE AGAINST THE KING.

[January 20, 164⅞.   Rushworth, vii. 1396.   See *Great Civil War*,
iv. 299.]

That the said Charles Stuart, being admitted King of England, and therein trusted with a limited power to govern by
and according to the laws of the land, and not otherwise; and
by his trust, oath, and office, being obliged to use the power
committed to him for the good and benefit of the people, and

for the preservation of their rights and liberties; yet, nevertheless, out of a wicked design to erect and uphold in himself an unlimited and tyrannical power to rule according to his will, and to overthrow the rights and liberties of the people, yea, to take away and make void the foundations thereof, and of all redress and remedy of misgovernment, which by the fundamental constitutions of this kingdom were reserved on the people's behalf in the right and power of frequent and successive Parliaments, or national meetings in Council; he, the said Charles Stuart, for accomplishment of such his designs, and for the protecting of himself and his adherents in his and their wicked practices, to the same ends hath traitorously and maliciously levied war against the present Parliament, and the people therein represented, particularly upon or about the 30th day of June, in the year of our Lord 1642, at Beverley, in the County of York; and upon or about the 24th day of August in the same year, at the County of the Town of Nottingham, where and when he set up his standard of war; and also on or about the 23rd day of October in the same year, at Edgehill or Keynton-field, in the County of Warwick; and upon or about the 30th day of November in the same year, at Brentford, in the County of Middlesex; and upon or about the 30th day of August, in the year of our Lord 1643, at the Caversham Bridge, near Reading, in the County of Berks; and upon or about the 30th day of October in the year last mentioned, at or upon the City of Gloucester; and upon or about the 30th day of November in the year last mentioned, at Newbury, in the County of Berks; and upon or about the 31st day of July, in the year of our Lord 1644, at Cropredy Bridge, in the County of Oxon; and upon or about the 30th day of September in the last year mentioned, at Bodmin and other places near adjacent, in the County of Cornwall; and upon or about the 30th day of November in the year last mentioned, at Newbury aforesaid; and upon or about the 8th day of June, in the year of our Lord 1645, at the Town of Leicester; and also upon the 14th day of the same month in the same year, at Naseby-field, in the County of Northampton. At which several times and places, or most of them, and at many other places in this land, at several other times within the years aforementioned, and in the year of our Lord 1646, he, the said Charles Stuart, hath caused and procured many thousands of the free people of this nation to be slain; and by divisions, parties, and insurrections within this land, by invasions from foreign parts, endeavoured and procured by him, and by many other evil ways and means, he, the said Charles Stuart, hath not only maintained and carried on the said war both by land and sea, during the years beforementioned, but also hath renewed, or caused to be renewed, the said war against the Parliament and good people of this nation in this present year 1648, in the Counties of Kent, Essex, Surrey, Sussex, Middlesex, and many other Counties and places in England and Wales, and also by sea. And particularly he, the said Charles Stuart, hath for that purpose given commission to his son the Prince, and others, whereby, besides multitudes of other persons, many such as were by the Parliament entrusted and employed for the safety of the nation (being by him or his agents corrupted to the betraying of their trust, and revolting from the Parliament), have had entertainment and commission for the continuing and renewing of war and hostility against the said Parliament and people as aforesaid. By which cruel and unnatural wars, by him, the said Charles Stuart, levied, continued, and renewed as aforesaid, much innocent blood of the free people of this nation hath been spilt, many families have been undone, the public treasure wasted and exhausted, trade obstructed and miserably decayed, vast expense and damage to the nation incurred, and many parts of this land spoiled, some of them even to desolation. And for further prosecution of his said evil designs, he, the said Charles Stuart, doth still continue his commissions to the said Prince, and other rebels and revolters, both English and foreigners, and to the Earl of Ormond, and the Irish rebels and revolters associated with him; from whom further invasions upon this land are threatened, upon the procurement, and on the behalf of the said Charles Stuart.

All which wicked designs, wars, and evil practices of him, the said Charles Stuart, have been, and are carried on for the advancement and upholding of a personal interest of will, power, and pretended prerogative to himself and his family, against the public interest, common right, liberty, justice, and peace of the people of this nation, by and from whom he was entrusted as aforesaid.

By all which it appeareth that the said Charles Stuart hath been, and is the occasioner, author, and continuer of the said unnatural, cruel and bloody wars; and therein guilty of all the treasons, murders, rapines, burnings, spoils, desolations, damages and mischiefs to this nation, acted and committed in the said wars, or occasioned thereby.

83. The King's reasons for declining the jurisdiction of the High Court of Justice.

[January 21, 164⅞.   Rushworth, vii. 1403.]

Having already made my protestations, not only against the illegality of this pretended Court, but also, that no earthly power can justly call me (who am your King) in question as a delinquent, I would not any more open my mouth upon this occasion, more than to refer myself to what I have spoken, were I in this case alone concerned: but the duty I owe to God in the preservation of the true liberty of my people will not suffer me at this time to be silent: for, how can any free-born subject of England call life or anything he possesseth his own, if power without right daily make new, and abrogate the old fundamental laws of the land which I now take to be the present case? Wherefore when I came hither, I expected that you would have endeavoured to have satisfied me concerning these grounds which hinder me to answer to your pretended impeachment. But since I see that nothing I can say will move you to it (though negatives are not so naturally proved as affirmatives) yet I will show you the reason why I am confident you cannot judge me, nor indeed the meanest man in England: for I will not (like you) without showing a reason, seek to impose a belief upon my subjects.

There is no proceeding just against any man, but what is warranted, either by God's laws or the municipal laws of the country where he lives.   Now I am most confident this day's proceeding cannot be warranted by God's laws; for, on the

contrary, the authority of obedience unto Kings is clearly
warranted, and strictly commanded in both the Old and New
Testament, which, if denied, I am ready instantly to prove.

And for the question now in hand, there it is said, that
'where the word of a King is, there is power; and who may
say unto him, what dost thou?' Eccles. viii. 4. Then for the
law of this land, I am no less confident, that no learned lawyer
will affirm that an impeachment can lie against the King, they
all going in his name : and one of their maxims is, that the
King can do no wrong.   Besides, the law upon which you
ground your proceedings, must either be old or new : if old,
show it ; if new, tell what authority, warranted by the fundamental laws of the land, hath made it, and when.   But how
the House of Commons can erect a Court of Judicature, which
was never one itself (as is well known to all lawyers) I leave
to God and the world to judge.   And it were full as strange,
that they should pretend to make laws without King or Lords'
House, to any that have heard speak of the laws of England.

And admitting, but not granting, that the people of England's
commission could grant your pretended power, I see nothing you
can show for that ; for certainly you never asked the question
of the tenth man in the kingdom, and in this way you manifestly
wrong even the poorest ploughman, if you demand not his free
consent; nor can you pretend any colour for this your pretended
commission, without the consent at least of the major part of
every man in England of whatsoever quality or condition,
which I am sure you never went about to seek, so far are you
from having it.   Thus you see that I speak not for my own
right alone, as I am your King, but also for the true liberty of
all my subjects, which consists not in the power of government,
but in living under such laws, such a government, as may
give themselves the best assurance of their lives, and property
of their goods; nor in this must or do I forget the privileges
of both Houses of Parliament, which this day's proceedings do
not only, violate, but likewise occasion the greatest breach of
their public faith that (I believe) ever was heard of, with which
I am far from charging the two Houses; for all the pretended
crimes laid against me bear date long before this Treaty at
Newport, in which I having concluded as much as in me lay,

and hopefully expecting the Houses' agreement thereunto, I was suddenly surprised and hurried from thence as a prisoner; upon which account I am against my will brought hither, where since I am come, I cannot but to my power defend the ancient laws and liberties of this kingdom, together with my own just right. Then for anything I can see, the higher House is totally excluded; and for the House of Commons, it is too well known that the major part of them are detained or deterred from sitting; so as if I had no other, this were sufficient for me to protest against the lawfulness of your pretended Court. Besides all this, the peace of the kingdom is not the least in my thoughts; and what hope of settlement is there, so long as power reigns without rule or law, changing the whole frame of that government under which this kingdom hath flourished for many hundred years? (nor will I say what will fall out in case this lawless, unjust proceeding against me do go on) and believe it, the Commons of England will not thank you for this change; for they will remember how happy they have been of late years under the reigns of Queen Elizabeth, the King my father, and myself, until the beginning of these unhappy troubles, and will have cause to doubt, that they shall never be so happy under any new: and by this time it will be too sensibly evident, that the arms I took up were only to defend the fundamental laws of this kingdom against those who have supposed my power hath totally changed the ancient government.

Thus, having showed you briefly the reasons why I cannot submit to your pretended authority, without violating the trust which I have from God for the welfare and liberty of my people, I expect from you either clear reasons to convince my judgment, showing me that I am in an error (and then truly I will answer) or that you will withdraw your proceedings.

This I intended to speak in Westminster Hall, on Monday, January 22, but against reason was hindered to show my reasons.

84. The Sentence of the High Court of Justice upon the King.

[January 27, 1648-9. Rushworth, vii. 1418. See *Great Civil War*, iv. 312.]

Whereas the Commons of England assembled in Parliament, have by their late Act intituled an Act of the Commons of England assembled in Parliament, for erecting an High Court of Justice for the trying and judging of Charles Stuart, King of England, authorised and constituted us an High Court of Justice for the trying and judging of the said Charles Stuart for the crimes and treasons in the said Act mentioned; by virtue whereof the said Charles Stuart hath been three several times convented before this High Court, where the first day, being Saturday, the 20th of January instant, in pursuance of the said Act, a charge of high treason and other high crimes was, in the behalf of the people of England, exhibited against him, and read openly unto him, wherein he was charged, that he, the said Charles Stuart, being admitted King of England, and therein trusted with a limited power to govern by, and according to the law of the land, and not otherwise; and by his trust, oath, and office, being obliged to use the power committed to him for the good and benefit of the people, and for the preservation of their rights and liberties; yet, nevertheless, out of a wicked design to erect and uphold in himself an unlimited and tyrannical power to rule according to his will, and to overthrow the rights and liberties of the people, and to take away and make void the foundations thereof, and of all redress and remedy of misgovernment, which by the fundamental constitutions of this kingdom were reserved on the people's behalf in the right and power of frequent and successive Parliaments, or national meetings in Council; he, the said Charles Stuart, for accomplishment of such his designs, and for the protecting of himself and his adherents in his and their wicked practices, to the same end hath traitorously and maliciously levied war against the present Parliament, and people therein represented, as with the circumstances of time and place is in the said charge more particularly set forth; and that he hath thereby caused and procured many thousands of the free people of this nation to be slain; and by divisions, parties, and insurrections within this land, by invasions from foreign parts, endeavoured and procured by him, and by many other evil ways and means, he, the said Charles Stuart, hath not only maintained and carried on the said war both by sea and land, but also hath renewed, or caused to be renewed, the said war against the Parliament and good people of this nation in this present year 1648, in several counties and places in this kingdom in the charge specified; and that he hath for that purpose given his commission to his son the Prince, and others, whereby, besides multitudes of other persons, many such as were by the Parliament entrusted and employed for the safety of this nation, being by him or his agents corrupted to the betraying of their trust, and revolting from the Parliament, have had entertainment and commission for the continuing and renewing of the war and hostility against the said Parliament and people: and that by the said cruel and unnatural war so levied, continued and renewed, much innocent blood of the free people of this nation hath been spilt, many families undone, the public treasure wasted, trade obstructed and miserably decayed, vast expense and damage to the nation incurred, and many parts of the land spoiled, some of them even to desolation; and that he still continues his commission to his said son, and other rebels and revolters, both English and foreigners, and to the Earl of Ormond, and to the Irish rebels and revolters associated with him, from whom further invasions of this land are threatened by his procurement and on his behalf; and that all the said wicked designs, wars, and evil practices of him, the said Charles Stuart, were still carried on for the advancement and upholding of the personal interest of will, power, and pretended prerogative to himself and his family, against the public interest, common right, liberty, justice, and peace of the people of this nation; and that he thereby hath been and is the occasioner, author, and continuer of the said unnatural, cruel, and bloody wars, and therein guilty of all the treasons, murders, rapines, burnings, spoils, desolations, damage, and mischief to this nation, acted and committed in the said wars, or occasioned thereby; whereupon the proceedings and judgment of this Court were prayed against him, as a tyrant, traitor, and murderer, and public enemy to the Commonwealth, as by the said charge more fully appeareth. To which charge, being read unto him as aforesaid, he, the said Charles Stuart, was required to give his answer; but he refused so to do, and upon Monday, the 22nd day of January instant, being again brought before this Court, and there required to answer directly to the said charge, he still refused so to do; whereupon his default and contumacy was entered; and the next day, being the third time brought before the Court, judgment was then prayed against him on the behalf of the people of England for his contumacy, and for the matters contained against him in the said charge, as taking the same for confessed, in regard of his refusing to answer thereto: yet notwithstanding this Court (not willing to take advantage of his contempt) did once more require him to answer to the said charge; but he again refused so to do; upon which his several defaults, this Court might justly have proceeded to judgment against him, both for his contumacy and the matters of the charge, taking the same for confessed as aforesaid.

Yet nevertheless this Court, for its own clearer information and further satisfaction, have thought fit to examine witnesses upon oath, and take notice of other evidences, touching the matters contained in the said charge, which accordingly they have done.

Now, therefore, upon serious and mature deliberation of the premises, and consideration had of the notoriety of the matters of fact charged upon him as aforesaid, this Court is in judgment and conscience satisfied that he, the said Charles Stuart, is guilty of levying war against the said Parliament and people, and maintaining and continuing the same; for which in the said charge he stands accused, and by the general course of his government, counsels, and practices, before and since this Parliament began (which have been and are notorious and public, and the effects whereof remain abundantly upon record) this Court is fully satisfied in their judgments and consciences, that he has been and is guilty of the wicked design and endeavours in the said charge set forth; and that the said war hath been levied, maintained, and continued by him as aforesaid, in prosecution, and for accomplishment of the said designs; and that he hath been and is the occasioner, author, and continuer of the said unnatural, cruel, and bloody wars, and therein guilty of high treason, and of the murders, rapines, burnings, spoils, desolations, damage, and mischief to this nation acted and committed in the said war, and occasioned thereby. For all which treasons and crimes this Court doth adjudge that he, the said Charles Stuart, as a tyrant, traitor, murderer, and public enemy to the good people of this nation, shall be put to death by the severing of his head from his body.

85. THE DEATH WARRANT OF CHARLES I.

[January 29, 164⅞. Rushworth, vii. 1426. See *Great Civil War*, iv. 309.]

At the High Court of Justice for the trying and judging of Charles Stuart, King of England, Jan. 29, Anno Domini 1648.

Whereas Charles Stuart, King of England, is, and standeth convicted, attainted, and condemned of high treason, and other high crimes; and sentence upon Saturday last was pronounced against him by this Court, to be put to death by the severing of his head from his body; of which sentence, execution yet remaineth to be done; these are therefore to will and require you to see the said sentence executed in the open street before Whitehall, upon the morrow, being the thirtieth day of this instant month of January, between the hours of ten in the morning and five in the afternoon of the same day, with full effect. And for so doing this shall be your sufficient warrant. And these are to require all officers, soldiers, and others, the good people of this nation of England, to be assisting unto you in this service.

To Col. Francis Hacker, Col. Huncks, and Lieut.-Col. Phayre, and to every of them.

Given under our hands and seals.

JOHN BRADSHAW.
THOMAS GREY.
OLIVER CROMWELL.
&c. &c.

PART V

THE COMMONWEALTH AND PROTECTORATE

86. ACT APPOINTING A COUNCIL OF STATE.

[February 13, 164⅘. Parliamentary Order Book, State Papers, Domestic Interregnum, 87. 1. See *Commonwealth and Protectorate*, i. 3–5.]

An Act of this present Parliament for constituting a Council of State for the Commonwealth of England.

Be it ordained and enacted by this present Parliament that Basil Earl of Denbigh, Edmund Earl of Mulgrave, &c., &c., or any nine of them shall be a Council of State, and have hereby power, and are authorised to put in execution the following instructions.

1. You are hereby authorised and required to oppose and suppress whomsoever shall endeavour or go about to set up or maintain the pretended title of Charles Stuart, eldest son to the late King, or any other of the said late King's issue or claiming under him or them, or the pretended title or claim of any other single person whomsoever to the Crown of England or Ireland, dominion of Wales, or to any of the dominions or territories to them or either of them belonging.

2. You are hereby authorised and empowered to order and direct all the militias and forces both by sea and land of England and Ireland and the dominions to them or either of them belonging, preserving the peace or safety thereof, and for preventing, resisting, and suppressing all tumults and insurrections that shall happen to rise in them or either of them, or any

invasions of them from abroad : and also upon any emergencies to raise and arm such forces as you shall judge necessary for the ends above expressed, and to give commissions under the seal of the Council to such officers as you shall judge necessary for the leading, conducting and commanding of the said forces, and for the prosecution and pursuance of these instructions, or of any other instructions you shall receive from the Parliament.

3. You are hereby authorised and required to use all good ways and means for the reducing of Ireland, the Isles of Jersey, Guernsey, Scilly, and the Isle of Man, and all other parts and places belonging to the Commonwealth of England not yet reduced.

4. You shall take care that the stores and magazines of all military provisions both for the land service and for the sea be from time to time well and sufficiently furnished, and that the same be issued as you shall by warrant direct : and you are also from time to time to take care of the repair of the shipping belonging to the Commonwealth of England, and to build such others as you shall judge necessary for the defence and safety thereof.

5. You are to use all good ways and means for the securing, advancement, and encouragement of the trade of England and Ireland and the dominions to them belonging, and to promote the good of all foreign plantations and factories belonging to this Commonwealth or any of the natives thereof.

6. You shall advise, order, and direct concerning the entertaining, keeping, renewing, or settling of amity and a good correspondency with foreign kingdoms and states, and for preserving the rights of the people of this nation in foreign parts, and composing of their differences there : and you are hereby authorised to send ambassadors, agents, or messengers to any foreign kingdom or state, and to receive ambassadors, agents, or messengers from them for the ends aforesaid.

7. You are to advise and consult of anything concerning the good of the Commonwealth, and report your opinion concerning the cause as you find occasion to the Parliament.

8. You are hereby authorised to send for any person or persons whatsoever to advise with them in pursuance of these or any other instructions that shall be given unto you.

9. You have hereby power and are authorised in case of danger to the Commonwealth to administer an oath to any person or persons for the discovery of the truth.

10. You are hereby authorised and empowered to send for and imprison or otherwise to secure by taking bond in recognizancy any such person or persons as shall be offenders against these or any other instructions which you shall receive from the Parliament; and all such as shall contemn or be refractory to any of your commands, directions, or orders in pursuance of the said instructions.

11. You have hereby power and are authorised to charge the public revenue by warrant under the seal of the Council with such sum or sums of money from time to time as you shall find necessary for defraying all charges of foreign negotiations, intelligence, and other incidencies, and for the salary of such subordinate officers and attendants as you shall judge fit to employ, and for the effectual carrying on of the service by those instructions committed to you, or by any other instructions hereafter to be given you from the Parliament.

12. You are also to observe and put in execution such further orders as you shall receive from time to time from the Parliament.

13. The power hereby committed to the Council of State shall continue for the space of one whole year from the day of passing hereof, unless it be otherwise ordered by the Parliament.

14. You have also hereby power to appoint committees or any person or persons for examinations, receiving of informations, and preparing of business for your debates or resolutions.

15. You are to meet at Derby House at four of the clock this afternoon, and from time to time and from place to place as you shall see cause, and in such manner as you shall think fit for the execution of your instructions.

87. Engagement taken by the members of the Council of State.

[February 22, 1649. Old Parliamentary History, xix. 38. See *Common-wealth and Protectorate*, i. 6, 7.]

I, A. B., being nominated a member of the Council of
State by this present Parliament, do testify that I do adhere
to this present Parliament, in the maintenance and defence
of the public liberty and freedom of this nation, as it is
now declared by this Parliament (by whose authority I am
constituted a member of the said Council) and in the maintenance and defence of their resolutions concerning the settling
of the government of this nation for the future in way of
a Republic, without King or House of Lords; and I do promise
in the sight of God that, through His grace, I will be
faithful in the performance of the trust committed to me
as aforesaid, and therein faithfully pursue the instructions
given to the said Council by this present Parliament; and
not reveal or disclose anything, in whole or in part, directly
or indirectly, that shall be debated or resolved upon in the
Council, without the command or direction of the Parliament,
or without the order or allowance of the major part of the
Council or of the major part of them that shall be present
at such debates or resolutions. In confirmation of the premises
I have hereto subscribed my name.

88. The Act abolishing the office of King.

[March 17, 1649. Scobell, ii. 7. See *Commonwealth
and Protectorate*, i. 39.]

Whereas Charles Stuart, late King of England, Ireland,
and the territories and dominions thereunto belonging, hath
by authority derived from Parliament been and is hereby
declared to be justly condemned, adjudged to die, and put to
death, for many treasons, murders, and other heinous offences
committed by him, by which judgment he stood, and is
hereby declared to be attainted of high treason, whereby
his issue and posterity, and all others pretending title under

him, are become incapable of the said Crowns, or of being
King or Queen of the said kingdom or dominions, or either
or any of them; be it therefore enacted and ordained, and
it is enacted, ordained, and declared by this present Parliament, and by authority thereof, that all the people of
England and Ireland, and the dominions and territories
thereunto belonging, of what degree or condition soever,
are discharged of all fealty, homage, and allegiance which is
or shall be pretended to be due unto any of the issue and
posterity of the said late King, or any claiming under him;
and that Charles Stuart, eldest son, and James called Duke
of York, second son, and all other the issue and posterity
of him the said late King, and all and every person and
persons pretending title from, by, or under him, are and be
disabled to hold or enjoy the said Crown of England and
Ireland, and other the dominions thereunto belonging, or
any of them; or to have the name, title, style, or dignity of
King or Queen of England and Ireland, Prince of Wales, or
any of them; or to have and enjoy the power and dominion
of the said kingdom and dominions, or any of them, or the
honors, manors, lands, tenements, possessions, and hereditaments belonging or appertaining to the said Crown of England
and Ireland, and other the dominions aforesaid, or to any
of them; or to the Principality of Wales, Duchy of Lancaster
or Cornwall, or any or either of them, any law, statute,
ordinance, usage, or custom to the contrary hereof in any
wise notwithstanding.

And whereas it is and hath been found by experience,
that the office of a King in this nation and Ireland, and to
have the power thereof in any single person, is unnecessary,
burdensome, and dangerous to the liberty, safety, and public
interest of the people, and that for the most part, use hath
been made of the regal power and prerogative to oppress and
impoverish and enslave the subject; and that usually and
naturally any one person in such power makes it his interest
to incroach upon the just freedom and liberty of the people,
and to promote the setting up of their own will and power
above the laws, that so they might enslave these kingdoms
to their own lust; be it therefore enacted and ordained by

this present Parliament, and by authority of the same, that the office of a King in this nation shall not henceforth reside in or be exercised by any one single person; and that no one person whatsoever shall or may have, or hold the office, style, dignity, power, or authority of King of the said kingdoms and dominions, or any of them, or of the Prince of Wales, any law, statute, usage, or custom to the contrary thereof in any wise notwithstanding.

And it is hereby enacted, that if any person or persons shall endeavour to attempt by force of arms or otherwise, or be aiding, assisting, comforting, or abetting unto any person or persons that shall by any ways or means whatsoever endeavour or attempt the reviving or setting up again of any pretended right of the said Charles, eldest son to the said late King, James called Duke of York, or of any other the issue and posterity of the said late King, or of any person or persons claiming under him or them, to the said regal office, style, dignity, or authority, or to be Prince of Wales; or the promoting of any one person whatsoever to the name, style, dignity, power, prerogative, or authority of King of England and Ireland, and dominions aforesaid, or any of them; that then every such offence shall be deemed and adjudged high treason, and the offenders therein, their counsellors, procurers, aiders and abettors, being convicted of the said offence, or any of them, shall be deemed and adjudged traitors against the Parliament and people of England, and shall suffer, lose, and forfeit, and have such like and the same pains, forfeitures, judgments, and execution as is used in case of high treason.

And whereas by the abolition of the kingly office provided for in this Act, a most happy way is made for this nation (if God see it good) to return to its just and ancient right, of being governed by its own representatives or national meetings in council, from time to time chosen and entrusted for that purpose by the people, it is therefore resolved and declared by the Commons assembled in Parliament, that they will put a period to the sitting of this present Parliament, and dissolve the same so soon as may possibly stand with the safety of the people that hath betrusted them, and with what is absolutely necessary for the preserving and upholding the Government

now settled in the way of a Commonwealth; and that they
will carefully provide for the certain choosing, meeting, and
sitting of the next and future representatives, with such other
circumstances of freedom in choice and equality in distribution
of members to be elected thereunto, as shall most conduce to
the lasting freedom and good of this Commonwealth.

And it is hereby further enacted and declared, notwithstanding any thing contained in this Act, no person or persons of
what condition and quality soever, within the Commonwealth
of England and Ireland, dominion of Wales, the islands of
Guernsey and Jersey, and town of Berwick-upon-Tweed, shall
be discharged from the obedience and subjection which he and
they owe to the Government of this nation, as it is now declared,
but all and every of them shall in all things render and perform
the same, as of right is due unto the supreme authority hereby
declared to reside in this and the successive representatives of
the people of this nation, and in them only.

89. An Act abolishing the House of Lords.

[March 19, 1649. Scobell, ii. 8. See *Commonwealth
and Protectorate*, i. 3.]

The Commons of England assembled in Parliament, finding
by too long experience that the House of Lords is useless
and dangerous to the people of England to be continued, have
thought fit to ordain and enact, and be it ordained and
enacted by this present Parliament, and by the authority of
the same, that from henceforth the House of Lords in Parliament shall be and is hereby wholly abolished and taken
away; and that the Lords shall not from henceforth meet or
sit in the said House called the Lords' House, or in any other
house or place whatsoever, as a House of Lords; nor shall
sit, vote, advise, adjudge, or determine of any matter or thing
whatsoever, as a House of Lords in Parliament: nevertheless
it is hereby declared, that neither such Lords as have demeaned
themselves with honour, courage, and fidelity to the Commonwealth, nor their posterities who shall continue so, shall
be excluded from the public councils of the nation, but shall
be admitted thereunto, and have their free vote in Parlia-

ment, if they shall be thereunto elected, as other persons of interest elected and qualified thereunto ought to have.

And be it further ordained and enacted by the authority aforesaid, that no Peer of this land, not being elected, qualified and sitting in Parliament as aforesaid, shall claim, have, or make use of any privilege of Parliament, either in relation to his person, quality, or estate, any law, usage, or custom to the conrtary notwithstanding.

90. An Act declaring England to be a Commonwealth.

[May 19, 1649. Scobell, ii. 30. See *Commonwealth and Protectorate*, i. 57.]

Be it declared and enacted by this present Parliament, and by the authority of the same, that the people of England, and of all the dominions and territories thereunto belonging, are and shall be, and are hereby constituted, made, established, and confirmed, to be a Commonwealth and Free State, and shall from henceforth be governed as a Commouwealth and Free State by the supreme authority of this nation, the representatives of the people in Parliament, and by such as they shall appoint and constitute as officers and ministers under them for the good of the people, and that without any King or House of Lords.

91. An Act declaring what offences shall be adjudged Treason.

[July 17, 1649. Scobell, ii. 65. See *Commonwealth and Protectorate*, i. 55.]

Whereas the Parliament hath abolished the kingly office in England and Ireland, and in the dominions and territories thereunto belonging; and having resolved and declared, that the people shall for the future be governed by its own representatives or national meetings in Council, chosen and entrusted by them for that purpose, hath settled the Government in the way of a Commonwealth and Free State, without King or House of Lords: be it enacted by this present Parliament, and by the authority of the same, that if any person

shall maliciously or advisedly publish, by writing, printing,
or openly declaring, that the said Government is tyrannical,
usurped, or unlawful; or that the Commons in Parliament
assembled are not the supreme authority of this nation; or
shall plot, contrive, or endeavour to stir up, or raise force
against the present Government, or for the subversion or alteration of the same, and shall declare the same by any open deed,
that then every such offence shall be taken, deemed, and adjudged by authority of this Parliament to be high treason.

And whereas the Keepers of the liberty of England, and
the Council of State, constituted, and to be from time to time
constituted by authority of Parliament, are to be under the
said representatives in Parliament, entrusted for the maintenance of the said Government, with several powers and authorities limited, given, and appointed unto them by the Parliament:
be it likewise enacted by the authority aforesaid, that if any
person shall maliciously and advisedly plot or endeavour the
subversion of the said Keepers of the liberty of England, or
the Council of State, and the same shall declare by any open
deed, or shall move any person or persons for the doing thereof,
or stir up the people to rise against them, or either of them,
their or either of their authorities, that then every such offence
and offences shall be taken, deemed, and declared to be high
treason.

And whereas the Parliament, for their just and lawful
defence, hath raised and levied the army and forces now
under the command of Thomas Lord Fairfax, and are at
present necessitated, by reason of the manifold distractions
within this Commonwealth, and invasions threatened from
abroad, to continue the same, which under God must be the
instrumental means of preserving the well-affected people of
this nation in peace and safety; be it further enacted by
the authority aforesaid, that if any person, not being an
officer, soldier, or member of the army, shall plot, contrive,
or endeavour to stir up any mutiny in the said army, or
withdraw any soldiers or officers from their obedience to their
superior officers, or from the present Government as aforesaid; or shall procure, invite, aid, or assist any foreigners
or strangers to invade England or Ireland; or shall adhere

to any forces raised by the enemies of the Parliament or Commonwealth, or Keepers of the liberty of England; or if any person shall counterfeit the Great Seal of England, for the time being, used and appointed by authority of Parliament, that then every such offence and offences shall be taken, deemed, and declared by authority of this Parliament to be high treason, and every such persons shall suffer pains of death; and also forfeit unto the Keepers of the liberty of England, to and for the use of the Commonwealth, all and singular his and their lands, tenements and hereditaments, goods and chattels, as in case of high treason hath been used by the laws and statutes of this land to be forfeit and lost.

Provided always, that no persons shall be indicted and arraigned for any of the offences mentioned in this Act, unless such offenders shall be indicted and prosecuted for the same within one year after the offence committed.

And be it further enacted by the authority aforesaid, that if any person shall counterfeit the money of this Commonwealth, or shall bring any false money into this land, counterfeit or other, like to the money of this Commonwealth, knowing the money to be false, to merchandize or make payment, in deceit of the people of this nation; or if any person shall hereafter falsely forge and counterfeit any such kind of coin of gold or silver, as is not the proper coin of this Commonwealth, and is or shall be current within this nation, by consent of the Parliament, or such as shall be by them authorised thereunto; or shall bring from the parts beyond the seas into this Commonwealth, or into any the dominions of the same, any such false and counterfeit coin of money, being current within the same, as is abovesaid, knowing the same money to be false and counterfeit, to the intent to utter or make payment with the same within this Commonwealth, by merchandize or otherwise; or if any person shall impair, diminish, falsify, clip, wash, round or file, scale or lighten, for wicked lucre or gain's sake, any the proper monies or coins of this Commonwealth, or the dominions thereof, or of the monies or coins of any other realm, allowed and suffered to be current within this Commonwealth, or the dominions thereof, that then all and every such offences above-mentioned,

shall be and are hereby deemed and adjudged high treason,
and the offenders therein, their councillors, procurers, aiders
and abettors, being convicted according to the laws of this
nation of any of the said offences, shall be deemed and adjudged
traitors against this Commonwealth, and shall suffer and have
such pains of death and forfeitures, as in case of high treason
is used and ordained.

Provided always, and be it enacted by the authority aforesaid, that this Act touching the monies and coins aforesaid,
or anything therein contained, nor any attainder of any person
for the same, shall in any wise extend or be judged to make
any corruption of blood, to any the heir or heirs of any such
offender, or to make the wife of any such offender to lose
or forfeit her dower, of or in any lands, tenements, or hereditaments, or her title, action, or interest in the same.

92. Engagement to be taken by all men of the age of eighteen.

[January 2, 1650. Civil War Tracts, E. 1060, No. 77. See *Commonwealth and Protectorate*, i. 193.]

I do declare and promise, that I will be true and faithful
to the Commonwealth of England, as it is now established,
without a King or House of Lords.

93. Act repealing several clauses in Statutes imposing penalties for not coming to church.

[September 27, 1650. Scobell, ii. 131. See *Commonwealth and Protectorate*, ii. 3.]

The Parliament of England taking into consideration several
Acts, made in the times of former Kings and Queens of this
nation, against recusants not coming to church, enjoining the
use of Common Prayer, the keeping and observing of holy
days, and some other particulars touching matters of religion;
and finding, that by the said Act divers religious and peaceable people, well-affected to the prosperity of the Commonwealth, have not only been molested and imprisoned, but also
brought into danger of abjuring their country, or in case of
return, to suffer death as felons. to the great disquiet and

utter ruin of such good and godly people, and to the detriment
of the Commonwealth, do enact, and be it enacted by this
present Parliament, and by authority of the same, that all
and every the branches, clauses, articles, and provisoes expressed and contained in the ensuing Acts of Parliament;
viz. in the Act of the first of Eliz. intituled, 'An Act for
uniformity of prayer, and administration of Sacraments'; and
in an Act of the thirty-fifth of Eliz. intituled, 'An Act for
punishing of persons obstinately refusing to come to church,
and persuading others to impugn the Queen's authority in
ecclesiastical causes'; and all and every the branches, clauses,
articles, and provisoes contained in an Act of Parliament of
the twenty-third of Eliz. intituled, 'An Act for retaining the
Queen's subjects in their due obedience'; hereafter expressed,
viz. 'Be it also further enacted by the authority aforesaid,
that every person above the age of sixteen years, which shall
not repair to some Church, Chapel, or usual place of Common
Prayer, but forbear the same, contrary to the tenor of a statute
made in the first year of her Majesty's reign, for uniformity
of Common Prayer, and being thereof lawfully convicted, shall
forfeit to the Queen's Majesty for every month, after the end
of this session of Parliament, which he or she shall so forbear,
£20 of lawful English money; and that over and besides the
said forfeitures, every person so forbearing by the space of
twelve months as aforesaid, shall for his or her obstinacy,
after certificate thereof in writing made into the Court, commonly called the King's Bench, by the Ordinary of the diocese,
a Justice of assize and gaol-delivery, or a Justice of Peace of
the county where such offender shall dwell, be bound with
two sufficient sureties, in the sum of £200 at the least, to
the good behaviour, and so to continue bound until such time
as the persons so bound do conform themselves and come to
the church, according to the true meaning of the said statute
made in the said first year of the Queen's Majesty's reign:
and be it further enacted, that if any person or persons, body
politic or corporate, after the feast of Pentecost next coming,
shall keep or maintain any schoolmaster, which shall not repair
to church as is aforesaid, or be allowed by the Bishop or
Ordinary of the diocese where such schoolmaster shall be so

kept, shall forfeit and lose for every month so keeping him, £10 : provided, that no such Ordinary or their Ministers shall take anything for the said allowance : and such schoolmaster or teacher presuming to teach contrary to this Act, and being thereof lawfully convict, shall be disabled to be a teacher of youth, and shall suffer imprisonment without bail or main-prize for one year. And be it likewise enacted, that all and every offences against this Act, or against the Acts of the first, fifth, or thirteenth years of her Majesty's reign, touching acknowledging of her Majesty's supreme Government in causes ecclesiastical, or other matters touching the service of God or coming to church, or establishment of true religion in this realm, shall and may be enquirable as well before justices of peace, as other justices named in the same statutes, within one year and a day after every such offence committed : anything in this Act, or in any other Act to the contrary not-withstanding' ; and all and every the branches, clauses, articles, and provisoes expressed and contained in any other Act or Ordinance of Parliament, whereby or wherein any penalty or punishment is imposed, or mentioned to be imposed on any person whatsoever, for not repairing to their respective parish churches, or for not keeping of holy days, or for not hearing Common Prayer, or for speaking or inveighing against the Book of Common Prayer, shall be, and are by the authority aforesaid, wholly repealed and made void.

And it is also hereby enacted and declared, that all pro-ceedings had or made by virtue of any the clauses, branches, or articles mentioned and contained in any of the aforesaid Acts, and hereby repealed, against any such person or persons as aforesaid, shall be fully and wholly superseded, made void and null.

Provided, that this Act, nor anything therein contained, shall extend to the taking away of any Act or Ordinance made by this present Parliament, concerning the due observation of the Lord's day, days of public thanksgiving and humiliation.

And to the end that no profane or licentious persons may take occasion by the repealing of the said laws (intended only for relief of pious and peaceably-minded people from the rigour of them) to neglect the performance of religious duties, be it further enacted by the authority aforesaid, that all and every person and persons within this Commonwealth and the territories thereof, shall (having no reasonable excuse for their absence) upon every Lord's day, days of public thanksgiving and humiliation, diligently resort to some public place where the service and worship of God is exercised, or shall be present at some other place in the practice of some religious duty, either of prayer, preaching, reading or expounding the scriptures, or conferring upon the same.

And be it further declared by the authority aforesaid, that every person and persons that shall not diligently perform the duties aforesaid, according to the true meaning hereof (not having reasonable excuse to the contrary) shall be deemed and taken to be offenders against this law, and shall be proceeded against accordingly.

94. ACT FOR THE SETTLEMENT OF IRELAND.

[August 12, 1652. Scobell, ii. 197. See *Commonwealth and Protectorate*, iv. 82–5.]

Whereas the Parliament of England, after the expense of much blood and treasure for suppression of the horrid rebellion in Ireland, have by the good hand of God upon their undertakings, brought that affair to such an issue, as that a total reducement and settlement of that nation may, with God's blessing, be speedily effected, to the end therefore that the people of that nation may know that it is not the intention of the Parliament to extirpate that whole nation, but that mercy and pardon, both as to life and estate, may be extended to all husbandmen, ploughmen, labourers, artificers, and others of the inferior sort, in manner as is hereafter declared; they submitting themselves to the Parliament of the Commonwealth of England, and living peaceably and obediently under their government; and that others also of higher rank and quality may know the Parliament's intention concerning them, according to the respective demerits and considerations under which they fall; be it enacted and declared by this present Parliament, and by the authority of the same, that all and every person and persons of the Irish nation, comprehended in any of the following qualifications, shall be liable unto the penalties and forfeitures therein mentioned and contained, or be made capable of the mercy and pardon therein extended respectively, according as is hereafter expressed and declared; that is to say,

I. That all and every person and persons, who at any time before the tenth day of November, 1642 (being the time of the sitting of the first General Assembly at Kilkenny in Ireland), have contrived, advised, counselled, promoted, or acted, the rebellion, murders, or massacres done or committed in Ireland, which began in the year 1641; or have at any time before the said tenth day of November, 1642, by bearing arms, or contributing men, arms, horse, plate, money, victual, or other furniture or hablements of war (other than such which they shall make to appear to have been taken from them by mere force and violence), aided, assisted, promoted, acted, prosecuted, or abetted the said rebellion, murders, or massacres, be excepted from pardon of life and estate.

II. That all and every Jesuit, priest, and other person or persons who have received orders from the Pope or See of Rome, or any authority derived from the same, that have any ways contrived, advised, counselled, promoted, continued, countenanced, aided, assisted, or abetted; or at any time hereafter shall any ways contrive, advise, counsel, promote, continue, countenance, aid, assist, or abet the rebellion or war in Ireland, or any the murders or massacres, robberies, or violences committed against the Protestants, English, or others there, be excepted from pardon for life and estate.

III. That James Butler Earl of Ormond, James Touchet Earl of Castlehaven, Ulick Bourke Earl of Clanricarde, Christopher Plunket Earl of Fingal, James Dillon Earl of Roscommon, Richard Nugent Earl of Westmeath, Morrogh O'Brien Baron of Inchiquin, Donogh MacCarthy Viscount Muskerry, Theobald Taaffe Viscount Taaffe of Corren, Richard Butler Viscount Mountgarret, &c., &c., be excepted from pardon for life and estate.

IV. That all and every person and persons (both principals and accessories) who since the first of October, 1641, have or shall kill, slay, or otherwise destroy any person or persons in Ireland, which at the time of their being so killed, slain, or destroyed, were not publicly entertained and maintained in arms as officers or private soldiers, for and on behalf of the English against the Irish; and all and every person and persons (both principals and accessories) who since the said first day of October, 1641, have killed, slain, or otherwise destroyed any person or persons entertained and maintained as officers or private soldiers, for and on the behalf of the English against the Irish (the said persons so killing, slaying, or otherwise destroying, not being then publicly entertained and maintained in arms as officer or private soldier under the command and pay of the Irish nation against the English), be excepted from pardon for life and estate.

V. That all and every person and persons in Ireland, that are in arms or otherwise in hostility against the Parliament of the Commonwealth of England, and shall not within eight and twenty days after publication hereof by the Commissioners for the Parliament, or Commander-in-Chief, lay down arms and submit to the power and authority of the said Parliament and Commonwealth, as the same is now established, be excepted from pardon for life and estate.

VI. That all other person and persons (not being comprehended in any of the former qualifications) who have borne command in the war of Ireland against the Parliament of England, or their forces, as general, lieutenant-general, major-general, commissary-general, colonel, governor of any garrison, castle, or fort, or who have been employed as receiver-general or treasurer of the whole nation or any province thereof, commissary-general of musters or provisions; marshal-general, or marshal of any province, advocate of the army, or secretary to the Council of War, or to any general of the army, or of any the several provinces, in order to the carrying on the war against the Parliament or their forces, be banished during the pleasure of the Parliament of the Commonwealth of England, and their estates forfeited and disposed of as followeth, viz. that two-third parts of their respective estates be had, taken, and disposed of for the use and benefit of the said Commonwealth; and that the other third part of their said respective estates or other lands, to the proportion and value thereof (to be assigned in such places in Ireland, as the Parliament, in order to the more effectual settlement of the peace of this nation, shall think fit to appoint for that purpose) be respectively had, taken, and enjoyed by the wives and children of the said persons respectively.

VII. That the Commissioners of Parliament and Commander-in-Chief have power to declare, that such person or persons as they shall judge capable of the Parliament's mercy (not being comprehended in any of the former qualifications), who have borne arms against the Parliament of England or their forces, and have laid down arms, or within eight and twenty days after publication hereof by the Commissioners for the Parliament, and the Commander-in-Chief, shall lay down arms and submit to the power and authority of the said Parliament and Commonwealth, as the same is now established (by promising and engaging to be true to the same), shall be pardoned for their lives, but shall forfeit their estates to the said Commonwealth, to be disposed of as followeth, viz. two third parts thereof (in three equal parts to be divided) for the use, benefit, and advantage of the said Commonwealth, and the other third part of the said respective estates or other lands, to the proportion or value thereof (to be assigned in such places in Ireland, as the Parliament, in order to the more effectual settlement of the peace of that nation shall think fit to appoint for that purpose), be enjoyed by the said persons, their heirs or assigns respectively, provided, that in case the Commissioners and Commander-in-Chief, or either of them, shall see cause to give any shorter time than twenty-eight days, unto any person or persons in arms, or in any garrison, castle, or fort in hostility against the Parliament, and shall give notice to such person or persons in arms, or in any garrison, castle, or fort, that all and every such person and persons who shall not within such time as shall be set down in such notice, surrender such garrison, castle, or fort to the power of the Parliament, and lay down arms, shall have no advantage of the time formerly limited in this qualification.

VIII. That all and every person and persons of the Popish Religion, who have resided in Ireland at any time from the first day of October, 1641, to the first of March, 1650, and have not manifested their constant good affection to the

interest of the Commonwealth of England (the said persons
not being comprehended in any of the former qualifications),
shall forfeit one third part of their estates in Ireland to the
said Commonwealth, to be disposed of for the use, benefit,
and advantage of the said Commonwealth ; and the other
two third parts of their respective estates or other lands, to
the proportion or value thereof, to be assigned in such place
in Ireland, as the Parliament, for the more effectual settlement
of the peace of that nation, shall think fit to appoint for that
purpose, be enjoyed by such person or persons, their heirs or
assigns respectively : and that all other persons who have
resided in Ireland within the time aforesaid, and have not
been in actual service for the Parliament, or otherwise manifested their good affection to the interests of the Parliament
of England, having opportunity to do the same, shall forfeit one
fifth part of their estates to the use of the said Commonwealth.

IX. That all and every person and persons (having no real
estate in Ireland, nor personal estate to the value of ten
pounds) that shall lay down arms, and submit to the power
and authority of the Parliament by the time limited in the
former qualifications, and shall take and subscribe the engagement, to be true and faithful to the Commonwealth of England,
as the same is now established, within such time and in such
manner as the Commissioners for the Parliament and Commander-in-Chief shall appoint and direct, such persons (not
being excepted from pardon, nor adjudged for banishment by
any of the former qualifications) shall be pardoned for life
and estate for any act or thing by them done in prosecution
of the war.

X. That all estates declared by the former qualifications concerning rebels or delinquents in Ireland to be forfeited, shall be
construed, adjudged, and taken, to all intents and purposes,
to extend to the forfeitures of all estates tail, and also of all
rights and titles thereunto, which since the five and twentieth
of March, 1639, have been or shall be in such rebels or delinquents, or any other in trust for them or any of them, or their
or any of their uses, with all reversions and remainders thereupon, in any other person or persons whatsoever . and also
to the forfeiture of all estates limited, appointed, conveyed,

settled, or vested in any person or persons declared by the said qualifications to be rebels or delinquents, with all reversions or remainders of such estates conveyed, vested, limited, declared, or appointed to any the heirs, children, or issues of such rebel or delinquent; which estate or estates, remainders, or reversions since the five and twentieth of March, 1639, have been or shall be in such rebels or delinquents, or in any their heirs, children, or issues of such rebels or delinquents, and to all estates granted, limited, appointed, or conveyed by any such rebels or delinquents, unto any their heirs, children, or issue, with all the reversions and remainders thereupon: provided, that this shall not extend to make void the estates of any English Protestants, who have constantly adhered to the Parliament, which were by them purchased for valuable consideration before the three and twentieth of October, 1641; or upon like valuable consideration mortgaged to them before that time, or to any person or persons in trust for them for satisfaction of debts owing to them.

Provided, that if any person or persons excepted by name or otherwise, comprehended in these qualifications, have been comprised within any articles granted unto them, or agreed upon between them and any commander of the Parliament's forces thereto authorised, that such person or persons shall nevertheless enjoy the benefit of those articles, in case the Commissioners of Parliament in Ireland shall adjudge them to be comprised therein; and that they have observed and kept, and continue to observe and keep the Articles on their parts, and that nevertheless it shall be in the power of the Parliament, or their Commissioners, if they see cause, to transplant such persons from the respective places of their usual habitation or residence, into such other places within that nation, as shall be judged most consistent with public safety, allowing them such proportion of land or estate in the parts to which they shall be transplanted, as they had or should have enjoyed of their own other where, in case they had not been so removed.

95. DECLARATION BY THE LORD GENERAL AND THE COUNCIL
ON THE DISSOLUTION OF THE LONG PARLIAMENT.

[April 22, 1653. Old Parliamentary History, xx. 137. See *Commonwealth and Protectorate*, ii. 271.]

Our intention is not to give an account, at this time, of the grounds which first moved us to take up arms, and engage our lives and all that was dear unto us in this cause; nor to mind, in this declaration, the various dispensations through which Divine Providence hath led us, or the witness the Lord hath borne, and the many signal testimonies of acceptance which He hath given, to the sincere endeavours of His unworthy servants, whilst they were contesting with the many and great difficulties, as well in the wars, as other transactions in the three nations; being necessitated, for the defence of the same cause they first asserted, to have recourse unto extraordinary actions, the same being evident by former declarations published on that behalf.

After it had pleased God not only to reduce Ireland and give in Scotland, but so marvellously to appear for His people at Worcester, that these nations were reduced to a great degree of peace, and England to perfect quiet, and thereby the Parliament had opportunity to give the people the harvest of all their labour, blood, and treasure, and to settle a due liberty both in reference to civil and spiritual things, whereunto they were obliged by their duty, their engagements, as also the great and wonderful things which God hath wrought for them; it was matter of much grief to the good and well-affected of the land to observe the little progress which was made therein, who thereupon applied to the army, expecting redress by their means; notwithstanding which, the army being unwilling to meddle with the civil authority in matters so properly appertaining to it, it was agreed that his Excellency and officers of the army which were members of Parliament, should be desired to move the Parliament to proceed vigorously in reforming what was amiss in government, and to the settling of the Commonwealth upon a foundation of justice and righteousness; which having done, we hoped that the Parliament would seasonably have answered our expectation: but finding, to our grief, delays therein, we renewed our desires in an humble petition to them,

which was presented in August last; and although they at that
time, signifying their good acceptance thereof, returned us thanks
and referred the particulars thereof to a Committee of the
House, yet no considerable effect was produced, nor any such
progress made, as might imply their real intentions to accomplish
what was petitioned for; but, on the contrary, there more and
more appeared amongst them an aversion to the things themselves, with much bitterness and opposition to the people of
God, and His spirit acting in them; which grew so prevalent,
that those persons of honour and integrity amongst them, who
had eminently appeared for God and the public good, both
before and throughout this war, were rendered of no further
use in Parliament, than by meeting with a corrupt party to
give them countenance to carry on their ends, and for effecting
the desire they had of perpetuating themselves in the supreme
government, for which purpose the said party long opposed,
and frequently declared themselves against having a new representative: and when they saw themselves necessitated to take
that Bill into consideration, they resolved to make use of it to
recruit the House with persons of the same spirit and temper,
thereby to perpetuate their own sitting; which intention divers
of the activest amongst them did manifest, labouring to persuade
others to a consent therein: and the better to effect this, divers
petitions, preparing from several counties for the continuance of
this Parliament, were encouraged, if not set on foot, by many
of them.

For obviating of these evils, the officers of the Army obtained
several meetings with some of the Parliament, to consider what
fitting means and remedy might be applied to prevent the
same: but such endeavours proving altogether ineffectual, it
became most evident to the Army, as they doubt not it also
is to all considering persons, that this Parliament, through the
corruption of some, the jealousy of others, the non-attendance
and negligence of many, would never answer those ends which
God, His people, and the whole nation expected from them;
but that this cause, which the Lord hath so greatly blessed
and borne witness to, must needs languish under their hands,
and, by degrees, be wholly lost; and the lives, liberties, and
comforts of His people delivered into their enemies' hands.

All which being sadly and seriously considered by the honest people of this nation, as well as by the Army, and wisdom and direction being sought from the Lord, it seemed to be a duty incumbent upon us, who had seen so much of the power and presence of God going along with us, to consider of some more effectual means to secure the cause which the good people of this Commonwealth had been so long engaged in, and to establish righteousness and peace in these nations.

And after much debate it was judged necessary, and agreed upon, that the supreme authority should be, by the Parliament, devolved upon known persons, men fearing God, and of approved integrity ; and the government of the Commonwealth committed unto them for a time, as the most hopeful way to encourage and countenance all God's people, reform the law, and administer justice impartially; hoping thereby the people might forget Monarchy, and, understanding their true interest in the election of successive Parliaments, may have the government settled upon a true basis, without hazard to this glorious cause, or necessitating to keep up armies for the defence of the same.   And being still resolved to use all means possible to avoid extraordinary courses, we prevailed with about twenty members of Parliament to give us a conference, with whom we freely and plainly debated the necessity and justness of our proposals on that behalf; and did evidence that those, and not the Act under their consideration, would most probably bring forth something answerable to that work, the foundation whereof God Himself hath laid, and is now carrying on in the world.

The which, notwithstanding, found no acceptance ; but, instead thereof, it was offered, that the way was to continue still this present Parliament, as being that from which we might reasonably expect all good things : and this being vehemently insisted upon, did much confirm us in our apprehensions, that not any love to a representative, but the making use thereof to recruit, and so perpetuate themselves, was their aim

They being plainly dealt with about this, and told that neither the nation, the honest interest, nor we ourselves would be deluded by such dealings, they did agree to meet again the next day in the afternoon for mutual satisfaction ; it being

consented unto by the members present that endeavours should
be used that nothing in the mean time should be done in
Parliament that might exclude or frustrate the proposals before
mentioned.

Notwithstanding this, the next morning the Parliament
did make more haste than usual in carrying on their said
Act, being helped on therein by some of the persons engaged
to us the night before; none of them which were then present
endeavouring to oppose the same ; and being ready to put
the main question for consummating the said Act, whereby
our aforesaid proposals would have been rendered void, and
the way of bringing them into a fair and full debate in
Parliament obstructed; for preventing thereof, and all the
sad and evil consequences which must, upon the grounds
aforesaid, have ensued ; and whereby, at one blow, the interest
of all honest men and of this glorious cause had been in
danger to be laid in the dust, and these nations embroiled in
new troubles at a time when our enemies abroad are watch-
ing all advantages against us, and some of them actually
engaged in war with us, we have been necessitated, though
with much reluctancy, to put an end to this Parliament ;
which yet we have done, we hope, out of an honest heart,
preferring this cause above our names, lives, families, or
interests, how dear soever; with clear intentions and real
purposes of heart, to call to the government persons of approved
fidelity and honesty ; believing that as no wise men will expect
to gather grapes of thorns, so good men will hope, that if
persons so qualified be chosen, the fruits of a just and righteous
reformation, so long prayed and wished for, will, by the blessing
of God, be in due time obtained, to the refreshing of all those
good hearts who have been panting after those things.

Much more might have been said, if it had been our desire
to justify ourselves by aspersing others, and raking into the
misgovernment of affairs ; but we shall conclude with this,
that as we have been led by necessity and Providence to
act as we have done, even beyond and above our own thoughts
and desires, so we shall and do in that part of this great
work which is behind, put ourselves wholly upon the Lord
for a blessing ; professing, we look not to stand one day

without His support, much less to bring to pass any of the things mentioned and desired, without His assistance; and therefore do solemnly desire and expect that all men, as they would not provoke the Lord to their own destruction, should wait for such issue as He should bring forth, and to follow their business with peaceable spirits, wherein we promise them protection by His assistance.

And for those who profess their fear and love to the name of God, that seeing in a great measure for their sakes, and for righteousness' sake, we have taken our lives in our hands to do these things, they would be instant with the Lord day and night on our behalfs, that we may obtain grace from Him; and seeing we have made so often mention of His name, that we may not do the least dishonour thereunto: which indeed would be our confusion, and a stain to the whole profession of Godliness.

We beseech them also to live in all humility, meekness, righteousness, and love one toward another, and towards all men, that so they may put to silence the ignorance of the foolish, who falsely accuse them, and to know that the late great and glorious dispensations, wherein the Lord hath so wonderfully appeared in bringing forth these things by the travail and blood of His children, ought to oblige them so to walk in the wisdom and love of Christ, as may cause others to honour their holy profession, because they see Christ to be in them of a truth.

We do further purpose, before it be long, more particularly to show the grounds of our proceedings, and the reasons of this late great action and change, which in this we have but hinted at.

And we do lastly declare, that all Judges, Sheriffs, Justices of the Peace, Mayors, Bailiffs, Committees, and Commissioners, and all other civil officers and public ministers whatsoever, within this Commonwealth, or any parts thereof, do proceed in their respective places and offices; and all persons whatsoever are to give obedience to them as fully as when Parliament was sitting.

Signed in the name, and by the appointment, of his Excellency the Lord General and his Council of Officers.

WILL. MALYN, Secretary.

96.   Summons to a Member of the so-called Barebones Parliament.

[June 6, 1653.   Old Parliamentary History, xx. 151.   See *Commonwealth and Protectorate*, ii. 283.]

Forasmuch as upon the dissolution of the late Parliament it became necessary that the peace, safety, and good government of this Commonwealth should be provided for; and, in order thereunto, divers persons fearing God, and of approved fidelity and honesty, are by myself, with the advice of my council of officers, nominated, to whom the great charge and trust of so weighty affairs is to be committed; and having good assurance of your love to, and courage for, God and the interest of His cause, and of the good people of this Commonwealth :

I, Oliver Cromwell, Captain-General and Commander-in-Chief of all the armies and forces raised, and to be raised, within this Commonwealth, do hereby summon and require you   (being one of the said persons nominated) personally to be and appear at the Council-Chamber, commonly known or called by the name of the Council-Chamber at Whitehall, within the City of Westminster, upon the 4th day of July next ensuing the date hereof; then and there to take upon you the said trust unto which you are hereby called and appointed, to serve as a member for the county of   And hereof you are not to fail.

Given under my hand and seal the 6th day of June, 1653.

O. Cromwell.

97.   The Instrument of Government.

[December 16, 1653.   Old Parliamentary History, xx. 248.   See *Commonwealth and Protectorate*, ii. 331–336.]

The government of the Commonwealth of England, Scotland, and Ireland, and the dominions thereunto belonging.

I. That the supreme legislative authority of the Commonwealth of England, Scotland, and Ireland, and the dominions thereunto belonging, shall be and reside in one person, and the people assembled in Parliament : the style of which person shall be the Lord Protector of the Commonwealth of England, Scotland, and Ireland.

II. That the exercise of the chief magistracy and the administration of the government over the said countries and dominions, and the people thereof, shall be in the Lord Protector, assisted with a council, the number whereof shall not exceed twenty-one, nor be less than thirteen.

III. That all writs, processes, commissions, patents, grants, and other things, which now run in the name and style of the keepers of the liberty of England by authority of Parliament, shall run in the name and style of the Lord Protector, from whom, for the future, shall be derived all magistracy and honours in these three nations; and have the power of pardons (except in case of murders and treason) and benefit of all forfeitures for the public use; and shall govern the said countries and dominions in all things by the advice of the council, and according to these presents and the laws.

IV. That the Lord Protector, the Parliament sitting, shall dispose and order the militia and forces, both by sea and land, for the peace and good of the three nations, by consent of Parliament; and that the Lord Protector, with the advice and consent of the major part of the council, shall dispose and order the militia for the ends aforesaid in the intervals of Parliament.

V. That the Lord Protector, by the advice aforesaid, shall direct in all things concerning the keeping and holding of a good correspondency with foreign kings, princes, and states; and also, with the consent of the major part of the council, have the power of war and peace.

VI. That the laws shall not be altered, suspended, abrogated, or repealed, nor any new law made, nor any tax, charge, or imposition laid upon the people, but by common consent in Parliament, save only as is expressed in the thirtieth article.

VII. That there shall be a Parliament summoned to meet at Westminster upon the third day of September, 1654, and that successively a Parliament shall be summoned once in every third year, to be accounted from the dissolution of the present Parliament.

VIII. That neither the Parliament to be next summoned, nor any successive Parliaments, shall, during the time of five months, to be accounted from the day of their first meeting, be adjourned, prorogued, or dissolved, without their own consent.

IX. That as well the next as all other successive Parliaments shall be summoned and elected in manner hereafter expressed; that is to say, the persons to be chosen within England, Wales, the Isles of Jersey, Guernsey, and the town of Berwick-upon-Tweed, to sit and serve in Parliament, shall be, and not exceed, the number of four hundred. The persons to be chosen within Scotland, to sit and serve in Parliament, shall be, and not exceed, the number of thirty ; and the persons to be chosen to sit in Parliament for Ireland shall be, and not exceed, the number of thirty.

X. That the persons to be elected to sit in Parliament from time to time, for the several counties of England, Wales, the Isles of Jersey and Guernsey, and the town of Berwick-upon-Tweed, and all places within the same respectively, shall be according to the proportions and numbers hereafter expressed : that is to say,

Bedfordshire	5	Tiverton	1
Bedford Town	1	Honiton	1
Berkshire	5	Dorsetshire	6
Abingdon	1	Dorchester	1
Reading	1	Weymouth and Melcomb-Regis	1
Buckinghamshire	5	Lyme-Regis	1
Buckingham Town	1	Poole	1
Aylesbury	1	Durham	2
Wycomb	1	City of Durham	1
Cambridgeshire	4	Essex	13
Cambridge Town	1	Malden	1
Cambridge University	1	Colchester	2
Isle of Ely	2	Gloucestershire	5
Cheshire	4	Gloucester	2
Chester	1	Tewkesbury	1
Cornwall	8	Cirencester	1
Launceston	1	Herefordshire	4
Truro	1	Hereford	1
Penryn	1	Leominster	1
East Looe and West Looe	1	Hertfordshire	5
Cumberland	2	St. Alban's	1
Carlisle	1	Hertford	1
Derbyshire	4	Huntingdonshire	3
Derby Town	1	Huntingdon	1
Devonshire	11	Kent	11
Exeter	2	Canterbury	2
Plymouth	2	Rochester	1
Clifton, Dartmouth, Hardness	1	Maidstone	1
Totnes	1	Dover	1
Barnstable	1	Sandwich	1

Queenborough	1
Lancashire	4
Preston	1
Lancaster	1
Liverpool	1
Manchester	1
Leicestershire	4
Leicester	2
Lincolnshire	10
Lincoln	2
Boston	1
Grantham	1
Stamford	1
Great Grimsby	1
Middlesex	4
London	6
Westminster	2
Monmouthshire	3
Norfolk	10
Norwich	2
Lynn-Regis	2
Great Yarmouth	2
Northamptonshire	6
Peterborough	1
Northampton	1
Nottinghamshire	4
Nottingham	2
Northumberland	3
Newcastle-upon-Tyne	1
Berwick	1
Oxfordshire	5
Oxford City	1
Oxford University	1
Woodstock	1
Rutlandshire	2
Shropshire	4
Shrewsbury	2
Bridgnorth	1
Ludlow	1
Staffordshire	3
Lichfield	1
Stafford	1
Newcastle-under-Lyne	1
Somersetshire	11
Bristol	2
Taunton	2
Bath	1
Wells	1
Bridgwater	1
Southamptonshire	8
Winchester	1
Southampton	1
Portsmouth	1
Isle of Wight	2

Andover	1
Suffolk	10
Ipswich	2
Bury St. Edmunds	2
Dunwich	1
Sudbury	1
Surrey	6
Southwark	2
Guildford	1
Reigate	1
Sussex	9
Chichester	1
Lewes	1
East Grinstead	1
Arundel	1
Rye	1
Westmoreland	2
Warwickshire	4
Coventry	2
Warwick	1
Wiltshire	10
New Sarum	2
Marlborough	1
Devizes	1
Worcestershire	5
Worcester	2

YORKSHIRE.

West Riding	6
East Riding	4
North Riding	4
City of York	2
Kingston-upon-Hull	1
Beverley	1
Scarborough	1
Richmond	1
Leeds	1
Halifax	1

WALES.

Anglesey	2
Brecknockshire	2
Cardiganshire	2
Carmarthenshire	2
Carnarvonshire	2
Denbighshire	2
Flintshire	2
Glamorganshire	2
Cardiff	1
Merionethshire	1
Montgomeryshire	2
Pembrokeshire	2
Haverfordwest	1
Radnorshire	2

The distribution of the persons to be chosen for Scotland and Ireland, and the several counties, cities, and places therein, shall be according to such proportions and number as shall be agreed upon and declared by the Lord Protector and the major part of the council, before the sending forth writs of summons for the next Parliament.

XI. That the summons to Parliament shall be by writ under the Great Seal of England, directed to the sheriffs of the several and respective counties, with such alteration as may suit with the present government, to be made by the Lord Protector and his council, which the Chancellor, Keeper, or Commissioners of the Great Seal shall seal, issue, and send abroad by warrant from the Lord Protector. If the Lord Protector shall not give warrant for issuing of writs of summons for the next Parliament, before the first of June, 1654, or for the Triennial Parliaments, before the first day of August in every third year, to be accounted as aforesaid ; that then the Chancellor, Keeper, or Commissioners of the Great Seal for the time being, shall, without any warrant or direction, within seven days after the said first day of June, 1654, seal, issue, and send abroad writs of summons (changing therein what is to be changed as aforesaid) to the several and respective Sheriffs of England, Scotland, and Ireland, for summoning the Parliament to meet at Westminster, the third day of September next ; and shall likewise, within seven days after the said first day of August, in every third year, to be accounted from the dissolution of the precedent Parliament, seal, issue, and send forth abroad several writs of summons (changing therein what is to be changed) as aforesaid, for summoning the Parliament to meet at Westminster the sixth of November in that third year. That the said several and respective Sheriffs shall, within ten days after the receipt of such writ as aforesaid, cause the same to be proclaimed and published in every market-town within his county upon the market-days thereof, between twelve and three of the clock ; and shall then also publish and declare the certain day of the week and month, for choosing members to serve in Parliament for the body of the said county, according to the tenor of the said writ, which shall be upon Wednesday five weeks after the date of the writ ; and shall likewise declare the place where the election shall be made : for which purpose he shall appoint the most convenient place for the whole county to meet in ; and shall send precepts for elections to be made in all and every city, town, borough, or place within his county, where elections are to be made by virtue of these presents, to the Mayor, Sheriff, or other head officer of such city, town, borough, or place, within three days after the receipt of such writ and writs; which the said Mayors, Sheriffs, and officers respectively are to make publication of, and of the certain day for such elections to be made in the said city, town, or place aforesaid, and to cause elections to be made accordingly.

XII. That at the day and place of elections, the Sheriff of each county, and the said Mayors, Sheriffs, Bailiffs, and other head officers within their cities, towns, boroughs, and places respectively, shall take view of the said elections, and shall make return into the chancery within twenty days after the said elections, of the persons elected by the greater number of electors, under their hands and seals, between him on the one part, and the electors on the other part ; wherein shall be contained, that the persons elected shall not have power to alter the government as it is hereby settled in one single person and a Parliament.

XIII. That the Sheriff, who shall wittingly and willingly make any false return, or neglect his duty, shall incur the penalty of 2000 marks of lawful English money ; the one moiety to the Lord Protector, and the other moiety to such person as will sue for the same.

XIV. That all and every person and persons, who have aided, advised, assisted, or abetted in any war against the Parliament, since the first day of January, 1641 (unless they have been since in the service of the Parliament, and given signal testimony of their good affection thereunto) shall be disabled and incapable to be elected, or to give any vote in the election of any members to serve in the next Parliament, or in the three succeeding Triennial Parliaments.

XV. That all such, who have advised, assisted, or abetted the rebellion of Ireland, shall be disabled and incapable for ever to be elected, or give any vote in the election of any member to serve in Parliament ; as also all such who do or shall profess the Roman Catholic religion.

XVI. That all votes and elections given or made contrary, or not according to these qualifications, shall be null and void; and if any person, who is hereby made incapable, shall give his vote for election of members to serve in Parliament, such person shall lose and forfeit one full year's value of his real estate, and one full third part of his personal estate; one moiety thereof to the Lord Protector, and the other moiety to him or them who shall sue for the same.

XVII. That the persons who shall be elected to serve in Parliament, shall be such (and no other than such) as are persons of known integrity, fearing God, and of good conversation, and being of the age of twenty-one years.

XVIII. That all and every person and persons seised or possessed to his own use, of any estate, real or personal, to the value of £200, and not within the aforesaid exceptions, shall be capable to elect members to serve in Parliament for counties.

XIX. That the Chancellor, Keeper, or Commissioners of the Great Seal, shall be sworn before they enter into their offices, truly and faithfully to issue forth, and send abroad, writs of summons to Parliament, at the times and in the manner before expressed: and in case of neglect or failure to issue and send abroad writs accordingly, he or they shall for every such offence be guilty of high treason, and suffer the pains and penalties thereof.

XX. That in case writs be not issued out, as is before expressed, but that there be a neglect therein, fifteen days after the time wherein the same ought to be issued out by the Chancellor, Keeper, or Commissioners of the Great Seal; that then the Parliament shall, as often as such failure shall happen, assemble and be held at Westminster, in the usual place, at the times prefixed, in manner and by the means hereafter expressed; that is to say, that the sheriffs of the several and respective counties, sheriffdoms, cities, boroughs, and places aforesaid within England, Wales, Scotland, and Ireland, the Chancellor, Masters, and Scholars of the Universities of Oxford and Cambridge, and the Mayor and Bailiffs of the borough of Berwick-upon-Tweed, and other places aforesaid respectively, shall at the several courts and places to be appointed as aforesaid, within thirty days after the said fifteen days, cause such members to be chosen for their said several and respective counties, sheriffdoms, universities, cities, boroughs, and places aforesaid, by such persons, and in such manner, as if several and respective writs of summons to Parliament under the Great Seal had issued and been awarded according to the tenor aforesaid : that if the sheriff, or other persons authorised, shall neglect his or their duty herein, that all and every such sheriff and person authorised as aforesaid, so neglecting his or their duty, shall, for every such offence, be guilty of high treason, and shall suffer the pains and penalties thereof.

XXI. That the clerk, called the clerk of the Commonwealth in Chancery for the time being, and all others, who shall afterwards execute that office, to whom the returns shall be made, shall for the next Parliament, and the two succeeding triennial Parliaments, the next day after such return, certify the names of the several persons so returned, and of the places for which he and they were chosen respectively, unto the Council ; who shall peruse the said returns, and examine whether the persons so elected and returned be such as is agreeable to the qualifications, and not disabled to be elected : and that every person and persons being so duly elected, and being approved of by the major part of the Council to be persons not disabled, but qualified as aforesaid, shall be esteemed a member of Parliament, and be admitted to sit in Parliament, and not otherwise.

XXII. That the persons so chosen and assembled in manner aforesaid, or any sixty of them, shall be, and be deemed the Parliament of England, Scotland, and Ireland ; and the supreme legislative power to be and reside in the Lord Protector and such Parliament, in manner herein expressed.

XXIII. That the Lord Protector, with the advice of the major part of the Council, shall at any other time than is before expressed, when the necessities of the State shall require it, summon Parliaments in manner before expressed, which shall not be adjourned, prorogued, or dissolved without their own consent, during the first three months of their sitting. And in case of future war with any foreign State, a Parliament shall be forthwith summoned for their advice concerning the same.

XXIV. That all Bills agreed unto by the Parliament, shall be presented to the Lord Protector for his consent; and in case he shall not give his consent thereto within twenty days after they shall be presented to him, or give satisfaction to the Parliament within the time limited, that then, upon declaration of the Parliament that the Lord Protector hath not consented nor given satisfaction, such Bills shall pass into and become laws, although he shall not give his consent thereunto; provided such Bills contain nothing in them contrary to the matters contained in these presents.

XXV. That Henry Lawrence, Esq., &c.[1], or any seven of them, shall be a Council for the purposes expressed in this writing; and upon the death or other removal of any of them, the Parliament shall nominate six persons of ability, integrity, and fearing God, for every one that is dead or removed; out of which the major part of the Council shall elect two, and present them to the Lord Protector, of which he shall elect one; and in case the Parliament shall not nominate within twenty days after notice given unto them thereof, the major part of the Council shall nominate three as aforesaid to the Lord Protector, who out of them shall supply the vacancy; and until this choice be made, the remaining part of the Council shall execute as fully in all things, as if their number were full. And in case of corruption, or other miscarriage in any of the Council in their trust, the Parliament shall appoint seven of their number, and the Council six, who, together with the Lord Chancellor, Lord Keeper, or Commissioners of the Great Seal for the time being, shall have power to hear and determine such corruption and miscarriage, and to award and inflict punishment, as the nature of the offence shall deserve, which punishment shall not be pardoned or remitted by the Lord Protector; and, in the interval of Parliaments, the major part of the Council, with the consent of the Lord Protector, may, for corruption or other miscarriage as aforesaid, suspend any of their number from the exercise of their trust, if they shall find it just, until the matter shall be heard and examined as aforesaid.

XXVI. That the Lord Protector and the major part of the Council aforesaid may, at any time before the meeting

[1] The names of fifteen members are given here.

of the next Parliament, add to the Council such persons as they shall think fit, provided the number of the Council be not made thereby to exceed twenty-one, and the quorum to be proportioned accordingly by the Lord Protector and the major part of the Council.

XXVII. That a constant yearly revenue shall be raised, settled, and established for maintaining of 10,000 horse and dragoons, and 20,000 foot, in England, Scotland and Ireland, for the defence and security thereof, and also for a convenient number of ships for guarding of the seas ; besides £200,000 per annum for defraying the other necessary charges of administration of justice, and other expenses of the Government, which revenue shall be raised by the customs, and such other ways and means as shall be agreed upon by the Lord Protector and the Council, and shall not be taken away or diminished, nor the way agreed upon for raising the same altered, but by the consent of the Lord Protector and the Parliament.

XXVIII. That the said yearly revenue shall be paid into the public treasury, and shall be issued out for the uses aforesaid.

XXIX. That in case there shall not be cause hereafter to keep up so great a defence both at land or sea, but that there be an abatement made thereof, the money which will be saved thereby shall remain in bank for the public service, and not be employed to any other use but by consent of Parliament, or, in the intervals of Parliament, by the Lord Protector and major part of the Council.

XXX. That the raising of money for defraying the charge of the present extraordinary forces, both at sea and land, in respect of the present wars, shall be by consent of Parliament, and not otherwise : save only that the Lord Protector, with the consent of the major part of the Council, for preventing the disorders and dangers which might otherwise fall out both by sea and land, shall have power, until the meeting of the first Parliament, to raise money for the purposes aforesaid ; and also to make laws and ordinances for the peace and welfare of these nations where it shall be necessary, which shall be binding and in force, until order shall be taken in Parliament concerning the same.

XXXI. That the lands, tenements, rents, royalties, jurisdictions and hereditaments which remain yet unsold or undisposed of, by Act or Ordinance of Parliament, belonging to the Commonwealth (except the forests and chases, and the honours and manors belonging to the same; the lands of the rebels in Ireland, lying in the four counties of Dublin, Cork, Kildare, and Carlow; the lands forfeited by the people of Scotland in the late wars, and also the lands of Papists and delinquents in England who have not yet compounded), shall be vested in the Lord Protector, to hold, to him and his successors, Lords Protectors of these nations, and shall not be alienated but by consent in Parliament. And all debts, fines, issues, amercements, penalties and profits, certain and casual, due to the Keepers of the liberties of England by authority of Parliament, shall be due to the Lord Protector, and be payable into his public receipt, and shall be recovered and prosecuted in his name.

XXXII. That the office of Lord Protector over these nations shall be elective and not hereditary; and upon the death of the Lord Protector, another fit person shall be forthwith elected to succeed him in the Government; which election shall be by the Council, who, immediately upon the death of the Lord Protector, shall assemble in the Chamber where they usually sit in Council; and, having given notice to all their members of the cause of their assembling, shall, being thirteen at least present, proceed to the election; and, before they depart the said Chamber, shall elect a fit person to succeed in the Government, and forthwith cause proclamation thereof to be made in all the three nations as shall be requisite; and the person that they, or the major part of them, shall elect as aforesaid, shall be, and shall be taken to be, Lord Protector over these nations of England, Scotland and Ireland, and the dominions thereto belonging. Provided that none of the children of the late King, nor any of his line or family, be elected to be Lord Protector or other Chief Magistrate over these nations, or any the dominions thereto belonging. And until the aforesaid election be past, the Council shall take care of the Government, and administer in all things as fully as the Lord Protector, or the Lord Protector and Council are enabled to do.

XXXIII. That Oliver Cromwell, Captain-General of the forces of England, Scotland and Ireland, shall be, and is hereby declared to be, Lord Protector of the Commonwealth of England, Scotland and Ireland, and the dominions thereto belonging, for his life.

XXXIV. That the Chancellor, Keeper or Commissioners of the Great Seal, the Treasurer, Admiral, Chief Governors of Ireland and Scotland, and the Chief Justices of both the Benches, shall be chosen by the approbation of Parliament; and, in the intervals of Parliament, by the approbation of the major part of the Council, to be afterwards approved by the Parliament.

XXXV. That the Christian religion, as contained in the Scriptures, be held forth and recommended as the public profession of these nations ; and that, as soon as may be, a provision, less subject to scruple and contention, and more certain than the present, be made for the encouragement and maintenance of able and painful teachers, for the instructing the people, and for discovery and confutation of error, hereby, and whatever is contrary to sound doctrine; and until such provision be made, the present maintenance shall not be taken away or impeached.

XXXVI. That to the public profession held forth none shall be compelled by penalties or otherwise ; but that endeavours be used to win them by sound doctrine and the example of a good conversation.

XXXVII. That such as profess faith in God by Jesus Christ (though differing in judgment from the doctrine, worship or discipline publicly held forth) shall not be restrained from, but shall be protected in, the profession of the faith and exercise of their religion; so as they abuse not this liberty to the civil injury of others and to the actual disturbance of the public peace on their parts : provided this liberty be not extended to Popery or Prelacy, nor to such as, under the profession of Christ, hold forth and practise licentiousness.

XXXVIII. That all laws, statutes and ordinances, and clauses in any law, statute or ordinance to the contrary of the aforesaid liberty, shall be esteemed as null and void.

XXXIX. That the Acts and Ordinances of Parliament made for the sale or other disposition of the lands, rents and hereditaments of the late King, Queen, and Prince, of Arch-bishops and Bishops, &c., Deans and Chapters, the lands of delinquents and forest-lands, or any of them, or of any other lands, tenements, rents and hereditaments belonging to the Commonwealth, shall nowise be impeached or made invalid, but shall remain good and firm; and that the securities given by Act and Ordinance of Parliament for any sum or sums of money, by any of the said lands, the excise, or any other public revenue; and also the securities given by the public faith of the nation, and the engagement of the public faith for satisfaction of debts and damages, shall remain firm and good, and not be made void and invalid upon any pretence whatsoever.

XL. That the Articles given to or made with the enemy, and afterwards confirmed by Parliament, shall be performed and made good to the persons concerned therein; and that such appeals as were depending in the last Parliament for relief concerning bills of sale of delinquents' estates, may be heard and determined the next Parliament, any thing in this writing or otherwise to the contrary notwithstanding.

XLI. That every successive Lord Protector over these nations shall take and subscribe a solemn oath, in the presence of the Council, and such others as they shall call to them, that he will seek the peace, quiet and welfare of these nations, cause law and justice to be equally administered; and that he will not violate or infringe the matters and things con-tained in this writing, and in all other things will, to his power and to the best of his understanding, govern these nations according to the laws, statutes and customs thereof.

XLII. That each person of the Council shall, before they enter upon their trust, take and subscribe an oath, that they will be true and faithful in their trust, according to the best of their knowledge; and that in the election of every successive Lord Protector they shall proceed therein impartially, and do nothing therein for any promise, fear, favour or reward.

98. An Ordinance by the Protector for the Union of England and Scotland.

[April 12, 1654. Scobell, ii. 293. See *Commonwealth and Protectorate*, ii. 103.]

His Highness the Lord Protector of the Commonwealth of England, Scotland and Ireland, &c., taking into consideration how much it might conduce to the glory of God and the peace and welfare of the people in this whole island, that after all those late unhappy wars and differences, the people of Scotland should be united with the people of England into one Commonwealth and under one Government, and finding that in December, 1651, the Parliament then sitting did send Commissioners into Scotland to invite the people of that nation unto such a happy Union, who proceeded so far therein that the shires and boroughs of Scotland, by their Deputies convened at Dalkeith, and again at Edinburgh, did accept of the said Union, and assent thereunto; for the completing and perfecting of which Union, be it ordained, and it is ordained by his Highness the Lord Protector of the Commonwealth of England, Scotland and Ireland, and the dominions thereto belonging, by and with the advice and consent of his Council, that all the people of Scotland, and of the Isles of Orkney and Shetland, and of all the dominions and territories belonging unto Scotland, are and shall be, and are hereby incorporated into, constituted, established, declared and confirmed one Commonwealth with England; and in every Parliament to be held successively for the said Commonwealth, thirty persons shall be called from and serve for Scotland.

And for the more effectual preservation of this Union, and the freedom and safety of the people of this Commonwealth so united, be it ordained, and it is ordained by the authority aforesaid, that all the people of Scotland and of the Isles of Orkney and Shetland, and of all the dominions and territories belonging unto Scotland, of what degree or condition soever, be discharged of all fealty, homage, service and allegiance, which is or shall be pretended due unto any of the issue and posterity of Charles Stuart, late King of England and Scotland,

or any claiming under him ; and that Charles Stuart, eldest
son, and James, called Duke of York, second son, and all other
the issue and posterity of the said late King, and all and every
person and persons pretending title from, by or under him,
are and be disabled to hold or enjoy the Crown of Scotland
and other the dominions thereunto belonging, or any of them ;
or to have the name, title, style or dignity of King or Queen
of Scotland ; or to have and enjoy the power and dominion of
the said kingdom and dominions, or any of them, or the
honours, manors, lands, tenements, possessions and hereditaments
belonging or appertaining to the said Crown of Scotland, or
other the dominions aforesaid, or to any of them, any law,
statute, usage, ordinance or custom in Scotland to the contrary
hereof in any wise notwithstanding.

And it is further ordained by the authority aforesaid, that
the said office, style, dignity, power and authority of King
of Scotland, and all right of the three Estates of Scotland
to convocate or assemble in any general Convocation or Parliament, and all conventional and Parliamentary authority in
Scotland, as formerly established, and all laws, usages and
customs, ordaining, constituting or confirming the same, shall
be and are hereby and from henceforth abolished and utterly
taken away and made null and void.

And that this Union may take its more full effect and intent,
be it further ordained by the authority aforesaid, that the
Arms of Scotland, viz. a cross, commonly called St. Andrew's
Cross, be received into and borne, from henceforth in the Arms
of this Commonwealth, as a badge of this Union ; and that all
the public seals, seals of office, and seals of bodies civil or
corporate, in Scotland, which heretofore carried the Arms of
the Kings of Scotland, shall from henceforth instead thereof
carry the Arms of this Commonwealth.

And be it further ordained by the authority aforesaid, that
all customs, excise and other imposts for goods transported
from England to Scotland, and from Scotland to England, by
sea or land, are and shall be so far taken off and discharged,
as that all goods for the future shall pass as free, and with
like privileges and with the like charges and burdens from
England to Scotland, and from Scotland to England, as goods

passing from port to port, or place to place in England; and that all goods shall and may pass between Scotland and any other part of this Commonwealth or dominions thereof, with the like privileges, freedom, charges and burdens as such goods do or shall pass between England and the said parts and dominions thereof, any law, statute, usage or custom to the contrary thereof in any wise notwithstanding, and that all goods prohibited by any law now in force in England to be transported out of England to any foreign parts, or imported, shall be and hereby are prohibited to be transported or imported by the same law, and upon the same penalties, out of Scotland to any foreign parts aforesaid, or from any foreign parts into Scotland.

And be it further ordained by the authority aforesaid, that all cesses, public impositions and taxations whatsoever, be imposed, taxed and levied from henceforth proportionably from the whole people of this Commonwealth so united.

And further, to the end that all dominion of tenures and superiorities importing servitude and vassalage may likewise be abolished in Scotland, be it further declared and ordained by the authority aforesaid, that all heritors, proprietors and possessors of lands in Scotland, or the dominions thereunto belonging, and their heirs, shall from and after the 12th day of April, in the year of our Lord 1654, hold their respective lands of the respective lord and lords by deed, charter, patent or enfeoffment, to be renewed upon the death of every heritor, proprietor or possessor (as now they do) to his heir or heirs, by and under such yearly rents, boons and annual services as are mentioned or due by any deeds, patents, charters or enfeoffments now in being, of the respective lands therein expressed, or by virtue thereof enjoyed without rendering, doing or performing any other duty, service, vassalage or demand whatsoever, by reason or occasion of the said lands, or any the clauses or covenants in the said deeds, charters, patents or enfeoffments contained, saving what is hereafter, herein and hereby particularly expressed and declared; that is to say, heriots, where the same are due, fines (certain where the same is already certain, and where the fine is uncertain, reasonable fines) upon the death of the lord, and upon the death or alienation of the tenant, or any of them, where the same have usually been paid, which said fine (not being already certain) shall not at any time exceed one year's value of the lands, and also doing suit and service to such Court and Courts Baron, as shall be constituted in Scotland, in such manner as is ordained by one other Ordinance, entitled, an Ordinance for erecting Courts Baron in Scotland.

And be it ordained by the authority aforesaid, that all and every the heritors, proprietors and possessors aforesaid, and their heirs, are and shall be from henceforth for ever discharged of all fealty, homage, vassalage and servitude, which is or shall be pretended due from them, or any of them, unto any their lords or superiors whatsoever, claiming dominion or jurisdiction over them, by virtue of the said patents, charters, deeds or enfeoffments, and other rights thereof, or of any clauses or conditions therein contained, other than is before declared and ordained. And that all the said superiorities, lordships and jurisdictions (other than as aforesaid) shall be, and are hereby abolished, taken off and discharged; and that all and every the said deeds, patents, charters and enfeoffments in that behalf be, and are hereby declared, and made so far void and null; and particularly, that all and every the heritors, and others the persons aforesaid, and their heirs, are and shall be for ever hereafter freed and discharged of, and from all suits, and appearing at or in any their lords' or superiors' courts of justiciary, regality, stuartry, barony, bailiary, heritable sheriff-ship, heritable admiralty, all which, together with all other offices heritable, or for life, are hereby abolished and taken away; and that all and every the heritors and persons aforesaid, and their heirs, are and shall be for ever hereafter freed and discharged of and from all military service, and personal attendance upon any their lords or superiors in expeditions or travels, and of all casualties of wards' lands formerly held of the King, or other superiors, and of the marriage, single and double avail thereof, non-entries, compositions for entries, and of all rights and casualties payable, if they be demanded, only or upon the committing of any clauses irritant. And that the said heritors and persons aforesaid be now, and from henceforth, construed, reputed, adjudged and declared free and acquitted thereof, and of and from all and all manner of holding suits, duties, services, personal or real, and demands whatsoever (other than is before declared and ordained), notwithstanding the present tenor of any their deeds, patents, enfeoffments, or any clauses, articles or covenants therein contained or mentioned to the contrary in any wise ; and that in time to come all and every clause, covenant, article, condition, or thing to the contrary hereof, shall be omitted out of all such deeds, patents, charters and enfeoffments.

And be it further ordained, that all forfeitures, escheats, simple, or of life, rent bastardy, and last heir, which heretofore escheated, forfeited and fell to the King, lords of regality, or other superiors, shall from henceforth fall, escheat, and forfeit to the Lord Protector of the Commonwealth for the time being.

Passed 12th April, 1654.   Confirmed Anno 1656, Cap. 10.

99.   An Ordinance by the Protector for Elections in Scotland.

[June 27, 1654.   Civil War Tracts, Press Mark E 1064, p. 431.
See *Commonwealth and Protectorate*, iii. 172.]

Whereas by the Government of the Commonwealth of England, Scotland and Ireland, publicly declared at Westminster, the 16th day of December, 1653 :

It is declared, that the distribution of the persons to be chosen for Scotland, and the several counties, cities and places within the same, shall be according to such proportions and numbers as shall be agreed upon and declared by the Lord Protector, and the major part of the Council, before the sending forth writs of summons for the next Parliament.   And whereas his Highness and the major part of the Council, before the sending forth of any writs of summons aforesaid, did agree and declare the distribution of the persons to be chosen for Scotland, according to the proportions and numbers hereafter mentioned ; it is therefore ordained, declared and agreed by his Highness the Lord Protector, with the consent of the Council, that the persons to be chosen for Scotland, and the several counties, cities and places within the same, shall be according to the proportions and numbers hereafter expressed ; that is to say, for the shires of Orkney, Shetland and Caithness, one, and the place of meeting for the election of such person shall be at Caithness; for the shires of Sutherland, Ross and Cromarty, one, and the place of meeting for the election of such person shall be at Ross; for the shire of Inverness, one, and the place of meeting for the election of such person shall be in the same shire; for the shires of Elgin and Nairn, one, and the place of meeting for the election of such person shall be at Elgin; for the shire of Banff, one, and the place of meeting for the election of such person shall be in the same shire; for the shire of Aberdeen, one, and the place of meeting for the election of such person shall be in the same shire; for the shires of Kincardine and Forfar, one, and the place of meeting for the election of such person shall be at Forfar; for the shires of Fife and Kinross, one, and the place of meeting for the election of such person shall be at Fife; for the shire of Perth, one, and the place of meeting for the election of such person shall be in the same shire; for the shires of Linlithgow, Stirling, and Clackmannan, one, and the place of meeting for the election of such person shall be at Stirling; for the shires of Dumbarton, Argyle, and Bute, one, and the place of meeting for the election of such person shall be at Dumbarton; for the shires of Ayr and Renfrew, one, and the place of meeting for the election of such person shall be in Ayrshire; for the shire of Lanark, one, and the place of meeting for the election of such person shall be in the same shire; for the shire of Mid-Lothian, one, and the place of meeting for the election of such person shall be in the same shire; for the shire of the Merse, one, and the place of meeting for the election of such person shall be in the same shire; for the shire of Roxburgh, one, and the place of meeting for the election of such person shall be in the same shire; for the shires of Selkirk and Peebles, one, and the place of meeting for the election of such person shall be at Peebles; for the shire of Dumfries, one, and the place of meeting for the election of such person shall be in the same shire; for the shire of Wigton, one, and the place of meeting for the election of such person shall be in the same shire; for the shire of East-Lothian, one, and the place of meeting for the election of such person shall be in the same shire; and for the boroughs of Dornoch, Tain, Inverness, Dingwall, Nairn, Elgin, and Fortrose, one, and the place of meeting for the election of such person shall be at Inverness; for the boroughs of Banff, Cullen, and Aberdeen, one, and the place of meeting for the election of such person shall be at Aberdeen ; for the boroughs of Forfar, Dundee, Arbroath, Montrose, and Brechin, one, and the place of meeting for the election of such person shall be at Dundee ; for the boroughs of Linlithgow, Queensferry, Perth, Culross, and Stirling, one, and the place of meeting for the election of such person shall be at Stirling; for the boroughs of St. Andrews, Dysart, Kirkcaldy, Cupar, Anstruther East, Pittenween, Crail, Dunfermline, Kinghorn, Anstruther West, Inverkeithing, Kilrenny, and Burnt Island, one, and the place of meeting for the election of such person shall be at Cupar in Fife ; for the boroughs of Edinburgh, two ; for the boroughs of Lanark, Glasgow, Rutherglen, Rothesay, Renfrew, Ayr, Irvine and Dumbarton, one, and the place of meeting for the election of such person shall be at Glasgow; for the boroughs of Dumfries, Sinclair, Lochmaben, Annandale, Wigton, Kirkcud-bright, Whithorn, and Galloway, one, and the place of meeting for the election of such person shall be at Dumfries; for the boroughs of Peebles, Selkirk, Jedburgh, Lauder, N. Berwick, Dunbar, and Haddington, one, and the place of meeting for the election of such person shall be at Lauder.   And it is further ordained by his said Highness the Lord Protector, with the consent of the Council, that for the effectual and orderly election of the persons aforesaid to be chosen to sit and serve in Parliament, as in the said Government is declared, several writs under the Great Seal of England shall issue, and be directed to the several and respective Sheriffs of the several and respective shires, wherein the respective elections are to be made of the respective persons to serve in Parliament for the respective shires, and to the respective Sheriffs of the county where the elections for the boroughs are hereby appointed to be made according to the distribution aforesaid; and that the respective Sheriffs to whom such writs shall be directed, are hereby authorised and impowered to make or cause proclamation to be made of such writ in all the counties, boroughs, and places respectively, for the making such election and elections, and to issue his warrant to the chief officer of the place, where

such election for boroughs is to be made, notwithstanding the
same be not within the shire whereof such person is Sheriff,
and to cause the elections to be made accordingly; which writs
the Chancellor, Keeper, or Commissioners of the Great Seal of
England, for the time being, shall seal, issue and send forth.

Tuesday, June 27th, 1654.

Ordered by his Highness the Lord Protector and his Council,
that this Ordinance be forthwith printed and published.

HENRY SCOBELL,

Clerk of the Council.

100. AN ORDINANCE BY THE PROTECTOR FOR ELECTIONS IN
IRELAND.

[June 27, 1654. Civil War Tracts, Press Mark E 1064, p. 439.
See *Commonwealth and Protectorate*, iii. 173.]

Whereas by the Government of the Commonwealth of England, Scotland and Ireland, publicly declared at Westminster
the 16th day of December, 1653, it is declared, that the distribution of the persons to be chosen for Ireland, and the
several counties, cities and places within the same, shall be
according to such proportions and number as shall be agreed
upon and declared by the Lord Protector and the major part
of the Council, before the sending forth writs of summons for
the next Parliament: And whereas his Highness and the
major part of the Council, before the sending forth of any writs
of summons aforesaid, did agree and declare the distribution
of the persons to be chosen for Ireland, according to the
proportions and numbers hereafter mentioned; it is therefore
ordained, declared and agreed by his Highness the Lord
Protector, with the consent of the Council, that the persons
to be chosen for Ireland, and the several counties, cities and
places within the same, shall be according to the proportion
and number hereafter expressed ; that is to say, for the province
of Leinster, ten; that is to say, for the counties of Meath and
Louth, two; and the place of meeting for the election of such
persons shall be at Drogheda.   For the counties of Kildare
and Wicklow, two; for the county and city of Dublin, two;
and the place of meeting for the election of such persons shall

be at Dublin. For the counties of Carlow, Wexford, Kilkenny and Queen's, two; and the place of meeting for the election of such persons shall be at Carlow. For the counties of Westmeath, Longford and King's, two; and the place of meeting for the election of such persons shall be at Mullingar. For the province of Ulster, seven, that is to say, for the counties of Down, Antrim and Armagh, two; for the towns of Carrickfergus and Belfast, one; and the place of meeting for the election of such persons shall be at Belfast. For the counties of Derry, Donegal and Tyrone, two; for the towns of Derry and Coleraine, one; and the place of meeting for the election of such persons shall be at Derry. For the counties of Cavan, Fermanagh and Monaghan, one; and the place of meeting for the election of such persons shall be at Enniskillen. For the province of Munster, nine; that is to say, for the counties of Kerry, Limerick and Clare, two; and the place of meeting for the election of such persons shall be at Rathkeale. For the city and county of the city of Limerick and Killmallock, one; and the place of meeting for the election of such persons shall be at Limerick. For the county of Cork, one; for the towns of Cork and Youghall, one; and the place of meeting for the election of such persons shall be at Cork. For the towns of Bandon and Kinsale, one; and the place of meeting for the election of such persons shall be at Bandon. For the counties of Waterford and Tipperary, two; and the place of meeting for the election of such persons shall be at Clonmel. For the cities of Waterford and Clonmel, one; and the place of meeting for the election of such persons shall be at Waterford. For the province of Connaught, except the county of Clare, four; that is to say, for the counties of Sligo, Roscommon and Leitrim, two; and the place of meeting for the election of such persons shall be at Jamestown. For the counties of Galway and Mayo, two; and the place of meeting for the election of such persons shall be at Galway.

And it is further ordained by his said Highness the Lord Protector, with the consent of the Council aforesaid, that for the effectual and orderly election of the persons aforesaid, to be chosen to sit and serve in Parliament, as in the said Government is declared, several writs under the Great Seal of England shall issue, and be directed to the several Sheriffs of the aforesaid counties and cities, to make the respective elections of the respective persons to serve in Parliament, for the said respective counties, cities, towns and boroughs, according to the distributions hereinbefore declared; which writs the Chancellor, Keeper, or Commissioners of the Great Seal of England for the time being shall seal, issue and send forth.

HEN. SCOBELL,
Clerk of the Council.

Tuesday, 27th June, 1654.

Ordered by his Highness the Lord Protector and the Council, that this Ordinance be forthwith printed and published.

HEN. SCOBELL,
Clerk of the Council.

101. THE CONSTITUTIONAL BILL OF THE FIRST PARLIAMENT OF THE PROTECTORATE.

[1654–5.   From a MS. in the possession of Lord Braye.   See *Commonwealth and Protectorate*, iii. 197–220, 234–245.]

An Act declaring and settling the government of the Commonwealth 11 Nov., *of England, Scotland, and Ireland, and the dominions* 1654. *thereto belonging.*

Be it enacted and declared by His Highness the Lord CAP. 1. Protector and the Parliament of the Commonwealth of England, Scotland, and Ireland, and the dominions thereto belonging; and it is hereby enacted and declared by the authority aforesaid, that the supreme legislative authority[1] of the Commonwealth of England, Scotland, and Ireland, and the dominions thereto belonging, is and shall reside in one person and the people assembled in Parliament in manner following, that is to say, All Bills agreed unto by the Parliament shall be presented to the said single person for his consent, and, in case he shall not give his consent thereunto within twenty days after they shall

---

[1] MS. authoritive.

be presented unto him, or give satisfaction to the Parliament within the time limited, that then such Bills shall pass into and become law, although he shall not consent thereunto; provided such Bills contain nothing in them contrary to such matters wherein the single person is hereby declared to have a negative.

14 Nov., 1654. CAP. 2.   That if any Bill be tendered at any time hereafter to alter the foundation and constitution of the government of this Commonwealth from a single person and a Parliament as aforesaid, that to such Bills the single person is hereby declared shall have a negative.

16 Nov., 1654. CAP. 3.   That the style of such single person is and shall be Lord Protector of the Commonwealth of England, Scotland, and Ireland, and the dominions thereunto belonging.

6 Dec., 1654. CAP. 4.   That the office of the Lord Protector over these nations shall be elective and not hereditary.

30 Nov., 1654. CAP. 5.   That the manner of electing the Protector, in the vacancy of a Protector (sitting the Parliament), shall be such as the Parliament shall think fit.

That the Protector dying in the intervals of Parliament, the Council, hereby to be constituted, shall immediately assemble in some convenient place, and having given notice to all their number, or to as many of them as conveniently they may, of the cause and time of their assembling, shall (being thirteen at least present) proceed to the election, and eleven of these or more shall agree who shall be the succeeding Protector, and before they depart shall declare such person so agreed upon to succeed in the government: the manner of election in all other things to be as the Council shall think fit.

CAP. 6.   That the person so to be elected Protector shall be such and no other than as, by his good conversation amongst the people of these nations, shall manifest himself to be a man of ability, truth, and courage, fearing God and hating covetousness: provided that he shall not be under the age of five-and-twenty years, no alien, nor Papist, nor any of the children of the late King Charles, nor such as shall have or may pretend to have title of inheritance unto the supreme government of these nations of England, Scotland, and Ireland; or any of them, or any other title than by election as aforesaid.

That the present Lord Protector shall take and subscribe a 15 Dec., solemn oath for the due calling of Parliaments, and the good $_{CAP. 7.}^{1654.}$ government of these nations, and every future Lord Protector, immediately after his election, and before he enter upon the government, shall take and subscribe the same solemn oath for the due calling of Parliament, and the good government of these nations; that such oath shall be taken in Parliament, if the Parliament be then sitting, and in the intervals of Parliament in such public place and manner as the Council shall appoint.

That this shall be the oath to be ministered to the Lord CAP. 8. Protector, viz.: 'I do, in the presence and by the name of God Almighty, promise and swear that to the uttermost of my power, I will uphold and maintain the true reformed Protestant Christian religion in the purity thereof, as it is contained in the Holy Scriptures of the Old and New Testament, and encourage the profession and professors of the same; and will duly cause Parliaments to be summoned and called; and that I will not wittingly or willingly violate nor infringe the liberties and privileges of Parliament, or any of the matters or things contained in the Act of Parliament declaring and settling the government of the Commonwealth of England, Scotland, and Ireland; and will in all things, to the best of my understanding, govern according to the laws, statutes, customs, and liberties of the people of these nations; and will seek their peace and welfare according to those laws, customs, and liberties; and cause justice and law to be equally and duly administered.'

That immediately after the death of every Lord Protector, 15 Dec. and after the election of a succeeding Lord Protector, a Par- $_{CAP. 9.}^{1654.}$ liament be summoned to meet, if a Parliament be not then sitting, or not to meet within four months by force of this Act, or not then already summoned.

That the exercise of the Chief Magistracy over this Common- 6 Dec., wealth and the people thereof shall be in the Lord Protector $_{CAP. 10.}^{1654.}$ assisted with the Council, the exercise of which power shall be according to the respective laws and customs of these nations of England, Scotland, and Ireland, and the dominions thereunto belonging.

That after the death of any Lord Protector, and until the 20 Dec., next Lord Protector shall be elected and sworn, the Council $_{CAP. 11.}^{1654.}$

shall take care of the government and administer in all things as fully as the Lord Protector or the Lord Protector and Council are enabled to do.

CAP. 12   That no writ of summons to any Parliament or any other writ, process, patents, commissions, nor any proceedings in law or justice shall be discontinued or made void by the death of any Lord Protector.

CAP. 13.   That all writs, process, patents, commissions, and proceedings in law or justice, issuing forth or being after any succeeding Lord Protector shall be elected and sworn, shall issue forth and be in the name of such Lord Protector, and are hereby declared to be of full force in law to all intents and purposes; and that all former writs, process, patents, commissions, offices, and officers, shall continue and be in full force as they should have been in if the said Lord Protector had been still living.

CAP. 14.   That all writs, process, commissions, patents, grants, and other things which heretofore did or might lawfully have passed or issued in the name or style of the Keepers of the Liberties of England by authority of Parliament, shall pass and issue in the name of the Lord Protector of the Commonwealth of England, Scotland, and Ireland, and the dominions thereunto belonging.

CAP. 15.   That such titles of honour as shall be hereafter conferred in this Commonwealth, shall be derived from the Lord Protector: and that no title of honour hereafter to be conferred by the said Protector shall be hereditary without consent in Parliament.

CAP. 16.   That it shall not be in the power of the said Lord Protector to pardon murder.

That it shall not be in the power of the said Lord Protector to pardon treason.

That the Lord Protector with the consent of the Council shall have power of pardon, except in case of murder and treason; provided that no pardon extend to exempt any Councillors of State, Judges, Officers, or other Ministers of State from being questioned or sentenced in Parliament for any maladministration or corruption in his office or employment, or for any sentence or judgment agreed upon in Parliament, or any execution thereof, nor shall extend to pardon any person for any breach of privilege of Parliament, nor any other sentence or judgment thereupon.

That Oliver Cromwell, Captain-General of the forces of England, Scotland and Ireland, is, and shall be, Lord Protector of the Commonwealth of England, Scotland and Ireland, and the dominions thereunto belonging for his life. 16 Nov., 1654.
CAP. 17.

That a constant yearly revenue of £200,000 by the year be settled and stablished upon the now Lord Protector, and the succeeding Lords Protectors, for the time being respectively, for defraying the necessary charges for administration of justice, and other expenses of the government, and for the support of his and their state and dignity as may be for the honour of this Commonwealth of England, Scotland, and Ireland: and that the said £200,000 by the year be constantly paid out of the public receipt of the Exchequer by warrant of the Lord Protector and the Council, and shall not be taken away nor diminished without the consent of the Lord Protector and the Parliament. 18 Dec., 1654.
CAP. 18.

That Whitehall, St. James' House and Park, the Mews, Somerset House, Greenwich House and Park, Hampton Court, and the Honour and Manor of Hampton Court, with the parks and grounds thereunto belonging, Windsor Castle, the little park there, and other the lands thereunto now belonging, and the house called the Manor near the city of York, with their and every of their appurtenances now unsold and undisposed of, be vested in the present Lord Protector, for the maintenance of his and their state and dignity, and shall not be aliened but by consent in Parliament. 19 Dec., 1654.
Cap. 19.

That a Parliament be summoned to meet and sit at Westminster the third Monday of October, 1656. 24 Nov., 1654.
CAP. 20.

That a Parliament shall be summoned to meet and sit at Westminster upon the third Monday in October, 1659, and so likewise on the third Monday in October in every third year successively. CAP. 21.

That neither this present Parliament, nor the Parliament which shall be summoned to meet on the third Monday of October, 1656, nor the Parliament that shall be summoned to meet on the third Monday in October in the year 1659, nor any succeeding triennial Parliament shall, during the time of CAP. 22.

twenty-six weeks, to be accounted from the day of their first meeting, be adjourned, prorogued, or dissolved without their own consent.

CAP. 23. That neither this present Parliament, which shall be summoned to meet on the third Monday in October, 1656, nor the Parliament that shall be summoned to meet on the third Monday in October, 1659, nor any successive triennial Parliament, shall continue above twenty-six weeks without the Lord Protector's consent, to be by Act of Parliament, in which Act there shall be a limited time for their sitting, not exceeding thirteen weeks.

CAP. 24. That the Lord Protector, with the advice of the major part of the Council, shall at any other time than is before expressed, when the necessities of the State shall require, summon Parliaments in manner hereby expressed, which shall not be adjourned, prorogued, or dissolved, without their own consent, during the space of thirteen weeks, to be accounted from the day of their first sitting, nor shall continue to sit beyond that time without the consent of the Lord Protector to be by Act of Parliament, in which Act there shall be a limited time for their sitting, not exceeding four weeks, provided that such Parliament shall end and be determined before the summoning of such Parliaments as are before hereby appointed.

CAP. 25. That the summons to Parliament shall be by writ under the Great Seal of England, directed to the Sheriffs and other officers (according to law) of the several and respective counties and places in manner and form following :—

'Oliver, Lord Protector of the Commonwealth of England, Scotland, and Ireland, and the dominions thereunto belonging, to the Sheriff of the County of   , greeting.   Whereas, in the Parliament holden at Westminster the third day of September, 1654, it is amongst other things enacted that Parliament shall be duly held in such manner as therein is expressed, and, to that end, that a Parliament be holden at the City of Westminster the   day of   next coming, there for us to consult with the knights, citizens, and burgesses of the said Commonwealth, of the weighty and urgent affairs concerning us, the state and defence of the said Commonwealth, and the maintenance of the true reformed Protestant Christian religion in purity thereof: we do command you firmly, enjoining that proclamation being made of the day and place aforesaid in every market town within your county, you cause, according to the form of the said statute, to be freely and indifferently chosen by them who shall be present at such election of the most fit and discreet persons to serve as knights with their swords girt, for the County of   and for the City of   , citizens of the most discreet and sufficient, and the names of the same knights, citizens, and burgesses so to be chosen, whether present or absent, you cause to be certified in certain indentures thereupon to be made between you and them who shall be present at such choice, and that you cause them to come at the day and place aforesaid; so that the knights severally may have full and sufficient power for themselves and the people of that county and borough aforesaid, to do and consent to those things which then and there by common counsel of the said Commonwealth in Parliament by God's blessing shall be ordained upon the weighty affairs aforesaid; so that for defect of such power, or by reason of improvident choice of the knights, citizens, and burgesses aforesaid, the said affairs may not be left undone in any wise, and we will that you be not chosen to serve as knight for your said county: and that the said choice in your full county distinctly and openly so to be made, you forthwith certify to us in our Chancery under your seals and the seals of them which shall be present at such choice, sending to us the other part of the said indentures annexed, together with this writ: and in your proceedings and execution hereof, we will that you pursue and observe the several directions limited and appointed by the said Act of Parliament. Witness ourselves, &c.,' which said writ the Chancellor, Keeper, or Commissioners of the Great Seal shall issue and send abroad by warrant from the Lord Protector.

That in case the Lord Protector shall not before the first of CAP. 26. July, 1656, give warrant for issuing out of writs of summons for a Parliament to meet the third Monday in October, 1656, and before the first day of July, 1659, give warrant for issuing forth of summons for a Parliament to meet the third Monday in October, 1659, and before the first day of July in every third year after that time give warrant for issuing writs of summons for a Parliament to meet every third Monday in October every third year successively, that then the Chancellor, Keeper, or Commissioner of the Great Seal for the time being, shall, without any warrant or direction, within seven days after the respective times aforesaid, seal, issue, and send abroad writs of summons to the several and respective Sheriffs of England, Scotland, and Ireland, and other officers for summoning another Parliament to meet at Westminster the third Monday in October, 1659, and for other Parliaments to meet at Westminster on the third Monday in October in every third year successively ; and that the said Sheriffs and other officers respectively shall, within ten days after the receipt of such writs as aforesaid, cause the same to be proclaimed and published in every market town in the said county upon the market days thereof, between twelve and three of the clock, and shall then also publish and declare the certain day of the week and month and the certain place for electing of members to serve in Parliament for the body of the said county according to the tenor of the said writ, which election shall be within six weeks after the date of the said writ; but not until fourteen days after all the proclamations made as aforesaid : for which purpose the Sheriff shall appoint some convenient day, and the usual or some other convenient and indifferent place for the electors of each county and place to meet in, and shall proceed to election between the hours of eight and eleven before noon : and shall send precepts for elections to be made in all and every city, town, borough, or place within his and their county and place where elections are to be made, to the Mayor, Sheriff, or other head officer, and officers of such city, town, borough, or place, within six days after the receipt of such writ and writs, which the said Mayor, Sheriff, and other officers respectively within eight days after the receipt of the said precept are to make publication of, and of the certain day for such elections to be made in the said city, town, or place aforesaid, and cause elections to be made accordingly within eight days after publication of the said precept made as aforesaid, provided that the usual place for elections for the county of Sussex shall be at Lewes.

That at the day and place of elections, the Sheriff of each

county, and the said Mayor, Sheriffs, and Bailiffs and other head officer and officers within the cities, towns, and boroughs and places respectively, shall take view of the said elections, and shall make return into the Chancery, within twenty days after the said elections, of the persons elected by the greater number of electors under the hands and seal of twelve or more of the said electors on the behalf of himself on the one part, and on the behalf of the electors on the other part, wherein shall be contained that the persons elected shall not have power to alter the government from one single person and a Parliament.

That the Sheriff who shall wittingly or willingly make any false return, or wittingly or willingly neglect his duty in execution of the premises, shall incur the penalty of £200 of lawful English money, and that every Mayor, Sheriff, or Bailiff, or other head-officer of any city, town, borough, or place aforesaid, who shall wittingly or wilfully make any false return, or wittingly or wilfully neglect his duty in the execution of the premises, shall incur the penalty of £100 of like lawful English money; the one moiety of all and every the penalties aforesaid to go to the Lord Protector, and the other moiety to such party grieved as shall sue for the same in any of the Courts of record at Westminster, by any action [of] debt, bill, plaint, or information, wherein shall be no wager of law, essoign, or protection allowed; which suit shall not be commenced until the Parliament hath adjudged the same to be such offence as aforesaid.

That all and every person and persons who have voluntarily aided, advised, assisted, or abetted in any war against the Parliament since the first day of October, 1641, unless they have been since in the service of the Parliament, and given signal testimony of their good affections thereunto; and also all and every person and persons whatsoever professing the Popish religion, or that did side, advise, assist, or abet in the Rebellion of Ireland before the 15th of September, 1643, shall during their lives be disabled and incapable to be elected or to give any vote in election of any members to serve in any Parliament.

That all votes and elections given or made contrary or not according to the aforesaid qualifications, shall be void and of none effect; and if any person who is by these aforesaid qualifications made incapable shall give his vote for election of members to serve in Parliament, such person shall lose and forfeit one full year's value of his real estate; and one full third part of his personal estate, one moiety thereof to the Lord Protector, and the other moiety to him or them who shall sue for the same in any of the Courts of record at Westminster by action of debt, bill, plaint, or information wherein shall be no wager of law, essoign, or protection allowed.

CAP. 31.   That the persons who shall be elected to serve in Parliament shall be such and none other than such as are persons of known integrity, fearing God, and of good conversation, and being of the age of one and twenty years, and not such as are disabled by the Act of the 17th of King Charles, intituled An Act for disabling all persons in Holy Orders to exercise any temporal jurisdiction or authority, nor such as are public ministers or public preachers of the Gospel, nor such as are guilty of any of the offences mentioned in an Act of Parliament bearing date the 9th of August, 1650, intituled An Act against several atheistical, blasphemous, and execrable opinions derogatory to the honour of God and destructive to human society; no common scoffer nor reviler of religion, or of any person or persons for professing thereof; nor persons that have married or shall marry a wife of the Popish religion, or hath trained or shall train up his child or children, or any other child or children under his tuition or government in the Popish religion; or that shall permit or suffer such child or children to be trained up in that said religion, or hath given or shall give his consent that his son or daughter shall marry any of that religion, no person that shall deny the Scriptures to be the word of God, or the sacraments, prayer, magistracy, and ministry to be the ordinances of God; no common profaner of the Lord's day, nor profane swearer, nor curser; no drunkard or common haunter[1] of taverns or ale-houses.

CAP. 32.   That all and every person and persons not within the aforesaid exceptions having an estate in freehold to the yearly value of forty shillings within any county, riding, limit, or place (to be declared upon oath by such person or persons, is

[1] hunter in MS.

required, and which said oath the Sheriffs or their deputies
are hereby empowered to give), shall be capable to give his
or their votes for the election of members for such county,
riding, limit, or place, where such land or estate doth lie,
provided this extends not to alter any ancient customs,
charters, privileges of any cities, boroughs, towns, or corporations who have hereby right to elect members of Parliament,
but the same to continue as formerly, anything in these presents
to the contrary notwithstanding.

That the now Lords Commissioners of the Great Seal shall   6 Jan.,
forthwith take a solemn oath in Parliament for the due issuing   1654/5.
and sending abroad writs of summoning to Parliament, accord-   CAP. 33.
ing to the tenor of the Act, which oath shall be in these words:
'I do, in the presence and in the name of Almighty God,
promise and swear that I will, to the utmost of my power,
truly and faithfully issue forth and send abroad writs of
summons to Parliament at such times and in such manner as
is expressed and enjoined by an Act of Parliament, intituled
An Act declaring and settling the government of the Commonwealth of England, Scotland, and Ireland, and the dominions
thereunto belonging'; and such Chancellor, Keeper, or Commissioner of the Great Seal as shall hereafter be, shall before
they enter unto their said office, take the same oath in
Parliament (sitting the Parliament), and in the interval of
Parliament the same shall be administered to them by the two
Chief Justices, and the Chief Baron for the time being, or one
of them.

That if the Lord Chancellor, Lord Keeper, or Lords Commissioners of the Great Seal for the time being shall not issue
and send abroad in manner and at the times hereby to them
limited and appointed, writs of summons to the several and
respective Sheriffs and other officers for England, Scotland,
and Ireland, for summoning a Parliament to meet at Westminster on the third Monday in October, 1656, and for
summoning another Parliament to meet at Westminster on the
third Monday in October, 1659; and for summoning other
Parliaments to meet at Westminster on the third Monday in
October, every third year successively; and shall not issue and
send abroad by authority hereof and without further warrant

like writs of summons (within ten days after the death of every Lord Protector and after the election of another Lord Protector) for the summoning of a Parliament to meet at Westminster within forty days the next following (if a Parliament be not then sitting, or not to meet within four months, or not then already summoned), every such wilful neglect and failure of issuing and sending out writ of summons as aforesaid, is hereby adjudged and declared to bo High Treason, and all and every Lord Chancellor, Lord Keeper, or Lord Commissioner of the Great Seal so neglecting or failing, shall be adjudged guilty of High Treason, and shall suffer the pains and penalties thereof. And in case writs be not issued out as is before expressed, but that there be a neglect therein fifteen days after the time wherein the same ought to be issued out by the Chancellor, Keeper, or Commissioners of the Great Seal, and in caso the Sheriff or other officer shall not receive such writs within fifteen days aforesaid, that then every such Sheriff or other officer shall within ten days after the said fifteen days, as fully to all intents and purposes as if such writs had been issued forth and received as aforesaid, cause proclamation to be made in every market town within his or their county or counties, riding, and places, upon the market days thereof between twelve and three of the clock, declaring the certain place and the day of the week and month for electing of members to serve Parliament for the body of the said county or counties, riding, or places respectively in such manner and form as is before provided, which said elections are to be made within twenty days after the said ten days, and shall send precepts for elections to be made in all and every city, town, borough, and place within his or their county or counties, riding, or place where elections are to be made, to the Mayor, Bailiff, or other officer or officers of such city, town, borough, or places within six days after the said fifteen days, which precept the said Mayors, Bailiffs, or other officer or officers respectively within eight days after the receipt of the said precept are to make publication of and of the certain day for such elections to be made accordingly within eight days after proclamation of the said precepts made as aforesaid, to the end there may be no failures, but that the Parliament may assemble and be

held at Westminster at the usual place, and at the same times
hereby appointed; and in case the said Sheriff, or Sheriffs, or
other officer or officers authorised as aforesaid shall neglect his
or their duty therein, so as through his or their neglect there
shall be a failure or disappointment of the said elections, and
all and every wilful neglect or failure by such Sheriff or Sheriffs,
officer or officers authorised as aforesaid is hereby adjudged and
declared to be High Treason, and every such Sheriff or Sheriffs,
officer or officers, shall be adjudged guilty of High Treason,
and shall suffer the pains and penalties thereof.

And in case by failure or neglect of the said Sheriffs and
other officers, elections shall not be made before the five and
twentieth day of August, 1656, of knights, citizens, and
burgesses, to meet in Parliament at Westminster in the third
Monday in October in the same year; and if like elections for
succeeding Parliaments shall not be made before the five and
twentieth day of August in every third year successively; that
in case of any such failure or neglect, the freeholders of the
said several and respective counties, ridings, and places, and
the citizens, burgesses, and other persons having voices in such
elections, and being qualified as aforesaid, within their several
cities, boroughs, towns, and places respectively shall by authority
hereof, without any other notice or warrant, assemble and meet
on the second Wednesday in September next following after
the five and twentieth day of August in every third year
successively at the places where they [met] formerly for the
selection of members to the then last preceding Parliament,
and there between the hours of eight and eleven in the forenoon, shall respectively proceed to the election of such fit and
discreet persons qualified as aforesaid to serve in Parliament
as knights, citizens, and burgesses for their said several counties,
ridings, cities, boroughs, towns and places respectively, as if
writs of summons had been issued and sent abroad; and at the
day and place of election such justices or justice of peace of
every the said counties, ridings, and places respectively who
shall be present at the said elections and not elected; and if
no such justices or justice of the peace be at the said election;
then the major part of the electors being present for the said
counties, ridings, and places, and the Mayor, Bailiff, or other

head officer of every the said cities, boroughs, towns, and places
who shall be present at the said election, and not elected, and
if no such head officer be present, then the major part of the
electors that shall be at the said election shall by authority
hereof respectively make returns into the Chancery within ten
days after the said elections of the persons elected by indentures under the hands and seals of the said electors or the
major part of them; wherein shall be contained that the persons
so elected shall not have power to alter the government from
one single person and a Parliament, and the Clerk of the
Commonwealth in Chancery, or such other officer or officers to
whom it appertains shall accept and receive the returns of such
elections, and file and record them according to law in like
manner as if writs of summons had issued and been executed,
as hath been used and accustomed, which persons so elected
and returned as aforesaid for knights, citizens, and burgesses,
shall have as full and sufficient power for themselves and the
people of their respective counties, cities, boroughs, towns, and
places, to sit and act in Parliament as if the said Sheriffs and
other officers had received writs of summons, and had made
such returns; and that such knights, citizens, and burgesses
so chosen shall appear and serve in Parliament at the times
and place aforesaid, and shall each of them be liable to such
pains and censures for his and their not appearing and serving
then and there in Parliament, as if he and they had been
elected and chosen by virtue of a writ under the Great Seal,
and shall be likewise subject unto such further pains and censures as by the rest of the knights, citizens, and burgesses
assembled in Parliament he or they shall be adjudged unto,
any writ, proclamation, edict, act, restraint, prohibition, order,
or warrant to the contrary in any wise notwithstanding; and
every county that shall neglect or fail to make such elections
and returns in manner and at the times aforesaid, shall forfeit
the sum of £1000 to the use of the Commonwealth; and every
city, borough, town, or place that shall neglect or fail to make
such elections and returns in manner and at the times aforesaid, shall forfeit £200 to the use of the Commonwealth, to be
sued for, recovered, and disposed of as the ensuing Parliament
shall direct.

That the Council be hereby empowered to examine upon CAP. 34. oath as touching any articles of popery or delinquency mentioned in Cap. 29 against any person or persons returned for members of Parliament, and, if they shall find such charge to be true, and shall certify the same to the Parliament, the first day of the sitting of the Parliament, that then such members shall not sit until the House have adjudged of the same.

That the persons chosen and assembled in manner aforesaid, CAP. 35. or any sixty of them, shall be and be deemed the Parliament of England, Scotland, and Ireland.

That the persons to be chosen within England, Wales, CAP. 36. and the Town of Berwick upon Tweed to sit and serve in Parliament shall be and not exceed the number of four hundred, viz. :—

[The list of constituencies with the number of members allotted to them follows here. It is, however, imperfect, many counties being omitted. The list, so far as it is given, is almost exactly the same as that in the Instrument of Government. The exceptions are that, in Kent, Hythe is to return one member in the place of Queenborough ; that, in Leicestershire, the city of Leicester is to return one member instead of two, the number of members allotted to the county being increased from four to five ; that, in Oxfordshire, Banbury is to return a member instead of Woodstock, and that the County of Carmarthen loses one member which is given to the borough.]

That the persons to be chosen within Scotland to sit and CAP. 37. serve in Parliament shall be and not exceed the number of thirty.

That the persons to be chosen within Ireland to sit and serve in Parliament shall be and not exceed the number of thirty.

That the Lord Protector for the time being shall be assisted CAP. 38. with a Council.

That the persons who shall be of the Council shall be such CAP. 39. as shall be nominated by the said Lord Protector, and approved by the Parliament.

That the number of the persons who shall be of the Council 5 Dec., shall be, and not exceed, one and twenty.   1654

That eleven of them shall be a council[1], and not under.

That no person shall continue to be of the Council longer than forty days after the meeting of each succeeding Parliament without a new approbation of the Parliament. That such persons as shall be of the Council before they shall take their trust upon them shall take a solemn oath for the faithful discharge of their duty in that employment; which oath shall be taken in Parliament (sitting the Parliament), and in the interval of Parliament, before the Lord Chancellor, Lord Keeper, or Lords Commissioners of the Great Seal for the time being, which oath shall be as follows, viz.: ' I do, in the presence and by the name of Almighty God, promise and swear that I will be true and faithful in performance of the trust committed unto me as one of the Council: and that I will not reveal or disclose anything in whole or in part, directly or indirectly, that shall be debated or resolved upon by the Council; wherein secrecy shall be enjoined by the said Council, without the direction of the Lord Protector or the Parliament, or leave of the Council: and that in the election of every successive Lord Protector, I will proceed thereon faithfully and impartially according to an Act of Parliament, intituled An Act declaring and settling the government of the Commonwealth of England, Scotland, and Ireland: and do nothing therein for any promise, fear, favour, or reward. I will to the best of my knowledge and understanding give faithful advice to the Lord Protector for the time being, in order to the good government, peace, and welfare of these nations, and will not advise, act, or consent unto anything to disadvantage the liberty, property, or interest of the people, contrary to the laws of the land, to the best of my understanding and knowledge, and I will faithfully pursue the instructions and directions which are or shall be given to the Council by the Parliament.'

That the true reformed Protestant Christian religion as it is contained in the Holy Scriptures of the Old and New Testament, and no other, shall be asserted and maintained as the public profession of these nations.

That in case any Bill shall be tendered to the Lord Protector by the Parliament to compel any person to the said

[1] † a quorum.

public profession by any penalty to such Bill, the said Lord Protector shall have a negative : provided that such Bills as hereafter shall be agreed upon by the Parliament, requiring from such ministers and preachers of the Gospel (as shall receive public maintenance for instructing the people) a submission and conformity to the public profession aforesaid, or enjoining attendance unto the preaching of the word and other religious duties on the Lord's day in some public church or chapel ; or at some other congregational and Christian meeting, shall pass into and become laws within twenty days after the presentation to the Lord Protector, although he shall not give his consent thereunto.

That without the consent of the Lord Protector and Parliament, no law or statute be made for the restraining of such tender consciences as shall differ in doctrine, worship, or discipline from the public profession aforesaid, and shall not abuse their liberty to the civil injury of others, or the disturbances of the public peace : provided that such bills as shall be agreed upon by the Parliament for restraining of damnable heresies particularly to be enumerated by *the Lord Protector and*[1] Parliament : and also such bills as shall be agreed upon by the Parliament for the restraining of atheism, blasphemy, popery, prelacy, licentiousness, and profaneness ; or such as shall preach, print, or publicly maintain anything contrary to the fundamental principles of doctrines held within the public profession which shall be agreed upon by the Lord Protector and the Parliament, or shall do any overt or public act to the disturbance thereof, shall pass into and become laws within twenty days after their presentation to the Lord Protector, although he shall not give his consent thereunto.

15 Dec., 1654. CAP. 43.

That until some better provision be made by the Parliament for the encouragement and maintenance of able, godly, and painful ministers and public preachers of the Gospel for instructing the people, and for discovery and confutation of errors, heresy, and whatsoever is contrary to sound doctrine, the present public maintenance shall not be taken away nor impeached.

CAP. 44.

---

[1] This clause was altered by the insertion of the words in italics on Jan. 12. See *Commonwealth and Protectorate*, iii. 241.

CAP. 45.   That Oliver Cromwell, the present Lord Protector, during
his life (the Parliament sitting) shall by consent of Parliament, and not otherwise, dispose and employ the forces of this
Commonwealth by sea and land for the peace and good of the
same.

17 Nov.,   That such of the standing forces of this Commonwealth as
1654.   shall be agreed to be continued upon the charge of the
CAP. 46.   Commonwealth in the intervals of Parliament shall be ordered
and disposed of for the ends aforesaid in the intervals of
Parliaments by the present Lord Protector during his life, by
and with the advice and consent of the said Council, and not
otherwise.

20 Nov.,   That the standing forces after the death of the present
1654.   Lord Protector in the intervals of Parliament shall be in the
CAP. 47.   disposition and ordering of the said Council for the ends
aforesaid, until a Parliament be assembled, and then the
disposal of the said forces to be made by the Parliament as
they shall think fit.

CAP. 48.   That the standing forces of this Commonwealth both by
sea and land during the life of the now Protector shall be no
more in number than shall be agreed upon from time to time
by the said Lord Protector and the Parliament.

16 Jan.,   That the sum of £400,000 arising by the customs and the
165$\frac{4}{5}$.   public receipts in England, Scotland, and Ireland, shall be
CAP. 49.   yearly paid out of the public receipts of the Exchequer by
warrant of the Lord Protector and the Council, for and towards
the maintenance of a convenient number of ships for guarding
of the seas, and securing and encouragement of trade; and
the maintenance of such garrisons as shall be necessary for
the defence of the Commonwealth of England, Scotland, and
Ireland, and the dominions thereunto belonging, which revenue
shall continue and not be altered without consent of the Lord
Protector and the Parliament; and that the yearly sum of
£700,000 more arising by excise or other public receipts in
England, Scotland, and Ireland, shall be provided by Parliament and paid out of the Exchequer by warrant of the Lord
Protector and the Council for the maintenance and full discharge of such field forces as shall be thought needful to be
kept up for the defence of this Commonwealth of England,

Scotland, and Ireland, and the dominions thereunto belonging; and for the payment and full discharge of such forces in garrisons, and naval charges, and all incident charges belonging to every of them as shall not be satisfied and paid out of the £400,000 aforesaid, which said £700,000 shall continue and be paid until the 25th of December, 1659, unless the Lord Protector and the Parliament shall agree to lessen the said sum before that time.

That such ordinances as heretofore were made by the Lord 23 Nov., Protector and his Council before this Parliament, for the raising, 1654. bringing in, and disposing of monies for the maintenance of the CAP. 50. forces of this Commonwealth by sea and land in England, Scotland, and Ireland; and for the necessary charges of the government, shall remain and continue to the end of this Parliament and no longer, unless the Parliament shall take further order to [the] contrary, or unless the said ordinances shall expire before that time.

That the laws of this Commonwealth shall not be altered, CAP. 51. suspended, abrogated, or repealed, nor any new law made, nor any tax, charge, or imposition laid upon the people but by common consent of the people assembled in Parliament.

That the power of making war is only in the Lord Protector CAP. 52. and the Parliament.

That sitting the Parliament, no peace shall be concluded, CAP. 53. but by consent of Parliament; and in the interval of Parliament the power of making peace shall be in the Lord Protector and the Council, with such reservations and limitations as the Parliament shall approve.

That the said Lord Protector, by the advice and consent of CAP. 54. the major part of the Council, shall direct in all things concerning the keeping and holding a good correspondence with foreign kings, princes, and states.

That the Chancellor, Keeper, or Commissioners of the Great CAP. 55. Seal, the Treasurer or Commissioners of the Treasury, Admiralty, or Commissioners exercising the power of the Lord Admiral; the Chief Governors of Ireland and Scotland; the Chief Justices and the rest of the Judges of both the benches; Chief Baron and the rest of the Barons of the Exchequer, shall be chosen by the approbation of Parliament, and in the interval of Parliament by the approbation of the major part of the Council, to be afterwards approved by the Parliament.

CAP. 56.   That the Chancellor, Keeper, or Commissioners for the Great Seal of Ireland, the Chief Justices and Judges of both benches, and Chief Baron and Barons of the Exchequer in Ireland, shall be chosen by the approbation of the Parliament, and in the interval of Parliament by the approbation of the major part of the Council, to be afterwards approved by the Parliament.

CAP. 57.   That the Judges of the public Courts of Justice in Scotland shall from henceforth be chosen by the approbation of Parliament, and in the intervals of the Parliament by the approbation of the major part of the Council, to be afterwards approved by the Parliament.

15 Dec., 1654. CAP. 58.   That the acts and ordinances of Parliament made for the sale or other disposition of the lands, rents, and hereditaments of the late King, Queen, and Prince, of Archbishops and Bishops, Deans and Chapters, the lands of delinquents, and forest lands, or any of them, or of any other lands, tenements, rents, and hereditaments belonging to the Commonwealth, shall no way be impeached or made invalid, but shall remain good and firm, and that the security given by act and ordinances of Parliament for any sum or sums of money by any of the said lands, the excise, or by any other public revenue; and also the securities given by the public faith of the nation, and the engagement of the public faith for satisfaction of the debts and damages shall remain firm and good, and not be made void or invalid upon any pretence whatsoever: provided that the articles given to, or made with the enemy, and afterwards confirmed by Parliament, shall be performed and made good to the persons concerned therein: provided also that all appeals or petitions that were made or exhibited to this Parliament before the first day of December, 1654, for relief concerning bills, may be heard and determined this Parliament.

CAP. 59.   That the articles herein contained, nor any of them, shall be altered, repealed, or suspended without the consent of the Lord Protector and the Parliament.

17 Jan., 1654.   Provided that this Bill, intituled An Act declaring and settling the government of the Commonwealth of England, Scotland, and Ireland, and the dominions thereunto belonging,

be ingrossed in order to its presentment to the Lord Protector for his consideration and consent; and that if the Lord Protector and the Parliament shall not agree thereunto, and to every article thereof, then this Bill shall be void and of none effect.

Provided that this Act for the government does not extend, nor be construed to extend, to abrogate, alter, or diminish any of the charters, customs, liberties, or franchises of the City of London, or any other cities, boroughs, towns corporate, or places within this Commonwealth, saving in such things wherein any alteration is hereby particularly made, but that the City of London, and all other the said cities, boroughs, towns corporate, and places, shall and may have and enjoy their said charters, customs, liberties, and franchises as aforesaid, the said Act or anything therein contained notwithstanding. 19 Jan, 165$\frac{6}{7}$.

Provided that whereas the militia of this Commonwealth ought not to be raised, formed, and made use of, but by common consent of the people assembled in Parliament: be it therefore enacted, that the said militia, consisting of trained forces, shall be settled as the Lord Protector and Parliament shall hereafter agree, in order to the peace and safety of the Commonwealth, and not otherwise. 20 Jan., 165$\frac{6}{7}$.

102. The Humble Petition and Advice.

[May 25, 1657. Scobell, ii. 378. See Masson's *Life of Milton*, v. 121.]

To his Highness the Lord Protector of the Commonwealth of England, Scotland and Ireland, and the dominions thereto belonging ; the Humble Petition and Advice of the Knights, Citizens and Burgesses now assembled in the Parliament of this Commonwealth.

We, the knights, citizens and burgesses in this present Parliament assembled, taking into our most serious consideration the present state of these three nations, joined and united under your Highness' protection, cannot but in the first place, with all thankfulness, acknowledge the wonderful mercy of Almighty God in delivering us from that tyranny and bondage, both in our spiritual and civil concernments, which the late King and his party designed to bring us under, and pursued the effecting thereof by a long and bloody war; and also that it hath pleased the same gracious God to preserve your person in many battles, to make you an instrument for preserving our peace, although environed with enemies abroad, and filled with turbulent, restless and unquiet spirits in our own bowels, that as in the treading down the common enemy, and restoring us to peace and tranquillity, the Lord hath used you so eminently, and the worthy officers and soldiers of the army (whose faithfulness to the common cause, we and all good men shall ever acknowledge, and put a just value upon): so also that he will use you and them in the settling and securing our liberties as we are men and Christians, to us and our posterity after us, which are those great and glorious ends which the good people of these nations have so freely, with the hazard of their lives and estates, so long and earnestly contended for : we consider likewise the continual danger which your life is in, from the bloody practices both of the malignant and discontented party (one whereof, through the goodness of God, you have been lately delivered from), it being a received principle amongst them, that no order being settled in your lifetime for the succession in the Government, nothing is wanting to bring us into blood and confusion, and them to their desired ends, but the destruction of your person; and in case things should thus remain at your death, we are not able to express what calamities would in all human probability ensue thereupon, which we trust your Highness (as well as we) do hold yourself obliged to provide against, and not to leave a people, whose common peace and interest you are intrusted with, in such a condition as may hazard both, especially in this conjuncture, when there seems to be an opportunity of coming to a settlement upon just and legal foundations: upon these considerations, we have judged it a duty incumbent upon us, to present and declare these our most just and necessary desires to your Highness.

1. That your Highness will be pleased by and under the name and style of Lord Protector of the Commonwealth of England, Scotland and Ireland, and the dominions and territories thereunto belonging, to hold and exercise the office of Chief Magistrate of these nations, and to govern according to this petition and advice in all things therein contained, and in all other things according to the laws of these nations, and not otherwise : that your Highness will be pleased during your

lifetime to appoint and declare the person who shall, immediately after your death, succeed you in the Government of these nations.

2. That your Highness will for the future be pleased to call Parliaments consisting of two Houses (in such manner and way as shall be more particularly afterwards agreed and declared in this Petition and Advice) once in three years at furthest, or oftener, as the affairs of the nation shall require, that being your great Council, in whose affection and advice yourself and this people will be most safe and happy.

3. That the ancient and undoubted liberties and privileges of Parliament (which are the birthright and inheritance of the people, and wherein every man is interested) be preserved and maintained; and that you will not break or interrupt the same, nor suffer them to be broken or interrupted; and particularly, that those persons who are legally chosen by a free election of the people to serve in Parliament, may not be excluded from sitting in Parliament to do their duties, but by judgment and consent of that House whereof they are members.

4. That those who have advised, assisted or abetted the rebellion of Ireland, and those who do or shall profess the Popish religion, be disabled and made incapable for ever to be elected, or to give any vote in the election of any member to sit or serve in Parliament; and that all and every person and persons who have aided, abetted, advised or assisted in any war against the Parliament, since the 1st day of Jan., 1641 (unless he or they have since borne arms for the Parliament or your Highness, or otherwise given signal testimony of his or their good affection to the Commonwealth, and continued faithful to the same), and all such as have been actually engaged in any plot, conspiracy or design against the person of your Highness, or in any insurrection or rebellion in England or Wales since the 16th day of December, 1653, shall be for ever disabled and made incapable to be elected, or give any vote in the election of any member to sit or serve in Parliament. That for Scotland none be capable to elect, or be elected to sit or serve in Parliament, who have been in arms against the Parliament of England, or against the Parliament in Scotland, before the 1st day of April, 1648 (except such as have since borne arms in the service of the

Parliament of England or your Highness, or given other signal testimony of their good affection), nor any that since the said 1st day of April, 1648, have been in arms, or otherwise aided, abetted, advised or assisted in any war against the Parliament of England or your Highness, except such as since the 1st day of March, 1651 (old style [1]), have lived peaceably, and thereby given testimony of their good affection to the Parliament and your Highness.

Provided, that nothing in this Article contained shall extend to put any incapacity upon any English or Scotch Protestants in Ireland, either to elect or be elected to serve in Parliament, who, before the 1st day of March, 1649, have borne arms for the Parliament or your Highness, or otherwise given signal testimony of their good affection to this Commonwealth, and continued faithful to the same; that all votes and elections, given or made contrary, or not according to the qualifications aforesaid, shall be void and of none effect; and that if any person or persons so incapable as aforesaid, shall give his or their vote for election of members to serve in Parliament, all and every such person or persons so electing shall lose and forfeit one year's value of his and their respective real estates, and one full third part of his and their respective personal estates; the one moiety to your Highness, and the other moiety to him or them who shall sue for the same in any Court of Record, by action of debt, bill, plaint or information, wherein no essoine, wager of law, or protection shall be allowed. And that the persons who shall be elected to serve in Parliament be such, and no other than such, as are persons of known integrity, fearing God, and of good conversation, and being of the age of twenty-one years, and not such as are disabled by the Act of the seventeenth year of the late King, entitled, 'An Act for disenabling all persons in Holy Orders to exercise any temporal jurisdiction or authority, nor such as are public ministers or public preachers of the Gospel.' Nor such as are guilty of any of the offences mentioned in an Act of Parliament bearing date the 9th of August, 1650, entitled, 'An Act against several atheistical, blasphemous, and execrable opinions derogatory to the honour of God, and destructive to

[1] i.e. 165½.

human society'; no common scoffer or reviler of religion, or of
any person or persons professing thereof; no person that hath
married or shall marry a wife of the Popish religion, or hath
trained or shall train up his child or children, nor any other
child or children under his tuition or government, in the Popish
religion, or that shall permit or suffer such child or children
to be trained up in the said religion, or that hath given or
shall give his consent that his son or daughter shall marry
any of that religion; no person that shall deny the Scriptures
to be the Word of God, or the sacraments, prayer, magistracy,
and ministry to be the Ordinances of God; no common profaner
of the Lord's day, no profane swearer or curser, no drunkard
or common haunter of taverns or alehouses.

And that these qualifications may be observed, and yet the
privilege of Parliament maintained, we desire that it may
be by your Highness' consent ordained, that forty-one Commissioners be appointed by Act of Parliament, who, or any
fifteen or more of them, shall be authorised to examine and
try whether the members to be elected for the House of
Commons in future Parliaments be capable to sit, according
to the qualifications mentioned in this Petition and Advice;
and in case they find them not qualified accordingly, then
to suspend them from sitting until the House of Commons
shall, upon hearing of their particular cases, admit them to
sit; which Commissioners are to stand so authorised for that
end, until the House of Commons in any future Parliament
shall nominate the like number of other Commissioners in their
places; and those other Commissioners so to be nominated in
any future Parliament, to have the same powers and authorities;
that the said Commissioners shall certify in writing to the House
of Commons, on the first day of their meeting, the causes and
grounds of their suspensions of any persons so to be elected as
aforesaid; that the accusation shall be upon the oath of the
informer, or of some other person, that a copy of the accusation
shall be left by the party accusing, in writing under his hand,
with the party accused, or, in his absence, at his house in the
county, city or town for which he shall be chosen, if he have
any such house, or if not, with the Sheriff of the county, if he
be chosen for a county, or with the Chief Magistrate of the city

or borough for which he is chosen; and that the number of persons to be elected and chosen to sit and serve in Parliament for England, Scotland and Ireland, and the distribution of the persons so chosen within the counties, cities and boroughs of them respectively, may be according to such proportions as shall be agreed upon and declared in this present Parliament.

5. That your Highness will consent, that none be called to sit and vote in the other House, but such as are not disabled, but qualified according to the qualifications mentioned in the former Article, being such as shall be nominated by your Highness, and approved by this House, and that they exceed not seventy in number, nor be under the number of forty (whereof the quorum to be one-and-twenty), who shall not give any vote by proxies; and that as any of them do die, or be legally removed, no new ones be admitted to sit and vote in their rooms, but by the consent of the House itself. That the other House do not proceed in any civil causes, except in writs of error, in cases adjourned from inferior courts into the Parliament for difficulty, in cases of petitions against proceedings in Courts of Equity, and in cases of privileges of their own House; that they do not proceed in any criminal causes whatsoever against any person criminally, but upon an impeachment of the Commons assembled in Parliament, and by their consent; that they do not proceed in any cause, either civil or criminal, but according to the known laws of the land, and the due course and custom of Parliament; that no final determinations or judgments be by any members of that House, in any cause there depending, either civil, criminal or mixed, as Commissioners or Delegates, to be nominated by that House; but all such final determinations and judgments to be by the House itself, any law or usage to the contrary notwithstanding.

6. That in all other particulars which concern the calling and holding of Parliaments, your Highness will be pleased that the laws and statutes of the land be observed and kept; and that no laws be altered, suspended, abrogated or repealed, or new law made, but by Act of Parliament.

7. And to the end there may be a constant revenue for support of the Government, and for the safety and defence

of these nations by sea and land; we declare our willingness to settle forthwith a yearly revenue of £1,300,000 pounds, whereof £1,000,000 for the navy and army, and £300,000 for the support of the Government, and no part thereof to be raised by a land tax; and this not to be altered without the consent of the three Estates in Parliament; and to grant such other temporary supplies, according as the Commons assembled in Parliament shall from time to time adjudge the necessities of these nations to require; and do pray your Highness that it be declared and enacted, that no charge be laid, nor no person be compelled to contribute to any gift, loan, benevolence, tax, tallage, aid, or other like charge without common consent by Act of Parliament, which is a freedom the people of these nations ought by the laws to inherit.

8. That none may be added or admitted to the Privy Council of your Highness or successors, but such as are of known piety, and undoubted affection to the rights of these nations, and a just Christian liberty in matters of religion, nor without consent of the Council to be afterwards approved by both Houses of Parliament, and shall not afterwards be removed but by consent of Parliament, but may in the intervals of Parliament be suspended from the exercise of his place by your Highness, or your successors and the Council, for just cause; and that the number of the Council shall not be above one-and-twenty, whereof the quorum to be seven, and not under; as also that after your Highness' death, the Commander-in-Chief under your successors of such army or armies as shall be necessary to be kept in England, Scotland or Ireland, as also all such field-officers at land or generals at sea, which, after that time shall be newly made and constituted by your successors, be by the consent of the Council, and not otherwise.

And that the standing forces of this Commonwealth shall be disposed of by the Chief Magistrate, by consent of both Houses of Parliament, sitting the Parliament; and in the intervals of Parliament, by the Chief Magistrate, by the advice of the Council; and also that your Highness and successors will be pleased to exercise your Government over these nations by the advice of your Council.

9. And that the Chancellor, Keeper or Commissioners of the Great Seal of England, the Treasurer or Commissioners of the Treasury there, the Admiral, the chief Governor of Ireland, the Chancellor, Keeper or Commissioners of the Great Seal of Ireland, the Chief Justices of both the Benches, and the Chief Baron in England and Ireland, the Commander-in-Chief of the forces in Scotland, and such officers of State there, as by Act of Parliament in Scotland, are to be approved by Parliament, and the Judges in Scotland hereafter to be made, shall be approved of by both Houses of Parliament.

10. And whereas your Highness out of your zeal to the glory of God, and the propagation of the gospel of the Lord Jesus Christ, hath been pleased to encourage a godly ministry in these nations, we earnestly desire that such as do openly revile them or their assemblies, or disturb them in the worship or service of God, to the dishonour of God, scandal of good men, or breach of the peace, may be punished according to law; and where the laws are defective, that your Highness will give consent to such laws as shall be made in that behalf.

11. That the true Protestant Christian religion, as it is contained in the Holy Scriptures of the Old and New Testament, and no other, be held forth and asserted for the public profession of these nations; and that a Confession of Faith, to be agreed by your Highness and the Parliament, according to the rule and warrant of the Scriptures, be asserted, held forth, and recommended to the people of these nations, that none may be suffered or permitted, by opprobrious words or writing, maliciously or contemptuously to revile or reproach the Confession of Faith to be agreed upon as aforesaid; and such who profess faith in God the Father, and in Jesus Christ His eternal Son, the true God, and in the Holy Spirit, God co-equal with the Father and the Son, one God blessed for ever, and do acknowledge the Holy Scriptures of the Old and New Testament to be the revealed Will and Word of God, and shall in other things differ in doctrine, worship or discipline, from the public profession held forth, endeavours shall be used to convince them by sound doctrine, and the example of a good conversation; but that they may not be compelled thereto by penalties, nor restrained from their profession, but protected

from all injury and molestation in the profession of the faith, and exercise of their religion, whilst they abuse not this liberty to the civil injury of others, or the disturbance of the public peace; so that this liberty be not extended to Popery or Prelacy, or to the countenancing such who publish horrible blasphemies, or practise or hold forth licentiousness or profaneness under the profession of Christ; and that those ministers or public preachers, who shall agree with the public profession aforesaid in matters of faith, although in their judgment and practice they differ in matters of worship and discipline, shall not only have protection in the way of their churches and worship respectively, but be esteemed fit and capable, notwithstanding such difference (being otherwise duly qualified and duly approved), of any trust, promotion or employment whatsoever in these nations, that any ministers who agree in doctrine, worship and discipline with the public profession aforesaid are capable of; and all others who agree with the public profession in matters of faith, although they differ in matters of worship and discipline as aforesaid, shall not only have protection as aforesaid, but be esteemed fit and capable (notwithstanding such difference, being otherwise duly qualified) of any civil trust, employment or promotion in these nations: but for such persons who agree not in matters of faith with the public profession aforesaid, they shall not be capable of receiving the public maintenance appointed for the ministry.

Provided, that this clause shall not be construed to extend to enable such ministers or public preachers, or pastors of congregations; but that they be disenabled, and they are hereby disenabled, to hold any civil employment, which those in Orders were or are disenabled to hold, by an Act, entitled, 'An Act for disenabling all persons in Holy Orders to exercise any temporal jurisdiction or authority.' And that your Highness will give your consent, that all laws, statutes, ordinances and clauses in any law, statute and ordinance, so far as they are contrary to the aforesaid liberty, be repealed.

12. That all Acts and Ordinances of Parliament made for the abolishing of Archbishops and Bishops, and for the abolishing of Deans, Deans and Chapters, Canons, Prebends, and other offices and titles of or belonging to any Cathedral,

or Collegiate Church or Chapel, and for the sale or other disposition of the lands, rents and hereditaments, unto any or either of them belonging, or for the sale or other disposition of the lands, rents and hereditaments of the late King, Queen, or Prince; or of the lands of delinquents, fee-farm, or other rents, forest-lands, or any of them; or any other lands, tenements, rents or hereditaments, lately belonging to the Commonwealth, shall no way be impeached, but that they do remain good and firm; and that the security given by Act and Ordinance of Parliament, for any sum or sums of monies, by any of the said lands, the excise, or by any other public revenue; and also the securities given by the public faith of the nation, and the engagement of the public faith for satisfaction of debts, may remain firm and good, and not be made void by any pretence whatsoever.

13. That all and every person and persons who have aided, abetted, advised or assisted in any war against the Parliament, since the 1st day of January, 1641 [1] (unless he or they have since borne arms for the Parliament or your Highness, or otherwise given signal testimony of his or their good affection to the Commonwealth, and continued faithful to the same); and all such as have been actually engaged in any plot, conspiracy or design, against the person of your Highness, or in any insurrection or rebellion, in England or Wales, since the 16th of December, 1653: and for Scotland, that all and every person and persons who have been in arms against the Parliament of England, or against the Parliament in Scotland, before the 1st day of April, 1648 (except such as have since borne arms in the service of the Parliament of England or your Highness, or given other signal testimony of their good affection); and every person or persons that since the said 1st day of April, 1648, have been in arms, or otherwise aided, abetted, advised or assisted in any war against the Parliament of England or your Highness (except such persons who having been in arms, or otherwise abetted, advised or assisted in any war against the Parliament of England or your Highness, since the 1st day of April, 1648), and were not in arms against the Parliament of England, or against the Parliament of Scotland, before the 1st

[1] i. e. 1641½.

day of April, 1648; and have since the 1st day of March, 1651 (old style), lived peaceably, and thereby given testimony of their good affection to the Parliament and your Highness, be made incapable for ever of holding or enjoying of any office or place of public trust, in these three nations, or any of them.

Provided, that nothing in this Article contained shall extend to put any incapacity in this Article mentioned upon any English or Scotch Protestants in Ireland, who, before the 1st day of March, 1649, have borne arms for the Parliament or your Highness, or otherwise given signal testimony of their good affection to this Commonwealth, and continued faithful to the same.

14. And that your Highness will be pleased to consent, that nothing in this Petition and Advice contained, nor your Highness' assent thereto, shall be construed to extend to the dissolving of this present Parliament, but that the same shall continue and remain, until such time as your Highness shall think fit to dissolve the same.

15[1]. And that nothing contained in this Petition and Advice, nor your Highness' consent thereunto, shall be construed to extend to the repealing or making void of any Act or Ordinance which is not contrary hereunto, or to the matters herein contained, but that the said Acts and Ordinances not contrary hereunto shall continue and remain in force, in such manner as if this present Petition and Advice had not at all been had or made, or your Highness' consent thereunto given.

16. And that all writs issued out of the Chancery, and all writs and patents of the Justices of the one Bench, and of the other, Barons of the Exchequer, Commissions of *oyer* and *terminer*, gaol-delivery, and Justices of the Peace, and all other commissions, patents, and grants, made and passed under the Great Seal of England, Scotland or Ireland, shall stand good and effectual in the law, notwithstanding this Petition and Advice, or your Highness' assent thereunto, or any law, statute or custom to the contrary; and that all writs, and all commissions, indictments, informations, process, actions, suits, bills or plaints, taken out, or now depending in any Court of Record

---

[1] In quoting the articles, it should be remembered that both Scobell and the official publication (B. M. Press Mark, E 1065, 18) number them wrongly from this point.

at Westminster, or any other Court of Record, in England, Scotland or Ireland, or in the town of Berwick-upon-Tweed; and all process, pleas, demurrers, continuances and proceedings, in every such writs, indictments, informations, actions, suits, bills and plaints, shall be returnable, stand good and effectual, and be prosecuted and sued forth, in such manner and form, and in the same state, condition and order, the style and test of proceedings, after passing of these presents, being made conformable thereunto, this present Petition and Advice, or your Highness' assent thereunto, or any law, custom or usage to the contrary thereof in any wise notwithstanding; and that any variance that shall be occasioned by reason thereof, touching any the said writs, process or proceedings in the name, style, test or otherwise, shall not be in any wise material as concerning any default or error to be alleged or objected thereunto.

17. And that your Highness and your successors will be pleased to take an oath, in such form as shall be agreed upon by your Highness and this present Parliament, to govern these nations according to the law.

18. And in case your Highness shall not be satisfied to give your consent to all the matters and things in this humble Petition and Advice, that then nothing in the same be deemed of force, to oblige the people of these nations in any the particulars therein contained.

And these our desires being granted by your Highness, we shall hope (through the rich mercy and goodness of God) that it will prove some remedy to those dangers, distractions, and distempers which these nations are now in, and be an effectual means to remove those jealousies and fears which remain in the minds of many men concerning the Government of this Commonwealth; and thereby we shall be enabled and encouraged with all cheerfulness to the settling of such things, which shall be further necessary for the good of these nations, and be most ready to join with you in promoting the work of reformation, happily begun by your Highness, the regulating courts of justice, and abridging both the delays and charges of law suits, and apply ourselves to such other courses and counsels as may be most like to heal our breaches and divisions, and to restore these poor nations to a union and consistency

with themselves, and to lay a foundation of further confidence
between your Highness and them, to the rejoicing of the hearts
of our friends and terror of our enemies.

Which Petition being presented the 25th day of May, 1657,
his Highness' answer thereunto was read by the Clerk of the
Parliament in these words,

The Lord Protector doth consent.

103. THE ADDITIONAL PETITION AND ADVICE.

[June 26, 1657.   Scobell, ii. 450.   See Masson's *Life of Milton*, v. 142.]

*To his Highness the Lord Protector of the Commonwealth of
England, Scotland and Ireland, and the dominions and
territories thereunto belonging; the humble additional and
explanatory Petition and Advice of the knights, citizens and
burgesses now assembled in the Parliament of this Commonwealth.*

Whereas upon the humble Petition and Advice of the said
knights, citizens and burgesses, now assembled in the Parliament of this Commonwealth, lately presented and consented
unto by your Highness, certain doubts and questions have
arisen, concerning some particulars therein comprised, for
explanation whereof m y it please your Highness to declare
and consent unto the additions and explanations hereafter mentioned, and may it be declared with your Highness' consent:

In the fourth Article.

That such person and persons as invaded England, under
Duke Hamilton, in the year 1648, or advised, consented,
assisted or voluntarily contributed unto that war, and were
for that cause debarred from public trust by the Parliament
of Scotland, be incapable to elect or be elected to sit and
serve as members of Parliament, or in any other place of public
trust, relating unto the fourth and thirteenth Articles in the
Petition and Advice, excepting such as since have borne arms
for your Highness or the Parliament, or have been admitted
to sit and serve in the Parliament of this Commonwealth, and
are of good life and conversation, or such as shall hereafter

be declared by your Highness, with the advice of your Council, to have given some signal testimony of their good affection and continuance in the same.

That the proviso in the said fourth Article be explained thus, viz. that such English and Scottish Protestants, who (since the defection of the Earl of Ormond, and the Lord Inchiquin, and before the 1st day of March, 1649 [1]) have borne arms for, and ever since continued faithful to the Parliament or your Highness, or have otherwise (before the said 1st day of March, 1649 [1]) given signal testimony of their good affection to this Commonwealth, and have ever since continued faithful to the same, shall not be debarred or deemed incapable of electing or being elected to serve in Parliament.

And whereas in the said fourth Article, public ministers or public preachers of the Gospel are disabled to be elected to serve in Parliament; it is hereby explained and declared to extend to such ministers and preachers only as have maintenance for preaching, or are pastors or teachers of congregations.

In the said fourth Article.

That instead of Commissioners to be appointed by Act of Parliament, to examine and try whether the members to be elected for the House of Commons in future Parliaments be capable to sit according to the qualifications mentioned in the said Petition and Advice, there shall be the penalty and fine of £1,000 laid and inflicted upon every such unqualified member (being so adjudged) by the said House of Commons, and imprisonment of his person until payment thereof.

And that the ensuing clauses in the said Article, viz. 'We desire that it may by your Highness' consent be ordained, that forty-one Commissioners be appointed by Act of Parliament, who, or five, or more of them, shall be authorised to examine and try whether the members to be elected for the House of Commons in future Parliaments be capable to sit, according to the qualifications mentioned in this Petition and Advice; and in case they find them not qualified accordingly, then to suspend them from sitting until the House of Commons shall, upon hearing their particular cases, admit them to sit; which Com-

[1] i. e. 16$\frac{48}{49}$.

missioners are to stand so authorised for that end, until the House of Commons in any future Parliament shall nominate the like number of other Commissioners in their places ; and those other Commissioners so to be nominated in any future Parliament, to have the same power and authority. That the said Commissioners shall certify in writing to the House of Commons, on the first day of their meeting, the cause and grounds of their suspensions of any person so to be elected as aforesaid ; that the accusation shall be upon oath of the informant, or of some other person. That a copy of the accusation shall be left by the party accusing, in writing under his hand, with the party accused, or, in his absence, at his house in the county, city or town for which he shall be chosen, if he have any such house, or if not, with the Sheriff of the county, if he be chosen for a county, or with the Chief Magistrate of the city or borough for which he is chosen ' ; shall not be put in execution or made use of, but shall be void, frustrate, null, and of none effect, and shall be so construed and taken to all intents and purposes whatsoever, anything contained in the said Petition and Advice to the contrary notwithstanding.

In the fifth Article.

That the nomination of the persons to supply the place of such members of the other House as shall die or be removed, shall be by your Highness and your successors.

In the seventh Article.

That the monies directed to be for the supply of the sea and land forces, be issued by advice of the Council; and that the Treasurer or Commissioners of the Treasury shall give an account of all the said money to every Parliament.

That the Officers of State and Judges, in the ninth Article of the said Petition and Advice mentioned, shall be chosen in the intervals of Parliament, by the consent of the Council, to be afterwards approved by Parliament.

That your Highness will be pleased, according to the usage of former Chief Magistrates in these nations, and for the better satisfaction of the people thereof, to take an oath in the form ensuing:

'I do in the presence, and by the name of God Almighty, promise and swear, that to the uttermost of my power I will uphold and maintain the true reformed Protestant Christian religion, in the purity thereof, as it is contained in the Holy Scriptures of the Old and New Testament, to the uttermost of my power and understanding, and encourage the profession and professors of the same; and that to the uttermost of my power I will endeavour, as Chief Magistrate of these three nations, the maintenance and preservation of the peace and safety, and of the just rights and privileges of the people thereof; and shall in all things according to my best knowledge and power, govern the people of these nations according to law.'

That your Highness' successors do, before they take upon them the government of these nations, take an oath in the form aforesaid.

That all such persons who now are or shall hereafter be of The Privy Council of your Highness or successors, before they or either of them do act as Councillors, shall respectively take an oath before persons to be authorised by your Highness and successors for that purpose, in the form following:

'I, A. B., do in the presence, and by the name of God Almighty, promise and swear, that to the uttermost of my power, in my place, I will uphold and maintain the true reformed Protestant Christian religion, in the purity thereof, as it is contained in the Holy Scriptures of the Old and New Testament, and encourage the profession and professors of the same; and that I will be true and faithful to His Highness the Lord Protector of the Commonwealth of England, Scotland, and Ireland and the dominions thereto belonging, as Chief Magistrate thereof; and shall not contrive, design or attempt any thing against the person or lawful authority of his said Highness, and shall keep secret all matters that shall be treated of in Council, and put under secrecy, and not reveal them but by command or consent of his Highness, the Parliament or the Council, and shall in all things faithfully perform the trust committed to me as a Councillor, according to the best of my understanding, in order to the good government, peace and welfare of these nations.'

That the same oath be taken by the members of your Highness' Council of Scotland and Ireland.

That every person who now is, or hereafter shall be, a member of either House of Parliament, before he sit in Parliament, shall, from and after the 1st day of July, 1657, take an oath before persons to be authorised and appointed by your Highness and successors for that purpose, in the form following:

' I, A. B., do in the presence, and by the name of God Almighty, promise and swear, that to the uttermost of my power, in my place, I will uphold and maintain the true reformed Protestant Christian religion, in the purity thereof, as it is contained in the Holy Scriptures of the Old and New Testament, and encourage the profession and professors of the same ; and that I will be true and faithful to the Lord Protector of the Commonwealth of England, Scotland, and Ireland, and the dominions and territories thereunto belonging, as Chief Magistrate thereof, and shall not contrive, design or attempt anything against the person or lawful authority of the Lord Protector, and shall endeavour as much as in me lies, as a member of Parliament, the preservation of the rights and liberties of the people.'

That your Highness would be pleased in convenient time, before the next meeting of this Parliament, to cause several summons in due form of law, to be issued forth to such persons as your Highness shall think fit (being qualified according to the humble Petition and Advice of the Parliament, whereto your Highness hath consented), to sit and serve as members in the other House of Parliament ; by which summons the said persons shall be respectively commanded to be, and personally to appear at a certain place and time, to be appointed by your Highness, to give their advice and assistance, and to do such things concerning the great and weighty affairs of this Commonwealth, as to the other House of Parliament doth appertain by the said humble Petition and Advice.

That the persons so summoned and assembled together, shall be, and are hereby declared to be, the other House of Parliament ; and shall, and may without further approbation of this House, from such time of their meeting, proceed to do and perform all such matters and things as the other House of Parliament ought to do and perform, and shall and may have and exercise all such privileges, powers and authorities as the other House of Parliament ought, by the aforesaid humble Petition and Advice to have and exercise; the said humble Petition and Advice, or anything therein contained to the contrary thereof notwithstanding.

Which Petition being presented the 26th day of June, 1657, his Highness' answer thereunto was read by the Clerk of the Parliament in these words,

The Lord Protector doth consent.

104. THE WRIT SUMMONING RICHARD CROMWELL TO THE HOUSE OF LORDS OF THE PROTECTORATE.

[December 10, 1657. Old Parliamentary History, xxi. 166.]

Oliver, Lord Protector of the Commonwealth of England, Scotland and Ireland, and the dominions and territories thereunto belonging: to our trusty and beloved son, Lord Richard Cromwell, greeting.

Whereas, by the advice and assent of our Council, for certain great and weighty affairs concerning us and the state and defence of the said Commonwealth, we ordained our present Parliament to be held at our city of Westminster, the 17th day of September, in the year of our Lord 1656, and there to consult and advise with the knights, citizens and burgesses of our said Commonwealth; which Parliament was then and there held, and continued until the 26th day of June last past, and then adjourned until the 20th day of January now next coming; therefore we command and firmly enjoin you, that, considering the difficulty of the said affairs and imminent dangers, all excuses being set aside, you be personally present at Westminster aforesaid, the said 20th day of January next coming there to treat, confer, and give your advice with us, and with the great men and nobles in and concerning the affairs aforesaid; and this, as you love our honour and safety, and the defence of the Commonwealth aforesaid, you shall in no wise omit.

Witness ourself at Westminster, the 10th day of December, 1657.

105. THE DECLARATION OF BREDA.

[April 4, 1660.   Old Parliamentary History, xxii. 238.   See Masson's
Life of Milton, v. 697.]

Charles R.

Charles, by the grace of God, King of England, Scotland,
France and Ireland, Defender of the Faith, &c. To all our
loving subjects, of what degree or quality soever, greeting.

If the general distraction and confusion which is spread over
the whole kingdom doth not awaken all men to a desire and
longing that those wounds which have so many years together
been kept bleeding, may be bound up, all we can say will be to
no purpose; however, after this long silence, we have thought
it our duty to declare how much we desire to contribute
thereunto; and that as we can never give over the hope, in
good time, to obtain the possession of that right which God and
nature hath made our due, so we do make it our daily suit to
the Divine Providence, that He will, in compassion to us and
our subjects, after so long misery and sufferings, remit and put
us into a quiet and peaceable possession of that our right, with
as little blood and damage to our people as is possible; nor do
we desire more to enjoy what is ours, than that all our
subjects may enjoy what by law is theirs, by a full and entire
administration of justice throughout the land, and by extending
our mercy where it is wanted and deserved.

And to the end that the fear of punishment may not engage
any, conscious to themselves of what is past, to a perseverance
in guilt for the future, by opposing the quiet and happiness
of their country, in the restoration of King, Peers and people
to their just, ancient and fundamental rights, we do, by these
presents, declare, that we do grant a free and general pardon,
which we are ready, upon demand, to pass under our Great
Seal of England, to all our subjects, of what degree or quality
soever, who, within forty days after the publishing hereof, shall

lay hold upon this our grace and favour, and shall, by any public act, declare their doing so, and that they return to the loyalty and obedience of good subjects; excepting only such persons as shall hereafter be excepted by Parliament, those only to be excepted. Let all our subjects, how faulty soever, rely upon the word of a King, solemnly given by this present declaration, that no crime whatsoever, committed against us or our royal father before the publication of this, shall ever rise in judgment, or be brought in question, against any of them, to the least endamagement of them, either in their lives, liberties or estates, or (as far forth as lies in our power) so much as to the prejudice of their reputations, by any reproach or term of distinction from the rest of our best subjects; we desiring and ordaining that henceforth all notes of discord, separation and difference of parties be utterly abolished among all our subjects, whom we invite and conjure to a perfect union among themselves, under our protection, for the re-settlement of our just rights and theirs in a free Parliament, by which, upon the word of a King, we will be advised.

And because the passion and uncharitableness of the times have produced several opinions in religion, by which men are engaged in parties and animosities against each other (which, when they shall hereafter unite in a freedom of conversation, will be composed or better understood), we do declare a liberty to tender consciences, and that no man shall be disquieted or called in question for differences of opinion in matter of religion, which do not disturb the peace of the kingdom; and that we shall be ready to consent to such an Act of Parliament, as, upon mature deliberation, shall be offered to us, for the full granting that indulgence.

And because, in the continued distractions of so many years, and so many and great revolutions, many grants and purchases of estates have been made to and by many officers, soldiers and others, who are now possessed of the same, and who may be liable to actions at law upon several titles, we are likewise willing that all such differences, and all things relating to such grants, sales and purchases, shall be determined in Parliament, which can best provide for the just satisfaction of all men who are concerned.

And we do further declare, that we will be ready to consent to any Act or Acts of Parliament to the purposes aforesaid, and for the full satisfaction of all arrears due to the officers and soldiers of the army under the command of General Monk; and that they shall be received into our service upon as good pay and conditions as they now enjoy.

> Given under our Sign Manual and Privy Signet, at our Court at Breda, this $\frac{4}{14}$ day of April, 1660, in the twelfth year of our reign.

APPENDIX

The Navigation Act.

[Oct. 9, 1651.   Scobell's Acts of Parliament, pt. ii, p. 176.   See *Commonwealth and Protectorate*, ii. 147.]

Cap. 22.

Goods from Foreign parts by whom to be imported.

For the increase of the shipping and the encouragement of the navigation of this nation, which [1] under the good providence and protection of God is so great a means of the welfare and safety of this Commonwealth: be it enacted by this present Parliament, and the authority thereof, that from and after the first day of December, one thousand six hundred fifty and one, and from thence forwards, no goods or commodities whatsoever of the growth, production or manufacture of Asia, Africa or America, or of any part thereof; or of any islands belonging to them, or which are described or laid down in the usual maps or cards of those places, as well of the English plantations as others, shall be imported or brought into this Commonwealth of England, or into Ireland, or any other lands, islands, plantations, or territories to this Commonwealth belonging, or in their possession, in any other ship or ships, vessel or vessels whatsoever, but only in such as do truly and without fraud belong only to the people of this Commonwealth, or the plantations thereof, as the proprietors or right owners thereof; and whereof the master and mariners are also for the most part of them of the people of this Commonwealth, under the penalty of the forfeiture and loss of all the goods that shall be imported contrary to this act; as also of the ship (with all her tackle, guns and apparel) in which the said goods or

[1] When this Act was re-enacted after the Restoration many changes were made, the most important being that the prohibition of importing in foreign bottoms was extended to exports (12 Car. II, cap. 18).

commodities shall be so brought in and imported; the one moiety to the use of the Commonwealth, and the other moiety to the use and behoof of any person or persons who shall seize the goods or commodities, and shall prosecute the same in any court of record within this Commonwealth.

And it is further enacted by the authority aforesaid, that no goods or commodities of the growth, production, or manufacture of Europe, or of any part thereof, shall after the first day of December, one thousand six hundred fifty and one, be imported or brought into this Commonwealth of England, or into Ireland, or any other lands, islands, plantations or territories to this Commonwealth belonging, or in their possession, in any ship or ships, vessel or vessels whatsoever, but in such as do truly and without fraud belong only to the people of this Commonwealth, as the true owners and proprietors thereof, and in no other, except only such foreign ships and vessels as do truly and properly belong to the people of that country or place, of which the said goods are the growth, production or manufacture ; or to such ports where the said goods can only be, or most usually are first shipped for transportation ; and that under the same penalty of forfeiture and loss expressed in the former branch of this Act, the said forfeitures to be recovered and employed as is therein expressed.

And it is further enacted by the authority aforesaid, that no goods or commodities that are of foreign growth, production or manufacture, and which are to be brought into this Commonwealth in shipping belonging to the people thereof, shall be by them shipped or brought from any other place or places, country or countries, but only from those of their said growth, production, or manufacture, or from those ports where the said goods and commodities can only, or are, or usually have been first shipped for transportation ; and from none other places or countries, under the same penalty of forfeiture and loss expressed in the first branch of this Act, the said forfeitures to be recovered and employed as is therein expressed.

And it is further enacted by the authority aforesaid, that no sort of cod-fish, ling, herring, pilchard, or any other kind of salted fish, usually fished for and caught by the people of this nation ; nor any oil made, or that shall be made of any kind of fish whatsoever, nor any whale-fins, or whale-bones, shall from henceforth be imported into this Commonwealth or into Ireland, or any other lands, islands, plantations, or territories thereto belonging, or in their possession, but only such as shall be caught in vessels that do or shall truly and properly belong to the people of this nation, as proprietors and right owners thereof; and the said fish to be cured, and the oil aforesaid made by the people of this Commonwealth, under the penalty and loss expressed in the first branch of this present Act; the said forfeit to be recovered and employed as is there expressed.

And it is further enacted by the authority aforesaid, that no sort of cod, ling, herring or pilchard, or any other kind of salted fish whatsoever, which shall be caught and cured by the people of this Commonwealth, shall be from and after the first of February, one thousand six hundred fifty three, exported from any place or places belonging to this Commonwealth, in any other ship or ships, vessel or vessels, save only in such as do truly and properly appertain to the people of this Commonwealth, as right owners; and whereof the master and mariners are for the most part of them English, under the penalty and loss expressed in the said first branch of this present Act; the said forfeit to be recovered and employed as is there expressed.

Provided always, that this Act, nor anything therein contained, extend not, or be meant to restrain the importation of any of the commodities of the Straits[1] or Levant seas, laden in the shipping of this nation as aforesaid, at the usual ports or places for lading of them heretofore, within the said Straits or Levant seas, though the said commodities be not of the very growth of the said places.

Provided also, that this Act nor anything therein contained, extend not, nor be meant to restrain the importing of any East India commodities laden in the shipping of this nation, at the usual port or places for lading of them heretofore in any part of those seas, to the southward and eastward of Cabo Bona Esperanza[2], although the said ports be not the very places of their growth.

---

[1] 'The Straits' are the Straits of Gibraltar, but the term includes the Mediterranean, or, as here, the western part of it.

[2] The Cape of Good Hope.

Provided also, that it shall and may be lawful to and for any of the people of this Commonwealth, in vessels or ships to them belonging, and whereof the master and mariners are of this nation as aforesaid, to load and bring in from any of the ports of Spain and Portugal, all sorts of goods or commodities that have come from, or any way belonged unto the plantations or dominions of either of them respectively.

Be it also further enacted by the authority aforesaid, that from henceforth it shall not be lawful to any person or persons whatsoever to load or cause to be laden and carried in any bottom or bottoms, ship or ships, vessel or vessels, whatsoever, whereof any stranger or strangers born (unless such be denizens or naturalized) be owners, or masters, any fish, victual, wares, or things of what kind or nature soever the same shall be, from one port or creek of this Commonwealth, to another port or creek of the same, under penalty to every one that shall offend contrary to the true meaning of this branch of this present Act, to forfeit all the goods that shall be so laden or carried, as also the ship upon which they shall be so laden or carried, the same forfeit to be recovered and employed as directed in the first branch of this present Act.

Lastly, that this Act nor anything therein contained, extend not to bullion, nor yet to any goods taken, or that shall be taken by way of reprisal by any ship or ships, having commission from this commonwealth.

Provided, that this Act, or anything therein contained, shall not extend, nor be construed to extend to any silk or silk wares which shall be brought by land from any part of Italy, and there bought with the proceed of English commodities, sold either for money or in barter; but that it shall and may be lawful for any of the people of this Commonwealth to ship the same in English vessels from Ostend, Nieuport, Rotterdam, Middelburg, Amsterdam, or any ports thereabouts, the owners and proprietors first making oath by themselves, or other credible witnesses, before the Commissioners of the Customs for the time being or their deputies, or one of the Barons of the Exchequer, that the goods aforesaid were so bought for his or their own proper account in Italy.

INDEX

Acts of Parliament: for triennial Parliaments, 144; for Strafford's attainder, 156; against dissolving the Long Parliament without its own consent, 158; for the grant of tonnage and poundage, 159; for the abolition of the Star Chamber, 179; for the abolition of the High Commission Court, 186; declaring the illegality of ship-money, 189; for the limitation of forests, 192; prohibiting knighthood fines, 196; imposing disabilities on the clergy, 241; for impressment, 242; navigation, 468.

Agreement of the People, the, xlix–liv, 359.

Arminians, the Commons complain of, 79; their tenets stated, 81; protestation of the Commons against, 82.

Army, votes for raising an, 261.

Array, commissions of, the King's letter sent with, 258.

Articles of Religion, the King's declaration prefixed to, 75.

Arundel, Earl of, documents relating to the restraint of, 44.

Attainder of Strafford, 156.

Barebones Parliament, the so-called, summons to a member of, 405.

Bates's case, xiii.

Benevolences, statute against levying, 66.

Bill on Church reform, 167.

Bishops, complaints against, 140; proposal to limit the authority of,

167; proposal to take away the votes of, 204; Act taking secular jurisdiction from, 241; proposal for the abolition of, 263, 275, 291.

Breda, the declaration of, 465.

Bristol, Earl of, documents relating to the restraint of, 44.

Buckingham, Duke of, documents relating to the impeachment of, 3.

Calvin, xxi–xxiii.

Charles I, incidents of his reign, xix, foll.; defends the Duke of Buckingham, 4; orders the collection of a Free Gift, 46; his answer to the Petition of Right, 70; claims tonnage and poundage, 74; his declaration on religion, 75; his declaration on the dissolution of his third Parliament, 83; comments on the session of 1629, 91; his declaration of sports, 99; is present at the decision of the Privy Council on the position of the Communion Table, 103; refers the legality of ship-money to the judges, 108; summons a Great Council, 136; his speech to the Recorder of the City, 201; his proclamation on religion, 232; his answer to the petition accompanying the Grand Remonstrance, 233; condemns the militia ordinance, 248; his answers to the Newcastle propositions, 306, 308, 311; suggested answer to be given by, 309; declares that he prefers the

Heads of Proposals to the Parliamentary propositions, 326; writes to Parliament after leaving Hampton Court, 328; erection of a High Court of Justice for the trial of, 357; charge against, 371; declines the jurisdiction of the High Court of Justice, 374; is sentenced to death, 377; warrant for the execution of, 380.

Charles II, issues the declaration of Breda, 465.

Church, Act repealing laws for not coming to, 391.

Church of England, the, the King's declaration prefixed to the articles of, 75; complaints of abuses in, 137; Bill for the reform of, 167; the Commons complain of innovations in, 197; order of the Lords on the services of, 199; Charles declares his intention of defending, 202; the King's proclamation for maintaining, 232; declaration of Parliament on the reform of, 247.

Clerical Disabilities Act, the, 241.

Clerkenwell, a college of Jesuits at, 79.

Commissions of Array, the King's letter sent with, 258.

Committee of both kingdoms, the, 271, 273.

Commons, House of, its protestation at the close of the session of 1625, 2; remonstrates against the King's defence of Buckingham, 6; impeaches Buckingham, 7; its protestation at the dissolution of 1629, 82; the King's declaration against the proceedings of, 83; the protestation of, 155; resolutions of, on ecclesiastical innovations, 197; proposes instructions to the Committee in Scotland, 199; declares the treatment of the five members to be a breach of privilege, 237; proposals for the reform of, 359, 407.

Commonwealth, the, engagement taken by the Council of State of, lii, 384; abolition of the office of

King in, 384; general engagement of fidelity to, 388.

Communion Table, the, position of, 103.

Cosins, Dr., his books complained of, 80.

Council of State, the, engagement taken by, 384.

Covenant, the Scottish National, 124; the Solemn League and, 267.

Cromwell, Oliver, his declaration on the dissolution of the Long Parliament, 400. *See* Protectorate.

Cromwell, Richard, summoned to the House of Lords of the Protectorate, 464.

Declaration of Breda, the, lxiii, 465.

Declaration of Sports, the, 99.

Delinquents, proposals made for dealing with, 278, 298.

Disbandment of the armies, proposals for the, 285.

Elections, proposals of the Agreement of the People relating to, 359; arrangements of the Instrument of Government for, 407; ordinance for the Scottish, 422; ordinance for the Irish, 425.

Engagement, the, 347.

Episcopacy. *See* Bishops.

Essex, Earl of, vote of Parliament to live and die with, 261.

Five Knights' Case, the, 57.

Five members, the, impeachment of, 236; declaration of the Commons on the breach of privilege in the treatment of, 237.

Forced Loan, the, Commission for raising, 51.

Forced loans, condemned, 67.

Forests, Act for the limitation of, 192.

Four Bills, the, xlviii, xlix, 335.

Free Gift, the, 46.

Goodman, bishop, his sermons complained of, 80.
Grand Remonstrance, the, 202 ; the King's Answer to the Petition accompanying, 233.
Great Council, the, the King's writ summoning, 136.

Heads of Proposals, the, 316 ; Charles expresses his preference for, 326.
Heath, Sir Robert, stays proceedings against recusants, 79.
High Commission, Court of, abolition of, xi, 186.
High Court of Justice, the, ordinance for erecting, 357 ; the King declines the jurisdiction of, 374 ; sentences the King, 377.
Hooker's *Ecclesiastical Polity*, xxvi.
Humble Petition and Advice, the, 447 ; the Additional, 459.

Impeachment of the five members, 236.
Impressment Act, the, 242.
Imprisonment without cause shewn, 67.
Innovations, ecclesiastical resolutions of the Commons on, 197 ; order of the Lords on, 199 ; proposed Bill for taking away, 263.
Instrument of Government, the, 405.
Ireland, instructions to the Committee in Scotland on the rebellion in, 200 ; statement made in the Grand Remonstrance about, 228 ; reply of the King about, 235 ; Act on impressment for service in, 242 ; proposal to make void the cessation in, 278 ; proposal to make war in, 283 ; Act for the settlement of, 394 ; ordinance for elections in, 425.

James I, King, incidents of his reign, xii, foll.

Jesuits, college of, 79.

King, abolition of the office of, 384.
Knighthood fines, Act prohibiting the exaction of, 196.

Lancashire, recreations in, 99.
Laud, Archbishop, xxii–xxiv.
Liberties of the subject, Bill on the, 65.
London, the City of, proposals in favour of, 285, 296, 304.
Long Parliament, the, legislation of, xi, xxxi ; Act against dissolving without its own consent, 158 ; declaration of the Protector on the dissolution of, 400.
Lords, House of, the, reading of a Bill on Church reform by, 167 ; makes an order on the services of the Church, 199 ; renunciation by the Commons of, 389 ; re-establishment, under the Protectorate, of, 449, 451 ; summons of Richard Cromwell to, 464.

Martial law, illegal exercise of, 68.
Militia, the, ordinance for placing under the authority of Parliament, 246 ; the King's declaration on the ordinance about, 248 ; declaration of the Houses on, 254 ; proposals made at the Treaty of Oxford on, 265 ; proposals made at the Treaty of Uxbridge on, 281 ; proposals made at Newcastle on, 293.
Militia ordinance, the, 245 ; is condemned by the King, 248 ; declaration of the Houses in defence of, 254.
Montague, Bishop, his books complained of, 79.

Navigation Act, 1651, 468.
Negative oath, the, 289.
Newcastle, the propositions of, 290 ; the King's answers to them, 306,

308, 311; answer suggested for
the King to give to, 309.
Nineteen Propositions, the, 249.
No Addresses, vote of, 356.

Oblivion, proposed Act of, 285.
Officials, proposals for the parliamentary nomination of, 251, 283,
304.
Ordinance, for the militia, 245;
appointing the first Committee
of both kingdoms, 271; appointing the second Committee, 273.
Oxford, propositions presented to
the King at, 262.

Parliament of 1628-9, proceedings
in, 65-83; the dissolution of, 83.
Parliament of 1620. *See* Long
Parliament, the.
Peace, propositions for. *See* Propositions.
Peers, the twelve, petition of, 134;
created since the removal of the
Great Seal, proposals to invalidate
the titles of, 283, 297.
Petition and Advice, the Humble,
447; the Additional, 459.
Petition of Right, xx, 66; of the
twelve peers, 134; the root and
branch, 137.
Popery, the Commons complain of
encouragement to, 78.
Privy Council, the, its decision on
the position of the Communion
Table, 103.
Propositions, the ten, 163; the
nineteen, 249; of Oxford, 262;
of Uxbridge, 275; of Newcastle,
290.
Protectorate, the, establishment of,
405; modification of, 447; House
of Lords of, 464.
Protestation, the, 155.

Recusancy laws, the, Act of the
Parliament of the Commonwealth
repealing, 391.
Recusants, stay of proceedings
against, 79.

Religion, the King's declaration
concerning, 75; resolutions of a
Sub-committee of the House of
Commons on, 77; the King explains his attitude towards 89;
assertions of the root and branch
petitions about, 138; the King's
proclamation on, 232; proposals
made in the Treaty of Uxbridge
on, 275; proposals made in the
propositions of Newcastle on,
292; Act for the toleration of,
391.
Remonstrance, the Grand, xxxv, 202.
Rich, Sir Nathaniel, speech of, 1.
Root and Branch Petition, the, 137.

St. John, Oliver, argues in the ship-
money case, 109.
Scotland, the National Covenant
of, 124; proposed instructions to
the Committee in, 199; ordinance
for uniting with England, 418;
ordinance for elections in, 422.
Self-denying Ordinance, the, 287.
Ship-money, xxv, xxxiii; the first
writ of, 105; opinion of the
judges on the King's right to,
108; speeches in the case of, 109;
argument of Sir R. Berkeley on,
115; its illegality declared by
Act of Parliament, 189.
Solemn League and Covenant, the,
267.
Sports, the Declaration of, 99.
Star Chamber, xi, xxxiii; abolition
of, xi, 179.
Strafford, attainder of, xxix, 156.

Tallage, alleged statute against
levying, 66.
Ten Propositions, the, 163.
Tonnage and Poundage, xxi-xxv;
commission for raising, 49; the
Commons' remonstrance against,
70; the King's claim to levy, 74;
protestation of the Commons
against, 82; the King explains
his claim to, 85; vindication of
the right of Parliament to grant,
159.

Treason, proviso in Strafford's attainder relating to, 157; Act of the Parliament of the Commonwealth defining, 388.

Treaties. *See* Propositions.

Triennial Act, the, xi, 144.

Tudor Monarchy, its constitution, &c., xi, foll.

Union of England and Scotland, 418.

Uxbridge, propositions prepared by Parliament to be discussed at, 275; propositions prepared by the King to be discussed at, 286.

Vote of No Addresses, 356.

Wardship, proposals at the Treaty of Uxbridge on, 277; order of the two Houses for taking away, 290.